The EU Regulatory Framework for Electronic Communications

Handbook

2007 Edition

Arnold & Porter LLP

London

25 Old Broad Street
London EC2N 1HQ
tel: +44 (0)20 7786 6100
fax: +44 (0)20 7786 6299

Brussels

11, Rue des Colonies
1000 Brussels
tel: +32-(0)2-517-6600
fax: +32-(0)2-517-6603

Washington, DC

555 12th Street NW
Washington, D.C. 20004-1206
tel: +1 202 942 5000
fax: +1 202 942 5999

New York

399 Park Avenue
New York, NY 10022-4690
tel: +1 212 715 1000
fax: +1 212 715 1399

Los Angeles

777 South Figueroa Street, 44th Floor
Los Angeles, CA 90017-5844
tel: +1 213 243 4000
fax: +1 213 243 4199

Denver

370 Seventeenth Street, Suite 4500
Denver, CO 80202-1370
tel: +1 303 863 1000
fax: +1 303 832 0428

Northern Virginia

1600 Tysons Boulevard, Suite 900
McLean, VA 22102-4865
tel: +1 703 720 7000
fax: +1 703 720 7399

Telecommunications Practice

Cranberg, Marcia A.
Cloke, Simon C.
Cook, Jr., William E.
Feira, Scott
Firestone, Richard M.
Frank, Theodore D.
Garrett, Robert A
Goshorn, Julie
Grant, Patrick J.
Hinchliff, Susan
Horton, Philip W.
Humes, Gary E.
Jeffreys, Maureen R.
Kirk, Sarah
Lee, Ronald D.
Mudge, Amy
Phillipps, Stephanie M.
Rosen, Richard L.
Ryan, Michael H.
Schildkraut, Peter J.
Sinel, Norman M.
Stepka, Donald T.
Wright, Emma L.

The EU Regulatory Framework for Electronic Communications

Handbook

2007 Edition

Michael H. Ryan

Arnold & Porter (UK) LLP, London

Published by:

Arnold & Porter (UK) LLP
25 Old Broad Street
London EC2N 1HQ
Tel: +44-20-7786 6100
Fax:: +44-20-7786 6299
E-mail: lontelecoms@aporter.com
http://aporter.pair.com

£35

ISBN 0-9543940-3-8 4th revised edition
(ISBN 0-9543940-2-X   3rd revised edition)
(ISBN 0-9543940-1-1   2nd revised edition)
(ISBN 0-9543940-0-3   1st edition)

TABLE OF CONTENTS

Other Instruments and Materials

Data Protection, Privacy, Data Retention

Equipment and Standards

Radio Spectrum

Competition Law

State Aid

Procedural Provisions

International Treaties

Measures of Transitional Relevance

Foreword

This is the fourth edition of Arnold & Porter LLP's Handbook on "The EU Regulatory Framework for Electronic Communications". Since the publication of the third edition two years ago, there have been significant developments, including publication of new ERG common positions on the concept of SMP and remedies, a new directive on data retention and new Commission recommendations on leased lines and accounting separation.

Inevitably, developments will continue. At the time we went to press, the Commission's '2006 Review' of the regulatory framework, which may result in amendments to key directives, was under way; a draft of a new recommendation on relevant product and service markets was the subject of consultation.

All instruments included in this book are reproduced with any subsequent amendments, as amended to-date. Some minor editorial changes have occasionally been made, and these are identified with square brackets ([]). Footnote references in number form appear in the original text, although in some cases for technical reasons the numbering does not always coincide with the original. Endnote references in letter form refer to Editors' Notes which can be found at the end of the main body of the relevant text.

I acknowledge with thanks the contributions of my colleagues at Arnold & Porter LLP to the realisation of this book, including Emma Wright and Simon Cloke. I co-edited previous editions of this book with Reinhard Schu. This edition benefits from the contributions he made to previous editions, and these are also acknowledged with thanks.

Michael H. Ryan
October 2006

DIRECTIVE 2002/21/EC OF THE EUROPEAN PARLIAMENT AND OF THE COUNCIL

of 7 March 2002[a]

on a common regulatory framework
for electronic communications networks and services

(Framework Directive)

THE EUROPEAN PARLIAMENT AND THE COUNCIL OF THE EUROPEAN UNION,

Having regard to the Treaty establishing the European Community, and in particular Article 95 thereof,

Having regard to the proposal from the Commission[1],

Having regard to the opinion of the Economic and Social Committee[2],

Acting in accordance with the procedure laid down in Article 251 of the Treaty[3],

Whereas:

(1)   The current regulatory framework for telecommunications has been successful in creating the conditions for effective competition in the telecommunications sector during the transition from monopoly to full competition.

(2)   On 10 November 1999, the Commission presented a communication to the European Parliament, the Council, the Economic and Social Committee and the Committee of the Regions entitled "Towards a new framework for electronic communications infrastructure and associated services – the 1999 communications review". In that communication, the Commission reviewed the existing regulatory framework for telecommunications, in accordance with its obligation under Article 8 of Council Directive 90/387/EEC of 28 June 1990 on the establishment of the internal market for telecommunications services through the implementation of open network provision[4]. It also presented a series of policy proposals for a new regulatory framework for electronic communications infrastructure and associated services for public consultation.

(3)   On 26 April 2000 the Commission presented a communication to the European Parliament, the Council, the Economic and Social Committee and the Committee of the Regions on the results of the public consultation on the 1999 communications review and orientations for the new regulatory framework. The communication summarised the public consultation and set out certain key orientations for the preparation of a new framework for electronic communications infrastructure and associated services.

(4)   The Lisbon European Council of 23 and 24 March 2000 highlighted the potential for growth, competitiveness and job creation of the shift to a digital, knowledge-based economy. In particular, it emphasised the importance for Europe's businesses and

---

[1]   OJ C 365 E, 19.12.2000, p. 198 and OJ C 270 E, 25.9.2001, p. 199.

[2]   OJ C 123, 25.4.2001, p. 56.

[3]   Opinion of the European Parliament of 1 March 2001 (OJ C 277, 1.10.2001, p. 91), Council Common Position of 17 September 2001 (OJ C 337, 30.11.2001, p. 34) and Decision of the European Parliament of 12 December 2001 [OJ C 177 E, 25.07.2002, p. 142]. Council Decision of 14 February 2002.

[4]   OJ L 192, 24.7.1990, p. 1. Directive as amended by Directive 97/51/EC of the European Parliament and of the Council (OJ L 295, 29.10.1997, p. 23).

citizens of access to an inexpensive, world-class communications infrastructure and a wide range of services.

(5)   The convergence of the telecommunications, media and information technology sectors means all transmission networks and services should be covered by a single regulatory framework. That regulatory framework consists of this Directive and four specific Directives: Directive 2002/20/EC of the European Parliament and of the Council of 7 March 2002 on the authorisation of electronic communications networks and services (Authorisation Directive)[5], Directive 2002/19/EC of the European Parliament and of the Council of 7 March 2002 on access to, and interconnection of, electronic communications networks and associated facilities (Access Directive)[6], Directive 2002/22/EC of the European Parliament and of the Council of 7 March 2002 on universal service and users' rights relating to electronic communications networks and services (Universal Service Directive)[7], Directive 97/66/EC of the European Parliament and of the Council of 15 December 1997 concerning the processing of personal data and the protection of privacy in the telecommunications sector[8], (hereinafter referred to as "the Specific Directives"). It is necessary to separate the regulation of transmission from the regulation of content. This framework does not therefore cover the content of services delivered over electronic communications networks using electronic communications services, such as broadcasting content, financial services and certain information society services, and is therefore without prejudice to measures taken at Community or national level in respect of such services, in compliance with Community law, in order to promote cultural and linguistic diversity and to ensure the defence of media pluralism. The content of television programmes is covered by Council Directive 89/552/EEC of 3 October 1989 on the coordination of certain provisions laid down by law, regulation or administrative action in Member States concerning the pursuit of television broadcasting activities[9]. The separation between the regulation of transmission and the regulation of content does not prejudice the taking into account of the links existing between them, in particular in order to guarantee media pluralism, cultural diversity and consumer protection.

(6)   Audiovisual policy and content regulation are undertaken in pursuit of general interest objectives, such as freedom of expression, media pluralism, impartiality, cultural and linguistic diversity, social inclusion, consumer protection and the protection of minors. The Commission communication "Principles and guidelines for the Community's audio-visual policy in the digital age", and the Council conclusions of 6 June 2000 welcoming this communication, set out the key actions to be taken by the Community to implement its audio-visual policy.

(7)   The provisions of this Directive and the Specific Directives are without prejudice to the possibility for each Member State to take the necessary measures to ensure the protection of its essential security interests, to safeguard public policy and public security, and to permit the investigation, detection and prosecution of criminal offences, including the establishment by national regulatory authorities of specific and proportional obligations applicable to providers of electronic communications services.

(8)   This Directive does not cover equipment within the scope of Directive 1999/5/EC of the European Parliament and of the Council of 9 March 1999 on radio equipment and

---

[5]   [OJ L 108, 24.4.2002, p. 21].
[6]   [OJ L 108, 24.4.2002, p. 7].
[7]   [OJ L 108, 24.4.2002, p. 51].
[8]   OJ L 24, 30.1.1998, p. 1.
[9]   OJ L 298, 17.10.1989, p. 23. Directive as amended by Directive 97/36/EC of the European Parliament and of the Council (OJ L 202, 30.7.1997, p. 60).

telecommunications terminal equipment and the mutual recognition of their conformity[10], but does cover consumer equipment used for digital television. It is important for regulators to encourage network operators and terminal equipment manufacturers to cooperate in order to facilitate access by disabled users to electronic communications services.

(9) Information society services are covered by Directive 2000/31/EC of the European Parliament and of the Council of 8 June 2000 on certain legal aspects of information society services, in particular electronic commerce, in the internal market (Directive on electronic commerce)[11].

(10) The definition of "information society service" in Article 1 of Directive 98/34/EC of the European Parliament and of the Council of 22 June 1998 laying down a procedure for the provision of information in the field of technical standards and regulations and of rules of information society services[12] spans a wide range of economic activities which take place on-line. Most of these activities are not covered by the scope of this Directive because they do not consist wholly or mainly in the conveyance of signals on electronic communications networks. Voice telephony and electronic mail conveyance services are covered by this Directive. The same undertaking, for example an Internet service provider, can offer both an electronic communications service, such as access to the Internet, and services not covered under this Directive, such as the provision of web-based content.

(11) In accordance with the principle of the separation of regulatory and operational functions, Member States should guarantee the independence of the national regulatory authority or authorities with a view to ensuring the impartiality of their decisions. This requirement of independence is without prejudice to the institutional autonomy and constitutional obligations of the Member States or to the principle of neutrality with regard to the rules in Member States governing the system of property ownership laid down in Article 295 of the Treaty. National regulatory authorities should be in possession of all the necessary resources, in terms of staffing, expertise, and financial means, for the performance of their tasks.

(12) Any party who is the subject of a decision by a national regulatory authority should have the right to appeal to a body that is independent of the parties involved. This body may be a court. Furthermore, any undertaking which considers that its applications for the granting of rights to install facilities have not been dealt with in accordance with the principles set out in this Directive should be entitled to appeal against such decisions. This appeal procedure is without prejudice to the division of competences within national judicial systems and to the rights of legal entities or natural persons under national law.

(13) National regulatory authorities need to gather information from market players in order to carry out their tasks effectively. Such information may also need to be gathered on behalf of the Commission, to allow it to fulfil its obligations under Community law. Requests for information should be proportionate and not impose an undue burden on undertakings. Information gathered by national regulatory authorities should be publicly available, except in so far as it is confidential in accordance with national rules on public access to information and subject to Community and national law on business confidentiality.

(14) Information that is considered confidential by a national regulatory authority, in accordance with Community and national rules on business confidentiality, may only

---

[10] OJ L 91, 7.4.1999, p. 10.

[11] OJ L 178, 17.7.2000, p. 1.

[12] OJ L 204, 21.7.1998, p. 37. Directive as amended by Directive 98/48/EC (OJ L 217, 5.8.1998, p. 18).

be exchanged with the Commission and other national regulatory authorities where such exchange is strictly necessary for the application of the provisions of this Directive or the Specific Directives. The information exchanged should be limited to that which is relevant and proportionate to the purpose of such an exchange.

(15) It is important that national regulatory authorities consult all interested parties on proposed decisions and take account of their comments before adopting a final decision. In order to ensure that decisions at national level do not have an adverse effect on the single market or other Treaty objectives, national regulatory authorities should also notify certain draft decisions to the Commission and other national regulatory authorities to give them the opportunity to comment. It is appropriate for national regulatory authorities to consult interested parties on all draft measures which have an effect on trade between Member States. The cases where the procedures referred to in Articles 6 and 7 apply are defined in this Directive and in the Specific Directives. The Commission should be able, after consulting the Communications Committee, to require a national regulatory authority to withdraw a draft measure where it concerns definition of relevant markets or the designation or not of undertakings with significant market power, and where such decisions would create a barrier to the single market or would be incompatible with Community law and in particular the policy objectives that national regulatory authorities should follow. This procedure is without prejudice to the notification procedure provided for in Directive 98/34/EC and the Commission's prerogatives under the Treaty in respect of infringements of Community law.

(16) National regulatory authorities should have a harmonised set of objectives and principles to underpin, and should, where necessary, coordinate their actions with the regulatory authorities of other Member States in carrying out their tasks under this regulatory framework.

(17) The activities of national regulatory authorities established under this Directive and the Specific Directives contribute to the fulfilment of broader policies in the areas of culture, employment, the environment, social cohesion and town and country planning.

(18) The requirement for Member States to ensure that national regulatory authorities take the utmost account of the desirability of making regulation technologically neutral, that is to say that it neither imposes nor discriminates in favour of the use of a particular type of technology, does not preclude the taking of proportionate steps to promote certain specific services where this is justified, for example digital television as a means for increasing spectrum efficiency.

(19) Radio frequencies are an essential input for radio-based electronic communications services and, in so far as they relate to such services, should therefore be allocated and assigned by national regulatory authorities according to a set of harmonised objectives and principles governing their action as well as to objective, transparent and non-discriminatory criteria, taking into account the democratic, social, linguistic and cultural interests related to the use of frequency. It is important that the allocation and assignment of radio frequencies is managed as efficiently as possible. Transfer of radio frequencies can be an effective means of increasing efficient use of spectrum, as long as there are sufficient safeguards in place to protect the public interest, in particular the need to ensure transparency and regulatory supervision of such transfers. Decision No 676/2002/EC of the European Parliament and of the Council of 7 March 2002 on a regulatory framework for radio spectrum policy in the European Community (Radio Spectrum Decision)[13] establishes a framework for harmonisation

---

[13] [OJ L 108, 24.4.2002, p. 1].

of radio frequencies, and action taken under this Directive should seek to facilitate the work under that Decision.

(20) Access to numbering resources on the basis of transparent, objective and non-discriminatory criteria is essential for undertakings to compete in the electronic communications sector. All elements of national numbering plans should be managed by national regulatory authorities, including point codes used in network addressing. Where there is a need for harmonisation of numbering resources in the Community to support the development of pan-European services, the Commission may take technical implementing measures using its executive powers. Where this is appropriate to ensure full global interoperability of services, Member States should coordinate their national positions in accordance with the Treaty in international organisations and fora where numbering decisions are taken. The provisions of this Directive do not establish any new areas of responsibility for the national regulatory authorities in the field of Internet naming and addressing.

(21) Member States may use, inter alia, competitive or comparative selection procedures for the assignment of radio frequencies as well as numbers with exceptional economic value. In administering such schemes, national regulatory authorities should take into account the provisions of Article 8.

(22) It should be ensured that procedures exist for the granting of rights to install facilities that are timely, non-discriminatory and transparent, in order to guarantee the conditions for fair and effective competition. This Directive is without prejudice to national provisions governing the expropriation or use of property, the normal exercise of property rights, the normal use of the public domain, or to the principle of neutrality with regard to the rules in Member States governing the system of property ownership.

(23) Facility sharing can be of benefit for town planning, public health or environmental reasons, and should be encouraged by national regulatory authorities on the basis of voluntary agreements. In cases where undertakings are deprived of access to viable alternatives, compulsory facility or property sharing may be appropriate. It covers inter alia: physical co-location and duct, building, mast, antenna or antenna system sharing. Compulsory facility or property sharing should be imposed on undertakings only after full public consultation.

(24) Where mobile operators are required to share towers or masts for environmental reasons, such mandated sharing may lead to a reduction in the maximum transmitted power levels allowed for each operator for reasons of public health, and this in turn may require operators to install more transmission sites to ensure national coverage.

(25) There is a need for ex ante obligations in certain circumstances in order to ensure the development of a competitive market. The definition of significant market power in the Directive 97/33/EC of the European Parliament and of the Council of 30 June 1997 on interconnection in telecommunications with regard to ensuring universal service and interoperability through application of the principles of open network provision (ONP)[14] has proved effective in the initial stages of market opening as the threshold for ex ante obligations, but now needs to be adapted to suit more complex and dynamic markets. For this reason, the definition used in this Directive is equivalent to the concept of dominance as defined in the case law of the Court of Justice and the Court of First Instance of the European Communities.

---

[14] OJ L 199, 26.7.1997, p. 32. Directive as amended by Directive 98/61/EC (OJ L 268, 3.10.1998, p. 37).

(26) Two or more undertakings can be found to enjoy a joint dominant position not only where there exist structural or other links between them but also where the structure of the relevant market is conducive to coordinated effects, that is, it encourages parallel or aligned anti-competitive behaviour on the market.

(27) It is essential that ex ante regulatory obligations should only be imposed where there is not effective competition, i.e. in markets where there are one or more undertakings with significant market power, and where national and Community competition law remedies are not sufficient to address the problem. It is necessary therefore for the Commission to draw up guidelines at Community level in accordance with the principles of competition law for national regulatory authorities to follow in assessing whether competition is effective in a given market and in assessing significant market power. National regulatory authorities should analyse whether a given product or service market is effectively competitive in a given geographical area, which could be the whole or a part of the territory of the Member State concerned or neighbouring parts of territories of Member States considered together. An analysis of effective competition should include an analysis as to whether the market is prospectively competitive, and thus whether any lack of effective competition is durable. Those guidelines will also address the issue of newly emerging markets, where de facto the market leader is likely to have a substantial market share but should not be subjected to inappropriate obligations. The Commission should review the guidelines regularly to ensure that they remain appropriate in a rapidly developing market. National regulatory authorities will need to cooperate with each other where the relevant market is found to be transnational.

(28) In determining whether an undertaking has significant market power in a specific market, national regulatory authorities should act in accordance with Community law and take into the utmost account the Commission guidelines.

(29) The Community and the Member States have entered into commitments in relation to standards and the regulatory framework of telecommunications networks and services in the World Trade Organisation.

(30) Standardisation should remain primarily a market-driven process. However there may still be situations where it is appropriate to require compliance with specified standards at Community level to ensure interoperability in the single market. At national level, Member States are subject to the provisions of Directive 98/34/EC. Directive 95/47/EC of the European Parliament and of the Council of 24 October 1995 on the use of standards for the transmission of television signals[15] did not mandate any specific digital television transmission system or service requirement. Through the Digital Video Broadcasting Group, European market players have developed a family of television transmission systems that have been standardised by the European Telecommunications Standards Institute (ETSI) and have become International Telecommunication Union recommendations. Any decision to make the implementation of such standards mandatory should follow a full public consultation. Standardisation procedures under this Directive are without prejudice to the provisions of Directive 1999/5/EC, Council Directive 73/23/EEC of 19 February 1973 on the harmonisation of the laws of Member States relating to electrical equipment designed for use within certain voltage limits[16] and Council Directive 89/336/EEC of 3 May 1989 on the approximation of the laws of the Member States relating to electromagnetic compatibility[17].

---

[15] OJ L 281, 23.11.1995, p. 51.
[16] OJ L 77, 26.3.1973, p. 29.
[17] OJ L 139, 23.5.1989, p. 19.

(31) Interoperability of digital interactive television services and enhanced digital television equipment, at the level of the consumer, should be encouraged in order to ensure the free flow of information, media pluralism and cultural diversity. It is desirable for consumers to have the capability of receiving, regardless of the transmission mode, all digital interactive television services, having regard to technological neutrality, future technological progress, the need to promote the take-up of digital television, and the state of competition in the markets for digital television services. Digital interactive television platform operators should strive to implement an open application program interface (API) which conforms to standards or specifications adopted by a European standards organisation. Migration from existing APIs to new open APIs should be encouraged and organised, for example by Memoranda of Understanding between all relevant market players. Open APIs facilitate interoperability, i.e. the portability of interactive content between delivery mechanisms, and full functionality of this content on enhanced digital television equipment. However, the need not to hinder the functioning of the receiving equipment and to protect it from malicious attacks, for example from viruses, should be taken into account.

(32) In the event of a dispute between undertakings in the same Member State in an area covered by this Directive or the Specific Directives, for example relating to obligations for access and interconnection or to the means of transferring subscriber lists, an aggrieved party that has negotiated in good faith but failed to reach agreement should be able to call on the national regulatory authority to resolve the dispute. National regulatory authorities should be able to impose a solution on the parties. The intervention of a national regulatory authority in the resolution of a dispute between undertakings providing electronic communications networks or services in a Member State should seek to ensure compliance with the obligations arising under this Directive or the Specific Directives.

(33) In addition to the rights of recourse granted under national or Community law, there is a need for a simple procedure to be initiated at the request of either party in a dispute, to resolve cross-border disputes which lie outside the competence of a single national regulatory authority.

(34) A single Committee should replace the "ONP Committee" instituted by Article 9 of Directive 90/387/EEC and the Licensing Committee instituted by Article 14 of Directive 97/13/EC of the European Parliament and of the Council of 10 April 1997 on a common framework for general authorisations and individual licences in the field of telecommunications services[18].

(35) National regulatory authorities and national competition authorities should provide each other with the information necessary to apply the provisions of this Directive and the Specific Directives, in order to allow them to cooperate fully together. In respect of the information exchanged, the receiving authority should ensure the same level of confidentiality as the originating authority.

(36) The Commission has indicated its intention to set up a European regulators group for electronic communications networks and services which would constitute a suitable mechanism for encouraging cooperation and coordination of national regulatory authorities, in order to promote the development of the internal market for electronic communications networks and services, and to seek to achieve consistent application, in all Member States, of the provisions set out in this Directive and the Specific Directives, in particular in areas where national law implementing Community law

---

[18] OJ L 117, 7.5.1997, p. 15.

gives national regulatory authorities considerable discretionary powers in application of the relevant rules.

(37) National regulatory authorities should be required to cooperate with each other and with the Commission in a transparent manner to ensure consistent application, in all Member States, of the provisions of this Directive and the Specific Directives. This cooperation could take place, inter alia, in the Communications Committee or in a group comprising European regulators. Member States should decide which bodies are national regulatory authorities for the purposes of this Directive and the Specific Directives.

(38) Measures that could affect trade between Member States are measures that may have an influence, direct or indirect, actual or potential, on the pattern of trade between Member States in a manner which might create a barrier to the single market. They comprise measures that have a significant impact on operators or users in other Member States, which include, inter alia: measures which affect prices for users in other Member States; measures which affect the ability of an undertaking established in another Member State to provide an electronic communications service, and in particular measures which affect the ability to offer services on a transnational basis; and measures which affect market structure or access, leading to repercussions for undertakings in other Member States.

(39) The provisions of this Directive should be reviewed periodically, in particular with a view to determining the need for modification in the light of changing technological or market conditions.

(40) The measures necessary for the implementation of this Directive should be adopted in accordance with Council Decision 1999/468/EC of 28 June 1999 laying down the procedures for the exercise of implementing powers conferred on the Commission[19].

(41) Since the objectives of the proposed action, namely achieving a harmonised framework for the regulation of electronic communications services, electronic communications networks, associated facilities and associated services cannot be sufficiently achieved by the Member States and can therefore, by reason of the scale and effects of the action, be better achieved at Community level, the Community may adopt measures in accordance with the principle of subsidiarity as set out in Article 5 of the Treaty. In accordance with the principle of proportionality, as set out in that Article, this Directive does not go beyond what is necessary for those objectives.

(42) Certain directives and decisions in this field should be repealed.

(43) The Commission should monitor the transition from the existing framework to the new framework, and may in particular, at an appropriate time, bring forward a proposal to repeal Regulation (EC) No 2887/2000 of the European Parliament and of the Council of 18 December 2000 on unbundled access to the local loop[20],

---

[19] OJ L 184, 17.7.1999, p. 23.
[20] OJ L 336, 30.12.2000, p. 4.

HAVE ADOPTED THIS DIRECTIVE:

CHAPTER I

SCOPE, AIM AND DEFINITIONS

Article 1

Scope and aim

1. This Directive establishes a harmonised framework for the regulation of electronic communications services, electronic communications networks, associated facilities and associated services. It lays down tasks of national regulatory authorities and establishes a set of procedures to ensure the harmonised application of the regulatory framework throughout the Community.

2. This Directive as well as the Specific Directives are without prejudice to obligations imposed by national law in accordance with Community law or by Community law in respect of services provided using electronic communications networks and services.

3. This Directive as well as the Specific Directives are without prejudice to measures taken at Community or national level, in compliance with Community law, to pursue general interest objectives, in particular relating to content regulation and audio-visual policy.

4. This Directive and the Specific Directives are without prejudice to the provisions of Directive 1999/5/EC.

Article 2

Definitions

For the purposes of this Directive:

(a) "electronic communications network" means transmission systems and, where applicable, switching or routing equipment and other resources which permit the conveyance of signals by wire, by radio, by optical or by other electromagnetic means, including satellite networks, fixed (circuit- and packet-switched, including Internet) and mobile terrestrial networks, electricity cable systems, to the extent that they are used for the purpose of transmitting signals, networks used for radio and television broadcasting, and cable television networks, irrespective of the type of information conveyed;

(b) "transnational markets" means markets identified in accordance with Article 15(4) covering the Community or a substantial part thereof;

(c) "electronic communications service" means a service normally provided for remuneration which consists wholly or mainly in the conveyance of signals on electronic communications networks, including telecommunications services and transmission services in networks used for broadcasting, but exclude services providing, or exercising editorial control over, content transmitted using electronic communications networks and services; it does not include information society services, as defined in Article 1 of Directive 98/34/EC, which do not consist wholly or mainly in the conveyance of signals on electronic communications networks;

(d) "public communications network" means an electronic communications network used wholly or mainly for the provision of publicly available electronic communications services;

(e) "associated facilities" means those facilities associated with an electronic communications network and/or an electronic communications service which enable and/or support the provision of services via that network and/or service. It includes conditional access systems and electronic programme guides;

(f) "conditional access system" means any technical measure and/or arrangement whereby access to a protected radio or television broadcasting service in intelligible form is made conditional upon subscription or other form of prior individual authorisation;

(g) "national regulatory authority" means the body or bodies charged by a Member State with any of the regulatory tasks assigned in this Directive and the Specific Directives;

(h) "user" means a legal entity or natural person using or requesting a publicly available electronic communications service;

(i) "consumer" means any natural person who uses or requests a publicly available electronic communications service for purposes which are outside his or her trade, business or profession;

(j) "universal service" means the minimum set of services, defined in Directive 2002/22/EC (Universal Service Directive), of specified quality which is available to all users regardless of their geographical location and, in the light of specific national conditions, at an affordable price;

(k) "subscriber" means any natural person or legal entity who or which is party to a contract with the provider of publicly available electronic communications services for the supply of such services;

(l) "Specific Directives" means Directive 2002/20/EC (Authorisation Directive), Directive 2002/19/EC (Access Directive), Directive 2002/22/EC (Universal Service Directive) and Directive 97/66/EC;

(m) "provision of an electronic communications network" means the establishment, operation, control or making available of such a network;

(n) "end-user" means a user not providing public communications networks or publicly available electronic communications services;

(o) "enhanced digital television equipment" means set-top boxes intended for connection to television sets or integrated digital television sets, able to receive digital interactive television services;

(p) "application program interface (API)" means the software interfaces between applications, made available by broadcasters or service providers, and the resources in the enhanced digital television equipment for digital television and radio services.

CHAPTER II

NATIONAL REGULATORY AUTHORITIES

Article 3

National regulatory authorities

1. Member States shall ensure that each of the tasks assigned to national regulatory authorities in this Directive and the Specific Directives is undertaken by a competent body.

2. Member States shall guarantee the independence of national regulatory authorities by ensuring that they are legally distinct from and functionally independent of all organisations providing electronic communications networks, equipment or services. Member States that retain ownership or control of undertakings providing electronic communications networks and/or services shall ensure effective structural separation of the regulatory function from activities associated with ownership or control.

3. Member States shall ensure that national regulatory authorities exercise their powers impartially and transparently.

4. Member States shall publish the tasks to be undertaken by national regulatory authorities in an easily accessible form, in particular where those tasks are assigned to more than one body. Member States shall ensure, where appropriate, consultation and cooperation between those authorities, and between those authorities and national authorities entrusted with the implementation of competition law and national authorities entrusted with the implementation of consumer law, on matters of common interest. Where more than one authority has competence to address such matters, Member States shall ensure that the respective tasks of each authority are published in an easily accessible form.

5. National regulatory authorities and national competition authorities shall provide each other with the information necessary for the application of the provisions of this Directive and the Specific Directives. In respect of the information exchanged, the receiving authority shall ensure the same level of confidentiality as the originating authority.

6. Member States shall notify to the Commission all national regulatory authorities assigned tasks under this Directive and the Specific Directives, and their respective responsibilities.

Article 4

Right of appeal

1. Member States shall ensure that effective mechanisms exist at national level under which any user or undertaking providing electronic communications networks and/or services who is affected by a decision of a national regulatory authority has the right of appeal against the decision to an appeal body that is independent of the parties involved. This body, which may be a court, shall have the appropriate expertise available to it to enable it to carry out its functions. Member States shall ensure that the merits of the case are duly taken into account and that there is an effective appeal mechanism. Pending the outcome of any such appeal, the decision of the national regulatory authority shall stand, unless the appeal body decides otherwise.

2. Where the appeal body referred to in paragraph 1 is not judicial in character, written reasons for its decision shall always be given. Furthermore, in such a case, its

decision shall be subject to review by a court or tribunal within the meaning of Article 234 of the Treaty.

Article 5

Provision of information

1. Member States shall ensure that undertakings providing electronic communications networks and services provide all the information, including financial information, necessary for national regulatory authorities to ensure conformity with the provisions of, or decisions made in accordance with, this Directive and the Specific Directives. These undertakings shall provide such information promptly on request and to the timescales and level of detail required by the national regulatory authority. The information requested by the national regulatory authority shall be proportionate to the performance of that task. The national regulatory authority shall give the reasons justifying its request for information.

2. Member States shall ensure that national regulatory authorities provide the Commission, after a reasoned request, with the information necessary for it to carry out its tasks under the Treaty. The information requested by the Commission shall be proportionate to the performance of those tasks. Where the information provided refers to information previously provided by undertakings at the request of the national regulatory authority, such undertakings shall be informed thereof. To the extent necessary, and unless the authority that provides the information has made an explicit and reasoned request to the contrary, the Commission shall make the information provided available to another such authority in another Member State.

    Subject to the requirements of paragraph 3, Member States shall ensure that the information submitted to one national regulatory authority can be made available to another such authority in the same or different Member State, after a substantiated request, where necessary to allow either authority to fulfil its responsibilities under Community law.

3. Where information is considered confidential by a national regulatory authority in accordance with Community and national rules on business confidentiality, the Commission and the national regulatory authorities concerned shall ensure such confidentiality.

4. Member States shall ensure that, acting in accordance with national rules on public access to information and subject to Community and national rules on business confidentiality, national regulatory authorities publish such information as would contribute to an open and competitive market.

5. National regulatory authorities shall publish the terms of public access to information as referred to in paragraph 4, including procedures for obtaining such access.

Article 6

Consultation and transparency mechanism

Except in cases falling within Articles 7(6), 20 or 21 Member States shall ensure that where national regulatory authorities intend to take measures in accordance with this Directive or the Specific Directives which have a significant impact on the relevant market, they give interested parties the opportunity to comment on the draft measure within a reasonable period. National regulatory authorities shall publish their national consultation procedures. Member States shall ensure the establishment of a single information point through which all current consultations can be accessed. The results of the consultation procedure shall be made publicly available by the national regulatory authority, except in the case of confidential information in accordance with Community and national law on business confidentiality.

Consolidating the internal market for electronic communications

1.   In carrying out their tasks under this Directive and the Specific Directives, national regulatory authorities shall take the utmost account of the objectives set out in Article 8, including in so far as they relate to the functioning of the internal market.

2.   National regulatory authorities shall contribute to the development of the internal market by cooperating with each other and with the Commission in a transparent manner to ensure the consistent application, in all Member States, of the provisions of this Directive and the Specific Directives. To this end, they shall, in particular, seek to agree on the types of instruments and remedies best suited to address particular types of situations in the market place.

3.   In addition to the consultation referred to in Article 6, where a national regulatory authority intends to take a measure which:

(a)   falls within the scope of Articles 15 or 16 of this Directive, Articles 5 or 8 of Directive 2002/19/EC (Access Directive) or Article 16 of Directive 2002/22/EC (Universal Service Directive), and

(b)   would affect trade between Member States,

it shall at the same time make the draft measure accessible to the Commission and the national regulatory authorities in other Member States, together with the reasoning on which the measure is based, in accordance with Article 5(3), and inform the Commission and other national regulatory authorities thereof. National regulatory authorities and the Commission may make comments to the national regulatory authority concerned only within one month or within the period referred to in Article 6 if that period is longer. The one-month period may not be extended.

4.   Where an intended measure covered by paragraph 3 aims at:

(a)   defining a relevant market which differs from those defined in the recommendation in accordance with Article 15(1), or

(b)   deciding whether or not to designate an undertaking as having, either individually or jointly with others, significant market power, under Article 16(3), (4) or (5),

and would affect trade between Member States and the Commission has indicated to the national regulatory authority that it considers that the draft measure would create a barrier to the single market or if it has serious doubts as to its compatibility with Community law and in particular the objectives referred to in Article 8, then the draft measure shall not be adopted for a further two months. This period may not be extended. Within this period the Commission may, in accordance with the procedure referred to in Article 22(2), take a decision requiring the national regulatory authority concerned to withdraw the draft measure. This decision shall be accompanied by a detailed and objective analysis of why the Commission considers that the draft measure should not be adopted together with specific proposals for amending the draft measure.

5.   The national regulatory authority concerned shall take the utmost account of comments of other national regulatory authorities and the Commission and may,

except in cases covered by paragraph 4, adopt the resulting draft measure and, where it does so, shall communicate it to the Commission.

6.   In exceptional circumstances, where a national regulatory authority considers that there is an urgent need to act, by way of derogation from the procedure set out in paragraphs 3 and 4, in order to safeguard competition and protect the interests of users, it may immediately adopt proportionate and provisional measures. It shall, without delay, communicate those measures, with full reasons, to the Commission and the other national regulatory authorities. A decision by the national regulatory authority to render such measures permanent or extend the time for which they are applicable shall be subject to the provisions of paragraphs 3 and 4.

CHAPTER III

TASKS OF NATIONAL REGULATORY AUTHORITIES

Article 8

Policy objectives and regulatory principles

1.   Member States shall ensure that in carrying out the regulatory tasks specified in this Directive and the Specific Directives, the national regulatory authorities take all reasonable measures which are aimed at achieving the objectives set out in paragraphs 2, 3 and 4. Such measures shall be proportionate to those objectives.

Member States shall ensure that in carrying out the regulatory tasks specified in this Directive and the Specific Directives, in particular those designed to ensure effective competition, national regulatory authorities take the utmost account of the desirability of making regulations technologically neutral.

National regulatory authorities may contribute within their competencies to ensuring the implementation of policies aimed at the promotion of cultural and linguistic diversity, as well as media pluralism.

2.   The national regulatory authorities shall promote competition in the provision of electronic communications networks, electronic communications services and associated facilities and services by inter alia:

(a)   ensuring that users, including disabled users, derive maximum benefit in terms of choice, price, and quality;

(b)   ensuring that there is no distortion or restriction of competition in the electronic communications sector;

(c)   encouraging efficient investment in infrastructure, and promoting innovation; and

(d)   encouraging efficient use and ensuring the effective management of radio frequencies and numbering resources.

3.   The national regulatory authorities shall contribute to the development of the internal market by inter alia:

(a)   removing remaining obstacles to the provision of electronic communications networks, associated facilities and services and electronic communications services at European level;

(b) encouraging the establishment and development of trans-European networks and the interoperability of pan-European services, and end-to-end connectivity;

(c) ensuring that, in similar circumstances, there is no discrimination in the treatment of undertakings providing electronic communications networks and services;

(d) cooperating with each other and with the Commission in a transparent manner to ensure the development of consistent regulatory practice and the consistent application of this Directive and the Specific Directives.

4. The national regulatory authorities shall promote the interests of the citizens of the European Union by inter alia:

(a) ensuring all citizens have access to a universal service specified in Directive 2002/22/EC (Universal Service Directive);

(b) ensuring a high level of protection for consumers in their dealings with suppliers, in particular by ensuring the availability of simple and inexpensive dispute resolution procedures carried out by a body that is independent of the parties involved;

(c) contributing to ensuring a high level of protection of personal data and privacy;

(d) promoting the provision of clear information, in particular requiring transparency of tariffs and conditions for using publicly available electronic communications services;

(e) addressing the needs of specific social groups, in particular disabled users; and

(f) ensuring that the integrity and security of public communications networks are maintained.

Article 9

Management of radio frequencies for electronic communications services

1. Member States shall ensure the effective management of radio frequencies for electronic communication services in their territory in accordance with Article 8. They shall ensure that the allocation and assignment of such radio frequencies by national regulatory authorities are based on objective, transparent, non-discriminatory and proportionate criteria.

2. Member States shall promote the harmonisation of use of radio frequencies across the Community, consistent with the need to ensure effective and efficient use thereof and in accordance with the Decision No 676/2002/EC (Radio Spectrum Decision).

3. Member States may make provision for undertakings to transfer rights to use radio frequencies with other undertakings.

4. Member States shall ensure that an undertaking's intention to transfer rights to use radio frequencies is notified to the national regulatory authority responsible for spectrum assignment and that any transfer takes place in accordance with procedures laid down by the national regulatory authority and is made public. National regulatory authorities shall ensure that competition is not distorted as a result of any such transaction. Where radio frequency use has been harmonised through the application of Decision No 676/2002/EC (Radio Spectrum Decision) or other

Community measures, any such transfer shall not result in change of use of that radio frequency.

Article 10

Numbering, naming and addressing

1. Member States shall ensure that national regulatory authorities control the assignment of all national numbering resources and the management of the national numbering plans. Member States shall ensure that adequate numbers and numbering ranges are provided for all publicly available electronic communications services. National regulatory authorities shall establish objective, transparent and non-discriminatory assigning procedures for national numbering resources.

2. National regulatory authorities shall ensure that numbering plans and procedures are applied in a manner that gives equal treatment to all providers of publicly available electronic communications services. In particular, Member States shall ensure that an undertaking allocated a range of numbers does not discriminate against other providers of electronic communications services as regards the number sequences used to give access to their services.

3. Member States shall ensure that the national numbering plans, and all subsequent additions or amendments thereto, are published, subject only to limitations imposed on the grounds of national security.

4. Member States shall support the harmonisation of numbering resources within the Community where that is necessary to support the development of pan European services. The Commission may, in accordance with the procedure referred to in Article 22(3), take the appropriate technical implementing measures on this matter.

5. Where this is appropriate in order to ensure full global interoperability of services, Member States shall coordinate their positions in international organisations and forums in which decisions are taken on issues relating to the numbering, naming and addressing of electronic communications networks and services.

Article 11

Rights of way

1. Member States shall ensure that when a competent authority considers:

    -   an application for the granting of rights to install facilities on, over or under public or private property to an undertaking authorised to provide public communications networks, or

    -   an application for the granting of rights to install facilities on, over or under public property to an undertaking authorised to provide electronic communications networks other than to the public,

    the competent authority:

    -   acts on the basis of transparent and publicly available procedures, applied without discrimination and without delay, and

    -   follows the principles of transparency and non-discrimination in attaching conditions to any such rights.

The abovementioned procedures can differ depending on whether the applicant is providing public communications networks or not.

2. Member States shall ensure that where public or local authorities retain ownership or control of undertakings operating electronic communications networks and/or services, there is effective structural separation of the function responsible for granting the rights referred to in paragraph 1 from activities associated with ownership or control.

3. Member States shall ensure that effective mechanisms exist to allow undertakings to appeal against decisions on the granting of rights to install facilities to a body that is independent of the parties involved.

Article 12

Co-location and facility sharing

1. Where an undertaking providing electronic communications networks has the right under national legislation to install facilities on, over or under public or private property, or may take advantage of a procedure for the expropriation or use of property, national regulatory authorities shall encourage the sharing of such facilities or property.

2. In particular where undertakings are deprived of access to viable alternatives because of the need to protect the environment, public health, public security or to meet town and country planning objectives, Member States may impose the sharing of facilities or property (including physical co-location) on an undertaking operating an electronic communications network or take measures to facilitate the coordination of public works only after an appropriate period of public consultation during which all interested parties must be given an opportunity to express their views. Such sharing or coordination arrangements may include rules for apportioning the costs of facility or property sharing.

Article 13

Accounting separation and financial reports

1. Member States shall require undertakings providing public communications networks or publicly available electronic communications services which have special or exclusive rights for the provision of services in other sectors in the same or another Member State to:

   (a) keep separate accounts for the activities associated with the provision of electronic communications networks or services, to the extent that would be required if these activities were carried out by legally independent companies, so as to identify all elements of cost and revenue, with the basis of their calculation and the detailed attribution methods used, related to their activities associated with the provision of electronic communications networks or services including an itemised breakdown of fixed asset and structural costs, or

   (b) have structural separation for the activities associated with the provision of electronic communications networks or services.

   Member States may choose not to apply the requirements referred to in the first subparagraph to undertakings the annual turnover of which in activities associated with electronic communications networks or services in the Member States is less than EUR 50 million.

2.   Where undertakings providing public communications networks or publicly available electronic communications services are not subject to the requirements of company law and do not satisfy the small and medium-sized enterprise criteria of Community law accounting rules, their financial reports shall be drawn up and submitted to independent audit and published. The audit shall be carried out in accordance with the relevant Community and national rules.

This requirement shall also apply to the separate accounts required under paragraph 1(a).

CHAPTER IV

GENERAL PROVISIONS

Article 14

Undertakings with significant market power

1.   Where the Specific Directives require national regulatory authorities to determine whether operators have significant market power in accordance with the procedure referred to in Article 16, paragraphs 2 and 3 of this Article shall apply.

2.   An undertaking shall be deemed to have significant market power if, either individually or jointly with others, it enjoys a position equivalent to dominance, that is to say a position of economic strength affording it the power to behave to an appreciable extent independently of competitors, customers and ultimately consumers.

In particular, national regulatory authorities shall, when assessing whether two or more undertakings are in a joint dominant position in a market, act in accordance with Community law and take into the utmost account the guidelines on market analysis and the assessment of significant market power published by the Commission pursuant to Article 15. Criteria to be used in making such an assessment are set out in Annex II.

3.   Where an undertaking has significant market power on a specific market, it may also be deemed to have significant market power on a closely related market, where the links between the two markets are such as to allow the market power held in one market to be leveraged into the other market, thereby strengthening the market power of the undertaking.

Article 15

Market definition procedure

1.   After public consultation and consultation with national regulatory authorities the Commission shall adopt a recommendation on relevant product and service markets (hereinafter "the recommendation"). The recommendation shall identify in accordance with Annex I hereto those product and service markets within the electronic communications sector, the characteristics of which may be such as to justify the imposition of regulatory obligations set out in the Specific Directives, without prejudice to markets that may be defined in specific cases under competition law. The Commission shall define markets in accordance with the principles of competition law.

The Commission shall regularly review the recommendation.

2. The Commission shall publish, at the latest on the date of entry into force of this Directive, guidelines for market analysis and the assessment of significant market power (hereinafter "the guidelines") which shall be in accordance with the principles of competition law.

3. National regulatory authorities shall, taking the utmost account of the recommendation and the guidelines, define relevant markets appropriate to national circumstances, in particular relevant geographic markets within their territory, in accordance with the principles of competition law. National regulatory authorities shall follow the procedures referred to in Articles 6 and 7 before defining the markets that differ from those defined in the recommendation.

4. After consultation with national regulatory authorities the Commission may, acting in accordance with the procedure referred to in Article 22(3), adopt a Decision identifying transnational markets.

Article 16

Market analysis procedure

1. As soon as possible after the adoption of the recommendation or any updating thereof, national regulatory authorities shall carry out an analysis of the relevant markets, taking the utmost account of the guidelines. Member States shall ensure that this analysis is carried out, where appropriate, in collaboration with the national competition authorities.

2. Where a national regulatory authority is required under Articles 16, 17, 18 or 19 of Directive 2002/22/EC (Universal Service Directive), or Articles 7 or 8 of Directive 2002/19/EC (Access Directive) to determine whether to impose, maintain, amend or withdraw obligations on undertakings, it shall determine on the basis of its market analysis referred to in paragraph 1 of this Article whether a relevant market is effectively competitive.

3. Where a national regulatory authority concludes that the market is effectively competitive, it shall not impose or maintain any of the specific regulatory obligations referred to in paragraph 2 of this Article. In cases where sector specific regulatory obligations already exist, it shall withdraw such obligations placed on undertakings in that relevant market. An appropriate period of notice shall be given to parties affected by such a withdrawal of obligations.

4. Where a national regulatory authority determines that a relevant market is not effectively competitive, it shall identify undertakings with significant market power on that market in accordance with Article 14 and the national regulatory authority shall on such undertakings impose appropriate specific regulatory obligations referred to in paragraph 2 of this Article or maintain or amend such obligations where they already exist.

5. In the case of transnational markets identified in the Decision referred to in Article 15(4), the national regulatory authorities concerned shall jointly conduct the market analysis taking the utmost account of the guidelines and decide on any imposition, maintenance, amendment or withdrawal of regulatory obligations referred to in paragraph 2 of this Article in a concerted fashion.

6. Measures taken according to the provisions of paragraphs 3, 4 and 5 of this Article shall be subject to the procedures referred to in Articles 6 and 7.

Article 17

Standardisation

1. The Commission, acting in accordance with the procedure referred to in Article 22(2), shall draw up and publish in the Official Journal of the European Communities a list of standards and/or specifications to serve as a basis for encouraging the harmonised provision of electronic communications networks, electronic communications services and associated facilities and services. Where necessary, the Commission may, acting in accordance with the procedure referred to in Article 22(2) and following consultation of the Committee established by Directive 98/34/EC, request that standards be drawn up by the European standards organisations (European Committee for Standardisation (CEN), European Committee for Electrotechnical Standardisation (CENELEC), and European Telecommunications Standards Institute (ETSI)).

2. Member States shall encourage the use of the standards and/or specifications referred to in paragraph 1, for the provision of services, technical interfaces and/or network functions, to the extent strictly necessary to ensure interoperability of services and to improve freedom of choice for users.

    As long as standards and/or specifications have not been published in accordance with paragraph 1, Member States shall encourage the implementation of standards and/or specifications adopted by the European standards organisations.

    In the absence of such standards and/or specifications, Member States shall encourage the implementation of international standards or recommendations adopted by the International Telecommunication Union (ITU), the International Organisation for Standardisation (ISO) or the International Electrotechnical Commission (IEC).

    Where international standards exist, Member States shall encourage the European standards organisations to use them, or the relevant parts of them, as a basis for the standards they develop, except where such international standards or relevant parts would be ineffective.

3. If the standards and/or specifications referred to in paragraph 1 have not been adequately implemented so that interoperability of services in one or more Member States cannot be ensured, the implementation of such standards and/or specifications may be made compulsory under the procedure laid down in paragraph 4, to the extent strictly necessary to ensure such interoperability and to improve freedom of choice for users.

4. Where the Commission intends to make the implementation of certain standards and/or specifications compulsory, it shall publish a notice in the Official Journal of the European Communities and invite public comment by all parties concerned. The Commission, acting in accordance with the procedure referred to in Article 22(3), shall make implementation of the relevant standards compulsory by making reference to them as compulsory standards in the list of standards and/or specifications published in the Official Journal of the European Communities.

5. Where the Commission considers that standards and/or specifications referred to in paragraph 1 no longer contribute to the provision of harmonised electronic communications services, or that they no longer meet consumers' needs or are hampering technological development, it shall, acting in accordance with the procedure referred to in Article 22(2), remove them from the list of standards and/or specifications referred to in paragraph 1.

6. Where the Commission considers that standards and/or specifications referred to in paragraph 4 no longer contribute to the provision of harmonised electronic

communications services, or that they no longer meet consumers' needs or are hampering technological development, it shall, acting in accordance with the procedure referred to in Article 22(3), remove them from this list of standards and/or specifications referred to in paragraph 1.

7. This Article does not apply in respect of any of the essential requirements, interface specifications or harmonised standards to which the provisions of Directive 1999/5/EC apply.

Article 18

Interoperability of digital interactive television services

1. In order to promote the free flow of information, media pluralism and cultural diversity, Member States shall encourage, in accordance with the provisions of Article 17(2) :

    (a) providers of digital interactive television services for distribution to the public in the Community on digital interactive television platforms, regardless of the transmission mode, to use an open API;

    (b) providers of all enhanced digital television equipment deployed for the reception of digital interactive television services on interactive digital television platforms to comply with an open API in accordance with the minimum requirements of the relevant standards or specifications.

2. Without prejudice to Article 5(1)(b) of Directive 2002/19/ EC (Access Directive), Member States shall encourage proprietors of APIs to make available on fair, reasonable and non-discriminatory terms, and against appropriate remuneration, all such information as is necessary to enable providers of digital interactive television services to provide all services supported by the API in a fully functional form.

3. Within one year after the date of application referred to in Article 28(1), second subparagraph, the Commission shall examine the effects of this Article. If interoperability and freedom of choice for users have not been adequately achieved in one or more Member States, the Commission may take action in accordance with the procedure laid down in Article 17(3) and (4).

Article 19

Harmonisation procedures

1. Where the Commission, acting in accordance with the procedure referred to in Article 22(2), issues recommendations to Member States on the harmonised application of the provisions in this Directive and the Specific Directives in order to further the achievement of the objectives set out in Article 8, Member States shall ensure that national regulatory authorities take the utmost account of those recommendations in carrying out their tasks. Where a national regulatory authority chooses not to follow a recommendation, it shall inform the Commission giving the reasoning for its position.

2. Where the Commission finds that divergence at national level in regulations aimed at implementing Article 10(4) creates a barrier to the single market, the Commission may, acting in accordance with the procedure referred to in Article 22(3), take the appropriate technical implementing measures.

Article 20

Dispute resolution between undertakings

1. In the event of a dispute arising in connection with obligations arising under this Directive or the Specific Directives between undertakings providing electronic communications networks or services in a Member State, the national regulatory authority concerned shall, at the request of either party, and without prejudice to the provisions of paragraph 2, issue a binding decision to resolve the dispute in the shortest possible time frame and in any case within four months except in exceptional circumstances. The Member State concerned shall require that all parties cooperate fully with the national regulatory authority.

2. Member States may make provision for national regulatory authorities to decline to resolve a dispute through a binding decision where other mechanisms, including mediation, exist and would better contribute to resolution of the dispute in a timely manner in accordance with the provisions of Article 8. The national regulatory authority shall inform the parties without delay. If after four months the dispute is not resolved, and if the dispute has not been brought before the courts by the party seeking redress, the national regulatory authority shall issue, at the request of either party, a binding decision to resolve the dispute in the shortest possible time frame and in any case within four months.

3. In resolving a dispute, the national regulatory authority shall take decisions aimed at achieving the objectives set out in Article 8. Any obligations imposed on an undertaking by the national regulatory authority in resolving a dispute shall respect the provisions of this Directive or the Specific Directives.

4. The decision of the national regulatory authority shall be made available to the public, having regard to the requirements of business confidentiality. The parties concerned shall be given a full statement of the reasons on which it is based.

5. The procedure referred to in paragraphs 1, 3 and 4 shall not preclude either party from bringing an action before the courts.

Article 21

Resolution of cross-border disputes

1. In the event of a cross-border dispute arising under this Directive or the Specific Directives between parties in different Member States, where the dispute lies within the competence of national regulatory authorities from more than one Member State, the procedure set out in paragraphs 2, 3 and 4 shall be applicable.

2. Any party may refer the dispute to the national regulatory authorities concerned. The national regulatory authorities shall coordinate their efforts in order to bring about a resolution of the dispute, in accordance with the objectives set out in Article 8. Any obligations imposed on an undertaking by the national regulatory authority in resolving a dispute shall respect the provisions of this Directive or the Specific Directives.

3. Member States may make provision for national regulatory authorities jointly to decline to resolve a dispute where other mechanisms, including mediation, exist and would better contribute to resolution of the dispute in a timely manner in accordance with the provisions of Article 8. They shall inform the parties without delay. If after four months the dispute is not resolved, if the dispute has not been brought before the courts by the party seeking redress, and if either party requests it, the national

regulatory authorities shall coordinate their efforts in order to bring about a resolution of the dispute, in accordance with the provisions set out in Article 8.

4.   The procedure referred to in paragraph 2 shall not preclude either party from bringing an action before the courts.

Article 22

Committee

1.   The Commission shall be assisted by a Committee ("the Communications Committee").

2.   Where reference is made to this paragraph, Articles 3 and 7 of Decision 1999/468/EC shall apply, having regard to the provisions of Article 8 thereof.

3.   Where reference is made to this paragraph, Articles 5 and 7 of Decision 1999/468/EC shall apply, having regard to the provisions of Article 8 thereof.

The period laid down in Article 5(6) of Decision 1999/468/EC shall be three months.

4.   The Committee shall adopt its rules of procedure.

Article 23

Exchange of information

1.   The Commission shall provide all relevant information to the Communications Committee on the outcome of regular consultations with the representatives of network operators, service providers, users, consumers, manufacturers and trade unions, as well as third countries and international organisations.

2.   The Communications Committee shall, taking account of the Community's electronic communications policy, foster the exchange of information between the Member States and between the Member States and the Commission on the situation and the development of regulatory activities regarding electronic communications networks and services.

Article 24

Publication of information

1.   Member States shall ensure that up-to-date information pertaining to the application of this Directive and the Specific Directives is made publicly available in a manner that guarantees all interested parties easy access to that information. They shall publish a notice in their national official gazette describing how and where the information is published. The first such notice shall be published before the date of application referred to in Article 28(1), second subparagraph, and thereafter a notice shall be published whenever there is any change in the information contained therein.

2.   Member States shall send to the Commission a copy of all such notices at the time of publication. The Commission shall distribute the information to the Communications Committee as appropriate.

Article 25

Review procedures

1.   The Commission shall periodically review the functioning of this Directive and report to the European Parliament and to the Council, on the first occasion not later than three years after the date of application referred to in Article 28(1), second subparagraph. For this purpose, the Commission may request information from the Member States, which shall be supplied without undue delay.

CHAPTER V

FINAL PROVISIONS

Article 26

Repeal

The following Directives and Decisions are hereby repealed with effect from the date of application referred to in Article 28(1), second subparagraph:

-      Directive 90/387/EEC,

-      Council Decision 91/396/EEC of 29 July 1991 on the introduction of a single European emergency call number[21],

-      Council Directive 92/44/EEC of 5 June 1992 on the application of open network provision to leased lines[22],

-      Council Decision 92/264/EEC of 11 May 1992 on the introduction of a standard international telephone access code in the Community[23],

-      Directive 95/47/EC,

-      Directive 97/13/EC,

-      Directive 97/33/EC,

-      Directive 98/10/EC of the European Parliament and of the Council of 26 February 1998 on the application of open network provision (ONP) to voice telephony and on universal service for telecommunications in a competitive environment[24].

Article 27

Transitional measures

Member States shall maintain all obligations under national law referred to in Article 7 of Directive 2002/19/EC (Access Directive) and Article 16 of Directive 2002/22/EC (Universal Service Directive) until such time as a determination is made in respect of those

---

[21]   OJ L 217, 6.8.1991, p. 31.
[22]   OJ L 165, 19.6.1992, p. 27. Directive as last amended by Commission Decision 98/80/EC (OJ L 14, 20.1.1998, p. 27).
[23]   OJ L 137, 20.5.1992, p. 21.
[24]   OJ L 101, 1.4.1998, p. 24.

obligations by a national regulatory authority in accordance with Article 16 of this Directive.

Operators of fixed public telephone networks that were designated by their national regulatory authority as having significant market power in the provision of fixed public telephone networks and services under Annex I, Part 1 of Directive 97/33/EC or Directive 98/10/EC shall continue to be considered "notified operators" for the purposes of Regulation (EC) No 2887/2000 until such a time as the market analysis procedure referred to in Article 16 has been completed. Thereafter they shall cease to be considered "notified operators" for the purposes of the Regulation.

Article 28

Transposition

1. Member States shall adopt and publish the laws, regulations and administrative provisions necessary to comply with this Directive not later than 24 July 2003. They shall forthwith inform the Commission thereof.

    They shall apply those measures from 25 July 2003.

2. When Member States adopt these measures, they shall contain a reference to this Directive or be accompanied by such a reference on the occasion of their official publication. The methods of making such a reference shall be laid down by the Member States.

3. Member States shall communicate to the Commission the text of the provisions of national law which they adopt in the field governed by this Directive and of any subsequent amendments to those provisions.

Article 29

Entry into force

This Directive shall enter into force on the day of its publication in the Official Journal of the European Communities.

Article 30

Addressees

This Directive is addressed to the Member States.

Editors' Notes:

[a] OJ L 108, 24.4.2002, p. 33. Some citations in the original text have been updated to the current and complete Official Journal citation.

<u>**ANNEX I**</u>

<u>List of markets to be included in the initial Commission recommendation on relevant
product and service markets referred to in Article 15</u>

1.   *Markets referred to in Directive 2002/22/EC (Universal Service Directive)*

   Article 16 – Markets defined under the former regulatory framework, where
   obligations should be reviewed.

   The provision of connection to and use of the public telephone network at fixed
   locations.

   The provision of leased lines to end users.

2.   *Markets referred to in Directive 2002/19/EC (Access Directive)*

   Article 7 – Markets defined under the former regulatory framework, where obligations
   should be reviewed.

   Interconnection (Directive 97/33/EC)

   > call origination in the fixed public telephone network

   > call termination in the fixed public telephone network

   > transit services in the fixed public telephone network

   > call origination on public mobile telephone networks

   > call termination on public mobile telephone networks

   > leased line interconnection (interconnection of part circuits)

   Network access and special network access (Directive 97/33/EC, Directive 98/10/EC)

   > access to the fixed public telephone network, including unbundled access to the
   > local loop

   > access to public mobile telephone networks, including carrier selection

   Wholesale leased line capacity (Directive 92/44/EEC)

   > wholesale provision of leased line capacity to other suppliers of electronic
   > communications networks or services

3.   *Markets referred to in Regulation (EC) No 2887/2000*

   Services provided over unbundled (twisted metallic pair) loops.

4.   *Additional markets*

   The national market for international roaming services on public mobile telephone
   networks.

<u>Criteria to be used by national regulatory authorities in making an assessment of
joint dominance in accordance with Article 14(2), second subparagraph</u>

Two or more undertakings can be found to be in a joint dominant position within the
meaning of Article 14 if, even in the absence of structural or other links between them, they
operate in a market the structure of which is considered to be conducive to coordinated
effects. Without prejudice to the case law of the Court of Justice on joint dominance, this is
likely to be the case where the market satisfies a number of appropriate characteristics, in
particular in terms of market concentration, transparency and other characteristics
mentioned below:

- mature market,

- stagnant or moderate growth on the demand side,

- low elasticity of demand,

- homogeneous product,

- similar cost structures,

- similar market shares,

- lack of technical innovation, mature technology,

- absence of excess capacity,

- high barriers to entry,

- lack of countervailing buying power,

- lack of potential competition,

- various kinds of informal or other links between the undertakings concerned,

- retaliatory mechanisms,

- lack or reduced scope for price competition.

The above is not an exhaustive list, nor are the criteria cumulative. Rather, the list is
intended to illustrate only the sorts of evidence that could be used to support assertions
concerning the existence of joint dominance.

DIRECTIVE 2002/20/EC OF THE EUROPEAN PARLIAMENT AND OF THE COUNCIL

of 7 March 2002[a]

on the authorisation of electronic communications networks and services

(Authorisation Directive)

THE EUROPEAN PARLIAMENT AND THE COUNCIL OF THE EUROPEAN UNION,

Having regard to the Treaty establishing the European Community, and in particular Article 95 thereof,

Having regard to the proposal from the Commission[1],

Having regard to the opinion of the Economic and Social Committee[2],

Acting in accordance with the procedure laid down in Article 251 of the Treaty[3],

Whereas:

(1)   The outcome of the public consultation on the 1999 review of the regulatory framework for electronic communications, as reflected in the Commission communication of 26 April 2000, and the findings reported by the Commission in its communications on the fifth and sixth reports on the implementation of the telecommunications regulatory package, has confirmed the need for a more harmonised and less onerous market access regulation for electronic communications networks and services throughout the Community.

(2)   Convergence between different electronic communications networks and services and their technologies requires the establishment of an authorisation system covering all comparable services in a similar way regardless of the technologies used.

(3)   The objective of this Directive is to create a legal framework to ensure the freedom to provide electronic communications networks and services, subject only to the conditions laid down in this Directive and to any restrictions in conformity with Article 46(1) of the Treaty, in particular measures regarding public policy, public security and public health.

(4)   This Directive covers authorisation of all electronic communications networks and services whether they are provided to the public or not. This is important to ensure that both categories of providers may benefit from objective, transparent, non-discriminatory and proportionate rights, conditions and procedures.

(5)   This Directive only applies to the granting of rights to use radio frequencies where such use involves the provision of an electronic communications network or service, normally for remuneration. The self-use of radio terminal equipment, based on the non-exclusive use of specific radio frequencies by a user and not related to an economic activity, such as use of a citizen's band by radio amateurs, does not consist of the provision of an electronic communications network or service and is therefore not covered by this Directive. Such use is covered by the Directive 1999/5/EC of the

---

[1]   OJ C 365 E, 19.12.2000, p. 230 and OJ C 270 E, 25.9.2001, p. 182.
[2]   OJ C 123, 25.4.2001, p. 55.
[3]   Opinion of the European Parliament of 1 March 2001 (OJ C 277, 1.10.2001, p. 116), Council Common Position of 17 September 2001 (OJ C 337, 30.11.2001, p. 18) and Decision of the European Parliament of 12 December 2001 [OJ C 177 E, 25.07.2002, p. 155]. Council Decision of 14 February 2002.

European Parliament and of the Council of 9 March 1999 on radio equipment and telecommunications terminal equipment and the mutual recognition of their conformity[4].

(6) Provisions regarding the free movement of conditional access systems and the free provision of protected services based on such systems are laid down in Directive 98/84/EC of the European Parliament and of the Council of 20 November 1998 on the legal protection of services based on, or consisting of, conditional access[5]. The authorisation of such systems and services therefore does not need to be covered by this Directive.

(7) The least onerous authorisation system possible should be used to allow the provision of electronic communications networks and services in order to stimulate the development of new electronic communications services and pan-European communications networks and services and to allow service providers and consumers to benefit from the economies of scale of the single market.

(8) Those aims can be best achieved by general authorisation of all electronic communications networks and services without requiring any explicit decision or administrative act by the national regulatory authority and by limiting any procedural requirements to notification only. Where Member States require notification by providers of electronic communication networks or services when they start their activities, they may also require proof of such notification having been made by means of any legally recognised postal or electronic acknowledgement of receipt of the notification. Such acknowledgement should in any case not consist of or require an administrative act by the national regulatory authority to which the notification must be made.

(9) It is necessary to include the rights and obligations of undertakings under general authorisations explicitly in such authorisations in order to ensure a level playing field throughout the Community and to facilitate cross-border negotiation of interconnection between public communications networks.

(10) The general authorisation entitles undertakings providing electronic communications networks and services to the public to negotiate interconnection under the conditions of Directive 2002/19/EC of the European Parliament and of the Council of 7 March 2002 on access to, and interconnection of, electronic communication networks and associated facilities (Access Directive)[6]. Undertakings providing electronic communications networks and services other than to the public can negotiate interconnection on commercial terms.

(11) The granting of specific rights may continue to be necessary for the use of radio frequencies and numbers, including short codes, from the national numbering plan. Rights to numbers may also be allocated from a European numbering plan, including for example the virtual country code "3883" which has been attributed to member countries of the European Conference of Post and Telecommunications (CEPT). Those rights of use should not be restricted except where this is unavoidable in view of the scarcity of radio frequencies and the need to ensure the efficient use thereof.

(12) This Directive does not prejudice whether radio frequencies are assigned directly to providers of electronic communication networks or services or to entities that use these networks or services. Such entities may be radio or television broadcast content providers. Without prejudice to specific criteria and procedures adopted by Member

---

[4]   OJ L 91, 7.4.1999, p. 10.
[5]   OJ L 320, 28.11.1998, p. 54.
[6]   [OJ L 108, 24.4.2002, p. 7].

States to grant rights of use for radio frequencies to providers of radio or television broadcast content services, to pursue general interest objectives in conformity with Community law, the procedure for assignment of radio frequencies should in any event be objective, transparent, non-discriminatory and proportionate. In accordance with case law of the Court of Justice, any national restrictions on the rights guaranteed by Article 49 of the Treaty should be objectively justified, proportionate and not exceed what is necessary to achieve general interest objectives as defined by Member States in conformity with Community law. The responsibility for compliance with the conditions attached to the right to use a radio frequency and the relevant conditions attached to the general authorisation should in any case lie with the undertaking to whom the right of use for the radio frequency has been granted.

(13) As part of the application procedure for granting rights to use a radio frequency, Member States may verify whether the applicant will be able to comply with the conditions attached to such rights. For this purpose the applicant may be requested to submit the necessary information to prove his ability to comply with these conditions. Where such information is not provided, the application for the right to use a radio frequency may be rejected.

(14) Member States are neither obliged to grant nor prevented from granting rights to use numbers from the national numbering plan or rights to install facilities to undertakings other than providers of electronic communications networks or services.

(15) The conditions, which may be attached to the general authorisation and to the specific rights of use, should be limited to what is strictly necessary to ensure compliance with requirements and obligations under Community law and national law in accordance with Community law.

(16) In the case of electronic communications networks and services not provided to the public it is appropriate to impose fewer and lighter conditions than are justified for electronic communications networks and services provided to the public.

(17) Specific obligations which may be imposed on providers of electronic communications networks and services in accordance with Community law by virtue of their significant market power as defined in Directive 2002/21/EC of the European Parliament and of the Council of 7 March 2002 on a common regulatory framework for electronic communications networks and services (Framework Directive)[7] should be imposed separately from the general rights and obligations under the general authorisation.

(18) The general authorisation should only contain conditions which are specific to the electronic communications sector. It should not be made subject to conditions which are already applicable by virtue of other existing national law which is not specific to the electronic communications sector. Nevertheless, the national regulatory authorities may inform network operators and service providers about other legislation concerning their business, for instance through references on their websites.

(19) The requirement to publish decisions on the granting of rights to use frequencies or numbers may be fulfilled by making these decisions publicly accessible via a website.

(20) The same undertaking, for example a cable operator, can offer both an electronic communications service, such as the conveyance of television signals, and services not covered under this Directive, such as the commercialisation of an offer of sound or television broadcasting content services, and therefore additional obligations can be imposed on this undertaking in relation to its activity as a content provider or

---

[7] [OJ L 108, 24.4.2002, p. 33].

distributor, according to provisions other than those of this Directive, without prejudice to the list of conditions laid in the Annex to this Directive.

(21) When granting rights of use for radio frequencies, numbers or rights to install facilities, the relevant authorities may inform the undertakings to whom they grant such rights of the relevant conditions in the general authorisation.

(22) Where the demand for radio frequencies in a specific range exceeds their availability, appropriate and transparent procedures should be followed for the assignment of such frequencies in order to avoid any discrimination and optimise use of those scarce resources.

(23) National regulatory authorities should ensure, in establishing criteria for competitive or comparative selection procedures, that the objectives in Article 8 of Directive 2002/21/EC (Framework Directive) are met. It would therefore not be contrary to this Directive if the application of objective, non-discriminatory and proportionate selection criteria to promote the development of competition would have the effect of excluding certain undertakings from a competitive or comparative selection procedure for a particular radio frequency.

(24) Where the harmonised assignment of radio frequencies to particular undertakings has been agreed at European level, Member States should strictly implement such agreements in the granting of rights of use of radio frequencies from the national frequency usage plan.

(25) Providers of electronic communications networks and services may need a confirmation of their rights under the general authorisation with respect to interconnection and rights of way, in particular to facilitate negotiations with other, regional or local, levels of government or with service providers in other Member States. For this purpose the national regulatory authorities should provide declarations to undertakings either upon request or alternatively as an automatic response to a notification under the general authorisation. Such declarations should not by themselves constitute entitlements to rights nor should any rights under the general authorisation or rights of use or the exercise of such rights depend upon a declaration.

(26) Where undertakings find that their applications for rights to install facilities have not been dealt with in accordance with the principles set out in Directive 2002/21/EC (Framework Directive) or where such decisions are unduly delayed, they should have the right to appeal against decisions or delays in such decisions in accordance with that Directive.

(27) The penalties for non-compliance with conditions under the general authorisation should be commensurate with the infringement. Save in exceptional circumstances, it would not be proportionate to suspend or withdraw the right to provide electronic communications services or the right to use radio frequencies or numbers where an undertaking did not comply with one or more of the conditions under the general authorisation. This is without prejudice to urgent measures which the relevant authorities of the Member States may need to take in case of serious threats to public safety, security or health or to economic and operational interests of other undertakings. This Directive should also be without prejudice to any claims between undertakings for compensation for damages under national law.

(28) Subjecting service providers to reporting and information obligations can be cumbersome, both for the undertaking and for the national regulatory authority concerned. Such obligations should therefore be proportionate, objectively justified and limited to what is strictly necessary. It is not necessary to require systematic and regular proof of compliance with all conditions under the general authorisation or

attached to rights of use. Undertakings have a right to know the purposes for which the information they should provide will be used. The provision of information should not be a condition for market access. For statistical purposes a notification may be required from providers of electronic communication networks or services when they cease activities.

(29) This Directive should be without prejudice to Member States' obligations to provide any information necessary for the defence of Community interests within the context of international agreements. This Directive should also be without prejudice to any reporting obligations under legislation which is not specific to the electronic communications sector such as competition law.

(30) Administrative charges may be imposed on providers of electronic communications services in order to finance the activities of the national regulatory authority in managing the authorisation system and for the granting of rights of use. Such charges should be limited to cover the actual administrative costs for those activities. For this purpose transparency should be created in the income and expenditure of national regulatory authorities by means of annual reporting about the total sum of charges collected and the administrative costs incurred. This will allow undertakings to verify that administrative costs and charges are in balance.

(31) Systems for administrative charges should not distort competition or create barriers for entry into the market. With a general authorisation system it will no longer be possible to attribute administrative costs and hence charges to individual undertakings except for the granting of rights to use numbers, radio frequencies and for rights to install facilities. Any applicable administrative charges should be in line with the principles of a general authorisation system. An example of a fair, simple and transparent alternative for these charge attribution criteria could be a turnover related distribution key. Where administrative charges are very low, flat rate charges, or charges combining a flat rate basis with a turnover related element could also be appropriate.

(32) In addition to administrative charges, usage fees may be levied for the use of radio frequencies and numbers as an instrument to ensure the optimal use of such resources. Such fees should not hinder the development of innovative services and competition in the market. This Directive is without prejudice to the purpose for which fees for rights of use are employed. Such fees may for instance be used to finance activities of national regulatory authorities that cannot be covered by administrative charges. Where, in the case of competitive or comparative selection procedures, fees for rights of use for radio frequencies consist entirely or partly of a one-off amount, payment arrangements should ensure that such fees do not in practice lead to selection on the basis of criteria unrelated to the objective of ensuring optimal use of radio frequencies. The Commission may publish on a regular basis benchmark studies with regard to best practices for the assignment of radio frequencies, the assignment of numbers or the granting of rights of way.

(33) Member States may need to amend rights, conditions, procedures, charges and fees relating to general authorisations and rights of use where this is objectively justified. Such changes should be duly notified to all interested parties in good time, giving them adequate opportunity to express their views on any such amendments.

(34) The objective of transparency requires that service providers, consumers and other interested parties have easy access to any information regarding rights, conditions, procedures, charges, fees and decisions concerning the provision of electronic communications services, rights of use of radio frequencies and numbers, rights to install facilities, national frequency usage plans and national numbering plans. The national regulatory authorities have an important task in providing such information and keeping it up to date. Where such rights are administered by other levels of

government the national regulatory authorities should endeavour to create a user-friendly instrument for access to information regarding such rights.

(35) The proper functioning of the single market on the basis of the national authorisation regimes under this Directive should be monitored by the Commission.

(36) In order to arrive at a single date of application of all elements of the new regulatory framework for the electronic communications sector, it is important that the process of national transposition of this Directive and of alignment of the existing licences with the new rules take place in parallel. However, in specific cases where the replacement of authorisations existing on the date of entry into force of this Directive by the general authorisation and the individual rights of use in accordance with this Directive would lead to an increase in the obligations for service providers operating under an existing authorisation or to a reduction of their rights, Member States may avail themselves of an additional nine months after the date of application of this Directive for alignment of such licences, unless this would have a negative effect on the rights and obligations of other undertakings.

(37) There may be circumstances under which the abolition of an authorisation condition regarding access to electronic communications networks would create serious hardship for one or more undertakings that have benefited from the condition. In such cases further transitional arrangements may be granted by the Commission, upon request by a Member State.

(38) Since the objectives of the proposed action, namely the harmonisation and simplification of electronic communications rules and conditions for the authorisation of networks and services cannot be sufficiently achieved by the Member States and can therefore, by reason of the scale and effects of the action, be better achieved at Community level, the Community may adopt measures in accordance with the principle of subsidiarity as set out in Article 5 of the Treaty. In accordance with the principle of proportionality, as set out in that Article, this Directive does not go beyond what is necessary for those objectives,

HAVE ADOPTED THIS DIRECTIVE:

Article 1

Objective and scope

1.   The aim of this Directive is to implement an internal market in electronic communications networks and services through the harmonisation and simplification of authorisation rules and conditions in order to facilitate their provision throughout the Community.

2.   This Directive shall apply to authorisations for the provision of electronic communications networks and services.

Article 2

Definitions

1.   For the purposes of this Directive, the definitions set out in Article 2 of Directive 2002/21/EC (Framework Directive) shall apply.

2.   The following definitions shall also apply:

(a)   "general authorisation" means a legal framework established by the Member State ensuring rights for the provision of electronic communications networks or services and laying down sector specific obligations that may apply to all or to specific types of electronic communications networks and services, in accordance with this Directive;

(b)   "harmful interference" means interference which endangers the functioning of a radionavigation service or of other safety services or which otherwise seriously degrades, obstructs or repeatedly interrupts a radiocommunications service operating in accordance with the applicable Community or national regulations.

Article 3

General authorisation of electronic communications networks and services

1.   Member States shall ensure the freedom to provide electronic communications networks and services, subject to the conditions set out in this Directive. To this end, Member States shall not prevent an undertaking from providing electronic communications networks or services, except where this is necessary for the reasons set out in Article 46(1) of the Treaty.

2.   The provision of electronic communications networks or the provision of electronic communications services may, without prejudice to the specific obligations referred to in Article 6(2) or rights of use referred to in Article 5, only be subject to a general authorisation. The undertaking concerned may be required to submit a notification but may not be required to obtain an explicit decision or any other administrative act by the national regulatory authority before exercising the rights stemming from the authorisation. Upon notification, when required, an undertaking may begin activity, where necessary subject to the provisions on rights of use in Articles 5, 6 and 7.

3.   The notification referred to in paragraph 2 shall not entail more than a declaration by a legal or natural person to the national regulatory authority of the intention to commence the provision of electronic communication networks or services and the submission of the minimal information which is required to allow the national regulatory authority to keep a register or list of providers of electronic communications networks and services. This information must be limited to what is necessary for the identification of the provider, such as company registration numbers, and the provider's contact persons, the provider's address, a short description of the network or service, and an estimated date for starting the activity.

Article 4

Minimum list of rights derived from the general authorisation

1.   Undertakings authorised pursuant to Article 3, shall have the right to:

(a)   provide electronic communications networks and services;

(b)   have their application for the necessary rights to install facilities considered in accordance with Article 11 of Directive 2002/21/EC (Framework Directive).

2.   When such undertakings provide electronic communications networks or services to the public the general authorisation shall also give them the right to:

(a)   negotiate interconnection with and where applicable obtain access to or interconnection from other providers of publicly available communications networks and services covered by a general authorisation anywhere in the

Community under the conditions of and in accordance with Directive 2002/19/EC (Access Directive);

(b) be given an opportunity to be designated to provide different elements of a universal service and/or to cover different parts of the national territory in accordance with Directive 2002/22/EC of the European Parliament and of the Council of 7 March 2002 on universal service and users' rights relating to electronic communications networks and services (Universal Service Directive)[8].

Article 5

Rights of use for radio frequencies and numbers

1. Member States shall, where possible, in particular where the risk of harmful interference is negligible, not make the use of radio frequencies subject to the grant of individual rights of use but shall include the conditions for usage of such radio frequencies in the general authorisation.

2. Where it is necessary to grant individual rights of use for radio frequencies and numbers, Member States shall grant such rights, upon request, to any undertaking providing or using networks or services under the general authorisation, subject to the provisions of Articles 6, 7 and 11(1)(c) of this Directive and any other rules ensuring the efficient use of those resources in accordance with Directive 2002/21/EC (Framework Directive).

   Without prejudice to specific criteria and procedures adopted by Member States to grant rights of use of radio frequencies to providers of radio or television broadcast content services with a view to pursuing general interest objectives in conformity with Community law, such rights of use shall be granted through open, transparent and non-discriminatory procedures. When granting rights of use, Member States shall specify whether those rights can be transferred at the initiative of the right holder, and under which conditions, in the case of radio frequencies, in accordance with Article 9 of Directive 2002/21/EC (Framework Directive). Where Member States grant rights of use for a limited period of time, the duration shall be appropriate for the service concerned.

3. Decisions on rights of use shall be taken, communicated and made public as soon as possible after receipt of the complete application by the national regulatory authority, within three weeks in the case of numbers that have been allocated for specific purposes within the national numbering plan and within six weeks in the case of radio frequencies that have been allocated for specific purposes within the national frequency plan. The latter time limit shall be without prejudice to any applicable international agreements relating to the use of radio frequencies or of orbital positions.

4. Where it has been decided, after consultation with interested parties in accordance with Article 6 of Directive 2002/21/EC (Framework Directive), that rights for use of numbers of exceptional economic value are to be granted through competitive or comparative selection procedures, Member States may extend the maximum period of three weeks by up to three weeks.

   With regard to competitive or comparative selection procedures for radio frequencies Article 7 shall apply.

---

[8] [OJ L 108, 24.4.2002, p. 51].

5.   Member States shall not limit the number of rights of use to be granted except where this is necessary to ensure the efficient use of radio frequencies in accordance with Article 7.

Article 6

Conditions attached to the general authorisation and to the rights of use for radio frequencies and for numbers, and specific obligations

1.   The general authorisation for the provision of electronic communications networks or services and the rights of use for radio frequencies and rights of use for numbers may be subject only to the conditions listed respectively in parts A, B and C of the Annex. Such conditions shall be objectively justified in relation to the network or service concerned, non-discriminatory, proportionate and transparent.

2.   Specific obligations which may be imposed on providers of electronic communications networks and services under Articles 5(1), 5(2), 6 and 8 of Directive 2002/19/EC (Access Directive) and Articles 16, 17, 18 and 19 of Directive 2002/22/EC (Universal Service Directive) or on those designated to provide universal service under the said Directive shall be legally separate from the rights and obligations under the general authorisation. In order to achieve transparency for undertakings, the criteria and procedures for imposing such specific obligations on individual undertakings shall be referred to in the general authorisation.

3.   The general authorisation shall only contain conditions which are specific for that sector and are set out in Part A of the Annex and shall not duplicate conditions which are applicable to undertakings by virtue of other national legislation.

4.   Member States shall not duplicate the conditions of the general authorisation where they grant the right of use for radio frequencies or numbers.

Article 7

Procedure for limiting the number of rights of use to be granted for radio frequencies

1.   Where a Member State is considering whether to limit the number of rights of use to be granted for radio frequencies, it shall inter alia:

    (a)   give due weight to the need to maximise benefits for users and to facilitate the development of competition;

    (b)   give all interested parties, including users and consumers, the opportunity to express their views on any limitation in accordance with Article 6 of Directive 2002/21/EC (Framework Directive);

    (c)   publish any decision to limit the granting of rights of use, stating the reasons therefor;

    (d)   after having determined the procedure, invite applications for rights of use; and

    (e)   review the limitation at reasonable intervals or at the reasonable request of affected undertakings.

2.   Where a Member State concludes that further rights of use for radio frequencies can be granted, it shall publish that conclusion and invite applications for such rights.

3.   Where the granting of rights of use for radio frequencies needs to be limited, Member States shall grant such rights on the basis of selection criteria which must be objective, transparent, non-discriminatory and proportionate. Any such selection criteria must give due weight to the achievement of the objectives of Article 8 of Directive 2002/21/EC (Framework Directive).

4.   Where competitive or comparative selection procedures are to be used, Member States may extend the maximum period of six weeks referred to in Article 5(3) for as long as necessary to ensure that such procedures are fair, reasonable, open and transparent to all interested parties, but by no longer than eight months.

   These time limits shall be without prejudice to any applicable international agreements relating to the use of radio frequencies and satellite coordination.

5.   This Article is without prejudice to the transfer of rights of use for radio frequencies in accordance with Article 9 of Directive 2002/21/EC (Framework Directive).

Article 8

Harmonised assignment of radio frequencies

Where the usage of radio frequencies has been harmonised, access conditions and procedures have been agreed, and undertakings to which the radio frequencies shall be assigned have been selected in accordance with international agreements and Community rules, Member States shall grant the right of use for such radio frequencies in accordance therewith. Provided that all national conditions attached to the right to use the radio frequencies concerned have been satisfied in the case of a common selection procedure, Member States shall not impose any further conditions, additional criteria or procedures which would restrict, alter or delay the correct implementation of the common assignment of such radio frequencies.

Article 9

Declarations to facilitate the exercise of rights to install facilities and rights of interconnection

At the request of an undertaking, national regulatory authorities shall, within one week, issue standardised declarations, confirming, where applicable, that the undertaking has submitted a notification under Article 3(2) and detailing under what circumstances any undertaking providing electronic communications networks or services under the general authorisation has the right to apply for rights to install facilities, negotiate interconnection, and/or obtain access or interconnection in order to facilitate the exercise of those rights for instance at other levels of government or in relation to other undertakings. Where appropriate such declarations may also be issued as an automatic reply following the notification referred to in Article 3(2).

Article 10

Compliance with the conditions of the general authorisation or of rights of use and with specific obligations

1.   National regulatory authorities may require undertakings providing electronic communications networks or services covered by the general authorisation or enjoying rights of use for radio frequencies or numbers to provide information necessary to verify compliance with the conditions of the general authorisation or of rights of use or with the specific obligations referred to in Article 6(2), in accordance with Article 11.

2. Where a national regulatory authority finds that an undertaking does not comply with one or more of the conditions of the general authorisation, or of rights of use or with the specific obligations referred to in Article 6(2), it shall notify the undertaking of those findings and give the undertaking a reasonable opportunity to state its views or remedy any breaches within:

    -   one month after notification, or

    -   a shorter period agreed by the undertaking or stipulated by the national regulatory authority in case of repeated breaches, or

    -   a longer period decided by the national regulatory authority.

3. If the undertaking concerned does not remedy the breaches within the period as referred to in paragraph 2, the relevant authority shall take appropriate and proportionate measures aimed at ensuring compliance. In this regard, Member States may empower the relevant authorities to impose financial penalties where appropriate. The measures and the reasons on which they are based shall be communicated to the undertaking concerned within one week of their adoption and shall stipulate a reasonable period for the undertaking to comply with the measure.

4. Notwithstanding the provisions of paragraphs 2 and 3, Member States may empower the relevant authority to impose financial penalties where appropriate on undertakings for failure to provide information in accordance with obligations imposed under Article 11(1)(a) or (b) of this Directive or Article 9 of Directive 2002/19/EC (Access Directive) within a reasonable period stipulated by the national regulatory authority.

5. In cases of serious and repeated breaches of the conditions of the general authorisation, the rights of use or specific obligations referred to in Article 6(2), where measures aimed at ensuring compliance as referred to in paragraph 3 of this Article have failed, national regulatory authorities may prevent an undertaking from continuing to provide electronic communications networks or services or suspend or withdraw rights of use.

6. Irrespective of the provisions of paragraphs 2, 3 and 5, where the relevant authority has evidence of a breach of the conditions of the general authorisation, rights of use or specific obligations referred to in Article 6(2) that represents an immediate and serious threat to public safety, public security or public health or will create serious economic or operational problems for other providers or users of electronic communications networks or services, it may take urgent interim measures to remedy the situation in advance of reaching a final decision. The undertaking concerned shall thereafter be given a reasonable opportunity to state its view and propose any remedies. Where appropriate, the relevant authority may confirm the interim measures.

7. Undertakings shall have the right to appeal against measures taken under this Article in accordance with the procedure referred to in Article 4 of Directive 2002/21/EC (Framework Directive).

Article 11

**Information required under the general authorisation,
for rights of use and for the specific obligations**

1. Without prejudice to information and reporting obligations under national legislation other than the general authorisation, national regulatory authorities may only require undertakings to provide information under the general authorisation, for rights of use

or the specific obligations referred to in Article 6(2) that is proportionate and objectively justified for:

(a) systematic or case-by-case verification of compliance with conditions 1 and 2 of Part A, condition 6 of Part B and condition 7 of Part C of the Annex and of compliance with obligations as referred to in Article 6(2);

(b) case-by-case verification of compliance with conditions as set out in the Annex where a complaint has been received or where the national regulatory authority has other reasons to believe that a condition is not complied with or in case of an investigation by the national regulatory authority on its own initiative;

(c) procedures for and assessment of requests for granting rights of use;

(d) publication of comparative overviews of quality and price of services for the benefit of consumers;

(e) clearly defined statistical purposes;

(f) market analysis for the purposes of Directive 2002/19/EC (Access Directive) or Directive 2002/22/EC (Universal Service Directive).

The information referred to in points (a), (b), (d), (e) and (f) of the first subparagraph may not be required prior to or as a condition for market access.

2. Where national regulatory authorities require undertakings to provide information as referred to in paragraph 1, they shall inform them of the specific purpose for which this information is to be used.

Article 12

Administrative charges

1. Any administrative charges imposed on undertakings providing a service or a network under the general authorisation or to whom a right of use has been granted shall:

(a) in total, cover only the administrative costs which will be incurred in the management, control and enforcement of the general authorisation scheme and of rights of use and of specific obligations as referred to in Article 6(2), which may include costs for international cooperation, harmonisation and standardisation, market analysis, monitoring compliance and other market control, as well as regulatory work involving preparation and enforcement of secondary legislation and administrative decisions, such as decisions on access and interconnection; and

(b) be imposed upon the individual undertakings in an objective, transparent and proportionate manner which minimises additional administrative costs and attendant charges.

2. Where national regulatory authorities impose administrative charges, they shall publish a yearly overview of their administrative costs and of the total sum of the charges collected. In the light of the difference between the total sum of the charges and the administrative costs, appropriate adjustments shall be made.

Article 13

Fees for rights of use and rights to install facilities

Member States may allow the relevant authority to impose fees for the rights of use for radio frequencies or numbers or rights to install facilities on, over or under public or private property which reflect the need to ensure the optimal use of these resources. Member States shall ensure that such fees shall be objectively justified, transparent, non-discriminatory and proportionate in relation to their intended purpose and shall take into account the objectives in Article 8 of Directive 2002/21/EC (Framework Directive).

Article 14

Amendment of rights and obligations

1. Member States shall ensure that the rights, conditions and procedures concerning general authorisations and rights of use or rights to install facilities may only be amended in objectively justified cases and in a proportionate manner. Notice shall be given in an appropriate manner of the intention to make such amendments and interested parties, including users and consumers, shall be allowed a sufficient period of time to express their views on the proposed amendments, which shall be no less than four weeks except in exceptional circumstances.

2. Member States shall not restrict or withdraw rights to install facilities before expiry of the period for which they were granted except where justified and where applicable in conformity with relevant national provisions regarding compensation for withdrawal of rights.

Article 15

Publication of information

1. Member States shall ensure that all relevant information on rights, conditions, procedures, charges, fees and decisions concerning general authorisations and rights of use is published and kept up to date in an appropriate manner so as to provide easy access to that information for all interested parties.

2. Where information as referred to in paragraph 1 is held at different levels of government, in particular information regarding procedures and conditions on rights to install facilities, the national regulatory authority shall make all reasonable efforts, bearing in mind the costs involved, to create a user-friendly overview of all such information, including information on the relevant levels of government and the responsible authorities, in order to facilitate applications for rights to install facilities.

Article 16

Review procedures

The Commission shall periodically review the functioning of the national authorisation systems and the development of cross-border service provision within the Community and report to the European Parliament and to the Council on the first occasion not later than three years after the date of application of this Directive referred to in Article 18(1), second subparagraph. For this purpose, the Commission may request from the Member States information, which shall be supplied without undue delay.

Article 17

Existing authorisations

1. Member States shall bring authorisations already in existence on the date of entry into force of this Directive into line with the provisions of this Directive by at the latest the date of application referred to in Article 18(1), second subparagraph.

2. Where application of paragraph 1 results in a reduction of the rights or an extension of the obligations under authorisations already in existence, Member States may extend the validity of those rights and obligations until at the latest nine months after the date of application referred to in Article 18(1), second subparagraph, provided that the rights of other undertakings under Community law are not affected thereby. Member States shall notify such extensions to the Commission and state the reasons therefor.

3. Where the Member State concerned can prove that the abolition of an authorisation condition regarding access to electronic communications networks, which was in force before the date of entry into force of this Directive, creates excessive difficulties for undertakings that have benefited from mandated access to another network, and where it is not possible for these undertakings to negotiate new agreements on reasonable commercial terms before the date of application referred to in Article 18(1), second subparagraph, Member States may request a temporary prolongation of the relevant condition(s). Such requests shall be submitted by the date of application referred to in Article 18(1), second subparagraph, at the latest, and shall specify the condition(s) and period for which the temporary prolongation is requested.

   The Member State shall inform the Commission of the reasons for requesting a prolongation. The Commission shall consider such a request, taking into account the particular situation in that Member State and of the undertaking(s) concerned, and the need to ensure a coherent regulatory environment at a Community level. It shall take a decision on whether to grant or reject the request, and where it decides to grant the request, on the scope and duration of the prolongation to be granted. The Commission shall communicate its decision to the Member State concerned within six months after receipt of the application for a prolongation. Such decisions shall be published in the Official Journal of the European Communities.

Article 18

Transposition

1. Member States shall adopt and publish the laws, regulations and administrative provisions necessary to comply with this Directive by 24 July 2003 at the latest. They shall forthwith inform the Commission thereof.

   They shall apply those measures from 25 July 2003.

   When Member States adopt these measures, they shall contain a reference to this Directive or be accompanied by such reference on the occasion of their official publication. The methods of making such reference shall be laid down by Member States.

2. Member States shall communicate to the Commission the text of the provisions of national law which they adopt in the field governed by this Directive and of any subsequent amendments to those provisions.

Article 19

Entry into force

This Directive shall enter into force on the day of its publication in the Official Journal of the European Communities.

Article 20

Addressees

This Directive is addressed to the Member States.

Editors' Notes:

[a] OJ L 108, 24.4.2002, p. 21. Some citations in the original text have been updated to the current and complete Official Journal citation.

ANNEX

The conditions listed in this Annex provide the maximum list of conditions which may be attached to general authorisations (Part A), rights to use radio frequencies (Part B) and rights to use numbers (Part C) as referred to in Article 6(1) and Article 11(1)(a).

A.   **Conditions which may be attached to a general authorisation**

1.   Financial contributions to the funding of universal service in conformity with Directive 2002/22/EC (Universal Service Directive).

2.   Administrative charges in accordance with Article 12 of this Directive.

3.   Interoperability of services and interconnection of networks in conformity with Directive 2002/19/EC (Access Directive).

4.   Accessibility of numbers from the national numbering plan to end-users including conditions in conformity with Directive 2002/22/EC (Universal Service Directive).

5.   Environmental and town and country planning requirements, as well as requirements and conditions linked to the granting of access to or use of public or private land and conditions linked to co-location and facility sharing in conformity with Directive 2002/21/EC[a] (Framework Directive) and including, where applicable, any financial or technical guarantees necessary to ensure the proper execution of infrastructure works.

6.   "Must carry" obligations in conformity with Directive 2002/22/EC (Universal Service Directive).

7.   Personal data and privacy protection specific to the electronic communications sector in conformity with Directive 97/66/EC of the European Parliament and of the Council of 15 December 1997 concerning the processing of personal data and the protection of privacy in the telecommunications sector[1].

8.   Consumer protection rules specific to the electronic communications sector including conditions in conformity with Directive 2002/22/EC (Universal Service Directive).

9.   Restrictions in relation to the transmission of illegal content, in accordance with Directive 2000/31/EC of the European Parliament and of the Council of 8 June 2000 on certain legal aspects of information society services, in particular electronic commerce, in the internal market[2] and restrictions in relation to the transmission of harmful content in accordance with Article 2a(2) of Council Directive 89/552/EEC of 3 October 1989 on the coordination of certain provisions laid down by law, regulation or administrative action in Member States concerning the pursuit of television broadcasting activities[3].

10.   Information to be provided under a notification procedure in accordance with Article 3(3) of this Directive and for other purposes as included in Article 11 of this Directive.

---

[1]   OJ L 24, 30.1.1998, p. 1.
[2]   OJ L 178, 17.7.2000, p. 1.
[3]   OJ L 298, 17.10.1989, p. 23. Directive as amended by Directive 97/36/EC of the European Parliament and of the Council (OJ L 202, 30.7.1997, p. 60).

11. Enabling of legal interception by competent national authorities in conformity with Directive 97/66/EC and Directive 95/46/EC of the European Parliament and of the Council of 24 October 1995 on the protection of individuals with regard to the processing of personal data and on the free movement of such data[4].

12. Terms of use during major disasters to ensure communications between emergency services and authorities and broadcasts to the general public.

13. Measures regarding the limitation of exposure of the general public to electromagnetic fields caused by electronic communications networks in accordance with Community law.

14. Access obligations other than those provided for in Article 6(2) of this Directive applying to undertakings providing electronic communications networks or services, in conformity with Directive 2002/19/EC (Access Directive).

15. Maintenance of the integrity of public communications networks in accordance with Directive 2002/19/EC (Access Directive) and Directive 2002/22/EC (Universal Service Directive) including by conditions to prevent electromagnetic interference between electronic communications networks and/or services in accordance with Council Directive 89/336/EEC of 3 May 1989 on the approximation of the laws of the Member States relating to electromagnetic compatibility[5].

16. Security of public networks against unauthorised access according to Directive 97/66/EC.

17. Conditions for the use of radio frequencies, in conformity with Article 7(2) of Directive 1999/5/EC, where such use is not made subject to the granting of individual rights of use in accordance with Article 5(1) of this Directive.

18. Measures designed to ensure compliance with the standards and/or specifications referred to in Article 17 of Directive 2002/21/EC (Framework Directive).

B. **Conditions which may be attached to rights of use for radio frequencies**

1. Designation of service or type of network or technology for which the rights of use for the frequency has been granted, including, where applicable, the exclusive use of a frequency for the transmission of specific content or specific audiovisual services.

2. Effective and efficient use of frequencies in conformity with Directive 2002/21/EC (Framework Directive), including, where appropriate, coverage requirements.

3. Technical and operational conditions necessary for the avoidance of harmful interference and for the limitation of exposure of the general public to electromagnetic fields, where such conditions are different from those included in the general authorisation.

4. Maximum duration in conformity with Article 5 of this Directive, subject to any changes in the national frequency plan.

---

[4] OJ L 281, 23.11.1995, p. 31.
[5] OJ L 139, 23.5.1989, p. 19. Directive as last amended by Directive 93/68/EEC (OJ L 220, 30.8.1993, p. 1).

5. Transfer of rights at the initiative of the right holder and conditions for such transfer in conformity with Directive 2002/21/EC (Framework Directive).

6. Usage fees in accordance with Article 13 of this Directive.

7. Any commitments which the undertaking obtaining the usage right has made in the course of a competitive or comparative selection procedure.

8. Obligations under relevant international agreements relating to the use of frequencies.

C. **Conditions which may be attached to rights of use for numbers**

1. Designation of service for which the number shall be used, including any requirements linked to the provision of that service.

2. Effective and efficient use of numbers in conformity with Directive 2002/21/EC (Framework Directive).

3. Number portability requirements in conformity with Directive 2002/22/EC (Universal Service Directive).

4. Obligation to provide public directory subscriber information for the purposes of Articles 5 and 25 of Directive 2002/22/EC (Universal Service Directive).

5. Maximum duration in conformity with Article 5 of this Directive, subject to any changes in the national numbering plan.

6. Transfer of rights at the initiative of the right holder and conditions for such transfer in conformity with Directive 2002/21/EC (Framework Directive).

7. Usage fees in accordance with Article 13 of this Directive.

8. Any commitments which the undertaking obtaining the usage right has made in the course of a competitive or comparative selection procedure.

9. Obligations under relevant international agreements relating to the use of numbers.

Editors' Notes:

[a] A numbering error in the Official Journal has been corrected.

DIRECTIVE 2002/19/EC OF THE EUROPEAN PARLIAMENT AND OF THE COUNCIL

of 7 March 2002[a]

on access to, and interconnection of, electronic communications
networks and associated facilities

(Access Directive)

THE EUROPEAN PARLIAMENT AND THE COUNCIL OF THE EUROPEAN UNION,

Having regard to the Treaty establishing the European Community, and in particular
Article 95 thereof,

Having regard to the proposal from the Commission[1],

Having regard to the opinion of the Economic and Social Committee[2],

Acting in accordance with the procedure laid down in Article 251 of the Treaty[3],

Whereas:

(1) Directive 2002/21/EC of the European Parliament and of the Council of 7 March 2002
on a common regulatory framework for electronic communications networks and
services (Framework Directive)[4] lays down the objectives of a regulatory framework
to cover electronic communications networks and services in the Community,
including fixed and mobile telecommunications networks, cable television networks,
networks used for terrestrial broadcasting, satellite networks and Internet networks,
whether used for voice, fax, data or images. Such networks may have been authorised
by Member States under Directive 2002/20/EC of the European Parliament and of the
Council of 7 March 2002 on the authorisation of electronic communications networks
and services (Authorisation Directive)[5] or have been authorised under previous
regulatory measures. The provisions of this Directive apply to those networks that are
used for the provision of publicly available electronic communications services. This
Directive covers access and interconnection arrangements between service suppliers.
Non-public networks do not have obligations under this Directive except where, in
benefiting from access to public networks, they may be subject to conditions laid
down by Member States.

(2) Services providing content such as the offer for sale of a package of sound or
television broadcasting content are not covered by the common regulatory framework
for electronic communications networks and services.

(3) The term "access" has a wide range of meanings, and it is therefore necessary to
define precisely how that term is used in this Directive, without prejudice to how it
may be used in other Community measures. An operator may own the underlying
network or facilities or may rent some or all of them.

---

[1] OJ C 365 E, 19.12.2000, p. 215 and OJ C 270 E, 25.9.2001, p. 161.
[2] OJ C 123, 25.4.2001, p. 50.
[3] Opinion of the European Parliament of 1 March 2001 (OJ C 277, 1.10.2001, p. 72), Council Common
Position of 17 September 2001 (OJ C 337, 30.11.2001, p. 1) and Decision of the European Parliament of 12
December 2001 [OJ C 177 E, 25.07.2002, p. 152]. Council Decision of 14 February 2002.
[4] [OJ L 108, 24.4.2002, p. 33].
[5] [OJ L 108, 24.4.2002, p. 21].

(4) Directive 95/47/EC of the European Parliament and of the Council of 24 October 1995 on the use of standards for the transmission of television signals[6] did not mandate any specific digital television transmission system or service requirement, and this opened up an opportunity for the market actors to take the initiative and develop suitable systems. Through the Digital Video Broadcasting Group, European market actors have developed a family of television transmission systems that have been adopted by broadcasters throughout the world. These transmissions systems have been standardised by the European Telecommunications Standards Institute (ETSI) and have become International Telecommunication Union recommendations. In relation to wide-screen digital television, the 16:9 aspect ratio is the reference format for wide-format television services and programmes, and is now established in Member States' markets as a result of Council Decision 93/424/EEC of 22 July 1993 on an action plan for the introduction of advanced television services in Europe[7].

(5) In an open and competitive market, there should be no restrictions that prevent undertakings from negotiating access and interconnection arrangements between themselves, in particular on cross-border agreements, subject to the competition rules of the Treaty. In the context of achieving a more efficient, truly pan-European market, with effective competition, more choice and competitive services to consumers, undertakings which receive requests for access or interconnection should in principle conclude such agreements on a commercial basis, and negotiate in good faith.

(6) In markets where there continue to be large differences in negotiating power between undertakings, and where some undertakings rely on infrastructure provided by others for delivery of their services, it is appropriate to establish a framework to ensure that the market functions effectively. National regulatory authorities should have the power to secure, where commercial negotiation fails, adequate access and interconnection and interoperability of services in the interest of end-users. In particular, they may ensure end-to-end connectivity by imposing proportionate obligations on undertakings that control access to end-users. Control of means of access may entail ownership or control of the physical link to the end-user (either fixed or mobile), and/or the ability to change or withdraw the national number or numbers needed to access an end-user's network termination point. This would be the case for example if network operators were to restrict unreasonably end-user choice for access to Internet portals and services.

(7) National legal or administrative measures that link the terms and conditions for access or interconnection to the activities of the party seeking interconnection, and specifically to the degree of its investment in network infrastructure, and not to the interconnection or access services provided, may cause market distortion and may therefore not be compatible with competition rules.

(8) Network operators who control access to their own customers do so on the basis of unique numbers or addresses from a published numbering or addressing range. Other network operators need to be able to deliver traffic to those customers, and so need to be able to interconnect directly or indirectly to each other. The existing rights and obligations to negotiate interconnection should therefore be maintained. It is also appropriate to maintain the obligations formerly laid down in Directive 95/47/EC requiring fully digital electronic communications networks used for the distribution of television services and open to the public to be capable of distributing wide-screen television services and programmes, so that users are able to receive such programmes in the format in which they were transmitted.

---

[6] OJ L 281, 23.11.1995, p. 51.
[7] OJ L 196, 5.8.1993, p. 48.

(9)   Interoperability is of benefit to end-users and is an important aim of this regulatory framework.   Encouraging interoperability is one of the objectives for national regulatory authorities as set out in this framework, which also provides for the Commission to publish a list of standards and/or specifications covering the provision of services, technical interfaces and/or network functions, as the basis for encouraging harmonisation in electronic communications.   Member States should encourage the use of published standards and/or specifications to the extent strictly necessary to ensure interoperability of services and to improve freedom of choice for users.

(10)   Competition rules alone may not be sufficient to ensure cultural diversity and media pluralism in the area of digital television.   Directive 95/47/EC provided an initial regulatory framework for the nascent digital television industry which should be maintained, including in particular the obligation to provide conditional access on fair, reasonable and non-discriminatory terms, in order to make sure that a wide variety of programming and services is available.   Technological and market developments make it necessary to review these obligations on a regular basis, either by a Member State for its national market or the Commission for the Community, in particular to determine whether there is justification for extending obligations to new gateways, such as electronic programme guides (EPGs) and application program interfaces (APIs), to the extent that is necessary to ensure accessibility for end-users to specified digital broadcasting services.   Member States may specify the digital broadcasting services to which access by end-users must be ensured by any legislative, regulatory or administrative means that they deem necessary.

(11)   Member States may also permit their national regulatory authority to review obligations in relation to conditional access to digital broadcasting services in order to assess through a market analysis whether to withdraw or amend conditions for operators that do not have significant market power on the relevant market.   Such withdrawal or amendment should not adversely affect access for end-users to such services or the prospects for effective competition.

(12)   In order to ensure continuity of existing agreements and to avoid a legal vacuum, it is necessary to ensure that obligations for access and interconnection imposed under Articles 4, 6, 7, 8, 11, 12, and 14 of Directive 97/33/EC of the European Parliament and of the Council of 30 June 1997 on interconnection in telecommunications with regard to ensuring universal service and interoperability through application of the principles of open network provision (ONP)[8], obligations on special access imposed under Article 16 of Directive 98/10/EC of the European Parliament and of the Council of 26 February 1998 on the application of open network provision (ONP) to voice telephony and on universal service for telecommunications in a competitive environment[9], and obligations concerning the provision of leased line transmission capacity under Council Directive 92/44/EEC of 5 June 1992 on the application of open network provision to leased lines[10], are initially carried over into the new regulatory framework, but are subject to immediate review in the light of prevailing market conditions.   Such a review should also extend to those organisations covered by Regulation (EC) No 2887/2000 of the European Parliament and of the Council of 18 December 2000 on unbundled access to the local loop[11].

(13)   The review should be carried out using an economic market analysis based on competition law methodology.   The aim is to reduce ex ante sector specific rules progressively as competition in the market develops.   However the procedure also

---

[8]   OJ L 199, 26.7.1997, p. 32. Directive as last amended by Directive 98/61/EC (OJ L 268, 3.10.1998, p. 37).
[9]   OJ L 101, 1.4.1998, p. 24.
[10] OJ L 165, 19.6.1992, p. 27. Directive as last amended by Commission Decision No 98/80/EC (OJ L 14, 20.1.1998, p. 27).
[11] OJ L 336, 30.12.2000, p. 4.

takes account of transitional problems in the market such as those related to international roaming and of the possibility of new bottlenecks arising as a result of technological development, which may require ex ante regulation, for example in the area of broadband access networks. It may well be the case that competition develops at different speeds in different market segments and in different Member States, and national regulatory authorities should be able to relax regulatory obligations in those markets where competition is delivering the desired results. In order to ensure that market players in similar circumstances are treated in similar ways in different Member States, the Commission should be able to ensure harmonised application of the provisions of this Directive. National regulatory authorities and national authorities entrusted with the implementation of competition law should, where appropriate, coordinate their actions to ensure that the most appropriate remedy is applied. The Community and its Member States have entered into commitments on interconnection of telecommunications networks in the context of the World Trade Organisation agreement on basic telecommunications and these commitments need to be respected.

(14) Directive 97/33/EC laid down a range of obligations to be imposed on undertakings with significant market power, namely transparency, non-discrimination, accounting separation, access, and price control including cost orientation. This range of possible obligations should be maintained but, in addition, they should be established as a set of maximum obligations that can be applied to undertakings, in order to avoid over-regulation. Exceptionally, in order to comply with international commitments or Community law, it may be appropriate to impose obligations for access or interconnection on all market players, as is currently the case for conditional access systems for digital television services.

(15) The imposition of a specific obligation on an undertaking with significant market power does not require an additional market analysis but a justification that the obligation in question is appropriate and proportionate in relation to the nature of the problem identified.

(16) Transparency of terms and conditions for access and interconnection, including prices, serve to speed-up negotiation, avoid disputes and give confidence to market players that a service is not being provided on discriminatory terms. Openness and transparency of technical interfaces can be particularly important in ensuring interoperability. Where a national regulatory authority imposes obligations to make information public, it may also specify the manner in which the information is to be made available, covering for example the type of publication (paper and/or electronic) and whether or not it is free of charge, taking into account the nature and purpose of the information concerned.

(17) The principle of non-discrimination ensures that undertakings with market power do not distort competition, in particular where they are vertically integrated undertakings that supply services to undertakings with whom they compete on downstream markets.

(18) Accounting separation allows internal price transfers to be rendered visible, and allows national regulatory authorities to check compliance with obligations for non-discrimination where applicable. In this regard the Commission published Recommendation 98/322/EC of 8 April 1998 on interconnection in a liberalised telecommunications market (Part 2-accounting separation and cost accounting)[12].

---

[12] OJ L 141, 13.5.1998, p. 6.

(19) Mandating access to network infrastructure can be justified as a means of increasing competition, but national regulatory authorities need to balance the rights of an infrastructure owner to exploit its infrastructure forits own benefit, and the rights of other service providers to access facilities that are essential for the provision of competing services. Where obligations are imposed on operators that require them to meet reasonable requests for access to and use of networks elements and associated facilities, such requests should only be refused on the basis of objective criteria such as technical feasibility or the need to maintain network integrity. Where access is refused, the aggrieved party may submit the case to the dispute resolutions procedure referred to in Articles 20 and 21 of Directive 2002/21/EC (Framework Directive). An operator with mandated access obligations cannot be required to provide types of access which are not within its powers to provide. The imposition by national regulatory authorities of mandated access that increases competition in the short-term should not reduce incentives for competitors to invest in alternative facilities that will secure more competition in the long-term. The Commission has published a Notice on the application of the competition rules to access agreements in the telecommunications sector[13] which addresses these issues. National regulatory authorities may impose technical and operational conditions on the provider and/or beneficiaries of mandated access in accordance with Community law. In particular the imposition of technical standards should comply with Directive 98/34/EC of the European Parliament and of the Council of 22 June 1998 laying down a procedure for the provision of information in the field of technical standards and regulations and of rules of Information Society Services[14].

(20) Price control may be necessary when market analysis in a particular market reveals inefficient competition. The regulatory intervention may be relatively light, such as an obligation that prices for carrier selection are reasonable as laid down in Directive 97/33/EC, or much heavier such as an obligation that prices are cost oriented to provide full justification for those prices where competition is not sufficiently strong to prevent excessive pricing. In particular, operators with significant market power should avoid a price squeeze whereby the difference between their retail prices and the interconnection prices charged to competitors who provide similar retail services is not adequate to ensure sustainable competition. When a national regulatory authority calculates costs incurred in establishing a service mandated under this Directive, it is appropriate to allow a reasonable return on the capital employed including appropriate labour and building costs, with the value of capital adjusted where necessary to reflect the current valuation of assets and efficiency of operations. The method of cost recovery should be appropriate to the circumstances taking account of the need to promote efficiency and sustainable competition and maximise consumer benefits.

(21) Where a national regulatory authority imposes obligations to implement a cost accounting system in order to support price controls, it may itself undertake an annual audit to ensure compliance with that cost accounting system, provided that it has the necessary qualified staff, or it may require the audit to be carried out by another qualified body, independent of the operator concerned.

(22) Publication of information by Member States will ensure that market players and potential market entrants understand their rights and obligations, and know where to find the relevant detailed information. Publication in the national gazette helps interested parties in other Member States to find the relevant information.

---

[13] OJ C 265, 22.8.1998, p. 2.
[14] OJ L 204, 21.7.1998, p. 37. Directive as amended by Directive 98/48/EC (OJ L 217, 5.8.1998, p. 18).

(23) In order to ensure that the pan-European electronic communications market is effective and efficient, the Commission should monitor and publish information on charges which contribute to determining prices to end-users.

(24) The development of the electronic communications market, with its associated infrastructure, could have adverse effects on the environment and the landscape. Member States should therefore monitor this process and, if necessary, take action to minimise any such effects by means of appropriate agreements and other arrangements with the relevant authorities.

(25) In order to determine the correct application of Community law, the Commission needs to know which undertakings have been designated as having significant market power and what obligations have been placed upon market players by national regulatory authorities. In addition to national publication of this information, it is therefore necessary for Member States to send this information to the Commission. Where Member States are required to send information to the Commission, this may be in electronic form, subject to appropriate authentication procedures being agreed.

(26) Given the pace of technological and market developments, the implementation of this Directive should be reviewed within three years of its date of application to determine if it is meeting its objectives.

(27) The measures necessary for the implementation of this Directive should be adopted in accordance with Council Decision 1999/468/EC of 28 June 1999 laying down the procedures for the exercise of implementing powers conferred on the Commission[15].

(28) Since the objectives of the proposed action, namely establishing a harmonised framework for the regulation of access to and interconnection of electronic communications networks and associated facilities, cannot be sufficiently achieved by the Member States and can therefore, by reason of the scale and effects of the action, be better achieved at Community level, the Community may adopt measures, in accordance with the principle of subsidiarity as set out in Article 5 of the Treaty. In accordance with the principle of proportionality, as set out in that Article, this Directive does not go beyond what is necessary in order to achieve those objectives,

HAVE ADOPTED THIS DIRECTIVE:

CHAPTER I

SCOPE, AIM AND DEFINITIONS

Article 1

Scope and aim

1. Within the framework set out in Directive 2002/21/EC (Framework Directive), this Directive harmonises the way in which Member States regulate access to, and interconnection of, electronic communications networks and associated facilities. The aim is to establish a regulatory framework, in accordance with internal market principles, for the relationships between suppliers of networks and services that will result in sustainable competition, interoperability of electronic communications services and consumer benefits.

---

[15] OJ L 184, 17.7.1999, p. 23.

2.   This Directive establishes rights and obligations for operators and for undertakings seeking interconnection and/or access to their networks or associated facilities. It sets out objectives for national regulatory authorities with regard to access and interconnection, and lays down procedures to ensure that obligations imposed by national regulatory authorities are reviewed and, where appropriate, withdrawn once the desired objectives have been achieved. Access in this Directive does not refer to access by end-users.

Article 2

Definitions

For the purposes of this Directive the definitions set out in Article 2 of Directive 2002/21/EC (Framework Directive) shall apply.

The following definitions shall also apply:

(a)   "access" means the making available of facilities and/or services, to another undertaking, under defined conditions, on either an exclusive or non-exclusive basis, for the purpose of providing electronic communications services. It covers inter alia: access to network elements and associated facilities, which may involve the connection of equipment, by fixed or non-fixed means (in particular this includes access to the local loop and to facilities and services necessary to provide services over the local loop), access to physical infrastructure including buildings, ducts and masts; access to relevant software systems including operational support systems, access to number translation or systems offering equivalent functionality, access to fixed and mobile networks, in particular for roaming, access to conditional access systems for digital television services; access to virtual network services;

(b)   "interconnection" means the physical and logical linking of public communications networks used by the same or a different undertaking in order to allow the users of one undertaking to communicate with users of the same or another undertaking, or to access services provided by another undertaking. Services may be provided by the parties involved or other parties who have access to the network. Interconnection is a specific type of access implemented between public network operators;

(c)   "operator" means an undertaking providing or authorised to provide a public communications network or an associated facility;

(d)   "wide-screen television service" means a television service that consists wholly or partially of programmes produced and edited to be displayed in a full height wide-screen format. The 16:9 format is the reference format for wide-screen television services;

(e)   "local loop" means the physical circuit connecting the network termination point at the subscriber's premises to the main distribution frame or equivalent facility in the fixed public telephone network.

CHAPTER II

GENERAL PROVISIONS

Article 3

General framework for access and interconnection

1. Member States shall ensure that there are no restrictions which prevent undertakings in the same Member State or in different Member States from negotiating between themselves agreements on technical and commercial arrangements for access and/or interconnection, in accordance with Community law. The undertaking requesting access or interconnection does not need to be authorised to operate in the Member State where access or interconnection is requested, if it is not providing services and does not operate a network in that Member State.

2. Without prejudice to Article 31 of Directive 2002/22/EC of the European Parliament and of the Council of 7 March 2002 on universal service and users' rights relating to electronic communications networks and services (Universal Service Directive)[16], Member States shall not maintain legal or administrative measures which oblige operators, when granting access or interconnection, to offer different terms and conditions to different undertakings for equivalent services and/or imposing obligations that are not related to the actual access and interconnection services provided without prejudice to the conditions fixed in the Annex of Directive 2002/20/EC (Authorisation Directive).

Article 4

Rights and obligations for undertakings

1. Operators of public communications networks shall have a right and, when requested by other undertakings so authorised, an obligation to negotiate interconnection with each other for the purpose of providing publicly available electronic communications services, in order to ensure provision and interoperability of services throughout the Community. Operators shall offer access and interconnection to other undertakings on terms and conditions consistent with obligations imposed by the national regulatory authority pursuant to Articles 5, 6, 7 and 8.

2. Public electronic communications networks established for the distribution of digital television services shall be capable of distributing wide-screen television services and programmes. Network operators that receive and redistribute wide-screen television services or programmes shall maintain that wide-screen format.

3. Without prejudice to Article 11 of Directive 2002/20/EC (Authorisation Directive), Member States shall require that undertakings which acquire information from another undertaking before, during or after the process of negotiating access or interconnection arrangements use that information solely for the purpose for which it was supplied and respect at all times the confidentiality of information transmitted or stored. The received information shall not be passed on to any other party, in particular other departments, subsidiaries or partners, for whom such information could provide a competitive advantage.

---

[16] [OJ L 108, 24.4.2002, p. 51].

Article 5

Powers and responsibilities of the national regulatory authorities with regard to access and interconnection

1. National regulatory authorities shall, acting in pursuit of the objectives set out in Article 8 of Directive 2002/21/EC (Framework Directive), encourage and where appropriate ensure, in accordance with the provisions of this Directive, adequate access and interconnection, and interoperability of services, exercising their responsibility in a way that promotes efficiency, sustainable competition, and gives the maximum benefit to end-users.

    In particular, without prejudice to measures that may be taken regarding undertakings with significant market power in accordance with Article 8, national regulatory authorities shall be able to impose:

    (a) to the extent that is necessary to ensure end-to-end connectivity, obligations on undertakings that control access to end-users, including in justified cases the obligation to interconnect their networks where this is not already the case;

    (b) to the extent that is necessary to ensure accessibility for end-users to digital radio and television broadcasting services specified by the Member State, obligations on operators to provide access to the other facilities referred to in Annex I, Part II on fair, reasonable and non-discriminatory terms.

2. When imposing obligations on an operator to provide access in accordance with Article 12, national regulatory authorities may lay down technical or operational conditions to be met by the provider and/or beneficiaries of such access, in accordance with Community law, where necessary to ensure normal operation of the network. Conditions that refer to implementation of specific technical standards or specifications shall respect Article 17 of Directive 2002/21/EC (Framework Directive).

3. Obligations and conditions imposed in accordance with paragraphs 1 and 2 shall be objective, transparent, proportionate and non-discriminatory, and shall be implemented in accordance with the procedures referred to in Articles 6 and 7 of Directive 2002/21/EC (Framework Directive).

4. With regard to access and interconnection, Member States shall ensure that the national regulatory authority is empowered to intervene at its own initiative where justified or, in the absence of agreement between undertakings, at the request of either of the parties involved, in order to secure the policy objectives of Article 8 of Directive 2002/21/EC (Framework Directive), in accordance with the provisions of this Directive and the procedures referred to in Articles 6 and 7, 20 and 21 of Directive 2002/21/EC (Framework Directive).

CHAPTER III

OBLIGATIONS ON OPERATORS AND MARKET REVIEW PROCEDURES

Article 6

Conditional access systems and other facilities

1. Member States shall ensure that, in relation to conditional access to digital television and radio services broadcast to viewers and listeners in the Community, irrespective of the means of transmission, the conditions laid down in Annex I, Part I apply.

2. In the light of market and technological developments, Annex I may be amended in accordance with the procedure referred to in Article 14(3).

3. Notwithstanding the provisions of paragraph 1, Member States may permit their national regulatory authority, as soon as possible after the entry into force of this Directive and periodically thereafter, to review the conditions applied in accordance with this Article, by undertaking a market analysis in accordance with the first paragraph of Article 16 of Directive 2002/21/EC (Framework Directive) to determine whether to maintain, amend or withdraw the conditions applied.

Where, as a result of this market analysis, a national regulatory authority finds that one or more operators do not have significant market power on the relevant market, it may amend or withdraw the conditions with respect to those operators, in accordance with the procedures referred to in Articles 6 and 7 of Directive 2002/21/EC (Framework Directive), only to the extent that:

(a) accessibility for end-users to radio and television broadcasts and broadcasting channels and services specified in accordance with Article 31 of Directive 2002/22/EC (Universal Service Directive) would not be adversely affected by such amendment or withdrawal, and

(b) the prospects for effective competition in the markets for:

(i) retail digital television and radio broadcasting services, and

(ii) conditional access systems and other associated facilities,

would not be adversely affected by such amendment or withdrawal.

An appropriate period of notice shall be given to parties affected by such amendment or withdrawal of conditions.

4. Conditions applied in accordance with this Article are without prejudice to the ability of Member States to impose obligations in relation to the presentational aspect of electronic programme guides and similar listing and navigation facilities.

Article 7

Review of former obligations for access and interconnection

1. Member States shall maintain all obligations on undertakings providing public communications networks and/or services concerning access and interconnection that were in force prior to the date of entry into force of this Directive under Articles 4, 6, 7, 8, 11, 12, and 14 of Directive 97/33/EC, Article 16 of Directive 98/10/EC, and Articles 7 and 8 of Directive 92/44/EC, until such time as these obligations have been reviewed and a determination made in accordance with paragraph 3.

2. The Commission will indicate relevant markets for the obligations referred to in paragraph 1 in the initial recommendation on relevant product and service markets and the Decision identifying transnational markets to be adopted in accordance with Article 15 of Directive 2002/21/EC (Framework Directive).

3. Member States shall ensure that, as soon as possible after the entry into force of this Directive, and periodically thereafter, national regulatory authorities undertake a market analysis, in accordance with Article 16 of Directive 2002/21/EC (Framework Directive) to determine whether to maintain, amend or withdraw these obligations. An appropriate period of notice shall be given to parties affected by such amendment or withdrawal of obligations.

Article 8

Imposition, amendment or withdrawal of obligations

1. Member States shall ensure that national regulatory authorities are empowered to impose the obligations identified in Articles 9 to 13.

2. Where an operator is designated as having significant market power on a specific market as a result of a market analysis carried out in accordance with Article 16 of Directive 2002/21/EC (Framework Directive), national regulatory authorities shall impose the obligations set out in Articles 9 to 13 of this Directive as appropriate.

3. Without prejudice to:

    -   the provisions of Articles 5(1), 5(2) and 6,

    -   the provisions of Articles 12 and 13 of Directive 2002/21/EC (Framework Directive), Condition 7 in Part B of the Annex to Directive 2002/20/EC (Authorisation Directive) as applied by virtue of Article 6(1) of that Directive, Articles 27, 28 and 30 of Directive 2002/22/EC (Universal Service Directive) and the relevant provisions of Directive 97/66/EC of the European Parliament and of the Council of 15 December 1997 concerning the processing of personal data and the protection of privacy in the telecommunications sector[17] containing obligations on undertakings other than those designated as having significant market power, or

    -   the need to comply with international commitments,

    national regulatory authorities shall not impose the obligations set out in Articles 9 to 13 on operators that have not been designated in accordance with paragraph 2.

    In exceptional circumstances, when a national regulatory authority intends to impose on operators with significant market power other obligations for access or interconnection than those set out in Articles 9 to 13 in this Directive it shall submit this request to the Commission. The Commission, acting in accordance with Article 14(2), shall take a decision authorising or preventing the national regulatory authority from taking such measures.

4. Obligations imposed in accordance with this Article shall be based on the nature of the problem identified, proportionate and justified in the light of the objectives laid down in Article 8 of Directive 2002/21/EC (Framework Directive). Such obligations shall only be imposed following consultation in accordance with Articles 6 and 7 of that Directive.

5. In relation to the third indent of the first subparagraph of paragraph 3, national regulatory authorities shall notify decisions to impose, amend or withdraw obligations on market players to the Commission, in accordance with the procedure referred to in Article 7 of Directive 2002/21/EC (Framework Directive).

Article 9

Obligation of transparency

1. National regulatory authorities may, in accordance with the provisions of Article 8, impose obligations for transparency in relation to interconnection and/or access,

---

[17] OJ L 24, 30.1.1998, p. 1.

requiring operators to make public specified information, such as accounting information, technical specifications, network characteristics, terms and conditions for supply and use, and prices.

2.	In particular where an operator has obligations of non-discrimination, national regulatory authorities may require that operator to publish a reference offer, which shall be sufficiently unbundled to ensure that undertakings are not required to pay for facilities which are not necessary for the service requested, giving a description of the relevant offerings broken down into components according to market needs, and the associated terms and conditions including prices. The national regulatory authority shall, inter alia, be able to impose changes to reference offers to give effect to obligations imposed under this Directive.

3.	National regulatory authorities may specify the precise information to be made available, the level of detail required and the manner of publication.

4.	Notwithstanding paragraph 3, where an operator has obligations under Article 12 concerning unbundled access to the twisted metallic pair local loop, national regulatory authorities shall ensure the publication of a reference offer containing at least the elements set out in Annex II.

5.	In the light of market and technological developments, Annex II may be amended in accordance with the procedure referred to in Article 14(3).

Article 10

Obligation of non-discrimination

1.	A national regulatory authority may, in accordance with the provisions of Article 8, impose obligations of non-discrimination, in relation to interconnection and/or access.

2.	Obligations of non-discrimination shall ensure, in particular, that the operator applies equivalent conditions in equivalent circumstances to other undertakings providing equivalent services, and provides services and information to others under the same conditions and of the same quality as it provides for its own services, or those of it subsidiaries or partners.

Article 11

Obligation of accounting separation

1.	A national regulatory authority may, in accordance with the provisions of Article 8, impose obligations for accounting separation in relation to specified activities related to interconnection and/or access.

	In particular, a national regulatory authority may require a vertically integrated company to make transparent its wholesale prices and its internal transfer prices inter alia to ensure compliance where there is a requirement for non-discrimination under Article 10 or, where necessary, to prevent unfair cross-subsidy. National regulatory authorities may specify the format and accounting methodology to be used.

2.	Without prejudice to Article 5 of Directive 2002/21/EC (Framework Directive), to facilitate the verification of compliance with obligations of transparency and non-discrimination, national regulatory authorities shall have the power to require that accounting records, including data on revenues received from third parties, are provided on request. National regulatory authorities may publish such information as would contribute to an open and competitive market, while respecting national and Community rules on commercial confidentiality.

Article 12

Obligations of access to, and use of, specific network facilities

1. A national regulatory authority may, in accordance with the provisions of Article 8, impose obligations on operators to meet reasonable requests for access to, and use of, specific network elements and associated facilities, inter alia in situations where the national regulatory authority considers that denial of access or unreasonable terms and conditions having a similar effect would hinder the emergence of a sustainable competitive market at the retail level, or would not be in the end-user's interest.

    Operators may be required inter alia:

    (a) to give third parties access to specified network elements and/or facilities, including unbundled access to the local loop;

    (b) to negotiate in good faith with undertakings requesting access;

    (c) not to withdraw access to facilities already granted;

    (d) to provide specified services on a wholesale basis for resale by third parties;

    (e) to grant open access to technical interfaces, protocols or other key technologies that are indispensable for the interoperability of services or virtual network services;

    (f) to provide co-location or other forms of facility sharing, including duct, building or mast sharing;

    (g) to provide specified services needed to ensure interoperability of end-to-end services to users, including facilities for intelligent network services or roaming on mobile networks;

    (h) to provide access to operational support systems or similar software systems necessary to ensure fair competition in the provision of services;

    (i) to interconnect networks or network facilities.

    National regulatory authorities may attach to those obligations conditions covering fairness, reasonableness and timeliness.

2. When national regulatory authorities are considering whether to impose the obligations referred in paragraph 1, and in particular when assessing whether such obligations would be proportionate to the objectives set out in Article 8 of Directive 2002/21/EC (Framework Directive), they shall take account in particular of the following factors:

    (a) the technical and economic viability of using or installing competing facilities, in the light of the rate of market development, taking into account the nature and type of interconnection and access involved;

    (b) the feasibility of providing the access proposed, in relation to the capacity available;

    (c) the initial investment by the facility owner, bearing in mind the risks involved in making the investment;

    (d) the need to safeguard competition in the long term;

(e)   where appropriate, any relevant intellectual property rights;

(f)   the provision of pan-European services.

Article 13

Price control and cost accounting obligations

1.   A national regulatory authority may, in accordance with the provisions of Article 8, impose obligations relating to cost recovery and price controls, including obligations for cost orientation of prices and obligations concerning cost accounting systems, for the provision of specific types of interconnection and/or access, in situations where a market analysis indicates that a lack of effective competition means that the operator concerned might sustain prices at an excessively high level, or apply a price squeeze, to the detriment of end-users. National regulatory authorities shall take into account the investment made by the operator and allow him a reasonable rate of return on adequate capital employed, taking into account the risks involved.

2.   National regulatory authorities shall ensure that any cost recovery mechanism or pricing methodology that is mandated serves to promote efficiency and sustainable competition and maximise consumer benefits. In this regard national regulatory authorities may also take account of prices available in comparable competitive markets.

3.   Where an operator has an obligation regarding the cost orientation of its prices, the burden of proof that charges are derived from costs including a reasonable rate of return on investment shall lie with the operator concerned. For the purpose of calculating the cost of efficient provision of services, national regulatory authorities may use cost accounting methods independent of those used by the undertaking. National regulatory authorities may require an operator to provide full justification for its prices, and may, where appropriate, require prices to be adjusted.

4.   National regulatory authorities shall ensure that, where implementation of a cost accounting system is mandated in order to support price controls, a description of the cost accounting system is made publicly available, showing at least the main categories under which costs are grouped and the rules used for the allocation of costs. Compliance with the cost accounting system shall be verified by a qualified independent body. A statement concerning compliance shall be published annually.

CHAPTER IV

PROCEDURAL PROVISIONS

Article 14

Committee

1.   The Commission shall be assisted by the Communications Committee set up by Article 22 of Directive 2002/21/EC (Framework Directive).

2.   Where reference is made to this paragraph, Articles 3 and 7 of Decision 1999/468/EC shall apply, having regard to the provisions of Article 8 thereof.

3.   Where reference is made to this paragraph, Articles 5 and 7 of Decision 1999/468/EC shall apply, having regard to the provisions of Article 8 thereof.

The period laid down in Article 5(6) of Decision 1999/468/EC shall be set at three months.

4.   The Committee shall adopt its rules of procedure.

Article 15

Publication of, and access to, information

1.   Member States shall ensure that the specific obligations imposed on undertakings under this Directive are published and that the specific product/service and geographical markets are identified. They shall ensure that up-to-date information, provided that the information is not confidential and, in particular, does not comprise business secrets, is made publicly available in a manner that guarantees all interested parties easy access to that information.

2.   Member States shall send to the Commission a copy of all such information published. The Commission shall make this information available in a readily accessible form, and shall distribute the information to the Communications Committee as appropriate.

Article 16

Notification

1.   Member States shall notify to the Commission by at the latest the date of application referred to in Article 18(1) second subparagraph the national regulatory authorities responsible for the tasks set out in this Directive.

2.   National regulatory authorities shall notify to the Commission the names of operators deemed to have significant market power for the purposes of this Directive, and the obligations imposed upon them under this Directive. Any changes affecting the obligations imposed upon undertakings or of the undertakings affected under the provisions of this Directive shall be notified to the Commission without delay.

Article 17

Review procedures

The Commission shall periodically review the functioning of this Directive and report to the European Parliament and to the Council, on the first occasion not later than three years after the date of application referred to in Article 18(1), second subparagraph. For this purpose, the Commission may request from the Member States information, which shall be supplied without undue delay.

Article 18

Transposition

1.   Member States shall adopt and publish the laws, regulations and administrative provisions necessary to comply with this Directive by not later than 24 July 2003. They shall forthwith inform the Commission thereof.

They shall apply those measures from 25 July 2003.

When Member States adopt these measures, they shall contain a reference to this Directive or be accompanied by such a reference on the occasion of their official publication. The methods of making such reference shall be laid down by Member States.

2.   Member States shall communicate to the Commission the text of the provisions of national law which they adopt in the field governed by this Directive and of any subsequent amendments to those provisions.

Article 19

Entry into force

This Directive shall enter into force on the day of its publication in the Official Journal of the European Communities.

Article 20

Addressees

This Directive is addressed to the Member States.

Editors' Notes:

[a] OJ L 108, 24.4.2002, p. 7. Some citations in the original text have been updated to the current and complete Official Journal citation.

CONDITIONS FOR ACCESS TO DIGITAL TELEVISION AND RADIO SERVICES
BROADCAST TO VIEWERS AND LISTENERS IN THE COMMUNITY

Part I: Conditions for conditional access systems to be applied in accordance with Article 6(1)

In relation to conditional access to digital television and radio services broadcast to viewers and listeners in the Community, irrespective of the means of transmission, Member States must ensure in accordance with Article 6 that the following conditions apply:

(a)   conditional access systems operated on the market in the Community are to have the necessary technical capability for cost-effective transcontrol allowing the possibility for full control by network operators at local or regional level of the services using such conditional access systems;

(b)   all operators of conditional access services, irrespective of the means of transmission, who provide access services to digital television and radio services and whose access services broadcasters depend on to reach any group of potential viewers or listeners are to:

-       offer to all broadcasters, on a fair, reasonable and non-discriminatory basis compatible with Community competition law, technical services enabling the broadcasters' digitally-transmitted services to be received by viewers or listeners authorised by means of decoders administered by the service operators, and comply with Community competition law,

-       keep separate financial accounts regarding their activity as conditional access providers.

(c)   when granting licences to manufacturers of consumer equipment, holders of industrial property rights to conditional access products and systems are to ensure that this is done on fair, reasonable and non-discriminatory terms. Taking into account technical and commercial factors, holders of rights are not to subject the granting of licences to conditions prohibiting, deterring or discouraging the inclusion in the same product of:

-       a common interface allowing connection with several other access systems, or

-       means specific to another access system, provided that the licensee complies with the relevant and reasonable conditions ensuring, as far as he is concerned, the security of transactions of conditional access system operators.

Part II: Other facilities to which conditions may be applied under Article 5(1)(b)

(a)   Access to application program interfaces (APIs);

(b)   Access to electronic programme guides (EPGs).

MINIMUM LIST OF ITEMS TO BE INCLUDED IN A REFERENCE OFFER FOR
UNBUNDLED ACCESS TO THE TWISTED METALLIC PAIR LOCAL LOOP
TO BE PUBLISHED BY NOTIFIED OPERATORS

For the purposes of this Annex the following definitions apply:

(a) "local sub-loop" means a partial local loop connecting the network termination point at the subscriber's premises to a concentration point or a specified intermediate access point in the fixed public telephone network;

(b) "unbundled access to the local loop" means full unbundled access to the local loop and shared access to the local loop; it does not entail a change in ownership of the local loop;

(c) "full unbundled access to the local loop" means the provision to a beneficiary of access to the local loop or local sub-loop of the notified operator authorising the use of the full frequency spectrum of the twisted metallic pair;

(d) "shared access to the local loop" means the provision to a beneficiary of access to the local loop or local sub-loop of the notified operator, authorising the use of the non-voice band frequency spectrum of the twisted metallic pair; the local loop continues to be used by the notified operator to provide the telephone service to the public;

A. **Conditions for unbundled access to the local loop**

   1. Network elements to which access is offered covering in particular the following elements:

      (a) access to local loops;

      (b) access to non-voice band frequency spectrum of a local loop, in the case of shared access to the local loop;

   2. Information concerning the locations of physical access sites[1], availability of local loops in specific parts of the access network;

   3. Technical conditions related to access and use of local loops, including the technical characteristics of the twisted metallic pair in the local loop;

   4. Ordering and provisioning procedures, usage restrictions.

B. **Co-location services**

   1. Information on the notified operator's relevant sites[1].

   2. Co-location options at the sites indicated under point 1 (including physical co-location and, as appropriate, distant co-location and virtual co-location).

   3. Equipment characteristics: restrictions, if any, on equipment that can be co-located.

---

[1] Availability of this information may be restricted to interested parties only, in order to avoid public security concerns.

4. Security issues: measures put in place by notified operators to ensure the security of their locations.

5. Access conditions for staff of competitive operators.

6. Safety standards.

7. Rules for the allocation of space where co-location space is limited.

8. Conditions for beneficiaries to inspect the locations at which physical co-location is available, or sites where co-location has been refused on grounds of lack of capacity.

C. Information systems

Conditions for access to notified operator's operational support systems, information systems or databases for pre-ordering, provisioning, ordering, maintenance and repair requests and billing.

D. Supply conditions

1. Lead time for responding to requests for supply of services and facilities; service level agreements, fault resolution, procedures to return to a normal level of service and quality of service parameters.

2. Standard contract terms, including, where appropriate, compensation provided for failure to meet lead times.

3. Prices or pricing formulae for each feature, function and facility listed above.

DIRECTIVE 2002/22/EC OF THE EUROPEAN PARLIAMENT AND OF THE COUNCIL

of 7 March 2002[a]

on universal service and users' rights relating to electronic communications networks and services

(Universal Service Directive)

THE EUROPEAN PARLIAMENT AND THE COUNCIL OF THE EUROPEAN UNION,

Having regard to the Treaty establishing the European Community, and in particular Article 95 thereof,

Having regard to the proposal from the Commission[1],

Having regard to the opinion of the Economic and Social Committee[2],

Having regard to the opinion of the Committee of the Regions[3],

Acting in accordance with the procedure laid down in Article 251 of the Treaty[4],

Whereas:

(1) The liberalisation of the telecommunications sector and increasing competition and choice for communications services go hand in hand with parallel action to create a harmonised regulatory framework which secures the delivery of universal service. The concept of universal service should evolve to reflect advances in technology, market developments and changes in user demand. The regulatory framework established for the full liberalisation of the telecommunications market in 1998 in the Community defined the minimum scope of universal service obligations and established rules for its costing and financing.

(2) Under Article 153 of the Treaty, the Community is to contribute to the protection of consumers.

(3) The Community and its Member States have undertaken commitments on the regulatory framework of telecommunications networks and services in the context of the World Trade Organisation (WTO) agreement on basic telecommunications. Any member of the WTO has the right to define the kind of universal service obligation it wishes to maintain. Such obligations will not be regarded as anti-competitive per se, provided they are administered in a transparent, non-discriminatory and competitively neutral manner and are not more burdensome than necessary for the kind of universal service defined by the member.

(4) Ensuring universal service (that is to say, the provision of a defined minimum set of services to all end-users at an affordable price) may involve the provision of some services to some end-users at prices that depart from those resulting from normal market conditions. However, compensating undertakings designated to provide such services in such circumstances need not result in any distortion of competition,

---

[1] OJ C 365 E, 19.12.2000, p. 238 and OJ C 332 E, 27.11.2001, p. 292.
[2] OJ C 139, 11.5.2001, p. 15.
[3] OJ C 144, 16.5.2001, p. 60.
[4] Opinion of the European Parliament of 13 June 2001 [OJ C 53 E, 28.02.2002, p. 195], Council Common Position of 17 September 2001 (OJ C 337, 30.11.2001, p. 55) and Decision of the European Parliament of 12 December 2001 [OJ C 177 E, 25.07.2002, p. 157]. Council Decision of 14 February 2002.

provided that designated undertakings are compensated for the specific net cost involved and provided that the net cost burden is recovered in a competitively neutral way.

(5)   In a competitive market, certain obligations should apply to all undertakings providing publicly available telephone services at fixed locations and others should apply only to undertakings enjoying significant market power or which have been designated as a universal service operator.

(6)   The network termination point represents a boundary for regulatory purposes between the regulatory framework for electronic communication networks and services and the regulation of telecommunication terminal equipment. Defining the location of the network termination point is the responsibility of the national regulatory authority, where necessary on the basis of a proposal by the relevant undertakings.

(7)   Member States should continue to ensure that the services set out in Chapter II are made available with the quality specified to all end-users in their territory, irrespective of their geographical location, and, in the light of specific national conditions, at an affordable price. Member States may, in the context of universal service obligations and in the light of national conditions, take specific measures for consumers in rural or geographically isolated areas to ensure their access to the services set out in the Chapter II and the affordability of those services, as well as ensure under the same conditions this access, in particular for the elderly, the disabled and for people with special social needs. Such measures may also include measures directly targeted at consumers with special social needs providing support to identified consumers, for example by means of specific measures, taken after the examination of individual requests, such as the paying off of debts.

(8)   A fundamental requirement of universal service is to provide users on request with a connection to the public telephone network at a fixed location, at an affordable price. The requirement is limited to a single narrowband network connection, the provision of which may be restricted by Member States to the end-user's primary location/residence, and does not extend to the Integrated Services Digital Network (ISDN) which provides two or more connections capable of being used simultaneously. There should be no constraints on the technical means by which the connection is provided, allowing for wired or wireless technologies, nor any constraints on which operators provide part or all of universal service obligations. Connections to the public telephone network at a fixed location should be capable of supporting speech and data communications at rates sufficient for access to online services such as those provided via the public Internet. The speed of Internet access experienced by a given user may depend on a number of factors including the provider(s) of Internet connectivity as well as the given application for which a connection is being used. The data rate that can be supported by a single narrowband connection to the public telephone network depends on the capabilities of the subscriber's terminal equipment as well as the connection. For this reason it is not appropriate to mandate a specific data or bit rate at Community level. Currently available voice band modems typically offer a data rate of 56 kbit/s and employ automatic data rate adaptation to cater for variable line quality, with the result that the achieved data rate may be lower than 56 kbit/s. Flexibility is required on the one hand to allow Member States to take measures where necessary to ensure that connections are capable of supporting such a data rate, and on the other hand to allow Member States where relevant to permit data rates below this upper limit of 56 kbits/s in order, for example, to exploit the capabilities of wireless technologies (including cellular wireless networks) to deliver universal service to a higher proportion of the population. This may be of particular importance in some accession countries where household penetration of traditional telephone connections remains relatively low. In specific cases where the connection to the public telephony network at a fixed

location is clearly insufficient to support satisfactory Internet access, Member States should be able to require the connection to be brought up to the level enjoyed by the majority of subscribers so that it supports data rates sufficient for access to the Internet. Where such specific measures produce a net cost burden for those consumers concerned, the net effect may be included in any net cost calculation of universal service obligations.

(9)   The provisions of this Directive do not preclude Member States from designating different undertakings to provide the network and service elements of universal service. Designated undertakings providing network elements may be required to ensure such construction and maintenance as are necessary and proportionate to meet all reasonable requests for connection at a fixed location to the public telephone network and for access to publicly available telephone services at a fixed location.

(10)   Affordable price means a price defined by Member States at national level in the light of specific national conditions, and may involve setting common tariffs irrespective of location or special tariff options to deal with the needs of low-income users. Affordability for individual consumers is related to their ability to monitor and control their expenditure.

(11)   Directory information and a directory enquiry service constitute an essential access tool for publicly available telephone services and form part of the universal service obligation. Users and consumers desire comprehensive directories and a directory enquiry service covering all listed telephone subscribers and their numbers (including fixed and mobile numbers) and want this information to be presented in a non-preferential fashion. Directive 97/66/EC of the European Parliament and of the Council of 15 December 1997 concerning the processing of personal data and the protection of privacy in the telecommunications sector[5] ensures the subscribers' right to privacy with regard to the inclusion of their personal information in a public directory.

(12)   For the citizen, it is important for there to be adequate provision of public pay telephones, and for users to be able to call emergency telephone numbers and, in particular, the single European emergency call number ("112") free of charge from any telephone, including public pay telephones, without the use of any means of payment. Insufficient information about the existence of "112" deprives citizens of the additional safety ensured by the existence of this number at European level especially during their travel in other Member States.

(13)   Member States should take suitable measures in order to guarantee access to and affordability of all publicly available telephone services at a fixed location for disabled users and users with special social needs. Specific measures for disabled users could include, as appropriate, making available accessible public telephones, public text telephones or equivalent measures for deaf or speech-impaired people, providing services such as directory enquiry services or equivalent measures free of charge for blind or partially sighted people, and providing itemised bills in alternative format on request for blind or partially sighted people. Specific measures may also need to be taken to enable disabled users and users with special social needs to access emergency services "112" and to give them a similar possibility to choose between different operators or service providers as other consumers. Quality of service standards have been developed for a range of parameters to assess the quality of services received by subscribers and how well undertakings designated with universal service obligations perform in achieving these standards. Quality of service standards do not yet exist in respect of disabled users. Performance standards and relevant

---

[5]   OJ L 24, 30.1.1998, p. 1.

parameters should be developed for disabled users and are provided for in Article 11 of this Directive. Moreover, national regulatory authorities should be enabled to require publication of quality of service performance data if and when such standards and parameters are developed. The provider of universal service should not take measures to prevent users from benefiting fully from services offered by different operators or service providers, in combination with its own services offered as part of universal service.

(14) The importance of access to and use of the public telephone network at a fixed location is such that it should be available to anyone reasonably requesting it. In accordance with the principle of subsidiarity, it is for Member States to decide on the basis of objective criteria which undertakings have universal service obligations for the purposes of this Directive, where appropriate taking into account the ability and the willingness of undertakings to accept all or part of the universal service obligations. It is important that universal service obligations are fulfilled in the most efficient fashion so that users generally pay prices that correspond to efficient cost provision. It is likewise important that universal service operators maintain the integrity of the network as well as service continuity and quality. The development of greater competition and choice provide more possibilities for all or part of the universal service obligations to be provided by undertakings other than those with significant market power. Therefore, universal service obligations could in some cases be allocated to operators demonstrating the most cost-effective means of delivering access and services, including by competitive or comparative selection procedures. Corresponding obligations could be included as conditions in authorisations to provide publicly available services.

(15) Member States should monitor the situation of consumers with respect to their use of publicly available telephone services and in particular with respect to affordability. The affordability of telephone service is related to the information which users receive regarding telephone usage expenses as well as the relative cost of telephone usage compared to other services, and is also related to their ability to control expenditure. Affordability therefore means giving power to consumers through obligations imposed on undertakings designated as having universal service obligations. These obligations include a specified level of itemised billing, the possibility for consumers selectively to block certain calls (such as high-priced calls to premium services), the possibility for consumers to control expenditure via pre-payment means and the possibility for consumers to offset up-front connection fees. Such measures may need to be reviewed and changed in the light of market developments. Current conditions do not warrant a requirement for operators with universal service obligations to alert subscribers where a predetermined limit of expenditure is exceeded or an abnormal calling pattern occurs. Review of the relevant legislative provisions in future should consider whether there is a possible need to alert subscribers for these reasons.

(16) Except in cases of persistent late payment or non-payment of bills, consumers should be protected from immediate disconnection from the network on the grounds of an unpaid bill and, particularly in the case of disputes over high bills for premium rate services, should continue to have access to essential telephone services pending resolution of the dispute. Member States may decide that such access may continue to be provided only if the subscriber continues to pay line rental charges.

(17) Quality and price are key factors in a competitive market and national regulatory authorities should be able to monitor achieved quality of service for undertakings which have been designated as having universal service obligations. In relation to the quality of service attained by such undertakings, national regulatory authorities should be able to take appropriate measures where they deem it necessary. National regulatory authorities should also be able to monitor the achieved quality of services

of other undertakings providing public telephone networks and/or publicly telephone services to users at fixed locations.

(18) Member States should, where necessary, establish mechanisms for financing the net cost of universal service obligations in cases where it is demonstrated that the obligations can only be provided at a loss or at a net cost which falls outside normal commercial standards. It is important to ensure that the net cost of universal service obligations is properly calculated and that any financing is undertaken with minimum distortion to the market and to undertakings, and is compatible with the provisions of Articles 87 and 88 of the Treaty.

(19) Any calculation of the net cost of universal service should take due account of costs and revenues, as well as the intangible benefits resulting from providing universal service, but should not hinder the general aim of ensuring that pricing structures reflect costs. Any net costs of universal service obligations should be calculated on the basis of transparent procedures.

(20) Taking into account intangible benefits means that an estimate in monetary terms, of the indirect benefits that an undertaking derives by virtue of its position as provider of universal service, should be deducted from the direct net cost of universal service obligations in order to determine the overall cost burden.

(21) When a universal service obligation represents an unfair burden on an undertaking, it is appropriate to allow Member States to establish mechanisms for efficiently recovering net costs. Recovery via public funds constitutes one method of recovering the net costs of universal service obligations. It is also reasonable for established net costs to be recovered from all users in a transparent fashion by means of levies on undertakings. Member States should be able to finance the net costs of different elements of universal service through different mechanisms, and/or to finance the net costs of some or all elements from either of the mechanisms or a combination of both. In the case of cost recovery by means of levies on undertakings, Member States should ensure that that the method of allocation amongst them is based on objective and non-discriminatory criteria and is in accordance with the principle of proportionality. This principle does not prevent Member States from exempting new entrants which have not yet achieved any significant market presence. Any funding mechanism should ensure that market participants only contribute to the financing of universal service obligations and not to other activities which are not directly linked to the provision of the universal service obligations. Recovery mechanisms should in all cases respect the principles of Community law, and in particular in the case of sharing mechanisms those of non-discrimination and proportionality. Any funding mechanism should ensure that users in one Member State do not contribute to universal service costs in another Member State, for example when making calls from one Member State to another.

(22) Where Member States decide to finance the net cost of universal service obligations from public funds, this should be understood to comprise funding from general government budgets including other public financing sources such as state lotteries.

(23) The net cost of universal service obligations may be shared between all or certain specified classes of undertaking. Member States should ensure that the sharing mechanism respects the principles of transparency, least market distortion, non-discrimination and proportionality. Least market distortion means that contributions should be recovered in a way that as far as possible minimises the impact of the financial burden falling on end-users, for example by spreading contributions as widely as possible.

(24) National regulatory authorities should satisfy themselves that those undertakings benefiting from universal service funding provide a sufficient level of detail of the

specific elements requiring such funding in order to justify their request. Member States' schemes for the costing and financing of universal service obligations should be communicated to the Commission for verification of compatibility with the Treaty. There are incentives for designated operators to raise the assessed net cost of universal service obligations. Therefore Member States should ensure effective transparency and control of amounts charged to finance universal service obligations.

(25) Communications markets continue to evolve in terms of the services used and the technical means used to deliver them to users. The universal service obligations, which are defined at a Community level, should be periodically reviewed with a view to proposing that the scope be changed or redefined. Such a review should take account of evolving social, commercial and technological conditions and the fact that any change of scope should be subject to the twin test of services that become available to a substantial majority of the population, with a consequent risk of social exclusion for those who can not afford them. Care should be taken in any change of the scope of universal service obligations to ensure that certain technological choices are not artificially promoted above others, that a disproportionate financial burden is not imposed on sector undertakings (thereby endangering market developments and innovation) and that any financing burden does not fall unfairly on consumers with lower incomes. Any change of scope automatically means that any net cost can be financed via the methods permitted in this Directive. Member States are not permitted to impose on market players financial contributions which relate to measures which are not part of universal service obligations. Individual Member States remain free to impose special measures (outside the scope of universal service obligations) and finance them in conformity with Community law but not by means of contributions from market players.

(26) More effective competition across all access and service markets will give greater choice for users. The extent of effective competition and choice varies across the Community and varies within Member States between geographical areas and between access and service markets. Some users may be entirely dependent on the provision of access and services by an undertaking with significant market power. In general, for reasons of efficiency and to encourage effective competition, it is important that the services provided by an undertaking with significant market power reflect costs. For reasons of efficiency and social reasons, end-user tariffs should reflect demand conditions as well as cost conditions, provided that this does not result in distortions of competition. There is a risk that an undertaking with significant market power may act in various ways to inhibit entry or distort competition, for example by charging excessive prices, setting predatory prices, compulsory bundling of retail services or showing undue preference to certain customers. Therefore, national regulatory authorities should have powers to impose, as a last resort and after due consideration, retail regulation on an undertaking with significant market power. Price cap regulation, geographical averaging or similar instruments, as well as non-regulatory measures such as publicly available comparisons of retail tariffs, may be used to achieve the twin objectives of promoting effective competition whilst pursuing public interest needs, such as maintaining the affordability of publicly available telephone services for some consumers. Access to appropriate cost accounting information is necessary, in order for national regulatory authorities to fulfil their regulatory duties in this area, including the imposition of any tariff controls. However, regulatory controls on retail services should only be imposed where national regulatory authorities consider that relevant wholesale measures or measures regarding carrier selection or pre-selection would fail to achieve the objective of ensuring effective competition and public interest.

(27) Where a national regulatory authority imposes obligations to implement a cost accounting system in order to support price controls, it may itself undertake an annual audit to ensure compliance with that cost accounting system, provided that it has the

necessary qualified staff, or it may require the audit to be carried out by another qualified body, independent of the operator concerned.

(28) It is considered necessary to ensure the continued application of the existing provisions relating to the minimum set of leased line services in Community telecommunications legislation, in particular in Council Directive 92/44/EEC of 5 June 1992 on the application of open network provision to leased lines[6], until such time as national regulatory authorities determine, in accordance with the market analysis procedures laid down in Directive 2002/21/EC of the European Parliament and of the Council of 7 March 2002 on a common regulatory framework for electronic communications networks and services (Framework Directive)[7], that such provisions are no longer needed because a sufficiently competitive market has developed in their territory. The degree of competition is likely to vary between different markets of leased lines in the minimum set, and in different parts of the territory. In undertaking the market analysis, national regulatory authorities should make separate assessments for each market of leased lines in the minimum set, taking into account their geographic dimension. Leased lines services constitute mandatory services to be provided without recourse to any compensation mechanisms. The provision of leased lines outside of the minimum set of leased lines should be covered by general retail regulatory provisions rather than specific requirements covering the supply of the minimum set.

(29) National regulatory authorities may also, in the light of an analysis of the relevant market, require mobile operators with significant market power to enable their subscribers to access the services of any interconnected provider of publicly available telephone services on a call-by-call basis or by means of pre-selection.

(30) Contracts are an important tool for users and consumers to ensure a minimum level of transparency of information and legal security. Most service providers in a competitive environment will conclude contracts with their customers for reasons of commercial desirability. In addition to the provisions of this Directive, the requirements of existing Community consumer protection legislation relating to contracts, in particular Council Directive 93/13/EEC of 5 April 1993 on unfair terms in consumer contracts[8] and Directive 97/7/EC of the European Parliament and of the Council of 20 May 1997 on the protection of consumers in respect of distance contracts[9], apply to consumer transactions relating to electronic networks and services. Specifically, consumers should enjoy a minimum level of legal certainty in respect of their contractual relations with their direct telephone service provider, such that the contractual terms, conditions, quality of service, condition for termination of the contract and the service, compensation measures and dispute resolution are specified in their contracts. Where service providers other than direct telephone service providers conclude contracts with consumers, the same information should be included in those contracts as well. The measures to ensure transparency on prices, tariffs, terms and conditions will increase the ability of consumers to optimise their choices and thus to benefit fully from competition.

(31) End-users should have access to publicly available information on communications services. Member States should be able to monitor the quality of services which are offered in their territories. National regulatory authorities should be able systematically to collect information on the quality of services offered in their territories on the basis of criteria which allow comparability between service

---

[6] OJ L 165, 19.6.1992, p. 27. Directive as last amended by Commission Decision No 98/80/EC (OJ L 14, 20.1.1998, p. 27).
[7] [OJ L 108, 24.4.2002, p. 33].
[8] OJ L 95, 21.4.1993, p. 29.
[9] OJ L 144, 4.6.1997, p. 19.

providers and between Member States. Undertakings providing communications services, operating in a competitive environment, are likely to make adequate and up-to-date information on their services publicly available for reasons of commercial advantage. National regulatory authorities should nonetheless be able to require publication of such information where it is demonstrated that such information is not effectively available to the public.

(32) End-users should be able to enjoy a guarantee of interoperability in respect of all equipment sold in the Community for the reception of digital television. Member States should be able to require minimum harmonised standards in respect of such equipment. Such standards could be adapted from time to time in the light of technological and market developments.

(33) It is desirable to enable consumers to achieve the fullest connectivity possible to digital television sets. Interoperability is an evolving concept in dynamic markets. Standards bodies should do their utmost to ensure that appropriate standards evolve along with the technologies concerned. It is likewise important to ensure that connectors are available on television sets that are capable of passing all the necessary elements of a digital signal, including the audio and video streams, conditional access information, service information, application program interface (API) information and copy protection information. This Directive therefore ensures that the functionality of the open interface for digital television sets is not limited by network operators, service providers or equipment manufacturers and continues to evolve in line with technological developments. For display and presentation of digital interactive television services, the realisation of a common standard through a market-driven mechanism is recognised as a consumer benefit. Member States and the Commission may take policy initiatives, consistent with the Treaty, to encourage this development.

(34) All end-users should continue to enjoy access to operator assistance services whatever organisation provides access to the public telephone network.

(35) The provision of directory enquiry services and directories is already open to competition. The provisions of this Directive complement the provisions of Directive 97/66/EC by giving subscribers a right to have their personal data included in a printed or electronic directory. All service providers which assign telephone numbers to their subscribers are obliged to make relevant information available in a fair, cost-oriented and non-discriminatory manner.

(36) It is important that users should be able to call the single European emergency number "112", and any other national emergency telephone numbers, free of charge, from any telephone, including public pay telephones, without the use of any means of payment. Member States should have already made the necessary organisational arrangements best suited to the national organisation of the emergency systems, in order to ensure that calls to this number are adequately answered and handled. Caller location information, to be made available to the emergency services, will improve the level of protection and the security of users of "112" services and assist the emergency services, to the extent technically feasible, in the discharge of their duties, provided that the transfer of calls and associated data to the emergency services concerned is guaranteed. The reception and use of such information should comply with relevant Community law on the processing of personal data. Steady information technology improvements will progressively support the simultaneous handling of several languages over the networks at a reasonable cost. This in turn will ensure additional safety for European citizens using the "112" emergency call number.

(37) Easy access to international telephone services is vital for European citizens and European businesses. "00" has already been established as the standard international telephone access code for the Community. Special arrangements for making calls between adjacent locations across borders between Member States may be established

or continued. The ITU has assigned, in accordance with ITU Recommendation E.164, code "3883" to the European Telephony Numbering Space (ETNS). In order to ensure connection of calls to the ETNS, undertakings operating public telephone networks should ensure that calls using "3883" are directly or indirectly interconnected to ETNS serving networks specified in the relevant European Telecommunications Standards Institute (ETSI) standards. Such interconnection arrangements should be governed by the provisions of Directive 2002/19/EC of the European Parliament and of the Council of 7 March 2002 on access to, and interconnection of, electronic communications networks and associated facilities (Access Directive)[10].

(38) Access by end-users to all numbering resources in the Community is a vital pre-condition for a single market. It should include freephone, premium rate, and other non-geographic numbers, except where the called subscriber has chosen, for commercial reasons, to limit access from certain geographical areas. Tariffs charged to parties calling from outside the Member State concerned need not be the same as for those parties calling from inside that Member State.

(39) Tone dialling and calling line identification facilities are normally available on modern telephone exchanges and can therefore increasingly be provided at little or no expense. Tone dialling is increasingly being used for user interaction with special services and facilities, including value added services, and the absence of this facility can prevent the user from making use of these services. Member States are not required to impose obligations to provide these facilities when they are already available. Directive 97/66/EC safeguards the privacy of users with regard to itemised billing, by giving them the means to protect their right to privacy when calling line identification is implemented. The development of these services on a pan-European basis would benefit consumers and is encouraged by this Directive.

(40) Number portability is a key facilitator of consumer choice and effective competition in a competitive telecommunications environment such that end-users who so request should be able to retain their number(s) on the public telephone network independently of the organisation providing service. The provision of this facility between connections to the public telephone network at fixed and non-fixed locations is not covered by this Directive. However, Member States may apply provisions for porting numbers between networks providing services at a fixed location and mobile networks.

(41) The impact of number portability is considerably strengthened when there is transparent tariff information, both for end-users who port their numbers and also for end-users who call those who have ported their numbers. National regulatory authorities should, where feasible, facilitate appropriate tariff transparency as part of the implementation of number portability.

(42) When ensuring that pricing for interconnection related to the provision of number portability is cost-oriented, national regulatory authorities may also take account of prices available in comparable markets.

(43) Currently, Member States impose certain "must carry" obligations on networks for the distribution of radio or television broadcasts to the public. Member States should be able to lay down proportionate obligations on undertakings under their jurisdiction, in the interest of legitimate public policy considerations, but such obligations should only be imposed where they are necessary to meet general interest objectives clearly defined by Member States in conformity with Community law and should be

---

[10]   [OJ L 108, 24.4.2002, p. 7].

proportionate, transparent and subject to periodical review. "Must carry" obligations imposed by Member States should be reasonable, that is they should be proportionate and transparent in the light of clearly defined general interest objectives, and could, where appropriate, entail a provision for proportionate remuneration. Such "must carry" obligations may include the transmission of services specifically designed to enable appropriate access by disabled users.

(44) Networks used for the distribution of radio or television broadcasts to the public include cable, satellite and terrestrial broadcasting networks. They might also include other networks to the extent that a significant number of end-users use such networks as their principal means to receive radio and television broadcasts.

(45) Services providing content such as the offer for sale of a package of sound or television broadcasting content are not covered by the common regulatory framework for electronic communications networks and services. Providers of such services should not be subject to universal service obligations in respect of these activities. This Directive is without prejudice to measures taken at national level, in compliance with Community law, in respect of such services.

(46) Where a Member State seeks to ensure the provision of other specific services throughout its national territory, such obligations should be implemented on a cost efficient basis and outside the scope of universal service obligations. Accordingly, Member States may undertake additional measures (such as facilitating the development of infrastructure or services in circumstances where the market does not satisfactorily address the requirements of end-users or consumers), in conformity with Community law. As a reaction to the Commission's e-Europe initiative, the Lisbon European Council of 23 and 24 March 2000 called on Member States to ensure that all schools have access to the Internet and to multimedia resources.

(47) In the context of a competitive environment, the views of interested parties, including users and consumers, should be taken into account by national regulatory authorities when dealing with issues related to end-users' rights. Effective procedures should be available to deal with disputes between consumers, on the one hand, and undertakings providing publicly available communications services, on the other. Member States should take full account of Commission Recommendation 98/257/EC of 30 March 1998 on the principles applicable to the bodies responsible for out-of-court settlement of consumer disputes[11].

(48) Co-regulation could be an appropriate way of stimulating enhanced quality standards and improved service performance. Co-regulation should be guided by the same principles as formal regulation, i.e. it should be objective, justified, proportional, non-discriminatory and transparent.

(49) This Directive should provide for elements of consumer protection, including clear contract terms and dispute resolution, and tariff transparency for consumers. It should also encourage the extension of such benefits to other categories of end-users, in particular small and medium-sized enterprises.

(50) The provisions of this Directive do not prevent a Member State from taking measures justified on grounds set out in Articles 30 and 46 of the Treaty, and in particular on grounds of public security, public policy and public morality.

(51) Since the objectives of the proposed action, namely setting a common level of universal service for telecommunications for all European users and of harmonising conditions for access to and use of public telephone networks at a fixed location and

---

[11] OJ L 115, 17.4.1998, p. 31.

related publicly available telephone services and also achieving a harmonised framework for the regulation of electronic communications services, electronic communications networks and associated facilities, cannot be sufficiently achieved by the Member States and can therefore by reason of the scale or effects of the action be better achieved at Community level, the Community may adopt measures in accordance with the principles of subsidiarity as set out in Article 5 of the Treaty. In accordance with the principle of proportionality, as set out in that Article, this Directive does not go beyond what is necessary in order to achieve those objectives.

(52) The measures necessary for the implementation of this Directive should be adopted in accordance with Council Decision 1999/468/EC of 28 June 1999 laying down the procedures for the exercise of implementing powers conferred on the Commission[12],

HAVE ADOPTED THIS DIRECTIVE:

CHAPTER I

SCOPE, AIMS AND DEFINITIONS

Article 1

Scope and aims

1. Within the framework of Directive 2002/21/EC (Framework Directive), this Directive concerns the provision of electronic communications networks and services to end-users. The aim is to ensure the availability throughout the Community of good quality publicly available services through effective competition and choice and to deal with circumstances in which the needs of end-users are not satisfactorily met by the market.

2. This Directive establishes the rights of end-users and the corresponding obligations on undertakings providing publicly available electronic communications networks and services. With regard to ensuring provision of universal service within an environment of open and competitive markets, this Directive defines the minimum set of services of specified quality to which all end-users have access, at an affordable price in the light of specific national conditions, without distorting competition. This Directive also sets out obligations with regard to the provision of certain mandatory services such as the retail provision of leased lines.

Article 2

Definitions

For the purposes of this Directive, the definitions set out in Article 2 of Directive 2002/21/EC (Framework Directive) shall apply.

The following definitions shall also apply:

(a) "public pay telephone" means a telephone available to the general public, for the use of which the means of payment may include coins and/or credit/debit cards and/or pre-payment cards, including cards for use with dialling codes;

---

[12] OJ L 184, 17.7.1999, p. 23.

(b)   "public telephone network" means an electronic communications network which is used to provide publicly available telephone services; it supports the transfer between network termination points of speech communications, and also other forms of communication, such as facsimile and data;

(c)   "publicly available telephone service" means a service available to the public for originating and receiving national and international calls and access to emergency services through a number or numbers in a national or international telephone numbering plan, and in addition may, where relevant, include one or more of the following services: the provision of operator assistance, directory enquiry services, directories, provision of public pay phones, provision of service under special terms, provision of special facilities for customers with disabilities or with special social needs and/or the provision of non-geographic services;

(d)   "geographic number" means a number from the national numbering plan where part of its digit structure contains geographic significance used for routing calls to the physical location of the network termination point (NTP);

(e)   "network termination point" (NTP) means the physical point at which a subscriber is provided with access to a public communications network; in the case of networks involving switching or routing, the NTP is identified by means of a specific network address, which may be linked to a subscriber number or name;

(f)   "non-geographic numbers" means a number from the national numbering plan that is not a geographic number. It includes inter alia mobile, freephone and premium rate numbers.

CHAPTER II

UNIVERSAL SERVICE OBLIGATIONS INCLUDING SOCIAL OBLIGATIONS

Article 3

Availability of universal service

1.   Member States shall ensure that the services set out in this Chapter are made available at the quality specified to all end-users in their territory, independently of geographical location, and, in the light of specific national conditions, at an affordable price.

2.   Member States shall determine the most efficient and appropriate approach for ensuring the implementation of universal service, whilst respecting the principles of objectivity, transparency, non-discrimination and proportionality. They shall seek to minimise market distortions, in particular the provision of services at prices or subject to other terms and conditions which depart from normal commercial conditions, whilst safeguarding the public interest.

Article 4

Provision of access at a fixed location

1.   Member States shall ensure that all reasonable requests for connection at a fixed location to the public telephone network and for access to publicly available telephone services at a fixed location are met by at least one undertaking.

2.   The connection provided shall be capable of allowing end-users to make and receive local, national and international telephone calls, facsimile communications and data

communications, at data rates that are sufficient to permit functional Internet access, taking into account prevailing technologies used by the majority of subscribers and technological feasibility.

Article 5

Directory enquiry services and directories

1. Member States shall ensure that:

    (a) at least one comprehensive directory is available to end-users in a form approved by the relevant authority, whether printed or electronic, or both, and is updated on a regular basis, and at least once a year;

    (b) at least one comprehensive telephone directory enquiry service is available to all end-users, including users of public pay telephones.

2. The directories in paragraph 1 shall comprise, subject to the provisions of Article 11 of Directive 97/66/EC, all subscribers of publicly available telephone services.

3. Member States shall ensure that the undertaking(s) providing the services referred to in paragraph 1 apply the principle of non-discrimination to the treatment of information that has been provided to them by other undertakings.

Article 6

Public pay telephones

1. Member States shall ensure that national regulatory authorities can impose obligations on undertakings in order to ensure that public pay telephones are provided to meet the reasonable needs of end-users in terms of the geographical coverage, the number of telephones, the accessibility of such telephones to disabled users and the quality of services.

2. A Member State shall ensure that its national regulatory authority can decide not to impose obligations under paragraph 1 in all or part of its territory, if it is satisfied that these facilities or comparable services are widely available, on the basis of a consultation of interested parties as referred to in Article 33.

3. Member States shall ensure that it is possible to make emergency calls from public pay telephones using the single European emergency call number "112" and other national emergency numbers, all free of charge and without having to use any means of payment.

Article 7

Special measures for disabled users

1. Member States shall, where appropriate, take specific measures for disabled end-users in order to ensure access to and affordability of publicly available telephone services, including access to emergency services, directory enquiry services and directories, equivalent to that enjoyed by other end-users.

2. Member States may take specific measures, in the light of national conditions, to ensure that disabled end-users can also take advantage of the choice of undertakings and service providers available to the majority of end-users.

Article 8

Designation of undertakings

1. Member States may designate one or more undertakings to guarantee the provision of universal service as identified in Articles 4, 5, 6 and 7 and, where applicable, Article 9(2) so that the whole of the national territory can be covered. Member States may designate different undertakings or sets of undertakings to provide different elements of universal service and/or to cover different parts of the national territory.

2. When Member States designate undertakings in part or all of the national territory as having universal service obligations, they shall do so using an efficient, objective, transparent and non-discriminatory designation mechanism, whereby no undertaking is a priori excluded from being designated. Such designation methods shall ensure that universal service is provided in a cost-effective manner and may be used as a means of determining the net cost of the universal service obligation in accordance with Article 12.

Article 9

Affordability of tariffs

1. National regulatory authorities shall monitor the evolution and level of retail tariffs of the services identified in Articles 4, 5, 6 and 7 as falling under the universal service obligations and provided by designated undertakings, in particular in relation to national consumer prices and income.

2. Member States may, in the light of national conditions, require that designated undertakings provide tariff options or packages to consumers which depart from those provided under normal commercial conditions, in particular to ensure that those on low incomes or with special social needs are not prevented from accessing or using the publicly available telephone service.

3. Member States may, besides any provision for designated undertakings to provide special tariff options or to comply with price caps or geographical averaging or other similar schemes, ensure that support is provided to consumers identified as having low incomes or special social needs.

4. Member States may require undertakings with obligations under Articles 4, 5, 6 and 7 to apply common tariffs, including geographical averaging, throughout the territory, in the light of national conditions or to comply with price caps.

5. National regulatory authorities shall ensure that, where a designated undertaking has an obligation to provide special tariff options, common tariffs, including geographical averaging, or to comply with price caps, the conditions are fully transparent and are published and applied in accordance with the principle of non-discrimination. National regulatory authorities may require that specific schemes be modified or withdrawn.

Article 10

Control of expenditure

1. Member States shall ensure that designated undertakings, in providing facilities and services additional to those referred to in Articles 4, 5, 6, 7 and 9(2), establish terms and conditions in such a way that the subscriber is not obliged to pay for facilities or services which are not necessary or not required for the service requested.

2.   Member States shall ensure that designated undertakings with obligations under Articles 4, 5, 6, 7 and 9(2) provide the specific facilities and services set out in Annex I, Part A, in order that subscribers can monitor and control expenditure and avoid unwarranted disconnection of service.

3.   Member States shall ensure that the relevant authority is able to waive the requirements of paragraph 2 in all or part of its national territory if it is satisfied that the facility is widely available.

Article 11

Quality of service of designated undertakings

1.   National regulatory authorities shall ensure that all designated undertakings with obligations under Articles 4, 5, 6, 7 and 9(2) publish adequate and up-to-date information concerning their performance in the provision of universal service, based on the quality of service parameters, definitions and measurement methods set out in Annex III. The published information shall also be supplied to the national regulatory authority.

2.   National regulatory authorities may specify, inter alia, additional quality of service standards, where relevant parameters have been developed, to assess the performance of undertakings in the provision of services to disabled end-users and disabled consumers. National regulatory authorities shall ensure that information concerning the performance of undertakings in relation to these parameters is also published and made available to the national regulatory authority.

3.   National regulatory authorities may, in addition, specify the content, form and manner of information to be published, in order to ensure that end-users and consumers have access to comprehensive, comparable and user-friendly information.

4.   National regulatory authorities shall be able to set performance targets for those undertakings with universal service obligations at least under Article 4. In so doing, national regulatory authorities shall take account of views of interested parties, in particular as referred to in Article 33.

5.   Member States shall ensure that national regulatory authorities are able to monitor compliance with these performance targets by designated undertakings.

6.   Persistent failure by an undertaking to meet performance targets may result in specific measures being taken in accordance with Directive 2002/20/EC of the European Parliament and of the Council of 7 March 2002 on the authorisation of electronic communications networks and services (Authorisation Directive)[13]. National regulatory authorities shall be able to order independent audits or similar reviews of the performance data, paid for by the undertaking concerned, in order to ensure the accuracy and comparability of the data made available by undertakings with universal service obligations.

Article 12

Costing of universal service obligations

1.   Where national regulatory authorities consider that the provision of universal service as set out in Articles 3 to 10 may represent an unfair burden on undertakings

---

[13]   [OJ L 108, 24.4.2002, p. 21].

designated to provide universal service, they shall calculate the net costs of its provision.

For that purpose, national regulatory authorities shall:

(a)   calculate the net cost of the universal service obligation, taking into account any market benefit which accrues to an undertaking designated to provide universal service, in accordance with Annex IV, Part A; or

(b)   make use of the net costs of providing universal service identified by a designation mechanism in accordance with Article 8(2).

2.   The accounts and/or other information serving as the basis for the calculation of the net cost of universal service obligations under paragraph 1(a) shall be audited or verified by the national regulatory authority or a body independent of the relevant parties and approved by the national regulatory authority. The results of the cost calculation and the conclusions of the audit shall be publicly available.

Article 13

Financing of universal service obligations

1.   Where, on the basis of the net cost calculation referred to in Article 12, national regulatory authorities find that an undertaking is subject to an unfair burden, Member States shall, upon request from a designated undertaking, decide:

(a)   to introduce a mechanism to compensate that undertaking for the determined net costs under transparent conditions from public funds; and/or

(b)   to share the net cost of universal service obligations between providers of electronic communications networks and services.

2.   Where the net cost is shared under paragraph 1(b), Member States shall establish a sharing mechanism administered by the national regulatory authority or a body independent from the beneficiaries under the supervision of the national regulatory authority. Only the net cost, as determined in accordance with Article 12, of the obligations laid down in Articles 3 to 10 may be financed.

3.   A sharing mechanism shall respect the principles of transparency, least market distortion, non-discrimination and proportionality, in accordance with the principles of Annex IV, Part B. Member States may choose not to require contributions from undertakings whose national turnover is less than a set limit.

4.   Any charges related to the sharing of the cost of universal service obligations shall be unbundled and identified separately for each undertaking. Such charges shall not be imposed or collected from undertakings that are not providing services in the territory of the Member State that has established the sharing mechanism.

Article 14

Transparency

1.   Where a mechanism for sharing the net cost of universal service obligations as referred to in Article 13 is established, national regulatory authorities shall ensure that the principles for cost sharing, and details of the mechanism used, are publicly available.

2.   Subject to Community and national rules on business confidentiality, national regulatory authorities shall ensure that an annual report is published giving the calculated cost of universal service obligations, identifying the contributions made by all the undertakings involved, and identifying any market benefits, that may have accrued to the undertaking(s) designated to provide universal service, where a fund is actually in place and working.

Article 15

Review of the scope of universal service

1.   The Commission shall periodically review the scope of universal service, in particular with a view to proposing to the European Parliament and the Council that the scope be changed or redefined. A review shall be carried out, on the first occasion within two years after the date of application referred to in Article 38(1), second subparagraph, and subsequently every three years.

2.   This review shall be undertaken in the light of social, economic and technological developments, taking into account, inter alia, mobility and data rates in the light of the prevailing technologies used by the majority of subscribers. The review process shall be undertaken in accordance with Annex V. The Commission shall submit a report to the European Parliament and the Council regarding the outcome of the review.

CHAPTER III

REGULATORY CONTROLS ON UNDERTAKINGS WITH SIGNIFICANT MARKET POWER IN SPECIFIC MARKETS

Article 16

Review of obligations

1.   Member States shall maintain all obligations relating to:

(a)   retail tariffs for the provision of access to and use of the public telephone network, imposed under Article 17 of Directive 98/10/EC of the European Parliament and of the Council of 26 February 1998 on the application of open network provision (ONP) to voice telephony and on universal service for telecommunications in a competitive environment[14];

(b)   carrier selection or pre-selection, imposed under Directive 97/33/EC of the European Parliament and of the Council of 30 June 1997 on interconnection in telecommunications with regard to ensuring universal service and interoperability through application of the principles of open network provision (ONP)[15];

(c)   leased lines, imposed under Articles 3, 4, 6, 7, 8 and 10 of Directive 92/44/EEC,

until a review has been carried out and a determination made in accordance with the procedure in paragraph 3 of this Article.

2.   The Commission shall indicate relevant markets for the obligations relating to retail markets in the initial recommendation on relevant product and service markets and the

---

[14]   OJ L 101, 1.4.1998, p. 24.
[15]   OJ L 199, 26.7.1997, p. 32. Directive as amended by Directive 98/61/EC (OJ L 268, 3.10.1998, p. 37).

Decision identifying transnational markets to be adopted in accordance with Article 15 of Directive 2002/21/EC (Framework Directive).

3. Member States shall ensure that, as soon as possible after the entry into force of this Directive, and periodically thereafter, national regulatory authorities undertake a market analysis, in accordance with the procedure set out in Article 16 of Directive 2002/21/EC (Framework Directive) to determine whether to maintain, amend or withdraw the obligations relating to retail markets. Measures taken shall be subject to the procedure referred to in Article 7 of Directive 2002/21/EC (Framework Directive).

Article 17

Regulatory controls on retail services

1. Member States shall ensure that, where:

   (a) as a result of a market analysis carried out in accordance with Article 16(3) a national regulatory authority determines that a given retail market identified in accordance with Article 15 of Directive 2002/21/EC (Framework Directive) is not effectively competitive, and

   (b) the national regulatory authority concludes that obligations imposed under Directive 2002/19/EC (Access Directive), or Article 19 of this Directive would not result in the achievement of the objectives set out in Article 8 of Directive 2002/21/EC (Framework Directive),

   national regulatory authorities shall impose appropriate regulatory obligations on undertakings identified as having significant market power on a given retail market in accordance with Article 14 of Directive 2002/21/EC (Framework Directive).

2. Obligations imposed under paragraph 1 shall be based on the nature of the problem identified and be proportionate and justified in the light of the objectives laid down in Article 8 of Directive 2002/21/EC (Framework Directive). The obligations imposed may include requirements that the identified undertakings do not charge excessive prices, inhibit market entry or restrict competition by setting predatory prices, show undue preference to specific end-users or unreasonably bundle services. National regulatory authorities may apply to such undertakings appropriate retail price cap measures, measures to control individual tariffs, or measures to orient tariffs towards costs or prices on comparable markets, in order to protect end-user interests whilst promoting effective competition.

3. National regulatory authorities shall, on request, submit information to the Commission concerning the retail controls applied and, where appropriate, the cost accounting systems used by the undertakings concerned.

4. National regulatory authorities shall ensure that, where an undertaking is subject to retail tariff regulation or other relevant retail controls, the necessary and appropriate cost accounting systems are implemented. National regulatory authorities may specify the format and accounting methodology to be used. Compliance with the cost accounting system shall be verified by a qualified independent body. National regulatory authorities shall ensure that a statement concerning compliance is published annually.

5. Without prejudice to Article 9(2) and Article 10, national regulatory authorities shall not apply retail control mechanisms under paragraph 1 of this Article to geographical or user markets where they are satisfied that there is effective competition.

Article 18

Regulatory controls on the minimum set of leased lines

1. Where, as a result of the market analysis carried out in accordance with Article 16(3), a national regulatory authority determines that the market for the provision of part or all of the minimum set of leased lines is not effectively competitive, it shall identify undertakings with significant market power in the provision of those specific elements of the minimum set of leased lines services in all or part of its territory in accordance with Article 14 of Directive 2002/21/EC (Framework Directive). The national regulatory authority shall impose obligations regarding the provision of the minimum set of leased lines, as identified in the list of standards published in the Official Journal of the European Communities in accordance with Article 17 of Directive 2002/21/EC (Framework Directive), and the conditions for such provision set out in Annex VII to this Directive, on such undertakings in relation to those specific leased line markets.

2. Where as a result of the market analysis carried out in accordance with Article 16(3), a national regulatory authority determines that a relevant market for the provision of leased lines in the minimum set is effectively competitive, it shall withdraw the obligations referred to in paragraph 1 in relation to this specific leased line market.

3. The minimum set of leased lines with harmonised characteristics, and associated standards, shall be published in the Official Journal of the European Communities as part of the list of standards referred to in Article 17 of Directive 2002/21/EC (Framework Directive). The Commission may adopt amendments necessary to adapt the minimum set of leased lines to new technical developments and to changes in market demand, including the possible deletion of certain types of leased line from the minimum set, acting in accordance with the procedure referred to in Article 37(2) of this Directive.

Article 19

Carrier selection and carrier pre-selection

1. National regulatory authorities shall require undertakings notified as having significant market power for the provision of connection to and use of the public telephone network at a fixed location in accordance with Article 16(3) to enable their subscribers to access the services of any interconnected provider of publicly available telephone services:

   (a) on a call-by-call basis by dialling a carrier selection code; and

   (b) by means of pre-selection, with a facility to override any pre-selected choice on a call-by-call basis by dialling a carrier selection code.

2. User requirements for these facilities to be implemented on other networks or in other ways shall be assessed in accordance with the market analysis procedure laid down in Article 16 of Directive 2002/21/EC (Framework Directive) and implemented in accordance with Article 12 of Directive 2002/19/EC (Access Directive).

3. National regulatory authorities shall ensure that pricing for access and interconnection related to the provision of the facilities in paragraph 1 is cost oriented and that direct charges to subscribers, if any, do not act as a disincentive for the use of these facilities.

CHAPTER IV

END-USER INTERESTS AND RIGHTS

Article 20

Contracts

1. Paragraphs 2, 3 and 4 apply without prejudice to Community rules on consumer protection, in particular Directives 97/7/EC and 93/13/EC, and national rules in conformity with Community law.

2. Member States shall ensure that, where subscribing to services providing connection and/or access to the public telephone network, consumers have a right to a contract with an undertaking or undertakings providing such services. The contract shall specify at least:

    (a)   the identity and address of the supplier;

    (b)   services provided, the service quality levels offered, as well as the time for the initial connection;

    (c)   the types of maintenance service offered;

    (d)   particulars of prices and tariffs and the means by which up-to-date information on all applicable tariffs and maintenance charges may be obtained;

    (e)   the duration of the contract, the conditions for renewal and termination of services and of the contract;

    (f)   any compensation and the refund arrangements which apply if contracted service quality levels are not met; and

    (g)   the method of initiating procedures for settlement of disputes in accordance with Article 34.

    Member States may extend these obligations to cover other end-users.

3. Where contracts are concluded between consumers and electronic communications services providers other than those providing connection and/or access to the public telephone network, the information in paragraph 2 shall also be included in such contracts. Member States may extend this obligation to cover other end-users.

4. Subscribers shall have a right to withdraw from their contracts without penalty upon notice of proposed modifications in the contractual conditions. Subscribers shall be given adequate notice, not shorter than one month, ahead of any such modifications and shall be informed at the same time of their right to withdraw, without penalty, from such contracts, if they do not accept the new conditions.

Article 21

Transparency and publication of information

1. Member States shall ensure that transparent and up-to-date information on applicable prices and tariffs, and on standard terms and conditions, in respect of access to and use of publicly available telephone services is available to end-users and consumers, in accordance with the provisions of Annex II.

2. National regulatory authorities shall encourage the provision of information to enable end-users, as far as appropriate, and consumers to make an independent evaluation of the cost of alternative usage patterns, by means of, for instance, interactive guides.

Article 22

Quality of service

1. Member States shall ensure that national regulatory authorities are, after taking account of the views of interested parties, able to require undertakings that provide publicly available electronic communications services to publish comparable, adequate and up-to-date information for end-users on the quality of their services. The information shall, on request, also be supplied to the national regulatory authority in advance of its publication.

2. National regulatory authorities may specify, inter alia, the quality of service parameters to be measured, and the content, form and manner of information to be published, in order to ensure that end-users have access to comprehensive, comparable and user-friendly information. Where appropriate, the parameters, definitions and measurement methods given in Annex III could be used.

Article 23

Integrity of the network

Member States shall take all necessary steps to ensure the integrity of the public telephone network at fixed locations and, in the event of catastrophic network breakdown or in cases of force majeure, the availability of the public telephone network and publicly available telephone services at fixed locations. Member States shall ensure that undertakings providing publicly available telephone services at fixed locations take all reasonable steps to ensure uninterrupted access to emergency services.

Article 24

Interoperability of consumer digital television equipment

In accordance with the provisions of Annex VI, Member States shall ensure the interoperability of the consumer digital television equipment referred to therein.

Article 25

Operator assistance and directory enquiry services

1. Member States shall ensure that subscribers to publicly available telephone services have the right to have an entry in the publicly available directory referred to in Article 5(1)(a).

2. Member States shall ensure that all undertakings which assign telephone numbers to subscribers meet all reasonable requests to make available, for the purposes of the provision of publicly available directory enquiry services and directories, the relevant information in an agreed format on terms which are fair, objective, cost oriented and non-discriminatory.

3. Member States shall ensure that all end-users provided with a connection to the public telephone network can access operator assistance services and directory enquiry services in accordance with Article 5(1)(b).

4.   Member States shall not maintain any regulatory restrictions which prevent end-users in one Member State from accessing directly the directory enquiry service in another Member State.

5.   Paragraphs 1, 2, 3 and 4 apply subject to the requirements of Community legislation on the protection of personal data and privacy and, in particular, Article 11 of Directive 97/66/EC.

Article 26

Single European emergency call number

1.   Member States shall ensure that, in addition to any other national emergency call numbers specified by the national regulatory authorities, all end-users of publicly available telephone services, including users of public pay telephones, are able to call the emergency services free of charge, by using the single European emergency call number "112".

2.   Member States shall ensure that calls to the single European emergency call number "112" are appropriately answered and handled in a manner best suited to the national organisation of emergency systems and within the technological possibilities of the networks.

3.   Member States shall ensure that undertakings which operate public telephone networks make caller location information available to authorities handling emergencies, to the extent technically feasible, for all calls to the single European emergency call number "112".

4.   Member States shall ensure that citizens are adequately informed about the existence and use of the single European emergency call number "112".

Article 27

European telephone access codes

1.   Member States shall ensure that the "00" code is the standard international access code.   Special arrangements for making calls between adjacent locations across borders between Member States may be established or continued.   The end-users of publicly available telephone services in the locations concerned shall be fully informed of such arrangements.

2.   Member States shall ensure that all undertakings that operate public telephone networks handle all calls to the European telephony numbering space, without prejudice to the need for an undertaking that operates a public telephone network to recover the cost of the conveyance of calls on its network.

Article 28

Non-geographic numbers

Member States shall ensure that end-users from other Member States are able to access non-geographic numbers within their territory where technically and economically feasible, except where a called subscriber has chosen for commercial reasons to limit access by calling parties located in specific geographical areas.

Article 29

Provision of additional facilities

1. Member States shall ensure that national regulatory authorities are able to require all undertakings that operate public telephone networks to make available to end-users the facilities listed in Annex I, Part B, subject to technical feasibility and economic viability.

2. A Member State may decide to waive paragraph 1 in all or part of its territory if it considers, after taking into account the views of interested parties, that there is sufficient access to these facilities.

3. Without prejudice to Article 10(2), Member States may impose the obligations in Annex I, Part A, point (e), concerning disconnection as a general requirement on all undertakings.

Article 30

Number portability

1. Member States shall ensure that all subscribers of publicly available telephone services, including mobile services, who so request can retain their number(s) independently of the undertaking providing the service:

   (a)   in the case of geographic numbers, at a specific location; and

   (b)   in the case of non-geographic numbers, at any location.

   This paragraph does not apply to the porting of numbers between networks providing services at a fixed location and mobile networks.

2. National regulatory authorities shall ensure that pricing for interconnection related to the provision of number portability is cost oriented and that direct charges to subscribers, if any, do not act as a disincentive for the use of these facilities.

3. National regulatory authorities shall not impose retail tariffs for the porting of numbers in a manner that would distort competition, such as by setting specific or common retail tariffs.

Article 31

"Must carry" obligations

1. Member States may impose reasonable "must carry" obligations, for the transmission of specified radio and television broadcast channels and services, on undertakings under their jurisdiction providing electronic communications networks used for the distribution of radio or television broadcasts to the public where a significant number of end-users of such networks use them as their principal means to receive radio and television broadcasts.   Such obligations shall only be imposed where they are necessary to meet clearly defined general interest objectives and shall be proportionate and transparent. The obligations shall be subject to periodical review.

2. Neither paragraph 1 of this Article nor Article 3(2) of Directive 2002/19/EC (Access Directive) shall prejudice the ability of Member States to determine appropriate remuneration, if any, in respect of measures taken in accordance with this Article while ensuring that, in similar circumstances, there is no discrimination in the treatment of undertakings providing electronic communications networks.   Where

remuneration is provided for, Member States shall ensure that it is applied in a proportionate and transparent manner.

CHAPTER V

GENERAL AND FINAL PROVISIONS

Article 32

Additional mandatory services

Member States may decide to make additional services, apart from services within the universal service obligations as defined in Chapter II, publicly available in its own territory but, in such circumstances, no compensation mechanism involving specific undertakings may be imposed.

Article 33

Consultation with interested parties

1. Member States shall ensure as far as appropriate that national regulatory authorities take account of the views of end-users, and consumers (including, in particular, disabled users), manufacturers, undertakings that provide electronic communications networks and/or services on issues related to all end-user and consumer rights concerning publicly available electronic communications services, in particular where they have a significant impact on the market.

2. Where appropriate, interested parties may develop, with the guidance of national regulatory authorities, mechanisms, involving consumers, user groups and service providers, to improve the general quality of service provision by, inter alia, developing and monitoring codes of conduct and operating standards.

Article 34

Out-of-court dispute resolution

1. Member States shall ensure that transparent, simple and inexpensive out-of-court procedures are available for dealing with unresolved disputes, involving consumers, relating to issues covered by this Directive. Member States shall adopt measures to ensure that such procedures enable disputes to be settled fairly and promptly and may, where warranted, adopt a system of reimbursement and/or compensation. Member States may extend these obligations to cover disputes involving other end-users.

2. Member States shall ensure that their legislation does not hamper the establishment of complaints offices and the provision of on-line services at the appropriate territorial level to facilitate access to dispute resolution by consumers and end-users.

3. Where such disputes involve parties in different Member States, Member States shall coordinate their efforts with a view to bringing about a resolution of the dispute.

4. This Article is without prejudice to national court procedures.

Article 35

Technical adjustment

Amendments necessary to adapt Annexes I, II, III, VI and VII to technological developments or to changes in market demand shall be adopted by the Commission, acting in accordance with the procedure referred to in Article 37(2).

Article 36

Notification, monitoring and review procedures

1.   National regulatory authorities shall notify to the Commission by at the latest the date of application referred to in Article 38(1), second subparagraph, and immediately in the event of any change thereafter in the names of undertakings designated as having universal service obligations under Article 8(1).

      The Commission shall make the information available in a readily accessible form, and shall distribute it to the Communications Committee referred to in Article 37.

2.   National regulatory authorities shall notify to the Commission the names of operators deemed to have significant market power for the purposes of this Directive, and the obligations imposed upon them under this Directive.   Any changes affecting the obligations imposed upon undertakings or of the undertakings affected under the provisions of this Directive shall be notified to the Commission without delay.

3.   The Commission shall periodically review the functioning of this Directive and report to the European Parliament and to the Council, on the first occasion not later than three years after the date of application referred to in Article 38(1), second subparagraph. The Member States and national regulatory authorities shall supply the necessary information to the Commission for this purpose.

Article 37

Committee

1.   The Commission shall be assisted by the Communications Committee, set up by Article 22 of Directive 2002/21/EC (Framework Directive).

2.   Where reference is made to this paragraph, Articles 5 and 7 of Decision 1999/468/EC shall apply, having regard to the provisions of Article 8 thereof.

      The period laid down in Article 5(6) of Decision 1999/468/EC shall be three months.

3.   The Committee shall adopt its rules of procedure.

Article 38

Transposition

1.   Member States shall adopt and publish the laws, regulations and administrative provisions necessary to comply with this Directive by 24 July 2003 at the latest. They shall forthwith inform the Commission thereof.

      They shall apply those measures from 25 July 2003.

2.   When Member States adopt these measures, they shall contain a reference to this Directive or be accompanied by such a reference on the occasion of their official

publication. The methods of making such a reference shall be laid down by the Member States.

3. Member States shall communicate to the Commission the text of the provisions of national law which they adopt in the field governed by this Directive and of any subsequent modifications to those provisions.

Article 39

Entry into force

This Directive shall enter into force on the day of its publication in the Official Journal of the European Communities.

Article 40

Addressees

This Directive is addressed to the Member States.

Editors' Notes:

[a] OJ L 108, 24.4.2002, p. 51. Some citations in the original text have been updated to the current and complete Official Journal citation.

DESCRIPTION OF FACILITIES AND SERVICES REFERRED TO IN ARTICLE 10 (CONTROL OF EXPENDITURE) AND ARTICLE 29 (ADDITIONAL FACILITIES)

Part A: Facilities and services referred to in Article 10

(a)   Itemised billing

Member States are to ensure that national regulatory authorities, subject to the requirements of relevant legislation on the protection of personal data and privacy, may lay down the basic level of itemised bills which are to be provided by designated undertakings (as established in Article 8) to consumers free of charge in order that they can:

(i)   allow verification and control of the charges incurred in using the public telephone network at a fixed location and/or related publicly available telephone services, and

(ii)   adequately monitor their usage and expenditure and thereby exercise a reasonable degree of control over their bills.

Where appropriate, additional levels of detail may be offered to subscribers at reasonabl₂ tariffs or at no charge.

Calls which are free of charge to the calling subscriber, including calls to helplines, are not to be identified in the calling subscriber's itemised bill.

(b)   Selective call barring for outgoing calls, free of charge

I.e. the facility whereby the subscriber can, on request to the telephone service provider, bar outgoing calls of defined types or to defined types of numbers free of charge.

(c)   Pre-payment systems

Member States are to ensure that national regulatory authorities may require designated undertakings to provide means for consumers to pay for access to the public telephone network and use of publicly available telephone services on pre-paid terms.

(d)   Phased payment of connection fees

Member States are to ensure that national regulatory authorities may require designated undertakings to allow consumers to pay for connection to the public telephone network on the basis of payments phased over time.

(e)   Non-payment of bills

Member States are to authorise specified measures, which are to be proportionate, non-discriminatory and published, to cover non-payment of telephone bills for use of the public telephone network at fixed locations. These measures are to ensure that due warning of any consequent service interruption or disconnection is given to the subscriber beforehand. Except in cases of fraud, persistent late payment or non-payment, these measures are to ensure, as far as is technically feasible, that any service interruption is confined to the service concerned. Disconnection for non-payment of bills should take place only after due warning is given to the subscriber. Member States may allow a period of limited service prior to complete disconnection, during which only calls that do not incur a charge to the subscriber (e.g. "112" calls) are permitted.

Part B: List of facilities referred to in Article 29

(a) Tone dialling or DTMF (dual-tone multi-frequency operation)

I.e. the public telephone network supports the use of DTMF tones as defined in ETSI ETR 207 for end-to-end signalling throughout the network both within a Member State and between Member States.

(b) Calling-line identification

I.e. the calling party's number is presented to the called party prior to the call being established.

This facility should be provided in accordance with relevant legislation on protection of personal data and privacy, in particular Directive 97/66/EC.

To the extent technically feasible, operators should provide data and signals to facilitate the offering of calling-line identity and tone dialling across Member State boundaries.

INFORMATION TO BE PUBLISHED IN ACCORDANCE WITH ARTICLE 21 (TRANSPARENCY AND PUBLICATION OF INFORMATION)

The national regulatory authority has a responsibility to ensure that the information in this Annex is published, in accordance with Article 21. It is for the national regulatory authority to decide which information is to be published by the undertakings providing public telephone networks and/or publicly available telephone services and which information is to be published by the national regulatory authority itself, so as to ensure that consumers are able to make informed choices.

1.   Name(s) and address(es) of undertaking(s)

     I.e. names and head office addresses of undertakings providing public telephone networks and/or publicly available telephone services.

2.   Publicly available telephone services offered

2.1. Scope of the publicly available telephone service

     Description of the publicly available telephone services offered, indicating what is included in the subscription charge and the periodic rental charge (e.g. operator services, directories, directory enquiry services, selective call barring, itemised billing, maintenance, etc.).

2.2. Standard tariffs covering access, all types of usage charges, maintenance, and including details of standard discounts applied and special and targeted tariff schemes.

2.3. Compensation/refund policy, including specific details of any compensation/refund schemes offered.

2.4. Types of maintenance service offered.

2.5. Standard contract conditions, including any minimum contractual period, if relevant.

3.   Dispute settlement mechanisms including those developed by the undertaking.

4.   Information about rights as regards universal service, including the facilities and services mentioned in Annex I.

QUALITY OF SERVICE PARAMETERS

Supply-time and quality-of-service parameters, definitions and measurement methods
referred to Articles 11 and 22

Parameter[1]	Definition	Measurement method
Supply time for initial connection	ETSI EG 201 769-1	ETSI EG 201 769-1
Fault rate per access line	ETSI EG 201 769-1	ETSI EG 201 769-1
Fault repair time	ETSI EG 201 769-1	ETSI EG 201 769-1
Unsuccessful call ratio[2]	ETSI EG 201 769-1	ETSI EG 201 769-1
Call set up time[2]	ETSI EG 201 769-1	ETSI EG 201 769-1
Response times for operator services	ETSI EG 201 769-1	ETSI EG 201 769-1
Response times for directory enquiry services	ETSI EG 201 769-1	ETSI EG 201 769-1
Proportion of coin and card operated public pay-telephones in working order	ETSI EG 201 769-1	ETSI EG 201 769-1
Bill correctness complaints	ETSI EG 201 769-1	ETSI EG 201 769-1

Note: Version number of ETSI EG 201769-1 is 1.1.1 (April 2000).

---

[1]   Parameters should allow for performance to be analysed at a regional level (i.e. no less than Level 2 in the Nomenclature of Territorial Units for Statistics (NUTS) established by Eurostat).
[2]   Member States may decide not to require that up-to-date information concerning the performance for these two parameters be kept, if evidence is available to show that performance in these two areas is satisfactory.

CALCULATING THE NET COST, IF ANY, OF UNIVERSAL SERVICE OBLIGATIONS AND ESTABLISHING ANY RECOVERY OR SHARING MECHANISM IN ACCORDANCE WITH ARTICLES 12 AND 13

Part A: Calculation of net cost

Universal service obligations refer to those obligations placed upon an undertaking by a Member State which concern the provision of a network and service throughout a specified geographical area, including, where required, averaged prices in that geographical area for the provision of that service or provision of specific tariff options for consumers with low incomes or with special social needs.

National regulatory authorities are to consider all means to ensure appropriate incentives for undertakings (designated or not) to provide universal service obligations cost efficiently. In undertaking a calculation exercise, the net cost of universal service obligations is to be calculated as the difference between the net cost for a designated undertaking of operating with the universal service obligations and operating without the universal service obligations. This applies whether the network in a particular Member State is fully developed or is still undergoing development and expansion. Due attention is to be given to correctly assessing the costs that any designated undertaking would have chosen to avoid had there been no universal service obligation. The net cost calculation should assess the benefits, including intangible benefits, to the universal service operator.

The calculation is to be based upon the costs attributable to:

(i) elements of the identified services which can only be provided at a loss or provided under cost conditions falling outside normal commercial standards.

This category may include service elements such as access to emergency telephone services, provision of certain public pay telephones, provision of certain services or equipment for disabled people, etc;

(ii) specific end-users or groups of end-users who, taking into account the cost of providing the specified network and service, the revenue generated and any geographical averaging of prices imposed by the Member State, can only be served at a loss or under cost conditions falling outside normal commercial standards.

This category includes those end-users or groups of end-users which would not be served by a commercial operator which did not have an obligation to provide universal service.

The calculation of the net cost of specific aspects of universal service obligations is to be made separately and so as to avoid the double counting of any direct or indirect benefits and costs. The overall net cost of universal service obligations to any undertaking is to be calculated as the sum of the net costs arising from the specific components of universal service obligations, taking account of any intangible benefits. The responsibility for verifying the net cost lies with the national regulatory authority.

PART B: Recovery of any net costs of universal service obligations

The recovery or financing of any net costs of universal service obligations requires designated undertakings with universal service obligations to be compensated for the services they provide under non-commercial conditions. Because such a compensation involves financial transfers, Member States are to ensure that these are undertaken in an objective, transparent, non-discriminatory and proportionate manner. This means that the transfers result in the least distortion to competition and to user demand.

In accordance with Article 13(3), a sharing mechanism based on a fund should use a transparent and neutral means for collecting contributions that avoids the danger of a double imposition of contributions falling on both outputs and inputs of undertakings.

The independent body administering the fund is to be responsible for collecting contributions from undertakings which are assessed as liable to contribute to the net cost of universal service obligations in the Member State and is to oversee the transfer of sums due and/or administrative payments to the undertakings entitled to receive payments from the fund.

———————————

ANNEX V

PROCESS FOR REVIEWING THE SCOPE OF UNIVERSAL SERVICE
IN ACCORDANCE WITH ARTICLE 15

In considering whether a review of the scope of universal service obligations should be undertaken, the Commission is to take into consideration the following elements:

-    social and market developments in terms of the services used by consumers,

-    social and market developments in terms of the availability and choice of services to consumers,

-    technological developments in terms of the way services are provided to consumers.

In considering whether the scope of universal service obligations be changed or redefined, the Commission is to take into consideration the following elements:

-    are specific services available to and used by a majority of consumers and does the lack of availability or non-use by a minority of consumers result in social exclusion, and

-    does the availability and use of specific services convey a general net benefit to all consumers such that public intervention is warranted in circumstances where the specific services are not provided to the public under normal commercial circumstances?

———————————

INTEROPERABILITY OF DIGITAL CONSUMER EQUIPMENT
REFERRED TO IN ARTICLE 24

1.   The common scrambling algorithm and free-to-air reception

All consumer equipment intended for the reception of digital television signals, for sale or rent or otherwise made available in the Community, capable of descrambling digital television signals, is to possess the capability to:

-     allow the descrambling of such signals according to the common European scrambling algorithm as administered by a recognised European standards organisation, currently ETSI;

-     display signals that have been transmitted in clear provided that, in the event that such equipment is rented, the rentee is in compliance with the relevant rental agreement.

2.   Interoperability for analogue and digital television sets

Any analogue television set with an integral screen of visible diagonal greater than 42 cm which is put on the market for sale or rent in the Community is to be fitted with at least one open interface socket, as standardised by a recognised European standards organisation, e.g. as given in the CENELEC EN 50049-1:1997 standard, permitting simple connection of peripherals, especially additional decoders and digital receivers.

Any digital television set with an integral screen of visible diagonal greater than 30 cm which is put on the market for sale or rent in the Community is to be fitted with at least one open interface socket (either standardised by, or conforming to a standard adopted by, a recognised European standards organisation, or conforming to an industry-wide specification) e.g. the DVB common interface connector, permitting simple connection of peripherals, and able to pass all the elements of a digital television signal, including information relating to interactive and conditionally accessed services.

CONDITIONS FOR THE MINIMUM SET OF LEASED LINES REFERRED TO IN ARTICLE 18

Note: In accordance with the procedure in Article 18, provision of the minimum set of leased lines under the conditions established by Directive 92/44/EC should continue until such time as the national regulatory authority determines that there is effective competition in the relevant leased lines market.

National regulatory authorities are to ensure that provision of the minimum set of leased lines referred to in Article 18 follows the basic principles of non-discrimination, cost orientation and transparency.

1.   Non discrimination

National regulatory authorities are to ensure that the organisations identified as having significant market power pursuant to Article 18(1) adhere to the principle of non-discrimination when providing leased lines referred to in Article 18.   Those organisations are to apply similar conditions in similar circumstances to organisations providing similar services, and are to provide leased lines to others under the same conditions and of the same quality as they provide for their own services, or those of their subsidiaries or partners, where applicable.

2.   Cost orientation

National regulatory authorities are, where appropriate, to ensure that tariffs for leased lines referred to in Article 18 follow the basic principles of cost orientation.

To this end, national regulatory authorities are to ensure that undertakings identified as having significant market power pursuant to Article 18(1) formulate and put in practice a suitable cost accounting system.

National regulatory authorities are to keep available, with an adequate level of detail, information on the cost accounting systems applied by such undertakings.   They are to submit this information to the Commission on request.

3.   Transparency

National regulatory authorities are to ensure that the following information in respect of the minimum set of leased lines referred to in Article 18 is published in an easily accessible form.

3.1.   Technical characteristics, including the physical and electrical characteristics as well as the detailed technical and performance specifications which apply at the network termination point.

3.2.   Tariffs, including the initial connection charges, the periodic rental charges and other charges.   Where tariffs are differentiated, this must be indicated.

Where, in response to a particular request, an organisation identified as having significant market power pursuant to Article 18(1) considers it unreasonable to provide a leased line in the minimum set under its published tariffs and supply conditions, it must seek the agreement of the national regulatory authority to vary those conditions in that case.

3.3.   Supply conditions, including at least the following elements:

-    information concerning the ordering procedure,

- the typical delivery period, which is the period, counted from the date when the user has made a firm request for a leased line, in which 95% of all leased lines of the same type have been put through to the customers.

  This period will be established on the basis of the actual delivery periods of leased lines during a recent time interval of reasonable duration. The calculation must not include cases where late delivery periods were requested by users,

- the contractual period, which includes the period which is in general laid down in the contract and the minimum contractual period which the user is obliged to accept,

- the typical repair time, which is the period, counted from the time when a failure message has been given to the responsible unit within the undertaking identified as having significant market power pursuant to Article 18(1) up to the moment in which 80% of all leased lines of the same type have been re-established and in appropriate cases notified back in operation to the users. Where different classes of quality of repair are offered for the same type of leased lines, the different typical repair times shall be published,

- any refund procedure.

In addition where a Member State considers that the achieved performance for the provision of the minimum set of leased lines does not meet users' needs, it may define appropriate targets for the supply conditions listed above.

———————————————

COMMISSION DIRECTIVE 2002/77/EC

of 16 September 2002[a]

on competition in the markets for electronic communications networks and services[b]

THE COMMISSION OF THE EUROPEAN COMMUNITIES,

Having regard to the Treaty establishing the European Community, and in particular Article 86(3) thereof,

Whereas:

(1) Commission Directive 90/388/EEC of 28 June 1990 on competition in the markets for telecommunications services[1], as last amended by Directive 1999/64/EC[2], has been substantially amended several times. Since further amendments are to be made, it should be recast in the interest of clarity.

(2) Article 86 of the Treaty entrusts the Commission with the task of ensuring that, in the case of public undertakings and undertakings enjoying special or exclusive rights, Member States comply with their obligations under Community law. Pursuant to Article 86(3), the Commission can specify and clarify the obligations arising from that Article and, in that framework, set out the conditions which are necessary to allow the Commission to perform effectively the duty of surveillance imposed upon it by that paragraph.

(3) Directive 90/388/EEC required Member States to abolish special and exclusive rights for the provision of telecommunications services, initially for other services than voice telephony, satellite services and mobile radiocommunications, and then it gradually established full competition in the telecommunications market.

(4) A number of other Directives in this field have also been adopted under Article 95 of the Treaty by the European Parliament and the Council aiming, principally, at the establishment of an internal market for telecommunications services through the implementation of open network provision and the provision of a universal service in an environment of open and competitive markets. Those Directives should be repealed with effect from 25 July 2003 when the new regulatory framework for electronic communications networks and services is applied.

(5) The new electronic communications regulatory framework consists of one general Directive, Directive 2002/21/EC of the European Parliament and of the Council of 7 March 2002 on a common regulatory framework for electronic communications networks and services (Framework Directive)[3] and four specific Directives: Directive 2002/20/EC of the European Parliament and of the Council of 7 March 2002 on the authorisation of electronic communications networks and services (Authorisation Directive)[4], Directive 2002/19/EC of the European Parliament and of the Council of 7 March 2002 on access to, and interconnection of, electronic communications networks and associated facilities (Access Directive)[5], Directive 2002/22/EC of the European Parliament and of the Council of 7 March 2002 on universal service and users' rights relating to electronic communications networks and services (Universal Service Directive)[6], and Directive 2002/58/EC of the European Parliament and of the Council

---

[1]   OJ L 192, 24.7.1990, p. 10.
[2]   OJ L 175, 10.7.1999, p. 39.
[3]   OJ L 108, 24.4.2002, p. 33.
[4]   OJ L 108, 24.4.2002, p. 21.
[5]   OJ L 108, 24.4.2002, p. 7.
[6]   OJ L 108, 24.4.2002, p. 51.

of 12 July 2002 concerning the processing of personal data and the protection of privacy in the electronic communications (Directive on privacy and electronic communications) sector[7].

(6)   In the light of the developments which have marked the liberalisation process and the gradual opening of the telecommunications markets in Europe since 1990, certain definitions used in Directive 90/388/EEC and its amending acts should be adjusted in order to reflect the latest technological developments in the telecommunications field, or replaced in order to take account of the convergence phenomenon which has shaped the information technology, media and telecommunications industries over recent years. The wording of certain provisions should, where possible, be clarified in order to facilitate their application, taking into account, where appropriate, the relevant Directives adopted under Article 95 of the Treaty, and the experience acquired through the implementation of Directive 90/388/EEC as amended.

(7)   This Directive makes reference to "electronic communications services" and "electronic communications networks" rather than the previously used terms "telecommunications services" and "telecommunications networks". These new definitions are indispensable in order to take account of the convergence phenomenon by bringing together under one single definition all electronic communications services and/or networks which are concerned with the conveyance of signals by wire, radio, optical or other electromagnetic means (i.e. fixed, wireless, cable television, satellite networks). Thus, the transmission and broadcasting of radio and television programmes should be recognised as an electronic communication service and networks used for such transmission and broadcasting should likewise be recognised as electronic communications networks. Furthermore, it should be made clear that the new definition of electronic communications networks also covers fibre networks which enable third parties, using their own switching or routing equipment, to convey signals.

(8)   In this context, it should be made clear that Member States must remove (if they have not already done so) exclusive and special rights for the provision of all electronic communications networks, not just those for the provision of electronic communications services and should ensure that undertakings are entitled to provide such services without prejudice to the provisions of Directives 2002/19/EC, 2002/20/EC, 2002/21/EC and 2002/22/EC. The definition of electronic communications networks should also mean that Member States are not permitted to restrict the right of an operator to establish, extend and/or provide a cable network on the ground that such network could also be used for the transmission of radio and television programming. In particular, special or exclusive rights which amount to restricting the use of electronic communications networks for the transmission and distribution of television signals are contrary to Article 86(1), read in conjunction with Article 43 (right of establishment) and/or Article 82(b) of the EC Treaty insofar as they have the effect of permitting a dominant undertaking to limit "production, markets or technical development to the prejudice of consumers". This is, however, without prejudice to the specific rules adopted by the Member States in accordance with Community law, and, in particular, in accordance with Council Directive 89/552/EEC of 3 October 1989[8], on the coordination of certain provisions laid down by law, regulation or administrative action in Member States concerning the pursuit of television broadcasting activities, as amended by Directive 97/36/EC of the European

[7]   OJ L 201, 31.7.2002, p. 37.
[8]   OJ L 298, 17.10.1989, p. 23.

Parliament and of the Council[9], governing the distribution of audiovisual programmes intended for the general public.

(9)   Pursuant to the principle of proportionality, Member States should no longer make the provision of electronic communications services and the establishment and provision of electronic communications networks subject to a licensing regime but to a general authorisation regime. This is also required by Directive 2002/20/EC, according to which electronic communications services or networks should be provided on the basis of a general authorisation and not on the basis of a license. An aggrieved party should have the right to challenge a decision preventing him from providing electronic communications services or networks before an independent body and, ultimately, before a court or a tribunal. It is a fundamental principle of Community law that an individual is entitled to effective judicial protection whenever a State measure violates rights conferred upon him by the provisions of a Directive.

(10) Public authorities may exercise a dominant influence on the behaviour of public undertakings, as a result either of the rules governing the undertaking or of the manner in which the shareholdings are distributed. Therefore, where Member States control vertically integrated network operators which operate networks which have been established under special or exclusive rights, those Member States should ensure that, in order to avoid potential breaches of the Treaty competition rules, such operators, when they enjoy a dominant position in the relevant market, do not discriminate in favour of their own activities. It follows that Member States should take all measures necessary to prevent any discrimination between such vertically integrated operators and their competitors.

(11) This Directive should also clarify the principle derived from Commission Directive 96/2/EC of 16 January 1996 amending Directive 90/388/EC with regard to mobile and personal communications[10], by providing that Member States should not grant exclusive or special rights of use of radio frequencies and that the rights of use of those frequencies should be assigned according to objective, non-discriminatory and transparent procedures. This should be without prejudice to specific criteria and procedures adopted by Member States to grant such rights to providers of radio or television broadcast content services with a view to pursuing general interest objectives in conformity with Community law.

(12) Any national scheme pursuant to Directive 2002/22/EC, serving to share the net cost of the provision of universal service obligations shall be based on objective, transparent and non-discriminatory criteria and shall be consistent with the principles of proportionality and of least market distortion. Least market distortion means that contributions should be recovered in a way that as far as possible minimises the impact of the financial burden falling on end-users, for example by spreading contributions as widely as possible.

(13) Where rights and obligations arising from international conventions setting up international satellite organisations are not compatible with the competition rules of the Treaty, Member States should take, in accordance with Article 307 of the EC Treaty, all appropriate steps to eliminate such incompatibilities. This Directive should clarify this obligation because Article 3 of Directive 94/46/EC[11], merely required Member States to "communicate to the Commission" the information they possessed on such incompatibilities. Article 11 of this Directive should clarify the obligation on

---

[9]   OJ L 202, 30.7.1997, p. 60.
[10] OJ L 20, 26.1.1996, p. 59.
[11] OJ L 268, 19.10.1994, p. 15.

Member States to remove any restrictions which could still be in force because of those international conventions.

(14) This Directive should maintain the obligation imposed on Member States by Directive 1999/64/EC, so as to ensure that dominant providers of electronic communications networks and publicly available telephone services operate their public electronic communication network and cable television network as separate legal entities.

(15) This Directive should be without prejudice to obligations of the Member States concerning the time limits set out in Annex I, Part B, within which the Member States are to comply with the preceding Directives.

(16) Member States should supply to the Commission any information which is necessary to demonstrate that existing national implementing legislation reflects the clarifications provided for in this Directive as compared with Directives 90/388/EC, 94/46/EC, 95/51/EC[12], 96/2/EC, 96/19/EC[13] and 1999/64/EC.

(17) In the light of the above, Directive 90/388/EC should be repealed,

HAS ADOPTED THIS DIRECTIVE:

Article 1

Definitions

For the purposes of this Directive the following definitions shall apply:

1. "electronic communications network" shall mean transmission systems and, where applicable, switching or routing equipment and other resources which permit the conveyance of signals by wire, by radio, by optical or by other electromagnetic means, including satellite networks, fixed (circuit - and packet - switched, including Internet) and mobile terrestrial networks, and electricity cable systems, to the extent that they are used for the purpose of transmitting signals, networks used for radio and television broadcasting, and cable television networks, irrespective of the type of information conveyed;

2. "public communications network" shall mean an electronic communications network used wholly or mainly for the provision of public electronic communications services;

3. "electronic communications services" shall mean a service normally provided for remuneration which consists wholly or mainly in the conveyance of signals on electronic communications networks, including telecommunications services and transmission services in networks used for broadcasting but exclude services providing or exercising editorial control over, content transmitted using electronic communications networks and services; it does not include information society services as defined in Article 1 of Directive 98/34/EC which do not consist wholly or mainly in the conveyance of signals on electronic communications networks;

4. "publicly available electronic communications services" shall mean electronic communications services available to the public;

5. "exclusive rights" shall mean the rights that are granted by a Member State to one undertaking through any legislative, regulatory or administrative instrument, reserving

---

[12] OJ L 256, 26.10.1995, p. 49.
[13] OJ L 74, 22.3.1996, p. 13.

it the right to provide an electronic communications service or to undertake an electronic communications activity within a given geographical area;

6. "special rights" shall mean the rights that are granted by a Member State to a limited number of undertakings through any legislative, regulatory or administrative instrument which, within a given geographical area:

   (a) designates or limits to two or more the number of such undertakings authorised to provide an electronic communications service or undertake an electronic communications activity, otherwise than according to objective, proportional and non-discriminatory criteria, or

   (b) confers on undertakings, otherwise than according to such criteria, legal or regulatory advantages which substantially affect the ability of any other undertaking to provide the same electronic communications service or to undertake the same electronic communications activity in the same geographical area under substantially equivalent conditions;

7. "satellite earth station network" shall mean a configuration of two or more earth stations which interwork by means of a satellite;

8. "cable television networks" shall mean any mainly wire-based infrastructure established primarily for the delivery or distribution of radio or television broadcast to the public.

Article 2

Exclusive and special rights for electronic communications networks and electronic communications services

1. Member States shall not grant or maintain in force exclusive or special rights for the establishment and/or the provision of electronic communications networks, or for the provision of publicly available electronic communications services.

2. Member States shall take all measures necessary to ensure that any undertaking is entitled to provide electronic communications services or to establish, extend or provide electronic communications networks.

3. Member States shall ensure that no restrictions are imposed or maintained on the provision of electronic communications services over electronic communications networks established by the providers of electronic communications services, over infrastructures provided by third parties, or by means of sharing networks, other facilities or sites without prejudice to the provisions of Directives 2002/19/EC, 2002/20/EC, 2002/21/EC and 2002/22/EC.

4. Member States shall ensure that a general authorisation granted to an undertaking to provide electronic communications services or to establish and/or provide electronic communications networks, as well as the conditions attached thereto, shall be based on objective, non-discriminatory, proportionate and transparent criteria.

5. Reasons shall be given for any decision taken on the grounds set out in Article 3(1) of Directive 2002/20/EC preventing an undertaking from providing electronic communications services or networks.

   Any aggrieved party should have the possibility to challenge such a decision before a body that is independent of the parties involved and ultimately before a court or a tribunal.

Article 3

Vertically integrated public undertakings

In addition to the requirements set out in Article 2(2), and without prejudice to Article 14 of Directive 2002/21/EC, Member States, shall ensure that vertically integrated public undertakings which provide electronic communications networks and which are in a dominant position do not discriminate in favour of their own activities.

Article 4

Rights of use of frequencies

Without prejudice to specific criteria and procedures adopted by Member States to grant rights of use of radio frequencies to providers of radio or television broadcast content services with a view to pursuing general interest objectives in conformity with Community law:

1.   Member States shall not grant exclusive or special rights of use of radio frequencies for the provision of electronic communications services.

2.   The assignment of radio frequencies for electronic communication services shall be based on objective, transparent, non-discriminatory and proportionate criteria.

Article 5

Directory services

Member States shall ensure that all exclusive and/or special rights with regard to the establishment and provision of directory services on their territory, including both the publication of directories and directory enquiry services, are abolished.

Article 6

Universal service obligations

1.   Any national scheme pursuant to Directive 2002/22/EC, serving to share the net cost of the provision of universal service obligations shall be based on objective, transparent and non-discriminatory criteria and shall be consistent with the principle of proportionality and of least market distortion. In particular, where universal service obligations are imposed in whole or in part on public undertakings providing electronic communications services, this shall be taken into consideration in calculating any contribution to the net cost of universal service obligations.

2.   Member States shall communicate any scheme of the kind referred to in paragraph 1 to the Commission.

Article 7

Satellites

1.   Member States shall ensure that any regulatory prohibition or restriction on the offer of space segment capacity to any authorised satellite earth station network operator are abolished, and shall authorise within their territory any space-segment supplier to verify that the satellite earth station network for use in connection with the space segment of the supplier in question is in conformity with the published conditions for access to such person's space segment capacity.

2. Member States which are party to international conventions setting up international satellite organisations shall, where such conventions are not compatible with the competition rules of the EC Treaty, take all appropriate steps to eliminate such incompatibilities.

Article 8

Cable television networks

1. Each Member State shall ensure that no undertaking providing public electronic communications networks operates its cable television network using the same legal entity as it uses for its other public electronic communications network, when such undertaking:

   (a) is controlled by that Member State or benefits from special rights; and

   (b) is dominant in a substantial part of the common market in the provision of public electronic communications networks and publicly available telephone services; and

   (c) operates a cable television network which has been established under special or exclusive right in the same geographic area.

2. The term "publicly available telephone services" shall be considered synonymous with the term "public voice telephony services" referred to in Article 1 of Directive 1999/64/EC.

3. Member States which consider that there is sufficient competition in the provision of local loop infrastructure and services in their territory shall inform the Commission accordingly.

   Such information shall include a detailed description of the market structure. The information provided shall be made available to any interested party on demand, regard being had to the legitimate interest of undertakings in the protection of their business secrets.

4. The Commission shall decide within a reasonable period, after having heard the comments of these parties, whether the obligation of legal separation may be ended in the Member State concerned.

5. The Commission shall review the application of this Article not later than 31 December 2004.

Article 9

Member States shall supply to the Commission not later than 24 July 2003 such information as will allow the Commission to confirm that the provisions of this Directive have been complied with.

Article 10

Repeal

Directive 90/388/EC, as amended by the Directives listed in Annex I, Part A, is repealed with effect from 25 July 2003, without prejudice to the obligations of the Member States in respect of the time limits for transposition laid down in Annex I, Part B.

References to the repealed Directives shall be construed as references to this Directive and shall be read in accordance with the correlation table in Annex II.

Article 11

This Directive shall enter into force on the 20th day following that of its publication in the Official Journal of the European Communities.

Article 12

This Directive is addressed to the Member States.

Editors' Notes:

[a] OJ L 249, 17.09.2002, p. 21.

[b] The Competition Directive consolidates previous liberalisation directives. (See the Introduction to the 2003 Edition of this book, Section 1(a), for a more detailed history of those measures.) The Commission press release that accompanied the release of the first draft of the Directive in July 2000 provides the following statement on the purpose of the Competition Directive:

> "The purpose of the Competition Directive is to recall the obligation imposed on Member States to abolish exclusive and special rights in the field of telecommunications which is an obligation deriving directly from the Treaty itself. In this sense, the Directives merely interprets and clarifies the scope of the Treaty's fundamental provisions.

> The new Competition Directive brings within one single, clear and convenient text all relevant provisions of Directive 90/388 which are to date scattered in six different Directives. The Directive does not impose new obligations on Member States. [...] Only those provisions which are still necessary for attaining the objectives of full competition in the telecommunications sector will be maintained. [...]

> Furthermore, certain definitions used in the consolidated Directive have been amended in order to reflect the latest technological developments in telecommunications, in general. Finally, the wording of certain provisions has been clarified in order to facilitate their application, taking into account the new six harmonisation Directives proposed by the Commission as well as the experience which the Commission has so far acquired through the implementation of Directive 90/388/EEC."

Part A:

List of Directives to be repealed

Directive 90/388/EEC (OJ L 192, 24.7.1990, p. 10)
Articles 2 and 3 of Directive 94/46/EC (OJ L 268, 19.1.1994, p. 15)
Directive 95/51/EC (OJ L 256, 26.10.1995, p. 49)
Directive 96/2/EC (OJ L 20, 26.1.1996, p. 59)
Directive 96/19/EC (OJ L 74, 22.3.1996, p. 13)
Directive 1999/64/EC (OJ L 175, 10.7.1999, p. 39)

Part B:

Transposition dates for the above Directives

Directive 90/388/EEC: transposition date: 31 December 1990
Directive 94/46/EC: transposition date: 8 August 1995
Directive 95/51/EC: transposition date: 1 October 1996
Directive 96/2/EC: transposition date: 15 November 1996
Directive 96/19/EC: transposition date: 11 January 1997
Directive 1999/64/EC: transposition date: 30 April 2000

Correlation Table

This Directive	Directive 90/388/EEC
Article 1 (Definitions)	Article 1
Article 2 (withdrawal of exclusive/special rights)	Article 2
Article 3 (vertically integrated public undertakings)	Article 3a (ii)
Article 4 (rights of use of radio frequencies	Article 3(b)
Article 5 (directory services)	Article 4(b)
Article 6 (universal service obligations)	Article 4(c)
Article 7 (satellites)	Article 3 of Directive 94/46/EC
Article 8 (cable networks)	Article 9

**COMMUNICATION COM(2006) 334 FINAL FROM THE COMMISSION TO THE
COUNCIL, THE EUROPEAN PARLIAMENT, THE EUROPEAN ECONOMIC
AND SOCIAL COMMITTEE AND THE COMMITTEE OF THE REGIONS**

of 29 June 2006

on the Review of the EU Regulatory Framework for electronic communications networks
and services

1.   SUMMARY

This Communication reports on the functioning of the five directives of the regulatory
framework for electronic communications networks and services, as required by these
directives[1]. This Communication also launches a public consultation on the future of the
electronic communications regulatory framework on which comments are requested by 27
October 2006. It explains how the framework has delivered on its objectives, and identifies
areas for change. The proposed changes are discussed in the associated Commission Staff
Working Document[a]. In keeping with the principles of better regulation, the opportunity has
been taken to propose reductions in administrative burdens and the repeal of outdated
measures. The associated Impact Assessment captures the broader range of options
considered prior to drawing the conclusions presented here. Taking account of the
comments received, the Commission will draw up legislative proposals for modification of
the framework, to be presented to the European Parliament and the Council, duly
accompanied by specific impact assessments.

2.   BACKGROUND

Creating a single European information space with an open and competitive internal market
is one of the key challenges for Europe[2], within the broader strategy for growth and jobs.
Electronic communications underpins the whole of the economy, and at EU level is
supported by a regulatory framework that entered into force in 2003. The aims of the
framework are to promote competition, consolidate the internal market for electronic
communications and benefit consumers and users. It is designed to take account of
convergence, in that it deals with markets and not technologies. Markets are defined
according to competition law principles, based on general demand and supply side
considerations, and are independent of changes in the underlying technology. The
framework provides for the progressive removal of regulation as and when competition
becomes effective. The markets in which the Commission considers regulation may be
justified, and the criteria used to identify such markets, are listed in a Commission
Recommendation[3], which is also being reviewed[4]. This overall approach allows the
framework to respond to changing technology and market conditions.

Given the special characteristics of mobile roaming in the Community, the Commission will
propose a European Parliament and Council Regulation to address this specific issue. The
revision of the Recommendation on relevant markets will take account of this.

Regulatory decisions are adopted by national regulatory authorities (NRAs) but a review
mechanism at EU level (known as the 'Article 7 procedure') safeguards the internal market

---

[1]   Directives 2002/19/EC, 2002/20/EC, 2002/21/EC, 2002/22/EC (OJ L 108, 24.4.2002, p. 7) and 2002/58/EC
     (OJ L 201, 31.7.2002, p. 37). See also Annex I of Impact Assessment.
[2]   COM(2005) 24, 2.2.2005.
[3]   Commission Recommendation on Relevant Product and Service Markets within the electronic
     communications sector susceptible to ex ante regulation, C(2003) 497.
[4]   Commission Staff Working Document on the Recommendation on relevant markets.

by helping to ensure the consistency of ex ante regulation across the EU. The Commission reported on the functioning of this procedure in February 2006[5].

In addition to the 'economic' regulation described above, the framework seeks to protect the consumer by laying down legal obligations in the areas of privacy and data protection, universal service and user rights. The framework does not deal with content services, which are subject to other rules at EU level, but it does give NRAs powers to deal with uncompetitive markets in situations where content services are bundled with electronic communications services.

3.   ASSESSMENT OF THE FRAMEWORK - ACHIEVEMENT OF OBJECTIVES

Market development

Electronic communications continue to be a success story for the EU. Since markets were fully opened up to competition in 1998, users and consumers have benefited from more choice, lower prices and innovative products and services. Mobile services have reached high penetration levels; broadband communications are growing rapidly. Overall growth in revenue terms in the sector continues to be strong, outpacing the growth of the EU economy. In 2005 the ICT sector was valued at €614bn, according to the Commission's 11th Implementation report which provides more information about these developments[6]. ICT also contributes macro-economically to productivity growth and increased competitiveness of the European economy as a whole, and thus is a factor in growth and job creation.

Stakeholder consultation

Responses to the Commission's 'Call for Input'[7] were generally positive about the impact of the regulatory framework, although some felt it was too early to draw definitive conclusions. Consumers and industry groups supported the framework's approach, albeit with criticisms concerning its implementation. Several stakeholders considered that, even if certain aspects needed updating, the framework brought greater regulatory robustness. Many called for a simplification of the market review procedures and generally welcomed the new institutional arrangements for spectrum harmonisation[8].

New entrants, cable operators, ISPs and software and equipment producers noted that the framework had allowed the development of competition and innovation across Europe, facilitating investment and broadband penetration. However, the majority of incumbents considered that ex-ante regulation hindered new investment and should be phased out by 2015.

Innovation, investment and competition

The available evidence indicates that European investment in this sector over recent years has been as high if not higher than in other world regions (€45bn in 2005)[9]. Both new entrants and incumbents, in response to competition, are investing to extend and upgrade fixed and wireless network infrastructure in order to provide innovative services. Relative to

---

[5]   COM(2006) 28, 6.2.2006.

[6]   COM(2006) 68, 20.2.2006.

[7]   The responses are available at:
     http://ec.europa.eu/information_society/policy/ecomm/info_centre/documentation/public_consult/review/ind ex_en.htm.

[8]   The Radio Spectrum Decision 676/2002/EC allows for technical harmonisation of spectrum usage conditions (via the Radio Spectrum Committee); strategic advice on radio spectrum policy via the Radio Spectrum Policy Group.

[9]   See footnote 6.

their turnover, new entrants are investing more than incumbents. Investment can flourish in a variety of regulatory situations, but competition remains the main driving force. According to a study commissioned by the Commission, countries that have applied the EU regulatory framework in an effective and pro-competitive manner have attracted most investment[10].

The correlation between investment in broadband and competition in infrastructure has become clear. Countries with strong competition between incumbents and cable operators tend to have the highest broadband penetration[11].

In this sector, the investments needed for network modernisation are substantial, but the operational savings from rationalisation and the use of modern technology are also considerable[12]. Some have called for regulatory forbearance to encourage investment in new network infrastructure, but there is little to show that regulatory 'holidays' generate new investment, absent other factors like competition.

The regulatory framework indicates that newly emerging markets should not be subject to inappropriate regulation[13]. The Commission regards as emerging markets those markets that are so new and fast-moving that it is premature to decide whether they satisfy the three criteria for ex-ante regulation identified in its Recommendation[14]. Once markets become more mature however, if they fulfil these criteria, the framework gives regulators considerable flexibility to reward innovative and risky investments[15]. Indeed, the framework explicitly recognises the need for regulators to allow adequate cost recovery on existing assets, and to properly reward innovation and new, risky investments by calling on NRAs to "take into account... the initial investment by the facility owner, bearing in mind the risks involved in making the investment"[16].

Summary

There is room for significant improvement in the way that spectrum is managed. Specifically, the Commission considers that more effective management of spectrum would release its full potential to contribute to offering innovative, diverse and affordable services to the European citizen and to strengthen the competitiveness of European ICT industries. In other respects, the Commission considers that the principles and flexible tools in the regulatory framework, when applied fully and effectively, offer the most appropriate means of encouraging investment, innovation and market development. There is nevertheless room for the Commission and NRAs to provide guidance on how the rules should be applied, so as to increase predictability for stakeholders.

4.   TECHNOLOGY AND MARKET EVOLUTION

The challenge for this review is to ensure that the framework continues to serve the needs of the sector for the next decade.

---

[10] London Economics in association with PricewaterhouseCoopers, study for DG Information Society and Media of the European Commission on 'An assessment of the Regulatory Framework for Electronic Communications - Growth and Investment in the EU e-communications sector' (to be published).
[11] See associated Commission Staff Working Document, section 2.
[12] ibid.
[13] Recital 27 Framework Directive.
[14] The 3 criteria are: a) the market is subject to high and non-transitory entry barriers; b) the market has characteristics such that it will not tend towards effective competition over time; c) competition law by itself is insufficient to deal with the market failure (absent ex ante regulation). See the Commission Staff Working Document on the Recommendation on relevant markets.
[15] Article 12(2) Access Directive.
[16] ibid.

Over this period, the main technological trends are expected to be a migration to 'all Internet Protocol (IP)' networks, growing use of wireless communications and wireless access platforms (e.g. 3G, WiFi, WiMAX and satellite), deployment of fibre in the local access network, and the transition to digital TV. Far-reaching impacts on existing network architectures, services and consumer devices can be expected. Market players are facing new competitors and are seeking new business models in the face of imminent changes to the electronic communications market of today.

All of this will lead to new and innovative services for users, with the current 'triple play' services (voice, internet and TV) being precursors of more sophisticated service bundles to come. Boundaries between electronic communications products and services will continue to blur; new forms of mobile and portable devices will appear with interactive and broadcasting features. Privacy and security will continue to be a concern for users.

So far, the framework has shown itself capable of addressing new technologies like Voice over Internet Protocol (VoIP), with a capacity to accommodate further technological and market evolutions. However the provisions governing the management of radio resources, which are critical to innovative wireless products and services and are shared with many other sectors, need to be adapted, in order to avoid inappropriate regulation.

5   CHANGES PROPOSED OVERALL

The current regulatory framework has produced considerable benefits, but it needs attention in a number of areas in order to remain effective for the coming decade. The two main areas for change are:

- application to electronic communications of the Commission's policy approach on spectrum management, as set out in the Communication of September 2005[17];

- reduction of the procedural burden associated with the reviews of markets susceptible to ex-ante regulation.

In addition to these two, the Communication identifies other changes that seek to:

- consolidate the single market,

- strengthen consumers and user interests,

- improve security and

- remove outdated provisions.

This Communication, and the staff working paper which accompanies it, set out the Commission's analysis and current ideas for change. These will be adjusted in the light of the public consultation, in particular those which deal with ways of strengthening effective competition during the transition from monopoly to full competition.

Many of the proposals entail the European Parliament and the Council defining regulatory objectives, leaving it to the Commission to adopt detailed technical measures in order to implement those objectives. This allows ex ante regulation to be responsive to changes in the sector while respecting the objectives and principles defined by the legislator.

---

[17] COM(2005) 411, 6.9.2005.

5.1   Improved approach to managing spectrum for electronic communications

Electronic communications services share spectrum with other sectors (aeronautical, maritime, space, security, defence, earth observation, etc). This calls for balancing these spectrum interests and considering the European dimension.

Rapid technological development and convergence have underlined the importance of spectrum as a valuable resource, but spectrum management within the EU has not kept pace with such evolution. It is estimated that the total value of electronic communications services that depend on use of the radio spectrum in the EU exceeds €200 billion, which equates to between 2% and 2.5% of the annual European GDP[18]. Maximising the social and economic potential of radio spectrum usage is essential to achieving the objectives of the EU's i2010 policy, and to support the renewed strategy for growth and jobs. In addition, improvements in the current system of spectrum management at EU level will allow operators to exploit the internal market more effectively.

A new system for spectrum management is needed that permits different models of spectrum licensing (the traditional administrative, unlicensed and new marked-based approaches) to coexist so as to promote economic and technical efficiency in the use of this valuable resource. Based on common EU rules, greater flexibility in spectrum management could be introduced by strengthening the use of general authorisations whenever possible. When not possible, owners of spectrum usage rights should not be unduly constrained but subject to certain safeguards, have the freedom to provide any type of electronic communications service ('service neutrality') using any technology or standard under common conditions ('technological neutrality').

Using criteria based on economic efficiency, selected bands agreed at EU level via a committee procedure would become available for use under general authorisations, or subject to secondary trading across the EU. Common authorisation conditions for the use of the radio spectrum would also be enacted with this procedure in appropriate cases (see 5.3.3).

The administrative model will remain important especially where, on balance, legal certainty and interference management issues are priorities and where public interest objectives are at stake.

5.2   Streamlining market reviews

In February 2006, the Commission reported on its experience with the 'Article 7' procedure[19] and concluded that the procedure represents an important step towards the creation of an internal market for electronic communications. As a follow-up to that report, this Communication proposes to reduce the administrative burden of the market review procedure by simplifying the notification requirements for certain draft national measures, given that by the time such changes are fully implemented, the NRAs will have considerably more experience with the process.

This approach accords with the Commission's Better Regulation Programme to achieve the same policy objectives in simpler ways. Regulators would still need to conduct market reviews and undertake national and European consultations, but for certain market analyses and notifications the current level of detail would no longer be required. In a number of predefined categories of cases, a simplified notification procedure would be introduced.

---

[18] See the study by Analysys et al. 'Conditions and options in introducing secondary trading of radio spectrum in the European Community' (2004), p. 12.
[19] See footnote 5.

This would allow the Commission and the NRAs to focus on cases where substantial problems may arise.

In the short term, it is proposed to issue a revised version of the procedural Recommendation in order to initiate the simplified notification procedures from 2007, and in the longer term, to modify the framework to allow all procedural elements to be gathered together into a single Regulation.

5.3   Consolidating the Internal Market

To attract investment and reap the benefits of the internal market, Europe must deliver a consistent regulatory approach in the 25 Member States. A unified single market offers EU suppliers a large home base for the development of innovative products, which is particularly important in areas like wireless communications where economies of scale count. Although progress has been made, an internal European market for electronic communications and for radio equipment[20] is not yet a reality, and further measures are proposed.

5.3.1   *Remedies under the 'Article 7' procedure*

The 'Article 7' procedure has enhanced consistency in terms of market definitions and the assessment of 'significant market power' by NRAs. However the Commission identified the need for greater consistency in the application of remedies[21].

Many comments made by the Commission on draft measures of NRAs have related to the appropriateness of the remedies proposed. The Commission has voiced concerns in particular regarding remedies that solved only part of the competition problem identified[22], remedies that appeared to be inadequate[23] and remedies that might have produced effective results too late[24]. To secure the benefits of the internal market, it is proposed to extend Commission veto powers to cover proposed remedies.

5.3.2   *Appeals*

A major difficulty with implementation of the framework is the judicial practice of routinely suspending regulatory decisions, despite the provisions of Article 4 of the Framework Directive. Courts vary widely in their treatment of interim relief. The proposal is to tackle the problem of routine suspension of regulatory decisions by some national courts during the appeal period by laying down EU level criteria for granting suspension of regulatory decisions.

5.3.3   *Common approach to the authorisation of services with pan-European or internal market dimension*

Member States are responsible for the authorisation of electronic communications networks and services. The conditions that apply to undertakings - including the rights of use for numbers and radio frequencies - vary between the Member States, making it burdensome to introduce services with a pan-European or an internal market dimension.

---

[20] The R&TTE Directive 1999/5/EC (OJ L 91 7.4.1999, p. 10) harmonises requirements on equipment but does not harmonise spectrum allocation.

[21] See footnote 5.

[22] As in a case where mobile termination rates were only regulated for calls originating on mobile networks or abroad, but not for calls originating on fixed networks.

[23] e.g. where price regulation was not based on the most appropriate cost model or where choices of cost model and cost accounting rules were left to the undertakings concerned.

[24] e.g. where cost-oriented mobile termination rates based on an LRIC cost model were left to private

For such services, a Community procedure is proposed, in order to reach EU-level agreement on common usage conditions as well as on common approaches to authorisation, to allow for co-ordinated deployment of services. This authorisation system would be complementary to the current system and would be applied in specific cases (e.g., satellite communication services). The Authorisation Directive would be amended to allow the Commission to adopt Decisions with the assistance of a committee, while monitoring and enforcement of compliance with the authorisation conditions for such services would continue to be handled by Member States at national level. Once authorisations are harmonised through this common mechanism, an authorisation granted in one Member State would be sufficient for the pan- European deployment of services.

5.3.4   *Other proposed changes*

Other changes designed to strengthen the internal market aim to: ensure that users can access information society services provided in other Member States (e.g. freephone numbers); strengthen the ability of NRAs to sanction a breach of regulatory obligations; extend the scope of the technical implementing measures that the Commission can take, e.g. in areas like numbering; introduce a mechanism for Commission approval of measures taken by NRAs under Article 5(1) of the Access and Interconnection Directive; require 'must carry' negotiations between operators first, before the regulator intervened in the context of dispute settlement. obligations to be reviewed by a specific deadline; and establish a procedure to facilitate agreement at EU level on common requirements on networks and services.

5.4   Strengthening consumers' and users' rights

A central goal of the regulatory framework is to deliver substantial consumer benefits. This is in large part achieved by relying on enhanced competition to provide choice, innovative services and value for money to consumers. This is complemented by specific consumer protection measures, including universal service obligations to safeguard users' needs.

Responses to the 'Call for Input' on the Review, together with contributions received on the Commission consultation on the scope of Universal Service[25], suggest a need for a fundamental reflection on the role and concept of universal service in the 21st century, and raise questions on the balance between sector specific and horizontal rules for protecting consumers, and the feasibility of a one-size-fits-all approach to universal service in a Union of 25 Member States. For these reasons, the Commission intends to publish a Green Paper on universal service in 2007, to launch a wide ranging debate.

Irrespective of the outcome of this debate, many of the provisions in the Universal Service Directive are linked to traditional telephone services, and need to be modernised. Other proposed changes will improve the quality of tariff information available to consumers, allow third parties to take legal action against 'spammers', ensure that caller location information is available to the emergency services, and facilitate access to emergency services by disabled users.

5.5   Improving Security

Security is identified in i2010 as one the four challenges for the creation of a Single European Information Space. Modern electronic communications networks and services are becoming essential for everyday life, in business and at home. The availability of communications services can be threatened by technical, organisational or human failure. The trend towards IP technology also means that networks are in general more open and vulnerable than in the past. The growth of spam, viruses, spyware and other forms of malware, which undermines users' confidence in electronic communications, is partly due

---

[25]   COM(2005) 203, 24.5. 2005.

to that openness, and partly due to the lack to appropriate security measures. The Communication on a strategy for a secure Information Society (COM(2006) 251) highlighted the need to ensure the right balance between technological development, self-regulation and regulatory measures. Specific regulatory measures are proposed in the context of this review.

In order to reinforce the trust and confidence of business and individual users in electronic communications, a series of measures is proposed: 1) to impose specific requirements on providers of electronic communications to notify certain breaches of security and to keep users informed; 2) to authorise competent national authorities to require specific security measures that implement Commission recommendations or decisions; and 3) to modernise the provisions on network integrity.

5.6 Better regulation: removing outdated provisions

It is proposed to withdraw the provisions on the minimum set of leased lines in the Universal Service Directive, since there are other provisions that allow NRAs to address problems in this area. The Regulation on unbundled access to the local loop[26] (ULL) is also due for repeal, since once all NRAs have completed their market analysis of the ULL market, the Regulation becomes unnecessary and can be withdrawn.

Other candidates for removal include the provisions on the European Telephony Numbering Space (ETNS) in the Universal Service Directive, and various other obsolete articles detailed in the associated Working Document.

6 CONCLUSION

The current regulatory framework has produced considerable benefits but it needs attention in a number of areas in order to remain effective for the coming decade. The two main proposals are to implement the Commission's policy approach on spectrum management, and to reduce the resources associated with the reviews of relevant markets by streamlining the procedures. Other changes proposed would strengthen the internal market, reinforce consumers' interests, improve security and generally update the framework.

The Staff Working Document describes these proposals in more detail. An evaluation of these changes as well as other options that were considered can be found in the associated Impact Assessment document.

Editors' Notes:

[a] Reproduced below.

---

[26] OJ L 336, 30.12.2000, p. 4.

COMMISSION GUIDELINES

on market analysis and the assessment of significant market power under the Community regulatory framework for electronic communications networks and services

(2002/C 165/03)[a]

1.   INTRODUCTION

1.1. Scope and purpose of the Guidelines

(1)   These guidelines set out the principles for use by national regulatory authorities (NRAs) in the analysis of markets and effective competition under the new regulatory framework for electronic communications networks and services.

(2)   This new regulatory framework comprises five Directives: Directive 2002/21/EC of the European Parliament and of the Council of 7 March 2002 on a common regulatory framework for electronic communications networks and services[1], hereinafter the framework Directive; Directive 2002/20/EC of the European Parliament and of the Council of 7 March 2002 on the authorisation of electronic communications networks and services[2], hereinafter the authorisation Directive; Directive 2002/19/EC of the European Parliament and of the Council of 7 March 2002 on access to, and interconnection of, electronic communications networks and associated facilities[3], hereinafter the access Directive; Directive 2002/22/EC of the European Parliament and of the Council of 7 March 2002 on universal service and users' rights relating to electronic communications networks and services[4], hereinafter the universal service Directive; a Directive of the European Parliament and of the Council concerning the processing of personal data and the protection of privacy in the electronic communications sector[5]. However, until this last Directive is formally adopted, Directive 97/66/EC of the European Parliament and the Council concerning the processing of personal data and protection of privacy in the telecommunications sector[6], hereinafter the data protection Directive, remains the relevant Directive.

(3)   Under the 1998 regulatory framework, the market areas of the telecommunications sector that were subject to ex-ante regulation were laid down in the relevant directives, but were not markets defined in accordance with the principles of competition law. In these areas defined under the 1998 regulatory framework, NRAs had the power to designate undertakings as having significant market power when they possessed 25 % market share, with the possibility to deviate from this threshold taking into account the undertaking's ability to influence the market, its turnover relative to the size of the market, its control of the means of access to end-users, its access to financial resources and its experience in providing products and services in the market.

(4)   Under the new regulatory framework, the markets to be regulated are defined in accordance with the principles of European competition law. They are identified by the Commission in its recommendation on relevant product and service markets pursuant to Article 15(1) of the framework Directive (hereinafter "the Recommendation"). When justified by national circumstances, other markets can also be identified by the NRAs, in accordance with the procedures set out in Articles 6 and 7 of the framework Directive. In case of transnational markets which are susceptible to ex-ante regulation, they will where appropriate be identified by the Commission in a decision on relevant transnational markets pursuant to Article 15(4) of the framework Directive (hereinafter "the Decision on transnational markets").

(5)   On all of these markets, NRAs will intervene to impose obligations on undertakings only where the markets are considered not to be effectively competitive[7] as a result of such undertakings being in a position equivalent to dominance within the meaning

of Article 82 of the EC Treaty[8]. The notion of dominance has been defined in the case-law of the Court of Justice as a position of economic strength affording an undertaking the power to behave to an appreciable extent independently of competitors, customers and ultimately consumers. Therefore, under the new regulatory framework, in contrast with the 1998 framework, the Commission and the NRAs will rely on competition law principles and methodologies to define the markets to be regulated ex-ante and to assess whether undertakings have significant market power ("SMP") on those markets.

(6)   These guidelines are intended to guide NRAs in the exercise of their new responsibilities for defining markets and assessing SMP. They have been adopted by the Commission in accordance with Article 15(2) of the framework Directive, after consultation of the relevant national authorities and following a public consultation, the results of which have been duly taken into account.

(7)   Under Article 15(3) of the framework Directive, NRAs should take the utmost account of these guidelines. This will be an important factor in any assessment by the Commission of the proportionality and legality of proposed decisions by NRAs, taking into account the policy objectives laid down in Article 8 of the framework Directive.

(8)   These guidelines specifically address the following subjects: (a) market definition; (b) assessment of SMP; (c) SMP designation; and (d) procedural issues related to all of these subjects.

(9)   The guidelines have been designed for NRAs to use as follows:

−   to define the geographical dimension of those product and service markets identified in the Recommendation. NRAs will not define the geographic scope of any transnational markets, as any Decision on transnational markets will define their geographic dimension,

−   to carry out, using the methodology set out in Section 3 of the guidelines, a market analysis of the conditions of competition prevailing in the markets identified in the Recommendation and Decision and by NRAs,

−   to identify relevant national or sub-national product and service markets which are not listed in the Recommendation when this is justified by national circumstances and following the procedures set out in Articles 6 and 7 of the framework Directive,

−   to designate, following the market analysis, undertakings with SMP in the relevant market and to impose proportionate ex-ante measures consistent with the terms of the regulatory framework as described in Sections 3 and 4 of the guidelines,

−   to assist Member States and NRAs in applying Article 11(1f) of the authorisation Directive, and Article 5(1) of the framework Directive, and thus ensure that undertakings comply with the obligation to provide information necessary for NRAs to determine relevant markets and assess significant market power thereon,

−   to guide NRAs when dealing with confidential information, which is likely to be provided by:

    •   undertakings under Article 11(1f) of the authorisation Directive and Article 5(1) of the framework Directive,

    •   national competition authorities (NCAs) as part of the cooperation foreseen in Article 3(5) of the framework Directive, and

    •   the Commission and a NRA in another Member State as part of the cooperation foreseen in Article 5(2) of the framework Directive.

(10)   The guidelines are structured in the following way:

Section 1 provides an introduction and overview of the background, purpose, scope and content of the guidelines. **Section 2** describes the methodology to be used by NRAs to define the geographic scope of the markets identified in the market Recommendation as well as to define relevant markets outside this Recommendation. **Section 3** describes the criteria for assessing SMP in a relevant market. **Section 4** outlines the possible conclusions that NRAs may reach in their market analyses and describes the possible actions that may result. **Section 5** describes the powers of investigation of NRAs, suggests procedures for coordination between NRAs and between NRAs and NCAs, and describes coordination and cooperation procedures between NRAs and the Commission. Finally, **Section 6** describes procedures for public consultation and publication of NRAs' proposed decisions.

(11)   The major objective of these guidelines is to ensure that NRAs use a consistent approach in applying the new regulatory framework, and especially when designating undertakings with SMP in application of the provisions of the regulatory framework.

(12)   By issuing these guidelines, the Commission also intends to explain to interested parties and undertakings operating in the electronic communications sector how NRAs should undertake their assessments of SMP under the framework Directive, thereby maximising the transparency and legal certainty of the application of the sector specific legislation.

(13)   The Commission will amend these guidelines, whenever appropriate, taking into account experience with the application of the regulatory framework and future developments in the jurisprudence of the Court of First Instance and the European Court of Justice.

(14)   These guidelines do not in any way restrict the rights conferred by Community law on individuals or undertakings. They are entirely without prejudice to the application of Community law, and in particular of the competition rules, by the Commission and the relevant national authorities, and to its interpretation by the European Court of Justice and the Court of First Instance. These guidelines do not prejudice any action the Commission may take or any guidelines the Commission may issue in the future with regard to the application of European competition law.

1.2. Principles and policy objectives of sector specific measures

(15)   NRAs must seek to achieve the policy objectives identified in Article 8(2), (3) and (4) of the framework Directive. These fall into three categories:

– promotion of an open and competitive market for electronic communications networks, services and associated facilities,

– development of the internal market, and

– promotion of the interests of European citizens.

(16)   The purpose of imposing ex-ante obligations on undertakings designated as having SMP is to ensure that undertakings cannot use their market power either to restrict or distort competition on the relevant market, or to leverage such market power onto adjacent markets.

(17)   These regulatory obligations should only be imposed on those electronic communications markets whose characteristics may be such as to justify sector-specific regulation and in which the relevant NRA has determined that one or more operators have SMP.

(18)   The product and service markets whose characteristics may be such as to justify sector-specific regulation are identified by the Commission in its Recommendation and, when the definition of different relevant markets is justified by national circumstances, by the NRAs following the procedures set out in Articles 6 and 7 of the framework Directive[9]. In addition, certain other markets are specifically identified in Article 6 of the access Directive and Articles 18 and 19 of the universal service Directive.

(19)   In respect of each of these relevant markets, NRAs will assess whether the competition is effective. A finding that effective competition exists on a relevant market is equivalent to a finding that no operator enjoys a single or joint dominant position on that market. Therefore, for the purposes of applying the new regulatory framework, effective competition means that there is no undertaking in the relevant market which holds alone or together with other undertakings a single or collective dominant position. When NRAs conclude that a relevant market is not effectively competitive, they will designate undertakings with SMP on that market, and will either impose appropriate specific obligations, or maintain or amend such obligations where they already exist, in accordance with Article 16(4) of the framework Directive.

(20)   In carrying out the market analysis under the terms of Article 16 of the framework Directive, NRAs will conduct a forward looking, structural evaluation of the relevant market, based on existing market conditions. NRAs should determine whether the market is prospectively competitive, and thus whether any lack of effective competition is durable[10], by taking into account expected or foreseeable market developments over the course of a reasonable period. The actual period used should reflect the specific characteristics of the market and the expected timing for the next review of the relevant market by the NRA. NRAs should take past data into account in their analysis when such data are relevant to the developments in that market in the foreseeable future.

(21)   If NRAs designate undertakings as having SMP, they must impose on them one or more regulatory obligations, in accordance with the relevant Directives and taking into account the principle of proportionality. Exceptionally, NRAs may impose obligations for access and interconnection that go beyond those specified in the access Directive, provided this is done with the prior agreement of the Commission, as provided by Article 8(3) of that Directive.

(22)   In the exercise of their regulatory tasks under Article 15 and 16 of the framework Directive, NRAs enjoy discretionary powers which reflect the complexity of all the relevant factors that must be assessed (economic, factual and legal) when identifying the relevant market and determining the existence of undertakings with SMP. These discretionary powers remain subject, however, to the procedures provided for in Article 6 and 7 of the framework Directive.

(23)   Regulatory decisions adopted by NRAs pursuant to the Directives will have an impact on the development of the internal market. In order to prevent any adverse effects on the functioning of the internal market, NRAs must ensure that they implement the provisions to which these guidelines apply in a consistent manner. Such consistency can only be achieved by close coordination and cooperation with other NRAs, with NCAs and with the Commission, as provided in the framework Directive and as recommended in Section 5.3 of these guidelines.

1.3. Relationship to Competition law

(24)   Under the regulatory framework, markets will be defined and SMP will be assessed using the same methodologies as under competition law. Therefore the definition of the geographic scope of markets identified in the Recommendation, the definition where necessary of relevant product/services markets outside the Recommendation, and the assessment of effective competition by NRAs should be consistent with competition case-law and practice. To ensure such consistency, these guidelines are based on (1) existing

case-law of the Court of First Instance and the European Court of Justice concerning market definition and the notion of dominant position within the meaning of Article 82 of the EC Treaty and Article 2 of the merger control Regulation[11]; (2) the "Guidelines on the application of EEC competition rules in the telecommunications sector"[12]; (3) the "Commission notice on the definition of relevant markets for the purposes of Community competition law"[13], hereinafter the "Notice on market definition"; and (4) the "Notice on the application of competition rules to access agreements in the telecommunications sector"[14], hereinafter the "Access notice".

(25)   The use of the same methodologies ensures that the relevant market defined for the purpose of sector-specific regulation will in most cases correspond to the market definitions that would apply under competition law. In some cases, and for the reasons set out in Section 2 of these guidelines, markets defined by the Commission and competition authorities in competition cases may differ from those identified in the Recommendation and Decision, and/or from markets defined by NRAs under Article 15(3) of the framework Directive. Article 15(1) of the framework Directive makes clear that the markets to be defined by NRAs for the purpose of ex-ante regulation are without prejudice to those defined by NCAs and by the Commission in the exercise of their respective powers under competition law in specific cases.

(26)   For the purposes of the application of Community competition law, the Commission's Notice on market definition explains that the concept of the relevant market is closely linked to the objectives pursued under Community policies. Markets defined under Articles 81 and 82 EC Treaty are generally defined on an ex-post basis. In these cases, the analysis will consider events that have already taken place in the market and will not be influenced by possible future developments. Conversely, under the merger control provisions of EC competition law, markets are generally defined on a forward-looking basis.

(27)   On the other hand, relevant markets defined for the purposes of sector-specific regulation will always be assessed on a forward looking basis, as the NRA will include in its assessment an appreciation of the future development of the market. However, NRAs' market analyses should not ignore, where relevant, past evidence when assessing the future prospects of the relevant market (see also Section 2, below). The starting point for carrying out a market analysis for the purpose of Article 15 of the framework Directive is not the existence of an agreement or concerted practice within the scope of Article 81 EC Treaty, nor a concentration within the scope of the Merger Regulation, nor an alleged abuse of dominance within the scope of Article 82 EC Treaty, but is based on an overall forward-looking assessment of the structure and the functioning of the market under examination. Although NRAs and competition authorities, when examining the same issues in the same circumstances and with the same objectives, should in principle reach the same conclusions, it cannot be excluded that, given the differences outlined above, and in particular the broader focus of the NRAs' assessment, markets defined for the purposes of competition law and markets defined for the purpose of sector-specific regulation may not always be identical.

(28)   Although merger analysis is also applied ex ante, it is not carried out periodically as is the case with the analysis of the NRAs under the new regulatory framework. A competition authority does not, in principle, have the opportunity to conduct a periodic review of its decision in the light of market developments, whereas NRAs are bound to review their decisions periodically under Article 16(1) of the framework Directive. This factor can influence the scope and breadth of the market analysis and the competitive assessment carried out by NRAs, and for this reason, market definitions under the new regulatory framework, even in similar areas, may in some cases, be different from those markets defined by competition authorities.

(29)   It is considered that markets which are not identified in the Recommendation will not warrant ex-ante sector specific regulation, except where the NRA is able to justify

such regulation of an additional or different relevant market in accordance with the procedure in Article 7 of the framework Directive.

(30)   The designation of an undertaking as having SMP in a market identified for the purpose of ex-ante regulation does not automatically imply that this undertaking is also dominant for the purpose of Article 82 EC Treaty or similar national provisions. Moreover, the SMP designation has no bearing on whether that undertaking has committed an abuse of a dominant position within the meaning of Article 82 of the EC Treaty or national competition laws. It merely implies that, from a structural perspective, and in the short to medium term, the operator has and will have, on the relevant market identified, sufficient market power to behave to an appreciable extent independently of competitors, customers, and ultimately consumers, and this, solely for purposes of Article 14 of the framework Directive.

(31)   In practice, it cannot be excluded that parallel procedures under ex-ante regulation and competition law may arise with respect to different kinds of problems in relevant markets[15]. Competition authorities may therefore carry out their own market analysis and impose appropriate competition law remedies alongside any sector specific measures applied by NRAs. However, it must be noted that such simultaneous application of remedies by different regulators would address different problems in such markets. Ex-ante obligations imposed by NRAs on undertakings with SMP aim to fulfil the specific objectives set out in the relevant directives, whereas competition law remedies aim to sanction agreements or abusive behaviour which restrict or distort competition in the relevant market.

(32)   As far as emerging markets are concerned, recital 27 of the framework Directive notes that emerging markets, where de facto the market leader is likely to have a substantial market share, should not be subject to inappropriate ex-ante regulation. This is because premature imposition of ex-ante regulation may unduly influence the competitive conditions taking shape within a new and emerging market. At the same time, foreclosure of such emerging markets by the leading undertaking should be prevented. Without prejudice to the appropriateness of intervention by the competition authorities in individual cases, NRAs should ensure that they can fully justify any form of early, ex-ante intervention in an emerging market, in particular since they retain the ability to intervene at a later stage, in the context of the periodic re-assessment of the relevant markets.

2.   MARKET DEFINITION

2.1. Introduction

(33)   In the Competition guidelines issued in 1991[16], the Commission recognised the difficulties inherent in defining the relevant market in an area of rapid technological change, such as the telecommunications sector. Whilst this statement still holds true today as far as the electronic communications sector is concerned, the Commission since the publication of those guidelines has gained considerable experience in applying the competition rules in a dynamic sector shaped by constant technological changes and innovation, as a result of its role in managing the transition from monopoly to competition in this sector. It should however be recalled that the present guidelines do not purport to explain how the competition rules apply, generally, in the electronic communications sector, but focus only on issues related to (i) market definition; and (ii) the assessment of significant market power within the meaning of Article 14 of the framework Directive (hereafter SMP).

(34)   In assessing whether an undertaking has SMP, that is whether it "enjoys a position of economic strength affording it the power to behave to an appreciable extent independently of its competitors, customers and ultimately consumers"[17], the definition of the relevant market is of fundamental importance since effective competition can only be assessed by reference to the market thus defined[18]. The use of the term "relevant market"

implies the description of the products or services that make up the market and the assessment of the geographical scope of that market (the terms "products" and "services" are used interchangeably throughout this text). In that regard, it should be recalled that relevant markets defined under the 1998 regulatory framework were distinct from those identified for competition-law purposes, since they were based on certain specific aspects of end-to-end communications rather than on the demand and supply criteria used in a competition law analysis[19].

(35)   Market definition is not a mechanical or abstract process but requires an analysis of any available evidence of past market behaviour and an overall understanding of the mechanics of a given sector. In particular, a dynamic rather than a static approach is required when carrying out a prospective, or forward-looking, market analysis[20]. In this respect, any experience gained by NRAs, NCAs and the Commission through the application of competition rules to the telecommunication sector clearly will be of particular relevance in applying Article 15 of the framework Directive. Thus, any information gathered, any findings made and any studies or reports commissioned or relied upon by NRAs (or NCAs) in the exercise of their tasks, in relation to the conditions of competition in the telecommunications markets (provided of course that market conditions have since remained unchanged), should serve as a starting point for the purposes of applying Article 15 of the framework Directive and carrying out a prospective market analysis[21].

(36)   The main product and service markets whose characteristics may be such as to justify the imposition of ex-ante regulatory obligations are identified in the Recommendation which the Commission is required to adopt pursuant to Article 15(1) of the framework Directive, as well as any Decision on transnational markets which the Commission decides to adopt pursuant to Article 15(4) of the framework Directive. Therefore, in practice the task of NRAs will normally be to define the geographical scope of the relevant market, although NRAs have the possibility under Article 15(3) of the framework Directive to define markets other than those listed in the Recommendation in accordance with Article 7 of the framework Directive (see below, Section 6).

(37)   Whilst a prospective analysis of market conditions may in some cases lead to a market definition different from that resulting from a market analysis based on past behaviour[22], NRAs should nonetheless seek to preserve, where possible, consistency in the methodology adopted between, on the one hand, market definitions developed for the purposes of ex-ante regulation, and on the other hand, market definitions developed for the purposes of the application of the competition rules. Nevertheless, as stated in Article 15(1) of the framework Directive and Section 1 of the guidelines, markets defined under sector-specific regulation are defined without prejudice to markets that may be defined in specific cases under competition law.

2.2. Main criteria for defining the relevant market

(38)   The extent to which the supply of a product or the provision of a service in a given geographical area constitutes the relevant market depends on the existence of competitive constraints on the price-setting behaviour of the producer(s) or service provider(s) concerned. There are two main competitive constraints to consider in assessing the behaviour of undertakings on the market, (i) demand-side; and (ii) supply-side substitution. A third source of competitive constraint on an operator's behaviour exists, namely potential competition. The difference between potential competition and supply-substitution lies in the fact that supply-side substitution responds promptly to a price increase whereas potential entrants may need more time before starting to supply the market. Supply substitution involves no additional significant costs whereas potential entry occurs at significant sunk costs[23]. The existence of potential competition should thus be examined for the purpose of assessing whether a market is effectively competitive within the meaning of the framework Directive, that is whether there exist undertakings with SMP[24].

(39)   Demand-side substitutability is used to measure the extent to which consumers are prepared to substitute other services or products for the service or product in question[25], whereas supply-side substitutability indicates whether suppliers other than those offering the product or services in question would switch in the immediate to short term their line of production or offer the relevant products or services without incurring significant additional costs.

(40)   One possible way of assessing the existence of any demand and supply-side substitution is to apply the so-called "hypothetical monopolist test"[26]. Under this test, an NRA should ask what would happen if there were a small but significant, lasting increase in the price of a given product or service, assuming that the prices of all other products or services remain constant (hereafter, "relative price increase"). While the significance of a price increase will depend on each individual case, in practice, NRAs should normally consider customers' (consumers or undertakings) reactions to a permanent price increase of between 5 to 10 %[27]. The responses by consumers or undertakings concerned will aid in determining whether substitutable products do exist and, if so, where the boundaries of the relevant product market should be delineated[28].

(41)   As a starting point, an NRA should apply this test firstly to an electronic communications service or product offered in a given geographical area, the characteristics of which may be such as to justify the imposition of regulatory obligations, and having done so, add additional products or areas depending on whether competition from those products or areas constrains the price of the main product or service in question. Since a relative price increase of a set of products[29] is likely to lead to some sales being lost, the key issue is to determine whether the loss of sales would be sufficient to offset the increased profits which would otherwise be made from sales made following the price increase. Assessing the demand-side and supply-side substitution provides a way of measuring the quantity of the sales likely to be lost and consequently of determining the scope of the relevant market.

(42)   In principle, the "hypothetical monopolist test" is relevant only with regard to products or services, the price of which is freely determined and not subject to regulation. Thus, the working assumption will be that current prevailing prices are set at competitive levels. If, however, a service or product is offered at a regulated, cost-based price, then such price is presumed, in the absence of indications to the contrary, to be set at what would otherwise be a competitive level and should therefore be taken as the starting point for applying the "hypothetical monopolist test"[30]. In theory, if the demand elasticity of a given product or service is significant, even at relative competitive prices, the firm in question lacks market power. If, however, elasticity is high even at current prices, that may mean only that the firm in question has already exercised market power to the point that further price increases will not increase its profits. In this case, the application of the hypothetical monopoly test may lead to a different market definition from that which would be produced if the prices were set at a competitive level[31]. Any assessment of market definition must therefore take into account this potential difficulty. However, NRAs should proceed on the basis that the prevailing price levels provide a reasonable basis from which to start the relevant analysis unless there is evidence that this is not in fact the case.

(43)   If an NRA chooses to have recourse to the hypothetical monopolist test, it should then apply this test up to the point where it can be established that a relative price increase within the geographic and product markets defined will not lead consumers to switch to readily available substitutes or to suppliers located in other areas.

2.2.1. The relevant product/service market

(44)   According to settled case-law, the relevant product/service market comprises all those products or services that are sufficiently interchangeable or substitutable, not only in terms of their objective characteristics, by virtue of which they are particularly suitable for satisfying the constant needs of consumers, their prices or their intended use, but also in terms of the conditions of competition and/or the structure of supply and demand on the

market in question[32]. Products or services which are only to a small, or relative degree interchangeable with each other do not form part of the same market[33]. NRAs should thus commence the exercise of defining the relevant product or service market by grouping together products or services that are used by consumers for the same purposes (end use).

(45)   Although the aspect of the end use of a product or service is closely related to its physical characteristics, different kind of products or services may be used for the same end. For instance, consumers may use dissimilar services such as cable and satellite connections for the same purpose, namely to access the Internet. In such a case, both services (cable and satellite access services) may be included in the same product market. Conversely, paging services and mobile telephony services, which may appear to be capable of offering the same service, that is, dispatching of two-way short messages, may be found to belong to distinct product markets in view of their different perceptions by consumers as regards their functionality and end use.

(46)   Differences in pricing models and offerings for a given product or service may also imply different groups of consumers. Thus, by looking into prices, NRAs may define separate markets for business and residential customers for essentially the same service. For instance, the ability of operators engaged in providing international retail electronic communications services to discriminate between residential and business customers, by applying different sets of prices and discounts, has led the Commission to decide that these two groups form separate markets as far as such services are concerned (see below). However, in order for products to be viewed as demand-side substitutes it is not necessary that they are offered at the same price. A low quality product or service sold at a low price could well be an effective substitute to a higher quality product sold at higher prices. What matters in this case is the likely responses of consumers following a relative price increase[34].

(47)   Furthermore, product substitutability between different electronic communications services will arise increasingly through the convergence of various technologies. Use of digital systems leads to an increasing similarity in the performance and characteristics of network services using distinct technologies. A packet-switched network, for instance, such as Internet, may be used to transmit digitised voice signals in competition with traditional voice telephony services[35].

(48)   In order, therefore, to complete the market-definition analysis, an NRA, in addition to considering products or services whose objective characteristics, prices and intended use make them sufficiently interchangeable, should also examine, where necessary, the prevailing conditions of demand and supply substitution by applying the hypothetical monopolist test.

2.2.1.1. Demand-side substitution

(49)   Demand-side substitution enables NRAs to determine the substitutable products or range of products to which consumers could easily switch in case of a relative price increase. In determining the existence of demand substitutability, NRAs should make use of any previous evidence of consumers' behaviour. Where available, an NRA should examine historical price fluctuations in potentially competing products, any records of price movements, and relevant tariff information. In such circumstances evidence showing that consumers have in the past promptly shifted to other products or services, in response to past price changes, should be given appropriate consideration. In the absence of such records, and where necessary, NRAs will have to seek and assess the likely response of consumers and suppliers to a relative price increase of the service in question.

(50)   The possibility for consumers to substitute a product or a service for another because of a small, but significant lasting price increase may, however, be hindered by considerable switching costs. Consumers who have invested in technology or made any other necessary investments in order to receive a service or use a product may be unwilling

to incur any additional costs involved in switching to an otherwise substitutable service or product. In the same vein, customers of existing providers may also be "locked in" by long-term contracts or by the prohibitively high cost of switching terminals. Accordingly, in a situation where end users face significant switching costs in order to substitute product A for product B, these two products should not be included in the same relevant market[36].

(51)   Demand substitutability focuses on the interchangeable character of products or services from the buyer's point of view. Proper delineation of the product market may, however, require further consideration of potential substitutability from the supply side.

2.2.1.2. Supply-side substitution

(52)   In assessing the scope for supply substitution, NRAs may also take into account the likelihood that undertakings not currently active on the relevant product market may decide to enter the market, within a reasonable time frame[37], following a relative price increase, that is, a small but significant, lasting price increase. In circumstances where the overall costs of switching production to the product in question are relatively negligible, then that product may be incorporated into the product market definition. The fact that a rival firm possesses some of the assets required to provide a given service is immaterial if significant additional investment is needed to market and offer profitably the services in question[38]. Furthermore, NRAs will need to ascertain whether a given supplier would actually use or switch its productive assets to produce the relevant product or offer the relevant service (for instance, whether their capacity is committed under long-term supply agreements, etc.). Mere hypothetical supply-side substitution is not sufficient for the purposes of market definition.

(53)   Account should also be taken of any existing legal, statutory or other regulatory requirements which could defeat a time-efficient entry into the relevant market and as a result discourage supply-side substitution. For instance, delays and obstacles in concluding interconnection or co-location agreements, negotiating any other form of network access, or obtaining rights of ways for network expansion[39], may render unlikely in the short term the provision of new services and the deployment of new networks by potential competitors.

(54)   As can been seen from the above considerations, supply substitution may serve not only for defining the relevant market but also for identifying the number of market participants.

2.2.2. Geographic Market

(55)   Once the relevant product market is identified, the next step to be undertaken is the definition of the geographical dimension of the market. It is only when the geographical dimension of the product or service market has been defined that a NRA may properly assess the conditions of effective competition therein.

(56)   According to established case-law, the relevant geographic market comprises an area in which the undertakings concerned are involved in the supply and demand of the relevant products or services, in which area the conditions of competition are similar or sufficiently homogeneous and which can be distinguished from neighbouring areas in which the prevailing conditions of competition are appreciably different[40]. The definition of the geographic market does not require the conditions of competition between traders or providers of services to be perfectly homogeneous. It is sufficient that they are similar or sufficiently homogeneous, and accordingly, only those areas in which the conditions of competition are "heterogeneous" may not be considered to constitute a uniform market[41].

(57)   The process of defining the limits of the geographic market proceeds along the same lines as those discussed above in relation to the assessment of the demand and supply-side substitution in response to a relative price increase.

(58)   Accordingly, with regard to demand-side substitution, NRAs should assess mainly consumers' preferences as well as their current geographic patterns of purchase. In particular, linguistic reasons may explain why certain services are not available or marketed in different language areas. As far as supply-side substitution is concerned, where it can be established that operators which are not currently engaged or present on the relevant market, will, however, decide to enter that market in the short term in the event of a relative price increase, then the market definition should be expanded to incorporate those "outside" operators.

(59)   In the electronic communications sector, the geographical scope of the relevant market has traditionally been determined by reference to two main criteria[42]:

(a) the area covered by a network[43]; and

(b) the existence of legal and other regulatory instruments[44].

(60)   On the basis of these two main criteria[45], geographic markets can be considered to be local, regional, national or covering territories of two or more countries (for instance, pan-European, EEA-wide or global markets).

2.2.3. Other issues of market definition

(61)   For the purposes of ex-ante regulation, in certain exceptional cases, the relevant market may be defined on a route-by-route basis. In particular, when considering the dimension of markets for international retail or wholesale electronic communications services, it may be appropriate to treat paired countries or paired cities as separate markets[46]. Clearly, from the demand side, the delivery of a call to one country is not a substitute for the delivery of the same to another country. On the other hand, the question of whether indirect transmission services, that is, re-routing or transit of the same call via a third country, represent effective supply-side substitutes depends on the specificities of the market and should be decided on a case-by-case basis[47]. However, a market for the provision of services on a bilateral route would be national in scope since supply and demand patterns in both ends of the route would most likely correspond to different market structures[48].

(62)   In its Notice on market definition, the Commission drew attention to certain cases where the boundaries of the relevant market may be expanded to take into consideration products or geographical areas which, although not directly substitutable, should be included in the market definition because of so-called "chain substitutability"[49]. In essence, chain substitutability occurs where it can be demonstrated that although products A and C are not directly substitutable, product B is a substitute for both product A and product C and therefore products A and C may be in the same product market since their pricing might be constrained by the substitutability of product B. The same reasoning also applies for defining the geographic market. Given the inherent risk of unduly widening the scope of the relevant market, findings of chain substitutability should be adequately substantiated[50].

2.3.   The Commission's own practice

(63)   The Commission has adopted a number of decisions under Regulation No 17 and the merger control Regulation relating to the electronic communications sector. These decisions may be of particular relevance for NRAs with regard to the methodology applied by the Commission in defining the relevant market[51]. As stated above, however, in a sector characterised by constant innovation and rapid technological convergence, it is clear that any current market definition runs the risk of becoming inaccurate or irrelevant in the near future[52]. Furthermore, markets defined under competition law are without prejudice to markets defined under the new regulatory framework as the context and the timeframe within which a market analysis is conducted may be different[53].

(64)   As stated in the Access notice, there are in the electronic communications sector at least two main types of relevant markets to consider, that of services provided to end users (services market) and that of access to facilities necessary to provide such services (access market) [54]. Within these two broad market definitions further market distinctions may be made depending on demand and supply side patterns.

(65)   In particular, in its decision-making practice, the Commission will normally make a distinction between the provision of services and the provision of underlying network infrastructure. For instance, as regards the provision of infrastructure, the Commission has identified separate markets for the provision of local loop, long distance and international infrastructure[55]. As regards fixed services, the Commission has distinguished between subscriber (retail) access to switched voice telephony services (local, long distance and international), operator (wholesale) access to networks (local, long distance and international) and business data communications services[56]. In the market for fixed telephony retail services, the Commission has also distinguished between the initial connection and the monthly rental[57]. Retail services are offered to two distinct classes of consumers, namely, residential and business users, the latter possibly being broken down further into a market for professional, small and medium sized business customers and another for large businesses[58]. With regard to fixed telephony retail services offered to residential users, demand and supply patterns seem to indicate that two main types of services are currently being offered, traditional fixed telephony services (voice and narrowband data transmissions) on the one hand, and high speed communications services (currently in the form of xDSL services) on the other hand[59].

(66)   As regards the provision of mobile communications services, the Commission has found that, from a demand-side point of view, mobile telephony services and fixed telephony services constitute separate markets[60]. Within the mobile market, evidence gathered from the Commission has indicated that the market for mobile communications services encompasses both GSM 900 and GSM 1800 and possibly analogue platforms[61].

(67)   The Commission has found that with regard to the "access" market, the latter comprises all types of infrastructure that can be used for the provision of a given service[62]. Whether the market for network infrastructures should be divided into as many separate submarkets as there are existing categories of network infrastructure, depends clearly on the degree of substitutability among such (alternative) networks[63]. This exercise should be carried out in relation to the class of users to which access to the network is provided. A distinction should, therefore, be made between provision of infrastructure to other operators (wholesale level) and provision to end users (retail level) [64]. At the retail level, a further segmentation may take place between business and residential customers[65].

(68)   When the service to be provided concerns only end users subscribed to a particular network, access to the termination points of that network may well constitute the relevant product market. This will not be the case if it can be established that the same services may be offered to the same class of consumers by means of alternative, easily accessible competing networks. For example, in its Communication on unbundling the local loop[66], the Commission stated that although alternatives to the PSTN for providing high speed communications services to residential consumers exist (fibre optic networks, wireless local loops or upgradable TV networks), none of these alternatives may be considered as a substitute to the fixed local loop infrastructure[67]. Future innovative and technological changes may, however, justify different conclusions[68].

(69)   Access to mobile networks may also be defined by reference to two potentially separate markets, one for call origination and another for call termination. In this respect, the question whether the access market to mobile infrastructure relates to access to an individual mobile network or to all mobile networks, in general, should be decided on the basis of an analysis of the structure and functioning of the market[69].

3.   ASSESSING SIGNIFICANT MARKET POWER (DOMINANCE)

(70)   According to Article 14 of the framework Directive "an undertaking shall be deemed to have significant market power if, either individually or jointly with others, it enjoys a position equivalent to dominance, that is to say a position of economic strength affording it the power to behave to an appreciable extent independently of competitors customers and ultimately consumers". This is the definition that the Court of Justice case-law ascribes to the concept of dominant position in Article 82 of the Treaty[70]. The new framework has aligned the definition of SMP with the Court's definition of dominance within the meaning of Article 82 of the Treaty[71]. Consequently, in applying the new definition of SMP, NRAs will have to ensure that their decisions are in accordance with the Commission's practice and the relevant jurisprudence of the Court of Justice and the Court of First Instance on dominance[72]. However, the application of the new definition of SMP, ex-ante, calls for certain methodological adjustments to be made regarding the way market power is assessed. In particular, when assessing ex-ante whether one or more undertakings are in a dominant position in the relevant market, NRAs are, in principle, relying on different sets of assumptions and expectations than those relied upon by a competition authority applying Article 82, ex post, within a context of an alleged committed abuse[73]. Often, the lack of evidence or of records of past behaviour or conduct will mean that the market analysis will have to be based mainly on a prospective assessment. The accuracy of the market analysis carried out by NRAs will thus be conditioned by information and data existing at the time of the adoption of the relevant decision.

(71)   The fact that an NRA's initial market predictions do not finally materialise in a given case does not necessarily mean that its decision at the time of its adoption was inconsistent with the Directive. In applying ex ante the concept of dominance, NRAs must be accorded discretionary powers correlative to the complex character of the economic, factual and legal situations that will need to be assessed. In accordance with the framework Directive, market assessments by NRAs will have to be undertaken on a regular basis. In this context, therefore, NRAs will have the possibility to react at regular intervals to any market developments and to take any measure deemed necessary.

3.1. Criteria for assessing SMP

(72)   As the Court has stressed, a finding of a dominant position does not preclude some competition in the market. It only enables the undertaking that enjoys such a position, if not to determine, at least to have an appreciable effect on the conditions under which that competition will develop, and in any case to act in disregard of any such competitive constraint so long as such conduct does not operate to its detriment[74].

(73)   In an ex-post analysis, a competition authority may be faced with a number of different examples of market behaviour each indicative of market power within the meaning of Article 82. However, in an ex-ante environment, market power is essentially measured by reference of the power of the undertaking concerned to raise prices by restricting output without incurring a significant loss of sales or revenues.

(74)   The market power of an undertaking can be constrained by the existence of potential competitors[75]. An NRA should thus take into account the likelihood that undertakings not currently active on the relevant product market may in the medium term decide to enter the market following a small but significant non-transitory price increase. Undertakings which, in case of such a price increase, are in a position to switch or extend their line of production/services and enter the market should be treated by NRAs as potential market participants even if they do not currently produce the relevant product or offer the relevant service.

(75)   As explained in the paragraphs below, a dominant position is found by reference to a number of criteria and its assessment is based, as stated above, on a forward-looking market analysis based on existing market conditions. Market shares are often used

as a proxy for market power. Although a high market share alone is not sufficient to establish the possession of significant market power (dominance), it is unlikely that a firm without a significant share of the relevant market would be in a dominant position. Thus, undertakings with market shares of no more than 25 % are not likely to enjoy a (single) dominant position on the market concerned[76]. In the Commission's decision-making practice, single dominance concerns normally arise in the case of undertakings with market shares of over 40 %, although the Commission may in some cases have concerns about dominance even with lower market shares[77], as dominance may occur without the existence of a large market share. According to established case-law, very large market shares - in excess of 50 % - are in themselves, save in exceptional circumstances, evidence of the existence of a dominant position[78]. An undertaking with a large market share may be presumed to have SMP, that is, to be in a dominant position, if its market share has remained stable over time[79]. The fact that an undertaking with a significant position on the market is gradually losing market share may well indicate that the market is becoming more competitive, but it does not preclude a finding of significant market power. On the other hand, fluctuating market shares over time may be indicative of a lack of market power in the relevant market.

(76)   As regards the methods used for measuring market size and market shares, both volume sales and value sales provide useful information for market measurement[80]. In the case of bulk products preference is given to volume whereas in the case of differentiated products (i.e. branded products) sales in value and their associated market share will often be considered to reflect better the relative position and strength of each provider. In bidding markets the number of bids won and lost may also be used as approximation of market shares[81].

(77)   The criteria to be used to measure the market share of the undertaking(s) concerned will depend on the characteristics of the relevant market. It is for NRAs to decide which are the criteria most appropriate for measuring market presence. For instance, leased lines revenues, leased capacity or numbers of leased line termination points are possible criteria for measuring an undertaking's relative strength on leased lines markets. As the Commission has indicated, the mere number of leased line termination points does not take into account the different types of leased lines that are available on the market - ranging from analogue voice quality to high-speed digital leased lines, short distance to long distance international leased lines. Of the two criteria, leased lines revenues may be more transparent and less complicated to measure. Likewise, retail revenues, call minutes or numbers of fixed telephone lines or subscribers of public telephone network operators are possible criteria for measuring the market shares of undertakings operating in these markets[82]. Where the market defined is that of interconnection, a more realistic measurement parameter would be the revenues accrued for terminating calls to customers on fixed or mobile networks. This is so because the use of revenues, rather than for example call minutes, takes account of the fact that call minutes can have different values (i.e. local, long distance and international) and provides a measure of market presence that reflects both the number of customers and network coverage[83]. For the same reasons, the use of revenues for terminating calls to customers of mobile networks may be the most appropriate means to measure the market presence of mobile network operators[84].

(78)   It is important to stress that the existence of a dominant position cannot be established on the sole basis of large market shares. As mentioned above, the existence of high market shares simply means that the operator concerned might be in a dominant position. Therefore, NRAs should undertake a thorough and overall analysis of the economic characteristics of the relevant market before coming to a conclusion as to the existence of significant market power. In that regard, the following criteria can also be used to measure the power of an undertaking to behave to an appreciable extent independently of its competitors, customers and consumers. These criteria include amongst others:

–   overall size of the undertaking,

- control of infrastructure not easily duplicated,

- technological advantages or superiority,

- absence of or low countervailing buying power,

- easy or privileged access to capital markets/financial resources,

- product/services diversification (e.g. bundled products or services),

- economies of scale,

- economies of scope,

- vertical integration,

- a highly developed distribution and sales network,

- absence of potential competition,

- barriers to expansion.

(79)   A dominant position can derive from a combination of the above criteria, which taken separately may not necessarily be determinative.

(80)   A finding of dominance depends on an assessment of ease of market entry. In fact, the absence of barriers to entry deters, in principle, independent anti-competitive behaviour by an undertaking with a significant market share. In the electronic communications sector, barriers to entry are often high because of existing legislative and other regulatory requirements which may limit the number of available licences or the provision of certain services (i.e. GSM/DCS or 3G mobile services). Furthermore, barriers to entry exist where entry into the relevant market requires large investments and the programming of capacities over a long time in order to be profitable[85]. However, high barriers to entry may become less relevant with regard to markets characterised by on-going technological progress. In electronic communications markets, competitive constraints may come from innovative threats from potential competitors that are not currently in the market. In such markets, the competitive assessment should be based on a prospective, forward-looking approach.

(81)   As regards the relevance of the notion of "essential facilities" for the purposes of applying the new definition of SMP, there is for the moment no jurisprudence in relation to the electronic communications sector. However, this notion, which is mainly relevant with regard to the existence of an abuse of a dominant position under Article 82 of the EC Treaty, is less relevant with regard to the ex-ante assessment of SMP within the meaning of Article 14 of the framework Directive. In particular, the doctrine of "essential facilities" is complementary to existing general obligations imposed on dominant undertaking, such as the obligation not to discriminate among customers and has been applied in cases under Article 82 in exceptional circumstances, such as where the refusal to supply or to grant access to third parties would limit or prevent the emergence of new markets, or new products, contrary to Article 82(b) of the Treaty. It has thus primarily been associated with access issues or cases involving a refusal to supply or to deal under Article 82 of the Treaty, without the presence of any discriminatory treatment. Under existing case-law, a product or service cannot be considered "necessary" or "essential" unless there is no real or potential substitute. Whilst it is true that an undertaking which is in possession of an "essential facility" is by definition in a dominant position on any market for that facility, the contrary is not always true. The fact that a given facility is not "essential" or "indispensable" for an economic activity on some distinct market, within the meaning of the existing case-law[86] does not mean that the owner of this facility might not be in a dominant position. For instance, a network operator can be in a dominant position despite the existence of alternative competing networks if the size or importance of its network affords him the possibility to behave independently from other network operators[87]. In other words, what matters is to establish whether a given facility affords its owner significant market power in

the market without thus being necessary to further establish that the said facility can also be considered "essential" or "indispensable" within the meaning of existing case-law.

(82)   It follows from the foregoing that the doctrine of the "essential facilities" is less relevant for the purposes of applying ex ante Article 14 of the framework Directive than applying ex-post Article 82 of the EC Treaty.

3.1.1. Leverage of market power

(83)   According to Article 14(3) of the framework Directive, "where an undertaking has significant market power on a specific market, it may also be deemed to have significant market power on a closely related market, where the links between the two markets are such as to allow the market power held in one market to be leveraged into the other market, thereby strengthening the market power of the undertaking".

(84)   This provision is intended to address a market situation comparable to the one that gave rise to the Court's judgment in Tetra Pak II[88]. In that case, the Court decided that an undertaking that had a dominant position in one market, and enjoyed a leading position on a distinct but closely associated market, was placed as a result in a situation comparable to that of holding a dominant position on the markets in question taken as a whole. Thanks to its dominant position on the first market, and its market presence on the associated, secondary market, an undertaking may thus leverage the market power which it enjoys in the first market and behave independently of its customers on the latter market[89]. Although in Tetra Pak the markets taken as a whole in which Tetra Pak was found to be dominant were horizontal, close associative links, within the meaning of the Court's case-law, will most often be found in vertically integrated markets. This is often the case in the telecommunications sector, where an operator often has a dominant position on the infrastructure market and a significant presence on the downstream, services market[90]. Under such circumstances, an NRA may consider it appropriate to find that such operator has SMP on both markets taken together. However, in practice, if an undertaking has been designated as having SMP on an upstream wholesale or access market, NRAs will normally be in a position to prevent any likely spill-over or leverage effects downstream into the retail or services markets by imposing on that undertaking any of the obligations provided for in the access Directive which may be appropriate to avoid such effects. Therefore, it is only where the imposition of ex-ante obligations on an undertaking which is dominant in the (access) upstream market would not result in effective competition on the (retail) downstream market that NRAs should examine whether Article 14(3) may apply.

(85)   The foregoing considerations are also relevant in relation to horizontal markets[91]. Moreover, irrespective of whether the markets under consideration are vertical or horizontal, both markets should be electronic communications markets within the meaning of Article 2 of the framework Directive and both should display such characteristics as to justify the imposition of ex-ante regulatory obligations[92].

3.1.2. Collective dominance

(86)   Under Article 82 of the EC Treaty, a dominant position can be held by one or more undertakings ("collective dominance"). Article 14(2) of the framework Directive also provides that an undertaking may enjoy significant market power, that is, it may be in a dominant position, either individually or jointly with others.

(87)   In the Access notice, the Commission had stated that, although at the time both its own practice and the case-law of the Court were still developing, it would consider two or more undertakings to be in a collective dominant position when they had substantially the same position vis-à-vis their customers and competitors as a single company has if it is in a dominant position, provided that no effective competition existed between them. The lack of competition could be due, in practice, to the existence of certain links between those

companies. The Commission had also stated, however, that the existence of such links was not a prerequisite for a finding of joint dominance[93].

(88)   Since the publication of the Access notice, the concept of collective dominance has been tested in a number of decisions taken by the Commission under Regulation No 17 and under the merger control Regulation. In addition, both the Court of First Instance (CFI) and the Court of Justice of the European Communities (ECJ) have given judgments which have contributed to further clarifying the exact scope of this concept.

3.1.2.1.   The jurisprudence of the CFI/ECJ

(89)   The expression "one or more undertakings" in Article 82 of the EC Treaty implies that a dominant position may be held by two or more economic entities which are legally and economically independent of each other[94].

(90)   Until the ruling of the ECJ in Compagnie maritime belge[95] and the ruling of the CFI in Gencor[96] (see below), it might have been argued that a finding of collective dominance was based on the existence of economic links, in the sense of structural links, or other factors which could give rise to a connection between the undertakings concerned[97]. The question of whether collective dominance could also apply to an oligopolistic market, that is a market comprised of few sellers, in the absence of any kind of links among the undertakings present in such a market, was first raised in Gencor. The case concerned the legality of a decision adopted by the Commission under the merger control Regulation prohibiting the notified transaction on the grounds that it would lead to the creation of a duopoly market conducive to a situation of oligopolistic dominance[98]. Before the CFI, the parties argued that the Commission had failed to prove the existence of "links" between the members of the duopoly within the meaning of the existing case-law.

(91)   The CFI dismissed the application by stating, inter alia, that there was no legal precedent suggesting that the notion of "economic links" was restricted to the notion of structural links between the undertakings concerned: According to the CFI, "there is no reason whatsoever in legal or economic terms to exclude from the notion of economic links the relationship of interdependence existing between the parties to a tight oligopoly within which, in a market with the appropriate characteristics, in particular in terms of market concentration, transparency and product homogeneity, those parties are in a position to anticipate one another's behaviour and are therefore strongly encouraged to align their conduct in the market, in particular in such a way as to maximise their joint profits by restricting production with a view to increasing prices. In such a context, each trader is aware that highly competitive action on its part designed to increase its market share (for example a price cut) would provoke identical action by the others, so that it would derive no benefit from its initiative. All the traders would thus be affected by the reduction in price levels"[99]. As the Court pointed out, market conditions may be such that "each undertaking may become aware of common interests and, in particular, cause prices to increase without having to enter into an agreement or resort to concerted practice"[100].

(92)   The CFI's ruling in Gencor was later endorsed by the ECJ in Compagnie maritime belge, where the Court gave further guidance as to how the term of collective dominance should be understood and as to which conditions must be fulfilled before such finding can be made. According to the Court, in order to show that two or more undertakings hold a joint dominant position, it is necessary to consider whether the undertakings concerned together constitute a collective entity vis-à-vis their competitors, their trading partners and their consumers on a particular market[101]. This will be the case when (i) there is no effective competition among the undertakings in question; and (ii) the said undertakings adopt a uniform conduct or common policy in the relevant market[102]. Only when that question is answered in the affirmative, is it appropriate to consider whether the collective entity actually holds a dominant position[103]. In particular, it is necessary to ascertain whether economic links exist between the undertakings concerned which enable

them to act independently of their competitors, customers and consumers. The Court recognised that an implemented agreement, decision or concerted practice (whether or not covered by an exemption under Article 81(3) of the Treaty) may undoubtedly result in the undertakings concerned being linked in a such way that their conduct on a particular market on which they are active results in them being perceived as a collective entity vis-à-vis their competitors, their trading partners and consumers[104].

(93)   The mere fact, however, that two or more undertakings are linked by an agreement, a decision of associations of undertakings or a concerted practice within the meaning of Article 81(1) of the Treaty does not, of itself, constitute a necessary basis for such a finding. As the Court stated, "a finding of a collective dominant position may also be based on other connecting factors and would depend on an economic assessment and, in particular, on an assessment of the structure of the market in question"[105].

(94)   It follows from the Gencor and Compagnie maritime belge judgments that, although the existence of structural links can be relied upon to support a finding of a collective dominant position, such a finding can also be made in relation to an oligopolistic or highly concentrated market whose structure alone in particular, is conducive to coordinated effects on the relevant market[106].

3.1.2.2. The Commission's decision-making practice and Annex II of the framework Directive

(95)   In a number of decisions adopted under the merger control Regulation, the Commission considered the concept of collective dominance. It sought in those cases to ascertain whether the structure of the oligopolistic markets in question was conducive to coordinated effects on those markets[107].

(96)   When assessing ex-ante the likely existence or emergence of a market which is or could become conducive to collective dominance in the form of tacit coordination, NRAs, should analyse:

(a)   whether the characteristics of the market makes it conducive to tacit coordination; and

(b)   whether such form of coordination is sustainable that is, (i) whether any of the oligopolists have the ability and incentive to deviate from the coordinated outcome, considering the ability and incentives of the non-deviators to retaliate; and (ii) whether buyers/fringe competitors/potential entrants have the ability and incentive to challenge any anti-competitive coordinated outcome[108].

(97)   This analysis is facilitated by looking at a certain number of criteria which are summarised in Annex II of the framework Directive, which have also been used by the Commission in applying the notion of collective dominance under the merger control Regulation. According to this Annex, "two or more undertakings can be found to be in a joint dominant position within the meaning of Article 14 if, even in the absence of structural or other links between them, they operate in a market, the structure of which is considered to be conducive to coordinated effects[109]. Without prejudice to the case-law of the Court of Justice on joint dominance, this is likely to be the case where the market satisfies a number of appropriate characteristics, in particular in terms of market concentration, transparency and other characteristics mentioned below:

—   mature market,

—   stagnant or moderate growth on the demand side,

—   low elasticity of demand,

—   homogeneous product,

—   similar cost structures,

– similar market shares,

– lack of technical innovation, mature technology,

– absence of excess capacity,

– high barriers to entry,

– lack of countervailing buying power,

– lack of potential competition,

– various kind of informal or other links between the undertakings concerned,

– retaliatory mechanisms,

– lack or reduced scope for price competition".

(98)   Annex II of the framework Directive expressly states that the above is not an exhaustive list, nor are the criteria cumulative. Rather, the list is intended to illustrate the sorts of evidence that could be used to support assertions concerning the existence of a collective (oligopolistic) dominance in the form of tacit coordination[110]. As stated above, the list also shows that the existence of structural links among the undertakings concerned is not a prerequisite for finding a collective dominant position. It is however clear that where such links exist, they can be relied upon to explain, together with any of the other abovementioned criteria, why in a given oligopolistic market coordinated effects are likely to arise. In the absence of such links, in order to establish whether a market is conducive to collective dominance in the form of tacit coordination, it is necessary to consider a number of characteristics of the market. While these characteristics are often presented in the form of the abovementioned list, it is necessary to examine all of them and to make an overall assessment rather than mechanistically applying a "check list". Depending on the circumstances of the case, the fact that one or another of the structural elements usually associated with collective dominance may not be clearly established is not in itself decisive to exclude the likelihood of a coordinated outcome[111].

(99)   In an oligopolistic market where most, if not all, of the abovementioned criteria are met, it should be examined whether, in particular, the market operators have a strong incentive to converge to a coordinated market outcome and refrain from reliance on competitive conduct. This will be the case where the long-term benefits of an anti-competitive conduct outweigh any short-term gains resulting from a resort to a competitive behaviour.

(100)   It must be stressed that a mere finding that a market is concentrated does not necessarily warrant a finding that its structure is conducive to collective dominance in the form of tacit coordination[112].

(101)   Ultimately, in applying the notion of collective dominance in the form of tacit coordination, the criteria which will carry the most sway will be those which are critical to a coordinated outcome in the specific market under consideration. For instance, in Case COMP/M.2499 - Norske Skog/Parenco/Walsum, the Commission came to the conclusion that even if the markets for newsprint and wood-containing magazine paper were concentrated, the products were homogeneous, demand was highly inelastic, buyer power was limited and barriers to entry were high, nonetheless the limited stability of market shares, the lack of symmetry in costs structures and namely, the lack of transparency of investments decisions and the absence of a credible retaliation mechanism rendered unlikely and unsustainable any possibility of tacit coordination among the oligopolists[113].

3.1.3.2. Collective dominance and the telecommunications sector

(102)   In applying the notion of collective dominance, NRAs may also take into consideration decisions adopted under the merger control Regulation in the electronic

communications sector, in which the Commission has examined whether any of the notified transactions could give rise to a finding of collective dominance.

(103) In MCI WorldCom/Sprint, the Commission examined whether the merged entity together with Concert Alliance could be found to enjoy a collective dominant position on the market for global telecommunications services (GTS). Given that operators on that market competed on a bid basis where providers were selected essentially in the first instances of the bidding process on the basis of their ability to offer high quality, tailor-made sophisticated services, and not on the basis of prices, the Commission's investigation was focused on the incentives for market participants to engage in parallel behaviour as to who wins what bid (and who had won what bids)[114]. After having examined in depth the structure of the market (homogenous product, high barriers of entry, customers countervailing power, etc.) the Commission concluded that it was not able to show absence of competitive constraints from actual competitors, a key factor in examining whether parallel behaviour can be sustained, and thus decided not to pursue further its objections in relation to that market[115].

(104) In BT/Esat[116], one of the issues examined by the Commission was whether market conditions in the Irish market for dial-up Internet access lent themselves to the emergence of a duopoly consisting of the incumbent operator, Eircom, and the merged entity. The Commission concluded that this was not the case for the following reasons. First, market shares were not stable; second, demand was doubling every six months; third, internet access products were not considered homogeneous; and finally, technological developments were one of the main characteristics of the market[117].

(105) In Vodafone/Airtouch[118], the Commission found that the merged entity would have joint control of two of the four mobile operators present on the German mobile market (namely D2 and E-Plus, the other two being T-Mobil and VIAG Interkom). Given that entry into the market was highly regulated, in the sense that licences were limited by reference to the amount of available radio frequencies, and that market conditions were transparent, it could not be ruled out that such factors could lead to the emergence of a duopoly conducive to coordinated effects[119].

(106) In France Telecom/Orange the Commission found that, prior to the entry of Orange into the Belgian mobile market, the two existing players, Proximus and Mobistar, were in a position to exercise joint dominance. As the Commission noted, for the four years preceding Orange's entry, both operators had almost similar and transparent pricing, their prices following exactly the same trends[120]. In the same decision the Commission further dismissed claims by third parties as to the risk of a collective dominant position of Vodafone and France Telecom in the market for the provision of pan-European mobile services to internationally mobile customers. Other than significant asymmetries between the market shares of the two operators, the market was considered to be emerging, characterised by an increasing demand and many types of different services on offer and on price[121].

4. IMPOSITION, MAINTENANCE, AMENDMENT OR WITHDRAWAL OF OBLIGATIONS UNDER THE REGULATORY FRAMEWORK

(107) Section 3 of these guidelines dealt with the analysis of relevant markets that NRAs must carry out under Article 16 of the framework Directive to determine whether a market is effectively competitive, i.e. whether there are undertakings in that market who are in a dominant position. This section aims to provide guidance for NRAs on the action they should take following that analysis, i.e. the imposition, maintenance, amendment or withdrawal, as appropriate, of specific regulatory obligations on undertakings designated as having SMP. This section also describes the circumstances in which similar obligations than those that can be imposed on SMP operators may, exceptionally, be imposed on undertakings who have not been designated as having SMP.

(108) The specific regulatory obligations which may be imposed on SMP undertakings can apply both to wholesale and retail markets. In principle, the obligations related to wholesale markets are set out in Articles 9 to 13 of the access Directive. The obligations related to retail markets are set out in Articles 17 to 19 of the universal service Directive.

(109) The obligations set out in the access Directive are: transparency (Article 9); non-discrimination (Article 10); accounting separation (Article 11), obligations for access to and use of specific network facilities (Article 12), and price control and cost accounting obligations (Article 13). In addition, Article 8 of the access Directive provides that NRAs may impose obligations outside this list. In order to do so, they must submit a request to the Commission, which will take a decision, after seeking the advice of the Communications Committee, as to whether the NRA concerned is permitted to impose such obligations.

(110) The obligations set out in the universal service Directive are: regulatory controls on retail services (Article 17), availability of the minimum set of leased lines (Article 18 and Annex VII) and carrier selection and preselection (Article 19).

(111) Under the regulatory framework, these obligations should only be imposed on undertakings which have been designated as having SMP in a relevant market, except in certain defined cases, listed in Section 4.3.

4.1. Imposition, maintenance, amendment or withdrawal of obligations on SMP operators

(112) As explained in Section 1, the notion of effective competition means that there is no undertaking with dominance on the relevant market. In other words, a finding that a relevant market is effectively competitive is, in effect, a determination that there is neither single nor joint dominance on that market. Conversely, a finding that a relevant market is not effectively competitive is a determination that there is single or joint dominance on that market.

(113) If an NRA finds that a relevant market is subject to effective competition, it is not allowed to impose obligations on any operator on that relevant market under Article 16. If the NRA has previously imposed regulatory obligations on undertaking(s) in that market, the NRA must withdraw such obligations and may not impose any new obligation on that undertaking(s). As stipulated in Article 16(3) of the framework Directive, where the NRA proposes to remove existing regulatory obligations, it must give parties affected a reasonable period of notice.

(114) If an NRA finds that competition in the relevant market is not effective because of the existence of an undertaking or undertakings in a dominant position, it must designate in accordance with Article 16(4) of the framework Directive the undertaking or undertakings concerned as having SMP and impose appropriate regulatory obligations on the undertaking(s) concerned. However, merely designating an undertaking as having SMP on a given market, without imposing any appropriate regulatory obligations, is inconsistent with the provisions of the new regulatory framework, notably Article 16(4) of the framework Directive. In other words, NRAs must impose at least one regulatory obligation on an undertaking that has been designated as having SMP. Where an NRA determines the existence of more than one undertaking with dominance, i.e. that a joint dominant position exists, it should also determine the most appropriate regulatory obligations to be imposed, based on the principle of proportionality.

(115) If an undertaking was previously subject to obligations under the 1998 regulatory framework, the NRA must consider whether similar obligations continue to be appropriate under the new regulatory framework, based on a new market analysis carried out in accordance with these guidelines. If the undertaking is found to have SMP in a relevant market under the new framework, regulatory obligations similar to those imposed

under the 1998 regulatory framework may therefore be maintained. Alternatively, such obligations could be amended, or new obligations provided in the new framework might also be imposed, as the NRA considers appropriate.

(116)   Except where the Community's international commitments under international treaties prescribe the choice of regulatory obligation (see Section 4.4) or when the Directives prescribe particular remedies as under Article 18 and 19 of the universal service Directive, NRAs will have to choose between the range of regulatory obligations set out in the Directives in order to remedy a particular problem in a market found not to be effectively competitive. Where NRAs intend to impose other obligations for access and interconnection than those listed in the access Directive, they must submit a request for Commission approval of their proposed course of action. The Commission must seek the advice of the Communications Committee before taking its decision.

(117)   Community law, and in particular Article 8 of the framework Directive, requires NRAs to ensure that the measures they impose on SMP operators under Article 16 of the framework Directive are justified in relation to the objectives set out in Article 8 and are proportionate to the achievement of those objectives. Thus any obligation imposed by NRAs must be proportionate to the problem to be remedied. Article 7 of the framework Directive requires NRAs to set out the reasoning on which any proposed measure is based when they communicate that measure to other NRAs and to the Commission. Thus, in addition to the market analysis supporting the finding of SMP, NRAs need to include in their decisions a justification of the proposed measure in relation to the objectives of Article 8, as well as an explanation of why their decision should be considered proportionate.

(118)   Respect for the principle of proportionality will be a key criterion used by the Commission to assess measures proposed by NRAs under the procedure of Article 7 of framework Directive. The principle of proportionality is well-established in Community law. In essence, the principle of proportionality requires that the means used to attain a given end should be no more than what is appropriate and necessary to attain that end. In order to establish that a proposed measure is compatible with the principle of proportionality, the action to be taken must pursue a legitimate aim, and the means employed to achieve the aim must be both necessary and the least burdensome, i.e. it must be the minimum necessary to achieve the aim.

(119)   However, particularly in the early stages of implementation of the new framework, the Commission would not expect NRAs to withdraw existing regulatory obligations on SMP operators which have been designed to address legitimate regulatory needs which remain relevant, without presenting clear evidence that those obligations have achieved their purpose and are therefore no longer required since competition is deemed to be effective on the relevant market. Different remedies are available in the new regulatory framework to address different identified problems and remedies should be tailored to these specified problems.

(120)   The Commission, when consulted as provided for in Article 7(3) of the framework Directive, will also check that any proposed measure taken by the NRAs is in conformity with the regulatory framework as a whole, and will assess the impact of the proposed measure on the single market.

(121)   The Commission will assist NRAs to ensure that as far as possible they adopt consistent approaches in their choice of remedies where similar situations exist in different Member States. Moreover, as noted in Article 7(2) of the framework Directive, NRAs shall seek to agree on the types of remedies best suited to address particular situations in the marketplace.

4.2. Transnational markets: joint analysis by NRAs

(122)   Article 15(4) of the framework Directive gives the Commission the power to issue a Decision identifying product and service markets that are transnational, covering the whole of the Community or a substantial part thereof. Under the terms of Article 16(5) of the framework Directive, the NRAs concerned must jointly conduct the market analysis and decide whether obligations need to be imposed. In practice, the European Regulators Group is expected to provide a suitable forum for such a joint analysis.

(123)   In general, joint analysis by NRAs would follow similar procedures (e.g. for public consultation) to those required when a single national regulatory authority is conducting a market analysis. Precise arrangements for collective analysis and decision-making will need to be drawn up.

4.3.   Imposition of certain specific regulatory obligations on non-SMP operators

(124)   The preceding parts of this section set out the procedures whereby certain specific obligations may be imposed on SMP undertakings, under Articles 7 and 8 of the access Directive and Article 16-19 of the universal service Directive. Exceptionally, similar obligations may be imposed on operators other than those that have been designated as having SMP, in the following cases, listed in Article 8(3) of the access Directive:

–   obligations covering inter alia access to conditional access systems, obligations to interconnect to ensure end-to-end interoperability, and access to application program interfaces and electronic programme guides to ensure accessibility to specified digital TV and radio broadcasting services (Article 5(1), 5(2) and 6 of the access Directive),

–   obligations that NRAs may impose for co-location where rules relating to environmental protection, health, security or town and country planning deprive other undertakings of viable alternatives to co-location (Article 12 of the framework Directive),

–   obligations for accounting separation on undertakings providing electronic communications services who enjoy special or exclusive rights in other sectors (Article 13 of the framework Directive),

–   obligations relating to commitments made by an undertaking in the course of a competitive or comparative selection procedure for a right of use of radio frequency (Condition B7 of the Annex to the authorisation Directive, applied via Article 6(1) of that Directive),

–   obligations to handle calls to subscribers using specific numbering resources and obligations necessary for the implementation of number portability (Articles 27, 28 and 30 of the universal service Directive),

–   obligations based on the relevant provisions of the data protection Directive, and

–   obligations to be imposed on non-SMP operators in order to comply with the Community's international commitments.

4.4.   Relationship to WTO commitments

(125)   The EC and its Member States have given commitments in the WTO in relation to undertakings that are "major suppliers" of basic telecommunications services[122]. Such undertakings are subject to all of the obligations set out in the EC's and its Member States' commitments in the WTO for basic telecommunications services. The provisions of the new regulatory framework, in particular relating to access and interconnection, ensure that NRAs continue to apply the relevant obligations to undertakings that are major suppliers in accordance with the WTO commitments of the EC and its Member States.

5.   POWERS OF INVESTIGATION AND COOPERATION PROCEDURES FOR THE PURPOSE OF MARKET ANALYSIS

5.1.   Overview

(126)   This section of the guidelines covers procedures in respect of an NRA's powers to obtain the information necessary to conduct a market analysis.

(127)   The regulatory framework contains provisions to enable NRAs to require undertakings that provide electronic communications networks and services to supply all the information, including confidential information, necessary for NRAs to assess the state of competition in the relevant markets and impose appropriate ex-ante obligations and thus to ensure compliance with the regulatory framework.

(128)   This section of the guidelines also includes guidance as to measures to ensure effective cooperation between NRAs and NCAs at national level, and among NRAs and between NRAs and the Commission at Community level. In particular this section deals with the exchange of information between those authorities.

(129)   Many electronic communication markets are fast-moving and their structures are changing rapidly. NRAs should ensure that the assessment of effective competition, the public consultation, and the designation of operators having SMP are all carried out within a reasonable period. Any unnecessary delay in the decision could have harmful effects on incentives for investment by undertakings in the relevant market and therefore on the interests of consumers.

5.2.   Market analysis and power of investigation

(130)   Under Article 16(1) of the framework Directive, NRAs must carry out an analysis of the relevant markets identified in the Recommendation and any Decision as soon as possible after their adoption or subsequent revision. The conclusions of the analysis of each of the relevant markets, together with the proposed regulatory action, must be published and a public consultation must be conducted, as described in Section 6.

(131)   In order to carry out their market analysis, NRAs will first need to collect all the information they consider necessary to assess market power in a given market. To the extent that such information needs to be obtained directly from undertakings, Article 11 of the authorisation Directive provides that undertakings are required by the terms of their general authorisation to supply the information necessary for NRAs to conduct a market analysis within the meaning of Article 16(2) of the framework Directive. This is reinforced by the more general obligation in Article 5(1) of the framework Directive which provides that Member States shall ensure that undertakings providing electronic communications networks and services provide all the information necessary for NRAs to ensure conformity with Community law.

(132)   When NRAs request information from an undertaking, they should state the reasons justifying the request and the time limit within which the information is to be provided. As provided for in Article 10(4) of the authorisation Directive, NRAs may be empowered to impose financial penalties on undertakings for failure to provide information.

(133)   In accordance with Article 5(4) of the framework Directive, NRAs must publish all information that would contribute to an open and competitive market, acting in accordance with national rules on public access to information and subject to Community and national rules on commercial confidentiality.

(134)   However, as regards information that is confidential in nature, the provisions of Article 5(3) of the framework Directive, require NRAs to ensure the confidentiality of such information in accordance with Community and national rules on business

confidentiality. This confidentiality obligation applies equally to information that has been received in confidence from another public authority.

5.3. Co-operation Procedures

Between NRAs and NCAs

(135) Article 16(1) of the framework Directive requires NRAs to associate NCAs with the market analyses as appropriate. Member States should put in place the necessary procedures to guarantee that the analysis under Article 16 of the framework Directive is carried out effectively. As the NRAs conduct their market analyses in accordance with the methodologies of competition law, the views of NCAs in respect of the assessment of competition are highly relevant. Cooperation between NRAs and NCAs will be essential, but NRAs remain legally responsible for conducting the relevant analysis. Where under national law the tasks assigned under Article 16 of the framework Directive are carried out by two or more separate regulatory bodies, Member States should ensure clear division of tasks and set up procedures for consultation and cooperation between regulators in order to assure coherent analysis of the relevant markets.

(136) Article 3(5) of the framework Directive requires NRAs and NCAs to provide each other with the information necessary for the application of the regulatory framework, and the receiving authority must ensure the same level of confidentiality as the originating authority. NCAs should therefore provide NRAs with all relevant information obtained using the former's investigatory and enforcement powers, including confidential information.

(137) Information that is considered confidential by an NCA, in accordance with Community and national rules on business confidentiality, should only be exchanged with NRAs where such exchange is necessary for the application of the provisions of the regulatory framework. The information exchanged should be limited to that which is relevant and proportionate to the purpose of such exchange.

Between the Commission and NRAs

(138) For the regulatory framework to operate efficiently and effectively, it is vital that there is a high level of cooperation between the Commission and the NRAs. It is particularly important that effective informal cooperation takes place. The European Regulators Group will be of great importance in providing a framework for such cooperation, as part of its task of assisting and advising the Commission. Cooperation is likely to be of mutual benefit, by minimising the likelihood of divergences in approach between different NRAs, in particular divergent remedies to deal with the same problem[123].

(139) In accordance with Article 5(2) of the framework Directive, NRAs must supply the Commission with information necessary for it to carry out its tasks under the Treaty. This covers information relating to the regulatory framework (to be used in verifying compatibility of NRA action with the legislation), but also information that the Commission might require, for example, in considering compliance with WTO commitments.

(140) NRAs must ensure that, where they submit information to the Commission which they have requested undertakings to provide, they inform those undertakings that they have submitted it to the Commission.

(141) The Commission can also make such information available to another NRA, unless the original NRA has made an explicit and reasoned request to the contrary. Although there is no legal requirement to do so, the Commission will normally inform the undertaking which originally provided the information that it has been passed on to another NRA.

Between NRAs

(142) It is of the utmost importance that NRAs develop a common regulatory approach across Member States that will contribute to the development of a true single market for electronic communications. To this end, NRAs are required under Article 7(2) of the framework Directive to cooperate with each other and with the Commission in a transparent manner to ensure the consistent application, in all Member States, of the new regulatory framework. The European Regulators' Group is expected to serve as an important forum for cooperation.

(143) Article 5(2) of the framework Directive also foresees that NRAs will exchange information directly between each other, as long as there is a substantiated request. This will be particularly necessary where a transnational market needs to be analysed, but it will also be required within the framework of cooperation in the European Regulators' Group. In all exchanges of information, the NRAs are required to maintain the confidentiality of information received.

6. PROCEDURES FOR CONSULTATION AND PUBLICATION OF PROPOSED NRA DECISIONS

6.1. Public consultation mechanism

(144) Except in the urgent cases as explained below, an NRA that intends to take a measure which would have a significant impact on the relevant market should give the interested parties the opportunity to comment on the draft measure. To this effect, the NRA must hold a public consultation on its proposed measure. Where the draft measure concerns a decision relating to an SMP designation or non-designation it should include the following:

— the market definition used and reasons therefor, with the exception of information that is confidential in accordance with European and national law on business confidentiality,

— evidence relating to the finding of dominance, with the exception of information that is confidential in accordance with European and national law on business confidentiality together with the identification of any undertakings proposed to be designated as having SMP,

— full details of the sector-specific obligations that the NRA proposes to impose, maintain, modify or withdraw on the abovementioned undertakings together with an assessment of the proportionality of that proposed measure.

(145) The period of the consultation should be reasonable. However, NRAs' decisions should not be delayed excessively as this can impede the development of the market. For decisions related to the existence and designation of undertakings with SMP, the Commission considers that a period of two months would be reasonable for the public consultation. Different periods could be used in some cases if justified. Conversely, where a draft SMP decision is proposed on the basis of the results of an earlier consultation, the length of consultation period for these decisions may well be shorter than two months.

6.2. Mechanisms to consolidate the internal market for electronic communications

(146) Where an NRA intends to take a measure which falls within the scope of the market definition or market analysis procedures of Articles 15 and 16 of the framework Directive, as well as when NRAs apply certain other specific Articles in the regulatory framework[124] and where the measures have an effect on trade between Member States, the NRAs must communicate the measures, together with their reasoning, to NRAs in other Member States and to the Commission in accordance with Article 7(3) of the framework Directive. It should do this at the same time as it begins its public consultation. The NRA must then give other NRAs and the Commission the chance to comment on the NRA's

proposed measures, before adopting any final decision. The time available for other NRAs and the Commission to comment should be the same time period as that set by the NRA for its national public consultation, unless the latter is shorter than the minimum period of one month provided for in Article 7(3). The Commission may decide in justified circumstances to publish its comments.

(147) With regard to measures that could affect trade between Member States, this should be understood as meaning measures that may have an influence, direct or indirect, actual or potential, on the pattern of trade between Member States in a manner which might create a barrier to the single European market[125]. Therefore, the notion of an effect on trade between Member States is likely to cover a broad range of measures.

(148) NRAs must make public the results of the public consultation, except in the case of information that is confidential in accordance with Community and national law on business confidentiality.

(149) With the exception of two specific cases, explained in the following paragraph, the NRA concerned may adopt the final measure after having taken account of views expressed during its mandatory consultation. The final measure must then be communicated to the Commission without delay.

6.3. Commission power to require the withdrawal of NRAs' draft measures

(150) Under the terms of Article 7(4) of the framework Directive, there are two specific situations where the Commission has the possibility to require an NRA to withdraw a draft measure which falls within the scope of Article 7(3):

– the draft measure concerns the definition of a relevant market which differs from that identified in the Recommendation, or

– the draft measure concerns a decision as to whether to designate, or not to designate, an undertaking as having SMP, either individually or jointly with others.

(151) In respect of the above two situations, where the Commission has indicated to the NRA in the course of the consultation process that it considers that the draft measure would create a barrier to the single European market or where the Commission has serious doubts as to the compatibility of the draft measure with Community law, the adoption of the measure must be delayed by a maximum of an additional two months.

(152) During this two-month period, the Commission may, after consulting the Communications Committee following the advisory procedure[126], take a decision requiring the NRA to withdraw the draft measure. The Commission's decision will be accompanied by a detailed and objective analysis of why it considers that the draft measure should not be adopted together with specific proposals for amending the draft measure. If the Commission does not take a decision within that period, the draft measure may be adopted by the NRA.

6.4. Urgent cases

(153) In exceptional circumstances, NRAs may act urgently in order to safeguard competition and protect the interest of users. An NRA may therefore, exceptionally, adopt proportionate and provisional measures without consulting either interested parties, the NRAs in other Member States, or the Commission. Where an NRA has taken such urgent action, it must, without delay, communicate these measures, with full reasons, to the Commission, and to the other NRAs. The Commission will verify the compatibility of those measures with Community law and in particular will assess their proportionality in relation to the policy objectives of Article 8 of the framework Directive.

(154) If the NRA wishes to make the provisional measures permanent, or extends the time for which it is applicable, the NRA must go through the normal consultation

procedure set out above. It is difficult to foresee any circumstances that would justify urgent action to define a market or designate an SMP operator, as such measure are not those that can be carried out immediately. The Commission therefore does not expect NRAs to use the exceptional procedures in such cases.

6.4. Adoption of the final decision

(155) Once an NRA's decision has become final, NRAs should notify the Commission of the names of the undertakings that have been designated as having SMP and the obligations imposed on them, in accordance with the requirements of Article 36(2) of the universal service Directive and Articles 15(2) and 16(2) of the access Directive. The Commission will thereafter make this information available in a readily accessible form, and will transmit the information to the Communications Committee as appropriate.

(156) Likewise, NRAs should publish the names of undertakings that they have designated as having SMP and the obligations imposed on them. They should ensure that up-to-date information is made publicly available in a manner that guarantees all interested parties easy access to that information.

---

[1] OJ L 108, 24.4.2002, p. 33.

[2] OJ L 108, 24.4.2002, p. 21.

[3] OJ L 108, 24.4.2002, p. 7.

[4] OJ L 108, 24.4.2002, p. 51.

[5] [OJ L 201, 31.07.2002, p. 37].

[6] OJ L 24, 30.1.1998, p. 1.

[7] Except where the new regulatory framework expressly permits obligations to be imposed independently of the competitive state of the market.

[8] Article 14 of the framework Directive.

[9] In addition, transnational markets whose characteristics may be such as to justify sector-specific regulation may be identified by the Commission in a Decision on transnational markets.

[10] Recital 27 of the framework Directive.

[11] Regulation (EEC) No 4064/89 on the control of concentrations between undertakings (OJ L 395, 30.12.1989, p. 1), as last amended by Regulation (EC) No 1310/97 of 30 June 1997 (OJ L 180, 9.7.1997, p. 1) (hereafter the merger control Regulation).

[12] Guidelines on the application of EEC competition rules in the telecommunications sector (OJ C 233, 6.9.1991, p. 2).

[13] Commission notice on the definition of relevant market for the purposes of Community competition law (OJ C 372, 9.12.1997, p. 5).

[14] Notice on the application of the competition rules to access agreements in the telecommunications sector (OJ C 265, 22.8.1998, p. 2).

[15] It is expected that effective cooperation between NRAs and NCAs would prevent the duplication of procedures concerning identical market issues.

[16] Guidelines on the application of EEC competition rules in the telecommunications sector (OJ C 233, 6.9.1991, p. 2).

[17] Article 14(2) of the framework Directive.

[18] Case C-209/98, Entreprenørforeningens Affalds [2000] ECR I-3743, paragraph 57, and Case C-242/95 GT-Link [1997] ECR I-4449, paragraph 36. It should be recognised that the objective of market definition is not an end in itself, but part of a process, namely assessing the degree of a firm's market power.

[19] See Directive 97/33/EC of the European Parliament and of the Council of 30 June 1997 on interconnection in telecommunications with regard to ensuring universal service and interoperability through application of the principles of open network provision (ONP) (OJ L 199, 26.7.1997, p. 32) (the interconnection Directive); Council Directive 90/387/EEC of 28 June 1990 on the establishment of the internal market for telecommunications services through the implementation of open network provision (OJ L 192, 24.7.1990,

p. 1) (the ONP framework Directive); Council Directive 92/44/EEC of 5 June 1992 on the application of open network provision to leased lines (OJ L 165, 19.6.1992, p. 27) (the leased lines Directive); Directive 95/62/EC of the European Parliament and of the Council of 13 December 1995 on the application of open network provision (ONP) to voice telephony (OJ L 321, 30.12.1995, p. 6), replaced by Directive 98/10/EC of the European Parliament and of the Council of 26 February 1998 on the application of open network provision (ONP) to voice telephony and on universal service for telecommunications in a competitive environment (OJ L 101, 1.4.1998, p. 24) (the ONP voice telephony Directive).

[20] Joined Cases C-68/94 and C-30/95, France and Others v Commission [1998] ECR I-1375. See, also, Notice on market definition, at paragraph 12.

[21] To the extent that the electronic communications sector is technology and innovation-driven, any previous market definition may not necessarily be relevant at a later point in time.

[22] Notice on market definition, paragraph 12.

[23] See, also, Notice on market definition, paragraphs 20-23, Case IV/M.1225 - Enso/Stora, (OJ L 254, 29.9.1999), paragraph 40.

[24] See Notice on market definition, paragraph 24. Distinguishing between supply-side substitution and potential competition in electronic communications markets may be more complicated than in other markets given the dynamic character of the former. What matters, however, is that potential entry from other suppliers is taken into consideration at some stage of the relevant market analysis, that is, either at the initial market definition stage or at the subsequent stage of the assessment of market power (SMP).

[25] It is not necessary that all consumers switch to a competing product; it suffices that enough or sufficient switching takes place so that a relative price increase is not profitable. This requirement corresponds to the principle of "sufficient interchangeability" laid down in the case-law of the Court of Justice; see below, footnote 32.

[26] See, also, Access notice, paragraph 46, and Case T-83/91, Tetra Pak v Commission, [1994] ECR II-755, paragraph 68. This test is also known as "SSNIP" (small but significant non transitory increase in price). Although the SSNIP test is but one example of methods used for defining the relevant market and notwithstanding its formal econometric nature, or its margins for errors (the so-called "cellophane fallacy", see below), its importance lies primarily in its use as a conceptual tool for assessing evidence of competition between different products or services.

[27] See Notice on market definition, paragraphs 17-18.

[28] In other words, where the cross-price elasticity of demand between two products is high, one may conclude that consumers view these products as close substitutes. Where consumer choice is influenced by considerations other than price increases, the SSNIP test may not be an adequate measurement of product substitutability; see Case T-25/99, Colin Arthur Roberts and Valerie Ann Roberts v Commission, [2001] ECR II-1881.

[29] Within the context of market definition under Article 82 of the EC Treaty, a competition authority or a court would estimate the "starting price" for applying the SSNIP on the basis of the price charged by the alleged monopolist. Likewise, under the prospective assessment of the effects which a merger may have on competition, the starting price would be based on the prevailing prices of the merging parties. However, where an NRA carries out a market analysis for the purposes of applying Article 14 of the framework Directive the service or product in question may be offered by several firms. In such a case, the starting price should be the industry "average price".

[30] It is worth noting that prices which result from price regulation which does not aim at ensuring that prices are cost-based, but rather at ensuring an affordable offer within the context of the provision of universal services, may not be presumed to be set at a competitive level, nor should they serve as a starting point for applying the SSNIP test.

[31] Indeed, one of the drawbacks of the application of the SSNIP test is that in some cases, a high-demand cross-price elasticity may mean that a firm has already exercised market power, a situation known in competition law and practice as the "cellophane fallacy". In such cases, the prevailing price does not correspond to a competitive price. Determining whether the prevailing price is set above the competitive level is admittedly one of the most difficult aspects of the SSNIP test. NRAs faced with such difficulties could rely on other criteria for assessing demand and supply substitution such as functionality of services, technical characteristics, etc. Clearly, if evidence exist to show that in the past a firm has engaged in anti-competitive behaviour (price-fixing) or has enjoyed market power, then this may serve as an indication that its prices are not under competitive constraint and accordingly are set above the competitive level.

[32] Case C-333/94 P, Tetra Pak v Commission [1996] ECR I-5951, paragraph 13, Case 31/80 L'Oréal [1980] ECR 3775, paragraph 25, Case 322/81, Michelin v Commission [1983] ECR 3461, paragraph 37, Case C-62/86, AkzoChemie v Commission [1991] ECR I-3359, Case T-504/93, Tiercé Ladbroke v Commission [1997] ECR II-923, paragraph 81, T-65/96, Kish Glass v Commission [2000] ECR II-1885, paragraph 62, Case C-475/99, Ambulanz Glöckner and Landkreis Südwestpfalz, [2001] ECR I-0000, paragraph 33. The test of sufficient substitutability or interchangeability was first laid down by the Court of Justice in Case

6/72, Europemballage and Continental Can v Commission, [1973] ECR 215, paragraph 32 and Case 85/76, Hoffmann La-Roche v Commission [1979] ECR 461, paragraph 23.

[33] Case C-333/94 P, Tetra Pak v Commission [1996] ECR I-5951, paragraph 13, Case 66/86, Ahmed Saeed [1989] ECR 803, paragraphs 39 and 40, Case United Brands v Commission [1978] ECR 207, paragraphs 22 and 29, and 12; Case T-229/94, Deutsche Bahn v Commission [1997] ECR II-1689, paragraph 54. In Tetra Pak, the Court confirmed that the fact that demand for aseptic and non-aseptic cartons used for packaging fruit juice was marginal and stable over time relative to the demand for cartons used for packaging milk was evidence of a very little interchangeability between the milk and the non-milk packaging sector, idem, paragraphs 13 and 15.

[34] For example, in the case of a relative price increase, consumers of a lower quality/price service may switch to a higher quality/price service if the cost of doing so (the premium paid) is offset by the price increase. Conversely, consumers of a higher quality product may no longer accept a higher premium and switch to a lower quality service. In such cases, low and high quality products would appear to be effective substitutes.

[35] Communication from the Commission - Status of voice on the Internet under Community law, and in particular, under Directive 90/388/EEC - Supplement to the Communication by the Commission to the European Parliament and the Council on the status and implementation of Directive 90/388/EEC on competition in the markets for telecommunications services (OJ C 369, 22.12.2000, p. 3). Likewise, it cannot be excluded that in the future. xDSL technology and multipoint video distribution services based on wireless local loops may be used for the transmission of TV materials in direct competition with other existing TV delivery systems based on cable systems, direct-to-home satellite transmission and terrestrial analogue or digital transmission platforms.

[36] Switching costs which stem from strategic choices by undertakings rather than from exogenous factors should be considered, together with some other form of entry barriers, at the subsequent stage of SMP assessment. Where a market is still growing, total switching costs for already "captured" consumers may not be significant and may not thus deter demand or supply-side substitution.

[37] The time frame to be used to assess the likely responses of other suppliers in case of a relative price increase will inevitably depend on the characteristics of each market and should be decided on a case-by-case basis.

[38] See, also, Case C-333/94, Tetra Pak v Commission, op. cit., paragraph 19. As mentioned above, the required investments should also be undertaken within a reasonable time frame.

[39] See, also, Case COMP/M.2574 - Pirelli/Edizione/Olivetti/Telecom Italia, paragraph 58.

[40] United Brands, op. cit., paragraph 44, Michelin, op. cit., paragraph 26, Case 247/86 Alsatel v Novasam [1988] ECR 5987, paragraph 15; Tiercé Ladbroke v Commission, op. cit., paragraph 102.

[41] Deutsche Bahn v Commission, op. cit., paragraph 92. Case T-139/98 AAMS v Commission, [2001] ECR 0000-II, paragraph 39.

[42] See, for instance, Case IV/M.1025 - Mannesmann/Olivetti/Infostrada, paragraph 17, and Case COMP/JV.23 - Telefónica Portugal Telecom/Médi Telecom.

[43] In practice, this area will correspond to the limits of the area in which an operator is authorised to operate. In Case COMP/M.1650 - ACEA/Telefónica, the Commission pointed out that since the notified joint venture would have a licence limited to the area of Rome, the geographical market could be defined as local; at paragraph 16.

[44] The fact that mobile operators can provide services only in the areas where they have been authorised to and the fact that a network architecture reflects the geographical dimension of the mobile licences explains why mobile markets are considered to be national in scope. The extra connection and communications costs that consumers face when roaming abroad, coupled with the loss of certain additional service functionalities (i.e. lack of voice mail abroad) further supports this definition; see Case IV/M.1439 - Telia/Telenor, paragraph 124, Case IV/M.1430 - Vodafone/Airtouch, paragraphs 13-17, Case COMP/JV.17 - Mannesmann/Bell Atlantic/Omnitel, paragraph 15.

[45] Physical interconnection agreements may also be taken into consideration for defining the geographical scope of the market, Case IV/M.570 - TBT/BT/TeleDanmark/Telenor, paragraph 35.

[46] Case IV/M.856 - British Telecom/MCI (II), paragraph 19s., Case IV/JV.15 - BT/AT & T, paragraph 84 and 92, Case COMP/M.2257 - France Telecom/Equant, paragraph 32, It is highly unlikely that the provision of electronic communications services could be segmented on the basis of national (or local) bilateral routes.

[47] Reference may be made, for instance, to the market for backhaul capacity in international routes (i.e. cable station serving country A to country E) where a potential for substitution between cable stations serving different countries (i.e., cable stations connecting Country A to B, A to C and A to D) may exist where a supplier of backhaul capacity in relation to the route A to E is or would be constrained by the ability of consumers to switch to any of the other "routes", also able to deal with traffic from or to country E.

[48] Where a market is defined on the basis of a bilateral route, its geographical scope could be wider than national if suppliers are present in both ends of the market and can satisfy demand coming from both ends of the relevant route.

[49] See Notice on market definition, paragraphs 57 and 58. For instance, chain substitutability could occur where an undertaking providing services at national level constraints the prices charged by undertakings providing services in separate geographical markets. This may be the case where the prices charged by undertakings providing cable networks in particular areas are constrained by a dominant undertaking operating nationally; see also, Case COMP/M.1628 - TotalFina/Elf (OJ L 143, 29.5.2001, p. 1), paragraph 188.

[50] Evidence should show clear price interdependence at the extremes of the chain and the degree of substitutability between the relevant products or geographical areas should be sufficiently strong.

[51] The Commission has, inter alia, made references in its decisions to the existence of the following markets: international voice-telephony services (Case IV/M.856 - British Telecommunications/MCI (II), OJ L 336, 8.12.1997), advanced telecommunications services to corporate users (Case IV/35.337, Atlas, OJ L 239, 19.9.1996, paragraphs 5-7, Case IV/35617, Phoenix/Global/One, OJ L 239, 19.9.1996, paragraph 6, Case IV/34.857, BT-MCI (I), OJ L 223, 27.8.1994), standardised low-level packet-switched data-communications services, resale of international transmission capacity (Case IV/M.975 - Albacom/BT/ENI, paragraph 24) audioconferencing (Albacom/BT/ENI, paragraph 17), satellite services (Case IV/350518 - Iridium, OJ L 16, 18.1.1997), (enhanced) global telecommunications services (Case IV/JV.15 - BT/AT & T, Case COMP/M.1741 - MCI WorldCom/Sprint, paragraph 84, Case COMP/M.2257 - France Telecom/Equant, paragraph 18), directory-assistance services (Case IV/M.2468 - SEAT Pagine Gialle/ENIRO, paragraph 19, Case COMP/M.1957 - VIAG Interkom/Telenor Media, paragraph 8), Internet-access services to end users (Case IV/M.1439 - Telia/Telenor, Case COMP/JV.46 - Blackstone/CDPQ/Kabel Nordrhein/Westfalen, paragraph 26, Case COMP/M.1838 - BT/Esat, paragraph 7), top-level or universal Internet connectivity (Case COMP/M.1741 - MCI WorldCom/Sprint, paragraph 52), seamless pan-European mobile telecommunications services to internationally mobile customers (Case COMP/M.1975 - Vodafone Airtouch/Mannesmann, Case COMP/M.2016 - France Telecom/Orange, paragraph 15), wholesale roaming services (Case COMP/M.1863 - Vodafone/Airtel, paragraph 17), and market for connectivity to the international signalling network (Case COMP/2598 - TDC/CMG/Migway JV, paragraphs 17-18).

[52] See, also, Joined Cases T-125/97 and T-127/97, The Coca-Cola Company and Others v Commission [2000] ECR II-1733, at paragraphs 81 and 82.

[53] See, also, Article 15 of the framework Directive.

[54] Access notice, paragraph 45.

[55] See Case COMP/M.1439 - Telia/Telenor.

[56] See Telia/Telenor, BT/AT & T, France Télécom/Equant, op. cit. See also Commission Decision of 20 May 1999, Cégétel + 4 (OJ L 218, 18.8.1999), paragraph 22. With regard to the emerging market for "Global broadband data communications services - GBDS", the Commission has found that such services can be supported by three main network architectures: (i) terrestrial wireline systems; (ii) terrestrial wireless systems; and (iii) satellite-based systems, and that from a demand side, satellite-based GBDS can be considered as a separate market, Case COMP/M.1564 - Astrolink, paragraphs 20-23.

[57] Directive 96/19/EC, recital 20 (OJ L 74, 22.3.1996, p. 13). See, also, communication from the Commission, "Unbundled access to the local loop: enabling the competitive provision of a full range of electronic communication services, including broadband multimedia and high speed Internet" (OJ C 272, 23.9.2000, p. 55). Pursuant to point 3.2, "While categories of services have to be monitored closely, particularly given the speed of technological change, and regularly reassessed on a case-by-case basis, these services are presently normally not substitutable for one another, and would therefore be considered as forming different relevant markets".

[58] The Commission has identified separate markets for services to large multinational corporations (MNCs) given the significant differences in the demand (and supply) of services to this group of customers compared to other retail (business) customers, see Case IV/JV.15 - BT/AT & T, Case COMP/M.1741 - MCI WorldCom/Sprint, Case COMP/M.2257 - France Télécom/Equant.

[59] See communication on "Unbundled access to the local loop", op.cit, point 3.2. The market for "high-speed" communications services could possibly be further divided into distinct segments depending on the nature of the services offered (i.e. Internet services, video-on-demand, etc.).

[60] Case COMP/M.2574 - Pirelli/Edizione/Olivetti/Telecom Italia, paragraph 33. It could also be argued that dial-up access to the Internet via existing 2G mobile telephones is a separate market from dial-up access via the public switched telecommunications network. According to the Commission, accessing the Internet via a mobile phone is unlikely to be a substitute for existing methods of accessing the Internet via a PC due to difference in sizes of the screen and the format of the material that can be obtained through the different platforms; see Case COMP/M.1982 - Telia/Oracle/Drutt, paragraph 15, and Case COMP/JV.48 Vodafone/Vivendi/Canal+.

[61] Case COMP/M.2469 - Vodafone/Airtel, paragraph 7, Case IV/M.1430 - Vodafone/Airtouch, Case IV/M.1669, Deutsche Telecom/One2One, paragraph 7. Whether this market can be further segmented into a carrier (network operator) market and a downstream service market should be decided on a case-by-case basis; see Case IV/M.1760 - Mannesmann/Orange, paragraphs 8-10, and Case COMP/M.2053 - Telenor/BellSouth/Sonofon, paragraphs 9-10.

[62] For instance, in British Interactive Broadcasting/Open, the Commission noted that for the provision of basic voice services to consumers, the relevant infrastructure market included not only the traditional copper network of BT but also the cable networks of the cable operators, which were capable of providing basic telephony services, and possibly wireless fixed networks, Case IV/36.359, (OJ L 312, 6.12.1999, paragraphs 33-38). In Case IV/M.1113 - Nortel/Norweb, the Commission recognised that electricity networks using "digital power line" technology could provide an alternative to existing traditional local telecommunications access loop, paragraphs 28-29.

[63] In assessing the conditions of network competition in the Irish market that would ensue following full liberalisation, the Commission also relied on the existence of what, at that period of time, were perceived as potential alternative infrastructure providers, namely, cable TV and electricity networks, Telecom Eireann, cit., paragraph 30. The Commission left open the question whether the provision of transmission capacity by an undersea network infrastructure constitutes a distinct market from terrestrial or satellite transmissions networks, Case COMP/M.1926 - Telefonica/Tyco/JV, at paragraph 8.

[64] Case COMP/M.1439, Telia/Telenor, paragraph 79. For instance, an emerging pan-European market for wholesale access (SMS) to mobile infrastructure has been identified by the Commission in Case COMP/2598 - TDC/CMG/Migway JV, at paragraphs 28-29.

[65] In applying these criteria, the Commission has found that, as far as the fixed infrastructure is concerned, demand for the lease of transmission capacity and the provision of related services to other operators occurs at wholesale level (the market for carrier's carrier services; see Case IV/M.683 - GTS-Hermes Inc./HIT Rail BV, paragraph 14, Case IV/M.1069 - WorldCom/MCI (OJ L 116, 4.5.1999, p. 1), Unisource (OJ L 318, 20.11.1997, p. 1), Phoenix/Global One (OJ L 239, 19.9.1996, p. 57), Case IV/JV.2 - Enel/FT/DT. In Case COMP/M.1439 - Telia/Telenor, the Commission identified distinct patterns of demand for wholesale and retail (subscriber) access to network infrastructure (provision or access to the local loop, and provision or access to long distance and international network infrastructure), paragraphs 75-83.

[66] See footnote 58.

[67] Fibre optics are currently competitive only on upstream transmission markets whereas wireless local loops which are still to be deployed will target mainly professionals and individuals with particular communications needs. With the exception of certain national markets, existing cable TV networks need costly upgrades to support two ways broadband communications, and, compared with xDLS technologies, they do not offer a guaranteed bandwidth since customers share the same cable channel.

[68] See also Case IV/JV.11 - @Home Benelux BV.

[69] For example, if a fixed operator wants to terminate calls to the subscribers of a particular network, in principle, it will have no other choice but to call or interconnect with the network to which the called party has subscribed. For instance, in light of the "calling party pays" principle, mobile operators have no incentives to compete on prices for terminating traffic to their own network. See also, OECD, "Competition issues in telecommunications-background note for the secretariat", DAFFE/CLP/WP2(2001)3, and Commission's press release IP/02/483.

[70] Case 27/76 United Brands v Commission [1978] ECR 207.

[71] See, also, recital 25 of the framework Directive.

[72] See Article 14, paragraph 2, and recital 28 of the framework Directive.

[73] It should be noted that NRAs do not have to find an abuse of a dominant position in order to designate an undertaking as having SMP.

[74] Case 85/76, Hoffmann-La Roche v Commission [1979] ECR 461, paragraph 39. It should be stressed here that for the purposes of ex-ante regulation, if an undertaking has already been imposed regulatory obligations, the fact that competition may have been restored in the relevant market as a result precisely of the obligations thus imposed, this does not mean that that undertaking is no longer in a dominant position and that it should no longer continue being designated as having SMP.

[75] The absence of any substitutable service or product may justify a finding of a situation of economic dependence which is characteristic of the existence of a dominant position. See Commission decisions, Decca Navigator System (OJ L 43, 15.2.1987, p. 27) and Magill TV Guide: ITP, BBC, RTE (OJ L 78, 21.3.1989, p. 43). See also, Case 22/78 Hugin v Commission 1979 [ECR] 1869, Case 226/84, British Leyland v Commission 1986 [ECR] p. 3263.

[76] See, also, recital 15 of Council Regulation (EEC) No 4064/89.

[77] United Brands v Commission, op. cit. The greater the difference between the market share of the undertaking in question and that of its competitors, the more likely will it be that the said undertaking is in a dominant position. For instance, in Case COMP/M.1741 - MCI WorldCom/Sprint it was found that the merged entity would have in the market for the provision of top-level Internet connectivity an absolute combined market share of more than [35-45] %, several times larger than its closest competitor, enabling it to behave independently of its competitors and customers (see paragraphs 114, 123, 126, 146, 155 and 196).

[78] Case C-62/86, AKZO v Commission, [1991] ECR I-3359, paragraph 60; Case T-228/97, Irish Sugar v Commission, [1999] ECR II-2969, paragraph 70, Case Hoffmann-La Roche v Commission, op. cit, paragraph 41, Case T-139/98, AAMS and Others v Commission [2001 ECR II-0000, paragraph 51. However, large market shares can become accurate measurements only on the assumption that competitors are unable to expand their output by sufficient volume to meet the shifting demand resulting from a rival's price increase.

[79] Case Hoffmann-La Roche v Commission, op. cit., paragraph 41, Case C-62/86, Akzo v Commission [1991] ECR I-3359, paragraphs 56, 59. "An undertaking which has a very large market share and holds it for some time, by means of the volume of production and the sale of the supply which it stands for - without holders of much smaller market shares being able to meet rapidly the demand from those who would like to break away from the undertaking which has largest market share - is by virtue of that share in a position of strength which makes it an unavoidable trading partner and which, because of this alone, secures for it, at the very least during relatively long periods, that freedom of action which is the special feature of a dominant position", Case AAMS and Others v Commission, op. cit., paragraph 51.

[80] Notice on market definition, op. cit., at p. 5.

[81] See Case COMP/M.1741 - MCI WorldCom/Sprint, paragraph 239-240. In bidding markets, however, it is important not to rely only on market shares as they in themselves may not be representative of the undertakings actual position, for further discussion, see, also, Case COMP/M.2201 - MAN/Aüwarter.

[82] See, Determination of organisations with significant power (SMP) for the implementation of the ONP Directive, DG XIII, 1 March 1999, at http://europa.eu.int/ISPO/infosoc/telecompolicy/en/SMPdeter.pdf, at paragraph 3.2.

[83] Idem, at paragraph 5.2.

[84] With regard to the interconnection market of fixed and mobile networks, the termination traffic to be measured should include own network traffic and interconnection traffic received from all other fixed and mobile networks, national or international.

[85] Hoffmann-La Roche v Commission, op. cit., at paragraph 48. One of the most important types of entry barriers is sunk costs. Sunk costs are particularly relevant to the electronic communications sector in view of the fact that large investments are necessary to create, for instance, an efficient electronic communications network for the provision of access services and it is likely that little could be recovered if a new entrant decides to exit the market. Entry barriers are exacerbated by further economies of scope and density which generally characterise such networks. Thus, a large network is always likely to have lower costs than a smaller one, with the result that an entrant in order to take a large share of the market and be able to compete would have to price below the incumbent, making it thus difficult to recover sunk costs.

[86] Joined Cases C-241/91 P and C-242/91 P, RTE and ITP v Commission, [1995] ECR I-743, Case C-7/97, Oscar Bronner [1998] ECR I-7791, and Joined Cases T-374/94, T-375/94, T-384/94 and T-388/94, European Night Services and others v Commission [1998] ECR II-3141.

[87] Case COMP/M.1741 - MCI WorldCom/Sprint, paragraph 196.

[88] Case C-333/94 P, Tetra Pak v Commission [1996] ECR I-5951.

[89] See, also, Case COMP/M.2146 - Tetra Laval/Sidel, paragraphs 325-389, sub judice, T-5/02.

[90] See Access notice, paragraph 65.

[91] In the case of horizontal markets, the market analysis should focus on establishing the existence of close associative links which will enable an undertaking dominant in one market to behave independently of its competitors in a neighbouring market. Such links may be found to exist by reference to the type of conduct of suppliers and users in the markets under consideration (same customers and/or suppliers in both markets, i.e. customers buying both retail voice calls and retail Internet access) or the fact that the input product or service is essentially the same (i.e. provision by a fixed operator of network infrastructure to ISPs for wholesale call origination and wholesale call termination); see, also, Case T-83/91, Tetra Pak v Commission, op. cit., paragraph 120 and Case COMP/M.2416 - Tetra Laval/Sidel.

[92] Article 14(3) of the framework Directive is not intended to apply in relation to market power leveraged from a "regulated" market into an emerging, "non-regulated" market. In such cases, any abusive conduct in the "emerging" market would normally be dealt with under Article 82 of the EC Treaty.

[93] See Access notice, paragraph 79.

94 Joined cases C-395/96 P and C-396/96 P, Compagnie maritime belge and others v Commission [2000] ECR I-1365.

95 Idem, at paragraph 39.

96 Case T102/96, Gencor v Commission [1999] ECR II-753.

97 See Joined Cases T-68/89, T-77/89 and T-78/89, SIV and Others v Commission [1992] ECR II-1403, paragraph 358, Case C-393/92 Almelo [1994] ECR I-1477, paragraph 43, Case C-96/94, Centro Servizi Spediporto [1995] ECR I-2883, paragraph 33, Joined Cases C-140/94, 141/94, and C-142/94, DIP, [1995] ECR I-3257, paragraph 62, Case C-70/95, Sodemare [1997] ECR I-3395, paragraph 46, and Joined Cases C-68/94 and C-30/95 France and Others v Commission [1998] ECR I-1375, paragraph 221.

98 Case IV/M.619 - Gencor Lonhro (OJ L 11, 14.1.1997, p. 30).

99 Gencor v Commission, op. cit., at paragraph 276.

100 Idem, at paragraph 277.

101 Compagnie maritime belge transports and Others, op. cit., at paragraph 39, see, also, Case T-342/99 Airtours/Commission [2002] ECR II-0000, paragraph 76.

102 See, in particular, France and Others v Commission, op. cit., paragraph 221.

103 Compagnie maritime belge, at paragraph 39.

104 Idem at paragraph 44.

105 Idem at paragraph 45.

106 The use here of the term "coordinated effects" is no different from the term "parallel anticompetitive behaviour" also used in Commission's decisions applying the concept of collective (oligopolistic) dominance.

107 See in particular, Cases COMP/M.2498 - UPM-Kymmene/Haindl, and COMP/M.2499 - Norske Skog/Parenco/Walsum, Case COMP/M.2201 - MAN/Auwärter, Case COMP/M.2097 - SCA/Matsä Tissue, Case COMP/M.1882 - Pirelli/BICC, Case COMP/M.1741 - MCI WorldCom/Sprint, sub judice, T-310/00 Case IV/M.1524 - Airtours/First Choice (OJ L 93, 13.4.2000, p. 1), sub judice T-342/99, Case IV/M.1383 - Exxon/Mobil, Case IV/M.1313 - Danish Crown/Vestjyske Slagterier (OJ L 20, 25.1.2000, p. 1), Case IV/M.1225 - Enso/Stora (OJ L 254, 29.9.1999, p. 9), Case IV/M.1016 - Price Waterhouse/Coopers & Lybrand (OJ L 50, 26.2.1999, p. 27), Case IV/M.619 - Gencor/Lonrho, cit., Case IV/M.308, Kali + Salz/MdK/Treuhand (OJ L 186, 21.7.1994, p. 38) and Case IV/M.190 - Nestlé/Perrier (OJ L 356, 5.12.1992, p. 1).

108 This is in essence the type of analysis carried out by the Commission in past decisions related to collective dominance, see, for instance, Case IV/M.190 - Nestlé/Perrier, (OJ L 356, 5.12.1992, p. 1), Gencor/Lonrho, cit., Case IV/M.1383 - Exxon/Mobil, paragraph 259, Case IV/M.1524 - Airtours/First Choice (OJ L 93, 13.4.2000, p. 1), and Case COMP/M.2499 - Norske Skog/Parenco/Walsum, paragraph 76; see, also, Airtours v Commission, op. cit., paragraph 62.

109 See, also, recital 26 of the framework Directive: 'two or more undertakings can be found to enjoy a joint dominant position not only where there exist structural or other links between them but also where the structure of the relevant market is conducive to coordinated effects, that is, it encourages parallel or aligned anticompetitive behaviour on the market'.

110 See Case COMP/M.2498 - UPM-Kymmene/Haindl, and Case COMP/M.2499 - Norske Skog/Parenco/Walsum, at paragraph 77.

111 See, for instance, Case COMP/M.2097 - SCA/Metsä Tissue.

112 For instance, in Case COMP/M.2201 - MAN/Auwärter, despite the fact that two of the parties present in the German city-bus market in Germany, MAN/Auwärter and EvoBus, would each supply just under half of that market, the Commission concluded that there was no risk of joint dominance. In particular, the Commission found that any tacit division of the market between EvoBus and MAN/Auwärter was not likely as there would be no viable coordination mechanism. Secondly, significant disparities between EvoBus and MAN/Auwärter, such as different cost structures, would make it likely that the companies would compete rather than collude. Likewise, in the Alcoa/British Aluminium case, the Commission found that despite the fact that two of the parties present in the relevant market accounted for almost 80 % of the sales, the market could not be said to be conducive to oligopolistic dominance since (i) market shares were volatile and unstable; and (ii) demand was quite irregular making it difficult for the parties to be able to respond to each other's action in order to tacitly coordinate their behaviour. Furthermore, the market was not transparent in relation to prices and purchasers had significant countervailing power. The Commission's conclusions were further reinforced by the absence of any credible retaliation mechanism likely to sustain any tacit coordination and the fact that competition in the market was not only based on prices but depended to a large extent on technological innovation and after-sales follow-up, Case COMP/M.2111 - Alcoa/British Aluminium.

[113] Likewise, in Case COMP/M.2348 - Outokumpu/Norzink, the Commission found that even if the zinc market was composed of few players, entry barriers were high and demand growth perspectives low, the likelihood of the emergence of a market structure conducive to coordinated outcome was unlikely if it could be shown that (i) parties could not manipulate the formation of prices; (ii) producers had asymmetric cost structures and there was no credible retaliation mechanism in place.

[114] See Case COMP/M.1741 - MCI WorldCom/Sprint, paragraph 263.

[115] Idem, paragraphs 257-302.

[116] Case COMP/M.1838 - BT/Esat.

[117] Idem, paragraphs 10 to 14.

[118] Case IV/M.1430 - Vodafone/Airtouch.

[119] Idem, at paragraph 28. The likely emergence of a duopolistic market concerned only the three largest mobile operators, that is D2 and E-Plus, on the one hand, and T-Mobil on the other hand, given that VIAG Interkom's market share was below 5 %. The Commission's concerns were finally removed after the parties proposed to divest Vodafone's entire stake in E-Plus.

[120] Case COMP/M.2016 - France Telecom/Orange, at paragraph 26.

[121] Idem, at paragraphs 39-40. In its working document "On the initial findings of the sector inquiry into mobile roaming charges", the Commission made reference to (i) the likely existence of a number of economic links between mobile operators, namely through their interconnection agreements, their membership of the GSM Association, the WAP and the UMTS forum, the fact that terms and conditions of roaming agreements were almost standardised; and (ii) the likely existence of high barriers to entry. In its preliminary assessment the Commission also stressed that the fact that the mobile market is, in general, technology driven, did not seem to have affected the conditions of competition prevailing on the wholesale international roaming market, see:
http://europa.eu.int/comm/competition/antitrust/others/sector_inquiries/roaming/, at pages. 24 and 25.

[122] GATS commitments taken by EC on telecommunications: http://gats-info.eu.int/gats-info/swtosvc.pl?&SECCODE=02.C.

[123] The Communications Committee in Article 22 of the framework Directive also aims at ensuring effective cooperation between the Commission and the Member States.

[124] The specific Articles covered are as follows: Articles 15 and 16 of the framework Directive (the latter of which refers to Articles 16-19 of the universal service Directive and Articles 7 and 8 of the access Directive), Articles 5 and 8 of the access Directive (the latter of which refers to the obligations provided for in Articles 9-13 of the access Directive) and Article 16 of the universal service Directive (which refers to Articles 17-19 of universal service Directive). In addition, Article 6 of the access Directive, although not explicitly referenced in Article 7 of the framework Directive, itself contains cross-reference to Article 7 of the framework Directive and is therefore covered by the procedures therein.

[125] Recital 38 of the framework Directive.

[126] As provided for in Article 3 of Council Decision 1999/468/EC laying the procedure for the exercising of implementing powers conferred on the Commission, the Commission shall take the utmost account of the opinion delivered by the Committee, but shall not be bound by the opinion.

Editors' Notes:

[a] OJ C 165, 11.07.2002, p. 6. Issued pursuant to Article 15(2) of the Framework Directive. Some citations in the original text have been updated to the current and complete Official Journal citation.

COMMISSION RECOMMENDATION 2003/311/EC

of 11 February 2003[a]

on relevant product and service markets within the electronic communications sector
susceptible to ex ante regulation in accordance with Directive 2002/21/EC of the European
Parliament and of the Council on a common regulatory framework for electronic
communication networks and services

THE COMMISSION OF THE EUROPEAN COMMUNITIES,

Having regard to the Treaty establishing the European Community,

Having regard to Directive 2002/21/EC of the European Parliament and of the Council on a
common regulatory framework for electronic communication networks and services[1], and in
particular Article 15 thereof,

Whereas:

(1) Directive 2002/21/EC (hereinafter the Framework Directive), establishes a new
legislative framework for the electronic communications sector that seeks to respond
to convergence trends by covering all electronic communications networks and
services within its scope The aim is to reduce ex ante sector-specific rules
progressively as competition in the market develops.

(2) The purpose of this Recommendation is to identify those product and service markets
in which ex ante regulation may be warranted. However, this first Recommendation
has to be consistent with the transition from the 1998 regulatory framework to the new
regulatory framework. Directive 2002/19/EC of the European Parliament and of the
Council on access to, and interconnection of, electronic communications networks and
associated facilities[2], hereinafter the Access Directive, and Directive 2002/22/EC of
the European Parliament and of the Council on universal service and users' rights
relating to electronic communications networks and services[3] hereinafter the
Universal service Directive already identify specific market areas which need to be
analysed by national regulatory authorities in addition to the markets listed in this
Recommendation. In accordance with the Framework Directive, it is for national
regulatory authorities to define relevant geographic markets within their territory.

(3) Under the 1998 regulatory framework, several areas in the telecommunications sector
are subject to ex ante regulation. These areas have been delineated in the applicable
directives, but are not always "markets" within the meaning of competition law and
practice. Annex I of the Framework Directive provides a list of such market areas to
be included in the initial version of the Recommendation.

(4) As the title of Annex I of the Framework Directive makes clear, all the market areas
listed therein need to be included in the initial version of the Recommendation in
order that NRAs can carry out a review of existing obligations imposed under the
1998 regulatory framework.

(5) Article 15(1) of the Framework Directive requires the Commission to define markets
in accordance with the principles of competition law. The Commission has therefore
defined markets (corresponding to the market areas listed in Annex I of the
Framework Directive) in accordance with competition law principles.

---

[1] OJ L 108, 24.4.2002, p. 33.
[2] OJ L 108, 24.4.2002, p. 7.
[3] OJ L 108, 24.4.2002, p. 51.

(6) There are in the electronic communications sector at least two main types of relevant markets to consider: markets for services or products provided to end users (retail markets), and markets for the inputs which are necessary for operators to provide services and products to end users (wholesale markets). Within these two types of markets, further market distinctions may be made depending on demand and supply side characteristics.

(7) The starting point for the definition and identification of markets is a characterisation of retail markets over a given time horizon, taking into account demand-side and supply-side substitutability. Having characterised and defined retail markets which are markets involving the supply and demand of end users, it is then appropriate to identify relevant wholesale markets which are markets involving the demand of products of, and supply of products to, a third party wishing to supply end users.

(8) Defining markets in accordance with the principles of competition law means that some of the market areas in Annex I of the Framework Directive comprise a number of separate individual markets on the basis of demand side characteristics. This is the case of products for retail access to the public telephone network at a fixed location and for telephone services provided at a fixed location. The market area in Annex I referring to wholesale leased lines is defined as separate markets for wholesale terminating segments and wholesale trunk segments on the basis of both demand side and supply side characteristics.

(9) In identifying markets in accordance with competition law principles, recourse should be had to the following three criteria. The first criterion is the presence of high and non-transitory entry barriers whether of structural, legal or regulatory nature. However, given the dynamic character and functioning of electronic communications markets, possibilities to overcome barriers within a relevant time horizon have also to be taken into consideration when carrying out a prospective analysis to identify the relevant markets for possible ex ante regulation. Therefore the second criterion admits only those markets the structure of which does not tend towards effective competition within the relevant time horizon. The application of this criterion involves examining the state of competition behind the barriers of entry. The third criterion is that application of competition law alone would not adequately address the market failure(s) concerned.

(10) In particular, as far as entry barriers are concerned, two types of entry barriers are relevant for the purpose of this Recommendation: structural barriers and legal or regulatory barriers.

(11) Structural barriers to entry result from original cost or demand conditions that create asymmetric conditions between incumbents and new entrants impeding or preventing market entry of the latter. For instance, high structural barriers may be found to exist when the market is characterised by substantial economies of scale and/or economies of scope and high sunk cost. To date, such barriers can still be identified with respect to the widespread deployment and/or provision of local access networks to fixed locations. A related structural barrier can also exist where the provision of service requires a network component that cannot be technically duplicated or only duplicated at a cost that makes it uneconomic for competitors.

(12) Legal or regulatory barriers are not based on economic conditions, but result from legislative, administrative or other state measures that have a direct effect on the conditions of entry and/or the positioning of operators on the relevant market. Examples are legal or regulatory barriers preventing entry into a market where there is a limit on the number of undertakings that have access to spectrum for the provision of underlying services. Other examples of legal or regulatory barriers are price controls or other price related measures imposed on undertakings, which affect not only entry but also the positioning of undertakings on the market.

(13) Entry barriers may also become less relevant with regard to innovation-driven markets characterised by ongoing technological progress. In such markets, competitive constraints often come from innovative threats from potential competitors that are not currently in the market. In such innovation-driven markets, dynamic or longer term competition can take place among firms that are not necessarily competitors in an existing "static" market. This Recommendation does not identify markets where entry barriers are not expected to persist over a foreseeable period.

(14) Even when a market is characterised by high barriers to entry, other structural factors in that market may mean that the market tends towards an effectively competitive outcome within the relevant time horizon. This may for instance be the case in markets with a limited, but sufficient, number of undertakings having diverging cost structures and facing price-elastic market demand. There may also be excess capacity in a market that would allow rival firms to expand output very rapidly in response to any price increase. In such markets, market shares may change over time and/or falling prices may be observed.

(15) The decision to identify a market as justifying possible ex ante regulation should also depend on an assessment of the sufficiency of competition law in reducing or removing such barriers or in restoring effective competition. Furthermore, new and emerging markets, in which market power may be found to exist because of "first-mover" advantages, should not in principle be subject to ex-ante regulation.

(16) In undertaking periodic reviews of the markets identified in this Recommendation, the three criteria should be used. These criteria should be applied cumulatively, so that failing any one of them means that the market should not be identified in subsequent recommendations. Thus, whether an electronic communications market continues to be identified by subsequent versions of the Recommendation as justifying possible ex ante regulation would depend on the persistence of high entry barriers, on the second criterion measuring the dynamic state of competitiveness and thirdly on the sufficiency of competition law (absent ex ante regulation) to address persistent market failures. A market could also be removed from a recommendation once there is evidence of sustainable and effective competition on that market within the Community, provided that the removal of existing regulation obligations would not reduce competition on that market.

(17) The Annex to this Recommendation indicates how each market in the Recommendation is linked to the market areas in Annex I to the Framework Directive. When reviewing existing obligations imposed under the previous regulatory framework, in order to determine whether to maintain, amend or withdraw them, NRAs should undertake the analysis on the basis of the markets identified in this Recommendation, in order to give effect to the requirement that market definition for the purposes of ex ante regulation should be based on competition law principles. Pending the first market analysis by NRAs under the new regulatory framework, existing obligations remain in force.

(18) The identification of markets in this Recommendation is without prejudice to markets that may be defined in specific cases under competition law.

(19) The range of different network topologies and technologies deployed across the Community means that in some cases national regulatory authorities must decide the precise boundaries between, or elements within, particular markets identified in the Recommendation, while adhering to competition law principles. National regulatory authorities may identify markets that differ from those of the Recommendation, provided they act in accordance with Article 7 of the Framework Directive. Since the imposition of ex ante regulation on a market could affect trade between Member States as described in recital 38 of the Framework Directive, the Commission considers that the identification of any market that differs from those of the

Recommendation are likely to be subject to the appropriate procedure in Article 7 of the Framework Directive. Failure to notify a market which affects trade between Member States may result in infringement proceedings being taken. Any market identified by national regulatory authorities should be based on the competition principles developed in the Commission Notice on the definition of relevant market for the purposes of Community competition law[4], and be consistent with the Commission Guidelines on market analysis and the assessment of significant market power and satisfy the three criteria set out above. Should an NRA consider that demand and supply patterns may justify an alternative market definition of a market listed in this Recommendation, it should then follow the appropriate procedures set out in Article 6 and 7 of the Framework Directive.

(20) The fact that this Recommendation identifies those product and service markets in which ex ante regulation may be warranted does not mean that regulation is always warranted or that these markets will be subject to the imposition of regulatory obligations set out in the specific Directives. Regulation will not be warranted if there is effective competition on these markets. In particular, regulatory obligations must be appropriate and be based on the nature of the problem identified, proportionate and justified in the light of the objectives laid down in the Framework Directive, in particular maximising benefits for users, ensuring no distortion or restriction of competition, encouraging efficient investment in infrastructure and promoting innovation, and encouraging efficient use and management of radio frequencies and numbering resources.

(21) The Commission will review the need for any update of this Recommendation no later than 30 June 2004 on the basis of market developments.

(22) This Recommendation has been subject to a public consultation and to consultation with national regulatory authorities and national competition authorities.

HAS ADOPTED THIS RECOMMENDATION:

1. In defining relevant markets in accordance with Article 15(3) of Directive 2002/21/EC, national regulatory authorities are recommended to analyse the product and service markets identified in the Annex.

2. This Recommendation is addressed to the Member States.

Editors' Notes:

[a] OJ L 114, 8.5.2003, p. 45. Notified under document number C(2003) 497

---

[4] OJ C 372, 9.12.1997, p. 5.

Retail level

1.   Access to the public telephone network at a fixed location for residential customers.

2.   Access to the public telephone network at a fixed location for non-residential customers.

3.   Publicly available local and/or national telephone services provided at a fixed location for residential customers.

4.   Publicly available international telephone services provided at a fixed location for residential customers.

5.   Publicly available local and/or national telephone services provided at a fixed location for non-residential customers.

6.   Publicly available international telephone services provided at a fixed location for non-residential customers.

These six markets are identified for the purpose of analysis in respect of Article 17 of the Universal Service Directive.

Together, markets 1 through 6 correspond to "the provision of connection to and use of the public telephone network at fixed locations", referred to in Annex I(1) of the Framework Directive. This combined market is also referred to in Article 19 of the Universal Service Directive (for possible imposition of carrier call-by-call selection or carrier selection).

7.   The minimum set of leased lines (which comprises the specified types of leased lines up to and including 2Mb/sec as referenced in Article 18 and Annex VII of the Universal Service Directive).

This market is referred to in Annex I(1) of the Framework Directive in respect of Article 16 of the Universal Service Directive (the provision of leased lines to end users).

A market analysis must be undertaken for the purposes of Article 18 of the Universal Service Directive which covers regulatory controls on the provision of the minimum set of leased lines.

Wholesale level

8.   Call origination on the public telephone network provided at a fixed location. For the purposes of this Recommendation, call origination is taken to include local call conveyance and delineated in such a way as to be consistent with the delineated boundaries for the markets for call transit and for call termination on the public telephone network provided at a fixed location.

This market corresponds to that referred to in Annex I(2) of the Framework Directive in respect of Directive 97/33/EC (call origination in the fixed public telephone network).

9.   Call termination on individual public telephone networks provided at a fixed location.

For the purposes of this Recommendation, call termination is taken to include local call conveyance and delineated in such a way as to be consistent with the delineated boundaries for the markets for call origination and for call transit on the public telephone network provided at a fixed location.

This market corresponds to the one referred to in Annex I(2) of the Framework Directive in respect of Directive 97/33/EC (call termination in the fixed public telephone network).

10. Transit services in the fixed public telephone network.

For the purposes of this Recommendation, transit services are taken as being delineated in such a way as to be consistent with the delineated boundaries for the markets for call origination and for call termination on the public telephone network provided at a fixed location.

This market corresponds to the one referred to in Annex I(2) of the Framework Directive in respect of Directive 97/33/EC (transit services in the fixed public telephone network).

11. Wholesale unbundled access (including shared access) to metallic loops and sub-loops for the purpose of providing broadband and voice services.

This market corresponds to that referred to in Annex I(2) of the Framework Directive in respect of Directive 97/33/EC and Directive 98/10/EC (access to the fixed public telephone network, including unbundled access to the local loop) and to that referred to in Annex I (3) of the Framework Directive in respect of Regulation No 2887/2000.

12. Wholesale broadband access.

This market covers "bit-stream" access that permit the transmission of broadband data in both directions and other wholesale access provided over other infrastructures, if and when they offer facilities equivalent to bit-stream access. It includes "Network access and special network access" referred to in Annex I(2) of the Framework Directive, but does not cover the market in point 11 above, nor the market in point 18.

13. Wholesale terminating segments of leased lines.

14. Wholesale trunk segments of leased lines.

Together, the wholesale markets 13 and 14 correspond to those referred to in Annex I(2) of the Framework Directive in respect of Directive 97/33/EC and Directive 98/10/EC (leased line interconnection) and to those referred to in Annex I(2) of the Framework Directive in respect of Directive 92/44/EEC (wholesale provision of leased line capacity to other suppliers of electronic communications networks or services).

15. Access and call origination on public mobile telephone networks, referred to (separately) in Annex I(2) of the Framework Directive in respect of Directives 97/33/EC and 98/10/EC.

16. Voice call termination on individual mobile networks.

This market corresponds to the one referred to in Annex I(2) of the Framework Directive in respect of Directive 97/33/EC (call termination on public mobile telephone networks).

17. The wholesale national market for international roaming on public mobile networks.

This market corresponds to the one referred to in Annex I(4) of the Framework Directive.

18.   Broadcasting transmission services, to deliver broadcast content to end users.

Note

National regulatory authorities have discretion with respect to the analysis of the market for "Conditional access systems to digital television and radio services broadcast" in accordance with Article 6(3) of the Access Directive. Article 6(3) of the Access Directive provides that Member States may permit their NRAs to review the market for conditional access system to digital television and radio services broadcast, irrespective of the means of transmission.

————————

**COMMISSION STAFF WORKING DOCUMENT AND
DRAFT COMMISSION RECOMMENDATION**

of 28 June 2006

On Relevant Product and Service Markets within the electronic communications sector susceptible to ex ante regulation in accordance with Directive 2002/21/EC of the European Parliament and of the Council on a common regulatory framework for electronic communication networks and services

(Second edition)

SEC(2006) 837

EXPLANATORY MEMORANDUM

1. INTRODUCTION

The Lisbon European Council of March 2000 highlighted the potential for growth, competitiveness and job creation of the shift to a digital, knowledge-based economy. In particular it emphasised the importance of access to inexpensive, world-class communications infrastructure and services. When the European Council revitalized the Lisbon strategy in March 2005, it re-emphasized the need to promote innovation and to spread the EU citizens' access to the information society. It called for better regulation and a reduced administrative burden for entrepreneurs and for a finalization of the internal market.

As part of the renewed Lisbon strategy for growth and jobs, the Commission proposed in June 2005 a new strategic framework, i2010 - European Information Society 2010, laying out broad policy orientations. The goal is to promote an open and competitive digital economy with an emphasis on ICT as a driver of inclusion and quality of life.

In tune with these goals, the legislative package for the electronic communications sector aims to establish a harmonised regulatory framework for networks and services across the EU and seeks to respond to convergence trends by covering all electronic communications networks and services within its scope. The EU legislative package had to be transposed into national law by 25th July 2003. Despite delays in several Member States, national implementation measures are now in place throughout the EU.

The regulatory framework for electronic communications networks and services comprises five Directives:

Directive of the European Parliament and of the Council on a common regulatory framework for electronic communications networks and services[1], hereinafter the Framework Directive

Directive of the European Parliament and of the Council on the authorisation of electronic communications networks and services[2], hereinafter the Authorisation Directive

---

[1] OJ L 108, 24.4.2002, p.33.
[2] OJ L 108, 24.4.2002, p.21.

Directive of the European Parliament and of the Council on access to, and interconnection of, electronic communications networks and associated facilities[3], hereinafter the Access Directive

Directive of the European Parliament and of the Council on universal service and user& rights relating to electronic communications networks and services[4], hereinafter the Universal service Directive

Directive of the European Parliament and of the Council concerning the processing of personal data and the protection of privacy in the electronic communications sector[5].

Article 15(1) of the Framework Directive requires the adoption of a Recommendation on Relevant Product and Service Markets. The Commission adopted the first edition of this Recommendation on 11 February 2003. The Recommendation identified those product and service markets within the electronic communications sector, the characteristics of which may be such as to justify the imposition of regulatory obligations set out in the specific directives. The markets identified in the Recommendation were defined in accordance with the principles of competition law, without prejudice to markets that may be defined in specific cases under competition law.

Article 15(1) of the Framework Directive requires that the Commission regularly reviews the Recommendation. On 25 November 2005, the Commission started the review process by issuing a 'Call for Input', which indicated that the Commission would review the Recommendation during the course of 2006. The views gathered in the call for input have provided input to the draft of the revised version of the Recommendation. This Explanatory Memorandum outlines in greater detail the reasoning behind the proposed changes to the Recommendation.

The Recommendation should be considered in conjunction with the 'Guidelines for market analysis and the assessment of market power' referred to in Article 15(2) of the Directive[6] (hereinafter, "the Guidelines"). National regulatory authorities ("NRAs") are required, taking utmost account of this Recommendation and the Guidelines, to define relevant markets appropriate to national circumstances, in particular relevant geographic markets within their territory, in accordance with the principles of competition law and to analyse those product and service markets, taking the utmost account of the Guidelines. On the basis of this market analysis, NRAs will determine whether these markets are effectively competitive or not and impose, amend, or withdraw regulatory obligations accordingly.

The regulatory framework aims at ensuring harmonisation across the single market and guaranteeing legal certainty. This Recommendation plays an important role in achieving both of these objectives, as it seeks to ensure that the same product and services markets will be subject to a market analysis in all Member States and that market players will be aware in advance of the markets to be analysed. It will only be possible for NRAs to regulate markets which differ from those identified in this Recommendation where this is justified by national circumstances and where the Commission does not raise any objections, in accordance with the procedures referred to in Articles 7(4) of the Framework Directive.

Competing network infrastructures are essential for achieving sustainable competition in networks and services in the long term. When there is effective competition, the framework

---

[3]   OJ L 108, 24.4.2002, p.7.
[4]   OJ L 108, 24.4.2002, p.51.
[5]   OJ L 201, 31.7.2000, P.37.
[6]   OJ 165; 11.7.2002, p.6.

requires ex-ante regulatory obligations to be lifted. Where competition is not yet effective granting others access to facilities in a way that levels the playing field but does not remove incentives for new infrastructure investment ensures that users enjoy choice and competition during the transition to a fully competitive market. Investment in new and competing infrastructure will bring forward the day when such transitional access obligations can be further relaxed.

NRAs define relevant markets appropriate to national circumstances, taking utmost account of the product markets listed in the Recommendation, in particular relevant geographic markets within their territory. The definition of relevant markets can and does change over time as the characteristics of products and services evolve and the possibilities for demand and supply substitution change. This is particularly important where the characteristics of products and services are continually evolving, where new products and services appear and where the way in which such products and services are produced and delivered evolves as a result of technological evolution. The convergence phenomenon where similar services can be delivered over different types of network is one example. This means that it will be necessary to continue periodically re-examining the markets identified in this revised Recommendation. At the same time the underlying purpose of the regulatory framework (and its ex ante market analysis and possible regulation) is to deal with predictable problems of lack of effective competition that have their origin in structural factors in the industry. The fact that the framework deals with situations where any lack of effective competition is durable means that a degree of continuity (as opposed to frequent revisions of this Recommendation) is warranted. After having been in force for more than 3 years, the time is now ripe to revise the first edition of the Recommendation on the basis of market developments.

2.   MARKET DEFINITION, IDENTIFYING MARKETS AND DEFINITION OF OTHER MARKETS

2.1   Methodologies used to define markets

In the regulatory framework, markets are defined in accordance with the principles of competition law, as explained in the Commission Notice on Market Definition[7] and the Guidelines.

The main purpose of market definition is to identify in a systematic way the competitive constraints that the undertakings face. The objective is to identify those actual and potential competitors of the undertakings that are capable of constraining their behaviour and of preventing them from behaving independently of an effective competitive pressure. The market definition arrived at can depend on the relative weight given to demand-side and supply-side substitutability, and can also depend on the prospective time horizon considered. It is important to recall that market definition for the purposes of the Recommendation is not an end in itself but is a means to assessing effective competition for the purposes of ex ante regulation.

As stated in the Commission's Guidelines and Access Notice[8], there are in the electronic communications sector at least two main types of relevant markets to consider, that of services or facilities provided to end users (retail markets) and that of access to facilities necessary to provide such services provided to operators (wholesale markets). Within these two types of markets, further market distinctions may be made depending on demand and supply side characteristics.

---

[7]   OJ C 372, 9.12.1997, p.5.
[8]   OJ C 265, 22.8.1998, p.2.

The starting point for the definition and identification of markets is a characterisation of retail markets over a given time horizon[9], taking into account demand-side and supply-side substitutability[10]. Having characterised and defined retail markets which are markets involving the supply and demand of end users, it is then appropriate to identify relevant wholesale markets which are markets involving the demand and supply of products to a third party wishing to supply end users.

As the market analyses carried out by NRAs have to be forward-looking, markets are defined prospectively[11]. Their definitions take account of expected or foreseeable technological or economic developments over a reasonable horizon linked to the timing of the next market review. Moreover, given the possibility to review a market at regular intervals, a NRA would be justified in taking into account past performance and existing market position as well as expectations concerning forthcoming developments[12].

Markets defined in the Recommendation are without prejudice to the markets defined in specific cases under competition law. Markets identified in the Recommendation, while based on competition law methodologies, will not necessarily be identical to markets defined in individual competition law cases. As explained in paragraph 27 of the Guidelines, the starting point for carrying out a market analysis for the purpose of Article 15 of the Framework Directive is not the existence of an agreement or concerted practice within the scope of Article 81 EC Treaty, nor a concentration within the scope of the Merger Regulation, nor an alleged abuse of dominance within the scope of Article 82 EC Treaty, but is based on an overall forward-looking assessment of the structure and the functioning of the market under examination. NRAs and competition authorities, when examining the same issues in the same circumstances and with the same objectives, should in principle reach the same conclusions. However it cannot be excluded that given the differences outlined above markets defined for the purposes of competition law and markets defined for the purpose of sector-specific regulation may not always be identical.

2.2 The basis for identifying markets that are susceptible to ex ante regulation in this Recommendation

Article 15(1) of the Framework Directive requires that the Recommendation identifies those product and service markets within the electronic communications sector, the characteristics of which may be such as to justify the imposition of regulatory obligations set out in the specific directives[13]. It is therefore appropriate first to consider the characteristics that may render a particular market susceptible to ex ante regulation.

In this context, it should be recalled that the Framework Directive is based on the premise that there is a need for ex ante obligations in certain circumstances in order to ensure the development of a competitive market (see e.g. recital 25).

So far the experience of liberalisation in the European Union has been that entry barriers often constitute a significant impediment to the development of competitive markets in the electronic communications sector. These barriers to entry may be legal or regulatory barriers. There are also structural barriers to entry which may, for example, result from continuing control over legacy infrastructure that is impossible or difficult to duplicate,

---

[9] Ex ante regulation addresses lack of effective competition that is expected to persist over a given horizon. Therefore, the time horizon for market definition and identification for the purposes of this Recommendation should be commensurate with the period during which possible ex ante regulatory remedies are likely to be imposed. The period may depend on whether an existing obligation is being maintained or reviewed, or a new obligation is being imposed.

[10] See section 2 of the SMP Guidelines.

[11] Framework Directive recital 27.

[12] See paragraph 20 of the SMP Guidelines.

[13] Whereas for the initial Recommendation Annex I to the Framework Directive listed a number of markets that were to be included, this is not anymore the case for the current second edition of the Recommendation.

network externalities or economies of scale and scope. Where barriers to entry are high, even an undertaking that is more efficient than the incumbent is unlikely to be able to enter markets and create competition to the benefit of the consumer in the absence of regulatory intervention. The existence of high barriers to entry in a market is therefore considered a first indication that regulatory intervention may be required in order to ensure the development of a competitive market.

In view of the character of electronic communications markets, for regulatory intervention to be justified, market characteristics should not only be analysed in a *static* but also in a *dynamic* manner. Does the market, in the absence of regulation, tend towards effective competition? Market dynamics may make barriers to entry disappear over time, for example as a result of technological developments. Convergence of previously distinct markets may increase competition. Or simply, there may be sufficient players active in the market for effective competition to emerge behind the barriers to entry. Possibilities for the market to tend towards a competitive outcome, in spite of high barriers to entry, need also to be taken into consideration in analysing whether market characteristics may justify ex ante regulation.

Thirdly, Recital 27 of the Framework Directive indicates that, in addition, ex ante regulatory obligations (with respect to electronic communications networks and services) should only be imposed where Community competition law remedies are not sufficient to address the problem[14]. Ex ante regulation and competition law serve as complementary instruments in achieving their respective policy objectives[15] in the electronic communications sector and in dealing with lack of effective competition. At the same time, a principle underlying the regulatory framework is that ex ante regulation should only be imposed where competition law remedies are insufficient and should be rolled back when it is no longer needed.

It is considered therefore that the criteria for identifying markets for the purposes of ex ante regulation should include an overall assessment of the effectiveness of competition law alone in addressing the market failures concerned. Such an assessment will draw on the experience gained from the application of competition law and the imposition of ex ante regulatory obligations in the electronic communications sector as a complementary instrument. Only markets where national and Community competition law is not considered sufficient by itself to redress market failures and to ensure effective and sustainable competition over a foreseeable time horizon should be identified for potential ex ante regulation.

For the aforementioned reasons, it is considered that the following specific cumulative criteria are appropriate to identify which electronic communications markets are susceptible to ex ante regulation.

The first criterion is that a market is subject to high and non-transitory entry barriers. The presence of high and non-transitory entry barriers, although a necessary condition, is not of itself a sufficient condition to warrant inclusion of a given defined market. Given the dynamic character of electronic communications markets, possibilities for the market to tend towards a competitive outcome, in spite of high and non-transitory barriers to entry, need also to be taken into consideration.

---

[14] Recital 27 also indicates that newly emerging markets, where de facto the market leader is likely to have a substantial market share, should not be subjected to inappropriate obligations. The Commission considers that 'emerging markets' are markets which are so new and volatile that it is not possible to determine whether or not the '3 criteria' test described below is met.

[15] Article 8 of the Framework Directive requires NRAs to pursue a number of objectives including: ensuring users derive maximum benefits in terms of choice, price and quality; ensuring there is no distortion or restriction of competition; encouraging efficient investment in infrastructure and promoting innovation; encouraging efficient use of and effective management of radio frequencies and numbering resources.

The second criterion, therefore, is that a market has characteristics such that it will not tend over time towards effective competition. This criterion is a dynamic one and takes into account a number of structural and behavioural aspects which on balance indicate whether or not, over the time period considered, the market has characteristics which may be such as to justify the imposition of regulatory obligations as set out in the specific directives of the new regulatory framework.

The third criterion considers the insufficiency of competition law by itself to deal with the market failure (absent ex ante regulation), taking account of the particular characteristics of the electronic communications sector.

(i).   Barriers to entry and to the development of competition

With respect to the first criterion, two types of barriers to entry and to the development of competition in the electronic communications sector appear to be relevant: structural barriers and legal or regulatory barriers.

A structural barrier to entry exists when the state of the technology, and its associated cost structure, and/or the level of the demand, are such that they create asymmetric conditions between incumbents and new entrants impeding or preventing market entry of the latter. For instance, high structural barriers may be found to exist when the market is characterised by absolute cost advantages, substantial economies of scale and/or economies of scope, capacity constraints, and high sunk cost. Such barriers can still be identified with respect to the widespread deployment and/or provision of local access networks to fixed locations.

An important qualification of the first criterion is whether high entry barriers are likely to be non-transitory in the context of a modified Greenfield approach (i.e. in the absence of regulation in the market concerned under this regulatory framework but including regulation which exists outside this framework). In this respect it is not sufficient to examine whether entry has occurred or is likely to occur in the market at all. The NRA will therefore examine whether the industry has experienced entry and whether entry has been or is likely in the future to be sufficiently immediate and persistent to limit market power. Small scale entry (e.g. in a limited geographic area) may not be considered sufficient since it may be unlikely to exercise any constraint on the dominant undertaking(s). Barriers to entry will also depend on the minimum efficient scale of output, and the fraction of costs which are sunk.

A specific and different type of barrier to the development of effective competition can also occur in the electronic communications sector where interconnection is required to enable a calling party to make a call to a specific subscriber number. In cases where a charge is levied for terminating the call, (which is passed on as a retail charge to the calling party), the terminating network operator can affect competition adversely by raising a rival's costs or by passing on inefficiencies to competitors.

This barrier by itself need not lead to an absence of competition. For example, where the receiver rather than the calling party is responsible for paying any charge associated with incoming calls or traffic, the incentive to raise termination charges above costs is absent. Technological solutions might also provide a way round the technical barrier.

Legal or regulatory barriers are not based on economic conditions, but result from legislative, administrative or other state measures that have a direct effect on the conditions of entry and/or the positioning of operators on the relevant market.

One example is the case of a legal limit on the number of undertakings that have access to spectrum. Such a limitation is typically linked to a related technical or technological barrier, e.g., a constraint on the amount of spectrum that can be assigned and consequently a limit on the number of licences given to undertakings seeking to enter a market. Additional entry is blocked unless additional spectrum becomes available or secondary trading of spectrum is permitted.

A significant legal or regulatory barrier to entry may also exist when entry into a particular market is rendered non-viable as a result of regulatory requirements, and in addition this situation is expected to persist for a foreseeable period. Regulatory requirements may lead to some services being provided at below cost or at rates of return that deter entry. One example is the retail pricing of access to the public telephone network (and local calls) at a fixed location or address. In cases where services fail to cover their forward-looking incremental costs, entry into local access is deterred. Tariff re-balancing will address such a barrier. However, broader policy concerns and objectives may mean that the situation persists for a significant period. For legal or regulatory barriers to be considered valid for the purposes of this three criteria test, such barriers should be necessary to manage a legitimate public policy objective. In the event that legal or regulatory barriers cannot be removed without significant negative effects on such legitimate public policy considerations and within a reasonable timeframe can a non-transitory entry barrier be said to exist.

(ii).   Dynamic aspects - no tendency to effective competition

The second criterion is that the market has characteristics such that it will not tend towards effective competition without ex ante regulatory intervention. The application of this criterion involves examining the state of competition behind the barrier to entry, taking account of the fact that even when a market is characterised by high barriers to entry, other structural factors or market characteristics and developments may mean that the market tends towards effective competition. This is for instance the case in markets with a limited, but sufficient, number of undertakings behind the entry barrier having diverging cost structures and facing price-elastic market demand. In such markets, market shares may change over time and/or falling prices may be observed.

There may also be excess capacity in a market that would allow rival firms to expand output very rapidly in response to any price increase, provided that there are no barriers to expansion behind the barriers to entry. Such barriers to expansion could exist, for example, if small scale entry does not allow firms to move from the fringe to the core of the market occupied by the established firm(s). Such barriers to expansion will just as the barriers to entry depend on the minimum efficient scale of output and the fraction of costs which are sunk.

Market dynamics may also be caused by technological developments or by the convergence of products and markets. Innovation-driven markets characterised by ongoing technological progress may indeed tend towards effective competition. In such markets, competitive constraints often come from innovative threats from potential competitors that are not currently in the market. In such innovation-driven and/or converging markets, dynamic or longer term competition can take place among firms that are not necessarily competitors in an existing "static" market.

The tendency towards effective competition does not necessarily imply that the market will reach the status of effective competition within the period of review. It simply means that there is clear evidence of dynamics in the market within the period of the review which indicates that the market will reach the status of effective competition in the longer-run without ex ante regulation in the market concerned. Where market dynamics are changing rapidly care should be taken in choosing the period of review so as to reflect the pertinent market developments. Anticipated events must be expected within a meaningful timeframe and on the basis of concrete elements (e.g. business plans, investments made, new technologies being rolled out) rather than something which may be theoretically possible.

The simple fact that market shares have begun to decrease in recent years or uncertain technological future developments are in themselves insufficient to find that the market tends towards effective competition.

In general, the later effective competition is expected to materialise in the future, the more likely it is that the second criterion is fulfilled.

(iii).   Relative efficiency of competition law and complementary ex ante regulation

The final decision to identify a market that fulfils the first two criteria (high and persistent entry barriers and absence of characteristics such that the market would tend towards effective competition) as justifying possible ex ante regulation, should depend on an assessment of the insufficiency of competition law by itself (absent ex ante regulation) to address the market failure.

Ex ante regulation would be considered to constitute an appropriate complement to competition law in circumstances where the application of competition law would not adequately address the market failures concerned. Such circumstances would for example include situations where the regulatory obligation necessary to remedy a market failure could not be imposed under competition law (e.g. access obligations under certain circumstances or specific cost accounting requirements), where the compliance requirements of an intervention to redress a market failure are extensive (e.g. the need for detailed accounting for regulatory purposes, assessment of costs, monitoring of terms and conditions including technical parameters etc) or where frequent and/or timely intervention is indispensable, or where creating legal certainty is of paramount concern (e.g. multi-period price control obligations). However, differences between the application of competition law and ex ante regulation in terms of resources required to remedy a market failure should not in themselves be relevant.

In practical application NRAs should consult with their National Competition Authority (NCA) and take into account that body's opinion when deciding whether use of both complementary regulatory tools is appropriate to deal with a specific issue, or whether competition law instruments are sufficient.

In summary, whether an electronic communications market is susceptible to ex ante regulation would depend on the persistence of high entry barriers, on the lack of a tendency towards effective competition and on the insufficiency of competition law by itself (absent ex ante regulation) to address persistent market failures. For those markets listed, the Recommendation creates a presumption for the NRA that the three criteria are met and therefore NRAs do not need to reconsider the three criteria. However, it is open to a NRA to assess the three criteria and whether they are satisfied for their specific market if the NRA believes that this would be appropriate. The results of any such analysis should follow the normal market notification procedure.

The three criteria test focuses on market characteristics. It is intended to screen where persistent market failures, that ultimately cause consumer harm, are most likely to exist. As such the three criteria test is different from the SMP assessment. Whereas the three criteria test focuses on the general structure and characteristics of a market in order to identify those markets the characteristics of which are such that they need to be analysed in more detail on a national basis by NRAs, the SMP assessment focuses on the market power of a specific operator in a given market with a view to determining whether that operator should or should not be made subject to ex ante regulation in that particular market. Meeting the three criteria test does not automatically mean that regulation is always warranted. Regulation will only be warranted if on a market meeting the three criteria test one or more operators are found to have significant market power[16]. NRAs should follow the same basic criteria and principles when they identify markets other than those appearing in this Recommendation. The Commission will use these criteria when making future revisions to this Recommendation.

---

[16]   See section 4 below for a market-by-market overview.

2.3   The definition by NRAs of other relevant markets

In this Recommendation, care has been taken to identify on an EU-wide basis markets whose characteristics may be such as to justify the imposition of regulatory obligations as set out in the specific directives. This list of relevant markets may not be exhaustive in the context of national circumstances, which may vary from Member State to Member State.

In the event that an NRA would identify an instance of consumer harm that cannot be addressed by imposing regulation on a market in the Recommendation they may consider defining a new market. NRAs should ensure that such a market (i) is defined on the basis of competition principles developed in the Commission Notice on the definition of relevant market for the purposes of Community competition law, (ii) is consistent with the Commission Guidelines on market analysis and the assessment of significant market power and (iii) satisfies the three criteria set out above. Since the imposition of *ex ante* regulation on a market would in most cases potentially affect trade between Member States as described in recital 38 of the Framework Directive, the Commission considers that the identification, analysis and regulation of a market that differs from those of the Recommendation is subject to the procedure foreseen in Article 7 of the Framework Directive.

There may moreover be a number of ways in which the borderlines of a specific product or service market may be drawn differently at a national level than set out in the Recommendation, for the purposes of market analysis. For example, in the first round of market analyses certain NRAs have, on the basis of specific national circumstances and consistent with competition law principles, segmented the wholesale terminating segments of leased lines into various product markets in function of the capacity of such leased lines. Likewise, so far all NRAs have in the first round of market analysis narrowed the definition of the wholesale market for broadcasting transmission services so as to identify a separate product market for transmission services over the predominant platform(s) in their country.

When NRAs consider redefining markets more narrowly or more broadly for reasons related to national market circumstances, such market definition must be consistent with competition law principles as set out in the guidelines. This also applies in relation to defining the geographic scope of a market. The Commission continues to see it in general as valid to define a market that spans the Member State, but it may be appropriate to differentiate the remedies imposed if the nature or degree of market failure differs within the national territory. However, NRAs will have to judge when it is more appropriate in their own national circumstances to define more limited geographic markets.

2.4   The analysis of markets identified as susceptible to ex ante regulation

Certain of the markets identified in the Recommendation are interrelated and for NRAs there is a logical sequence in analysing these markets.

In general, the market to be analysed first is that market which is most upstream in the vertical supply chain. Taking into account the ex ante regulation imposed on that market (if any), it should then be assessed whether there still is SMP on a forward-looking basis on the related downstream market(s). This methodology has become known as the "modified greenfield approach". Thus the NRA should work its way further down the vertical supply chain until it reaches the stage of the retail market(s). A retail market should only be made subject to direct regulation if competition on that retail market still exhibits SMP in the presence of wholesale regulation in the related upstream market(s).

For example, with regard to wholesale broadband access, it is recommended that NRAs first analyse the market for local loop unbundling. Taking into account regulation imposed on that market, the market for wholesale broadband access should then be analysed. If that market continues to exhibit significant market power on a prospective basis despite the presence of LLU regulation (unless the NRA finds that the market no longer fulfils the three criteria test and excludes it from regulation on that basis), appropriate regulation on the wholesale broadband access market should be imposed.

Likewise, NRAs should take into account regulation imposed on the market for local loop unbundling when analysing the wholesale market for fixed origination. Remedies imposed on the markets for local loop unbundling should then be taken into account when assessing SMP on a forward looking basis on the retail fixed access market.

Given that the analysis of these markets must be conducted within the context of the entire value chain from the wholesale input market through to the final output market, it is imperative that, for NRAs to be in position to carry out their tasks, they should have access to data at all levels in the value chain. This is particularly pertinent in relation to the retail level. As noted elsewhere by the Commission[17] NRAs have all the necessary powers under the current framework to ensure that they are in a position to obtain such data. Such data requirements may be extensive given the extent of joint and common costs which may transcend both SMP and non-SMP markets and so accounting separation may cover markets where the operator does not have SMP to ensure the coherence of data etc. Therefore an accounting separation obligation may require the preparation and disclosure of information for markets where an operator does not have SMP

The interrelationship of markets should also be taken into account when determining and implementing remedies on the respective markets in order to ensure the effectiveness and consistency of the remedies imposed.

2.5   Remedies

Remedies are the final part of a process which starts with market definition and identification as a market susceptible to ex ante regulation, which is followed by market analysis and, in the event of an SMP designation, moves to corrective action. Markets susceptible to ex-ante regulation are selected on the basis of the criteria set out in section 2.2. The identification of a market for analysis does not of itself mean that that market requires regulatory intervention. It is only where NRAs find that there is the absence of effective competition on that market that they impose remedies. Even then there needs to be careful consideration of which remedy should be applied. The regulatory framework is very flexible. NRAs have a suite of regulatory tools at their disposal, as set out in Directive 2002/19/EC and Directive 2002/22/EC. When imposing a specific obligation on an undertaking with significant market power, the NRA will need to demonstrate the obligation in question is based on the nature of the problem identified, proportionate and justified in the light of the NRA's basic objectives as set out in Article 8 of the Framework Directive.

These basic objectives require NRAs to:

-         promote competition in the provision of electronic communications networks, electronic communications services and associated facilities and services;.

-         contribute to the development of the internal market;

-         promote the interests of the citizens of the European Union.

The Framework Directive also requires NRAs to seek to agree between themselves on the types of instruments and remedies best suited to address particular types of situations in the marketplace. In particular, as noted in the Guidelines on market analysis, in order to establish that a proposed remedy is compatible with the principle of proportionality, the

---

[17] 2005/698/EC Commission Recommendation of 19 September 2005 on Accounting Separation and Cost Accounting Systems Under the Regulatory Framework for Electronic Communications.

action to be taken must pursue a legitimate aim and the means employed to achieve the aim must be both necessary and the least burdensome, i.e. it must be the minimum necessary to achieve the aim.

A number of considerations are set out in the Directives qualifying the use of specific remedies. In particular, before imposing the more onerous remedies, NRAs need to be mindful of the initial investment by the facility owner, bearing in mind the risks involved in making the investment. The NRAs have a duty to safeguard competition in the long term which will inter alia be a function of the need to assess the technical and economic viability of using or installing competing facilities and the effect of such an intervention on possible investment in such competing facilities. This is especially important where new technologies or networks are being deployed in unproven markets.

In principle, the proposed obligations should pertain to the relevant product market in which SMP has been found. However, in dealing with lack of effective competition arising from a position of SMP in an identified market, it may be necessary to impose several obligations to remedy the competition problem relating to services both inside and outside the market. In principle, an NRA may impose obligations in an area outside but closely related to the relevant market under review, provided such imposition constitutes

(a)   the most appropriate, proportionate and efficient means of remedying the lack of effective competition found on the relevant market; and

(b)   an essential element in support of obligation(s) imposed on the relevant SMP market without which those obligations would be ineffective.

For instance, an obligation of accounting separation may cover the disclosure of information related to non-SMP products, which are closely associated with SMP-products.

3.   GENERAL ISSUES

In the course of the notification process and in the public call for input many of the following themes were dealt with. These include the issues of self-supply, bundling, next generation networks (NGNs) and emerging markets. How these general issues are treated in this draft Recommendation is outlined below.

3.1   Self Supply

The issue of how to take into account the self provision of wholesale inputs arises frequently in delineating markets. In some cases, what is under consideration is the self supply of the incumbent operators. In others, it is the self supply of alternative operators.

In many cases the incumbent is the only firm in a position to provide a potential wholesale service. It is likely that there will be no merchant market as this in not in the interest of the incumbent operator. Where there is no merchant market and where there is consumer harm, there is the need to construct a notional market when pent-up demand exists. Here the implicit self supply of this input by the incumbent to itself should be taken into account.

In other contexts there are alternative firms that also self supply the necessary inputs. In these cases, third party access seekers could potentially move their business to such alternative operators. However, this is normally limited by capacity constraints, the potential lack of ubiquity of these networks, and the likelihood of the alternative providers entering the merchant market quickly. In general self supply by alternative operators will only be considered where these constraints are not present, which is unlikely in practice.

3.2   Bundling

Communications companies provide a multitude of services to their customers, which are often sold as a bundle or a cluster. In most cases the individual services in a cluster are not good substitutes for each other yet can be considered to be part of the same relevant market. In the future converged offerings between mobile and fixed services may emerge but this is not expected to be a widespread phenomenon during the life of the revised Recommendation. Such clusters are often sold as such due to economies of scope in the supply function. Some of these economies of scope are related to the marketing and billing functions and are, as such, independent of the context. Others relate to the actual technology used where a given network can be configured to provide a large range of services.

On the demand side, consumers may have a preference for a bundle/cluster if there are significant transactional costs. In this case, consumer preferences may be such that the vast majority prefer to purchase the whole bundle from a single supplier and hence the bundle may become the relevant product market.

Whilst certain bundles are well established (voice and SMS on mobile), others are at a much earlier stage of development. In many circumstances such bundling is to the advantage of consumers without impacting negatively on competition.

As yet, there is little evidence to consider triple or quadruple plays as a bundle that should be analysed as a single market. An important part of this is that the consumer is able to "unpick" the bundle and obtain a particular service from another provider if they so desire. For the same reason, access and calls markets in the fixed arena would still be viewed as separate markets.

3.3   Next Generation Networks (NGNs)

Many firms are planning or in the process of updating the core of their networks to both provide new and innovative services and to provide existing services more efficiently. These plans are normally referred to as the next generation networks (NGNs). A smaller number of operators also plan to update parts of their local access network using fibre. These changes will continue over a much longer period than that covered by this draft Recommendation.

Incentives to upgrade the network can be attributed in part to the need for operators to make cost savings and in part to the need for them to be able to provide advanced services as voice revenues decline. The use of more efficient technology to provide existing regulated services does not alter the justification for that regulation; the move to NGNs does not provide an opportunity to roll back regulation on existing services if the competitive conditions have not changed.

It is recognised that some market definitions may change in the face of the new service offerings that NGNs could bring. The 'all IP' network could have a knock-on effect on business models; for example, the introduction of a 'bill-and-keep' model for interconnection of voice calls on IP networks would have a major impact on the market for call termination.

However, the final impact of these technological developments on defined markets is unclear at a European level and will be further assessed in subsequent editions of this Recommendation.

3.4   Emerging Markets

The framework states that emerging markets should not be subject to inappropriate regulation. The framework aims to take into account the risks inherent in making investments to create new and innovative services, whilst at the same time guarding against the re-emergence of monopolies. The Commission considers that 'emerging markets' are markets which are so new and volatile that it is not possible to determine whether or not the '3 criteria' test is met. Only markets which satisfy the three criteria warrant consideration for ex-ante economic regulation, although consumer protection rules may nonetheless apply.

When the first products are introduced to the market, it is unclear whether the same service could be provided in some other manner. As a market matures however, there will be sufficient certainty to conclude on the nature of entry barriers and how long they are likely to persist. If there are no entry barriers and the service matures successfully and starts to become a mass market, entry should be expected under normal circumstances. Announcements that firms intend to enter independently would certainly point to the fact that entry barriers are not high. However, caution must be taken in relation to making the opposite conclusion as announcements may not be made in advance of market entry.

Even when entry barriers can be identified and their non-transitory nature confirmed, there is still the question of the dynamic behind the entry barrier. It may be that new services are associated with considerable expenditure both on networks, content and other services. This may lead to a firm realising that the only way to recoup this investment over a reasonable period of time is to allow third party access. Provided that it is offered in an open and pro-competitive way, such access could help to provide a level of service competition and move the market away from an outcome that causes considerable harm to consumers. Notwithstanding, the normal considerations relating to the second criterion also apply.

4.   EXAMINATION OF MARKETS IN ORDER TO IDENTIFY RELEVANT MARKETS FOR THE PURPOSES OF THE RECOMMENDATION

This section examines the broad market areas within the electronic communications sector, analyses briefly the general market structure of the relevant retail and wholesale markets within those broad areas, and identifies the specific markets that are susceptible to ex ante regulation.

A key aim of the new regulatory framework is to enhance user and consumer benefits in terms of choice, price and quality by promoting and ensuring effective competition. It is only where consumer harm could be expected absent a regulatory intervention that a market should be susceptible to ex ante regulation. The starting point is therefore a characterisation of retail markets, followed by a description and definition of related wholesale markets.

NRAs have powers as a last resort and after due consideration to impose retail regulation on an undertaking with significant market power. However, regulatory controls on retail services should only be imposed where NRAs consider that relevant wholesale or related measures would fail to achieve the objective of ensuring effective competition[18]. In principle, lack of effective competition may occur at the retail level or the wholesale level or both. That means that NRAs may need to examine the overall degree of market power of undertakings and the impact on effective competition. The identification of a retail market (as part of the value chain) for the purposes of ex ante market analysis does not imply, where there is a finding of a lack of effective competition by a NRA, that regulatory remedies would be applied to a retail market. Regulatory controls on retail services can only be imposed where relevant wholesale measures would fail to achieve the objective of ensuring effective competition at retail level.

Markets should be examined in a way that is independent of the network or infrastructure being used to provide services, as well as in accordance with the principles of competition law. For the purposes of the second edition of the Recommendation, the starting point for market definition and identification is those markets that were identified in the initial Recommendation.

---

[18]   Universal Service Directive recital 26.

4.1   Product and service markets in the electronic communications sector

Electronic communications networks and services are defined in the Framework Directive. Electronic communications services include telecommunications services and transmission services in networks used for broadcasting, but exclude services providing or exercising editorial control over content transmitted using electronic communications networks and services. They do not include information society services, as defined in Directive 98/34/EC, which do not consist wholly or mainly in the conveyance of signals on electronic communications networks[19].

In the initial Recommendation, a general division was made between services provided at fixed locations and those provided to non-fixed locations. Overwhelmingly, despite some moves towards converged offerings, this distinction remains valid. A general distinction was also made between voice services and non-voice (data) services. These distinctions for the purposes of analysing markets do not imply an advance judgement that these services constitute separate markets. However, at the current time voice and data services are still considered overall to be sufficiently distinct in terms of demand substitution that they are analysed separately. At a wholesale level, this distinction between voice and non-voice services may be less easy. For example a transmission channel may carry (or be capable of carrying) both voice and non-voice services[20]. These issues are dealt with in the relevant analysis sections.

Across the EU different Member States have communication network topologies which differ significantly from each other. Since the adoption of the initial Recommendation, diversity has even increased as a consequence of the accession of ten new Member States and different speeds of incumbents rolling out NGNs based on IP in network cores. Diverging national circumstances may lead NRAs to adopt a different market definition than foreseen in the Recommendation, subject to the conditions set out in section 2.3 above.

4.2   Services provided at fixed locations

4.2.1   *Public telephone services provided at fixed locations*

The aim of this section is to (i) describe and define relevant retail markets for voice services provided at fixed locations[21], (ii) define the linked wholesale markets and (iii) identify those markets which warrant ex-ante regulation.

The initial Recommendation identified the following fixed telephony markets as susceptible to ex ante regulation:

- two retail markets for access to the public network at a fixed location, based on a distinction between residential and non-residential customers;

- two retail markets for local and/or national calls, based on a distinction between residential and non-residential customers;

- two retail markets for international calls, based on a distinction between residential and non-residential customers;

- a wholesale market for call origination at a fixed location;

---

[19] Framework directive Article 2.

[20] This raises the question of technical neutrality with respect to the treatment of services and the means by which they are delivered. As well as recognising that some services may constitute substitutes, irrespective of technical provision, it is also necessary to recognise that different services may be characterised by different technical requirements within a given network, for example in terms of delay (real-time or not) and bandwidth (and the level and variance of these technical requirements).

[21] Dial-up Internet services are treated in section 4.2.2 on access to data and related services.

- a wholesale market for call termination at a fixed location (single-network markets for call termination to end-users);

- a wholesale market for transit.

In addition, the initial Recommendation identified the wholesale market for unbundled access to metallic loops and sub-loops as a market susceptible to ex ante regulation. LLU allows alternative operators to provide retail access and voice services at a fixed location, as well as wholesale origination and termination services at a fixed location. Generally, however, alternative operators primarily invest in LLU to provide data services (mainly broadband Internet access), with voice services as a possible addition. Therefore, LLU was in the initial Recommendation and is also in this draft revised Recommendation primarily examined in the context of data services.

Retail Markets

The retail market at a general level can be described as the provision of a connection or access (at a fixed location or address) to the public telephone network for the purpose of making and/or receiving telephone calls and related services. Such access and services may be supplied by several possible means in respect of the undertaking providing the service and the technology that is used. The most common technology currently employed still is via traditional telephone networks using metallic twisted pairs. Alternatives include cable TV networks offering telephone service, mobile cellular networks that have been adapted to provide service to fixed locations or which are confined to a limited radius around a fixed location and other wireless based networks.

Broadband connections are also capable of facilitating delivery of narrowband services, though generally consumers will not upgrade to a broadband service solely for the purposes of accessing voice services. Consumers switch from narrowband to broadband connections primarily to get access to higher speed Internet services. Such migration appears to be independent of the price difference between both products; cross-price elasticity appears to be limited. So far most customers when switching to a broadband connection have kept their narrowband connection, indicating that both access products are used as complements rather than substitutes. There are various reasons for this, including the absence in some Member States of DSL-only connections (so-called "naked DSL") and the pricing structure of naked DSL offers where such offers are available, numbering and emergency call regulation of VoIP. Also from the supply-side, substitution between fixed narrowband access and fixed broadband access is limited.

Households which choose fixed narrowband access either have no demand for Internet access or their demand for Internet access is such that they would not respond to a small non- transitory price increase by upgrading to broadband. While households with broadband connections may be prepared to switch off their narrowband connections, those who are not broadband customers are not likely to switch given the focus of their demand. Therefore from such a starting point, i.e. fixed narrowband access in order to avail of narrowband services, broadband access is clearly not a substitute. For the time being, therefore, it is considered that fixed broadband access is not in the same market as fixed narrowband access.

For locations where there is demand for a large number of user connections, some form of dedicated access, such as leased lines, may be used. In general, as with broadband access, leased lines are generally not substitutable with fixed narrowband access. The retail and wholesale leased lines markets will be analysed in section 4.2.3 below.

In the initial Recommendation, a distinction was made between residential and non-residential access. However, the experience so far of market analyses and notifications under the Framework Directive has shown that the contractual terms of access do not significantly and systematically differ between residential and non-residential access.

Operators do not generally seek to classify different demand categories and do not normally register whether a particular access service is supplied to a residential or non-residential customer, so that collecting separate data for both groups of customers has in practice often appeared to be difficult. From a supply perspective, since similar products (in particular PSTN access lines) are often used by residential and non-residential users, suppliers to non-residential customers could generally divert their supplies to residential customers should prices to residential customers rise, and vice versa. On this basis, the Commission proposes in the draft revised Recommendation to define one single narrowband access market for residential and non-residential customers.

NRAs may, however, decide on the basis of national circumstances and in line with competition law principles to segment this market further where this would be appropriate (for example identifying distinct product markets for different types of access lines such as PSTN, ISDN2 and ISDN3O where it is found that no or very limited demand-side and supply-side substitution between such products exist).

Telephone services are usually supplied as overall packages of access and usage. Various options and packages may be available to end users depending on their typical usage or calling patterns[22]. Although many end users appear to prefer to purchase both access and outgoing calls from the same undertaking, others choose alternative undertakings from the one providing access (and the receipt of calls) in order to make some or all of their outgoing calls. An undertaking that attempted to raise the price of outgoing calls above the competitive level would face the prospect of end users substituting alternative service providers. End users can relatively easily choose alternative undertakings by means of short access codes, (via contractual or pre-paid means) or by means of carrier pre-selection. Whilst undertakings that provide access compete on the market for outgoing calls, it does not appear to be the case that undertakings supplying outgoing calls via carrier selection or pre-selection would systematically enter the access market in response to a small but significant non-transitory increase in the price of access. Therefore, it is possible to identify separate retail markets for access and outgoing calls.

As regards outgoing calls, the initial Recommendation distinguished between local and national calls on the one hand and international calls on the other hand, essentially on the basis of supply-side substitution. Such distinction remains valid. Also on the basis of supply- substitution both markets include fixed-to-fixed as well as fixed-to-mobile calls.

The experience so far under the market review procedure indicates that voice over broadband (VoB) services has increasingly become available across the EU. Substitutability between VoB and narrowband telephony depends on a number of factors such as product characteristics, numbering, quality of service, prices, broadband penetration etc. In countries where broadband penetration is significant, VoB services may exercise a competitive constraint on narrowband telephony services, provided that it is not possible for the incumbent operator to price discriminate between consumers that only have a narrowband connection and consumers that also have a broadband connection. Where substitutability exists, VoB services should be treated as part of the retail calls markets. On the basis of quality differences and product characteristics (e.g. whether conventional handsets can be used and whether the computer must be switched on to receive calls) unmanaged VoB services appear for the time being to be less of a substitute for narrowband telephony than managed VoB, but that distinction may disappear over time as quality of unmanaged VoB services improves and technical features change.

In the absence of any regulation (at retail or wholesale level), the incumbent PSTN operator(s) would face little competitive constraint in terms of price or quality of services

---

[22] The question of whether metered and unmetered (flat-rate) access to Internet are in the same or separate markets is considered in section 4.2.2.

and customers would have little choice of supplier either in relation to access or calls (with the possible exception of large business users). In the following sections we highlight the wholesale inputs that should be identified so as to influence the competitive outcome at the retail level. Finally, we examine if wholesale regulation alone could render the retail markets effectively competitive and in so doing see if the retail markets continue to be susceptible to ex ante regulation.

Related Wholesale Markets

Wholesale call termination

Call termination is the least replicable element in the suite of inputs required to provide retail call services and is therefore analysed first. Wholesale call termination is required in order to terminate calls to called locations or subscribers. Undertakings owning or operating networks to provide telephone services may interconnect at relatively high levels in the network, i.e. at a few interconnect points. Consequently call termination arrangements may in practice comprise call conveyance as well as local call termination. However, undertakings faced by a price increase in say national call termination could purchase local call termination separately from the call conveyance part. Therefore, it makes sense to focus on local call termination as the relevant call termination market.

In using demand and supply substitution possibilities to define a relevant market for competition analysis, it is normal to start with a narrow definition and expand it as appropriate. In this case, the starting point is call termination to a specified location, subscriber or number. However, it is difficult for an undertaking that supplies wholesale call termination to other undertakings wishing to terminate calls to price discriminate between termination charges to different subscribers or locations on its network. Therefore the relevant market is at least as wide as each network operator.

In considering whether a wider definition is appropriate, it is necessary to examine the possibilities for demand and supply substitution that might constrain the setting of termination charges on a given network[23]. If all (or at least a substantial number of) fixed locations or subscribers in a given geographical area were connected by two or more networks, then alternative possibilities would exist for terminating calls to given locations. Another possible source of supply substitution would occur if it was possible technically for calls to a given location or end user to be terminated by an undertaking other than the one operating the network that serves the given location. Currently no such supply substitution is possible.

Call termination charges at a wholesale level on a given network might be constrained via demand substitution but there is currently no potential for demand substitution at the wholesale level. However, there are possibilities for demand substitution at the retail level. Examples could comprise any means of communication that constituted a reasonable alternative to making a call to the location or subscriber number concerned. Such alternatives might include terminating the call to the person concerned via a mobile network, a call using a call-back arrangement, a call that does not involve a specific call termination arrangement (e.g. where parties call via IP based links) or communication via messages of varying kinds (e.g. email, voicemail, paging). It is also necessary that the alternative possibility leads to an effective constraint on the setting of call termination charges by making it unprofitable for a network to raise call termination charges.

Such alternatives for demand or supply substitution do not appear currently to provide sufficient discipline on call termination at fixed locations or an argument in favour of a

---

[23] It is also important to examine countervailing market power, in this case countervailing buyer power in negotiating call termination charges, but this is part of the effective competition analysis once the relevant market is defined.

wider market definition, so that the relevant market appears to be call termination on individual networks with the consequent satisfaction of the first criterion (i.e. high and non-transitory barriers to entry). Each market for call termination on an individual fixed network is a monopolistic market with no tendency towards effective competition, hence satisfying the second criterion. Effective regulation of termination services moreover requires frequent intervention on a coordinated basis and a detailed cost assessment. Termination rates should also be regulated ex ante in order to provide legal certainty to other operators when setting their retail tariffs which are inter alia in function of the terminating cost. Competition law is therefore insufficient to address the market failure on this market.

However, such a market definition - call termination on individual networks - does not automatically mean that every network operator has significant market power; this depends on the degree of any countervailing buyer power[24] and other factors potentially limiting that market power. Small networks will normally face some degree of buyer power that will limit their associated market power. Absent any regulatory rules on interconnection, a small network may have very little market power relative to a larger one in respect of call termination. The existence of a regulatory requirement to negotiate interconnection in order to ensure end-to-end connectivity (as required by the regulatory framework) redresses this imbalance of market power. However, such a regulatory requirement would not endorse any attempt by a small network to set excessive termination charges. The existence of buyer power and the ability of small network operators to raise termination rates above the competitive level should be examined on a case-by-case basis in the context of the SMP assessment on this market. Thereby, one should not only examine the ability of smaller network operators to raise termination rates vis-à-vis the incumbent fixed network operator but also vis-à-vis other operators that may have less buying power.

Wholesale access and call origination

After termination, access and call origination are the next least replicable elements of the wholesale inputs required to provide retail call services. At the retail level, a distinction has been made between access and outgoing calls. An undertaking may make a decision to enter the combined market for access and calls or simply enter part or all of the calls market. In assessing the relevant linked wholesale markets, it is necessary, therefore, to bear in mind that there are a number of means of addressing the retail markets.

With respect to access, the main alternatives are between building (i.e. duplicating the existing local access network) or buying (i.e. using existing local access network) as indicated below. The latter option potentially includes any transmission path that is capable of supporting voice services, e.g. a leased circuit, an unbundled local loop or the wholesale provision of a digital subscriber line (DSL) or bit-stream services. Such alternatives are also capable of supporting the provision of data services or multiple voice channels and are considered in more detail below.

With respect to calls services, the main elements required to produce such services are call origination, call conveyance (including routing and switching) of varying kinds and call termination. Related elements include signalling and the ancillary services needed, for example, for billing purposes. An undertaking that supplies retail telephone service could purchase these inputs separately or together, or produce all of them by constructing an extensive network, or purchase some and produce others.

---

[24] Considerations of relative market power are not limited to networks (of differing size or coverage) serving end users at a fixed location or address but also networks such as mobile cellular networks serving non fixed locations. In circumstances where a 'fixed' network with significant market power is subject to a regulatory remedy (beyond the basic one to negotiate interconnect) such as regulated prices for call termination, market power relative to mobile networks would be affected.

One direct alternative to the purchase of call origination is to establish an access network (cable, fibre to the home,...) to the end user location. Another alternative is to purchase or lease an established network connection to the end user location (for example through local loop unbundling). Both alternatives entail considerable time and investments, a large proportion of which are sunk. Incumbents continue to enjoy, as regards the local access network, absolute cost advantages due to economies of scale and density. The market for fixed call origination hence continues to expose high and non-transitory barriers to entry. Both the development of alternative access networks (cable, fibre to the home,...) and the degree of local loop unbundling remain, for the time being, limited on a European scale. Where market entry has occurred, it has often been limited to particular geographical areas or to particular customer groups. Market entrance has not occurred and is within the coming years not foreseen to occur on such a scale as to make this market tend towards effective competition. Finally, the remedies necessary to address the market failure (in particular access obligations) could not be imposed on the basis of competition law.

Wholesale call origination services (originating access or interconnection) can be provided in the form of minutes or in the form of capacity. It may also be supplied together with switching and/or call conveyance services (see below). The market identified for the purpose of this Recommendation is wholesale call origination services. The relevant market is considered to comprise call origination for telephone calls and for the purposes of accessing dial-up Internet service provision. Therefore the market is defined as call origination on the public telephone network provided at a fixed location.

Wholesale Transit Services

In addition to wholesale call origination and call termination, call conveyance or transit will be needed in order to complete a call. Call conveyance or transit interconnection involves transmission and/or switching or routing. For an undertaking providing services to a limited number of end users, an alternative to using wholesale call conveyance services could be to use interconnected leased lines or dedicated trunk capacity. Transit services refer to the (long distance) conveyance of switched calls on the public telephone network provided at a fixed location. This is a different product from say the provision of dedicated capacity of itself, even if some transit services are provided over leased circuits or links. The difference is that leased lines provide dedicated capacity between two fixed points whereas transit refers instead to switched calls on the public telephone network provided at a fixed location. Transit services therefore compromise both conveyance between tandem switches on a given network, between tandem switches on different networks and including pure conveyance across a third network. Some parts of this transit service market are likely to become more competitive more quickly than others, but there cannot be a presumption that some switched call conveyance (from an incumbent to an entrant's network) is automatically different from other switched call conveyance (between two entrants' networks).

The provision of transit interconnection can be bought either directly or the elements necessary for the provision of such services can be bought separately and the services can be self-provided. The range of operators providing services or indeed the necessary network elements (both self-supplied and to third parties) is almost entirely dependent on the traffic volumes on particular transit routes. While for certain busy routes self provision or even merchant offers by alternative operators are more likely, for other less busy or thinner routes this is not the case, meaning that the ability to provide geographically ubiquitous transit services still normally depend on incumbent provided transit services.

In a large number of Member States, new entrants are still dependent on the incumbent for the provision of transit services on many routes. Due to such scale advantages of incumbent operators and large (sunk) investments, in particular as regards thin routes, there continue to be high and non-transitory barriers to entry on the transit market. Depending inter alia on the roll out of alternative infrastructure and the proportion between thin routes and thick routes in a given Member State, one may see a certain tendency towards effective competition behind the barriers to entry, in particular where alternative operators are providing transit services on the merchant market in competition with the incumbent. Where the presence of such alternative sources of supply constraints the incumbent's behaviour even as regards thinner routes, the transit market may on a case by case basis be found not to meet the second criterion and hence not to be susceptible to ex ante regulation in certain Member States. On a European scale such a tendency towards effective competition however does not yet exist and is not foreseeable in the coming years so that inclusion of this market in the revised draft Recommendation remains warranted. Competition law is in such cases insufficient, as the compliance requirements of an intervention to redress the market failure would be extensive, including for example detailed accounting rules, assessment of costs and monitoring of terms and conditions including technical parameters.

The market defined in the context of this Recommendation is Wholesale Transit Services in the Public Telephone Network. Depending on network topologies, the delineation between call origination and transit services can vary and it is left to NRAs to define those elements constituting each part. It should be noted by the NRAs that while there is a degree of discretion in deciding the appropriate elements constituting call origination, call termination and transit services, these elements are additive, the sum of the three making the whole. This means for instance that if call origination and call termination are already defined that then transit is also defined by default.

Retail Regulation

In the initial Recommendation, in line with Annex I of the Framework Directive, two access markets and four calls markets were identified as being susceptible to ex ante regulation. Retail regulation can only be justified if, with all regulatory remedies on wholesale markets including Carrier Selection and Carrier Pre-Selection in place, there remains a lack of effective competition at the retail level.

Regarding retail access to the public telephone network at a fixed location, the only wholesale regulation that could potentially impact on competition in this market is local loop unbundling, as local loop unbundling enables new entrants to provide narrowband access services to retail customers. However, local loop unbundling requires time and high investments, a large portion of which are sunk. Moreover, new entrants in principle do not unbundle local loops to provide narrowband access only. Local loop unbundling therefore does not remove the high and non-transitory barriers to enter the retail access market at a fixed location, nor does it make this market tend towards effective competition. Even in combination with the development of other infrastructures such as cable and fibre-to-the-home, such a tendency is not envisaged yet on a European basis. Therefore, even in the presence of wholesale regulation, the retail market for access to the public telephone network at a fixed location remains susceptible to ex ante regulation.

As regards the retail calls markets at a fixed location, the conclusion is different. Wholesale regulation, including Carrier Selection and Carrier Pre-Selection obligations, significantly reduce the barriers to enter these markets. This is evidenced by large scale market entry of alternative operators across Europe, to the detriment on the incumbents which overall are losing significant market share. Market entry of Carrier Select and Carrier Pre-Select operators, in combination with VoB services in Member States with significant broadband penetration, imply that overall in the EU, retail fixed calls markets tend towards effective competition. Potential restrictions of competition may still arise, for example through price squeeze strategies of incumbent operators that remain dominant on related upstream markets, but where such strategies constitute an abuse of dominance, competition law provides the appropriate instruments to deal with such market failures. Therefore, the retail calls markets are no longer considered susceptible to ex ante regulation on a European basis. However, in case an NRA finds that national circumstances require a different conclusion, it is open to that NRA to demonstrate that (some of) the retail calls markets in its country continue to meet the three criteria test. This may for example be the case in

Member States where Carrier Select and Carrier Pre-Select obligations have only recently been introduced or so far remain ineffective (e.g. because of particular consumer habits) and where broadband penetration is low and VoB offerings insignificant.

Conclusion

On the basis of the above, it is considered that the following specific markets related to the provision of public telephone services at fixed locations should be included in the revised Recommendation:

Retail level

(1)   Access to the public telephone network at a fixed location

Wholesale level

(2)   Call origination or capacity (on all networks serving a fixed location).

(3)   Call termination on individual networks.

(4)   Transit services in the public telephone network.

4.2.2   Access to data and related services at fixed locations

The aim of this section is to (i) describe and define relevant markets for access to generic data services (in particular the provision of Internet service) at fixed locations at a retail level, (ii) define the linked wholesale markets and (iii) identify the relevant markets which warrant ex-ante regulation.

In the area of data services at fixed locations, the initial Recommendation identified the following markets as susceptible to ex ante regulation:

-         Wholesale unbundled access (including shared access) to metallic loops and sub-loops (or equivalent);

-         Wholesale broadband access.

Retail Markets

The increased use of Internet for a mix of communications services has created potentially wide-ranging retail markets for access to data and related services at fixed locations. In general, the provision of retail Internet access consists of two parts: (i) the network or transmission service to and from the end-user's location and (ii) the provision of Internet services, in particular end to end connectivity with other end users or hosts. These two services may be bundled together.

At the current time, it is possible to identify three commonly available forms of Internet access (i) dial-up service, (ii) high bandwidth services using digital subscriber line (DSL) technologies (or equivalents) or cable modems and (iii) dedicated access[25].

In the period since the initial Recommendation large numbers of residential subscribers and small business users accessing Internet from fixed locations have switched from narrowband to broadband access either through cable modems or more widely via xDSL modems. Although so far consumers have switched to varying degrees across the Member

---

[25] Higher bandwidth or broadband Internet services may be characterised as allowing downstream capacity to end-users in excess of 128 kbits/sec. The bandwidth of the service supplied may be asymmetric or symmetric. Dedicated access would typically involve the provision of symmetric bandwidth.

States, the trend is obvious and appears set to continue. Nevertheless, a significant number of users continue to have narrowband connections, including dial-up access via analogue telephone lines and ISDN.

From the demand-side, substitutability between narrowband and broadband Internet access seems limited. There are a number of technical characteristics of broadband access that imply certain applications are just not viable on dial-up access. On this technical basis and from the standpoint of broadband, therefore, narrowband would be a separate market, because the services and/or the quality features of those services (including their uplink and downlink speed) which can be offered over a narrowband connection would not be seen as viable substitutes from the point of view of an end user which is making use of a broadband connection[26]. In addition, a flat-rate or un-metered narrowband dial-up service may not be considered to be an 'always-on' service in the way that a broadband service could be, as the service is likely to be interrupted if un-used for a given period. For a specific group of customers, in particular those which are less sensitive to bandwidth and speed, broadband access may be a substitute for narrowband access, but evidence shows that once customers have migrated from narrowband to broadband access, they are unlikely to switch back, even in response to a small but non-transitory increase in price. Substitutability therefore is at most in one direction, from narrowband to broadband.

Also from the supply-side, a provider cannot readily switch from offering narrowband Internet access to offering broadband Internet access and vice versa.

A range of broadband access possibilities at a fixed location exist, including DSL networks and cable TV networks that have been upgraded to provide a return path[27]. Satellite and terrestrial TV networks (provided they have adequate capacity and are linked to a return path) are also capable of providing data services and access to Internet[28]. In certain Member States fibre-to-the-home networks are being rolled out on a limited scale. In the future, other wireless technologies and power-line technologies may be exploited for access at fixed locations. Experience under the market analysis and Article 7 review procedures so far indicates that at retail level broadband access services over these platforms, where available, generally belong to a single product market. Likewise, within the category of DSL based services, there is no evidence suggesting that ADSL, ADSL2, ADSL2+, VDSL and future other DSL based retail broadband access services would not be part of a single product market. But when defining markets taking into account the Recommendation, NRAs should analyse on a case-by-case basis substitutability of services provided using these various technologies, thereby taking the principle of technology neutral regulation as a starting point.

Price differentials can be observed between narrowband and broadband access but these can vary and they may be a function of the specific data-rate or qualitative features of services offered, whether flat-rate narrow-band offers are available or not, whether there is competition between different forms of broadband access or for other reasons. It is not

---

[26] The above analysis may well lead to different results were the starting point to be services offered on narrowband connections. In other words, it may exist for this type of markets asymmetric substitutability: for example, under certain conditions a broadband connection may be a viable substitute for a narrowband connection, since it offers additional features, whereas a narrowband connection may not be a viable substitute for a broadband connection. As broadband offers gradually become available at higher average speeds, substitutability with narrowband access further decreases.

[27] DSL remains the main technology for broadband access across the EU. The DSL share of fixed broadband lines in 2005 was 80.4% compared to 16.8% of lines provided by cable and 2.8% by other technologies. DSL continues to gain in importance compared to cable. See the Commission Staff Working Paper attached to the 11th Implementation Report, p. 34.

[28] Internet access via the TV is becoming more common, although there are often limitations with respect to the content that can be accessed and the applications that can be used. In most cases a standard modem on a telephone line is used. However, the broadcast path could also be used in which case access would more closely resemble other higher speed access methods.

therefore easy, at the current time, simply on the basis of price differentials, to discern whether separate retail markets exist.

At the same time, for the purposes of deriving wholesale markets, there are important distinguishing characteristics from a demand perspective between broadband services and dial-up or narrow-band service. At a retail level customers in the broadband market have a range of options to purchase connectivity at these speeds. Consumers can buy service from cable operators with upgraded networks using cable modems, they can buy service from new entrants using either unbundled local loops that the entrant has modified or which have been modified for them, or the customer can buy these services directly from the incumbent. Other technologies such as wireless local loops are not widely available, but are capable of providing equivalent services. Between these options, provided prices are comparable, a consumer will be indifferent.

In the narrowband market, dial-up services may be paid for on the basis of a subscription, usage or a combination of the two. Un-metered or flat-rate retail (subscription only) service is widely available in the Community.

Metered and un-metered (flat-rate) access can be considered to be part of the same market for a number of reasons. Firstly, the only difference between the products is the way in which tariffs are structured. Secondly, the two products appear to be substitutable for end-users, although there appears to be little evidence of end-users substituting metered service in response to a price increases in un-metered service. Thirdly, if obligations exist to allow operators to buy wholesale call origination on an un-metered basis supply substitution will be possible in that a hypothetical monopolist that raised the price of un-metered access would induce other providers (of metered products) to offer an un-metered product at a lower, competitive price level. Therefore metered and un-metered call origination do not constitute distinct markets.

It would be open to NRAs to impose requirements on the broader call origination market which included a requirement to offer un-metered call origination, provided this obligation is proportionate as stated in Article 8(4) of the Access Directive.

On the basis of the above, two retail markets are identified: narrowband (dial-up) Internet access and broadband Internet access. It will be examined further hereafter to what extent wholesale and/or retail regulation are warranted in order to ensure effective competition on these markets. The relevant market for dedicated access is treated separately in section 2.2.3 below.

Wholesale inputs to broadband Internet access

In order for broadband access to Internet and related data services to be supplied to an end user at a fixed location, an appropriate transmission channel is required, that is capable of passing data in both directions and at rates that are appropriate for the service demanded. Therefore, an undertaking providing services to end users needs to build, establish or obtain access to a transmission channel to an end user location.

The least replicable element in the establishment of an access transmission channel to an end user location is the local loop. There are major obstacles, in terms of cost, time and legal barriers to duplicate the incumbent's local access network. Barriers to enter the local loop market are indeed high and non-transitory. Behind the barriers to entry, there is no tendency towards effective competition. While upgraded cable systems have become more widely developed and deployed in some parts of the Community, such systems overall still have a limited coverage. Moreover, the unbundling of cable networks at this stage does not appear technologically possible, or economically viable, so that an equivalent service to local loop unbundling cannot be provided over cable networks. Other access technologies including wireless local loops, digital broadcast systems and power-line systems are starting to become available, but only on such a marginal scale that they do not exercise any constraint on the local loop operators. Thirdly, competition law would be insufficient to redress the market failure on the local loop market, as the compliance requirements of intervention in this market are extensive (including the need for detailed accounting, assessment of costs and monitoring of terms and conditions including technical parameters). The local loop market hence meets the three criteria test and continues to be susceptible to ex ante regulation.

The question then arises whether in addition to LLU, the market for wholesale broadband access constitutes a distinct market and, if so, whether it warrants ex ante regulation. An operator using unbundled local loops will not normally consider wholesale broadband access to be a substitute even if the service provided by the wholesale broadband access provider allowed the supply of all the same services that were provided over the unbundled loops. Once an operator has invested in local loop unbundling, it is unlikely to switch to wholesale broadband access as a large part of its unbundling investment would be sunk. Equally, it is questionable as to whether an entrant using wholesale broadband access to deliver retail broadband services to the final user market could easily switch to using unbundled local loops to provide an equivalent service. From a demand perspective, a retail provider using wholesale broadband access will only consider unbundled local loops a substitute if it has all the other network elements needed to self-provide an equivalent wholesale service. The supply substitution possibilities depend on the same condition. Therefore, unbundled local loops and wholesale broadband access constitute distinct markets.

The local loop market is situated upstream from the wholesale broadband access market and regulation on the local loop market may facilitate market entry on the wholesale broadband access market. However, in view of the investment required for LLU and the absolute cost advantages of the incumbent resulting from economies of density and scale, high barriers to enter the wholesale broadband access market remain even in the presence of regulated LLU. The wholesale broadband access market hence continues to meet the first criterion under the modified Greenfield approach. Experience under the market analysis and Article 7 notification procedures so far indicates that the coverage of LLU in a given Member State, in combination with the existence of alternative broadband access networks such as cable and/or fibre, may imply that in a limited number of Member States the market for wholesale broadband access may tend towards effective competition behind the barriers to entry. This may in particular be the case where both broadband penetration and unbundling rates are very high, and in particular where alternative operators have started to provide wholesale broadband access services in large parts of the country in competition with the incumbent[29]. Across the EU, however, this is not the case yet and is not foreseeable within the next years. Therefore the wholesale broadband access market continues to meet the second criterion. Where there is no tendency towards effective regulation on the wholesale broadband access market in a given Member State and the incumbent operator continues to have SMP, competition law is not sufficient to redress the market failure as under competition law the provision of wholesale broadband access services could in principle not be mandated and compliance requirements would be high (including detailed monitoring of cost and technical conditions). Moreover, co-ordination should be ensured between regulation of wholesale broadband access and regulation of local loop unbundling in order to ensure consistency in the regulatory interventions. Since the third criterion is also met, the wholesale broadband access market continues to warrant inclusion in the revised draft Recommendation as a market susceptible to ex ante regulation.

In the initial Recommendation, the wholesale broadband access market was said to cover 'bitstream'[30] access that permit the transmission of broadband data in both directions and

[29]   See case NL12005/0281.
[30]   For the purpose of this Recommendation bitstream is a service which depends in part on the PSTN and may include other networks such as the ATM network.

other wholesale access provided over other infrastructures, if and when they offer facilities equivalent to bitstream access. In this context, the question has arisen whether wholesale access to cable networks that provide a return path, is part of the relevant market. Across the EU, cable represents 16,8% of broadband connections only, compared to 80,4% of DSL-lines and its relative importance continues to decrease. Experience under the market analysis and Article 7 notification procedures so far has indicated that, where cable networks exist, their geographical coverage is often limited and wholesale access to such networks does not constitute a direct substitute for DSL based wholesale access products from the demand or the supply side, so that inclusion in the same product market is not justified[31]. The presence of cable in a given Member State may, however, exercise an indirect constraint on the provider of DSL based wholesale broadband access, through the substitutability between both products at retail level. Such indirect pricing constraint, where it is found to exist, should be taken into account when assessing if the incumbent DSL operator has SMP on the relevant market.

Another question that has arisen is whether wholesale broadband access services using DSL technologies other than ADSL are part of the relevant market. The speeds which DSL technologies are capable of providing are evolving continuously with higher speed service availability depending on the network topology, proximity to exchange points and so on. DSL technologies are currently capable of supplying up to 20 Mbit/see to end users providing the ancillary elements are suitable and the future roll-out of VDSL allows for speeds up to 50 Mbit/sec. For the time being, end users using DSL technologies typically expect to receive service in the range of 2-10 Mbits and there are no indications that this will change dramatically over the next one to two years, unless in certain Member States, TV over DSL would develop rapidly. To satisfy such retail demand, wholesale broadband access services over any DSL technology appear to be substitutable, provided that switching between such technologies for the customer does not entail switching costs. It remains open to individual NRAs to examine this issue in further detail on the basis of national circumstances.

On the basis of the above, the relevant markets identified for the purposes of this revised draft Recommendation as being susceptible to ex ante regulation are:

-        unbundled access (including shared access) to metallic loops and sub-loops (including shared access); and

-        wholesale broadband access. The point in the network at which the wholesale broadband access market will need to be supplied will depend on the market analysis and in particular on the network topology and the state of network competition.

Wholesale inputs to dial-up Internet access and services - wholesale call origination

Despite the growth of broadband access, narrowband dial-up access to the Internet remains an important end user product[32]. An Internet service provider (ISP) supplying dial-up Internet access requires wholesale call origination and wholesale call termination as inputs as well as wholesale Internet connectivity. A wholesale product corresponding to the retail product for access to the public telephone network at a fixed location would be necessary for the provision of dial-up Internet services. Users encountering a hypothetical monopolist

---

[31] For existing wholesale customers, migrating from DSL based access to cable-based access would cause substantial switching costs so that switching is unlikely to occur in reaction to a small but significant non-transitory price increase. Suppliers would also be in a position to price discriminate between existing wholesale customers and wholesale customers that have not committed yet to a particular technology so that existing customers would not benefit from any constraining effect of uncommitted customers.

[32] In most Member States, dial-up still represents more than half of total fixed Internet access (see Commission Staff Working Paper annexed to 1 1 Implementation Report, p. 32).

on the call origination market would be able to easily switch service provider through the use of Carrier Pre Selection (CPS) or Carrier Selection (CS). Switching call origination service providers is in general both easy and cheap. This may result in there being more separate bills to be paid as the access provider and the service provider(s) cease to be the same entity or entities. While there is undoubtedly a range of customers who value the ease of single billing, it is not clear that this population would be significantly large to mitigate the disciplining role of those not concerned with single billing. Whether service is supplied on a metered basis or on an un-metered basis (or a combination of the two), call origination frequently takes place using appropriate number ranges which route calls to the network used by an ISP for onward connectivity with the public Internet. Depending on the specific call origination arrangements used, ISPs may compensate the originating network operators on behalf of their end-users or call origination may be paid for directly by end-users.

In general, end-users accessing the Internet via dial-up means at a fixed location use the undertaking that provides access to the public telephone network. The relevant market includes both call origination for the purpose of speech communications and for other forms of communication such as fax or data. Therefore, the relevant market for wholesale call origination for dial-up Internet service is call origination on the public telephone network provided at a fixed location (the same market defined in section 4.2.1).

Wholesale call termination

In order to provide dial-up end-users with Internet access and connectivity, ISPs need to ensure that dial-up calls are terminated; i.e. go through a terminating operator en route to the ISPs server.

Wholesale call termination as part of Internet service provision is different from call termination on fixed or mobile networks for the completion of calls between two end-users. In the case of call termination for Internet service provision, end-users have a contractual relationship (implicit or explicit) with an ISP but normally have no notion of the undertaking terminating dial-up calls. The ISP chooses the terminating operator (or operators) that receives the dial-in calls and may itself pay the terminating charge[33]. Since any terminating charge is incorporated into the overall amount that is charged by the ISP (and faced by the end-user), and end-users can switch between competing ISPs, ISPs have an incentive to minimise the termination charges that they pay.

In general, ISPs will have a wide choice with respect to terminating operators since entry into this market is relatively easy and there is evidence of ISPs switching terminating operators. Switching terminating operators is easy provided that such alternatives exist. However, in certain Member States it may be that there is less choice of terminating operators or that one or more operators that have market power on originating access are in a position to more fully exert that market power with respect to call termination. The more limited choice may occur because operators may need to build out networks in order to terminate dial-up calls under unmetered arrangements. Therefore if NRAs consider it necessary to define an Internet termination market they can do so by following the Art. 7 procedure.

Whilst the relevant wholesale call origination market fulfils the criteria to warrant identification in the Recommendation, the relevant wholesale call termination market does not for the purpose of this Recommendation.

Wholesale Internet connectivity

---

[33] A number of actual business models may exist. In the metered approach, a portion of the retail usage charge may be passed from the originating to the terminating operator and on to the ISP. In a subscription model, the terminating operator may compensate the originating operator and charge this to the ISP.

Irrespective of whether end-users access Internet via dial-up or broadband means, ISPs still need to ensure connectivity with other ISPs and their end-users.

To ensure that data packets sent by end-users reach the intended destinations and also that incoming traffic is received, undertakings need to make the necessary arrangements to permit connectivity with all other Internet end users or at least with the networks that they use. This global connectivity can be arranged in a number of ways. It can be purchased from a network that is in a position by its own arrangements to guarantee such connectivity. It can be obtained by interconnecting and exchanging traffic with a sufficiently large number of networks that all possible destinations are covered. Alternatively it can be arranged by a combination of interconnecting with certain networks and purchasing the remaining connectivity that is needed.

Two questions arise for the purposes of the Recommendation. Is it necessary to identify a market for Internet connectivity or packet delivery for the purposes of ex ante market analysis, and if so, what is the relevant market? There are a number of differences between the typical arrangements for terminating calls on the public telephone network and delivering packets to destination addresses on the public Internet. In the latter case, end users are implicitly paying to both send and receive packets. It is not automatically or typically the case that incoming traffic is charged for and that this charge is passed to the traffic sender via the sender's network. As indicated above, traffic connectivity can be arranged in a number of ways.

Entry barriers to this market are low and although there is evidence of economies of scale and that the ability to strike mutual traffic exchange (peering) agreements is helped by scale, this alone can not be construed as inhibiting competition. Therefore, unlike the case of call termination in section 4.2.1, there is no a priori presumption that ex ante market analysis is required. Therefore, no market for wholesale Internet connectivity (or delivery of incoming packets) is identified for the purposes of the Recommendation.

Conclusion

Therefore it is considered that the following specific markets related to access to data and related services at fixed locations should be included in the revised Recommendation:

Wholesale level

-        Wholesale unbundled access (including shared access) to metallic loops and sub-loops (or equivalent)

-        Wholesale broadband access.

-        Call origination on the public telephone network at a fixed location.

4.2.3   *Dedicated connections and capacity (leased lines)*

The markets related to dedicated connections and capacity have a link to some of the markets defined with respect to access at fixed locations and the provision of services at fixed locations. For example, dedicated connections may be an alternative to unbundled local loops and vice versa in certain circumstances. Also dedicated trunk or long distance connections may be an alternative to long distance call conveyance. Lower speed leased lines may be replaced in certain instances by standard broadband connections based on DSL or cable modems depending on quality of service requirements.

Dedicated capacity or leased lines may be required by end users to construct networks or link locations or be required by undertakings that in turn provide services to end users. Therefore it is possible to define retail and wholesale markets that are broadly parallel.

The key elements in the demand and supply for dedicated connections are service guarantees, bandwidth, distance and the location or locations to be served. There may also be qualitative characteristics because in some cases distinctions are still made between voice grade and data grade circuits.

At the retail level, specific reference is made in the Universal Service Directive to the provision of the minimum set of leased lines[34]. The minimum set of leased lines refers to specified leased circuits with harmonised characteristics that must be made available under particular conditions throughout the national territory. In line with the approach set out for the identification of markets it is clear that there would be consumer harm at the retail level absent a regulatory intervention. However, whether there is a need to regulate at both retail and a wholesale level in the market is not clear.

At the wholesale level, it is possible to distinguish separate markets, in particular between the terminating segments of a leased circuit (sometimes called local tails or local segments) and the trunk segments. What constitutes a terminating segment will depend on the network topology specific to particular Member States and will be decided upon by the relevant NRA.

While many trunk segments on major routes are likely to be effectively competitive in certain geographic areas in Member States, other trunk segments may not support alternative suppliers. Depending on the proportion of such routes in a given Member State, one may see a tendency towards effective competition behind the barriers to entry where alternative operators have made sufficient investments in alternative infrastructures and are in competition with the incumbent on the merchant market. The trunk segment leased line market has so far been found not to meet the second criterion in one Member State and hence not to be susceptible to ex ante regulation. In a number of other Member States, the NRA has found the market for trunk segments of leased lines to be effectively competitive. This trend is likely to continue. However, across the EU a tendency towards effective competition does not yet exist and seems not imminent so that inclusion of this market in the revised draft Recommendation remains warranted on the basis of the first and second criteria. Given that across the EU a vast number of routes continue to be only served by a single operator, there will be little incentive to open these up to other parties on a commercial basis. In this way, new entrants cannot compete with the established operator throughout a large proportion of the territory. Whilst it might be considered that competition law can address the failure on a route by route basis, it is unrealistic for competition law to be able to do so as long as the number of unduplicated trunk routes in a country remains high considering the general costing and pricing principles that would have to be applied throughout the network. For the aforementioned reasons trunk segments of leased lines continue to be susceptible to ex ante regulation on an overall European basis, but individual NRAs may come to a different conclusion on the basis of national circumstances.

In relation to terminating segments the existence of high and non-transitory entry barriers and the absence of a tendency towards effective competition across the EU are more obvious. Often the terminating segments of leased lines rely in one form or another on the former incumbent's ubiquitous access network. The control over that ubiquitous access network continues to provide the incumbent with a legacy advantage on the terminating segments of leased line market that new entrants, across the EU, have not yet overcome. Even more than with trunk segments, there is little dynamic towards effective competition and competition law cannot alone address the failures on the trunk segments market.

With SMP regulation applied at the wholesale level, there is not likely to be consumer harm on the retail leased lines market. Wholesale regulation, where appropriate, should be sufficient to ensure that there is competitive supply at the retail level. The minimum set of

---

[34] OJ C 339, 7.11.1998, p. 6.

leased lines was included in the initial Recommendation in line with Annex 1 of the Framework Directive. However, it is not clear that there is any significant residual market failure that would be required in order for this market to warrant ex-ante regulation. Putting consideration of its inclusion in the text of the directives to one side we can examine whether this market satisfies the three criteria.

With wholesale regulation in place there should be little barriers to market entry into the retail market. Firms can make tenders to provide a widely based leased line offer to the customer's premises. Having overcome the problem of making a ubiquitous offer, then entry barriers into this market are no longer high. Thus, the retail market for the minimum set of leased lines will not be identified in this draft revised Recommendation. Consequently the Commission will propose to make the Minimum Set of Leased Lines a null set.

Conclusion

Therefore it is considered that the following specific markets related to the provision of dedicated connections and capacity (leased lines) should be included in the Recommendation:

Wholesale level

Wholesale terminating segments of leased lines.

Wholesale trunk segments of leased lines.

4.3   Services provided at non-fixed locations

The aim of this section is to (i) describe and define relevant markets for mobile services at a retail level, (ii) define the linked wholesale markets and (iii) identify the relevant markets which are susceptible to ex-ante regulation.

In the area of services provided at non-fixed locations (mobile services), the initial Recommendation identified the following markets as susceptible to ex ante regulation:

-        Wholesale access and call origination on public mobile networks;

-        Wholesale voice call termination on individual mobile networks;

-        Wholesale national market for international roaming on public mobile networks.

Retail markets

Customers use mobile phones for different purposes, such as making a voice call or sending an SMS. Rather than using different providers of these services, customers appreciate the ease and convenience of having only one handset and SIM card. Thus, consumers purchase a bundle or "cluster" of services from one mobile operator which usually includes local national and international (and roamed) calls and SMS. In this manner mobile firms benefit from economies of scope and consumers benefit from a reduction in transaction costs. Thus, the relevant market should include a "cluster" of products, where non-substitutable services are included in the same market.

With respect to the overall retail mobile market, it remains unclear whether residential and most business customers can be considered to be part of the same market or not as there does not appear to be a clear way to separate them, even if there may be significant differential pricing of services in order to attract certain types of customer or use[35]. With respect to demand substitution, end users may be indifferent between tariff packages designed for business or residential users provided the terms suit their usage profile. With respect to supply substitution, an undertaking serving the business market may easily switch to supplying residential users in response to a small but non-transitory price increase by a hypothetical monopolist.

However, it is clear that large business users are in a position to demand and get personalised offerings. These firms often tender to have their mobile communications needs fulfilled, and the contract terms are private information. Moreover, these users are closed user groups who care about both making and receiving calls. They internalise the externality caused by the Calling Party Pays (CPP) convention. For this reason, business users that individually negotiated rates are explicitly excluded from the remainder of the analysis. The actual boundary between this group of business users and other business users may differ between Member States and it will be for NRAs to properly delineate where this lies.

Pre- and post-pay mobile services can also be considered to be part of the same market. Supply substitutability is relatively easy, as is demand substitutability (in particular from prepay to contractual terms).

Mobile telephone users have no apparent substitute for mobile access and there is no supply substitute unless new spectrum becomes available. Therefore it seems that access could be considered as a market that is separate from the supply of services over the network at a retail level. However, every end-user purchases access to a mobile network with the objective of making calls or receiving calls (and using SMS etc.) or both (nationally or whilst roaming internationally). Even if a user purchasing service chose not to originate calls, their decision to have service must be based on a need for call termination (to receive calls) otherwise access would be meaningless. This has implications for the definition of corresponding wholesale market for termination.

Similar considerations exist for international roaming at a retail level. Retail international roaming services include the ability to make and to receive calls whilst in a country other than the one where the end user has established his or her network subscription. From a demand perspective, the retail provision of international roaming services could be examined to see if it is a separate market. However, it is a standard part of the bundle of services offered by mobile operators. Moreover, roaming is likely to be even more marked by transactional complementarities than other services offered by mobile operators (where a consumer might like to sign contracts with different operators for different countries and for different times of the day etc.). Thus, retail roaming is part of the cluster of services purchased. Moreover, a domestic supplier of other mobile telephony services could respond to a price increase by a hypothetical monopolist by making agreements with foreign operators so as to supply retail roaming services.

Therefore it is possible to define a single cluster retail market that includes access, national, international and roaming calls and SMS.

Since the adoption of the initial Recommendation, mobile services have continued to spread with mobile penetration reaching 92.8% of the EU population in 2005. Mobile number portability has become compulsory since 2003. Despite a slow start number porting has increased dramatically in 2005, with 28 million mobile number ports. Most of these happened, however, in only a number of countries. In over half of the Member States, mobile network operators concluded wholesale access agreements with service providers and mobile virtual network operators (MVNOs) and in countries where this happened

---

[35] One area where a specific business market might be identified is in the retail provision of national and international services (including international roaming) for large corporate customers. Such a market is not identified for the purpose of ex ante regulatory analysis.

competition tends to be more intense. The sector shows a trend towards consolidation, with transactions integrating competing mobile networks within certain Member States (the Netherlands, Austria) as well as pan-European transactions such as TelefonicalO2. At the same time, 3G operators are entering the market.

Related Wholesale Markets

In order to provide retail mobile services, operators need various wholesale inputs, including termination services, access and call origination services and international roaming services.

Wholesale call and SMS termination on mobile networks

As for fixed telephony, termination services are the least replicable input for retail mobile services. Mobile call termination is an input both to the provision of mobile calls (that terminate on other mobile networks) but also to calls that are originated by callers on networks serving fixed locations that terminate on mobile networks. This also applies to SMS termination, though very few messages currently originate directly on the fixed network but more and more come via the Internet. Since the termination charge is set by the called network, which is chosen by the called subscriber, the calling party in general does not have the ability to affect or influence termination charges. This is the case under the calling party pays (CPP) principle which is currently common in Europe. As the market failure is the same for both call and SMS termination and as both services are sold as part of the same mobile cluster both at retail and wholesale level, it seems appropriate to deal with them as part of a single termination market per operator.

The CCP convention allows the terminating operator to raise its prices without a constraint from either party to the call. The calling party pays a bundled fee and will not see a direct price signal. The receiving party makes no payment by convention so cannot constrain the ability of their terminating operator. To the extent that the increased price reduces the number of calls that a person receives they are made worse off. However, this may not be really noticed and the person will not be able to attribute this fall off in calls to a higher termination rate. Thus, M1'40s can raise the price of reaching one of its subscribers readily.

This externality, whereby the called party may independently and adversely affect the calling party, can potentially be internalised, so that the ability for a network to set excessive termination charges is constrained. Whether such a process can be expected to occur does affect both how a relevant termination market is defined and whether a relevant termination market should be identified for the purposes of the Recommendation. These issues are examined in more detail below.

At a retail level a call/SMS to a given user or user's terminal is not a substitute for a call/SMS to another user and this limitation on demand substitution follows through at the wholesale level. In respect of supply substitution, if the supplier of call/SMS termination raises its price, it is not easy for alternative suppliers to switch to supply that market because they would need the SIM card details of that user to do so. However, the market is wider than call/SMS termination on a given user terminal because it is not possible for an operator to readily price discriminate between termination charges to different users across their network. Therefore the relevant market is at least as wide as termination for each operator.

However, with such a starting point in market definition, the supplier and the product are perfectly linked. It is important therefore to consider the possibilities for demand and supply substitution that might constrain termination charges and also the behaviour of network operators in setting termination charges. A constraint would exist if, when a network operator tried to raise termination charges (or resisted lowering them), the overall impact were unprofitable. Such supply side substitution is not currently possible but may become feasible at some point in the future.

This could become the case with software enabled SIM cards, comparable to cases where operators establish preferred arrangements for their end-users when they are roaming internationally.

Nonetheless, it is clear that the first criterion of a high and non-transitory entry barrier is met for mobile termination of voice calls and SMS messages. The fact that a mobile operator has a collection of customers for which it has a monopoly for terminating traffic cannot be overcome by other operators regardless of their size.

In principle mobile termination charges might be constrained via demand substitution, but there is no potential for demand substitution at a wholesale level. Demand at the wholesale level is inextricably linked to supply. The operator (of the caller) is unable to purchase call or SMS termination on a given network from an alternative source (as indicated above).

However, there are various possibilities for demand substitution at the retail level. It may be that other forms of calls or communications are reasonably close substitutes for the calls considered above, such as call back and call forwarding but in order for that potential substitution to broaden the market it would need to constrain the behaviour of the operator setting termination charges by lowering its overall profitability. Similar considerations apply for SMS messaging.

There may be substitutes for different classes of call, for instance a possible substitute for a fixed to mobile call is a mobile to mobile call[36]. The substitute call would need to be on net to lower profitability and constrain behaviour. In conjunction with the possibility for closed groups of users to exert buyer power (as described below), the potential substitution has a stronger impact because it could lead not only to the loss of termination charges but also to the loss of subscribers from one network to another.

A possible substitute for an off-net mobile call could be a mobile to fixed call. This would result in the loss of the termination charges but it is likely that the alternative call is only a close substitute in specific circumstances (e.g. knowing that the called party is close to a given fixed phone).

To summarise, some of these potential substitutions could constrain termination charges but empirical evidence does not seem to indicate that in practice they do so. In practice, none of the demand substitutes above seem to operate a level that would constrain the mobile operator's behaviour.

Another specific way in which end-users and their operators can avoid excessive termination charges is by tromboning (traffic re-file) or re-routing. In particular, it is possible to re-originate traffic so that it appears that it is coming from the mobile network on which calls are due to terminate. The latter practice is only viable for end-users that originate a significant amount of traffic for termination on a mobile network. In addition, it is possible for mobile operators to design differentiated tariff services in order to separate such user groups.

Another possible constraint on the ability of operators to set excessive termination charges may come from buyer power at the retail level. Two main types of buyer power may arise.

The first is where users of mobile phones are sufficiently concerned about receiving incoming calls that the price of incoming calls and SMS affects their choice of supplier. For this to exert a constraint on the pricing of termination it is necessary that such a factor is as important to users as the pricing of other services such as outgoing calls, rental subscriptions etc. Under the calling party pays (CPP) principle, the calling party pays for the

---

call, and the called party does not, therefore there is no direct relationship between the charges applied and demand for the service by the user of the mobile network who receives the call. Mobile users have shown little price sensitivity to how much it costs others to call them.

A second type of buyer power can come from closed user groups where a particular group of users (whether or not they pay for part of the bill associated with incoming calls) make sufficient calls/SMS between them that intra-group calls/SMS constitute a significant proportion of their bill. If a given network raised termination charges and thereby increased the price of incoming calls, group members could switch networks to be on a given network and take advantage of lower on net prices. However, mobile operators are able to price-discriminate among the various categories of users and (through the use of on-net tariffs) offer closed economic user groups discounts for calls to particular mobile etc. Thus, for on-net calls there is no market failure as the mobile operator has an incentive to encourage intensive use of its network.

In general therefore, whilst it is apparent that end-users who subscribe to mobile services have a choice about the network to which they subscribe and that it is relatively easy to switch between networks, there is limited evidence of widespread constraints on the pricing of wholesale call and SMS termination.

The conclusion at the current time (under a calling party pays system) is that call and SMS termination by third parties on individual networks is the appropriate relevant market.

A market definition for call and SMS termination on each mobile network would imply that currently each mobile network operator is a single supplier on each market. However, whether every operator then has market power still depends on whether there is any countervailing buyer power, which would render any non-transitory price increase un-profitable.

It is, of course, open to NRAs to treat calls and SMS separately. However, as the market failure is the same and they are sold as part of the same mobile cluster it may be more appropriate to deal with them as part of a single termination market per operator.

The decisions of some national appeals bodies have highlighted the potential bargaining that may occur due to countervailing buyer power. Whilst not stating that the level of termination rates is the result of a bargaining process, these decision point to the need to fully examine the issue of countervailing buyer power on a case-by-case basis when analysing the existence on SMP on this market.

Access and Call Origination

Besides call termination, the key elements required to produce a retail service are network access and call origination. Network access and call origination are typically supplied together by a network operator so that both services can be considered as part of the same market at a wholesale level[37].

The relevant wholesale market is access and call origination on mobile networks. This market is still subject to entry barriers. Undertakings without spectrum assignments can only enter this market on the basis of future spectrum allocations and assignment or secondary trading of spectrum. This may not be an absolute entry barrier, however, in case operators voluntarily share spectrum.

---

[37] In fact it could be argued that access, call origination and call termination constitute one wholesale market and on the other hand that call termination is a separate stand-alone wholesale product. The former is sold to the retail arm of a network operator; the latter is sold to other networks.

An additional factor when considering entry barriers is that the number of mobile network operators that a national market can sustain from an economic perspective might be limited. Barriers to entry for a new network operator may be high and possibly non-transitory in certain countries irrespective of the availability of spectrum if the minimum economies of scale which are sustainable in view of the network roll out costs restrict the number of entrants and technological development does not overcome these scale restrictions.

The degree of competition generally observed in this market at the retail level indicates that ex-ante regulatory intervention at a wholesale level may not be warranted in all countries alike. In addition, in most Member States the wholesale mobile access and call origination market is effectively competitive as mobile network operators conclude access agreements on commercial terms. In some Member States, however, there are no mobile virtual network operators (MVNOs) or service providers on the market. As indicated above, retail markets where there are MVNO access agreements tend to be more competitive. There are two possible interpretations of this phenomenon (which are not mutually exclusive): the first is that the introduction of MVNOs brings more competition to the market; the second is that competitive markets deliver voluntary wholesale access as a natural outcome.

In competitive markets, operators may have an incentive to conclude voluntary access agreements as can be observed in many Member States today. This may in particular be the case where operators have excess capacity and can identify market segments where they perform less well. In such circumstances, it may be in the individual interest of an MNO to sign an access agreement with a partner than can sell to these market segments more effectively. This in turn increases the intensity of competition on the retail market and such a market dynamic has been seen in the majority of Member States.

In other Member States, however, it has been observed that firms have an incentive to tacitly collude so as to dilute the normal competitive dynamic. In certain circumstances in the mobile sector, by refusing to grant access to their networks, mobile network operators may seek to prevent MVNOs or service providers from entering the retail market in order to protect market share and rents at the retail level.

In such circumstances, although individually they have incentives to provide MVNO access, collectively Ml'40s may be better off if none of them grants such access as this could enable them to protect rents and they may tacitly collude to this effect.

In such as situation, mandating access to MVNO/service providers could be an effective means to break the tacit collusion and thereby deliver effective competition at the retail level.

On balance, there seem to be arguments both in favour and against maintaining this market in the revised Recommendation. The starting point is that the Commission indicated in the Explanatory Memorandum of its initial Recommendation that it was not anticipated that this market would be included in future revisions of this Recommendation. The level of competition generally observed at the retail level in most Member States could also plead against regulating this wholesale market. However, in a limited number of Member States mobile network operators, by refusing wholesale mobile access despite pent-up demand for such access, MNO's may seek to protect retail market share and rents and thereby cause consumer harm. This may justify regulatory intervention in such cases.

In view of the complexity of the issues that this market presents and in view of the fact that the market analysis in a number of Member States is still ongoing so that the Commission's overview for the time being is not yet complete, the Commission seeks in particular the views of stakeholders on the need to maintain the wholesale mobile access and call origination market in the revised Recommendation. In any event, if the market were removed from the list, this would not preclude individual NRAs from finding on the basis of national circumstances that the market meets the three criteria test and is susceptible to ex ante regulation. Similarly, if the market is maintained in the list, this does not require

NRAs to regulate this market as they may find the market in their country effectively competitive as a number of NRAs have concluded so far.

Wholesale international roaming

The wholesale international roaming market was included in the first version of the Recommendation. Experience with market analysis has revealed that this market has exceptional characteristics which make it different from all the other markets discussed.

Wholesale international roaming services provide access and capacity (airtime minutes) to a foreign mobile network operator for the purposes of enabling its subscribers to make and receive calls while on another operator's network abroad. International wholesale roaming services are thus provided by a domestic mobile network operator (visited network) to a mobile network operator in another country (home network). Wholesale international roaming satisfies a demand by foreign mobile network operators whose main objective is to offer their own subscribers a seamless service, not limited to the territory in which they have their own physical network. This operators' demand results from a demand from their subscribers to be able to make and receive calls and SMSs on their mobile terminals abroad without having to acquire a new SIM card, or enter into another subscription with a foreign GSM operator, or change their number.

The result is a market with very particular characteristics: wholesale minutes sold to an operator in one geographic market are sold on to retail consumers in another, separate geographic market. Any economic analysis has to examine a market where retail and wholesale markets have different operators, different structures, different data requirements and come under different jurisdictions, giving rise to problems of co-ordination for NRAs when analysing this market.

Further difficulties concern the level and nature of retail demand in this market. Roaming services are generally considered to constitute part of a broader retail services market. In this broader market, the proportion of roaming services is uncertain or unknown at the time of subscription, and consumers have great difficulty interpreting retail roaming prices. At the time of purchase, prices for roaming services may therefore be ascribed a low weighting in the user's purchasing decision. Neither do operators have clear incentives to bargain for lower roaming rates, since they are at the same time buyers and sellers of roaming minutes to foreign operators and the relative bargaining position will depend on size and net traffic flow between operators.

The overall result is a situation where very high consumer prices persist and where the market is characterised by rigidity in its pricing and structure. The work undertaken by the national regulatory authorities (both individually and in the European Regulators Group) in analysing the wholesale national markets for international roaming in accordance with the 2002 framework, has demonstrated that it has not yet been possible for a national regulator acting alone to effectively address the high level of wholesale international roaming charges on the basis of the normal market analyses procedures.

In order to address the excessively high level of wholesale international roaming charges and to respond to the difficulties faced by NRAs identified above, the Commission is simultaneously pursuing various antitrust cases, including an ex-officio investigation into the competitive effects of roaming alliances, as well as considering a proposal for an EP and Council Regulation to lower international roaming rates both at wholesale and retail level across the EU. In this very exceptional case of the normal market analysis procedure not being adequate, the question of whether or not this market fulfils the 3 criteria is not considered.

In these circumstances and depending on the outcome of the other initiatives mentioned above to address the issue, the Commission will need to decide whether it would be appropriate to continue to include the market for Wholesale international roaming in the revised version of the Recommendation.

Other Mobile data services

In addition to voice and SMS services mobile or wireless cellular networks can be used to access data and related services including Internet, mobile TV etc.

Such retail services are currently less developed than their equivalent provision to fixed locations and it remains to be seen how services will be supplied and priced in the context of third generation networks. It remains difficult at this stage to foresee how data services and access to Internet will develop, and also how voice and non-voice services will develop in the context of third generation networks. Much of the services that may be accessed through these networks are also available on a nomadic basis through other technologies. Even though the mobile element may be missing, for the majority of uses even the mobile phone may be used more in a nomadic fashion. At this stage these issues remain unresolved. Thus, there remains great uncertainty at this stage as to whether the first criterion will apply. Moreover, it is not clear how competition will develop behind any entry barrier. Will 3G mobile firms attempt to create a walled garden or will they take an expansive approach to allowing their subscribers to use their networks to obtain services?

Most of these issues can currently be dealt with only with a high degree of uncertainty. Thus, no retail or wholesale markets are identified still for the purposes of the revised draft Recommendation.

Conclusion

Therefore it is considered that the following specific markets related to the provision of Voice Services provided at non-fixed locations should be included in the Recommendation:

Wholesale level

-        Voice call and SMS termination from third parties on individual mobile networks.

-        Wholesale national market for international roaming on public mobile networks.

The Commission seeks, in particular, stakeholders' views on the continued need for inclusion of:

-        Access and call origination on public mobile telephone networks.

4.4   **Markets related to Broadcasting Transmission**

Electronic communications services exclude services providing or exercising control over content transmitted using electronic communications networks and services. The provision of broadcasting content therefore lies outside the scope of this regulatory framework. On the other hand, the transmission of content constitutes an electronic communication service and networks used for such transmission likewise constitute electronic communications networks and therefore these services and networks are within the scope of the regulatory framework.

We first outline the structure of the retail market. The overall retail market(s) consist(s) of the delivery of radio and television broadcasting and includes free-to-air broadcasting, pay broadcasting, as well as pay platforms and also the delivery or transmission of interactive services.

We first outline the structure of the retail market. The overall retail market(s) consist(s) of the delivery of radio and television broadcasting and includes free-to-air broadcasting, pay broadcasting, as well as pay platforms and also the delivery or transmission of interactive services.

Free-to-air broadcasting is a further example of a two sided market. Householders want to see (or listen to) content. Free-to-air broadcasters produce content but use advertising income and/or state contribution to cover their costs. Advertisers, in turn, want to reach households. For advertisers a prerequisite, in a free-to-air broadcaster, is that they reach the maximum number of householders as possible. Thus, free-to-air broadcasters are driven by their commercial need to satisfy the demands of advertisers to sign transmission agreements with any transmission platform that has been chosen by even a small (but significant) number of households. Failure to do this will result in an automatic fall in advertising revenue.

Pay broadcasters have a direct commercial relationship with the viewer (listener) as a subscriber. Similarly to free-to-air broadcasters, pay broadcasters are also interested in being on most transmission platforms possible as that increases the maximum number of potential subscribers.

Pay platforms aggregate free-to-air and pay channels into package offerings to the public for subscriptions and transmit this package of channels through their own platform (for example, in case of a vertically integrated cable operator acting both as a pay platform and as a transmission service provider) or through a third party's transmission platform (for example, a satellite transmission service provider). Whereas the transmission services a pay platform purchases (captively or on the merchant market) are electronic communications services and fall under the regulatory framework, the relationship between the individual broadcasters and the pay platform concerns a content aggregating service and does not fall under the regulatory framework.

Currently, end users, depending on their particular circumstance, may receive radio and television broadcasting via (analogue or digital) terrestrial, (analogue or digital) cable, (analogue or digital) satellite or DSL networks. Whether services broadcast over these transmission systems constitute separate retail markets or not depends on a number of factors, such as their price, the coverage or availability of the different transmission systems and the ability of end-users to switch between broadcasting or transmission platforms.

In particular, it is important to note that many households have free-to-air terrestrial broadcasts available comprising the most popular channels or stations. In terms of TV, free-to-air terrestrial broadcasts are chosen by almost 40% of EU households. Given the role of regulation - in particular 'must-carry' which is discussed in greater detail below - this allows households the possibility of receiving an adequate service without an on-going subscription. This may place a limit on the prices that subscription services provided over any platform can charge without losing a significant number of subscriptions.

A significant and increasing proportion of EU households are deciding to subscribe to either a satellite or cable pay platform. Across the EU 25 this amounts to over 60% of households in total. This has risen from 41% in the old EU-15 in the year 2000, and has increased markedly in recent years. There are individual Member States that do not exhibit such a pattern (Greece and Cyprus for example). At the other extreme are Member States such as Austria and the Netherlands where the vast majority of households have cable pay platform subscriptions. However, it is not clear that this trend will continue into the future as digital terrestrial is launched, TV over DSL takes up and as more and more companies move their content "into the clear" on satellite.

Increasingly cable and satellite services carry radio broadcasts too. In addition, radio broadcasts are very often made available as live streams on the websites of the radio stations.

Although satellite coverage covers most of the area of the Member States there are often rules that inhibit the adoption of this reception technology. Local planning rules are such an example. The Commission has taken action against a number of Member States to enforce the individual's right to install a satellite dish. Indeed cable is strongest where such restrictions used to apply.

Satellite companies are now making arrangements to minimise inadvertent spill-over, which makes this technology a more and more attractive proposition for broadcasters as they are less likely to become mired in IPR disputes. This, in turn, may increase the degree of excess capacity in the satellite sector.

In all but a handful of Member States the majority of households have normally up to three potential means of receiving broadcast content. With technological developments in the area of digital terrestrial broadcasting and broadcasting over DSL networks the number of alternative transmission channels from the point of view of the households is expected to further increase. Consequently no retail market is identified for the purposes of the Recommendation. The remaining paragraphs deal with the related wholesale markets.

At the wholesale level, as indicated above, buyers of broadcasting transmission services (i.e. free-to-air broadcasters, pay broadcasters and pay platforms) consider broadcasting transmission services provided over different platforms (i.e. terrestrial, cable, satellite or DSL, where available) as complementary rather than substitutes. Thus, in line with the notifications that the Commission has received so far, this market can be segmented by platform.

When analysing these markets under the SMP regime laid down in the Framework Directive, the following types of regulation that may be in place within the Member States should be taken into account, in line with the modified green-field approach.

Must carry rules can be imposed in line with Article 31 of the Universal Service Directive. Member States can impose a must carry obligation when a significant number of end users use a network as their principal means of receiving radio and television broadcasts. The approach to must carry differs across the Community, and in some cases channels designated as must carry take up a significant proportion of the available channels available. Much of this difference can be traced back to the requirement that a significant number of end users must use a network as their primary means of receiving broadcasts. In many countries analogue terrestrial is the only candidate, in others cable networks need only be considered.

Article 5 of the Access Directive enables NRAs in certain specific and limited circumstances to impose access and interconnection on all undertakings without regard to their SMP status. Specifically in the context of broadcasting, under Article 5.1(b) of the Access Directive the NRA may, to achieve its objectives in terms of ensuring accessibility for end-users to digital radio and television broadcasting services specified by the Member State, impose obligations on operators to provide access to Application Program Interfaces (APIs) and Electronic Programme Guides (EPGs) on fair, reasonable and non-discriminatory terms.

So far only the UK has invoked Article 5 in the context of broadcasting. Oftel imposed a general obligation on all digital interactive TV companies to provide access to APIs. Remedies in relation to EPGs were only placed on BSkyB, as other platforms (cable and digital terrestrial) were seen as closed access systems. In the UK, access to the EPG has had an immediate impact on the number of channels available on the main satellite system. In recent times many of the "must have" channels and their digital off-shoots have moved into the clear and are now available without on-going charge. Even though this does not cover closed access systems such as cable it will have an indirect effect through the vehicle of household choice. It is likely that similar measures could be taken with respect to IPTV.

According to Article 12 of the Framework Directive, where undertakings are deprived of access to viable alternatives because of the need to protect the environment, public health, public security or to meet town and country planning objectives, Member States may impose the sharing of facilities or property (including physical co-location) on an undertaking operating an electronic communications network. Such sharing or coordination arrangements may include rules for apportioning the costs of facility or property sharing.

Absent any such regulation there are likely to be high and non-transitory entry barriers in this market. Firstly, there is the limited economic incentive to duplicate any given existing platform. Sunk costs are potentially a formidable barrier to entry into the wholesale market. This applies to all platforms. In relation to terrestrial it is very difficult to build a network due to very tight planning restrictions related to heights of towers etc. In relation to cable the insurmountable barrier of building (on an economically rational basis) a de novo network in a brown-field site where there is already a strong incumbent cable operator. On the other hand, a quarter of all EU households have broadband access and an increasing number of operators are offering IPTV. In relation to satellite the issues are somewhat different. There are two providers of satellite capacity (which are characterised by excess capacity) but the normal commercial relationship is with a content aggregator that has purchased satellite capacity. Potentially it is open to a broadcaster to deal directly with the satellite provider. However, there remain high barriers to entry into the retail market absent regulated access to APIs and EPGs. One of the open issues is the degree to which broadcast transmission over satellite meets the first criterion. The Commission invites, in particular, views on whether wholesale broadcast transmission over satellite meets the first criterion.

The dynamic behind the high and non-transitory entry barriers are complex in relation to broadcast transmission. As indicated above, broadcasting is subject to many other forms of regulation unrelated to SMP. These include must carry rules, access under Article 5 of the Access Directive and Article 12 of the Framework Directive. The particular implementation of each of these (must carry in particular) vary considerably across Member States. From that perspective, it is difficult to assess on an EU-wide basis the market dynamic behind the barriers to entry[38].. Whilst there is a view that the dynamic may be towards effective competition in relation to cable and satellite in most Member States, there is also a view that the situation is different in relation to terrestrial broadcast transmission (and possibly cable transmission in certain Member States). Further input on this on a Member State by Member State basis will be critical before a firm determination can be made either way.

Competition law on its own cannot be effective in this case. The remedies that may be required may not be readily imposed and monitored using competition law alone.

On this basis, it remains open as to whether this market will be included at all (or indeed if only part of the original market should be included) in the revised Recommendation. The views from the public consultation will be helpful in this regard.

Conclusion

In view of the diversity of non-SMP regulation in this market as described above and limited experience so far under the market reviews and Article 7 notification procedures, the stakeholders' views would be most welcomed on whether the following market (or part thereof) should be maintained in the revised Recommendation:

-       Broadcasting transmission services over individual transmission platforms to deliver broadcast content to end users

---

[38] For this market, a limited number of notifications under the Article 7 procedure has been received so far.

5.   TRANSITION TO THE NEW RECOMMENDATION

Note. The present document is a working paper for consultation, and does not affect the status of the current Recommendation, which remains fully applicable.

The transition between editions of the Recommendation raises issues for all stakeholders. This is particularly the case when a market is being removed as this may happen in the middle of an on-going market analysis by an NRA.

The removal of a market from the Recommendation (i.e. once the second edition of the Recommendation is published) means that the Commission no longer believes that this market satisfies the three criteria in most circumstances. However, there may be Member States where particular market conditions mean that the three criteria remain satisfied. In those circumstances, NRAs should append to their analysis detailed reasoning outlining why, in their particular circumstances, the three criteria are satisfied. In these cases the NRA can draw on the reasoning in the initial Recommendation. In the interim period between publication of this working document and the final adoption of the revised Recommendation, there will be markets where there may be uncertainty as to whether the three criteria are still satisfied. In the case of a market that is being considered for removal from this Recommendation, NRAs should first determine that the three criteria are satisfied before they engage in a market analysis. Once the second edition of Recommendation is adopted and applied, NRAs will not have to demonstrate to the Commission that, in relation to the markets identified in this Recommendation, the three criteria are met.

6.   PUBLICATION   OF   RECOMMENDATION   AND   SUBSEQUENT REVISION

The Recommendation will be periodically reviewed by the Commission depending on the speed of market developments, the period needed by NRAs to undertake market analysis, the principle set out in section 1 that the imposition of ex-ante regulation to address lack of effective competition implies a degree of continuity, and the need for predictability and legal security for market players.

National regulatory authorities will regularly review their market analysis on the basis of the market identified in any updating of the Recommendation, as stated in Article 16 of the Framework Directive.

In reviewing the Recommendation, the Commission will consult Member States, NRAs and NCAs, and all interested parties via a public consultation.

DRAFT COMMISSION RECOMMENDATION

On Relevant Product and Service Markets within the electronic communications sector susceptible to ex ante regulation in accordance with Directive 2002/21/EC of the European Parliament and of the Council on a common regulatory framework for electronic communication networks and services
(Text with EEA relevance).

THE COMMISSION OF THE EUROPEAN COMMUNITIES,

Having regard to the Treaty establishing the European Community,

Having regard to Directive 2002/21/EC of the European Parliament and of the Council on a common regulatory framework for electronic communication networks and services[39], and in particular Article 15(1) thereof,

Whereas:

(1) Directive 2002/21/EC (hereinafter the Framework Directive), establishes a legislative framework for the electronic communications sector that seeks to respond to convergence trends by covering all electronic communications networks and services within its scope. The aim is to reduce ex-ante sector-specific rules progressively as competition in the market develops.

(2) The purpose of this Recommendation is to identify those product and service markets in which ex ante regulation may be warranted. The objective of any ex-ante regulatory intervention is ultimately to produce benefits for end users by making retail markets sustainably competitive.

(3) Article 15(1) of the Framework Directive requires the Commission to define markets in accordance with the principles of competition law. Markets are therefore defined using competition law principles to set the product market boundaries within the electronic communications sector, while the identification or selection of defined markets for ex ante regulation depends on those markets having the characteristics which may be such as to justify the imposition of ex ante regulatory obligations. In accordance with the Framework Directive, it is for national regulatory authorities to define relevant markets appropriate to national circumstances, in particular relevant geographic markets within their territory.

(4) Recourse should be had to a test of three criteria to identify markets that are susceptible to ex ante regulation. The first criterion is the presence of high and non-transitory entry barriers. These may be of structural, legal or regulatory nature. However, given the dynamic character and functioning of electronic communications markets, possibilities to overcome barriers within the period of the review have also to be taken into consideration when carrying out a prospective analysis to identify the relevant markets for possible ex ante regulation. Therefore the second criterion admits only those markets the structure of which does not tend towards effective competition within the period of the review. The application of this criterion involves examining the state of competition behind the barriers of entry. The third criterion is that application of competition law alone would not adequately address the market failure(s) concerned. Thus, in addition to being defined in accordance with the principles of competition law, markets should also be identified on the basis of these three criteria. Any market which satisfies the three criteria in the absence of ex ante regulation is susceptible to ex-ante regulation.

---

[39] OJ L 108, 24.4.2002, p. 33.

(5) Emerging markets, i.e. markets where due to their novelty it is impossible to apply the 3 criteria, should not in principle be subject to ex ante regulation even if there is a first mover advantage.

(6) As far as entry barriers are concerned, two types of entry barriers are relevant for the purpose of this Recommendation: structural barriers and legal or regulatory barriers.

(7) Structural barriers to entry result from original cost or demand conditions that create asymmetric conditions between incumbents and new entrants impeding or preventing market entry of the latter. For instance, high structural barriers may be found to exist when the market is characterised by absolute cost advantages, substantial economies of scale and/or economies of scope, capacity constraints and high sunk costs. To date, such barriers can still be identified with respect to the widespread deployment and/or provision of local access networks to fixed locations. A related structural barrier can also exist where the provision of service requires a network component that cannot be technically duplicated or only duplicated at a cost that makes it uneconomic for competitors.

(8) Legal or regulatory barriers are not based on economic conditions, but result from legislative, administrative or other state measures that have a direct effect on the conditions of entry and/or the positioning of operators on the relevant market. Examples are legal or regulatory barriers preventing entry into a market where there is a limit on the number of undertakings that have access to spectrum for the provision of underlying services. Other examples of legal or regulatory barriers are price controls or other price related measures imposed on undertakings, which affect not only entry but also the positioning of undertakings on the market.

(9) Entry barriers may also become less relevant with regard to innovation-driven markets characterised by ongoing technological progress. In such markets, competitive constraints often come from innovative threats from potential competitors that are not currently in the market. In such innovation-driven markets, dynamic or longer term competition can take place among firms that are not necessarily competitors in an existing "static" market. This Recommendation does not identify markets where entry barriers are not expected to persist over a foreseeable period. In assessing whether entry barriers are likely to be persistent absent regulation, it must be examined whether the industry has experienced frequent and successful entry and whether entry has been or is likely in the future to be sufficiently immediate and persistent to limit market power. Such barriers to entry will depend inter alia on the minimum efficient scale of output and the costs which are sunk.

(10) Even when a market is characterised by high barriers to entry, other structural factors in that market may mean that the market tends towards an effectively competitive outcome within the period of the review. Market dynamics may for instance be caused by technological developments, or by the convergence of products and markets which may give rise to competitive constraints being exercised between operators active in distinct product markets. This may also be the case in markets with a limited - but sufficient - number of undertakings having diverging cost structures and facing price-elastic market demand. There may also be excess capacity in a market that would normally allow rival firms to expand output very rapidly in response to any price increase. In such markets, market shares may change over time and/or falling prices may be observed. Where market dynamics are changing rapidly care should be taken in choosing the period of review so as to reflect the pertinent market developments.

(11) The decision to identify a market as justifying possible ex ante regulation should also depend on an assessment of the sufficiency of competition law to address the market failures that result from the first two criteria being met. Competition law interventions are unlikely to be sufficient where the compliance requirements of an intervention to

redress a market failure are extensive or where frequent and/or timely intervention is indispensable, or where creating legal certainty is of paramount concern.

(12) The application of the three criteria would limit the number of markets within the electronic communications sector where ex ante regulatory obligations are imposed and thereby contribute to the aim of the regulatory framework to reduce ex ante sector specific rules progressively as competition in the markets develops. These criteria should be applied cumulatively, so that failing any one of them would indicate that the market should not be identified as susceptible to ex ante regulation.

(13) There are in the electronic communications sector at least two main types of relevant markets to consider: markets for services or products provided to end users (retail markets), and markets for the inputs which are necessary for operators to provide services and products to end users (wholesale markets).

(14) Regulatory controls on retail services should only be imposed where national regulatory authorities consider that relevant wholesale measures or measures regarding carrier selection or pre-selection would fail to achieve the objective of ensuring effective competition and public interest. By intervening at the wholesale level member states can ensure that as much of the value chain is open to normal competition processes as possible, thereby delivering the best outcomes for end users. Should a national regulatory authority have reason to consider that wholesale interventions would prove unsuccessful, retail regulation may be imposed.

(15) The process of identifying markets in this Recommendation is without prejudice to markets that may be defined in specific cases under competition law. Moreover, the scope of ex ante regulation is without prejudice to the scope of activities that may be analysed under competition law.

(16) National regulatory authorities can assume that the 3 criteria are met in relation to markets identified in this Recommendation, but for markets not listed in the Recommendation national regulatory authorities should undertake the 3 criteria test. For markets listed in this Recommendation a national regulatory authority may choose not to analyse a market if it determines that the three criteria are not satisfied in the particular situation. National regulatory authorities may identify markets that differ from those of the Recommendation, provided that they act in accordance with Article 7 of the Framework Directive. Failure to notify a market which affects trade between Member States may result in infringement proceedings being taken. Markets that differ from those listed in this Recommendation should be defined on the basis of competition principles developed in the Commission Notice on the definition of relevant market for the purposes of Community competition law and be consistent with the Commission Guidelines on market analysis and the assessment of significant market power whilst satisfying the three criteria set out above.

(17) The fact that this Recommendation identifies those product and service markets in which ex ante regulation may be warranted does not mean that regulation is always warranted or that these markets will be subject to the imposition of regulatory obligations set out in the specific Directives. In particular, regulation cannot be imposed or must be withdrawn if there is effective competition on these markets absent regulation, i.e. if no operator has significant market power in the sense of Article 14 of the Framework Directive. Regulatory obligations must be appropriate and be based on the nature of the problem identified, proportionate and justified in the light of the objectives laid down in the Framework Directive, in particular maximising benefits for users, ensuring no distortion or restriction of competition, encouraging efficient investment in infrastructure and promoting innovation, and encouraging efficient use and management of radio frequencies and numbering resources.

(18) This Recommendation has been subject to a public consultation and to consultation with national regulatory authorities and national competition authorities.

HAS ADOPTED THIS RECOMMENDATION:

1.   In defining relevant markets in accordance with Article 15(3) of Directive 2002/21/EC, national regulatory authorities are recommended to analyse the product and service markets identified in the Annex.

2.   The markets included in this Recommendation have been identified on the basis of the following 3 criteria:

(a)   The first criterion is the presence of high and non-transitory entry barriers. These may be of structural, legal or regulatory nature,

(b)   The second criterion admits only those markets the structure of which does not tend towards effective competition within the period of the review. The application of this criterion involves examining the state of competition behind the barriers of entry.

(c)   The third criterion is that application of competition law alone would not adequately address the market failure(s) concerned.

For the wholesale markets listed, the related retail markets are characterised by consumer harm absent regulation.

3.   When defining markets other than those identified in the Annex, national regulatory authorities should ensure that the three criteria are met.

4.   This Recommendation is without prejudice to market definitions, results of market analyses and regulatory obligations adopted by national regulatory authorities in accordance with Articles 15(3) and 16 of Directive 2002/21/EC prior to its entry into force.

5.   This Recommendation is addressed to the Member States.

Retail level

1. Access to the public telephone network at a fixed location for residential and non-residential customers.

Wholesale level

2. Call termination on individual public telephone networks provided at a fixed location.

    For the purposes of this Recommendation, call termination is taken to include local call conveyance and delineated in such a way as to be consistent with the delineated boundaries for the markets for call origination and for call transit on the public telephone network provided at a fixed location.

3. Call origination on the public telephone network provided at a fixed location.

    For the purposes of this Recommendation, call origination is taken to include local call conveyance and delineated in such a way as to be consistent with the delineated boundaries for the markets for call transit and for call termination on the public telephone network provided at a fixed location.

4. Transit services in the fixed public telephone network

    For the purposes of this Recommendation, the boundaries of this market should be delineated in such a way as to be consistent with the delineated boundaries for the markets for call origination and for call termination on the public telephone network provided at a fixed location.

5. Wholesale unbundled access (including shared access) to metallic loops and subloops (or equivalent) for the purpose of providing broadband and voice services.

6. Wholesale broadband access.

    This market covers 'bit-stream' access that permit the transmission of broadband data in both directions and other wholesale access provided over other infrastructures, if and when they offer facilities equivalent to bit-stream access.

7. Wholesale terminating segments of leased lines

8. Wholesale trunk segments of leased lines

9. Voice call and SMS termination on individual mobile networks

10. Access and call origination on public mobile telephone networks*

11. Wholesale national market for international roaming on public mobile networks.

12. Broadcasting transmission services, to deliver broadcast content to end users*

    *   The Commission notes that the number of notifications for these markets has been relatively limited (various analyses by the NRAs are still on-going). In view thereof and the complexity of issues raised, the Commission seeks particularly the stakeholders' view on whether these markets should be retained in the revised version on the Recommendation.

REVISED ERG WORKING PAPER[1]
ON THE SMP CONCEPT FOR THE NEW REGULATORY FRAMEWORK

September 2005

ERG (03) 09rev3

Table of Contents

1. Scope of the paper

The ERG Work Programme for 2004, identified the need for further work on a common position on the concept of significant market power. In this context the Work Programme stated: There is already an ERG working paper (ERG (03)09) on the concept of SMP. The goal is to arrive at a common ERG position on SMP designation. Further work will be done on the theoretical implications of the SMP-criteria as set out in §78 and 97 of the SMP-guidelines. Specific attention will be given to the theoretic economic background, and its practical implications on market analysis in the new regulatory framework. This work will be integrated with ERG (03) 09.

In fulfilling this mandate a document was set up on the basis of the ERG Working paper ERG (03)09. After internal agreement within IRG the document was discussed with the services of the European Commission in order to find general acceptance within ERG. In December 2004 Plenary, a Public Consultation on the document was decided and several responses were received. The following document takes into account those responses.

On content: This paper identifies criteria for the assessment of effective competition and describes their implication for the assessment of market power. In so doing, the report builds on the criteria listed in the Commission SMP-guidelines (section 3) and the Annex to the Framework Directive, which in turn are the result of jurisprudence of the European Courts and the practice of the European Commission,. Nevertheless, it has to be taken into account, that this document is merely a starting point and cannot prejudice the interpretation or weight attributed to certain criteria by NRAs in the market analysis procedure, nor the interpretation of the concept of SMP of Article 14, paragraph 2 of the Framework Directive as interpreted by the Court of Justice. In this respect, it is important to note that this document only serves as guidance for NRAs and is not a substitute for the Commission SMP Guidelines.

The deliverable consists of the following four chapters:

*   Chapter 2 provides an introduction and some background information

*   Chapter 3 lists and explains the common understanding on single dominance criteria as provided through the SMP-guidelines (§ 78) of the European Commission

---

[1] The paper reflects the current status of discussion within ERG. ERG documents do not necessarily reflect the views of the European Commission.

- Chapter 4 lists and explains the common understanding on joint dominance criteria as provided through the SMP-guidelines (§ 97) of the European Commission. It also takes into account relevant jurisprudence of European Courts on Joint Dominance.

- Chapter 5 finally, discusses some indicators that can provide some useful information to support a thorough and overall analysis of the economic characteristics of the relevant market.

2.   Introduction and General Background

1.   The new framework obliges NRAs to carry out analyses of the relevant markets with the purpose to determine whether there is effective competition on a relevant market or not. If an NRA comes to the conclusion that there is no effective competition, one or several operators are deemed to have significant market power (SMP). According to Art 14 (2) of the Framework Directive "an undertaking shall be deemed to have significant market power if, either individually or jointly with others, it enjoys a position equivalent to dominance, that is to say a position of economic strength affording it the power to behave to an appreciable extent independently of competitors, customers and ultimately consumers". Art 14 (3) introduces leveraging of market power and states, that "where an under-taking has significant market power on a specific market, it may also be deemed to have significant market power on a closely related market, where the links between the two markets are such as to allow the market power held in one market to be leveraged into the other market, thereby strengthening the market power of the undertaking." Art 14 (2) follows the definition that the Court of Justice case law ascribes to the concept of dominant position in Art. 82 of the treaty. (§ 70 SMP guidelines). Consequently, in applying the new definition of SMP, NRAs will have to ensure that their decisions are in accordance with Commission's practice and the relevant jurisprudence of the Court of Justice and the Court of First Instance (CFI) on dominance.

2.   Annex II to the Framework Directive and the SMP-Guidelines[2] contain a number of demonstrative criteria which should be taken into account when NRAs conduct market analyses and decide if there is effective competition or single/joint dominance in a relevant market. However, while the guidelines provide explanation on several methodological aspects of market definition and market analysis, it only explains the relevance of some criteria for market analysis and the assessment of SMP (particularly in section 3). Chapter 3 and 4 of this document aim to provide additional information on the criteria for single and joint dominance.

3.   Hence, the document aims

   i)   to make the concept of SMP more concrete,

   ii)   to explain further the criteria which are provided in the SMP-Guidelines and in Annex II of the FD,

   iii) to support thereby consistency in the interpretation and application of the criteria among NRAs,

   iv)   to provide a basis for making the criteria operational (in order to support a harmonised understanding amongst NRAs in case of Art. 7 procedures and – where applicable – for international comparisons)

---

[2]   The relevant section of the SMP-guidelines is chapter 3 "Assessing Market Power (Dominance). Paragraph 78 of the guidelines lists amongst others a set of criteria to be relevant for single dominance. Paragraph 97 on the other hand provides a not exhaustive list of criteria relevant to evaluate the existence of Joint Dominance.

v)   to add some indicators that are considered to be relevant in the context of market analyses.

4.   Concerning the last mentioned aspect, the Guidelines explicitly state that the criteria listed on single-and joint dominance are demonstrative and other criteria may also be considered when assessing the effectiveness of competition. Chapter 5 takes this into account and adds (and explains) some further indicators to support a thorough and overall analysis of the economic characteristics of the relevant market.

5.   The Guidelines do not specifically state that the criteria identified for evaluation of single dominance are also relevant for assessing joint dominance. However, it is in line with standard competition analysis that when an assessment is made on the existence of joint dominance, single dominance criteria have to be taken into account.

6.   The criteria listed below are not to be regarded as a simple checklist to evaluate whether an SMP position (dominance) exists. Market analyses have to be considered as an overall forward looking approach of analysing the economic characteristics of a given relevant market (§ 78 SMP-guidelines) taking into account the specific facts of the individual case. Accordingly, a dominant position will only be found by reference to and assessment against a number of criteria. For this reason and because of the diversity of the markets under consideration, it is not considered appropriate to set priorities (put weights) on the criteria. What (set of) criteria is of particular importance has always to be considered in the context of a certain market taking into account the specific facts of the individual case. In order to evaluate the relevance of criteria to assess the existence of a dominant position, it is also useful to consider them against the background of the respective market phase: concentration processes, the mixture of behavioural parameters and the resulting performance indicators etc. are often different, depending on the particular market phase. In fact this is the only approach which is in line with the relevant jurisprudence of the European Court of Justice/Court of First instance in relation to the assessment of a single or joint dominant position.

3.   Criteria for assessing single dominance

This chapter highlights the main criteria considered to be relevant when assessing dominance in a given market. As mentioned above, it shall not be considered as covering all relevant criteria; some further indicators to support a thorough and overall analysis of the economic characteristics of the relevant market are provided in chapter 5. Again it has to be mentioned that a dominant position cannot derive from a single criterion but from any combination of the criteria. The explanations and examples given under the criteria are not intended to represent a full description of all the factors that might be taken into account, rather they are intended to provide a better understanding of some of the main points that can be considered in the analysis.

7.   *Market shares (§ 75-78 SMP-guidelines).* Market shares, important as they may be, are – as any other criterion – not conclusive on their own. The economic relevance of market shares as an indicator for the assessment of single dominance derives from economic theory and empirical evidence on the relation between market shares and profitability (in terms of price-cost margins)[3]. Although theory and empirics indicate that there is a positive correlation between market shares and individual price cost margin, there is no clear-cut relation between a certain market share and the existence of dominance. According to the EC's competition law practise suppliers with market

---

[3]   Theoretically this can be (most easily) demonstrated by the relation between the Lerner index (price cost margin) and the market-share in oligopolistic markets with Cournot competition. In this case the Lerner-Index can be described as follows $\dfrac{P - MC}{P} = \dfrac{s_i}{\varepsilon}$ whereas P stands for the price, MC for marginal costs, S_i for the market share and ε for the price elasticity of demand.

shares below 25 % are not likely to enjoy single dominance. According to case law a market share over 50 % would lead to a rebuttable presumption of dominance. In the European Commission's decision-making practice, single dominance concerns normally arise where an undertaking has at least 40 % market share. However, there may even be concerns about dominance where an undertaking has less than 40 %, depending on the size of that undertaking's market share relative to its competitors[4].

In addition, a snap shot on market shares has less meaning then the development of market shares over time. While persistence of a high market share over time can indicate dominance, declining market shares on the other hand may provide evidence of entry and increasing competition (although this may not preclude a finding of dominance). The fact that, in the beginning of a liberalisation process, the market share of the monopolist decreases does not mean that there is no longer dominance. This may be indeed the "natural" effect of opening the market for competitors. In emerging or fast growing markets, high market shares are less indicative of market power than in mature or slow-growing markets[5]. Fluctuations in market shares may also indicate a lack of market power. The market share's significance in the competitive environment also depends on the distance from the other competitors and the division of market shares between them. Apart from the more common analysis of market shares, appropriate measures to evaluate market concentration are the Hirschmann-Herfindahl Index (HHI) or concentration ratios, like CR3 or CR5[6].

Market shares may be assessed either on the basis of volume (capacity, minutes, number of termination points etc.) or value of sales. The criteria to be used to measure market shares of undertakings concerned will depend on the characteristics of the relevant market. In general it is likely that the most appropriate measures will be volume for bulk products (e.g. wholesale conveyance minutes), and value for differentiated (branded) products. Hence volume data should be used if there are no large differences in prices, since this minimises the differences between results based on volume and value data. If there were significant differences in prices, calculations based on volume data would not paint a realistic picture of the position and economic significance of market players. In practice, therefore, market shares are usually calculated using sales revenues instead of volumes although in most cases it might be appropriate to analyse both for a proper assessment[7]. Where – concerning a fairly homogenous product or service – a firm has a higher market share by value than by volume, this might be an indication that it can price above rivals and make super normal profits. Such a pricing behaviour might be a sign of significant market power. In general therefore, the comparison of volume/revenue based market shares can provide some indirect and useful information on market power.

---

[4] The converse is also possible, as was seen in the Finnish case, where SMP was not found by the Commission despite a market share of over 50%.

[5] Recital 27 of the Framework Directive (2002/21/EC) highlights on this when it states: "…Those guidelines will also address the issue of newly growing markets, where de facto the market leader is likely to have a substantial market share but should not be subjected to inappropriate obligations." A further discussion on dominance and emerging markets can be found in the ERG common Position 2004.

[6] In its comments on Case No UK/2003/0001 on mobile network access and call origination, the Commission highlighted: "Moreover, while HHI ratios are an accepted measure of market concentration in evaluating the increase in concentration resulting from a merger, for example, the Commission considers that HHI indices are not the only appropriate ones in assessing the current level of concentration in narrow oligopolies, especially for the purposes of assessing SMP. Concentration ratios, in particular, can provide an additional relevant view of market concentration."

[7] In its decision to the cases FI/2003/0024 and FI/2003/0027 on publicly available telephone services provided at a fixed location for residential and non-residential customers, the Commission noticed in its conclusions, that "The evolution of market shares over time provides information about the dynamics of market structure as a result of both competitive interaction between the suppliers and the subsequent change in market performance. In this context, market shares for several consecutive years, calculated both in terms of volumes and revenues, is another appropriate means to obtain a picture of the evolution of competitive forces in the relevant markets."

8. *Overall size of the undertaking (§ 78 SMP-guidelines).* This refers to the potential advantages, and the sustainability of those advantages, that may arise from the large size of an undertaking relative to its competitors. Areas where such advantages may exist include economies of scale (see also separate criterion below, paragraph 14); finance (see also separate criterion below, paragraph 12); purchasing; production capacities; distribution and marketing. Such advantages may accrue in part due to other activities of the under-taking outside the market under consideration.

9. *Control of infrastructure not easily duplicated (§ 78, 81, 82 SMP-guidelines).* This indicator refers to a situation in which the availability of a certain infrastructure is

    i)   necessary to produce a particular product/service,

    ii) the required infrastructure is exclusively or overwhelmingly under control of a certain undertaking and

    iii) there are high and non-transitory barriers to substitute the infrastructure in question.

    In such a situation, the control of infrastructure not easily duplicated can make it feasible for the undertaking in question to behave independently from other suppliers (network operators) and to exercise market power (in absence of significant countervailing power), as there is almost no actual or potential competition. One example is control/ownership of a large network that a competitor would find costly and time-consuming to build in order to provide the service in question. Such control may hence represent a significant barrier to entry. In addition it might be possible for the supplier to lever its market power horizontally (to adjacent markets) or vertically (downstream markets).

10. *Technological advantages or superiority (§ 78 SMP-guidelines).* Such advantages may represent a barrier to entry as well as an advantage over existing competitors due to lower production costs or product differentiation. Doing a forward-looking analysis, however, NRAs will have to take into account that some technological advantages might only be temporary and may therefore not be a permanent source of market power.

11. *Absence of or low countervailing power (§ 78 SMP-guidelines).* The existence of customers with a strong negotiating position, which is exercised to produce a significant impact on competition, will tend to restrict the ability of providers to act independently of their customers. The extent of countervailing buyer power largely depends on whether customers can credibly threaten to switch to other suppliers, to self-provide the service, to significantly reduce consumption or to cease to use the service at all in case of a price increase. Many factors play a role in determining the scale of countervailing power on the part of the buyers. The higher the amount of purchase of services by customers or the higher the proportion of the producer's total output that is bought by a certain customer, the stronger the countervailing power might be. The higher the portion of the costs for a service in relation to their total expenditure and the better informed, the more sensitive consumers are to the price and quality of the service and the more ready they might be to switch suppliers or to reduce demand. Further to this, the higher a seller's locked-in investment in specific customers (asset specificity), the more willing he will be to negotiate. Overall, this criterion is more meaningful in wholesale markets, because providers purchasing network services from other providers are in general more visible and powerful than retail customers.

12. *Easy or privileged access to capital markets/financial resources (§ 78 SMP-guidelines).* Easy or privileged access to capital markets may represent a barrier to entry as well as an advantage over existing competitors. Aside from internal sources

(e.g. as indicated by the cash flow or revenue) the ability to procure outside capital, a firms capital structure and its ability to increase equity capital (e.g. structure of shareholders) might be considered. Further to this access to capital might be influenced if a firm has links with other companies (e.g. affiliated companies belonging to the same group) that are favourable for its activities in the market in question. However when doing the analysis one also has to look at the intercompany links the competitors may have.

13. *Product/services diversification (e.g. bundled products or services); (§ 78 SMP-guidelines).* Diversification is where a firm produces a range of products/services (which may or may not be in separate markets). Product or service diversification can be observed particularly in more mature markets and is characterised by the fact that an undertaking is able to provide a "portfolio" of related products and services, which, especially when combined with bundling, may have the consequence of making competitive entry into the supply of one or more of the services potentially more difficult. In that sense product/services diversification may enable the undertaking in question to secure and maintain its client basis.

14. *Economies of scale (§ 78 SMP-guidelines).* Economies of scale arise when increasing production causes average costs (per unit of output) to fall. Economies of scale are common where the production process involves high fixed costs, which is often the case in communication markets. One other way in which increasing scale can lower unit costs is by allowing greater specialisation, and in turn higher productivity. Although economies of scale on their own do not create entry barriers (given a certain level of demand, technology and cost function, entrants can exhaust the same economies if they are able to produce the same volumes), they can de-facto amount to an entry barrier if further factors, such as sunk costs, switching costs etc. exist[8] so that economies of scale create an asymmetry between the incumbent and new entrants or smaller competitors. If this is the case, economies of scale can act as a barrier to entry as well as an advantage over existing competitors.

15. *Economies of scope (§ 78 SMP-guidelines).* Economies of scope exist where average costs for one product are lower as a result of it being produced jointly with other products by the same firm. Cost savings may be made where common processes are used in production. Economies of scope are common where networks exist, as the capacity of the network can be shared across multiple products. Similar to the economies of scale discussed above, economies of scope can be a barrier to entry as well as an advantage over existing competitors. If the existence of economies of scope requires entrants to enter in more than one market simultaneously, this may require additional expertise, more capital etc., which may sum up to higher costs, thus hampering ease of market entry.

16. *Vertical integration (§ 78 SMP-guidelines).* Vertical integration while normally efficient, can strengthen dominance by making new market entry harder due to control of upstream or downstream markets. As such, vertical integration may give an advantage to the integrated firm (over its competitors), as access to sales and supply markets might be more easily attainable for the integrated firm (through better prices, service levels, lead times and development of new products). Vertical integration potentially creates conditions for leverage of market power from (say) upstream to downstream markets, due to both the incentive and ability for vertically integrated firms to limit entry into downstream markets.. Also relevant in this context is the fact that vertically integrated multi product operators often have a clear competitive advantage over their competitors if they are in a position to bundle products (e.g.

---

[8] See e.g. Carlton, D.W./Perloff, J.M. (2000), p. 79ff for the relation between economies of scale and sunk costs.

access and voice traffic or voice traffic and internet access etc.) which may either not be replicable for the competitors due to a lack of corresponding wholesale products which might increase the cost of entry.

17. *A highly developed distribution and sales network (§ 78 SMP-guidelines).* Well-developed distribution systems are costly to replicate and maintain, and may even be incapable of duplication. They may represent a barrier to entry as well as an advantage over existing competitors.

18. *Absence of potential competition (§ 74, 78, 80 SMP-guidelines).* This refers to the prospect of new competitors (which are in the position to switch or extend their line of production) entering the market (e.g. due to a hypothetical price increase) within the timeframe considered by the review. The record of past entry is one factor that can be looked at, as well as potential (structural, legal or regulatory) barriers to entry. Some of them are discussed under "Ease of market entry" below.

19. *Barriers to expansion (§ 78 SMP-guidelines).* There may be more active competition where there are lower barriers to growth and expansion. While growth and expansion is easier to achieve for individual firms (and in particular for new entrants) in growing markets, it might be inhibited in mature, saturated markets, where customers are already locked in with a certain supplier and have to be induced to switch.

20. *Excessive pricing.* As stated in paragraph 4 above, the SMP-guidelines explicitly state that criteria other than the ones listed in that document may be considered when assessing effective competition. In this context, the ability to price at a level that keeps profits persistently and significantly above the competitive level is an important indicator for market power. The SMP-Guidelines (§ 73) refer to the importance, when assessing market power on an ex-ante basis, of considering the power (or ability) of undertakings to raise prices without incurring a significant loss of sales or revenue. In a competitive market, individual firms should not be able to persistently raise prices above costs and sustain excess profits. As costs fall, prices should be expected to fall too, if competition is effective. Although the existence of prices at a level that keeps profits persistently and significantly above the competitive level is an important indicator for the existence of SMP it is not a necessary condition for finding SMP given the ex ante character of the regulatory framework.

Factors that may explain excessive prices, such as greater innovation and efficiency, or unexpected changes in demand, should however be considered in interpreting high profit figures. Conversely, low profits may be more an indicator of the inefficiency of the firm than of effective competition. Excessive prices in principle can be detected by an analysis of Price Cost Margins (PCM) which measure directly the deviation of prices from costs[9]. However, although valuable from a theoretic perspective, in many cases necessary data to calculate PCM will not be available at a disaggregated product or market level. In addition, the fact that in communication markets usually there are multi-product undertakings with high joint and common costs that have to be attributed to certain services may make the calculation of PCM even more difficult

21. *Ease of market entry (§ 80 SMP-guidelines).* The threat of potential entry may prevent firms from raising prices above competitive levels, leading thereby to a situation in which no market power is exercised. However, if there are significant barriers to entry, this threat may be weak or absent. Operators may then be able to raise prices and make persistent excess profits without attracting additional competition that would reduce them again. The impact of these barriers is likely to be greater where the market is

---

[9] More formally, price cost margins can be described as $(P-C)/P$, whereas C (cost) can e.g. be marginal, incremental or fully allocated costs; see also footnote 3 above.

growing slowly and is initially dominated by one large supplier, as entrants will be able to grow only by attracting customers from the dominant firm. However, barriers to entry may become less relevant where markets are associated with ongoing technological change and innovation.

Structural barriers plus any evidence of both potential and actual entry are relevant to the assessment, although lack of entry may also be a rational decision given price signals and potential profits. For example, not enough customers may be willing to switch given the level of potential savings available. Market reviews might consider whether there is evidence that new competitors have a significant impact within the time frame considered by the review. There are two broad categories of barriers to entry – strategic and absolute. Absolute barriers exist where firms own, have access to, or are granted privileged use of important assets or resources which are not similarly accessible to potential entrants. Strategic barriers arise due to the strategic behaviour of existing market players, for example through pricing behaviour (such as predatory pricing, price-squeezing, cross-subsidies and price discrimination) or through non-price behaviour (such as increased investment, promotion and distribution). Whilst structural and behavioural aspects can be interwoven, making the absolute-strategic distinction blurred, the distinction may help to indicate appropriate remedies to address dominance. Sunk costs can be an important barrier to entry. These are costs which are needed to enter an industry but which cannot be recovered on exit. Existing firms, which only have to cover ongoing costs, could set prices too low to allow entrants to both recover sunk costs and compete. Several other potential barriers to entry were already introduced above. Further examples are: patents and other intellectual property rights; brand image (including high advertising); distribution agreements etc.

22. *Costs and barriers to switching.* When considering a switch to new services in place of existing services, there are three possible cases. First, consumers will remain with current services if satisfied. Second, if not satisfied after a comparison of information, they will substitute services in question for new services, unless significant barriers exist (such as uncertainty about the quality of service and reputation of alternative suppliers). If consumers already have a considerable investment in equipment necessary for the services, are locked into long-term contracts or are concerned about disruptions and inconveniences in so doing, they will stick to current services and show inertia in the choice of services and carriers. Related to significant barriers to switching suppliers are high connection/disconnection fees, lengthy contracts with penalty clauses, additional costs for new peripheral equipment, billing arrangements including separate bills, the existence and effectiveness of number portability etc. Consumers' reluctance to switching suppliers can subsequently work as a potential barrier to entry and/or expansion. Consumer surveys can ask detailed questions on the extent and substance of such barriers to switching. One of the proxies for measuring this variable is the percentage of actual switching to new service or suppliers after receiving relevant information. If the level of consumer satisfaction drops over time but the rate of switching suppliers stay relatively low, this implies a high level of switching barriers exists in the relevant market.

23. The determination that a company has a dominant market position requires a wider assessment of all the competitive conditions of significance for the market in question. If this assessment reveals an imbalance in the relevant characteristics to one company's advantage, this could mean that the company's scope for using competitive parameters or market strategies can no longer be adequately constrained by its competitors.

4.   Criteria for assessing joint dominance[10]

24.   Joint (or collective) dominance refers to a situation where a dominant position (in the sense of Art 14 (2) FD) is held by two or more undertakings that are legally and economically independent of each other (§ 89 SMP-guidelines). Without prejudice to the case law of the Court of Justice on joint dominance, this is likely to be the case where the market satisfies a number of characteristics, in particular in terms of market concentration, transparency and other characteristics mentioned below. Again there is no specific ranking of importance amongst the criteria and NRAs are requested to consider and examine these criteria and make an overall assessment rather than mechanistically applying a check-list (§ 98 SMP-guidelines). What does need to be established is that market operators have a strong incentive to converge to a co-ordinated market outcome and refrain from reliance on competitive conduct (§ 99 SMP-guidelines). However, if an NRA intends to assess collective (or joint) dominance in a particular case, it will be necessary to take into account the Commissions practice and the European Courts jurisprudence.

25.   There have been three cases in particular which provide useful guide to the tests that must be satisfied in order to find a position of joint dominance. These are: Compagnie Maritime Belge Transports SA v Commission, Gencor and the CFI's decision in the Air-tours/First Choice merger case. In the last mentioned case the Court of First Instance (CFI) overturned the Commission's findings and outlined certain criteria that must be given to determine undertakings as oligopolistic jointly dominant (such oligopolistic joint dominance can be distinguished from a situation in which joint dominance might be found on the basis of structural links between undertakings). Since the case law on joint dominance is continually evolving, this shall not be interpreted as the final definitive statement on joint dominance, but it has to be taken into account when assessing joint dominance. The CFI's judgement defines collective dominance as a situation in which it is possible, economically rational and preferable for firms to adopt, on a lasting basis, a common policy in the market with the aim of selling at above competitive prices. In the Airtours/First Choice merger decision the CFI set out three necessary conditions for a collective dominance position:

i)   Each member of the dominant oligopoly must have the ability to know how the other members are behaving in order to monitor whether or not they are adopting the common strategy. It is therefore necessary for sufficient transparency for all firms in the oligopoly to be aware, sufficiently precisely and quickly, of the way in which the other firms' market conduct is evolving. The most important criteria from those listed below to meet this condition are: Market concentration (paragraph 26), transparency (paragraph 27), mature market (paragraph 28), predictable growth on the demand side (paragraph 29) and homogeneity of products (paragraph 31).

ii)   Any tacit co-ordination must be sustainable over time. Implicit in this is the view that a retaliatory mechanism of some kind is necessary, so that any firm that deviates from the co-ordinated practice would be met by competitive reactions (not necessarily only addressing the cheating firm) by other firms. The most important criterion listed below to meet this condition: Retaliatory mechanisms (paragraph 40).

iii)   It is necessary that existing and future competitors, as well as customers, do not undermine the results expected from the common policy. Particularly relevant in this context is whether there are fringe competitors and, if they are able to

---

[10]   As already mentioned in paragraph 5 above, the criteria identified for the evaluation of single dominance are also relevant for assessing Joint Dominance and should therefore be taken into account.

counteract a collective dominant position. Important criteria to be considered in this context are the existence of high barriers to entry (see below paragraph 36), differences in cost structures (paragraph 32) and demand elasticities (paragraph 30).

26. *Market concentration (§ 97, 99 SMP-guidelines).* Collective dominance is more likely in a highly concentrated market in which a few market players (facilitates co-ordination by reducing transaction and monitoring costs) have a high market share. However, even where a market is highly concentrated it does not necessarily warrant a finding that the structure of the market is conducive to collective dominance in the form of tacit co-ordination.

27. *Transparency (§ 97 SMP-guidelines).* For the evaluation of this indicator one has to make a distinction between transparency between competitors and transparency between suppliers and consumers. A situation where companies can easily obtain good knowledge of their competitors' prices and customers is more conducive to collective dominance. If there is transparent information on rival's prices and output, a quick detection of cheating rivals is possible and essential for the maintenance of collusion. From this perspective, publications of prices, pre-announcements of price changes, and similar communications, can support transparency as they may facilitate tacit collusion whereas secret price cutting to certain customers is the most common form of cheating. On the other hand, transparency between consumers and suppliers could be a pro-competitive indicator as well-informed customers will in general be more price sensitive.

28. *Mature market (§ 97 SMP-guidelines).* In more mature markets, it is harder to enter the market and attract new customers.

29. *Stagnant or moderate growth on demand side (§ 97 SMP-guidelines).* The faster and more predictably demand is growing, the more likely providers are to compete aggressively due to the potentially higher returns available in terms of future market shares and profits. However, economic theory also indicates that (long term) future profits from collusive behaviour increases with growing demand whereas short-term profits from cheating are independent from demand growth (assuming that cheating will lead to a competitive outcome). Whenever short-term gains from cheating are small compared with the cost of future retaliation, collusion is easier to sustain. In a ceteris paribus analysis with a fixed number of market participants, this leads to the economic conclusion that collusion in a situation with strong demand growth (frequently given in an early market stage) is more likely than in a situation with moderate growth[11]. Thus the interpretation of this criterion with respect to its meaning for collective dominance is ambiguous.

30. *Low elasticity of demand (§ 97 SMP-guidelines).* Demand elasticity is an ambivalent criterion in context of the assessment of joint dominance. Both a high as well as a low elasticity of demand can enforce collusion. Where customer demand does not change much in response to price changes, there is less incentive to reduce prices in order to undercut competitors; hence it would require substantial price cuts to attract further demand. If oligopolists – on the other hand -face a highly elastic demand curve, they might feel an incentive to undercut the collusive price level, since already small reductions of prices cause a large expansion of demand (the price-effect is more then compensated by an increase in volume – leading to a net revenue effect). If the interaction of oligopolists however lasts for several periods, the cheating firm has to expect punishment by the competitors. They may react by cutting down their prices

---

[11] See Ivaldi, M. et.al: The economics of tacit collusion, Final report for DG Competition, p. 26f., European Commission, March 2003

with the result that in the end of this process none of the oligopolists might be better off. A high elasticity of demand implies that rivals can react very effectively to cheating. The collusive outcome in general becomes more sustainable, the more severe the punishment is (this phenomenon is known as Topsy-Turvy principle in super games).

31. *Homogeneous product (§ 97 SMP-guidelines).* The more similar the products, or the more similar they are perceived by customers, the stronger the potential for price competition between providers and the easier the mutual control; both aspects may increase the incentive and ability to collude. In differentiated product markets, on the other hand, competition does not focus on price alone, but takes place along multiple dimensions, and agreements (tacit or otherwise) are more difficult to reach.

32. *Similar cost structures (§ 97 SMP-guidelines).* Similar cost structures would make muted price competition easier, as for a given price level similar costs will produce similar levels of profit. If firms have different marginal cost functions, their individual price preferences will differ at any given output level. This makes agreeing on a common profit-maximising price more difficult. .]

33. *Similar market shares (§ 97 SMP-guidelines).* Large imbalances of market shares between suppliers may make collective dominance less likely. Behaviour that limits competition may be more likely where market shares are similar. A situation of stable market shares over time may result from collusion or muted competition.

34. *Lack of technical innovation, mature technology (§ 97 SMP-guidelines).* The more mature the technology, the lower the scope for providers to compete by being differentiated on technology grounds. The situation is completely different as long as technical innovation takes place. First, technical innovation comes along with product differentiation and in the context with differentiated products competition takes place along several dimensions; the consequence is that an agreeing on a joint-profit maximising outcome is harder to achieve. Second, sitting back and enjoying high profits may increase the likelihood of new competitors coming in with innovative products. Third, because of uncertainty over future market conditions, competitors in innovative markets may wish to compete fiercely and gain market share now, in order to have a strong starting position in the next market phase.

35. *Absence of excess capacity (§ 97 SMP-guidelines).* Absence of excess capacity would tend to make it easier to maintain an anti-competitive agreement, as providers would not have an incentive to deviate from an agreement by using their excess capacity to produce at a lower price, and in so doing make more profit overall.

36. *High Barriers to entry (§ 97 SMP-guidelines).* For an explanation on the implication for the assessment of market power see in particular paragraph 21 "Ease of market entry" above.

37. *Lack of countervailing power (§ 97 SMP-guidelines).* The existence of customers with a strong negotiating position, which is exercised to produce a significant impact on competition, will tend to restrict the ability of providers to act independently of their customers. For an explanation on the implication for the assessment of market power see paragraph 11 "Absence of or low countervailing power" above.

38. *Lack of potential competition (§ 97 SMP-guidelines).* This refers to the prospect of new competitors entering the market within the timeframe considered by the review. For an explanation on the implication for the assessment of market power see in particular paragraph 21 "Ease of market entry" above.

39. *Various kinds of informal or other links between the undertakings concerned (§ 97 SMP-guidelines).* Evidence of such links will inform an assessment of the potential for

collusion. However such evidence is not a pre-requisite for finding a collectively dominant position. For example, links may exist to legitimately resolve common issues through self-regulation. Patterns of price movements are one piece of evidence that might indicate concerted action by firms, although this has to be interpreted carefully, as other reasons (e.g. increasing input prices) might be the cause for that development.

40. *Retaliatory mechanisms (§ 97 and § 99 SMP-guidelines).* The likely existence of such mechanisms can deter action that might break collective agreements, as they will make it not worthwhile for any member of the potential dominant oligopoly to depart from the common course of conduct to the detriment of the other oligopolists. An example of such a mechanism would be a credible threat of stronger price competition that would impact unequally upon providers.

41. *Lack or reduced scope of price competition (§ 97 SMP-guidelines).* If competition were effective, one would generally expect to see prices close to or moving towards cost. But the potential for tough price competition can create an incentive not to compete actively. An assessment of some of the other collective dominance criteria may also indicate limited scope for price competition. So a potential result of collective dominance is evidence of a history of market price movements within a narrow range.

5.   Further possible indicators to identify market problems

The above criteria serve to assess the existence of single or joint dominance. However in most cases such an assessment will be triggered by a NRA's overall concerns as to the general state of competitiveness prevailing in a given market. The indicators discussed below are among those that often prompt an NRA to carry out a further and more detailed analysis of a given market.

42. *Evidence of previous anti competitive behaviour.* Effectively competitive markets lack any form of collusion be it explicit or tacit[12] among suppliers and anti-competitive behaviour, e.g. predatory pricing and other anti-competitive practices such as market foreclosure, refusals to deal, delaying tactics etc. The indicator can be judged on the grounds that economically feasible and fair transactions are achievable. NRAs can collect information on the number of applications for such services and agreements and on the length of average period of time between the applications and agreements for these services. A more obvious indicator of previous anti-competitive behaviour is the existence of past binding decisions finding a breach of competition law.

43. *Active competition on other parameters.* Aside of pricing other strategic competition parameters, such as marketing, innovation etc. exist. Another parameter is the rate of growth in geographic/service coverage by competitors. An indirect way of measuring the level of active competition as well as the ease of entry might be to look at the number of recent entries and exits in the relevant market. Concerning competition in innovation, measures include the number and nature of services offered by providers and the degree of innovation in terms of service packaging, bundling and exploitation of technological convergence. This can be also measured through the speed and varieties with which innovative services are brought to the market. However, the measurement of this parameter is hard to standardize and the practical difficulties of monitoring retail offerings may limit the analysis on this indicator to a very general level.

---

[12]   The incentive to tacitly collude is generally greater the lower is market concentration (i.e. the benefits of collusion are highest when the market is effectively competitive), but the ability to tacitly collude is greater the more concentrated is the market.

44. *Existence of standards/conventions.* Useful background information not only for market delineation but also for the assessment of product homogeneity/heterogeneity, the existence of market barriers for potential entrants and for the assessment of dominance can be obtained by considering the existence and consequences of standards and conventions. The extent of technical standardization may determine the potential for product differentiation as well as the ease of market entry (availability of a certain technology; compatibility with other firms' products/technologies). Moreover, reliance upon conventions like the "calling-party-pays" principle or the adoption of the standard international roaming agreement by the GSM Association, may help to interpret the other indicators mentioned in this document and/or to understand the source of a market failure or competition problems.

45. *Customers ability to access and use information.* Limited customer access to and use of reliable information on prices and other aspects of the services can dampen competition by reducing the degree to which customers act upon differences between providers. As a result, providers are better able to act independently of customers. However, it is possible for active behaviour by relatively more aware customer segments to produce competitive effects disproportionate to the number of customers involved. This indicator is distinct from "costs and barriers to switching" in that switching does not cover first time purchasers of a product. These customers may be more numerous than switchers at certain stages of a product's life cycle. The measurement of this indicator can be conducted through consumer awareness surveys (on a regular basis) across a range of important issues in communications markets, including the availability of quality of service offers. For this indicator, directly measurable data may include information on prices and avail-able service options to consumers by service providers, the level of content contained in information on services via Internet, the provision of requested information in a timely manner and others.

46. *Price trends and pricing behaviour.* Pricing patterns substantially determine the welfare of customers, and thereby overall welfare. The degree of competition in a relevant market (and its dynamic) might be observed through time series of price movements (possibly linked to international benchmarks)[13], the reactions on price setting of single providers and prevailing differences in prices over time (for homogenous products). If for example competitors cut their prices whereas a particular undertaking (or group of undertakings) leaves its prices unchanged, economic theory would conclude that this should lead to a loss in sales to this (group of) undertaking(s). If therefore a (group of) undertaking(s) can sustain its (their) prices permanently at a higher level, this can be seen as an indication that this (group of) undertaking(s) is free to behave independently from its rivals. Further insights can be gained by an extension of the observation period, which may reveal whether a certain undertaking (group of undertakings) is forced to react to its competitors' price cuts with a lag. The shorter the

---

[13] In cases FI/2003/0024 and FI/2003/0027 on publicly available international telephone services provided at a fixed location for residential and non-residential customers, the European Commission claimed a lack of evidence to support the finding of a lack of SMP. With respect to prices the EC noticed: "Concerning prices, Ficora states that prices have decreased by 50% since 1994, without any specific information on the degree of changes on a yearly basis or their absolute levels. This must be read against the background that, according to data collected within the framework of the 9th implementation report, Finland appears to be amongst the Member States with the highest retail tariffs for international calls both for non-residential and residential users." Furthermore the Commission notes in its conclusions: "In particular, the evolution of price levels over time is a good indicator of market performance, and thus reflects the development of the competitive conditions in the relevant market." On this basis price trends and international comparisons provide relevant back-ground information for the SMP analysis. Fair enough to add, that FICORA explained that the price basket applied does not reflect the structure of Finnish international calls, that calls to the nearest EU country in Finland are below the EU average and that the minimum cost of an international call in Finland is well below the average cost in the EU: (data referring to tables of the 9th implementation report).

lag and the sharper the price response in reaction to price cuts of rivals, the fiercer competition can be assumed to be[14]. Pricing patterns might therefore provide important additional information on the effectiveness of competition and might be taken into account as pricing is central to economic conduct.

47.   International benchmarking. For many of the criteria listed above additional valuable information can be obtained if these are benchmarked with the corresponding criteria in comparable economies[15, 16].It has to be recognised, however, that international benchmarking will only be useful if benchmarks are not influenced by the exercise of market power.

---

[14]   In its comments to case UK/2003/0040: Wholesale mobile voice call termination the Commission states with respect to Oftel's proposed designation of Inquam as an operator having SMP: "Without questioning Oftel's conclusion, the Commission would like to point out that Ofcom may want to consider strengthening its SMP analysis with regard to Inquam by taking into account for example Inquam's pricing behaviour in the past."

[15]   See also footnote 11 above.

[16]   In its comments to Case No UK/2003/0001 on mobile network access and call origination the Commission noted: "In its market concentration analysis, Oftel relies on a comparison of the Herfindahl-Hirschmann Index ("HHI") score in the UK market with that in other large Member States. The Commission considers that the fact that the UK market has a lower HHI score than markets in other Member States is not in itself an indication of its propensity towards, or away form, collective (or indeed single-firm) dominance."

COMMISSION RECOMMENDATION 2003/561/EC

of 23 July 2003[a]

on notifications, time limits and consultations provided for in Article 7 of Directive 2002/21/EC of the European Parliament and of the Council on a common regulatory framework for electronic communications networks and services

THE COMMISSION OF THE EUROPEAN COMMUNITIES,

Having regard to the Treaty establishing the European Community,

Having regard to Directive 2002/21/EC of the European Parliament and of the Council of 7 March 2002 on a common regulatory framework for electronic communications networks and services (Framework Directive)[1] and in particular Article 19(1) thereof,

Whereas:

(1) Under the new regulatory framework for electronic communications networks and services, national regulatory authorities have an obligation to contribute to the development of the internal market by, inter alia, cooperating with each other and with the Commission in a transparent manner to ensure the development of consistent regulatory practice and the consistent application of the Directives making up the new regulatory framework.

(2) In order to ensure that decisions at national level do not have an adverse effect on the single market or the objectives pursued by the new regulatory framework, national regulatory authorities must notify to the Commission and other national regulatory authorities those draft measures identified in Article 7(3) of Directive 2002/21/EC (Framework Directive).

(3) As an additional requirement, national regulatory authorities must obtain Commission authorisation for obligations covered by the second subparagraph of Article 8(3) of Directive 2002/19/EC of the European Parliament and of the Council (Access Directive)[2], which constitutes a separate process.

(4) The Commission will give national regulatory authorities, if they so request, an opportunity to discuss any draft measure, before formal notification thereof under Article 7 of Directive 2002/21/EC (Framework Directive) and Article 8(3) of Directive 2002/19/EC (Access Directive). If, pursuant to Article 7(4) of Directive 2002/21/EC (Framework Directive), the Commission has indicated to the national regulatory authority that it considers that the draft measure would create a barrier to the single market or if it has serious doubts as to its compatibility with the Community law, the national regulatory authority concerned will be given an early opportunity to express its views in relation to the issues raised by the Commission.

(5) Directive 2002/21/EC (Framework Directive) lays down certain binding time limits for the consideration of notifications under Article 7.

(6) In order to facilitate and ensure the effectiveness of the cooperation and consultation mechanism set out in Article 7 of Directive 2002/21/EC (Framework Directive) and in the interests of legal certainty, clear rules are needed for the notification process and the examination by the Commission of a notification and for calculating the legal time limits referred to above.

---

[1] OJ L 108, 24.4.2002, p. 33.
[2] OJ L 108, 24.4.2002, p. 7.

(7)   It would likewise be beneficial to clarify procedural arrangements in the context of the second subparagraph of Article 8(3) of Directive 2002/19/EC (Access Directive).

(8)   In order to simplify and expedite the examination of a notified draft measure, it is desirable for national regulatory authorities to use a standard format for notifications (summary notification form).

(9)   The European Regulators Group established by Commission Decision 2002/627/EC[3] has recognised the need for these arrangements.

(10)   In order to comply with the objectives laid down in Article 8 of Directive 2002/21/EC (Framework Directive), and in particular with the need to ensure the development of consistent regulatory practices and the consistent application of that Directive, it is essential that the notification mechanism laid down in Article 7 thereof is fully respected and as effective as possible.

(11)   The Communications Committee has delivered its opinion in accordance with Article 22(2) of Directive 2002/21/EC (the Framework Directive),

HEREBY RECOMMENDS THAT:

1.   Terms defined in Directive 2002/21/EC (Framework Directive) and the specific directives have the same meaning when used in this Recommendation. In addition:

-    "recommendation on relevant markets" means Commission Recommendation 2003/311/EC on relevant product and service markets within the electronic communications sector susceptible to ex ante regulation in accordance with Directive 2002/21/EC of the European Parliament and of the Council on a common regulatory framework for electronic communications networks and services[4];

-    "Notification" means the notification to the Commission by a national regulatory authority of a draft measure pursuant to Article 7(3) of Directive 2002/21/EC (Framework Directive) or a request pursuant to the second subparagraph of Article 8(3) of Directive 2002/19/EC (Access Directive), accompanied by the summary notification form as provided in this Recommendation (Annex I).

2.   Notifications should be effected, where possible, by electronic mail with a request for acknowledgement of receipt.

Documents sent by electronic mail will be presumed to have been received by the addressee on the day on which they were sent.

Subject to point 6 below, notifications and supporting documents will be registered in the order in which they have been received.

3.   Notifications will become effective on the date on which the Commission registers them ("date of registration"). The date of registration will be the date on which a complete notification is received by the Commission.

---

[3]   OJ L 200, 30.7.2002, p. 38.
[4]   OJ L 114, 8.5.2003, p. 45.

Notice will be given on the Commission's website and by electronic means to all national regulatory authorities of the date of registration of the notification, the subject matter of the notification and of any supporting documentation received.

4.   Notifications should be in any of the official languages of the Community. The accompanying summary notification form (Annex) may be in a language other than that of the draft measure in order to facilitate the effective consultation of all other national regulatory authorities.

Any comments made or decision adopted by the Commission pursuant to Article 7 of Directive 2002/21/EC (Framework Directive) will be in the language of the notified draft measure, translated where possible into the language used in the summary notification form.

5.   Draft measures notified by a national regulatory authority should be accompanied by the documentation necessary for the Commission to carry out its tasks. Draft measures should be sufficiently reasoned.

6.   Notifications should include each of the following where applicable:

(a)   the relevant product or service market;

(b)   the relevant geographic market;

(c)   the main undertaking(s) active on the relevant market;

(d)   the results of the analysis of the relevant market, in particular the findings as to the presence or absence of effective competition therein, together with the reasons therefore;

(e)   where appropriate, the undertaking(s) to be designated as having, individually or jointly with others, significant market power within the meaning of Article 14 of Directive 2002/21/EC (Framework Directive) and the reasoning, evidence and/or any other relevant factual information in support of such designation;

(f)   the results of prior public consultation carried out by the national regulatory authority;

(g)   the opinion issued by the national competition authority, where provided;

(h)   elements to show that at the time of notification to the Commission, appropriate steps have been taken to notify the draft measure to national regulatory authorities in all other Member States;

(i)   in the case of notification of draft measures which fall within the scope of Articles 5 or 8 of Directive 2002/19/EC (Access Directive) or Article 16 of Directive 2002/22/EC of the European Parliament and of the Council (Universal Service Directive)[5], the specific regulatory obligation(s) proposed to address the lack of effective competition in the relevant market concerned or, in the case where a relevant market is found to be effectively competitive and such obligations have already been imposed in relation to it, the measures proposed to withdraw those obligations.

7.   Where a draft measure defines, for the purposes of the market analysis, a relevant market which differs from those in the Recommendation on relevant markets, national

---

[5]   OJ L 108, 24.4.2002, p. 51.

regulatory authorities should provide sufficient reasoning as to the criteria relied upon for such a market definition.

8.   Notifications made in accordance with the second paragraph of Article 8(3) of Directive 2002/19/EC (Access Directive) should also contain adequate reasoning as to why obligations other than those listed in Articles 9 to 13 thereof should be imposed on operators with significant market power.

9.   Notifications falling within the scope of Article 8(5) of Directive 2002/19/EC (Access Directive) should also contain adequate reasoning as to why the intended measures are required in order to comply with international commitments.

10. Notifications that include the applicable information within the meaning of point 6 will be presumed complete. Where the information, including documents, contained in the notification is incomplete in a material respect, the Commission will within five working days of receipt inform the national regulatory authority concerned and specify the extent to which it considers the notification to be incomplete. The notification will not be registered for so long as the national regulatory authority concerned has not provided the necessary information. In such cases for the purposes of Article 7 of Directive 2002/21/EC (Framework Directive) the notification will become effective on the date on which the Commission receives the complete information.

11. Without prejudice to point 6 above, following registration of a notification, the Commission, in accordance with Article 5(2) of Directive 2002/21/EC (Framework Directive), may seek further information or clarification from the national regulatory authority concerned. National regulatory authorities should endeavour to provide the information requested within three working days, where this is readily available.

12. Where the Commission makes comments in accordance with Article 7(3) of Directive 2002/21/EC (Framework Directive), it will notify the national regulatory authority concerned by electronic means and publish such comments on its website.

13. Where a national regulatory authority makes comments in accordance with Article 7(3) of Directive 2002/21/EC (Framework Directive), it shall communicate those comments by electronic means to the Commission and the other national regulatory authorities.

14. Where the Commission in applying Article 7(4) of Directive 2002/21/EC (Framework Directive) considers that a draft measure would create a barrier to the single market or it has serious doubts as to its compatibility with Community law, and in particular the objectives referred to in Article 8 of Directive 2002/21/EC (Framework Directive); or subsequently

     (a)   withdraws the objections mentioned above, or

     (b)   takes a decision requiring a national regulatory authority to withdraw the draft measure,

     it will notify the national regulatory authority concerned by electronic means and post a notice on its website.

15. With regard to notifications made pursuant to the second paragraph of Article 8(3) of Directive 2002/19/EC (Access Directive), the Commission, acting in accordance with Article 14(2) thereof will normally take a decision authorising or preventing the national authority from adopting the proposed draft measure within a period not exceeding three months. The Commission may decide to extend this period for a further two months in view of the difficulties raised.

16. A national regulatory authority may at any time decide to withdraw the notified draft measure, in which case the notified measure will be removed from the register. The Commission will publish an appropriate notice to that effect on its website.

17. Where a national regulatory authority that has received comments from the Commission or another national regulatory authority made in accordance with Article 7(3) of Directive 2002/21/EC (Framework Directive), adopts the draft measure, on the Commission's request it shall provide information to the Commission and other national regulatory authorities of the manner in which it took the utmost account of the comments made.

18. When requested by a national regulatory authority, the Commission will informally discuss a draft measure prior to notification.

19. In accordance with Council Regulation (EEC, Euratom) No 1182/71[6], any period of time referred to in Directive 2002/21/EC (Framework Directive) or in this Recommendation will be calculated as follows:

   (a) where a period expressed in days, weeks or months is to be calculated from the moment at which an event occurs, the day during which that event occurs shall not be counted as falling within the period in question;

   (b) a period expressed in weeks or in months shall end with the expiry of whichever day in the last week or month is the same day of the week or falls on the same date as the day during which the event from which the period is to be calculated occurred. If in a period expressed in months the day on which it should expire does not occur in the last month, the period shall end with the expiry of the last day of that month;

   (c) time periods shall include official holidays, Saturdays and Sundays;

   (d) working days means all days other than official and/or public holidays, Saturdays and Sundays.

   Where the time period would end on a Saturday, Sunday or official holiday, it shall be extended until the end of the first following working day. The list of official holidays as determined by the Commission is published in the Official Journal of the European Union before the beginning of each year.

20. The Commission, together with the national regulatory authorities, will evaluate the necessity of reviewing these rules, in principle no earlier than 25 July 2004.

21. This Recommendation is addressed to the Member States.

Editors' Notes:

[a] OJ 190, 30.7.2003, p. 13. Notified under document number C(2003) 2647.

---

[6] OJ L 124, 8.6.1971, p. 1.

FORM RELATING TO NOTIFICATIONS OF DRAFT MEASURES PURSUANT TO
ARTICLE 7 OF DIRECTIVE 2002/21/EC (FRAMEWORK DIRECTIVE)

("Summary Notification Form")

Introduction

This form specifies the summary information to be provided by national regulatory
authorities to the Commission when notifying draft measures in accordance with Article 7
of Directive 2002/21/EC (Framework Directive).

The Commission intends to discuss with national regulatory authorities issues related to the
implementation of Article 7, especially during pre-notification meetings. Accordingly,
national regulatory authorities are encouraged to consult the Commission on any aspect of
this form and in particular on which kind of information they are requested to supply or
conversely the possibility to dispense with the obligation to provide certain information in
relation to the market analysis carried out by national regulatory authorities pursuant to
Articles 15 and 16 of Directive 2002/21/EC (Framework Directive).

Correct and complete information

All information submitted by national regulatory authorities should be correct and complete
and reproduced in a summarised manner in the form prescribed below. The form does not
intend to replace the notified draft measure but should enable the Commission and the
national regulatory authorities of other Member States to verify that the notified draft
measure does indeed contain, by reference to the information contained in the form, all
information which is necessary in order for the Commission to carry out its tasks under
Article 7 of Directive 2002/21/EC (Framework Directive) within the time period prescribed
therein.

The information required by this form should be set out in the sections and paragraph
numbers of the form with cross-references to the body of the draft measure where this
information is to be found.

Language

The form should be completed in one of the official languages of the European Community
and may be different from the language used in the notified draft measure. Any opinion
issued or decision taken by the Commission in accordance with Article 7 of Directive
2002/21/EC (Framework Directive) will be in the language of the notified draft measure,
translated where possible into the language used in the summary notification form.

SUMMARY NOTIFICATION FORM

SECTION 1

Market definition

Please state where applicable:

1.1. the affected relevant product/service market. Is this market mentioned in the recommendation on relevant markets?

1.2. the affected relevant geographic market;

1.3. a brief summary of the opinion of the national competition authority where provided;

1.4. a brief overview of the results of the public consultation to date on the proposed market definition (for example, how many comments were received, which respondents agreed with the proposed market definition, which respondents disagreed with it);

1.5. where the defined relevant market is different from those listed in the recommendation on relevant markets, a summary of the main reasons which justified the proposed market definition by reference to Section 2 of the Commission's Guidelines on the definition of the relevant market and the assessment of significant market power[1], and the three main criteria mentioned in recitals 9 to 16 of the recommendation on relevant markets and Section 3.2 of the accompanying Explanatory Memorandum.

SECTION 2

Designation of undertakings with significant market power

Please state where applicable:

2.1. the name(s) of the undertaking(s) designated as having individually or jointly significant market power.

Where applicable, the name(s) of the undertaking(s) which is (are) considered to no longer have significant market power;

2.2. the criteria relied upon for deciding to designate or not an undertaking as having individually or jointly with others significant market power;

2.3. the name of the main undertakings (competitors) present/active in the relevant market;

2.4. the market shares of the undertakings mentioned above and the basis of their calculation (e.g., turnover, number of subscribers).

Please provide a brief summary of:

2.5. the opinion of the national competition authority, where provided;

---

[1] Commission guidelines on market analysis and the assessment of significant market power under the Community regulatory framework for electronic communications and services, OJ C 165, 11.7.2002, p. 6.

2.6. the results of the public consultation to date on the proposed designation(s) as undertaking(s) having significant market power (e.g., total number of comments received, numbers agreeing/disagreeing).

SECTION 3

Regulatory obligations

Please state where applicable:

3.1. the legal basis for the obligations to be imposed, maintained, amended or withdrawn (Articles 9 to 13 of Directive 2002/19/EC (Access Directive));

3.2. the reasons for which the imposition, maintenance or amendment of obligations on undertakings is considered proportional and justified in the light of the objectives laid down in Article 8 of Directive 2002/21/EC (Framework Directive). Alternatively, indicate the paragraphs, sections or pages of the draft measure where such information is to be found;

3.3. if the remedies proposed are other than those set out in Articles 9 to 13 of Directive 2002/19/EC (Access Directive), please indicate which are the "exceptional circumstances" within the meaning of Article 8(3) thereof which justify the imposition of such remedies. Alternatively, indicate the paragraphs, sections or pages of the draft measure where such information is to be found.

SECTION 4

Compliance with international obligations

In relation to the third indent of the first subparagraph of Article 8(3) of Directive 2002/19/EC (Access Directive), please state where applicable:

4.1. whether the proposed draft measure intends to impose, amend or withdraw obligations on market players as provided for in Article 8(5) of Directive 2002/19/EC (Access Directive);

4.2. the name(s) of the undertaking(s) concerned;

4.3. which are the international commitments entered by the Community and its Member States that need to be respected.

COMMISSION DECISION C(2004)527 FINAL

of 20 February 2004

pursuant to Article 7(4) of Directive 2002/21/EC
("Request of withdrawal of a notified draft measure")

Cases FI/2003/0024 and FI/2003/0027: publicly available international telephone services provided at a fixed location for residential and non-residential customers

THE COMMISSION OF THE EUROPEAN COMMUNITIES,

Having regard to the Treaty establishing the European Community,

Having regard to Directive 2002/21/EC of the European Parliament and of the Council of 7 March 2002 on a common regulatory framework for electronic communications networks and services (the "Framework Directive") and in particular Article 7 thereof[1],

Having regard to the Commission Recommendation 2003/561/EC of 23 July 2003 on notifications, time limits and consultations provided for in Article 7 of Directive 2002/21/EC (the "Procedural Recommendation")[2],

Having regard to the notifications submitted by Viestintävirasto (Finnish Communications Regulatory Authority) ("Ficora") pursuant to Article 7 of the Framework Directive,

After consulting the Communications Committee,

Whereas:

I.   PROCEDURE

(1)   On 21 November 2003 the Commission registered notifications by Ficora, concerning markets for publicly available international telephone services provided at a fixed location for residential and non-residential customers in Finland under case numbers FI/2003/0024 and FI/2003/0027, respectively.

(2)   On 25 and 28 November the Commission requested Ficora to provide additional information and clarifications regarding the assessment of significant market power (SMP) in these markets. Ficora replied on 28 November and 3 December 2003, respectively.

(3)   On 18 December 2003 the Commission, pursuant to Article 7(4) of the Framework Directive, informed Ficora that it had serious doubts as to the compatibility of the draft measures with Community law (the "serious doubts letter").

(4)   On 9 January 2004 the Commission posted a notice on its website inviting third parties to submit observations on the Commission's serious doubts letter within five working days (the "notice").

(5)   On 22 January 2004 the Commission requested Ficora to provide additional information and clarifications regarding the submissions of third parties and the assessment of SMP in the markets concerned. Ficora replied on 27 January 2004.

---

[1]   OJ L 108, 24.4.2002, p.33.
[2]   OJ L 190, 30.7.2003, p.13.

(6) On 11 February 2004 the Communications Committee was consulted on the draft decision in accordance with the procedure referred to in Article 22(2) of the Framework Directive.

II. DESCRIPTION OF THE DRAFT MEASURES

(7) The draft measures notified concern the Finnish markets for (retail) publicly available international telephone services provided at a fixed location for residential customers (case FI/2003/0024) and for non-residential customers (case FI/2003/0027). In both cases, Ficora considers the relevant geographic markets to be nation-wide and to cover the territory of Finland.

(8) Ficora's market analyses conclude that there are no SMP operators in either of the two defined markets. In both cases, Ficora bases its findings on three factors: (i) the fact that there are several (approximately 10) providers of publicly available international telephone services provided at a fixed location, (ii) the fact that there are low barriers to entry, and (iii) the fact that subscribers may easily acquire publicly available international telephone services from operators other than the undertaking providing the subscriber connection (i.e. the access to the public telephone network at a fixed location).

(9) As a consequence, Ficora states that, despite the high market shares[3] of TeliaSonera Finland Oyj (TeliaSonera)[4] (i.e. about 55% of the residential market and about 50% of the non-residential market), the latter does not have SMP in either of the two markets. However, Ficora also states in its notifications that *"TeliaSonera holds such market power that affords it the possibility to restrict competition"*. The second and third largest operators in the two defined markets, namely Finnet International Oy (with about 30% in the residential market and about 27% of the non-residential market) and Song Networks Oy (with about 7% of both markets), are considered also not to have SMP. Ficora does not assess the possibility of collective dominance between the two largest operators[5] in the defined markets.

(10) In its notification under case number FI/2003/0027, Ficora also refers to a decision of Kilpailuvirasto[6], the Finnish Competition Authority, dated 30 April 1999, according to which Sonera Oyj ("Sonera") is found to have market power in the market for international telephone services to business customers, but is not found to be dominant.

III. OBSERVATIONS SUBMITTED BY THIRD PARTIES

(11) Following the publication of the notice of the Commission on its website, three interested third parties and Ficora submitted observations to the Commission. All observations were carefully considered to the extent that they reflected genuine and relevant concerns. The Commission's consideration of the observations received is presented in Part IV of this Decision.

IV. ASSESSMENT

(12) In order to ensure that decisions at national level do not have an adverse effect on the single market or other Treaty objectives, measures taken by NRAs should be

---

[3] Market shares are calculated from the volume of international calls in minutes.

[4] A merged company of former Telia Ab and Sonera Oyj, TeliaSonera started its operations on 1 January 2003.

[5] In terms of market shares.

[6] Decision Dno 746/61/97

compatible with Community law, and in particular with the objectives and principles of the new regulatory framework. Although NRAs are accorded discretionary powers correlative to the complex character of the economic, factual and legal situations, these factors must be assessed in line with the requirements of Article 15 and 16 of the Framework Directive. Therefore, when carrying out the market analysis, NRAs should conduct a forward looking evaluation of the relevant market, based on existing market conditions. NRAs should determine whether the market is prospectively competitive, and thus whether any lack of effective competition is durable, by taking into account expected or foreseeable market developments over the course of a reasonable period. However, the discretionary powers of NRAs remain subject to the procedure provided for in Article 7 of the Framework Directive.

(13) Ficora's draft measures concerning the markets for publicly available international telephone services provided at a fixed location for residential and non-residential customers fall within Article 7(4)(b) of the Framework Directive and would affect trade between Member States[7]. A draft measure designating or not an undertaking with SMP and the regulatory obligations that may or may not be imposed in Finland for the provision of publicly available international telephone services may have an influence, direct or indirect, actual or potential, on the ability of undertakings established in other Member States to provide such electronic communications services.

(14) The draft measures are not compatible with Community law and in particular with the objectives referred to in Article 8 of the Framework Directive. Pursuant to Article 8(2)(b) of the Framework Directive, national regulatory authorities ("NRAs") shall promote competition in the provision of electronic communications services by ensuring that there is no distortion or restriction of competition in the electronic communications sector. The information available does not warrant the conclusion that Ficora has undertaken the assessment in accordance with Articles 14 and 16 of the Framework Directive, in particular with regard to Article 8(2)(b) of the Framework Directive read in conjunction with Articles 10 and 82 of the EC Treaty. The Commission's view is based on the following reasons:

A.   Lack of evidence to support the finding of the absence of SMP

(15) Ficora does not analyse to what extent TeliaSonera is in a position to behave to an appreciable extent independently of its competitors, customers and ultimately its consumers.

1.   *Market shares*

(16) Although market shares alone are not in themselves indicative of the presence or lack of market power, according to established case-law under EC competition rules[8] a market share in excess of 50% is, in the absence of exceptional circumstances, in itself

---

[7]   See Recital 38 of the Framework Directive. In particular, the lack of SMP concerning TeliaSonera may affect the ability of undertakings established in other Member States to offer such services.

[8]   Commission Guidelines on market analysis and the assessment of significant market power under the Community regulatory framework for electronic communications networks and services (the "Guidelines on market analysis"), OJ C 165, 11.7.2002, p. 6, point 75. For example, in the relevant market for the judgment of 13 February 1979 in Case 85/76 *Hoffmann-La Roche v Commission*, [1979] ECR 461, Roche had 47%, competitors had 27%, 18%, 7%, and 1%. The ECJ pointed out that "Roche's share, which is equal to the aggregate of the shares of its two next largest competitors, proves that it is entirely free to decide what attitude to adopt when confronted by competition" (at point 51). The case here is quite similar: TeliaSonera's market share is almost double the size of its next competitor and it is more than all of its competitors' market shares combined.

evidence of a dominant position[9]. In the present cases, Ficora has submitted neither sufficient facts nor sufficient reasoning to the contrary, or to eradicate doubts as to the solidity of the results of its market analyses. The statement in Ficora's notification that *"TeliaSonera has such market power that may allow it to restrict competition"*[10] is not further elaborated.

(17) In its notifications, Ficora failed to provide any market data related to the exact degree of changes in market shares over the past years. In its response to a request for information, dated 3 December 2003, Ficora claimed that it was impossible to provide market shares for the past ten years, and that the only available information was the market shares prior to liberalisation (i.e. 100%) and those presented in the draft measure (i.e. 55% and 50%). Nevertheless, Ficora provided information on 16 January 2004 indicating that the market share of Sonera dropped from 100% in 1993 to 48,1% in 1999. However, this information does not relate to the relevant markets defined in the draft measures, but to the broader overall market for international calls (which includes calls made by both residential and non-residential users). Ficora confirms in its reply to a request for information, dated 27 January 2004, that it has not collected separate data on the international calls market from the years prior to 2002 related to residential and non-residential customers, and that no assessment of the eventual impacts of the merger between Telia and Sonera on the markets concerned was yet available since the merged group TeliaSonera only started its operations on 1 January 2003.

(18) Furthermore, even if it was demonstrated that the significant drop in the market shares of Sonera up to 1999 relating to the overall market for international calls was equally true for the relevant markets notified in the draft measures, there seems not to be enough information to conclude that further substantial decrease has taken place between 1999 and 2003.[11] In its response to a request for information, dated 27 January 2004, Ficora failed to provide potential reasons based on economic analysis for such a relative slowdown in the decrease in, or even stagnation in the level of, market shares since 1999.

2. *Prices*

(19) In its notifications, Ficora failed to provide any market data related to price levels. In its response to a request for information, dated 3 December 2003, Ficora stated that prices of international calls have decreased by 50% since 1994. However, this information again does not relate to the relevant markets defined in the draft measure, but to an overall market for international calls. This must be read against the background that, according to data collected within the framework of the 9th Implementation Report[12] Finland appears to be amongst the Member States with the

---

[9] See for instance CFI judgment of 30 September 2003 in joined cases T-191/98, T-212/98 to T-214/98, *Atlantic Container Line AB and Ors v Commission* (not yet reported), at point 907 with further references.

[10] See the seventh paragraph of Part 2, "Market analysis and decision on significant market power", for the non-residential market, and the seventh paragraph of Part 2, "Market analysis and decision on significant market power", for the residential market (translations into English language from original notification in Finnish). Ficora also states in the same Part of both draft decisions that TeliaSonera has, in comparison to other enterprises in the sector, considerable financial resources that it can exploit in all its operations

[11] An undertaking with a large market share may be presumed to have SMP, if its market share has remained stable over time. Case *Hoffmann-La Roche v Commission*, op. cit., at point 41, Case C-62/86, *Akzo v Commission* [1991] ECR I-3359, at points 56, 59

[12] Commission Communication COM(2003)715 of 19.11.2003 on "European Electronic Communications Regulation and Markets 2003; Report on the Implementation of the EU Electronic Communications Regulatory Package".

highest retail tariffs for international calls both for non-residential and residential users.[13]

(20) In its submission of 16 January 2004, Ficora refers to an OECD report[14] according to which international standard calling rates in Finland are below the OECD-average. This, however, does not contradict the market data set out in the Implementation Report and must be read together with data from the same report, according to which, compared with other Member States, Finland is the second most expensive Member State for international calls at peak times and the third most expensive Member State for international calls at off-peak times. Moreover, the average cost of one-minute international calls at peak times to other OECD countries between 1993 and 2003 dropped by 70% at an EU average compared with a drop of only 39% in Finland.

(21) However, it is the task of the NRA to ensure the consistent interpretation of sources for evidence presented in, and methodologies applied in the context of its market analyses. Only slight differences in the definition of variables (e.g. residential and non-residential consumers grouped together, calling rates calculated separately for onpeak and off-peak times), together with different sources, can lead to substantially different results.

3.   Other market data

(22) In its notifications, Ficora failed to provide any market data related to other factors which are relevant to the assessment of market power. Following a request for information related to the conditions under which undertakings active in the markets for international calls have access to capital markets and/or financial resources, data concerning the profitability and cost structure, and the distribution and sales network of undertakings active in the markets for international calls, Ficora, in its reply dated 27 January 2004, states that information on the above issues was not easily available.

(23) In its notifications, Ficora refers to a decision of the Finnish Competition Authority, dated 30 April 1999, according to which Sonera is found to have market power in the market for international telephone services to business customers, but is not found to be dominant. However, the investigation carried out by the Finnish Competition Authority only relates to one of the two markets notified by Ficora, and its results relate to 1999, that is, before the merger of Telia and Sonera, and more than four years before the market conditions analysed in the draft measures. In its submission of 9 January 2004 the Finnish Competition Authority observes that since 1999 it has not investigated whether dominant players exist in the market in question.

(24) In its submission of 16 January 2004, Ficora states that *"over the 10 years of competition in the international telephone service market there have been no complaints made to Ficora or to the Finnish Competition Authority"* and that *"this can be seen as an indication of a competitive market"*. However, the mere fact that no complaints have been made does not mean that there would not be SMP in these markets.

B.   Lack of consideration of existing remedies

(25) It is not clear how Ficora reaches the conclusion that barriers to entry to the market for publicly available international telephony services provided at fixed locations are low. One of the reasons why this market had been identified in the Recommendation on

---

[13] See in particular Figures 88, 89, 92 and 93 in the 9th Implementation Report.
[14] "Trends in international calling prices in OECD countries", 19 December 2003, (DSTI/ICCP/TISP(2003)2/FINAL), available at: http://www.oecd.org/dataoecd/52/9/23901905.pdf

relevant markets[15] as a market suitable for *ex ante* regulation is the presumption that high barriers to entry exist in these markets in the absence of any regulation. Ficora's claims that barriers to entry into these markets are low, that end users have access to more than one undertaking providing international telephone services, and that some degree of competition has developed, as well as the resulting conclusion of a lack of SMP, seem to rely entirely on existing regulation, such as carrier selection, carrier preselection, or, at earlier stages of the liberalisation process, the obligation to interconnect and to provide access.

(26) In its submission of 16 January 2004, Ficora provided data indicating a significant drop in the market shares of Sonera between 1994 and 1998, when the international telephony services had already been liberalised but carrier pre-selection was not yet mandatory.[16] Following a request for information concerning the legal background of the markets in question for the period between 1994 and 1998, with specific emphasis on any form of regulation (not limited to carrier selection or carrier pre-selection) that could have rendered it possible or mandatory for telephone network operators to allow electronic communications service providers to supply, for example, international calls over their networks, Ficora, in its reply dated 27 January 2004, did not indicate whether it considered that these markets would have exhibited the same tendency towards competition in the absence of existing regulatory obligations. In fact, Ficora referred to a decision issued by the Ministry of Transport and Communications on the interconnection of service operators, which was in force from 1 December 1995 to 1 August 1996, and also to a modification of the Act on Telecommunications Activity on 1 August 1996, which rendered it mandatory for public telephone network operators to allow other service providers to provide telephone services in their networks.

(27) However, a key principle for market analyses is to assess whether effective competition is or is not entirely or primarily a result of regulation in place, and whether the status of competition in the defined market is likely to be different in the absence of such regulation. Against this background, Ficora did not justify its conclusions in light of existing regulatory obligations, and did not consider what the outcome of the market analysis is likely to be in the absence of such obligations. Conversely, Ficora did not consider how the justification for existing regulatory obligations, which are imposed on undertakings in the same or other closely related markets, and which may have a substantial competitive effect on markets for publicly available international telephone services provided at a fixed location, would be affected by the conclusions of its market analyses.

V. CONCLUSION AND PROPOSALS FOR AMENDING THE DRAFT MEASURES

(28) Following detailed examination of Ficora's notified draft measures, of its submission and of its replies to the Commission's requests for information and clarification, and for the reasons given in Part IV, it is concluded that the evidence provided by Ficora is not sufficient to support the conclusion of its market analyses, and thus Ficora's draft measures are not compatible with Community law. Ficora is therefore requested to withdraw the draft measures.

---

[15] Commission Recommendation 2003/311/EC of 11 February 2003 on relevant product and services markets within the electronic communications sector susceptible for ex ante regulation in accordance with Directive 2002/21/EC of the European Parliament and of the Council of 7 March 2002 on a common regulatory framework for electronic communications networks and services, OJ L 114, 8.5.2003, p. 45.

[16] Based on the data available, carrier pre-selection does not seem to have delivered the expected results in the decrease of retail tariffs for end-users, despite the fact that there are about ten providers for international services (alleged low barriers to entry). However, as noted above, this information does not relate to the relevant markets defined in the draft measure, but to the broader market for international calls.

(29) NRAs are accorded discretionary powers correlative to the complex character of the economic, factual and legal situations that need to be assessed. Therefore, the Commission cannot prejudice the outcome of a further market analysis.

(30) Ficora is encouraged to analyse to what extent TeliaSonera is in a position to behave to an appreciable extent independently of its competitors, customers and ultimately its consumers.

(31) Ficora should undertake, in accordance with the Guidelines on market analysis, a thorough and complete analysis of the economic characteristics of the relevant markets before coming to a conclusion as to the existence of significant market power. In that regard, and in respect of the international calls markets, Ficora should consider using a number of indicators to discern the degree of market power of undertakings and inform its regulatory intervention. In particular, the evolution of price levels over time is a good indicator of market performance, and thus reflects the development of the competitive conditions in the relevant markets.

(32) The evolution of market shares over time provides information about the dynamics of market structure as a result of both competitive interaction between the suppliers and the subsequent change in market performance. In this context, market shares for several consecutive years, calculated both in terms of volumes and revenues, is another appropriate means to obtain a picture of the evolution of competitive forces in the relevant markets. The outcome of the market analysis of the relevant markets should not rely solely on a snapshot of the market share distribution. The fewer the observations contained in the data set, the less robust the results of the market analysis are likely to be.

(33) Examination of the nature and of the intensity of barriers to market entry, both in the absence and in the presence of regulatory intervention, is also recommended. To this end, prevailing cost structures can be examined, including economies of scale and scope. Also, information on an undertakings' underlying costs in providing the specific services in question, when data are available and appropriate cost modelling techniques are used, are particularly useful in that they can provide information on an undertaking's level of profits.

(34) In addition to the above, Ficora should not hesitate to consider several other criteria to measure the power of an undertaking to behave to an appreciable extent independently of its competitors, customers and consumers, which are referred to in the Guidelines on market analysis.

(35) Ficora should make clear in its notified draft measures whether a finding of lack of SMP in a defined retail market relies principally on existing regulatory obligations. If this is the case, Ficora should make clear on which basis the existing regulatory obligations in the same or other closely related markets will continue to exist for the relevant period of forward-looking assessment.

(36) Ficora is encouraged to ensure the consistent interpretation of sources for evidence both in the methodology and in the analysis. The data mentioned above will enable Ficora to have an assessment of the situation in the markets concerned which is more accurate than any analysis carried out several years ago.

(37) Ficora is encouraged to use its powers under national law to obtain all the information, including financial information, from undertakings providing electronic communications networks and services that are necessary for Ficora to ensure conformity with the provisions of the Framework Directive. Such information can be requested for the current period as well as for past periods.

HAS ADOPTED THIS DECISION:

Article 1

Pursuant to Article 7 of the Framework Directive, Ficora is required to withdraw the notified draft measures described in Part II above.

Article 2

This Decision is addressed to:

Viestintävirasto
Itämerenkatu 3 A
FIN-00180 Helsinki
Finland

COMMISSION DECISION C(2004)3682 FINAL

of 5 October 2004

pursuant to Article 7(4) of Directive 2002/21/EC
("Withdrawal of a notified draft measure")

Case FI/2004/0082: Access and call origination
on public mobile telephone networks in Finland

THE COMMISSION OF THE EUROPEAN COMMUNITIES,

Having regard to the Treaty establishing the European Community,

Having regard to Directive 2002/21/EC of the European Parliament and of the Council of 7 March 2002 on a common regulatory framework for electronic communications networks and services (the "Framework Directive") and in particular Article 7(4) thereof[1],

Having regard to the Commission Recommendation 2003/561/EC of 23 July 2003 on notifications, time limits and consultations provided for in Article 7 of Directive 2002/21/EC (the "Procedural Recommendation")[2],

Having regard to the opening of Phase II investigations pursuant to Article 7(4) of the Framework Directive (the "serious doubts letter") issued on 3 August 2004,

Having regard to the additional information provided by the Finnish Communications Regulatory Authority ("Ficora"),

Having regard to the notice posted on its website on 10 August 2004 inviting third parties to submit observations on the Commission's serious doubts letter (the "notice"),

After consulting the Communications Committee,

Whereas:

I. PROCEDURE

(1) On 5 July 2004 the Commission registered a notification by Ficora pursuant to Article 7(3) of the Framework Directive, concerning a market for access and call origination on public mobile telephone networks in Finland under a case number FI/2004/0082.

(2) On 14 July the Commission requested Ficora to provide additional information. Ficora replied on 16 July 2004.

(3) On 3 August 2004 the Commission, pursuant to Article 7(4) of the Framework Directive, informed Ficora that it had serious doubts as to the compatibility of the draft measures with Community law (the "serious doubts letter").

(4) On 10 August 2004 the Commission posted a notice on its website inviting third parties to submit observations on the Commission's serious doubts letter within five working days (the "notice").

(5) On 2 September 2004 Ficora sent additional information and clarifications regarding the assessment of SMP in the market concerned.

---

[1] OJ L 108, 24.4.2002, p.33.
[2] OJ L 190, 30.7.2003, p.13.

(6)   On 28 September 2004 the Communications Committee was consulted on the draft decision in accordance with the procedure referred to in Article 22(2) of the Framework Directive.

II.   DESCRIPTION OF THE DRAFT MEASURES

(7)   The draft measure notified concerns the Finnish market for access and call origination on public mobile telephone networks. The market for access and call origination consists of providing access to the networks of mobile network operators ("MNO"), call origination on a mobile telephone network and interconnection products and services that are necessary for the implementation of access and call origination. Regarding access, the products and services necessary for service providers ("SP"[3]) or mobile virtual network operators ("MVNO"[4]) who have been granted access rights to a mobile network, include, for instance, the right to use the SIM[5] card of the subscriber connection, the number of the subscriber connection and the necessary products and services for the use of the connection, such as call minutes, short messages (SMS) and invoicing services. For call origination, the necessary services include, for instance, routing and channelling services (i.e. opening of general operator prefixes, network and service number prefixes, opening of access-priced prefixes, and changing an established prefix) and other products and services that may be necessary for call origination. Ficora considers the relevant geographic market to be nationwide.

(8)   Ficora's market analysis concludes that Sonera Mobile Networks Oy ("TeliaSonera") has significant market power ("SMP") in the defined market. Ficora bases its findings mainly on the following factors: (i) high market share (TeliaSonera's market share of all calls from nationwide mobile networks is in excess of 60%), (ii) the fact that the most significant independent service provider ("SP") operates in TeliaSonera's network, (iii) the lack of countervailing buying power and (iv) network effects, economies of scale and scope, and financial strength.

(9)   In order to remedy market power in the market for access and call origination on public mobile telephone networks, Ficora proposes to impose on TeliaSonera the following remedies: (i) obligation to relinquish access rights to its mobile network, (ii) interconnection obligation, (iii) non-discrimination obligations concerning pricing and other terms, and (iv) obligation to negotiate on national roaming with a network operator that has a license for a third generation mobile network.

III.   OBSERVATIONS SUBMITTED BY THIRD PARTIES

(10)   Following the publication of the notice of the Commission on its website, eight interested third parties and Ficora submitted observations to the Commission. All observations were carefully considered.

IV.   ASSESSMENT

(11)   In order to ensure that decisions at national level do not have an adverse effect on the single market or other Treaty objectives, measures taken by National Regulatory

---

[3]   A service provider can be either a vertically integrated part of a MNO or an independent service provider which does not constitute an integrated part of a MNO. "SP" later in this decision means an independent service provider.

[4]   Contrary to a service provider, an MVNO uses a network element belonging to its own network system, i.e. the Home Location Register (HLR), instead of that of a MNO. Therefore, an MVNO's possibilities to offer its own services to end-users are more varied than those of a service provider.

[5]   Subscriber Identification Module.

Authorities ("NRAs") should be compatible with Community law, and in particular with the objectives and principles of the new regulatory framework. Although NRAs are accorded discretionary powers correlative to the complex character of the economic, factual and legal situations, these factors must be assessed in line with the requirements of the Framework Directive, in particular, its Articles 14 to 16. When determining whether operators have SMP on the relevant market, NRAs must apply the notion of SMP as set out in Article 14(2) of the Framework Directive. Furthermore, when carrying out an analysis of the relevant market, NRAs must take utmost account of the guidelines on market analysis.[6] Therefore, in carrying out the market analysis, NRAs should conduct a forward-looking evaluation of the relevant market, based on existing market conditions. NRAs should determine whether the market is prospectively competitive, and thus whether any lack of effective competition is durable, by taking into account expected or foreseeable market developments over the course of a reasonable period. The NRAs' findings in this respect remain subject to the procedure provided for in Article 7 of the Framework Directive.

(12) Ficora's draft measures fall within Article 7(4)(b) of the Framework Directive and would affect trade between Member States. In particular, the conditions for access to mobile network infrastructure and wholesale services determine the ability of other operators, SPs and MVNOs who require such access to provide their own services, and consequently may affect the pattern of trade between Member States[7].

(13) The draft measure is not compatible with Community law for the reasons set out below. In particular, the draft measure does not meet the objectives referred to in Article 8 of the Framework Directive. Pursuant to Article 8(2)(b) of the Framework Directive, NRAs shall promote competition in the provision of electronic communications services by ensuring that there is no distortion or restriction of competition in the electronic communications sector. The information available does not warrant the conclusion that Ficora has undertaken the assessment in accordance with Articles 14 and 16 of the Framework Directive, in particular with regard to Article 8(2)(b) of the Framework Directive read in conjunction with Articles 10 and 82 of the EC Treaty. The Commission's view is based on the following reasons:

(14) In its examination Ficora had to ensure on a forward-looking basis whether TeliaSonera is in a position to behave to an appreciable extent independently of its competitors, customers and ultimately consumers in the relevant market. The evidence provided by Ficora does not provide a sufficient basis for concluding that this is so.

(15) Despite the fact that the market share of TeliaSonera in the relevant market[8] is in excess of 60%, other factors relevant for the assessment of SMP must also be taken into account. In the circumstances of the given case, in the absence of a full assessment of the dynamics of competition, there is not sufficient evidence as to the existence of SMP.

1.   Lack of taking into consideration the apparent market dynamics

(16) In addition to TeliaSonera, there are two other mobile network operators operating a nationwide network in Finland i.e. Elisa Oyj and Finnet Verkot Oy[9]. Further to

---

[6]   Commission guidelines on market analysis and the assessment of significant market power under the Community regulatory framework for electronic communications networks and services, OJ C 165, 11.7.2002, p. 6.
[7]   See also Recital 38 of the Framework Directive.
[8]   Call origination minutes used as a proxy for market share in the relevant market.
[9]   Elisa Oyj's market share of all calls from nationwide mobile networks was between [20-30%] in the first half of 2004 and that of Finnet Verkot [5-15%].

vertically-integrated MNOs there are over 10 SPs in the market which altogether increased their market share to more than 10% of all mobile subscribers by mid 2004. At least three MVNO agreements have been concluded between SPs and MNOs. The fact that one SP has concluded an MVNO agreement with two MNOs suggests that these agreements may not be exclusive and therefore permit SPs to buy capacity from different MNOs.

(17) Even though there is currently no regulatory obligation for MNOs to provide access[10], both SPs and MVNOs have been able to conclude agreements on a commercial basis with each of the three nationwide-operating MNOs in the relevant market, enabling them in turn to provide mobile services to their own customers in the Finnish retail mobile market. On the basis of the information available in the notification documents and the submissions of third parties, it is apparent that there are economic incentives for MNOs to provide access to SPs, mainly due to the fact that they seek to increase traffic on their networks in order to improve capacity utilisation ratios[11].

(18) Whereas previously 100% of the retail market was supplied by vertically-integrated MNOs, this has changed considerably following the market entry of the first SPs in 2000. The recent developments in the retail market[12] indicate that SPs and MVNOs, on the basis of their wholesale agreements with MNOs, have succeeded in gaining subscribers from the retail arms of the vertically integrated MNOs. In particular, two SPs have increased their market shares over the past 18 months to a considerable extent.[13] One of these SPs has recently succeeded in concluding MVNO agreements with network operators. In this market, where approximately 90% of the retail market is supplied by vertically integrated MNOs, the dynamics observed in the retail market are likely to have a significant impact on the competitive conditions of the relevant wholesale market, due to the strengthened position that SPs thereby achieved on the demand side of the relevant market.

(19) SPs have strengthened their demand side position in the relevant market, as they have apparently been able to build their own market reputation vis-à-vis retail customers and consequently increased their market shares in the Finnish retail mobile market very rapidly. Given this, each MNO has a strong incentive either to keep successful SPs on its own network or to convince others to switch to its network under a service provider or MVNO agreement. Moreover, in case of losing retail customers, a vertically-integrated MNO is either (i) increasing its market share at the wholesale level in case of customers switching to an SP operating in its network or (ii) freeing capacity in its network, which it can use to offer services to SPs in the relevant market in case of customers switching to an SP operating outside its network.

(20) The elements provided by third parties subsequent to the Commission's serious doubts letter indicate that SPs usually negotiate with all MNOs and compare prices and other terms. On the basis of the same information, MNOs were apparently able to conclude agreements with different SPs due to their ability "to provide flexible offers" or "types of services that are not provided by other MNOs". These factors are indicative of dynamics in the relevant market and potential competitive pressure from

---

[10] Previously, in accordance with section 5 of Decision 1997/1393, a MNO that had concluded a service provision agreement had an obligation to provide the service provider with a possibility to open, manage and close its subscriber connection.

[11] See also point 32 below.

[12] The introduction of mobile number portability in June 2003 has proven to act as a strong means to induce competition in the retail market. As indicated by Ficora, there have been important wins and losses of customers by suppliers over the past six months, with a pattern of "large companies are losing, new and small ones are winning". The two most successful service providers were able to attract in a very short period of time a considerable part of the retail market.

[13] All service providers taken together have increased their market share to more than 10% in total by mid 2004, whereas their market share at the end of 2003 was only less than 4%.

other MNOs, who also have a strong incentive to provide SPs with access to their networks. This is borne out by the fact that they are, according to information available to the Commission from both the notification documents and submissions of third parties, faced with significantly lower capacity utilisation rates than TeliaSonera.

(21) Provided that MNOs are not subject to capacity constraints[14] of their networks and SPs are not locked in to their suppliers as a result of high switching costs and the absence of countervailing buying power, the competitive threat of other MNOs' attracting SPs or MVNOs which proved to be successful at retail level is likely to limit TeliaSonera's market power in the relevant market. As a matter of fact, given the increase of SPs' market shares in the retail market, any switch by a successful SP from TeliaSonera's network to another MNO would automatically lead to a significant change in the market share distribution in the relevant market. This reduces considerably the importance of the high market share of TeliaSonera currently observed.

2. *Lack of evidence of capacity constraints*

(22) In its submission of 2 September 2004, Ficora provides further information on factors which could possibly prevent TeliaSonera's competitors in the relevant market from making competitive bids to SPs and MVNOs.

(23) When assessing the capacity constraints in mobile networks, Ficora concludes that despite high costs, it is possible to extend mobile networks and increase capacity. Ficora also concludes that "*the possibility to increase capacity does not play a significant role in the current market situation in the context of estimating the market power of network operators in the Finnish market in question*". Therefore, there is not sufficient evidence as to the existence of barriers to expansion in the relevant market.

(24) Moreover, given, and as stated by Ficora, that TeliaSonera's competitors have lower capacity utilisation rates, there seems to be no immediate impediment for them to take more traffic on their networks, i.e. to conclude service provision agreements with SPs or MVNOs, as they can improve utilisation of their capacity currently installed.

3. *Lack of evidence as to high switching costs and the absence of countervailing buying power*

(25) Taking into account the market shares gained so far by SPs and the overall dynamics resulting from mobile number portability in the retail mobile market, it is crucial to analyse thoroughly the ability of SPs to use their successful market entry at retail level for negotiating favourable wholesale agreements and avoiding any lock-ins with MNOs.

(26) In its submission of 2 September 2004, Ficora provides further information on switching costs and the countervailing buyer power of SPs. Ficora concludes that since, under the current service provider model, the MNO owns the SIM cards used by the SP's end-users, SPs are relatively tied to their wholesale provider. Ficora estimates that the risk of losing a significant part of customers in the context of switching is a more considerable barrier to switching than the actual costs incurred from the switch itself.

(27) In assessing the commercial risk of switching, Ficora refers to a switch which has taken place in the past, and in which context the switched operator lost 25% of its customers. This switch, however, took place in 2002 when mobile number portability

---

[14] See section 2 below.

was not yet in place and consequently, as a result of the switch, subscriber numbers have changed, which in turn caused inconvenience to end-users, also resulting in some customers choosing another operator. Therefore, the past experience of switching is not fully relevant in the current market situation. Furthermore, Ficora does not consider the incentives of MNOs to bear the costs of switching themselves, taking into account the apparent incentives for MNOs to provide access to SPs. On the basis of the information provided by third parties, some MNOs had already considered paying costs to be incurred by an SP ready to switch to their networks.

(28)   Furthermore, compared to the current service provider model, MVNO agreements give SPs even more flexibility as, for example, they are not tied to MNOs' SIM cards. This flexibility is also confirmed by Ficora in its submission stating that "*it may be easier to switch network operators in MVNO operations*". The flexible nature of MVNO agreements is also evidenced by the fact that the largest SP has made an MVNO agreement with two MNOs. Nevertheless, no analysis is provided on how the transition to the MVNO-model affects the bargaining position of SPs. In this context, it is not relevant that – as Ficora states – the most significant SP currently operates in TeliaSonera's network.

(29)   In this context, it must be emphasized that in carrying out the market analysis under the terms of Article 16 of the Framework Directive, NRAs should determine whether the market is prospectively competitive, and thus whether any lack of competition is durable, by taking into account expected or foreseeable market developments over the course of a reasonable period.

(30)   The elements presented above, together with the fact that SPs ask for competing offers from different MNOs, support the view that SPs and MVNOs possess a significant degree of bargaining power vis-à-vis MNOs.

4.   *Undue weight given to evidence of network effects, economies of scale and scope, and substantial financial advantages*

(31)   While not contesting that network effects and economies of scale and scope resulting from the overall size of a network may be taken into account as indicators of SMP, in this case these factors are themselves – in the absence of more detailed evidence as explained above – insufficient to substantiate a finding of SMP.

(32)   While some economies of scale may exist due to a difference in size and coverage of TeliaSonera's network compared to that of its competitors, TeliaSonera's competitive advantage seems to stem primarily from its superior capacity utilisation, i.e. a currently much larger number of customers on its nationwide network[15]. Thus, and based on the information received subsequent to the Commission's serious doubts letter, advantages of TeliaSonera would not primarily relate to (scale) economies resulting from a better positioning on the long-run average cost curve, but to cost savings resulting from lower short-run average costs.

(33)   As opposed to differences in scale, *ceteris paribus*, differences in capacity utilisation do not offer a sustainable competitive advantage to an operator and can be overcome by attracting a larger number of customers onto existing capacity.

(34)   The specificities of the market for mobile access and call origination are such that MNOs can improve their capacity utilisation considerably by allowing SPs onto their network, which is what TeliaSonera appears to have been doing successfully. Due to

---

[15]   Although each of the three nationwide mobile networks covers in practice the whole of the population, there are differences in geographic coverage.[...]

the asymmetries in capacity utilisation, the remaining MNOs have an even stronger incentive to attract SPs or MVNOs onto their networks by offering attractive conditions. This situation points towards a functioning market for mobile access and call origination.

(35) As far as network effects are concerned, these are claimed to be particularly strong due to differences in prices for on-net and off-net calls. However, such differences are mainly relevant for the assessment of the retail mobile market. Moreover, depending on the nature of the underlying market structures and regulations in place, such price differences might be addressed in other (wholesale) mobile markets. In any event, and given the absence of capacity constraints, all MNOs can take advantage of such network effects by attracting more customers onto their networks.

(36) As to the financial advantages, no evidence is provided that – taking into account the fact that TeliaSonera's competitors are also parts of large vertically and horizontally integrated telecommunications groups - these are of such a degree that could serve as the basis of an SMP finding.

V. CONCLUSION AND PROPOSALS FOR AMENDING THE DRAFT MEASURE

(37) Following the detailed examination of Ficora's notified draft measure, of its submission and of its replies to the Commission's requests for information and clarification, and for the reasons stated above, the Commission concludes that the evidence in the present case does not support the conclusion that TeliaSonera has SMP in the market for access and call origination on public mobile telephone networks, and the draft measure is thus not compatible with Community law. The Commission therefore requires Ficora to withdraw the draft measure.

(38) The above findings are based in particular on the recent developments in the Finnish retail mobile market and on the fact that SPs have been able to conclude wholesale agreements, including MVNO agreements, on a commercial basis with all MNOs in the relevant market. It is for Ficora to analyse the development in the relevant market and review this market in light of future developments at both the wholesale and retail level, with a view to assessing on a forward-looking basis whether TeliaSonera is in a position to behave to an appreciable extent independently of its competitors, customers and ultimately its consumers in the relevant market.

(39) In such an assessment the incentives and the ability of each MNO to provide SPs with access to their network, absent strict access regulation, should be examined in detail. The assessment should also extend to any dynamics observed in the retail market, the bargaining power of SPs vis-à-vis MNOs (taking into account *inter alia* the market shares acquired by SPs in the retail market), the characteristics and structure of negotiations between SPs and MNOs, the impact of MVNO-agreements on the conditions of switching and the changes in price levels on the relevant market.

(40) NRAs are accorded discretionary powers correlative to the complex character of the economic, factual and legal situations that need to be assessed. Therefore, the Commission cannot prejudice the outcome of a future market analysis.

HAS ADOPTED THIS DECISION:

Article 1

The Finnish Communications Regulatory Authority is required to withdraw the draft measures concerning the market for access and call origination on public mobile telephone networks in Finland, notified to the Commission on 5 July 2004 and registered under case number FI/2004/0082.

Article 2

This Decision is addressed to Viestintävirasto (the Finnish Communications Regulatory Authority):

Viestintävirasto
ltämerenkatu 3 A
FIN-00180 Helsinki
Finland

COMMISSION DECISION C(2004)4070 FINAL

of 20 October 2004[a]

pursuant to Article 7(4) of Directive 2002/21/EC
("Withdrawal of a notified draft measure")

Case AT/2004/0090: transit services in the fixed public telephone network in Austria

THE COMMISSION OF THE EUROPEAN COMMUNITIES,

Having regard to the Treaty establishing the European Community,

Having regard to Directive 2002/21/EC of the European Parliament and of the Council of 7 March 2002 on a common regulatory framework for electronic communications networks and services (the "Framework Directive") and in particular Article 7(4) thereof[1],

Having regard to the Commission Recommendation 2003/561/EC of 23 July 2003 on notifications, time limits and consultations provided for in Article 7 of Directive 2002/21/EC (the "Procedural Recommendation")[2],

Having regard to the opening of Phase II investigations pursuant to Article 7(4) of the Framework Directive (the "serious doubts letter") issued on 20 August 2004,

Having regard to the additional information provided by Telekom-Control-Kommission (Austrian Telecommunications Regulatory Authority) ("TKK"),

Having regard to the notice posted on its website on 25 August 2004 inviting third parties to submit observations on the Commission's serious doubts letter (the "notice"),

After consulting the Communications Committee,

Whereas:

I.   PROCEDURE

(1)   On 20 July 2004 the Commission registered a notification by TKK[3], concerning the market for transit services in the fixed public telephone network in Austria under case number AT/2004/0090.

(2)   On 30 July 2004 the Commission requested TKK to provide additional information and clarifications regarding TKK′s preliminary market definition and third party comments.

(3)   On 20 August 2004 the Commission, pursuant to Article 7(4) of the Framework Directive, informed TKK that it had serious doubts as to the compatibility of the draft measure with Community law (the "serious doubts letter").

(4)   On 25 August 2004 the Commission posted a notice on its website inviting third parties to submit observations on the Commission's serious doubts letter within five working days (the "notice").

---

[1]   OJ L 108, 24.4.2002, p.33.
[2]   OJ L 190, 30.7.2003, p.13.
[3]   TKK and Rundfunk und Telekom Regulierungs-GmbH ("RTR") are notified to the Commission as the relevant bodies of the national regulatory authority ("NRA"). Their duties are listed in Section 115 to 117 of the Austrian Telecommunications Act 2003.

(5)   On 3 September 2004 the Commission held a meeting with TKK to obtain from TKK additional information and clarification regarding the submissions of third parties and the definition of the market concerned.

(6)   On 13 October 2004 the Communications Committee was consulted on the draft decision in accordance with the procedure referred to in Article 22(2) of the Framework Directive.

II.   DESCRIPTION OF THE DRAFT MEASURE

(7)   The draft measure concerns the market for transit services in the fixed public telephone network in Austria.[4] TKK considers the relevant geographic market to be nationwide and to cover the territory of Austria.

(8)   Telekom Austria (TA) is the incumbent operator which owns the traditional nationwide fixed telephony network. TA's network consists of seven tandem exchanges, and 43 interconnectable exchanges at the local level (also referred to as local exchanges). Two operators, UTA and Tele.ring are interconnected with TA at all local exchanges.

(9)   While TKK considers there to be only one market for transit services, two types of product are analysed separately: unbundled and bundled transit services. Unbundled transit services concern all traffic above the level of local interconnectable exchanges, i.e. on the mere transit level. Bundled transit services are offered together with call origination and/or call termination services.

(10)   TKK states that any two network operators which directly interconnect no longer need to buy unbundled transit services. In this case self-provided transit would replace unbundled transit services. TKK has witnessed an increasing number of direct interconnections specifically between mobile operators as well as fixed to mobile interconnections. According to TKK, more than 30 Alternative Network Operators (ANOs) are now directly interconnected with each other.

(11)   Because of TA's extensive national network, most network operators directly interconnect with TA either at the tandem or local (interconnectable) exchanges. The minimum configuration for an ANO who wants to terminate calls on TA's network consists of at least one interconnection at the level of the tandem exchange. This operator would buy bundled transit including termination from TA. A call originating on the network of such an ANO would be transferred first from TA's tandem exchange to TA's local (interconnectable) exchange using *transit* services, and then be *terminated* on TA's network. ANOs which expect a significant traffic volume at the level of specific local (interconnectable) exchanges would also interconnect there. This would allow them to provide their own transit and buy termination only.

(12)   TKK's market analysis concludes that there are no SMP operators in the defined market. TKK bases its findings mainly on three factors: (i) that self-provision of transit services through direct interconnection should be included in the market as a demand side substitute. According to TKK, TA holds a share of just under 90% of call minutes relating to "unbundled" transit services, and a share in excess of 90% relating to "bundled" transit services. Having defined the market in a broader way by

---

[4]   As set down in the Commission Recommendation 2003/311/EC of 11 February 2003 on relevant product and services markets within the electronic communications sector susceptible for *ex ante* regulation in accordance with the Framework Directive (the "Recommendation"), the market for transit services in the fixed public telephone network is "delineated in such a way as to be consistent with the delineated boundaries for the markets for call origination and for call termination on the public telephone network provided at a fixed location."

including self-provision through direct interconnection, TA's share falls to just under 50% of unbundled, and 25% of bundled transit services; (ii) that self-provision through direct interconnection is also a supply-side substitute which should be considered part of the market; (iii) that the market share of the largest operator TA is only 45% if self provision through direct interconnection is taken into consideration.

(13) As a consequence, TKK states that TA does not have SMP in the market. However, TKK also states that there are high barriers to market entry and that network roll-out for self-provision would require high investments as well as substantial planning and time. TKK points to the fact that unregulated tariffs for the provision of transit services would be to the advantage of larger operators which are able to substitute those services through self-provision. Conversely, TKK states that this would lead to competitive disadvantages for smaller operators with limited traffic and infrastructure.

III. OBSERVATIONS SUBMITTED BY THIRD PARTIES

(14) Following the publication of the notice of the Commission on its website, five interested third parties and TKK submitted observations to the Commission. All observations were carefully considered.

IV. ASSESSMENT

(15) In order to ensure that decisions at national level do not have an adverse effect on the single market or other Treaty objectives, measures taken by NRAs should be compatible with Community law, and in particular with the objectives and principles of the new regulatory framework. Although NRAs are accorded discretionary powers correlative to the complex character of the economic, factual and legal situations, these factors must be assessed in line with the requirements of the Framework Directive, in particular, its Articles 14 to 16. Pursuant to Article 15 of the Framework Directive NRAs shall take the utmost account of the Commission guidelines on market analysis[5] and define a relevant market according to national circumstances in accordance with the principles of competition law. According to the guidelines on market analysis when defining a relevant market, NRAs should determine the substitutable products to which wholesale customers could easily switch in case of a relative price increase. Where wholesale customers face significant switching costs in order to substitute product A for product B, these two products should not be included in the same relevant market. NRAs should also ascertain whether a given supplier would actually use or switch its productive assets to produce the relevant product or offer the relevant service in the foreseeable future. Mere hypothetical supply-side substitution is not sufficient for the purposes of market definition. The NRAs' findings in this respect remain subject to the procedure provided for in Article 7 of the Framework Directive.

(16) TKK's draft measure concerning the market for transit services in the fixed public telephone network in Austria falls within Article 7(4)(a) and (b) of the Framework Directive and would affect trade between Member States. A draft measure designating or not an undertaking with SMP and the regulatory obligations that may or may not be imposed in Austria for the provision of transit services in the fixed public telephone network may have an influence, direct or indirect, actual or potential, on the ability of undertakings established in other Member States to provide electronic communications services dependent on transit[6]. In particular, the failure to designate

---

[5] The Commission guidelines on market analysis and the assessment of significant market power under the Community regulatory framework for electronic communications network and service (the "Guidelines on market analysis"). OJ C 165 of 11.7.2002, p. 6.

[6] See also Recital 38 of the Framework Directive.

Telekom Austria with SMP may affect the ability of undertakings established in other Member States to offer such services.

(17) The draft measure is not compatible with Community law and in particular cannot be considered as a reasonable measure aimed at achieving the objectives referred to in Article 8 of the Framework Directive. Pursuant to Article 8(2)(b) of the Framework Directive, NRAs shall promote competition in the provision of electronic communications services by ensuring that there is no distortion or restriction of competition in the electronic communications sector. The information available does not support the conclusion that TKK has undertaken the assessment in accordance with Articles 14 and 16 of the Framework Directive, in particular with regard to Article 8(2)(b) of the Framework Directive read in conjunction with Articles 10 and 82 of the EC Treaty. The Commission's view is based on the following grounds:

A.   Insufficient evidence for the inclusion of self-provision through direct interconnection in the market

(18) According to the Commission's Recommendation regulatory authorities should decide on the elements to be included within particular markets identified in the Recommendation, while adhering to competition law principles. There is not sufficient evidence to justify the inclusion of self-provision through direct interconnection in the relevant market. On the basis of the information currently available to the Commission, it regards self-provision through direct interconnection to be outside the relevant market.

(19) In this regard, in determining the existence of demand-side substitutability, there is insufficient evidence that network operators purchasing transit services could promptly shift to other products or services in response to price changes. In its notification TKK finds that self-provision through direct interconnection requires network roll-out associated with high investments as well as substantial planning and time. Given these findings, it is not readily apparent from the notification and the additional information provided how network operators could promptly shift to self-provision through direct interconnection, and thus "demand" their self-provided transit services.[7]

(20) In its submission of 1 September 2004 TKK emphasises the fact that the availability of leased lines lowers the barriers for the self-provision of transit services through direct interconnection. However, this argument is questionable for two reasons. First, TKK finds in its notification regarding wholesale trunk segments of leased lines from 9 June 2004 (AT/2004/0074) that such leased lines are in a distinct market from transit services in the fixed public telephone network. Given TKK's exclusion of leased lines from the transit market in case AT/2004/0074 and that the Commission did not oppose this view, the Commission has reservations as to an approach that would indirectly include leased lines in the transit market. Secondly, the same notification has also shown that in certain regions TA is the sole supplier of leased lines[8].

(21) As far as supply-side substitutability is concerned, there is no substantiation of the claim that network operators which replaced the purchase of transit services by self-

---

[7] In case FI/2004/0075, the Finnish regulator (Ficora) found that direct interconnection, although always possible, is not a competitive substitute to the transit services provided within the Finnish telecommunication areas. The fact that Ficora did not regard direct interconnection as a substitute for transit services was to a substantial extent based on the costs for the respective network roll-out. In case UK/2003/0016, OFTEL pointed to insufficient traffic volume to establish direct interconnections with all operators.

[8] In five regions, TA is the only supplier of leased lines.

provision through direct interconnection use their productive assets, i.e. the newly-created capacity, to offer on a systematic basis the relevant transit services to third parties. In the notification and additional information no evidence is provided that network operators that ceased to purchase transit services subsequent to self-provision through direct interconnection would, in the short term, be willing and consider it economically viable to supply systematically transit services to third parties. Mere hypothetical supply-side substitution is not sufficient for the purposes of market definition[9].

(22) In its submission to the Commission's serious doubts letter, TKK itself confirms that none of the alternative network operators that are directly interconnected at TA's local exchanges offers single or double tandem transit services to third parties[10]. According to TKK these operators may potentially enter the market depending on the level of future bundled transit charges, which are however not further specified by TKK. Subsequently, TKK alleged that there were three operators offering transit services on the market. However, this information was not further substantiated, and, according to all the information available to the Commission, these operators were already taken into account in the residual (non-TA) market share[11].

(23) The evidence thus provided does not indicate that directly interconnected operators would systematically offer transit services to third parties and hence TKK should not automatically include all self-provision through direct interconnection in the relevant market.

(24) In any event, to the extent that self-provision through direct interconnection may provide a potential source of competition, it should fall to be considered in terms of the SMP assessment and not the market definition with the corresponding effect on market share.

(25) On the basis of the evidence presently available to the Commission, the notified market definition is therefore not tenable. Moreover, the Commission notes from TKK's notification and the additional information provided that TA's share of a market which does not include self-provision through direct interconnection is nearer 90%. Such a market share would presumably not support its finding of absence of SMP.

B.   The importance of applying a thorough green field analysis

(26) A green field analysis should examine whether the market conditions that would prevail in the absence of regulation would indeed reflect those characteristic of the existence of effective competition in the relevant market. In this case, such an analysis should focus on the effects any withdrawal of obligations may have on TA's actual supply of transit services. In terms of TKK's analysis, TKK finds that the proposed withdrawal of regulation may lead to competitive disadvantages to operators with relatively small networks. TKK qualifies this finding with the suggestion that such an outcome would provide incentives for further network roll-outs of such operators, although it states further that direct interconnection for all operators would constitute, in economic terms, a waste of resources.

(27) Therefore, as indeed TKK states in its submission, small operators for whom infrastructure investment or infrastructure rental are not economical will rely on undertakings which are actually offering transit services. It is on this market that TA

---

[9]   See further the Guidelines on market analysis, paragraph 52.
[10] Submission of TKK of 1st September 2004, pp. 4-5.
[11] See paragraph 12 above of this Decision.

has a market share of 90% which in all likelihood will affect the ability of operators to offer their own telecommunications services at competitive rates.

V. CONCLUSION AND PROPOSALS FOR AMENDING THE DRAFT MEASURES

(28) Following detailed examination of TKK's notified draft measure, of its submission and of its replies to the Commission's requests for information and clarification, and for the reasons stated above, the Commission concludes that the evidence provided by TKK is not sufficient to support the conclusions of its market analysis, and thus its draft measure is not compatible with Community law. The Commission therefore requires TKK to withdraw the draft measure.

(29) TKK should undertake, in accordance with the Guidelines on market analysis, a thorough and complete analysis of the economic characteristics of the relevant market. Evidence should be provided as to undertakings that are *actually* offering transit services to third parties or those which would, in the short term, be willing and consider it economically viable to offer such services to third parties. Following from the evidence presented so far, self-provision through direct interconnection appears only to provide a *potential* source of competition. Hence it should fall to be considered in terms of the SMP assessment and not the market definition with the corresponding effect on market share.

(30) Further to that, more information is required on how business models of alternative operators (namely, all operators other than TA, whether fixed or mobile or operating on the basis of any other technologies) are affected by a possible withdrawal of remedies and how this may affect competition in the provision of the relevant electronic communications services.

(31) NRAs are accorded discretionary powers correlative to the complex character of the economic, factual and legal situations that need to be assessed. Therefore, the Commission cannot prejudice the outcome of a future market analysis.

HAS ADOPTED THIS DECISION:

Article 1

The Telekom-Control-Kommission is required to withdraw the draft measures concerning the market for transit services in the fixed public telephone network in Austria, notified to the Commission on 20 July 2004 and registered under case number AT/2004/0090.

Article 2

This Decision is addressed to:

Telekom-Control-Kommission
Mariahilferstraße 77–79
A–1060 Wien
Österreich

and

Rundfunk und Telekom Regulierungs-GmbH
Mariahilferstraße 77–79
A–1060 Wien
Österreich

Editors' Notes:

[a] In June 2005 the Austrian regulator, TKK, requested a preliminary ruling by the European Court of Justice on the European Commission veto of TKK's analysis of the wholesale market for transit services in the fixed public telephone network: see 2005/C 205/23. In Case C-256/05, 2006/C 10/15, the Fifth Chamber ruled that "the Court of Justice of the European Communities clearly has no jurisdiction to answer the question referred by the Telekom-Control-Kommission in its decision of 13 June 2005."

COMMISSION COMMENTS PURSUANT TO ARTICLE 7(3)
OF THE FRAMEWORK DIRECTIVE

of 17 December 2003

Case FI/2003/0031 : Market for voice call termination on individual mobile networks

[Excerpts][a]

I. PROCEDURE

On 21 November 2003, the Commission registered notifications by Viestintävirasto, the Finnish Communications Regulatory Authority (Ficora), concerning the market for voice call termination on individual mobile networks. The national consultation[1] took place between 9 October and 12 November 2003.

On 25 November and on 28 November, the Commission services requested Ficora to submit further information and clarification in order to be able to make a full assessment of the notified measure. Ficora provided the requested information and clarification on 28 November and 3 December 2003, respectively.

Pursuant to Article 7(3) of the Framework Directive, national regulatory authorities (NRAs) and the Commission may make comments on notified draft measures to the NRA concerned.

II. DESCRIPTION OF THE DRAFT MEASURE

Ficora defines the relevant product market as the market for voice call termination on individual mobile networks[2]. Based on the draft measures and the additional information provided by Ficora, the Commission concludes that the product market definition is in conformity with the Commission's Recommendation on relevant markets[3].

As far as the relevant geographic markets regarding call termination on an individual mobile network are concerned, Ficora considers that the area of each mobile network providing this service constitutes a separate relevant market.

The criteria used by Ficora to assess whether operators have significant market power (SMP) in the provision of mobile call termination services are high market shares, control over network and horizontal integration of operators, lack of actual and potential competition and financial strength. Each provider has 100% market share in the market for termination on its own network. There is no actual or potential competition on this market due to the fact that the call termination service on a certain mobile network cannot be provided by any operator other than the owner of the network.

On the basis of these criteria and its market analysis, Ficora intends to designate the following mobile network operators as having SMP in voice call termination on mobile networks:

(1)   Sonera Mobile Networks Oy;

(2)   Radiolinja Origo Oy;

---

[1]   In accordance with Article 6 of the Framework Directive.
[2]   According to Ficora, this market also includes interconnection products and services necessary for the implementation of call termination.
[3]   Commission Recommendation 2003/311/EC of 11 February 2003 on relevant product and service markets within the electronic communications sector susceptible to ex ante regulation [...], market 16 of the Annex.

(3)   Finnet Verkot Oy;

(4)   Ålands Mobiltelefon Ab.

The Communication Market Act (CMA)[4] empowers Ficora to impose the following obligations on SMP operators:

(1)   interconnection obligation;

(2)   obligations to publish delivery terms and tariff information;

(3)   obligations concerning pricing and other terms (cost-orientation and nondiscrimination);

(4)   obligation to use cost-accounting procedures;

(5)   accounting separation obligation.

[...]

Despite the fact that termination of fixed-to-mobile calls is included in the product market definition and that SMP is found by Ficora on the markets thus defined, the scope of the remedies that Ficora proposes is limited with regard to the termination of such calls originating on a fixed network in Finland. In the draft measures and in the additional information provided by Ficora, it is stated that Article 43 of the CMA restricts the obligation of mobile network operators to price terminating traffic originating on fixed networks, so that there is no obligation to specify a wholesale price for this traffic. More precisely, Section 3 of this Article states that a telecommunications operator shall specify a separate price when another operator uses the telephone network to establish a connection where this connection is from another operator's network to the telecommunications operator's network. However, according to Section 4 it is not necessary to set a separate price for traffic terminated on a mobile network when the connection is made from a fixed network to a mobile network.

III. COMMENTS

The Commission has examined the notification and the additional information provided by Ficora, and has the following comments[5]:

(1)   **The limitation of the remedies to the termination of calls originating on mobile networks in Finland or originating abroad:** Article 16(4) of the Framework Directive provides that when a NRA determines that a relevant market is not effectively competitive, it shall identify undertakings with significant market power on that market and impose on such undertakings appropriate specific regulatory obligations. In accordance with Article 8(4) of the Access Directive, the obligations imposed on SMP operators shall be based on the nature of the problem identified, proportionate and justified in the light of the regulatory objectives laid down in Article 8 of the Framework Directive.

The Commission considers that the proposed measures contravene the aforementioned provisions.

First, the problem identified in the market for voice call termination on individual mobile networks is the SMP of mobile network operators for call termination

---

[4]   Communications Market Act (CMA) N° 323 of 23 May 2003.
[5]   Pursuant to Article 7(3) of the Framework Directive.

regardless of the network on which the terminated traffic originates. Therefore, the remedies imposed should not be limited on the basis of the originating network. By limiting the remedies as is proposed, the Commission considers that Ficora does not base the remedy on the nature of the problem identified.

Secondly, the Commission notes that the measures proposed by Ficora are also not proportionate or justified in the light of the regulatory objectives laid down in Article 8 of the Framework Directive, for the following reasons:

–   the measures do not ensure maximum benefit to the users, as fixed telephony subscribers in Finland will be excluded (without justification) from benefiting from the measures[6];

–   the measures maintain a discrimination between fixed network operators and mobile network operators in Finland, which potentially distorts competition and impedes the creation of an internal market for electronic communications[7]; and

–   the measures fail to remove a remaining obstacle to the provision of retail fixed-to-mobile services in Finland, namely the absence of a wholesale call termination product. The absence of a wholesale call termination product for fixed-to-mobile calls deters the market entry of fixed operators in Finland[8].

Since the proposed measures discriminate fixed telephone networks vis-à-vis mobile networks, they moreover cannot be considered technologically neutral contrary to what is required in Article 8(1) of the Framework Directive.

Finally, Article 4(2) of the Authorisation Directive and Article 4(1) of the Access Directive guarantee undertakings providing electronic communications networks or services the right to negotiate interconnection with and where applicable obtain access to or interconnection from other providers of publicly available communications networks and services. The proposed measures deny this right to operators of fixed networks in Finland.

The Commission recognizes that the basis for excluding calls originating on a fixed network in Finland from the proposed remedies is Article 43, Section 4, of the CMA. Ficora can be assured that the Commission envisages using its powers in accordance with Article 226 of the Treaty with respect to this provision which Ficora perceives as limiting its powers. However, it should also be pointed out that, according to standing case law of the Court of Justice: *"It is appropriate to bear in mind [...] that in accordance with settled case-law the primacy of Community law requires any provision of national law which contravenes a Community rule to be disapplied, regardless of whether it was adopted before or after that rule. The duty to disapply national legislation which contravenes Community law applies not only to national courts but also to all organs of the State, including administrative authorities. [...], which entails, if the circumstances so require, the obligation to take all appropriate measures to enable Community law to be fully applied [...].*[9]*"*

[...]

---

6   Contrary to Article 8(2)(a) of the Framework Directive.
7   Contrary to Article 8(3)(c) of the Framework Directive.
8   Contrary to Article 8(3)(a) of the Framework Directive.
9   Judgment of the ECJ of 9 September 2003 in case C-198/01, *Consorzio Industrie Fiammiferi (CIF) v contra Autorità Garante della Concorrenza e del Mercato* (not yet reported), par. 48 and 49, confirming earlier case law of the ECJ.

Pursuant to Article 7(5) of the Framework Directive, Ficora must take the utmost account of comments of other national regulatory authorities and the Commission and may adopt the resulting draft measures and, where it does so, shall communicate them to the Commission.

The above comments reflect the Commission's position on this particular notification, and are without prejudice to any position it may take vis-à-vis other notified draft measures.

Editors' Notes:

[a] Whilst no formal veto decision pursuant to Article 7(4) of the Framework Directive was made in this case, these Commission comments made pursuant to Article 7(3) of the Framework Directive, in particular those made at paragraph III.(1), are regarded as significant and are therefore reproduced here. Minor omissions in the text and footnotes have been made for editorial reasons.

COMMISSION DECISION C(2005)1442 FINAL

of 17 May 2005

pursuant to Article 7(4) of Directive 2002/21/EC
("Withdrawal of notified draft measures")

Case DE/2005/0144: Call termination on individual public telephone networks provided
at a fixed location

THE COMMISSION OF THE EUROPEAN COMMUNITIES,

Having regard to the Treaty establishing the European Community,

Having regard to Directive 2002/21/EC of the European Parliament and of the Council of 7
March 2002 on a common regulatory framework for electronic communications networks
and services (the "Framework Directive") and in particular Article 7(4) thereof[1],

Having regard to the Commission Recommendation 2003/561/EC of 23 July 2003 on
notifications, time limits and consultations provided for in Article 7 of the Framework
Directive (the "Procedural Recommendation")[2],

Having regard to the opening of Phase II investigations pursuant to Article 7(4) of the
Framework Directive on 11 March 2005,

Having regard to the additional information provided by the German Telecommunications
Regulatory Authority ("Regulierungsbehörde für Telekommunikation und Post"-"RegTP"),

Having regard to the notice posted on the Commission's website on 15 March 2005 inviting
third parties to submit observations on the Commission's serious doubts letter (the
"notice"),

After consulting the Communications Committee,

Whereas:

I.　PROCEDURE

(1)　On 15 February 2005 the Commission registered a notification by RegTP, concerning
the markets for call termination on individual public telephone networks provided at a
fixed location in Germany, under case number DE/2005/0144.

(2)　On 22 February 2005 the Commission requested RegTP to provide additional
information and clarifications regarding RegTP's preliminary market definition,
significant market power ("SMP") assessment under the regulation currently in place.
A response by RegTP was received on 25 February 2005.

(3)　On 11 March 2005 the Commission, pursuant to Article 7(4) of the Framework
Directive, informed RegTP that it had serious doubts as to the compatibility of the
draft measures with Community law (the "serious doubts letter").

(4)　On 15 March 2005 the Commission posted a notice on its website inviting third parties
to submit observations on the Commission's serious doubts letter within five working
days.

---

[1]　OJ L 108, 24.4.2002, p.33.
[2]　OJ L 190, 30.7.2003, p.13.

(5) On 17 March 2005 the Commission held a meeting with RegTP to obtain additional information and clarifications regarding regulation currently in place and the SMP assessment of alternative network operators ("ANOs"). A further request for information was sent to RegTP on 6 April 2005, to which a response was received on 11 April 2005.

(6) On 29 April 2005 the Communications Committee was consulted on the draft decision in accordance with the procedure referred to in Article 22(2) of the Framework Directive.

II. DESCRIPTION OF THE DRAFT MEASURES

(7) RegTP defines and analyses the markets for call termination on individual public telephone networks provided at a fixed location including local call conveyance[3]. RegTP identifies a total number of 54 separate operators to be active on such markets, and defines 54 separate markets for call termination on individual public telephone networks. Of these, Deutsche Telekom AG ("DTAG") is the incumbent network operator and 53 operators are alternative network operators.

(8) RegTP considers the geographic scope of the 54 markets to follow the area covered by the single operator's fixed telephone network. RegTP's market definition is in line with the Commission Recommendation on Relevant Markets[4] (market no. 9).

(9) RegTP mainly considers market shares and countervailing buyer power to decide whether or not an undertaking has SMP on the markets concerned. Further criteria considered such as the overall size of the undertakings, technological advantages or superiority, product/services diversification, economies of scale/scope, vertical integration and a highly developed distribution and sales network are in RegTP's view not decisive for the SMP assessment on the markets concerned.

(10) In the markets for call termination on individual public telephone networks provided at a fixed location, RegTP finds that each operator has a 100% market share on its respective network. RegTP designates DTAG with SMP on the market for call termination on its network. However, RegTP concludes that the 53 ANOs do not have SMP for call termination on their respective networks, despite their 100% market share. In RegTP's view, DTAG has countervailing buyer power which does not allow each of the alternative network operators to behave to an appreciable extent independently of its competitors (at the retail level) and customers (at the wholesale level, in the relevant market) when offering call termination services.

(11) RegTP recognizes in its notification that its position deviates from the position taken by other national regulatory authorities (NRAs) that have analysed market 9 so far[5]. Generally, NRAs indeed consider that the incumbent's buyer power vis-à-vis the ANOs is limited by the incumbent's obligation to interconnect with the ANOs and by the fact that its own termination tariffs are regulated. The Commission has not opposed these arguments[6].

---

[3] Local call conveyance is the conveyance of calls from the interconnection point nearest to the end user to the end user.

[4] Commission Recommendation 2003/311/EC of 11 February 2003 on relevant product and service markets within the electronic communications sector susceptible to ex ante regulation in accordance with the Framework Directive.

[5] P. 105 of the non-confidential version of the notification referring to the positions taken by Oftel (UK), ICP-ANACOM (Portugal), ComReg (Ireland) and RTR (Austria). Also Ficora (Finland), PTS (Sweden), NHH (Hungary) and NITA (Denmark) in their notifications came to the conclusion that ANOs have SMP.

[6] See e.g. the Commission's comments letter of 22 September 2003 in case UK/2003/0003 (SG(2003)D/231920) and the Commission's no comments letter of 25 June 2004 in case PT/2004/0061

(12) RegTP argues its finding of non-SMP for ANOs on the basis of two Greenfield approaches, the so-called "strict Greenfield approach" and the so-called "modified Greenfield approach".

(13) RegTP considers under the "strict Greenfield approach" a scenario under which DTAG is not obliged to interconnect with each of the ANOs. In such a scenario, DTAG could, be it in general or in price negotiations, credibly threaten each ANO not to interconnect or to disconnect and thereby exercise countervailing buyer power.

(14) Under the "modified Greenfield approach", RegTP proceeds on the basis of a scenario in which DTAG is generally obliged to interconnect with ANOs. According to RegTP, such obligation is however imposed on account of the imbalance of power in interconnection negotiations between DTAG and each ANO. It would therefore be methodologically wrong, in RegTP's view, to take this obligation of DTAG into account in the assessment of market power of each ANO[7]. Moreover, the obligation of DTAG to interconnect with and purchase termination services from each ANO would in RegTP's view solely prohibit a refusal to interconnect at reasonable conditions but not oblige DTAG to accept unreasonable conditions for interconnections. Hence, while DTAG would be under an interconnection obligation, it could still refuse unacceptably high call termination rates demanded by an ANO in (price) negotiations, limit the single ANO's freedom to behave to an appreciable extent independently of its competitors or customers and thereby exercise countervailing buyer power[8].

(15) RegTP only indirectly considers the relationship between individual ANOs or between ANOs and mobile network operators ("MNOs") as far as call termination services are concerned. In RegTP's view the extent of market power of an ANO on the market for call termination services is mainly determined by its position vis-à-vis DTAG and not vis-à-vis other ANOs or MNOs. According to RegTP, ANOs and MNOs only play a marginal role on the demand side of these markets as most of the traffic originating on their networks is terminated indirectly on ANOs' networks, using the transit and termination services offered by DTAG. RegTP also points out that it has so far never received a request to order interconnection against an ANO.

III. OBSERVATIONS SUBMITTED BY THIRD PARTIES

(16) Following the publication of the notice of the Commission on its website, eleven interested third parties submitted observations to the Commission. All observations were carefully considered.

IV. ASSESSMENT

(17) In order to ensure that decisions at national level do not have an adverse effect on the single market or other Treaty objectives, measures taken by NRAs should be compatible with Community law, and in particular with the objectives and principles of the new regulatory framework. Although NRAs are accorded discretionary powers correlative to the complex character of the economic, factual and legal situations, these factors must be assessed in line with the requirements of the Framework Directive, in particular, its Articles 14 to 16. Therefore an undertaking should be designated to have SMP, if either individually or jointly with others, it enjoys a position of economic strength affording it the power to behave to an appreciable extent independently of competitors, customers and ultimately consumers. The 100% market share of network

---

(SG(2004)D/202508). See also the Explanatory Memorandum to the Recommendation on relevant markets, p. 20.

[7] P. 106 and 107 of the non-confidential version of the notification, further clarified by RegTP in section IV. 1 of its response to the request for information submitted on 11 April 2005.

[8] P. 107 and 108 of the non-confidential version of the notification.

operators in the market for call termination on their individual public telephone network provided at a fixed location raises a strong presumption of SMP, save in exceptional circumstances which need to be clearly and unambiguously demonstrated by the NRA. RegTP therefore has not provided sufficient evidence to support a finding of absence of SMP of each ANO on the market for call termination on its individual public telephone networks.

(18) RegTP's draft measures concerning the markets for call termination on individual public telephone networks provided at a fixed location in Germany fall within Article 7(4)(b) of the Framework Directive and would affect trade between Member States. A draft measure designating or not an undertaking with SMP and as a consequence imposing or not imposing regulatory obligations for the provision of call termination services on individual public telephone networks provided at a fixed location in Germany may have a direct or indirect, actual or potential influence on the ability of undertakings established in other Member States to provide electronic communications services dependent on such call termination[9].

(19) It cannot reliably be concluded on the basis of the notified market analysis that the draft measures relating to ANOs are compatible with Community law and in particular with the objectives referred to in Article 8 of the Framework Directive. Pursuant to Article 8.2 (a) and (b) of the Framework Directive, NRAs shall promote competition in the provision of electronic communications services by ensuring that users derive maximum benefit in terms of choice, price and quality and by ensuring that there is no distortion or restriction of competition in the electronic communications sector. According to Article 8.3 (b), NRAs are to contribute to the development of the internal market by encouraging the establishment and development of trans-European networks and the interoperability of pan-European services, and end-to-end connectivity. The information available does not support the conclusion that RegTP has undertaken the assessment in accordance with Articles 14 and 16 of the Framework Directive, in particular with regard to Article 8.2(a) and (b), and Article 8.3(b) of the Framework Directive read in conjunction with Articles 10 and 82 of the EC Treaty.

(20) The Commission considers that RegTP has not provided convincing evidence that, despite a 100% market share, each of the 53 ANOs in Germany would not have SMP on the markets for call termination on their individual networks. This view is based on the following considerations.

A.   No justification for the considered strict Greenfield approach

(21) Under the so-called "strict Greenfield approach", RegTP considers a scenario under which DTAG is not obliged to interconnect with each of the ANOs[10]. In such a scenario, DTAG could, according to RegTP, credibly threaten each ANO not to interconnect or to disconnect and thereby exercise countervailing buyer power.

---

[9]   See Recital 38 of the Framework Directive. In particular, the conditions for call termination services on individual public telephone networks provided at a fixed location in Germany determine the costs and the ability of other operators and service providers to compete, including those established in other Member States, who require such termination services to provide their own services. Consequently, they may affect the pattern of trade between Member States.

[10]   In its serious doubts letter of 11 March 2005, the Commission indicated at p. 4 that *"under the strict Greenfield approach. RegTP considers a scenario absent all sector-specific regulation in all electronic communications markets, irrespective of whether such regulation is based on an SMP finding or not"* RegTP clarified in its reply to the request for information submitted on 11 April 2005 in footnote 1, that *"the strict Greenfield approach is based on a scenario in which (only) the markets for termination services of ANOs are unregulated".*

(22) The Commission is, however, of the view that there is no legal or economic basis for such a strict Greenfield approach. On the basis of competition rules, applicable under Article 14 and 16 of the Framework Directive, in particular Article 82 of the EC Treaty, an analysis of dominance (i.e. SMP) requires taking into account the concrete economic circumstances including legislative and administrative acts. In economic terms, it is not appropriate to exclude regulatory obligations that exist independently of a SMP finding on the market under consideration but that can have an impact on the SMP finding on the markets under consideration. From a methodological viewpoint obligations flowing from existing regulation, other than the specific regulation imposed on the basis of SMP status in the analysed market, must be taken into consideration when assessing the ability of an undertaking to behave independently of its competitors and customers on that market. In the Commission's view, this could only be otherwise where it is uncertain whether the regulation concerned will continue to exist throughout the period of the forward- looking assessment[11].

(23) The purpose of a Greenfield approach is indeed to avoid circularity in the market analysis by avoiding that, when as a result of existing regulation a market is found to be effectively competitive, which could result in withdrawing that regulation, the market may return to a situation where there is no longer effective competition. In other words, any Greenfield approach must ensure that absence of SMP is only found and regulation only rolled back where markets have become sustainably competitive, and not where the absence of SMP is precisely the result of the regulation in place. This implies that regulation which will continue to exist throughout the period of the forward-looking assessment independently of a SMP finding on the market concerned, must be taken into account[12].

(24) RegTP has informed the Commission that it intends to impose an interconnection obligation[13] on DTAG as a consequence of DTAG having SMP on the market for termination on its own network[14]. Such a regulatory obligation, together with any other regulatory obligation imposed on a market other than the one for which the SMP assessment is conducted[15], must be taken into account.

(25) Accordingly, there is no justification for the proposed strict Greenfield approach.

(26) RegTP has not demonstrated that DTAG can credibly threaten to cut off its existing interconnection with each of the ANOs. Under the European regulatory framework, each public network operator has a right and, when requested, an obligation to negotiate interconnection agreements in order to ensure provision and interoperability of services[16]. NRAs may also order operators controlling access to end-users to

---

[11] See in this respect the cases FI/2003/0024 and FI/2003/0027 in which the Commission considered that the Finnish NRA, Ficora, had failed to analyse the potential impact of its market analyses on the existing regulatory obligations. In that case, Ficora had based its finding of absence of SMP on the international calls markets on existing regulation (i.e. carrier select and pre-select obligations). In its veto decision of 20 February 2004, the Commission stated that if Ficora wanted to rely primarily on regulatory obligations to conclude that the incumbent operator had no SMP, "Ficora should make clear on which basis the existing regulatory obligations in the same or closely related markets will continue to exist for the relevant period of forward-looking assessment." (paragraph 35 of the veto decision)

[12] "In carrying out the market analysis under the terms of Article 16 of the Framework Directive, NRAs will conduct a forward looking, structural evaluation of the relevant market, based on the existing market conditions" (Point 20 of the Commission Guidelines on market analysis and the assessment of significant market power under the Community regulatory framework for electronic communications networks and services).

[13] On the basis of sec. 3 no. 34 new TKG and RegTP's previous decision practice, the obligation to interconnect seems to include the obligation to purchase termination services from ANOs.

[14] As set out in RegTP's reply to the request for information submitted on 11 April 2005.

[15] Provided that it may have an impact on the markets under investigation and that it will continue to exist throughout the period of the forward-looking assessment.

[16] Article 4(1) of the Access Directive.

interconnect where necessary to ensure end-to-end connectivity[17]. Further NRAs are to contribute to the development of the internal market by encouraging inter alia end-to-end connectivity[18]. If an operator, such as DTAG, were unwilling to interconnect at the request of an ANO or were to cut off an existing interconnection[19], the ANO could turn to RegTP to seek an interconnection order[20]. These requirements are not dependent on a finding of SMP.

(27) Regardless of the existing regulatory framework set out above[21], DTAG has little economic incentive either to cut off current interconnection with, or to stop buying termination services from, any particular ANO. According to DTAG, offering its customers the possibility to call all retail customers irrespective of whether they are subscribed to DTAG or an ANO is an important selling point for DTAG[22]. If DTAG decided not to purchase termination from a certain ANO, this would conversely result in customer dissatisfaction, reputation damage and pressure from consumer organisations as DTAG's retail customers would no longer be ensured end-to-end connectivity.

(28) In addition, if DTAG were to cease to purchase termination from ANOs, this may have the effect of stimulating substitution via carrier selection. There are several long distance carrier (pre-) select operators on the German retail calls markets which are eager to capture market share[23]. In the presence of such carrier (pre-) select operators, a refusal by DTAG to offer its customers certain retail calls services - namely calls to the subscribers of ANOs which DTAG no longer wants to purchase termination services from - could lead DTAG's retail customers to switch to these carrier (pre-) select operators for making such calls. DTAG's retail customers could thus use such carrier (pre-) selection operators to by-pass calls - whose ubiquitous coverage is no longer guaranteed by DTAG - provided of course that those operators are directly or indirectly interconnected with the ANO in question. In such a case, DTAG would lose market share in a core area of its business.

(29) Finally, RegTP has confirmed that DTAG has in practice never ceased to purchase termination services from an ANO, even where ANOs had - against the will of DTAG - on the basis of regulatory intervention raised their termination rates and some of them had cancelled their existing interconnection agreement with DTAG. According to RegTP, DTAG continued to purchase these services voluntarily, without any explicit buying obligation having been imposed on it[24].

(30) Under the present regulatory framework and prevailing economic circumstances in Germany, the Commission considers it therefore not correct to assess the market power of each of the ANOs as if DTAG would not, through regulation or otherwise, be obliged to interconnect with each of them. RegTP has not provided evidence of DTAG having effectively used buyer power in the face of these regulatory and economic

---

[17] Article 5(1) of the Access Directive.

[18] Article 8.3(b) of the Framework Directive.

[19] Which according to standard interconnection contract of DT seems to be in any event subject to a 6 months notice period.

[20] Article 5(1) of the Access Directive read together with Article 8.3(b) of the Framework Directive

[21] RegTP has maintained that the interconnection obligations on DTAG are only applicable insofar as the ANO's prices are reasonable.

[22] See T-Com's submission to the Commission of 7 April 2005.

[23] According to the draft measures notified to the Commission on 15 February 2005 and registered by the Commission under case number DE/2005/0143, RegTP intends to designate DTAG as a SMP operator on the market for wholesale call origination on the public telephone network provided at fixed location. It can therefore be assumed that DTAG will also in the time-frame of the forward-looking assessment of this notification continue to be obliged to enable its subscribers to access the services of carrier (pre-) selection operators.

[24] Section IV.2 of RegTP's response to the request for information submitted on 11 April 2005.

constraints. On the contrary, it seems that DTAG continues to buy termination services voluntarily, even at rates that it does not agree with and that it (at least in part) continues to challenge in court.

B.   No convincing evidence of absence of SMP under the so-called "modified Greenfield approach"

(31) Under the modified Greenfield approach, RegTP proceeds on the basis of a scenario that there is an obligation to interconnect on DTAG or that such an obligation will be imposed on the basis of DTAG's SMP status on the market for termination of calls on its own network. RegTP, however, questions whether this obligation can be taken into account for assessing the market power of each of the ANOs, as the obligation would be imposed precisely to redress the equilibrium in interconnection negotiations between DTAG and each ANO. RegTP considers that taking the interconnection obligation into account could under such circumstances be circular.

(32) The Commission does not share RegTP's view. The source of an ANO's market power for termination on its own network is not the regulatory requirement on DTAG to interconnect, but the ANO's 100% market share and the control over its network and over a service for which no substitute exists[25]. Whether that market power is constrained to such an extent that the ANO cannot behave independently of its competitors (at the retail level) and of consumers should then be assessed on the basis of the concrete economic circumstances, in particular DTAG's buyer power. This approach does not lead to circularity, because ANOs' SMP does not result from interconnection obligation, but rather from their 100% market shares. Therefore, when assessing DTAG's buyer power its interconnection obligation must be taken into account.

(33) The Commission acknowledges that the market definition - call termination on individual networks - does not automatically mean that every network operator has significant market power; this depends on the degree of any countervailing buyer power and other factors potentially limiting that market power. While small networks will normally face greater buyer power than large networks, the regulatory requirements referred to in paragraph 26 above will normally redress this imbalance of market power. However, this would not endorse any attempt by a small ANO to set excessive termination rates. It may still be easier for a large network than for a small network to initiate a price raise, but this risk is essentially removed if the large network operator's termination rates are regulated (as is the case for DTAG)[26].

(34) Contrary to other NRAs that have notified market 9 so far[27], RegTP asserts that DTAG's buyer power limits the ability of each ANO to behave independently of its customers and competitors (at the retail level). RegTP does, however, not present concrete evidence that DTAG has effectively exercised such buyer power. In fact what appears to have constrained the individual ANOs' call termination rates in the past is not the countervailing buyer power on the part of DTAG, but the regulatory regime under which RegTP has introduced a de facto ex ante price regulation for ANOs' termination rates.

---

[25] In other words, a particular ANO's market power derives from the fact that: (i) there is no substitute for a particular ANO's (termination) network, and (ii) as (an operator such as) DTAG is committed to delivering calls of its customers to all networks, it has no choice but to buy termination from that (ANO's) network. See further paragraph 27 above.

[26] See further Explanatory Memorandum, p. 20.

[27] Other NRAs have under similar circumstances argued that countervailing buyer power of an incumbent operator is sufficiently weakened by the obligation to purchase call termination services of ANOs (interconnection obligation) so that subsequently the ANOs were found to have SMP on their respective networks.

(35) Presently, under the German law, it seems that the interconnection charges (i.e. also call termination rates) of a non-SMP operator may be price regulated in case of failure of private interconnection negotiations and without the need for any prior SMP finding[28]. Against this regulatory background and following applications by at least 37 ANOs, RegTP has since mid September 2004 ruled that each requesting ANO is allowed to charge 25% more for the call termination on its respective network than DTAG[29]. This implies that call termination rates of (a large proportion of) ANOs are constrained by a regulatory ceiling[30] rather than DTAG exercising countervailing buyer power. Such a regulatory price ceiling preventing ANOs from unilaterally raising their call termination charges appears to support the notion of ANOs attempting to set call termination charges independently of their customers and competitors (at the retail level) and might indicate that the designation of SMP status not only with regard to DTAG but also for these alternative operators would be warranted.

(36) It is generally considered that countervailing buyer power of a large operator is essentially lost if its call termination rates are additionally regulated in the separate market for call termination on that operator's individual public telephone network[31]. DTAG's call termination rates are currently regulated and it is the Commission's understanding that they will continue to be regulated as a consequence of RegTP's finding that DTAG has SMP on the market for call termination on its network. In view of DTAG's own termination rates being regulated and given that it cannot realistically threaten to stop purchasing termination services (as set out above), DTAG would therefore be deprived of any bargaining tool in the form of a corresponding increase in its own tariffs when negotiating termination rates on that ANO's network.

(37) RegTP does not contest that DTAG's own termination rates will (continue to) be price regulated, nor does it contest that, even in a Greenfield approach, this element is to be taken into account when assessing DTAG's buyer power. In RegTP's view, price regulation of DTAG's own termination rates does however not significantly limit its buyer power. RegTP argues to the contrary that it reduces the risk of collusion whereby both DTAG and each ANO would have a joint interest in raising termination rates. It may indeed be correct that DTAG's own price regulation could lower the risk of potential collusion, and DTAG could thus from this perspective have a greater incentive to exercise buyer power. However, as regards the ability rather than the incentive of DTAG to exert buyer power, the regulation of DTAG's own termination rates undisputedly removes a potential instrument of buyer power.

(38) For the above reasons, the Commission considers that also under the modified Greenfield approach, RegTP has not provided convincing evidence to support the absence of SMP of each ANO.

C.   No analysis of ANOs' market power vis-à-vis each other and vis-à-vis MNOs

(39) RegTP has limited its SMP analysis for ANOs mainly to an analysis of negotiation powers between DTAG and each of the ANOs. However, it appears that a number of direct interconnection agreements between ANOs exist and, as the Commission

---

[28] RegTP bases its respective decisions on §25 (5) TKG in conjunction with §30 (4) TKG and §38 (2)-(4) TKG.

[29] From this follows that in line with §28 TKG charges in excess of DTAG+25% are considered abusive by RegTP. Further cases of this kind are pending.

[30] It indeed appears that the termination rates sought by several ANOs were significantly higher than the rates that were ultimately set by RegTP.

[31] This is the view taken also by the Austrian regulator Telekoni Control Kommission ("TKK") in its notification AT/2004/0106, Entwurf der Vollziehungshandlung gemäß § 128 Abs. 1 TKG 2003, p. 18

pointed out in its serious doubts letter, an analysis of these agreements could have provided further information on the market power of ANOs.

(40) In the course of the second phase, RegTP and a number of operators argued that the pricing behaviour of ANOs vis-à-vis each other (and MNOs) is indirectly constrained by DTAG's buyer power. As ANOs (and MNOs) could always terminate traffic indirectly on each other's network, via the transit plus termination services offered by DTAG, the termination rates applied to them could defacto not rise above DTAG's (regulated) transit plus termination rates.

(41) This argument is not convincing for the following reasons. In the first place, it implies defacto that ANOs seem to be in a position to raise their termination rates vis-à-vis each other (and MNOs) above the competitive level and assume for themselves as profit the price which DTAG charges for its (pure) transit service. Secondly, such behaviour may lead to a perpetuated dominance of DTAG on the transit market, as the competitive conditions on the transit market are directly influenced by the pricing conditions on the wholesale termination markets. Wholesale termination services are indeed on the one hand a necessary upstream input for the provision of transit services, and on the other hand a potential substitute for such transit services (as direct interconnection can be a potential substitute for indirect interconnection). If the termination rates of an ANO would be higher, equal or close to DTAG's transit plus termination rate, the incentive for an ANO (or MNO) to invest in and switch to direct interconnection may be reduced. Moreover, the level playing field between DTAG and each ANO for offering transit plus termination services would be distorted, as DTAG would be able to purchase the necessary wholesale input at more favourable conditions than the ANOs. RegTP seems to have been aware of this risk since, when it allowed the requesting ANOs to increase their termination up to 25% above DTAG's rates, it imposed on them a non-discrimination obligation (again absent a prior SMP finding). The Commission is aware of at least one operator who has not sought regulatory intervention to increase its termination rates and still maintains reciprocal tariffs with DTAG, while having raised its tariffs by 25% vis-à-vis those ANOs which have increased their rates following regulatory intervention.

(42) Such autonomy in pricing behaviour and ability to price discriminate also points towards SMP status of ANOs.

(43) The fact that RegTP has so far not received any request for a regulatory interconnection order against an ANO seems also not decisive. This may at least partly have been caused by a common interest of ANOs to rather put pressure on DTAG's and MNO's termination rates.

V.   CONCLUSION AND PROPOSALS FOR AMENDING THE DRAFT MEASURES

(44) Following detailed examination of RegTP's notified draft measures, of its submission and of its replies to the Commission's requests for information and clarification, and for the reasons stated above, the Commission concludes that the evidence provided by RegTP does not support its finding of an absence of SMP for each ANO, and the draft measures are thus not compatible with Community law. The Commission therefore requires RegTP to withdraw the notified draft measures to the extent that they relate to the markets for call termination on the individual networks of the 53 alternative network operators in Germany. Since the Commission does not question RegTP's finding of SMP of Deutsche Telekom AG (DTAG) on the market for call termination on its individual public telephone network provided at a fixed location in Germany, the notified draft measure with regard to DTAG can be adopted.

(45) The above conclusion is based on the fact that each ANO's market share of 100% on its own networks raises a strong presumption of its holding a position of SMP and the

evidence in the present case does not rebut this presumption. This is because there is no concrete demonstration of how DTAG's alleged countervailing buyer power has in fact constrained and will continue to constrain the ANOs' behaviour on their markets. No due account was taken of the regulatory situation that will continue to exist throughout the period of RegTP's forward-looking assessment which seems to limit DTAG's countervailing buyer power (in particular the regulatory provisions on interconnection and the price regulation of DTAG's own termination), or of DTAG's economic incentives. Finally, RegTP has failed to take properly into account the constraints on each ANO's behaviour vis-à-vis each other.

(46) RegTP should fully reflect the Commission's conclusions, set out above, when carrying out a new analysis of the markets for call termination services on individual public telephone networks of ANOs provided at a fixed location. Regulatory obligations on DTAG to interconnect with other operators with a view to ensuring end-to-end connectivity, the regulation of DTAG's own call termination charges as well as DTAG's economic incentives should be fully taken into consideration when assessing DTAG's countervailing buyer power and each ANO's ability to act independently of its customers and competitors (at retail level) on the market for call termination on its respective network. RegTP should also assess ANOs ability to raise call termination charges vis-à-vis other ANOs or MNOs when assessing their SMP status.

HAS ADOPTED THIS DECISION:

Article 1

This Decision concerns the draft measures relating to the markets for call termination on the 54 individual public telephone networks provided at a fixed location in Germany notified to the Commission on 15 February 2005 and registered under case number DE/2005/0144 (the "draft measures").

Article 2

(1) The Regulierungsbehörde für Telekommunikation und Post shall withdraw the draft measures.

(2) Paragraph 1 shall not apply to the draft measure relating to termination on the individual network of Deutsche Telekom AG.

Article 3

This Decision is addressed to:

Regulierungsbehörde für Telekommunikation und Post
Tulpenfeld 4
D-531 13 Bonn
Germany

REVISED ERG COMMON POSITION ON THE APPROACH TO APPROPRIATE REMEDIES IN THE ECNS REGULATORY FRAMEWORK

May 2006

ERG (06)33

This document is an ERG Common Position, expressing the position of the members of the ERG. The document was approved at the ERG8 Plenary on 1 April 2004. The document does not necessarily reflect the official position of the European Commission. The European Commission accepts no responsibility or liability whatsoever with regard to any information or data referred to in this document.

<u>Table of Contents</u>

Executive summary

This document sets out the Common Position of the European Regulators Group of National Regulatory Authorities (NRAs) and the European Commission Services of DG Information Society and DG Competition on remedies under the new regulatory framework for electronic communications. It is a revised version of the Common Position (ERG (03) 30 Rev1) published in 2004 and reflects comments received during the public consultation on a revised text (ERG (05) 70 Rev1), launched in November 2005. It aims to ensure a consistent and harmonised approach to the application of remedies by NRAs in line with the Community law principle of proportionality, and with the new framework's key objectives of promoting competition, contributing to the development of the internal market and promoting the interests of EU citizens (Art 8 Framework Directive[1]). The document is organised in five chapters following the underlying logic of a remedy selection process: an introductory discussion of purpose and context is followed by (i) the identification and categorization of standard competition problems; (ii) a catalogue of the available standard remedies; (iii) the principles to guide NRAs in selecting appropriate remedies; (iv) a matching between the standard competition problems and the remedies available.

1. **Purpose and context (Chapter 1)**

Consistent with standard economic analysis, public policy increasingly intervenes in markets only to address clearly identified market failures or in the light of some overriding public policy concern. In the context of the new regulatory framework, the most important market failure is that associated with market power. The underlying source of most of the competition problems related to market power in communications markets, in turn, are barriers to entry. Wherever high barriers to entry exist and where the cost and demand structure is such that it supports only a limited number of firms, incumbent undertakings may have significant market power.

---

[1] Directive 2002/21/EC.

The aim of the new regulatory framework is to provide a harmonised approach for the regulation of electronic communications that will result in sustainable competition, interoperability of services and provide consumer benefits.

The imposition of remedies represents the third stage of the process set out in the new regulatory framework with respect to regulatory obligations linked to significant market power[2]. The three steps are the following.

1.　*Market Definition:* NRAs define markets susceptible to ex ante regulation, appropriate to national circumstances. In order to filter or select from the large number of markets, which could be defined at the first stage, the Commission has identified three criteria[3]:

- High and non-transitory entry barriers;

- The dynamic state of competitiveness behind entry barriers; and

- The sufficiency of competition law (absent ex ante regulation).

The three criteria, which are described in the Recommendation, were and will be used by the European Commission and the NRAs to identify those markets the characteristics of which may be such as to justify the imposition of regulatory obligations set out in the specific Directives[4]. Thus, there is a presumption that ex ante regulation is appropriate on the 18 markets in the Recommendation if a position of SMP is found. It is therefore not necessary for national authorities themselves to determine whether competition law by itself would be sufficient to deal with competition problems in the markets included in the Recommendation.

2.　*Market analysis* represents the second stage. Once a market is defined (which implies a specific action by a NRA), it must be analysed to assess the degree of competition on that market in a manner consistent with the SMP Guidelines[5]. NRAs will intervene to impose obligations on undertakings only where the markets are considered not to be effectively competitive as a result of such undertakings being in a position equivalent to dominance within the meaning of Article 82 of the EC Treaty[6].

3.　*Remedies:* Where market analysis reveals that competition on the market is not effective, and the NRA designates one or more operators as having SMP on that market, at least one appropriate ex ante remedy must be applied[7]; this is the third and final stage.

The three stage process enables regulation to be re-focussed on areas where it is actually required. It also follows the logic of NRAs' decision making when selecting a remedy to address an identified competition problem. This has numerous benefits over the previous framework where markets were defined, SMP established and remedies imposed rather mechanistically while the new framework enables regulation to be re-focussed on areas where it is actually required. Throughout the document it is assumed that the markets under consideration have satisfied the first two stages of the process.

Policy objectives and regulatory principles for NRAs are set out in Art 8 of the Framework Directive. These objectives are to:

---

[2]　Directive 2002/21/EC, Arts 15 and 16.
[3]　Commission Recommendation on relevant markets, OJ 8.5.2003 L 114/45.
[4]　Directive 2002/21/EC, Article 15.
[5]　Commission Guidelines on market analysis and assessment of significant market power under the Community regulatory framework for electronic communications networks and services 2002/C 165/03
[6]　Treaty establishing the European Community OJ 2002 C325/33. Article 82 prohibits abuse of dominant position within a common market or in a substantial part of it.
[7]　Directive 2002/21/EC, Article 16.

- Promote competition

- Contribute to the development of the internal market

- Promote the interests of the citizens of the European Union

These goals are reflected in the remedies from the Access Directive and the Universal Service Directive which together should allow NRAs to pursue these goals in a balanced manner.

2.   Standard competition problems (Chapter 2)

In the field of sector-specific ex ante regulation, national regulatory authorities will have to deal with undertakings which have significant market power (SMP) on one or several communications markets. In such situations, the following problems may arise: The dominant undertaking may attempt to drive competitors out of the SMP market or a related market and the dominant undertaking may engage in practices which are otherwise to the detriment of end users, such as excessive pricing, the provision of low quality, and inefficient production. The four basic market constellations relevant to such competition problems are:

Vertical leveraging: This applies where a dominant firm seeks to extend its market power from a wholesale market to a vertically related wholesale or retail market. Horizontal leveraging: This applies where an SMP operator seeks to extend its market power to another market that is not vertically related.

- *Single market dominance:* The problems which may occur within the context of a single market are entry deterrence, exploitative pricing practices, and productive inefficiencies.

- *Termination (Two-way access):* This relates to the link between price setting in termination markets and in the related retail markets that may be competitive.

Using this typology, 27 potential competition problems are described. Each of these competition problems may be identified in the course of the market analysis as a problem that has to be addressed by the NRA. Of course, not all problems will arise in every case in practice. This list of competition problems is a guide only and does not preclude NRAs from identifying other potential problems.

3.   Standard remedies (Chapter 3)

The standard remedies provided by the new regulatory framework are set out in articles 9 to 13 of the Access Directive and 17 to 19 of the Universal Service Directive.

The following wholesale obligations are set out in the Access Directive:

- Transparency

- Non-discrimination

- Accounting separation

- Access

- Price control and cost accounting

In addition, the Access Directive enables NRAs to impose remedies other than the standard remedies enumerated in the Directive in exceptional circumstances. These exceptional remedies are not covered by the present document.

The list of possible retail obligations mentioned in the Universal Service Directive is not exhaustive. However, it includes specific mentioning of the prohibition of excessive or predatory pricing, undue price discrimination or unreasonable bundling of services, which may be implemented inter alia by means of price caps or individual price controls. Regulatory controls on retail services can only be imposed where relevant wholesale or related measures would fail to achieve the objective of ensuring effective competition.

4.   Principles for imposing remedies (Chapter 4)

Article 8 of the Access Directive requires that remedies must be based on the underlying (competition) problem identified, proportionate and justified in light of the objectives set out for NRAs in Article 8 of the Framework Directive[8]. The purpose of this chapter is to put flesh on these concepts and to give guidance to NRAs on how to fulfil the aims of the framework while, at the same time, respecting these requirements.

The first principle is that the NRA must produce reasoned decisions in line with their obligations under the Directives. This incorporates the need that the remedy selected be based on the nature of the problem identified. The problem(s) in the market will have already been identified in the market analysis procedure. Decisions must include a discussion on the proportionality of the remedy. These decisions should include, for any given problem, consideration of alternative remedies where possible, so that the least burdensome effective remedy can be selected. The decisions should also take into account the potential effect of the proposed remedies on related markets.

A second principle is that where infrastructure competition is not likely to be feasible, due to the persistent presence of bottlenecks associated with significant economies of scale or scope or other entry restrictions, NRAs will need to ensure that there is sufficient access to wholesale inputs. Thus, consumers may enjoy the maximum benefits possible. In this instance, NRAs should also protect against the potential behavioural abuses that might occur.

A third principle is that, where as part of the market definition and analysis process, replication of the incumbent's infrastructure is viewed as feasible, the available remedies should assist in the transition process to a sustainable competitive market[9]. Where there is sufficient certainty that replication is feasible these markets should be treated in an analogous manner to those markets where replication is known to be feasible. In other cases with more marked uncertainty the NRA should keep an open mind and engage in on-going monitoring and discussion with the industry to continually re-assess their views.

A fourth principle is that remedies should be designed, where possible, to be incentive compatible. Thus, NRAs should, wherever possible, formulate remedies in such a way that the advantages to the regulated party of compliance outweigh the benefits of evasion. Incentive compatible remedies are likely to be both effective and require a minimum of on-going regulatory intervention. This may be difficult to achieve in practice, especially as the legal power to develop incentives for compliance is likely to vary greatly across Member States.

---

[8]   Directive 2002/19/EC. Article 8 of Directive 2002/21/EC (the Framework Directive) sets out the objectives of the NRA, which are to promote competition, to contribute to the development of the internal market and to promote the interests of EU citizens.

[9]   When referring to replication in this document, what is really being referred to is other infrastructure that is capable of delivering the same services. Thus, the replication needs not be on the basis of the same technology and, even if it is, there is no assumption that it will be configured in the same manner.

5.   Matching remedies to competition problems (Chapter 5)

This final chapter attempts to match the remedies available to NRAs as set out in Chapter 3 to the standard competition problems identified in Chapter 2. Underlying this match are the general principles as discussed in Chapter 4. The analysis of the chapter is made on a general level, abstracting from conditions which NRAs usually will face and will have to take into account when taking decisions about remedies. Therefore, the conclusions drawn should not be seen as advocating a mechanistic approach or preclude NRAs from coming to different conclusions based on their market analysis. This summary does not intend to give an overview of this exercise for all the 27 problems which have been identified, but will only highlight the most important issues.

When imposing ex ante remedies NRAs frequently cannot actually observe a certain type of anti-competitive behaviour but will have to anticipate the appearance of a particular competition problem based on the incentives of an SMP undertaking to engage in such behaviour which in turn will be investigated in the market analysis. However as the imposition of remedies will follow the market definition and market analysis stage, regulators will have detailed market knowledge, and, where a market is not effectively competitive, will have determined SMP and identified the source of market power as well as actual and potential competition problems.

If markets have the characteristics of natural monopolies (significant economies of scale and/or scope at the relevant level of output) and significant barriers to entry exist (e.g. because of large sunk costs), effective competition is unlikely to emerge on its own, and regulators will have to deal directly with the adverse effects of market power, such as excessive pricing, price discrimination, lack of investment, inefficiencies, and low quality. In other markets, where no significant economies of scale or scope, and only limited structural (and thus exogenous) barriers to entry exist, concerns about the market power are reduced, however, SMP positions may result from endogenous barriers to entry, i.e., barriers to entry following from the behaviour of the dominant undertaking (foreclosure). In such cases, the NRA is called upon to prevent such behaviour in order to promote market entry and enable competition to develop.

In order to promote sustainable, infrastructure-based competition, NRAs have to set investment incentives such that the dominant undertaking's infrastructure is replicated wherever this is technically feasible and economically efficient within a reasonable period of time. Investment incentives are particularly relevant in the context of access regulation. By the decision as to if and on which level of the infrastructure access has to be provided by the SMP undertaking and by setting the access price, NRAs will influence investment incentives of both the SMP undertaking and alternative operators. Given that the cost structure and investment incentives of alternative operators are likely to change over time as they develop their trademark and a customer base, NRAs may consider to give them the possibility to take their investments in a step-by-step manner. This approach, where two or more access products at different levels of the network hierarchy are simultaneously available to alternative operators has been called the 'ladder of investment'.

If there is sufficient certainty that efficient replication is possible, NRAs may signal in their reviews that they view some remedies as bridging a gap and/or consider adopting dynamic access pricing rules in order to promote investments. By changing the incentive properties of regulation over time, NRAs can induce operators to 'climb the ladder', which will in the long run allow them to phase out regulation in those markets where replication has occurred.

Where uncertainty about replicability exists, NRAs will have to weigh the benefits of infrastructure competition against the risk of inefficient duplication and the risk of having neither infrastructure nor service competition in the end, if replication does not occur. Wherever the latter is likely to prevail, NRAs should adopt a more 'neutral' approach, set the prices for the relevant access products at some measure of costs, monitor the market outcome and keep up discussion with the industry. Investment incentives may also change over time due to market dynamics, leading to replication without additional regulatory incentives. In segments where infrastructure competition is unlikely to develop, NRAs should set the access price such that the incumbent has incentives to maintain and upgrade its network while at the same time ensuring efficient entry at the retail level.

With regard to emerging markets, which as such will usually not be subject to ex ante regulation, there may be the need for regulatory action if a failure to act will lead to the complete foreclosure of the emerging market. This can occur where the emerging market depends upon inputs that cannot be replicated or substituted within a reasonable period of time. In these circumstances, there may be grounds for early regulatory intervention in the market from which the market power could be leveraged to guarantee access to this input in the normal manner, in order to allow competition to develop in the emerging market. In this way, the distinct nature of the emerging market is maintained whilst at the same time preventing foreclosure by applying regulation only on the necessary input market.

Another important issue which is dealt with is the question of the regulatory approach to termination rates. Where there is a danger that an SMP operator on a termination market exploits its market power to set above cost termination rates resulting into distorted pricing structures, NRAs may consider the obligation of transparency, non-discrimination or price control to address the problem. Although transparency may in some cases lead to increased customer awareness, and non-discrimination would make the costs of terminating on-net calls visible, both remedies do not address the problem directly, and therefore in most cases are likely to be inappropriate.

An obligation by which the termination charge can be targeted directly is by setting a cost-oriented price based on a price control and cost accounting obligation. This may have to be backed by an obligation of accounting separation. With a cost-oriented access price, excessive pricing is made impossible and distortions are reduced. In cases where an immediate implementation of charge control that sets charges at the competitive level could cause disproportionate problems for operators on the relevant market, NRAs may apply a price cap system or a glide path to achieve a competitive level over a reasonable period of years.

In cases where different remedies are considered appropriate in order to allow for cost differences due to different economies of scale and the ability to reach economies of scale, this may lead to using glide path schemes or delayed reciprocity. While in principle the same considerations apply in the case of both fixed and mobile termination, the nature of the market dynamic and the ability to reach minimum efficient scale may in practice lead to different outcomes with regard to the appropriate period of any possible glide path. Nevertheless, where glide paths are to be used, NRAs should construct glide paths which encourage greater efficiency over time.

6. Conclusion

While NRAs have to protect consumers against exploitative behaviour and inefficiencies where significant market power exists, the ultimate goal is to promote self-sustaining competition and to focus regulation on those parts of the market where the replication of the incumbent's assets is infeasible or economically undesirable. NRAs can pursue this goal by preventing the SMP undertaking from leveraging its market power into potentially competitive markets and by designing access products and access prices such that incumbents and alternative operators face – over time – the right incentives to invest.

1. Purpose and Context

This document sets out the common position of the European Regulators Group (ERG), which has been prepared in close cooperation with the European Commission Services in Directorate General Information Society and Media, and Directorate General Competition, on remedies imposed on firms that have been designated to have significant market power (SMP) in specific markets under the new regulatory framework. The document only deals with obligations for which an SMP designation is a necessary precondition and situations where ex ante regulation is needed, given that the sufficiency of ex post intervention has already been considered.

The aim of this document is to set out the views of national regulatory authorities (NRAs) on imposing remedies in a manner that contributes to the development of the internal market and ensures a consistent application of the new regulatory framework. Under the new regulatory framework NRAs have been set the objective of contributing to the development of the internal market. This document is one of the concrete steps that they are taking to fulfil this obligation.

This document is part of a process of seeking to agree on the instruments and remedies that are best suited to address particular types of situations on the market place. In this, NRAs are required to co-operate with each other and with the Commission in a transparent manner to ensure consistent application, in all Member States, of the new regulatory framework[10].

It is a living document that will be updated regularly in the light of developments in the marketplace and the experience that NRAs accumulate in applying remedies.

1.1 Background

Before delving into the detail of the new regulatory framework and how remedies are applied to firms with SMP in specific markets, it is worthwhile to re-state the reasons why (and how) policymakers intervene in markets.

Consistent with standard economic analysis, public policy increasingly intervenes in markets only to address clearly identified market failures or in the light of some overriding public policy concern. In the context of the new framework the most important market failure is that associated with market power. Policymakers are concerned with market power as it allows firms to act independently of other players on the market, its suppliers and its customers. Narrowly defined, market power is the ability to raise prices above the competitive level.

Under EC competition law market power is addressed in a number of ways. Firstly, there is ex post control via the abuse of a dominant position provisions under Article 82 of the Treaty. This involves a three stage process of defining the relevant market, determining that a position of dominance is held on this market and finally an assessment of whether an actual abuse has occurred. Thus, Article 82 EC is about placing controls on market power that currently exists[11]. Competition cases, including those involving dominance, must always be seen as case specific. Competition policy also serves to act prospectively through merger regulation to stop a dominant position on a market emerging (or a position of dominance being extended) that would likely lead to a serious detriment to consumers[12]. This intervention, which is a once-off intervention, can be in the form of allowing the merger through with conditions or in exceptional cases outright prohibition. Generally the provisions of EC competition law apply across all sectors of the economy.

In key sectors of the economy, such as telecommunications and energy, the entrenched privileged position of the previously state owned vertically integrated monopolies presents a particular challenge. These companies started out with a monopoly on certain key

---

[10] Directive 2002/21/EC, Arts 7.2 and 8.3(d).
[11] Article 81 of the Treaty controls agreements or other practices (e.g. a cartel), which have the object or the effect of preventing, restricting or distorting competition.
[12] The proposed standard that will apply from the 1st of May 2004 is that a merger must not significantly impede effective competition on the market.

infrastructures that are necessary in order to deliver services to consumers. Given the complexity of these networks, and given that under the liberalisation policy there exists the need to mandate access, to set and regulate tariffs, policymakers have from the outset of liberalisation of electronic communications networks and services decided that until effective competition emerges, the competition issues in these markets are best tackled through a combination of ex ante sector specific regulation and ex post application of the competition rules.

Economic theory and technological development have challenged the former assumption that these services could only be delivered by a vertically integrated monopoly. It is now recognised that not only is competition feasible in many of the layers of the value chain but that this competition delivers static and dynamic benefits to consumers.

Under the previous EU framework, the legislation itself directly defined the markets, set a strict and mechanistic rule for defining an operator as having SMP (i.e. 25% market share), and identified the remedies to be imposed. The main innovation of the new framework is to intrinsically link regulation to the concepts and principles of competition law in the EU. This means that the remedies have to be determined by the NRAs, taking into account the principle of proportionality, depending on the specific circumstances at hand. This reflects the importance of the role of economic analysis in being capable to identify the types of competition problems and the remedies to these problems in an effective and self-sustaining manner. Hence, regulation under the new framework is imposed on relevant markets that are defined consistent with economic theory and competition law practice when a firm (or a set of firms) have a position equivalent to dominance on this market (SMP). Thus, the absence of dominance is the trigger for removing obligations. The trigger is the same as for assessing dominance under Article 82 of the Treaty but the analysis is prospective. Unlike the regulation of mergers, ex ante regulation involves on-going reviews so that remedies can be tailored in the light of experience.

The underlying source of most of the competition problems related to market power in communications markets are barriers to entry. Where such barriers do not exist or are sufficiently low, actual or potential market entry will lead to a situation of overall allocative and productive efficiency with prices following costs at a socially desired level of output. However, these circumstances rarely exist in communications markets, as barriers to entry, which may be either structural or legal/regulatory, exist in many areas. These barriers have been identified in the Commission Recommendation[13] as the first (of three cumulatively applied) criteria when deciding whether a market could be considered relevant for ex ante regulation.

Structural barriers - according to the Recommendation – '... exist when the state of the technology, and its associated cost structure, as well as the level of the demand, are such that they create asymmetric conditions between incumbents and new entrants impeding or preventing market entry of the latter. For instance, high structural barriers may be found to exist when the market is characterised by substantial economies of scale, scope and density and high sunk cost'[14].

Legal or regulatory barriers to entry, on the other hand, '... are not based on economic conditions, but may result from legislative, administrative or other state measures that have a direct effect on the conditions of entry and/or the positioning of operators on the relevant market. One example is the case of a legal limit on the number of undertakings that have

---

[13] Commission Recommendation of 11 February 2003 on relevant product and service markets within the electronic communications sector susceptible to ex ante regulation in accordance with Directive 2002/21/EC of the European Parliament and of the Council on a common regulatory framework for electronic communications networks and services, OJ 8.5.2003 L 114/45. Henceforth referred to as Commission Recommendation on relevant markets.

[14] Commission Recommendation on relevant markets, p. 10.

access to spectrum. Such a limitation is typically linked to a related technical or technological barrier, e.g., a constraint on the amount of spectrum that can be assigned and consequently a limit on the number of licences given to undertakings seeking to enter a market. A significant legal or regulatory barrier to entry may also exist when entry into a particular market is rendered non-viable as a result of regulatory requirements, and in addition this situation is expected to persist for a foreseeable period'[15].

NRAs can, by means of the remedies of the new regulatory framework, address certain aspects of market structure, such as barriers to entry. The structural barriers which are mentioned in the Commission Recommendation (economies of scale, scope and density; sunk costs), however, are factors which cannot be influenced by regulatory intervention, and in any case necessitate of long periods of time to be influenced. The new regulatory framework and other obligations on Member States (which were already part of the previous ONP-framework) also aim to limit legal and/or regulatory barriers (e.g. through general authorisation, frequency trading or a stronger requirement to harmonise).

Wherever high barriers to entry exist and where the cost and demand structure is such that it supports only a limited number of firms[16], incumbent undertakings may have significant market power. Under such circumstances, three issues arise for the regulator: First, the dominant undertaking may attempt to transfer (leverage) its market power to an adjacent vertically or horizontally related market; second, the undertaking may engage in practices to defend its SMP market; and finally it might engage in what might be called 'textbook monopoly behaviour', such as excessive pricing, the provision of low quality, and inefficient production.

1.2 The new regulatory framework

The aim of the Directives is to achieve a harmonised framework for the regulation of electronic communications that will result in sustainable competition, interoperability of services and provide consumer benefits.

The new framework operates on the basis of technological neutrality and draws upon competition law principles. It is a major step in the transition path between the vertically integrated monopolies of the past and the normal competition process (governed exclusively, where appropriate, by competition law). Member States can proceed at a speed determined by conditions in their own market, whilst at the same time applying the uniform framework that is necessary for the functioning of the internal market.

The scope of the new framework is all electronic communications products and services.

1.2.1 Remedies in the context of the new regulatory framework

The imposition of remedies represents the third stage of the process set out in the new regulatory framework (with respect to regulatory obligations linked to significant market power – SMP)[17]. The three steps are summarised below. Remedies can be imposed on firms with SMP in specified markets under both the Access Directive and (in specific circumstances) under the Universal Service Directive.

---

[15] Commission Recommendation on relevant markets, p. 11.
[16] In the extreme case, the cost and demand structure supports only a single undertaking, which is referred to as the case of natural monopoly (or a sub-additive cost structure).
[17] Directive 2002/21/EC, Arts 15 and 16.

1. *Market Definition:* NRAs define markets susceptible to ex ante regulation, appropriate to national circumstances. In so doing, they must take the utmost account of the markets identified in the Commission Recommendation on relevant markets[18].

In order to filter or select from the large number of markets, which could be defined at the first stage, the Commission has identified three criteria. The three criteria which are described in the Recommendation to identify the markets the characteristics of which may be such as to justify the imposition of regulatory obligations set out in the Specific Directives[19] are:

- High and non-transitory entry barriers;

- The dynamic state of competitiveness behind entry barriers; and

- The sufficiency of competition law (absent ex ante regulation).

These three criteria were used by the Commission in identifying markets in the current Recommendation and will be used in future versions of the Recommendation. Thus, there is a presumption that ex ante regulation is appropriate on the 18 markets in the Recommendation if a position of SMP is found. It is therefore not necessary for national authorities themselves to determine whether competition law by itself would be sufficient to deal with competition issues in the markets included in the Recommendation. NRAs must however apply all three criteria when determining whether a market not included in the Recommendation, or otherwise defined with respect to those included in the Recommendation, should be considered eligible for ex ante regulation. Accordingly, the Commission will also use these criteria when NRAs notify markets that differ from those in the Recommendation.

Textbox 1: Emerging markets

The concept of an emerging market is introduced in the Framework Directive, where it says that although the "de facto the market leader is likely to have a substantial market share" it "should not be subject to inappropriate obligations"[20]. In the SMP Guidelines it is made clear that in the case of emerging markets a more flexible approach is warranted as the premature imposition of ex ante regulation may unduly influence the competitive conditions taking shape within a new and emerging market[21]. Furthermore, the Guidelines note that Article 14 (3) of the Framework Directive (leveraging of an undertaking with significant market power) is not intended to apply in relation to market power leveraged from a "regulated" market into an emerging, "non regulated" market. Any abusive conduct in an emerging market will normally be dealt with under the dominance provisions of Article 82 of the Treaty[22]. At the same time, to the extent that there is a real threat of market power being leveraged, foreclosure of such emerging markets by the leading undertaking should be prevented through effective regulation of the market(s) from which market power may be leveraged.

In the Recommendation on relevant markets the Commission outlines the markets that are susceptible to ex ante regulation[23]. If a market is to be subject to regulation it must be a properly defined market in accordance with the principles of competition law, as explained

---

[18] Commission Recommendation on relevant markets, OJ 8.5.2003 L 114/45
[19] Directive 2002/21/EC, Article 15.
[20] Directive 2002/21/EC, Recital 27.
[21] This paragraph draws heavily from the Commission Guidelines on market analysis and the assessment of significant market power, 2002/C 165/03, paragraphs 83-85.
[22] Commission Guidelines on market analysis and the assessment of SMP, footnote 92.
[23] 2003/311/EC.

in the Commission's Notice on Market Definition[24]. This also applies to an emerging market. An emerging market must also be distinct from a market that is already susceptible to ex ante regulation from both a demand and a supply perspective. This means that consumers of the new service should not move their custom to currently available services, in response to a small but significant non-transitory increase in the price of the new service. In a similar manner, firms currently providing existing services should not be in a position to quickly enter the new service market in response to such a price increase[25]. For example, the mere bundling of distinct retail products does not in itself give rise to the existence of a new retail product belonging to a separate market.

Correct application of the regulatory framework does not require NRAs to assess whether or not a particular market which is being considered for ex-ante regulation is "emerging". This is because, in the Commission's view, its three criteria provide the definitive test of the susceptibility of a market to ex-ante regulation. These criteria, that must be satisfied cumulatively, are that there are high and non-transitory entry barriers, that there is no dynamic behind the entry barriers towards effective competition and that competition law on its own is not sufficient to remedy the problem. There is no generally accepted definition of an "emerging market". But in the view of ERG, the distinguishing feature of such a market is that it is immature which implies that there is high degree of demand uncertainty and entrants to the market bear higher risk. Where these characteristics are present, it will not be possible to make definitive findings on whether or not the three criteria are met in relation to the emerging market.. Even if a firm makes non-trivial investments to be able to provide a new service, there is no guarantee that, in an innovative and fast moving sector, a cheaper alternative mechanism for delivering the service will not be found. It is also difficult to assess the dynamic of competition behind any entry barrier, as many potential entrants will not make firm plans to enter a new service area until the market is seen to be a commercial proposition. Many new initiatives on the marketplace fail but successful ones create incentives for other firms to enter the market. In discussing the second criteria, in the Explanatory Memorandum to the Recommendation, it is stated that "entry barriers may also become less relevant with regard to innovation-driven markets characterised by ongoing technological progress. In such markets, competitive constraints often come from innovative threats from potential competitors that are not currently in the market. In such innovation-driven markets, dynamic or longer term competition can take place among firms that are not necessarily competitors in an existing "static" market." It is only with the elapse of a sufficient amount of time that these questions can be answered.

There are however two other important points to be made concerning emerging markets. While robust assessment of the three criteria may not be possible early on, close monitoring of the situation by NRAs is appropriate. This is particularly important in situations where emerging markets are in some way linked to established markets on which there is SMP, for instance where entry into an emerging market depends upon inputs of the SMP market that cannot be replicated or substituted within a reasonable period of time (see section 5.2.2.3).

Second, it is by no means the case that every new service offer or every large investment constitutes an emerging market. For example, a technological upgrade to an existing network which will be used mainly to provide equivalent or incrementally improved services to the situation before the upgrade, is unlikely to affect the application of the three criteria. Moreover, a mere upgrade of an existing service is not considered in itself to constitute a new market[26]. If the relevant markets were susceptible to ex-ante regulation before the upgrade, that is likely to remain the case.

---

[24] OJ C 372, 9.12.1997.
[25] In such a case, it would not be possible to sustain a definition different from a currently regulated market.
[26] See Commission's comments in case DE/2005/0262.

An example of an emerging market could be the future provision of next generation mobile broadband data services. In such markets operators would provide end users with access to the Internet through a fast connection and with the added feature of mobility. As is said in the Explanatory Memorandum to the Commission's Recommendation on relevant markets, many important issues in these markets "can currently be dealt with only with a high degree of uncertainty". On this basis no retail or wholesale markets in this area were identified in the Recommendation.

2. *Market analysis* represents the second stage. Once a market is defined (which implies a specific action by a NRA), it must be analysed to assess the degree of competition on that market in a manner consistent with the SMP Guidelines[27]. NRAs will intervene to impose obligations on undertakings only where the markets are considered not to be effectively competitive as a result of such undertakings being in a position equivalent to dominance within the meaning of Article 82 of the EC Treaty[28]. The notion of dominance has been defined in the case-law of the Court of Justice as a position of economic strength affording an undertaking the power to behave to an appreciable extent independently of competitors, customers and ultimately consumers.

3. *Remedies:* Where market analysis reveals that competition on the market is not effective, and the NRA designates one or more operators as having SMP on that market, at least one appropriate ex ante remedy must be applied[29]; this is the third and final stage.

Throughout the remainder of this document it is assumed that the markets under consideration have satisfied the first two stages of the process. This is without prejudice to the analysis that individual NRAs will undertake. Nor does this necessarily mean that a market identified in the Recommendation will be always characterised by the existence of SMP. However, satisfying the tests set out at step 1 and 2 does establish the presumption that some form of ex ante regulation is warranted, and that therefore at least one remedy will have to be applied to the undertaking(s) identified as having SMP.

The definition of markets susceptible to ex ante regulation (stage 1) is distinct from the assessment of effective competition in individual markets (stage 2). It is also distinct from the application of remedies in particular markets (stage 3). This document is intended to assist NRAs in stage 3 and complements guidance already provided by the Commission on stages 1 and 2[30]. There will nevertheless be a strong relationship between each of the three stages. For example, the effects of remedies will be monitored and evaluated in future market reviews, and when assessing whether a market is effectively competitive the effects of existing remedies should be taken into account.

This document analyses remedies issues on a general level, abstracting from conditions which NRAs usually will face and will have to take into account when taking their decisions. Therefore the conclusions drawn should be viewed as guidelines and in no way aim at advocating a mechanistic approach or preclude NRAs from coming to different conclusions based on a thorough market analysis and taking into account the particular circumstances at hand.

The three stage process enables regulation to be re-focussed on areas where it is actually required. It also follows the logic of NRAs' decision making when selecting a remedy to address an identified competition problem. This has numerous benefits over the previous framework where markets were defined, SMP established and remedies imposed

---

[27] Commission Guidelines on market analysis and the assessment of significant market power, 2002/C 165/03.
[28] Treaty establishing the European Community OJ 2002 C325/33. Article 82 prohibits abuse of dominant position within a common market or in a substantial part of it.
[29] Directive 2002/21/EC, Art 16.
[30] Directive 2002/21/EC, Arts 15 & 16.

mechanistically. The old framework was designed for opening communications markets for competition, but, as competition develops in many areas, would run the risk of both regulating where it was not necessary and of not regulating where it was necessary.

Both of these errors are harmful to welfare, both from the point of view of producers and from that of consumers. Under the new framework, the goal is to first re-focus regulation on where it is truly required and then to regulate so as to deliver sustainable effective competition over the medium term, where this possible.

A consequence of the approach taken by the new framework is that it is consistent with competition law, the economic principles of which are of universal validity. Thus the new framework, when applied properly, ensures that regulation will target only those markets and those situations where it is strictly needed. In particular, any perceived proliferation of markets to be subject to ex ante regulation is readily apparent. While under the old framework entire areas of the economy were subject to the same level of regulation, under the new framework each market will be subject to an appropriate regulatory response to specific, clearly identified problems. The result is that the overall level of regulation will be, with time, lower, more targeted at the competition problems, and conducive to a situation in which regulation will be needed increasingly less.

The new framework comes with a not insignificant set-up cost, but this cost will ultimately result in greater benefits from the re-focussing of regulation at a finer level of granularity. The new framework will continue to pay off into the future as effective competition becomes established and more and more markets are freed from ex ante regulation. As such it facilitates the transition to ex post controls based on general competition law, as markets where sustainable effective competition has taken hold are identified in periodic reviews and removed from the scope of ex ante regulation.

1.2.2   The objectives of NRAs

As set out in Article 8 of the Access Directive, obligations must be based on the nature of the problem identified, proportionate and justified in light of the objectives of NRAs as outlined in the Framework Directive. The same applies to those particular circumstances under Article 17(2) of the Universal Service Directive where obligations can be placed on a retail market. These objectives are to:

*   *Promote competition* in the provision of electronic communications networks, electronic communications services and associated facilities and services facilities. This can be achieved inter alia by ensuring the best price, choice and quality for consumers through effective competition, efficient investment in infrastructure and resource management;

*   *Contribute to the development of the internal market.* This can be achieved inter alia by removing obstacles to pan European networks and services and ensuring a consistent regulatory practice across the community; and to

*   *Promote the interests of the citizens of the European Union.* This can be achieved inter alia by ensuring universal access and protecting the rights of consumers and in particular those with special needs. The Universal Service Directive sets out the powers that NRAs have to ensure that these objectives are met.

These goals are reflected in the remedies from the Access Directive and the Universal Service Directive to different degrees. Whereas the Access Directive primarily focuses on promoting competition (from a static as well as from a dynamic point of view by encouraging efficient investment and innovation), consumer interests and the internal market are at the heart of the Universal Service Directive. However, the borders between the two are blurred to the extent that promoting competition will, in general, lead to lower prices, better quality, more innovation and more variety, which is in the consumer's best interest, whereas the instruments of the Universal Service Directive also have the effect of promoting competition.

The whole process of consistent application of the framework and harmonisation is how NRAs ensure that they are meeting the objective to contribute to the development of the internal market. Ensuring the consistency of regulatory practice across the EU is the responsibility of each NRA, subject to particular conditions in national markets. NRAs should co-operate with each other and with the Commission in a transparent manner to ensure consistent application of the framework in all Member States[31].

In particular, as outlined in Articles 7(2) and 8(3)d of the Framework Directive, NRAs shall seek to agree on the types of instruments and remedies best suited to address particular types of situations in the market place, and shall cooperate in a transparent manner to ensure the development of consistent regulatory practice and application of the Directives. This Common Position is an effort to ensure such consistency of approaches in relation to remedies. Thus, the production of the Common Position is part of the process of NRAs contributing to the development of the internal market. However, specific national circumstances may arise which could justify a different approach to the application of remedies in individual cases. In such cases NRAs shall set out the reasons for their approach. As with all proposed remedies, any such approach will be subject to the notification and consultation procedures of Article 7[32].

The earlier stages of market definition and market analysis are already harmonised. This has been achieved through the Commission Guidelines on market analysis and SMP and the Commission Recommendation on relevant markets. All market reviews are subject to the Article 7 procedure[33].

In some instances the impact of a particular measure may be felt in other Member States. In these instances, NRAs should be mindful of the potential to cause a distortion of trade, given their duty to contribute to the development of the internal market[34]. The European Regulators Group (ERG) was specifically set up in order to deal with this and other issues[35]. Thus, in addition to the processes outlined in Article 7 of the Framework Directive, NRAs (through the ERG) should remain in close contact with each other (and with the Commission) when they are considering regulatory measures that have the potential to influence the pattern of trade between Member States in a manner that might create a barrier to the single market.

1.3 The structure of the document

This document is not based on abstract economic analysis alone, but also on reports and studies informed by market data and by the combined practical experience of the NRAs with competition problems in their respective markets, and with the means best suited to resolving these problems. This is only the first version of what must be regarded as a living document. This document will be revised continually in the light of the experience that NRAs gain in applying remedies and on the basis of developments in the market place. The ERG's work programme for 2004 envisages that this process of review of this document will start as early as the last quarter of 2004.

---

[31] Directive 2002/21/EC, Article 7.
[32] Although remedies are not subject to the veto power of the European Commission.
[33] Under the terms of Article 7, national regulation authorities are required to notify the Commission when they seek to define a new market and for each designation of an operator who occupies a dominant position when this would affect trade between Member States. All other NRAs are also consulted.
[34] Article 8(3) of the Framework Directive [Directive 2002/21/EC].
[35] Article 3, Commission Decision 2002/627/EC.

The rest of the document is structured along four Chapters, which follow the logic of an NRA's approach with regard to remedies: Chapter 2 reviews the areas where, through experience and from reviewing the economic literature, issues of market power arise in relations to communications networks and services markets. This chapter abstracts from the Recommendation on relevant markets and highlights what problems are likely to be raised on these markets. Chapter 3 summarises briefly for reference purposes the available remedies. Chapter 4 expounds a set of over-arching principles that NRAs will use in applying remedies. This chapter sets out how NRAs can best achieve their objectives under the new framework in selecting remedies to tackle SMP. The final chapter integrates the work of the previous chapters of the document and gives a detailed overview of the likely reasoning that an NRA may undertake in a particular circumstance. This guidance is provided at a very high level as the examples considered lack the rich context that normal market analyses in Member States throw up. Thus, the final chapter should be used as a guide to analysis rather than any definitive statement.

2.   Generalization of competition problems

2.1   Introduction

This chapter aims to provide an analytical framework within which competition problems of the communications sector can be described and classified. The term 'competition problem' here refers to any practice of an SMP[36] undertaking which is aimed either at driving competitors out of the market (or prevent them from entering the market) or at exploiting consumers. As the imposition of remedies in the new regulatory framework does not presuppose that an abuse of market power has actually occurred, the problems identified should be regarded as potential or possible competition problems which can be assumed to emerge under particular circumstances.

The remedy-discussion in the following chapters, however, does not assume that each of the problems automatically occurs in a particular situation. Rather, Chapter 5 includes an incentive-discussion on a general level, where the incentives of an SMP operator to engage in a certain type of exclusionary or exploitative behaviour are elaborated. Of course, regulatory intervention will always have to be based on the particular (national) circumstances at hand, which are identified in the course of a detailed market analysis but are beyond the scope of this document.

Within the framework, 27 standard competition problems are identified. Such a classification should allow – in a second step, dealt with in Chapter 5 – to match these standard competition problems to standard remedies of the new regulatory framework. The framework focuses on the behavioural dimension of competition problems, as it is above all the behaviour of a dominant undertaking which can be addressed by the remedies of the new regulatory framework. However, this does not mean that structural or legal/regulatory barriers to entry as described in Chapter 1 will not be taken into account in the following consideration nor does it mean that they are not relevant when NRAs make their decisions on regulatory intervention. In order to impose the least burdensome and most effective remedy based on the principles set out in Chapter 4, it is essential to identify the source of market power, giving rise to the existence of a particular competition problem. This is only possible if the NRA is aware of structural and/or regulatory barriers to entry in a particular market.

---

[36] The notion of SMP in the context of this document must not be confused with the notion of SMP in the ONP framework, where an SMP position automatically triggered a series of remedies. As argued in Chapter 3 of this document, remedies under the new framework will always have to be based on the nature of the problem identified, proportionate and justified. Also SMP is now defined as dominance in line with the European Jurisprudence.

This chapter is structured as follows: First, the framework within which the standard competition problems are classified will be explained. Second, the identified competition problems as well as the effects they may entail will be described in detail.

The framework is quite general and might not only be suited to deal with the 'old, well-known' competition problems with all their peculiarities, but might also prove helpful when approaching new unforeseen ones. It is an analytical approach and does not only aim at providing a classification scheme but also at unravelling relations and causalities between certain types of behaviour and phenomena commonly referred to as 'competition problems'.

2.2 The classification framework

In the field of sector-specific ex ante regulation, national regulatory authorities will have to deal with undertakings which have significant market power (SMP) on one or several communications markets. Three kinds of problems may arise in such situations: First, the dominant undertaking may attempt to transfer (leverage) its market power to an adjacent vertically or horizontally related market; second, the undertaking may engage in practices to defend its SMP position by building up barriers to entry (e.g. increasing consumers switching costs) and finally it might engage in what might be called 'textbook monopoly behaviour', such as excessive pricing, the provision of low quality, and inefficient production.

A competition problem in this context can usually best be described in terms of the behaviour of one or more undertaking(s) with market power. The behaviour in turn rests on one or more strategic variables the undertaking has at its disposal.

To prevent anti-competitive or exploitative behaviour by ex ante regulation, a remedy usually will prescribe the behaviour an undertaking is supposed and not supposed to engage in[37]. By preventing the SMP undertaking from leveraging its market power into adjacent markets or from erecting barriers to entry on the SMP market, NRAs can promote market entry and competition in those markets. Where entry is unlikely to occur or where market power persists due to first mover advantages, NRAs have to protect consumers against exploitative behaviour and inefficiencies. Thus, to be able to choose a suitable remedy and to recognize the root causes of a competition problem, knowledge about the global market constellation and the source of market power is vital. This knowledge will be gained in the market definition and analysis stage of the process.

Against this background, competition problems are fitted into two dimensions: One of them is the market-dimension. Here, four cases are distinguished:

- *Case 1 - Vertical Leveraging:* An undertaking is operating on both a wholesale and a vertically related retail market[38] (i.e., is vertically integrated) and has SMP on the upstream (i.e., wholesale) market. This is by far the most prevalent case in communications markets, at least as far as fixed networks are concerned. The SMP operator owns some essential upstream input and may attempt to transfer its market power onto the potentially competitive retail market. If leveraging is successful, the undertaking will then have market power on both, the wholesale and the retail market.

- *Case 2 - Horizontal Leveraging (retail or wholesale):* An undertaking is operating on two not vertically related markets, and has SMP in one of them. Under certain

---

[37] This prescription might be more or less precise. In some cases, a specific price is set or a detailed access obligation is imposed. In other cases an obligation not to unduly discriminate might suffice (see also the discussion in section 3.2.1.).

[38] In the following, the upstream market is referred to as the wholesale market and the downstream market as the retail market. The same considerations apply, however, for any two vertically related markets, i.e., also two wholesale markets.

circumstances (no perfect competition on the linked market and/or high barriers to entry) it may then try to transfer its market power from the market where it has SMP to the related market. Horizontal leveraging may occur between retail markets as well as between wholesale markets or between a wholesale and a (not vertically related) retail market.

- *Case 3 - Single market dominance (retail or wholesale):* Competition problems may also pertain to only one market (although the undertaking might be operating on two or more markets). Here, the company having SMP in the market may engage in the erection of entry barriers in order to protect its dominant position, or, if its position is sufficiently safe, may engage in 'textbook monopoly behaviour', i.e., excessive pricing, price discrimination, productive inefficiencies, etc., leading to losses in overall welfare. Such behaviour may pertain to a wholesale as well as to a retail market.

- *Case 4 - Termination:* This refers to a situation of two-way access (as opposed to one-way access dealt with in case 1) in which two or several networks in a first step negotiate interconnection agreements at the wholesale level and in a second step set their prices on the retail market where they may or may not be in competition with one another. The problems discussed in this case may arise in particular if undertakings have SMP on their individual call termination markets. Although the problems described in this context may also be subsumed under the other three constellations, due to its particularities and its particular practical importance it is considered as an own case here.

The other dimension attributed to the competition problems is a 'cause-and-effect' type dimension. Thereby, each competition problem is depicted in the following way: In order to leverage or exploit its market power, an undertaking will engage in a certain type of behaviour. The behaviour, on the one hand, rests on one or more strategic variables the undertaking can dispose of and, on the other hand, will lead to certain effects, affecting either the dominant undertaking's competitors (or potential competitors) or directly the dominant firm's consumers. The 'cause-effect' dimension is therefore made up of the following parts:

Strategic variables: price, quality, time, information, etc. Behaviour: price discrimination, quality discrimination, delaying tactics, withholding of information, etc. Effects: raising rivals' costs, restriction of competitors' sales, margin squeeze, foreclosure, etc. In practice, there is – beside the market constellation and the (possible) behaviour of the dominant undertaking – a range of other circumstances like national particularities, links to other markets, or transnational effects, which have to be taken into account by NRAs when designing remedies as well, but as this chapter aims at developing a general framework, they are not further considered in this context.

Of course, the framework adopted is only one of many possibilities to approach competition problems. Frequently it will be difficult to distinguish between causes and effects, and sometimes even the distinction between behaviour and effect might be ambiguous (e.g. in the case of margin squeeze, which can be either regarded as a behaviour in itself or as a result of – primarily – price discrimination on the wholesale market and/or predatory pricing on the retail market). This does not mean that the approach adopted is arbitrary, however. Rather, it has been attempted to depict standard competition problems in a way which allows them to be addressed with the remedies of the new regulatory framework.

2.3 Standard competition problems

In the framework described above, and based on experiences of NRAs, 27 standard competition problems have been identified and outlined in Table 1. They are based on a stock-taking exercise performed by the IRG working groups, on the inputs received in course of the ERG consultation in June/July 2003,[39] and on several documents dealing with competition problems and/or regulation[40]. Most of the problems identified therefore are based on NRA's experience and reflect communications markets reality. In addition, some problems are considered which are frequently discussed in the literature related to telecommunications markets and competition policy. The list is guide only and does not preclude NRAs from identifying other (potential) problems which may be addressed by remedies of the new regulatory framework. The 27 competition problems rest on the behaviour-dimension of the framework, as a competition problem usually can best be described in terms of the behaviour of one or more undertaking(s) with market power. Furthermore, the remedies of the new regulatory framework (Art 9-13 of the Access Directive and Art 17-19 of the Universal Service Directive) are primarily designed to address the behaviour of SMP undertakings.

The standard competition problems are such that each of them can potentially be identified as a competition problem which has to be addressed by the NRA in course of the market analysis. Whereas most competition problems are dealing with endogenous entry barriers, i.e., behaviour leading to market foreclosure, some problems are dealing with exploitative behaviour or inefficiencies, which do not aim at lessening competition but nevertheless result into welfare losses due to allocative and/or productive inefficiencies.

Table 1: Standard competition problems

Market constellation	Competition problems
Case 1: vertical leveraging	1.1. refusal to deal/denial of access 1.2. discriminatory use or withholding of information 1.3. delaying tactics 1.4. bundling/tying 1.5. undue requirements 1.6. quality discrimination 1.7. strategic design of product 1.8. undue use of information about competitors 1.9. price discrimination 1.10. cross-subsidisation 1.11. predatory pricing
Case 2: horizontal leveraging	2.1. bundling/tying 2.2. cross-subsidisation
Case 3: single market dominance	3.1. strategic design of product to raise consumers' switching costs 3.2. contract terms to raise consumers' switching costs 3.3. exclusive dealing 3.4. over-investment 3.5. predatory pricing 3.6. excessive pricing 3.7. price discrimination 3.8. lack of investment 3.9. excessive costs/inefficiency 3.10. low quality
Case 4: termination	4.1. tacit collusion 4.2. excessive pricing 4.3. price discrimination 4.4. refusal to deal/denial to interconnect

---

[39] Public call for input on regulatory remedies, see http://www.erg.eu.int/documents/index_en.htm.
[40] See, e.g., European Commission (1998), Oxera (2002), Cave (2002) or OFT (1999a).

2.3.1 Case 1: Vertical leveraging

Case 1 deals with competition problems arising in the context of vertical leveraging. Leveraging, in general, can be described as any behaviour by which an undertaking with SMP on one market transfers its market power to another, potentially competitive market. As leveraging is an attempt to drive rivals out of the potentially competitive market, to limit their sales or profits, or to prevent them from entering the market, it can also be regarded as a form of foreclosure.

Vertical leveraging can be defined as '... any dominant firm's practice that denies proper access to an essential input it produces to some users of this input, with the intent of extending monopoly power from one segment of the market (the bottleneck segment) to the other (the potentially competitive segment)'[41]. Leveraging is not explicitly depicted in the framework set out above, but can be thought of as a 'heading' for all competition problems in case 1 and 2. As leveraging creates market power in a potentially competitive market, it is usually detrimental to overall welfare.

With regard to remedies, it is helpful to distinguish three types of vertical leveraging strategies:

- An outright refusal to deal/denial of access

- Leveraging by means of non-price variables

- Leveraging by means of pricing

2.3.1.1 Refusal to deal/denial of access

An undertaking with SMP on the wholesale market may attempt to leverage its market power by denying access to or refusing to deal with undertakings operating downstream and competing with the incumbent's retail affiliate. 'Refusal to deal can create competitive harm when a firm with SMP controls an input or inputs which are essential for other players to be able to operate/compete in (downstream) markets. In particular, a firm which operates in two vertically related markets and which has SMP in the upstream market may (unfairly) strengthen its position in the downstream market if it refuses to supply downstream competitors'[42].

In European case law refusal to deal covers not only situations where a dominant undertaking absolutely refuses to supply a customer, but also those circumstances in which the supplier is only prepared to supply a good or a service on unreasonable terms. The approach chosen in this document will deal separately with plain refusal to deal and 'unreasonable terms' on information, quality, price, etc.

Under standard economic analysis, 'for refusal to deal to constitute an abuse of a dominant position, it must not only harm a consumer or a competitor, but must also substantially weaken competition in the relevant downstream market'[43]. Taking into account the effects on retail markets is not only standard in merger analysis but is also emphasized in Art 12 (1) of the Access Directive.

---

[41] Rey/Tirole (1997, p. 1).
[42] Oxera (2003, p. 7).
[43] Oxera (2003, p. 8).

Refusal to deal/denial of access can lead directly to foreclosure if the wholesale product is a necessary input, but may alternatively lead to raising rivals' costs if bypass (e.g. in-house production) is possible but associated with higher production costs.

2.3.1.2 Non-price issues

Discriminatory use or withholding of information refers to a discriminatory practice where the SMP operator on the wholesale market provides its retail arm with information it does not provide to other downstream-undertakings or refuses to supply other information which is necessary to take up the wholesale offer and/or to supply the retail service. An example here would be a fixed network operator refusing to provide its retail competitors information about future changes in the network topology. In the worst case, the independent retail-undertakings are not able to provide the retail service, which then amounts to the case of refusal to deal. In other cases the lack of information will 'only' increase rivals' costs.

Delaying tactics, sometimes also referred to as 'provisioning squeeze', denominates a behaviour where the SMP undertaking does not refuse to supply a certain input to its downstream competitors but the independent undertakings are supplied at a later point in time compared to the retail affiliate of the SMP undertaking. Delaying tactics may come in various forms, such as lengthy negotiations or pretended technical problems. The motivation for such a behaviour can be twofold: First, if an established retail market is opened up to competition which would erode the dominant undertaking's margins on that market, the dominant undertaking may attempt to delay entry as long as possible in order to protect its monopoly rents. Second, if a new retail product or service is introduced by the incumbent, delaying tactics will, in addition to the first point, result into a first mover advantage, which is not achieved if the required wholesale product is provided to all retail undertakings at the same point in time. A first mover advantage may increase rivals' costs relative to the first mover and may also restrict competitors' sales.

Bundling/Tying: Tying refers to the practice of conditioning the sale of one product on the sale of another product. Bundling is usually referred to as a special case of tying, where the products are sold in fixed proportions. In the case of two vertically related markets, an SMP undertaking on the wholesale market can condition the sale of a necessary input on the sale of other, not necessary products or services and in this way can raise the costs of its downstream rivals. If the price of the wholesale bundle is larger than the retail price minus the retail costs of an efficient operator, tying amounts to a margin squeeze.

Undue requirements are any contract terms, which require a particular behaviour of the downstream competitor, which is unnecessary for the provision of the upstream product but raises rivals' costs or restricts rivals' sales. Examples for such undue requirements are the stipulation of a particular (more expensive) technology, bank guarantees, security payments, or information requirements, for example data about the competitors' customers beyond the extent which might be economically or technically justified in certain cases. Customer data may be used by the incumbent to target competitors' customers with tailor-made retail offers and induce them to switch (see also 'undue use of information about competitors' below).

By quality discrimination, the dominant firm can either raise rivals' costs or restrict its rivals' sales. The costs are raised if additional efforts or investments are required to offset the quality-disadvantage, whereas demand is reduced if the difference in quality cannot be offset and is perceived by retail consumers. An example for the second instance would be an incumbent who gives priority to its own traffic at network bottlenecks or, in case of network breakdowns, gives priority to its own customers when fixing the problem.

The strategic design of product characteristics is another possibility for the upstream SMP undertaking to put its downstream competitors on a disadvantage. Strategic design can embrace all types of product characteristics like design, compatibility, norms and standards, etc. and can either raise rivals' costs or restrict competitors' sales. The SMP undertaking may, for example, use standards which are easy to meet for their own retail arm but not for alternative operators, which may have to make additional investments to ensure compatibility or make access/ interconnection technically possible.

Issues of undue use of information about competitors may arise when a dominant undertaking on the wholesale market provides access to a competitor on the retail market and obtains certain information about the customers of the retail undertaking. Based on this information, the retail arm of the dominant undertaking can target its competitors' customers with tailor-made offers and so can restrict its competitors' sales and/or raise its rivals' costs (as competitors might have to increase their marketing efforts). If the dominant undertaking receives planning information from a potential downstream competitor it might even be able to build 'Chinese walls' around the customer and so prevent its rival from entry.

2.3.1.3 Pricing issues

Price discrimination can be used by a vertically integrated undertaking with SMP on the wholesale market to raise its rivals' costs downstream and induce a margin squeeze. This is achieved by charging a higher price (which usually is above costs) to downstream competitors than implicitly charged to the own retail affiliate, i.e. discrimination between internal and external provision.

Cross-subsidisation involves two prices in two markets. Whereas in one market (the SMP market) a price above costs is charged, in the other market (the market where the SMP-position is leveraged to) a price below costs (predatory pricing) is charged. Cross-subsidisation is not anti-competitive in itself. However, if one price is excessive and the other price is predatory, it can be used to leverage market power and foreclose a related, potentially competitive market. If the market where the high price is charged is a wholesale market and the market where the predatory price is charged is a retail market and the dominant undertaking is vertically integrated (case 1), cross-subsidisation will result in a margin squeeze.

'Predatory pricing' occurs, inter alia, where a dominant firm sells a good or service below costs of production for a sustained period of time, with the intention of deterring entry, or putting a rival out of business, enabling the dominant firm to further increase its market power and later its accumulated profits'[44]. According to economic analysis, predatory pricing has the following characteristics: (i) the price charged is below costs,

(ii) competitors are either driven out of the market or excluded, and (iii) the undertaking is able to recoup its losses. Predation thus involves a trade-off for the predator between the short-run and the long-run. Consumers will benefit in the short run from low prices but will suffer in the long rung from the elimination of competitors. In practice, predation is hard to prove, especially in dynamic markets with high fixed costs, multi-product firms and long-run business cases.

A vertically integrated undertaking with SMP upstream supplying a necessary input to its retail competitors might engage in predatory pricing on the retail level to expose its downstream rivals to a margin squeeze, restrict their sales, and drive them out of the market.

2.3.2 Case 2: Horizontal leveraging

Bundling/Tying: In the case of two horizontally related markets, bundling/tying of an SMP product with a potentially competitive product may reduce rivals' demand or increase the

---

[44] See Notice on the application of the competition rules to access agreements in the telecommunications sector (98/C 265/02) p. 16.

costs of entry in the potentially competitive market and thus may lead to foreclosure. Bundling/Tying can also be used by a dominant undertaking to defend its dominant position in the SMP market[45]. In particular, bundling/tying can have anti-competitive effects if the implicit price of the tied good is below cost and/or if the bundle cannot be replicated by competitors and the bundled goods are positively correlated in demand.

An example for anti-competitive bundling might be an operator with SMP on the retail market for access to the public (fixed) telephone network, bundling the access product with a package of call minutes. As this is a bundle between an SMP product (access) and a potentially competitive product (call services), the two products are positively correlated in demand, and as the bundle cannot be replicated by (most) alternative operators, competitive concerns may arise.

Cross-subsidization: Leveraging by cross-subsidisation as discussed above (Section 2.3.1.3.) may also occur between two non vertically related markets. Here, the SMP undertaking may attempt to drive its competitors out of the market by setting a price below costs in the potentially competitive market, while the losses are covered by profits from the SMP market. Thus, cross-subsidisation may – in the same way as a predation strategy – lead to a restriction of competitors' sales in the potentially competitive market.

2.3.3 Case 3: Single market dominance

Besides the leveraging issues as discussed above, three different types of behaviour are of concern to regulators in the case of an SMP position on a particular market:

- Entry deterrence: The SMP undertaking might engage in practices to erect barriers to entry in order to protect its SMP position against potential entrants.

- Exploitative behaviour: The SMP undertaking may exploit customers by setting an excessive price and/or by engaging in price discrimination.

- Productive inefficiencies: The SMP undertaking might fail to produce efficiently.

2.3.3.1 Entry deterrence

Strategic design of product to raise consumers' switching costs: If only one market is involved, strategic design of a product by an SMP undertaking can target raising consumers' switching costs, for example by compatibility with complementary products produced by the SMP undertaking (lock-in effect).

Contract terms to raise consumers' switching costs can be used by a dominant undertaking to raise the costs of competitors and new entrants, which have to increase their efforts to persuade customers to switch. Examples for such contract designs are lengthy contract duration and excessive penalties in case of premature termination, loyalty programs, or special rates for closed user groups. The SMP undertaking may also attempt to raise high charges on number portability and to impose administrative barriers on customers willing to switch. Such practices will also restrict competitors' sales.

Exclusive dealing refers to an exclusive vertical relation between the SMP undertaking and another undertaking. It can be of two forms: (i) The SMP undertaking on the wholesale market has an exclusive contract with a retailer, stating that the retailer is allowed to buy only from the SMP undertaking; (ii) the SMP undertaking on the retail market has an exclusive contract with a wholesale company stating that this company is only allowed to sell its products to the SMP undertaking. Although exclusive vertical relations can increase

---

[45] A number of economic models exist which explore if and under which conditions bundling/tying is profitable. For a summary see Nalebuff (2003) or Inderst (2003).

efficiency (e.g. by the internalisation of negative external effects or by the resolution of hold-up problems, i.e., in general, by synergistic effects) they also can be used as an instrument of foreclosing the SMP market: Exclusive contracts of the form (i), for example, '... can make it more difficult for existing competitors at the upstream level to expand their sales, or for potential competitors at the upstream level to obtain access to retail service customers'[46]. Exclusive dealing can thus lead to a restriction of competitors' sales or can increase rival's costs and in this way can foreclose the SMP market.

Over-investment: In the presence of economies of scale, the incumbent may – under certain circumstances – deter entry by investing in excess capacity. If the investments are sunk it can commit itself to an aggressive entry response, i.e., to increase output. With the increased output, prices fall and entry will be unprofitable. The circumstances under which such a strategy is viable are rather specific, however[47].

Predatory pricing: As discussed in Section 2.3.1.3., predatory pricing may lead – under certain circumstances – to a restriction of competitors' sales and thus to foreclosure.

2.3.3.2   Exploitative behaviour

Excessive pricing: According to economic analysis, prices can be considered excessive if they allow the undertaking to sustain profits higher than it could expect to earn in a competitive market (super-normal profits). Undertakings with market power will usually set their prices above costs, at a level which maximizes their profits given consumers' demand. As quantity, consumer surplus, and total surplus (total welfare) fall short of their values under competitive conditions in such a case, there is potential for regulatory intervention.

Price discrimination: Economic analysis[48] suggests that price discrimination occurs when two or more similar goods are sold at prices, which are in different ratios to costs of production. This includes cases where similar goods produced at the same costs are sold at different prices as well as cases where products are sold at the same price although the costs of production differ. In order to be able to discriminate on price, three conditions have to be fulfilled: (i) the undertaking has to have (at least some) market power, (ii) it has to be able to sort customers, and (iii) it has to be able to prevent resale.

If only one SMP market is involved (as in case 3), the effects of price discrimination are ambiguous. In some cases, price discrimination may increase welfare compared to situations without price discrimination, especially when total output rises. In the presence of large fixed costs, for example, where marginal cost pricing is not viable, price discrimination can be desirable[49]. Nevertheless, as long as market power exists, one or all prices are likely to be above costs, and welfare will usually fall short of its maximum value under competition. Regulatory intervention might then be justified.

2.3.3.3   Productive inefficiencies

Lack of investment, excessive costs/inefficiency, and low quality: As J. R. Hicks already noted in 1935, 'the best of all monopoly profits is a quiet life'. Whereas undertakings exposed to the pressure of competition constantly have to strive to reduce costs and improve quality (and make the necessary investments to achieve these goals), a dominant undertaking with no or insignificant actual and potential competition may fail to do so. This may result in inefficiencies, inferior quality and lack of investment, results which have negative welfare effects (productive inefficiencies) compared to a hypothetical competitive situation.

---

[46] Oxera (2003, p. 13).
[47] See, for example Gilbert (1989).
[48] See Varian (1989, pp. 599, 600).
[49] See Laffont/Tirole (2000, p. xv).

Lack of investment might also occur in situations where the dominant undertaking is operating two potentially competing platforms, as for example in the case of broadband internet access via cable networks and xDSL. This problem in particular has been addressed by Art 8 of the Directive 2002/77/EC[50].

2.3.4 Case 4: Termination

With regard to termination, two cases have to be distinguished: (i) the case of interconnection between networks which are competing for customers at the retail market, such as fixed-to-fixed (F2F) and mobile-to-mobile (M2M) telephony, and (ii) the case of two networks which are not (yet) competing for customers at the retail market, e.g. fixed-to-mobile (F2M) or mobile-to-fixed (M2F) telephony[51].

Excessive pricing: The main source of this competition problem is that network operators may have significant market power over the termination of calls on their networks. This is likely to be the case whenever a calling-party-pays principle is in force, recipients of the call do not sufficiently care about the costs other parties have when calling them, and there is no significant countervailing buyer power. Operators then have incentives to charge an excessive price on their termination services. This is likely to lead to allocative inefficiencies and a distorted pricing structure. This holds even true if the profits made on incoming calls are competed away on the retail market.

This problem may particularly arise in the F2M and F2F situation. In the case of F2M termination with regulated fixed networks and unregulated mobile networks, mobile operators with SMP on the market for call termination may exploit their market power and charge an excessive price to fixed network operators while, at the same time, they may cross-subsidize their retail business, e.g. in the form of free handsets. Economic theory suggests that, if retail tariffs are cross-subsidized with profits from the termination business, welfare might be increased to the extent that fixed network customers are able to reach more mobile customers than without cross-subsidisation and mobile customers benefit from lower prices. Without regulation, however, mobile termination charges may nevertheless be too high from an overall-welfare point of view. The negative effect from the increased prices particularly to fixed network customers is likely to outweigh the positive effects mentioned above[52]. The problem is likely to be exacerbated if fixed network customers cannot distinguish between different mobile networks and thus are unaware of the actual costs of the call. In such situations, mobile operators may raise the price of termination even above the monopoly level[53]. The case of M2F is under the prevailing (regulatory) circumstances less crucial, although potentially similar distortions as in the F2M case may arise. Regulatory decisions in one sector will, of course, always have an impact on the other sector, which has to be taken into account by NRAs when evaluating the effects of regulatory action.

The excessive pricing problem is less likely to occur in an M2M situation. As long as traffic between networks is reasonably balanced and cost structures are symmetric, termination charges are likely to be reciprocal and therefore termination payments may cancel out. Even if networks are asymmetric, the fact that they are competing at the retail market leads to other considerations when negotiating interconnection agreements compared to a F2M situation. This is reflected in the other competition problems of section 2.3.4.

---

[50] Commission Directive 2002/77/EC of 16 September 2002 on competition in the markets for electronic communications networks and services, OJ 17.9.2003 L 249/21.
[51] Whether fixed and mobile networks are in competition on the retail market or not has to be determined in course of the market definition/market analysis.
[52] See Armstrong (2002) and Wright (2000).
[53] See Gans/King (1999).

Tacit collusion: Economic theory suggests that – under certain circumstances – the setting of reciprocal high or low termination charges can be used as an instrument of tacit collusion between networks which are in competition on the retail market[54]. This problem thus may occur in situations of M2M or F2F interconnection. Tacit collusion leads to prices above costs and thus to allocative inefficiencies. The conditions under which this result emerges are rather specific, however, and therefore this type of tacit collusion may not often be observed in practice, in particular if networks are of different size and have different cost structures.

Price discrimination: The problem of price discrimination to foreclose the market pertains mainly to the M2M situation. The incumbent operator(s) may seek to foreclose the retail market by charging a high (above-cost) termination charge to other networks whereas implicitly charging a lower price internally. This leads to high costs for off-net calls for other operators at the wholesale level and thus to high prices for off-net calls at the retail level. On-net calls, on the other hand, are associated with lower costs and thus with lower retail prices. Such a price structure creates network externalities ('tariff-mediated network externalities'[55]) and thus puts small networks with few participants at a disadvantage. The disadvantage is larger the higher the termination charge and thus the higher the difference between the price of an on-net and an off-net call is.

Refusal to deal/Denial to interconnect: As with the previous competition problem, a refusal to deal / denial to interconnect is targeted at foreclosing the market to new entrants. This problem could be observed in the M2M as well as in the F2F or F2M situation. Whereas it is vital for the entrant to be connected to established networks, the incumbent(s) can manage easily without interconnecting to the entrant as long as the number of the entrant's subscribers is low enough. A refusal to deal restricts competitors' sales and thus is likely to lead to foreclosure. As foreclosure may substantially lessen competition, it is likely to be detrimental to overall welfare. For example, the F2F situation is usually characterized by an incumbent operator who holds most of the access lines and a number of smaller firms most of whom only hold a few access lines each. The primary concern in this case is a denial to interconnect by the incumbent operator leading to foreclosure of the retail market, which is dealt with in the competition problem 'refusal to deal/denial to interconnect'. Once the dominant operator is subject to an obligation to interconnect and a regulated termination charge, however, alternative operators may have incentives to exploit their market power on the termination markets and set prices above costs.

2.3.5 Possible effects

The 'effects' described in this section result from one or more standard competition problems as discussed in the previous section. The causal relations between effects and competition problems are depicted in figure 1 at the end of this section.

First mover advantage: The term first mover advantage refers to the economic advantage the company which is first in a market has over other companies which enter this market at a later point in time. First mover advantages can pertain to the supply side (the cost function) as well as to the demand side. Supply side first mover advantages include network externalities and learning by making cost reductions, whereas demand side advantages primarily result from customer lock-in effects. A first mover advantage thus can be said to raise rivals' costs (relative to the first mover) or restrict competitors' sales. A first mover advantage only is a problem if it is artificially achieved, e.g. by delaying tactics on the wholesale market. If first mover advantages are strong, they can lead to foreclosure of the retail market.

---

[54] See Laffont/Tirole (2000), Armstrong (2002) or Gans/King (2000).
[55] See Laffont/Tirole (2000).

Margin squeeze: A margin squeeze, sometimes also referred to as price squeeze, occurs when:

- a dominant provider supplies an 'upstream' product A which is itself (or is closely related to) a component of a 'downstream' product A+B (product B is supplied by the dominant provider only to itself: those who compete against A+B will supply their own alternative to B).

- the implicit charge by the dominant provider to itself for B (i.e. the difference between the prices at which it supplies A+B and A only) is so low that a reasonably efficient competitor cannot profitably compete against A+B[56].

A margin squeeze can be effected in three ways[57]: (i) The SMP undertaking can charge a price above costs for the wholesale product to its competitors but (implicitly) a lower price to its own retail arm; (ii) it can charge a cost-based price to all retail undertakings but may set a predatory price on the retail market; finally (iii) it might charge a price above costs on the wholesale market, and at the same time charge a predatory price on the retail market. This behaviour may also result in cross-subsidisation.

Although the dominant undertaking may set a margin between its downstream retail price and upstream wholesale charge (paid by downstream competitors) that is insufficient to cover its downstream costs, on an 'end-to-end' basis, i.e. aggregating across the firm's upstream and downstream activities, the firm may be profitable (in contrast to the case of predatory pricing where the firm suffers short-term losses). An equally (or more efficient) downstream competitor could be unable to compete, because, in effect, it is being charged a higher price for the upstream input than its competitor, the vertically integrated firm's own downstream arm.

Exposed to a margin squeeze, a retail competitor in general will not be able to cover its costs and will be driven out of the market. If the competitor has some market power on the retail market (for example because of product differentiation) or if it is sufficiently more efficient than the dominant undertaking, a margin squeeze might result in partial foreclosure (losses of market share and/or profits) only.

Although margin squeeze also has a behavioural aspect it is classified as an effect here, as it can be the result of different behaviours of the dominant undertaking. When designing remedies it might be important to be aware of the particular behaviour leading to a margin squeeze (i.e., in particular, price discrimination upstream and/or predatory pricing downstream).

Raising rivals' costs is a quite general expression for all practices, which – in one form or another – negatively influence competitors' and potential competitors' cost functions. As can be seen from figure 1, most anti-competitive behaviour will increase rivals' costs.

Restriction of competitors' sales is defined here as the result of any behaviour of the dominant undertaking, which does not (or not only) negatively impact the cost function of its rivals, but their demand function. As depicted in figure 1, there are several ways in which an SMP undertaking can restrict its competitors' sales.

Foreclosure is any behaviour of a dominant firm, which aims at excluding competitors from the market. Foreclosure can be 'complete', in which case competitors are driven out of the market or do not enter the market, or 'partial', whereby competitors do survive, but suffer losses of market share or profits. An undertaking will exert foreclosure only if it can – in the

---

[56] In the event that the price paid for A is not transparent, accounting separation might be needed to establish the price paid by the incumbent's retail arm.

[57] See Canoy, et al (2002, pp. 26-31).

short or in the long run – increase its profits by doing so. As foreclosure reduces or eliminates competition and creates market power in potentially competitive markets, it is usually also detrimental to overall welfare. Behaviour leading to foreclosure is frequently referred to as 'anti-competitive behaviour' throughout this document.

Negative welfare effects here denotes the result of a certain behaviour which does not lead to foreclosure and/or leveraging, i.e., is not targeted towards competitors, but still has a negative impact on total welfare. Two cases can be distinguished here: allocative inefficiency, which leads to deadweight welfare losses (i.e. consumer and total welfare could be increased by increasing total output), and productive inefficiency, where the dominant undertaking falls short of producing a given output with the minimum of inputs. Allocative inefficiency results from excessive pricing and may also result from price discrimination; productive inefficiency may become manifest in excessive costs, low quality or lack of investment. As discussed above, price discrimination may not always be detrimental to welfare and thus should be subject to analysis on a case-by-case basis.

Figure 1 finally depicts each of the identified competition problems together with the strategic variable(s) it is based on, as well as with the anti-competitive and welfare effects it may entail. Therefore, the effects-side has been divided into two stages: The 'immediate effects' (first mover advantage, margin squeeze, raising rivals' costs, and restriction of competitors' sales) and the 'ultimate effect', which is 'foreclosure' in many cases.

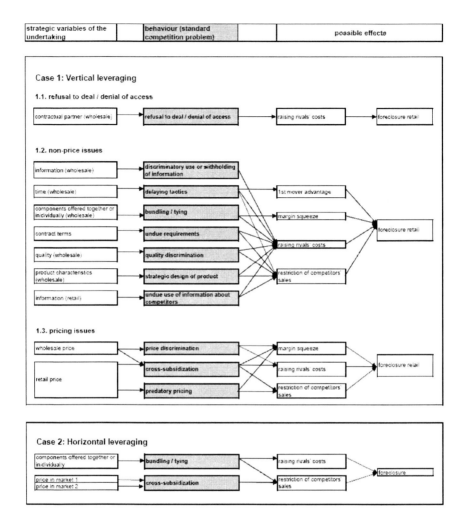

Figure 1a: Overview of standard competition problems, cases 1 and 2

strategic variables of the undertaking		behaviour (standard competition problem)		possible effects

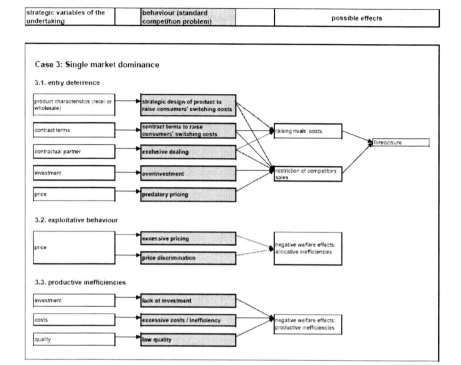

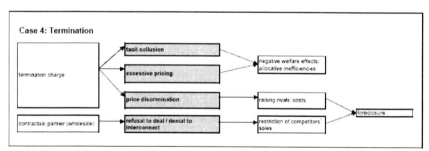

Figure 1b: Overview of standard competition problems, cases 3 and 4

3.   Remedies Available

3.1   Introduction

The aim of the Access Directive is establish a regulatory framework, in accordance with internal market principles, for the relationships between suppliers of networks and services that will result in sustainable competition, interoperability of electronic communications services and consumer benefits.

As outlined in the introduction, when we are considering remedies, there is a presumption that SMP has been identified on a market that is susceptible to ex ante regulation. Throughout this document remedies are synonymous with the concept of obligations under the Directives.

The Access Directive and the Universal Services Directive contain a list of obligations that may be imposed on operators with SMP in wholesale and retail markets respectively, but also provide for NRAs to impose access obligations not explicitly listed, subject to the prior agreement with the Commission[58]. Due to the exceptional nature of these remedies, the specific circumstances in which they may be considered and the veto power of the Commission it is not possible to provide any guidance on this issue in this document.

Obligations listed in the Access Directive include:

- a *transparency* obligation (Art 9) making public specified information (accounting information, technical specification, network characteristics, prices etc.);

- a *non-discrimination* obligation (Art 10), that is to apply equivalent conditions in equivalent circumstances, and not to discriminate in favour of the regulated firm's own subsidiaries or partners;

- an *accounting separation* obligation (Art 11) to make transparent the internal transfer prices to the regulated firm's own downstream operation in order to ensure compliance with a non-discrimination obligation or to prevent unfair cross-subsidies;

- an *access* obligation (Art 12) that consists of obligations to meet reasonable requests for access or interconnection or use specific network elements. These may include a range of obligations, including an obligation to negotiate in good faith over terms and conditions of providing access; and

- a *price control and cost accounting* obligation (Art 13), which can require operators to set cost-oriented access charges or the imposition of a price control on the regulated firm. This is restricted to cases where the market analysis suggests that otherwise access charges might be sustained at an excessively high level, or where the firm might engage in a margin squeeze to the detriment of consumers[59].

The Universal Service Directive provides for inter alia the imposition of obligations on undertakings with SMP in specific markets. The aim of the Universal Service Directive is to ensure the availability throughout the Community of good quality publicly available services through effective competition and choice and to deal with circumstances in which the needs of end users are not satisfactorily met by the market.

Obligations mentioned in the Universal Service Directive as being capable under certain circumstances of being placed on undertakings with SMP in specific markets include the prohibition of excessive or predatory pricing, undue price discrimination and the unreasonable bundling of services. NRAs may apply retail price caps, individual price controls or measures to orient prices towards costs in order to protect end users whilst promoting effective competition.

All of the above remedies must be based on the nature of the problem identified, proportionate and justified in the light of the basic regulatory objectives of promoting competition, contributing to the development of the internal market, and promoting the interest of citizens.

The remainder of this chapter seeks to examine the predetermined remedies that are available for use by NRAs, how remedies interact and may be mutually dependant, and finally some practical issues surrounding implementation. There is no automatic remedy solution for any given situation and certainly no automatic linking of obligations to construct a particular remedy. The appropriate remedy will at all times be dictated by the specific problems identified by the NRA in any given market.

---

[58] See Article 8, Access Directive [Directive 2002/19/EC].

[59] Article 13(1) of the Access Directive also notes that NRAs shall take into account the investment made by the operator and allow him a reasonable rate of return, taking into account the risks involved.

3.2 Remedies available

The Access and Universal Service Directives give a considerable amount of guidance regarding the use and linkages between the different remedies.

3.2.1 Transparency

Looking first at the transparency obligation[60] it is stated that transparency may be used in relation to 'interconnection and/or access, requiring operators to make public specified information, such as accounting information, technical specifications, network characteristics, terms and conditions for supply and use, and prices.'

This implies that there is a natural linkage between any access or interconnection obligation and a transparency requirement making publicly available any critical technical and/or financial information to make such access or interconnection obligations feasible. Similarly there is a logical linking between the transparency requirements and accounting separation and to non-discrimination[61].

To achieve transparency NRAs may require that operators publish a reference offer for services giving the terms and conditions available at a level of detail dictated by the NRA. In addition there are specific provisions for information regarding unbundled local loop information[62].

It is difficult to see many situations relating to access and interconnection where transparency by itself is likely to be an effective remedy, although it might help identify anti-competitive behaviour that could be dealt with by competition law or deter such behaviour by supporting an implicit threat of regulation. Potentially, NRAs will want to make some of the internal transactions of the SMP firm and the conditions relation to access and interconnections as transparent as possible.

Notwithstanding this, it is logical to assume and indeed the presentation of the transparency obligation seems to suggest that it is really an accompanying obligation with and to other obligations in order to make the overall remedy more effective. For instance, the requirement to behave in a non-discriminatory manner towards competitors requires that parties can observe and compare easily the factors over which discrimination could take place. Additionally, accounting separation as an obligation is a natural complement to transparency in pricing and costing matters. Transparency is a very important obligation as it is a significant counterweight to possible SMP undertakings' strategies in reaction to regulatory obligations. Economic literature[63] observes that where access is given at particular prices, access requirements can be rendered significantly less effective through the use of selected standards, quality degradation, late delivery etc. Transparency, which allows NRAs to specify the precise information to be made available, can render such actions less likely to succeed by at least making such behaviour observable.

3.2.2 Non-discrimination

In general non-discrimination[64] requires that the SMP undertaking 'applies equivalent conditions in equivalent circumstances to other undertakings providing equivalent services, and provides services and information to others under the same conditions and of the same quality as it provides for its own services, or those of its subsidiaries or partners.' This shows that the scope of the non-discrimination obligation clearly covers a firm's internal

---

[60] Directive 2002/19/EC, Article 9.
[61] Directive 2002/19/EC, Articles 9(1) and 9(2).
[62] Directive 2002/19/EC, Article 9(4).
[63] See, e.g., Laffont/Tirole (2000).
[64] Directive 2002/19/EC, Article 10.

processes. The general non-discrimination obligation requires that third party access seekers are treated no less favourably than the operators internal divisions.

Non-discrimination is again an obligation that could be imposed by itself as remedy but in order to be an effective remedy it is likely to need to be combined with a number of other obligations. Transparency is a natural complement to this obligation as the ability to identify behaviour, which could be detrimental through the use of discriminatory practices, depends on the ability to detect such behaviour.

Non-discrimination could be used to get a SMP undertaking to justify self-supplying inputs at greatly reduced prices because of scale where significant scale economies are exhausted much earlier in the production process. Thus, differences in terms and conditions, even where transactions are not necessarily exactly the same, should be justified so that anti-competitive discrimination can be prohibited.

Another problem with non-discrimination is that together with the transparency obligation it can also facilitate and indeed encourage tacit collusion among operators.

In markets which meet many or all of the criteria[65] which would indicate the presence of possible joint dominance, consideration should be given to the extent that such obligations may have adverse consequences, possibly to the extent that alternative or modified obligations might be considered.

3.2.3   Accounting separation

The obligation of accounting separation may impose obligations in relation to specified activities related to interconnection and/or access. This obligation is specifically put in place to support the obligations of transparency and non-discrimination. It may also act to support the NRA in implementing price control and cost accounting obligations. Accounting separation should ensure that a vertically integrated company makes transparent its wholesale prices and its internal transfer prices especially where there is a requirement for non-discrimination. Where necessary, accounting separation may identify cases in which a vertically integrated company engages in unfair cross-subsidy. Unfair cross subsidy would occur where an unjustifiably low price in one product market was facilitated by (excessive) charges in another product market. In addition, in order to obtain a complete overview, accounting separation may, in certain circumstances, cover one or more markets, including markets where the operator does not have SMP[66].

NRAs have discretion to specify the format and accounting methodology to be used. While such accounting information could also be required of any firm through the use of the more general Article 5 of the Framework Directive, such information may not always be available in the normal course of business operations and may need to be specifically required. Information provision under this obligation can provide information which facilitates ongoing monitoring of market situations rather than for the specific purpose of market analysis.

Problems similar to that identified in relation to transparency and non-discrimination also apply in this area regarding co-ordinating effects and the possible promotion or facilitation of tacit collusion. The revelation of business processes, efficiencies and indeed strategies to competitors can be mitigated by appropriate control of the information. Therefore the publication of information by NRAs is conditioned in the sense that it has to contribute to

[65]   See SMP Guidelines, OJ C 165, 11.7.2002, p.6.
[66]   See EC Recommendation C(2005)3480 Recital 5.

an open and competitive market, while national and Community rules on commercial confidentiality are respected[67].

The identification of cross subsidy through the use of accounting separation will often require finely balanced decisions regarding the allocation of joint and common costs in electronic communication markets. Detailed guidance can be found in the Commission Recommendation on accounting separation and cost accounting under the regulatory framework for electronic communications[68] and the ERG Common Position on cost accounting and accounting separation[69].

3.2.4   Access to, and use of, specific network facilities

In an open and competitive market, there should be no restrictions that prevent undertakings from negotiating access and interconnection arrangements between themselves, subject to competition rules. Undertakings which receive requests for access or interconnection should in principle conclude such agreements on a commercial basis, and negotiate in good faith. That this should be the case is envisaged in Article 3 of the Access Directive.

However, the experience of NRAs shows that commercial negotiation is the exception rather than the rule. The Access Directive thus provides that in markets where there continue to be large differences in negotiating power between undertakings, and where some undertakings rely on infrastructure provided by others for delivery of their services, it is appropriate to establish a framework to ensure that the market functions effectively. National regulatory authorities should have the power to secure, where commercial negotiation fails, adequate access and interconnection and interoperability of services in the interest of end-users.

Mandating reasonable requests for access to network infrastructure can be justified as a means of increasing competition, but NRAs need to balance the rights of an infrastructure owner to exploit its infrastructure for its own benefit, and the rights of other service providers to access facilities that are necessary for the provision of competing services. However an important principle is that the imposition of mandated access that increases competition in the short-term should not reduce incentives for competitors to invest in alternative facilities that will secure more competition in the long-term[70].

Obligations can be imposed on operators 'to meet reasonable requests for access to, and use of, specific network elements and associated facilities, inter alia in situations where the national regulatory authority considers that denial of access or unreasonable terms and conditions having a similar effect would hinder the emergence of a sustainable competitive market at the retail level, or would not be in the end-user's interest[71].

Significant detail is given regarding a non-exhaustive set of requirements that may be imposed. There is a broad requirement to give access to specific network elements or facilities including unbundled access to the local loop, to negotiate in good faith, to maintain supply, to provide wholesale services for resale. In addition there are technical, collocation, interoperability, operational support and general interconnection requirements which operators may be required to provide or adhere to.

NRAs may attach conditions covering fairness, reasonableness and timeliness, conditions which are set out in the access requirement and which, as always, are bound by consideration of Article 8 Framework Directive and Article 8(4) of the Access Directive.

---

[67] Art. 11 (2) Access Directive.
[68] EC Recommendation C(2005)3480.
[69] ERG Common Position ERG(05) 29.
[70] Directive 2002/19/EC, Recital 19.
[71] Directive 2002/19/EC, Article 12 (1).

Such requirements may be particularly useful to protect against strategies aimed at covert rather than overt attempts to deny access. Terms which amount to a refusal to grant access can be generalised as being terms which by their monetary level mean that no efficient competitor can be reasonably expected to enter the market bearing in mind that alternative tactics such as delaying access or degrading quality of supply simply raises the effective cost of access for the entrant. Quality of service obligations can be useful to protect against the unreasonable raising of rival's costs through such mechanisms.

Given the scope of this obligation there are a number of considerations that an NRA is explicitly required to take into account when imposing an access requirement[72]. It is worth noting here the general considerations. The obligation imposed must of course be consistent with the provisions of Article 8 and must take into account the feasibility of the action, the viability of using or installing competing infrastructures and the maintenance of the initial investment decision so that long term competition is safeguarded to the greatest extent possible. There is also a requirement on NRAs to take intellectual property rights into consideration as well as the development of any pan-European services.

In terms of the Directives this is by far the most extensively described of any of the obligations reflecting the importance of this obligation and its central role in effecting competitive markets. This obligation can be a stand alone remedy with a general provision to provide access and to negotiate in good faith being the only requirement or it may be accompanied by the full suite of predefined remedies in Articles 9 to 13 of the Access Directive where cost control and non-discrimination obligations are required. In general it will rarely operate as a stand alone remedy; instead it is likely to be accompanied by a transparency obligation, perhaps in the form of a Reference offer or some other mechanism which sets out availability, the technical and financial terms and conditions for such access. Non-discrimination is also likely to accompany such an obligation as often where access is required vertically integrated entities are capable of acting in ways so as to leverage market power from the upstream to the downstream firm's advantage. Imposition of a non-discrimination obligation would protect against such behaviour. NRAs would then have to consider whether sufficient information is available to ensure efficient monitoring of the non-discrimination requirement or whether additional obligations in terms of accounting separation are necessary to ensure effective compliance. Finally, it may often be the case that the actual level of charges for access must be set by the NRA and so a cost control may be imposed. There is a logical sequencing to the remedies that might be required but there is no way to say beforehand which combination or combinations would be appropriate. Such a decision depends on the specific problems identified by the NRA for correction in a specific market.

The access requirements are both broad and extensive; ranging from the provision of services on a wholesale basis for resale by third parties to the provision of access to specific network components and various technical and interoperability requirements. Due to the extensive nature and serious effects attached to this obligation there is explicit reference within the obligation that the NRAs give careful consideration to the investment decisions of both entrants and incumbents to ensure, where possible, that self sustaining competition is encouraged.

3.2.5 Price Control and Cost accounting Obligations

Price control may be necessary when market analysis in a particular market reveals inefficient competition. The regulatory intervention may be relatively light, such as an obligation that prices are reasonable, or much heavier such as an obligation that prices are cost oriented to provide full justification for those prices where competition is not sufficiently strong to prevent excessive pricing. In particular, operators with significant

---

[72] Directive 2002/19/EC, Article 12 (2).

market power should avoid a price squeeze whereby the difference between their retail prices and the access/interconnection prices charged to competitors who provide similar retail services is not adequate to ensure sustainable competition. When a NRA calculates costs the method used should be appropriate to the circumstances taking account of the need to promote efficiency and sustainable competition and maximise consumer benefits[73].

The obligation concerning price control and cost accounting allows that an NRA may impose obligations relating to cost recovery and price controls (including cost orientation of prices and details of the cost accounting methodology to allow their calculation). This obligation is qualified to apply where a lack of effective competition means that the operator concerned might apply either excessive prices or implement a price squeeze with anti-competitive intent (i.e. to the detriment of end-users). In particular, operators with significant market power must avoid a price squeeze whereby the difference between their retail prices and the interconnection/access prices charged to competitors who provide similar retail services is not adequate to ensure sustainable competition.

The burden of proof to demonstrate that charges are derived from costs including a reasonable rate of return on investment rests with the operator. Furthermore, the NRA may require a full justification of the operator's prices and may require their adjustment if appropriate. The freedom of the NRA to use a methodology or a particular cost model to calculate an appropriate charge is unrestricted except to comply with Article 8, general competition law and the requirement that it serves to promote efficiency, sustainable competition and maximise consumer benefits.

NRAs should specify the costing methodology underpinning a price control obligation. Leaving it up to each operator to decide the cost-accounting procedures it wishes to use would limit the measure's contribution to consumer benefit, the enhancement of competition and the development of the internal market[74]. Furthermore, by specifying the costing methodology, NRAs provide adequate transparency and legal certainty for market players[75].

NRAs must ensure that where a cost accounting system is mandated in order to support price controls a description of the cost accounting system is made publicly available, showing at least the main categories under which costs are grouped and the rules used for the allocation of costs.

Compliance with the cost accounting system shall be verified by a qualified independent body, which can be the NRA provided that it has the necessary qualified staff. A statement concerning compliance shall be published annually.

Just as with the access obligation there are implicit references to Article 8 obligations and the need to promote efficiency. It is necessary to take into account all relevant factors when setting the rate of return to ensure investment is maintained, to ensure long term competition and ensuring maximum consumer benefits. It is suggested that guidance can be derived from observing what happens in comparable competitive markets. Such cross-country comparisons require careful analysis as many key cost factors may vary from Member State to Member State (e.g. physical topology). It may also be useful for comparisons within a geographic market to compare related markets within the ICT sector[76].

---

[73] Directive 2002/19/EC, Recital 20.
[74] See Commission's comments in cases FI/2003/0028-0029, FI/2003/0030, FI/2003/0031.
[75] SK/2004/0107, SK/2005/0136.
[76] Cost benchmarks are widely used in the identification of a problem that might require regulatory intervention: a difference between prices and some notion of underlying costs is taken as an indication of market power. This procedure is based on the assumption that, in a competitive market, prices correspond to

The key problem with this obligation would appear to be identifying a price control level which facilitates services competition without reinforcing network market power and the distortions which can result from setting charges too low or too high. This is discussed at more length in Chapters 4 and 5.

3.2.6 Retail Obligations

The Universal Service Directive's aim is to ensure the availability of good quality publicly available services through effective competition and choice and to deal with circumstances in which the needs of end-users are not satisfactorily met by the market[77].

Under the Universal Service Directive regard is given to interventions specifically concerning retail markets that are characterised by the existence of SMP. As a general rule, regulatory controls on retail services should only be imposed where NRAs consider that relevant wholesale measures under the Access Directive or measures regarding carrier selection or pre-selection would fail to achieve the objectives that have been set for NRAs in the Framework Directive[78]. This is a common theme in the new regulatory framework and the Recommendation on relevant markets states, that interventions on the wholesale market are preferable to interventions on the retail market.

'Regulatory controls on retail services can only be imposed where relevant wholesale or related measures would fail to achieve the objective of ensuring effective competition'[79].

Article 17(1)(b) suggests that if measures at the wholesale level taken under the Access Directive or the use of a carrier selection or pre-selection obligation on these markets are not capable of resolving the problems on the market that other obligations on the retail level can be applied. It is clear that the obligations available in the Access Directive may, if appropriate, be available to tackle problems at the retail level[80]. Since the wording of Article 17(2) is deliberately non-exhaustive, the specific retail obligations are not limited to but may include requirements that the identified undertakings do not charge excessive prices, inhibit market entry or restrict competition by setting predatory prices, show undue preference to specific end-users or unreasonably bundle services.

NRAs may apply to such undertakings appropriate retail price cap measures, measures to control individual tariffs, or measures to orient tariffs towards costs or prices on comparable markets, in order to protect end-user interests whilst promoting effective competition.

Where price controls are being put in place at a retail level the necessary and appropriate cost accounting systems must be implemented and the format and accounting methodology used to be specified by the NRA to ensure compliance. A qualified independent body must verify compliance with the cost accounting system, which as mentioned earlier can be the NRA so long as it has the necessary qualified staff. Finally a statement concerning compliance must be published each year.

The problem with imposing obligations at the retail level is that given it is only appropriate to impose such obligations where obligations at the wholesale level are not effective, there is a danger that, even where wholesale controls may be ultimately effective, such controls

---

costs. However the assumption that market prices correspond to costs does not necessarily hold where competition takes place over a bundle of services which are provided subject to economies of scale and scope. In the presence of fixed and common costs, competing firms will structure their relative mark-ups in response to demand conditions.

[77] Directive 2002/22/EC, Article 1.

[78] Directive 2002/22/EC, Recital 26, Article 17. These objectives are to promote competition, to contribute to the development of the internal market and to protect the interests of EU citizens.

[79] Page 15 Recommendation on Relevant Markets.

[80] This would allow for instance, if appropriate, for wholesale line rental (Article 12(1d) of the Access Directive) to be imposed in relation to an identified problem on the retail access market.

may take a prolonged period of time to take effect. In the meantime and in the interest of consumers' welfare it may be necessary to impose some retail price controls. In assessing the need for retail measures, NRAs therefore have to take into account the effects of wholesale measures on competition in the related retail market and vice versa. NRAs need to take particular attention to the possibility of price or margin squeezes and appropriate measuring and monitoring mechanisms may need to be put in place.

Under the Universal Service Directive transparency obligations in relation to tariffs etc, are applied at the retail level. However, transparency measures at a retail level can create a situation where parties to the market could be facilitated in engaging in anti-competitive practices. NRAs must ensure that any transparency measures imposed do not lead inadvertently to anti-competitive behaviour.

3.2.7 Leased Lines and Carrier Selection/Pre-selection

There are two other articles in the Universal Service Directive that are addressed at firms with SMP. These relate to controls on the minimum set of leased lines and carrier selection and carrier pre-selection. These obligations, whilst using the trigger of SMP to be imposed, are not designed exclusively to address market power and, where applicable, they must be imposed by the NRA. For this reason, the principles outlined in the next chapter do not apply directly. The obligation on leased lines is to ensure that a harmonised offering is available throughout the Community, and as such, relates to the imperative of the internal market. While promoting competition on retail markets, the provision of carrier selection and carrier pre-selection is also motivated on the basis of benefiting subscribers.

There are specific provisions in the Universal Service Directive concerning regulatory controls on the minimum set of leased lines and these are set out in some detail in Annex VII of the Universal Service Directive. Those obligations mean SMP undertakings must provide leased lines in the minimum set in a non-discriminatory manner, at cost orientated price (with associated cost accounting) where appropriate, a transparency requirement and according to certain quality parameters.

In addition, undertakings with SMP for connection to and use of the public fixed network at a fixed location must provide carrier selection by means of a carrier selection code and carrier pre-selection combined with carrier selection at cost orientated prices. In addition, their direct charges to subscribers, e.g. line rentals, should not act as a disincentive to the use of such facilities.

4.   Principles to guide Regulators in choosing appropriate remedies

4.1 Introduction

This chapter outlines the high level principles that should guide NRAs in the decisions on remedies. The chapter takes as given what the framework is designed to achieve. In particular the aim of the Access Directive is to establish a regulatory framework, in accordance with internal market principles, for the relationships between suppliers of networks and services that will result in sustainable competition, interoperability of electronic communications services and consumer benefits.

At the heart of framework is the welfare of consumers. Competition is the process that guarantees that markets work to deliver enhanced consumer benefits. Competition delivers greater choice, quality and lower prices to consumers, which in turn make consumers better off. It is recognised in the Access Directive that in an open and competitive market there should be no restrictions, other than normal competition rules, on normal commercial negotiations for access and interconnection.

However, it is also made clear that in markets where there continue to be large differences in negotiating power between undertakings, and where some undertakings rely on infrastructure provided by others for delivery of their services, it is appropriate to establish a framework to ensure that the market functions effectively. National regulatory authorities should have the power to secure, where commercial negotiation fails, adequate access and interconnection and interoperability of services in the interest of end-users[81]. Within the confines of these circumstances, policymakers have given NRAs a presumption that regulatory intervention is warranted in order to enhance the welfare of consumers.

In imposing remedies to tackle SMP, NRAs have to ensure that the remedies are based on the nature of the problem identified, proportionate and justified in light of the objectives of NRAs as outlined in the Framework Directive. NRAs have been set the following objectives to guide them as they carry out the task specified for them in the Directives:

- Promote competition;

- Contribute to the development of the internal market; and to

- Promote the interests of the citizens of the European Union.

As argued in Chapter 1, not of all of these objectives arise when considering remedies that are designed to tackle SMP. Clearly the objective of promoting competition is of critical importance given the nature of the problem identified. The Directives make clear that this is a dynamic view of competition as NRAs have to ensure that competition is promoted by encouraging efficient investment and innovation. This is made concrete in relation to mandating access where it is stated that the imposition of mandated access that increases competition in the short-term should not reduce incentives for competitors to invest in alternative facilities that will secure more competition in the long-term[82]. Of course, when imposing obligations on SMP firms under the Universal Service Directive, NRAs must also keep in mind the objective of protecting the interests of EU citizens.

The remainder of Chapter 4 goes on to outline principles that should guide NRAs when they are at the remedies stage of the process. The first principle looks at what elements should be included in the decisions of NRAs in order that they meet their objectives and respect their obligations under the Directives. The next two principles tackle the approach the NRA should take when competition over infrastructure is and is not likely. The final principle deals with ensuring that, where possible, SMP undertakings are given incentives to comply.

4.2 The Principles

Article 8 of the Access Directive requires that remedies must be based on the underlying (competition) problem identified, proportionate and justified in light of the objectives set out for NRAs in Article 8 of the Framework Directive[83]. The purpose of this chapter is to put flesh on these concepts and to give guidance to NRAs on how, at the same time as respecting these requirements, to fulfil the aims of the framework.

The first principle is that the NRA must produce reasoned decisions in line with their obligations under the Directives. This incorporates the need that the remedy selected be based on the nature of the problem identified. The problem(s) in the market will have already been identified in the market analysis procedure. Decisions must include a discussion on the proportionality of the remedy. These decisions should include, for any given problem, consideration of alternative remedies where possible, so that the least

---

[81] Directive 2002/19/EC, Recitals 5 and 6.
[82] Directive 2002/29/EC, Recital 19.
[83] Directive 2002/19/EC. Article 8 of Directive 2002/21/EC (the Framework Directive) sets out the objectives of the NRA, which are to promote competition, to contribute to the development of the internal market and to promote the interests of EU citizens.

burdensome effective remedy can be selected. The decisions should also take into account the potential effect of the proposed remedies on related markets.

A second principle is that where infrastructure competition is not likely to be feasible, due to the persistent presence of bottlenecks associated with significant economies of scale or scope or other entry restrictions, NRAs will need to ensure that there is sufficient access to wholesale inputs. Thus, consumers may enjoy the maximum benefits possible. In this instance, NRAs should also protect against the potential behavioural abuses that might occur.

A third principle is that, where as part of the market definition and analysis process, replication of the incumbent's infrastructure is viewed as feasible, the available remedies should assist in the transition process to a sustainable competitive market[84]. Where there is sufficient certainty that replication is feasible these markets should be treated in an analogous manner to those markets where replication is known to be feasible. In other cases with more marked uncertainty the NRA should keep an open mind and engage in on-going monitoring to continually re-assess their views. In these circumstances, no action should be taken that might delay or otherwise stop investment in competing infrastructure where this is efficient. In coming to these views on the feasibility of replication the NRA will need to be mindful of the possibility of inefficient investment.

A fourth principle is that remedies should be designed, where possible, to be incentive compatible. Thus, NRAs should, wherever possible, formulate remedies in such a way that the advantages to the regulated party of compliance outweigh the benefits of evasion. Incentive compatible remedies are likely to be both effective and require a minimum of on-going regulatory intervention. This may be difficult to achieve in practice, especially as the legal power to develop incentives for compliance is likely to vary greatly across Member States.

4.2.1 NRAs should produce reasoned decisions in line with their obligations under the Directives

As outlined in Article 8(4) of the Access Directive, remedies "shall be based on the nature of the problem identified, proportionate and justified in light of the objectives laid down" for NRAs in the Framework Directive. This is an obligation that NRAs face when they impose remedies on SMP undertakings under the Access Directive[85]. NRAs have experience of engaging in transparent public consultations and producing reasoned decisions. This is a proper discipline that all NRAs must work under.

It is an important principle that NRAs should clearly demonstrate their compliance with these obligations in their decisions.

The decisions of NRAs should also be transparent and well argued. This is important to improve the consistency of regulation both over time and across jurisdictions and to assist in providing clear signals to market players. Decisions should include, for any given problem, a consideration of alternative remedies wherever possible, so that the least burdensome effective remedy that best meets the objectives can be selected[86].

---

[84] When referring to replication in this chapter, what is really being referred to is other infrastructure that is capable of delivering the same services. Thus, the replication need not be on the basis of the same technology and, even if it is, there is no assumption that it will be configured in the same manner.

[85] An identical obligation applies to remedies applied to retail markets under Article 17 of the Universal Service Directive [2002/22/EC].

[86] The SMP firm primarily feels the burden of any given remedy. These include such issues as the administrative burden associated with compliance etc. However, the burdens also include the need for on-going monitoring on the part of the NRA.

Ensuring the consistency of regulatory practice across the EU is the responsibility of each NRA, subject to particular conditions in national markets. NRAs should co-operate with each other and with the Commission in a transparent manner to ensure consistent application of the framework in all Member States[87]. It is also important, in order to promote the consistent application of the framework, that NRAs start from a common understanding of what each element of this obligation entails.

Harmonisation will be required in the process of analysis across all Member States. This will produce significant benefits to market players in terms of regulatory certainty and predictability but will not automatically result in harmonised outcomes across the EU as the outcomes in each Member State will depend on national circumstances (which will be mainly captured at the market definition and SMP assessment stages of the process).

NRAs must seek to agree between themselves and the Commission on the types of instruments and remedies best suited to address particular types of situations in the marketplace[88]. As the new framework envisages on-going interactions between the NRA and the National Competition Authority, the NRA may wish to keep the NCA informed as to the remedies that it proposes to implement. This would be of assistance to the National Competition Authority if they were ever to become involved in a complementary manner in relation to the same issue.

The first issue that will be tackled in the NRA's decision will be an identification of the issue to be addressed. NRAs will have considered and identified the nature of the market problem(s) to be addressed in the course of the market definition and market analysis stages of the process[89]. This gives the NRA a clear insight to the nature of the market failure that they are considering. NRAs can then apply the available remedy (or the series of remedies) that most clearly addresses the core of the problem – the competitive effects[90]. As outlined earlier these problems arise due to the factors that enable the SMP firm to possess market power. When choosing the most effective remedy and in order to avoid over-regulation, NRAs should focus their attention on the anti-competitive behaviour that is most likely to occur in the specific market situation, otherwise the situation might be dealt with inadequately.

By tackling the underlying cause of the problem the NRA will attempt to do two things. Firstly, to best reign in the market power of the SMP firm with a view to obtaining the best deal for consumers. Secondly, in those areas where the NRA believes that effective competition may be generated, it will attempt also to encourage new entrants in progressively rolling out competing infrastructure. Of course, if self-sustaining effective competition is not feasible, then NRAs must attempt to control the effects of the market power in the most efficient manner possible. Both of these cases are discussed in the principles below.

It is appropriate at this stage to discuss what the remedies are hoping to achieve. This is in line with the requirement that NRAs justify the remedies in light of the objectives laid down for them.

These objectives as laid out in Article 8 of the Framework Directive are to:

- *Promote competition* in the provision of electronic communications networks, electronic communications services and associated facilities and services facilities. This can be achieved *inter-alia* by ensuring the best price, choice and quality for

---

[87] Directive 2002/21/EC, Article 7.
[88] Directive 2002/21/EC Article 7(2) Framework Directive.
[89] Directive 2002/21/EC, Articles 14, 15 and 16.
[90] See Directive 2002/19/EC, Article 8(4) for obligations under the Access Directive and Directive 2002/22/EC, Article 17(2) for obligations under the Universal Service Directive.

consumers through fair competition, efficient investment in infrastructure and resource management;

- *Contribute to the development of the internal market.* This can be achieved inter-alia by removing obstacles to pan European networks and services and ensuring a consistent regulatory practice across the community; and to

- *Promote the interests of the citizens of the European Union.* This can be achieved inter-alia by ensuring universal access and protecting the rights of consumers and in particular those with special needs. The Universal Service Directive sets out the powers that NRAs have to ensure that these objectives are met.

In carrying out their regulatory tasks specified in the Directives NRAs shall take all reasonable measures that are aimed at achieving these objectives[91]. These are global objectives and in dealing with specific issues, one or more of these objectives comes to the fore.

In terms of selecting remedies in the Access Directive to address the competitive effects associated with market power (which is the problem that has been identified) it is clear that the main objective that the NRA has to bear in mind is that of the promotion of competition. This includes (when considering access remedies) that NRAs seek to ensure the following:

- ensuring that users, including disabled users, derive maximum benefit in terms of choice, price, and quality;

- ensuring that there is no distortion or restriction of competition in the electronic communications sector;

- encouraging efficient investment in infrastructure, and promoting innovation[92].

It is also clear from Article 8(2) of the Framework Directive that this is not just a static view of competition as the NRA has to ensure that competition is promoted by encouraging efficient investment and innovation. The differences in remedies in situations where a NRA is attempting to promote competition in a static and dynamic sense is dealt with later in the document when principles 2 and 3 are discussed. Imposing obligations on SMP firms under the Universal Service Directive requires that NRAs also keep in mind the objective of protecting citizen's interests. In applying remedies, NRAs will need to bear in mind how effective these remedies are in achieving their objectives. This will be important when NRAs come to consider the issue of proportionality as the negative impacts of a remedy need to be balanced against how effective it is.

The whole process of consistent application of the framework and harmonisation is how NRAs ensure that they are meeting the objective to contribute to the development of the internal market. As outlined in Article 7(2) of the Framework Directive, NRAs shall seek to agree on the types of instruments and remedies best suited to address particular types of situations in the market place, and shall cooperate in a transparent manner to ensure the development of consistent regulatory practice and application of the Directives. This paper and the process of seeking to agree on remedies is a concrete step in meeting this objective of NRAs.

Proportionality is one of the over-arching general principles of European law. It is described as the minimum intervention required, to achieve the objective set out. Guidance from case law tells us that[93]:

---

[91]   Directive 2002/21/EC, Article 8(1).
[92]   Directive 2002/21/EC, Article 8(2).

'In accordance with the principle of proportionality, which is one of the general principles of Community law, the lawfulness of the prohibition of an economic activity is subject to the condition that the prohibitory measures are appropriate and necessary in order to achieve the objectives legitimately pursued by the legislation in question, it being understood that when there is a choice between several appropriate measures recourse must be had to the least onerous, and the disadvantages caused must not be disproportionate to the aims pursued.'

In considering proportionality it is important to bear in mind that when SMP is found on a properly identified market some form of regulatory action is warranted. This is provided for in the Directives and is in line with the view that remedies, in these circumstances, lead to welfare improvements. Thus, there is a presumption that remedies increase welfare. This implies that there is no requirement to demonstrate that remedies are globally welfare improving. The issue is to select amongst those remedies that achieve the NRA's intention that which are the most proportionate. The impact on market players might also have to be considered if there is strong evidence to believe that the immediate introduction of a remedy might cause excessive adjustment costs. In these cases, a short time-limited glide path could be followed.

Decisions should include, for any given problem, a consideration of alternative remedies wherever relevant, so that the least burdensome effective remedy that best meets the objectives can be selected. Each remedy may also achieve the objective of the NRA to a varying degree. This also needs to be considered. Second, in order to assess whether a remedy is proportionate and justified in the light of the objectives set out in the Framework Directive, NRAs should balance the burden of the remedy imposed on the undertaking with SMP and other costs which the imposition of a remedy may entail against its prospective benefits. Both assessments are already required by some national systems of administrative law and form part of the proportionality assessment under Community law. However, in order to make the choices involved more transparent, NRAs may carry out an assessment of the regulatory options available, including a qualitative assessment of the anticipated benefits and potential costs of the option selected ("regulatory options assessment").

When carrying out a regulatory options assessment, the justification of regulatory measures will generally be based on a qualitative analysis taking into account economic theory and market experience. Further to this, NRAs can where reliable data is readily available also use quantitative methods to support the assessment. However, predictions of future market developments are difficult to quantify due to uncertainty about the behaviour of market parties, limited availability of data and statistically significant estimates, second-order effects of intervention, and the impact of exogenous factors. This means any prospective quantification will necessarily be of a partial character and can in the best case only provide estimates of limited value e.g. indicating general trends such as the direction and in some cases the order of magnitude of expected effects. Hence, quantitative analysis where at all feasible will at best play a supportive role.

Even the best-designed remedies may take a period of time to take effect. At the same time the incumbent is likely to have a strong incentive to ensure that the new entrant does not reach the critical mass in terms of market presence to roll out competing infrastructure. In those circumstances it will be necessary to ensure that the short term exercise of market power is controlled by a series of remedies that ensure that the objectives of regulation are not frustrated.

In considering the imposition of several remedies the NRA will also have to consider the potential interaction of the series of remedies to ensure that there are no unintended

---

[93] Case C-331/88, 13 November 1990, FEDESA.

consequences that would frustrate the regulatory goals or lead to a disproportionate burden being placed on the market players.

It is very important to maintain consistency between remedies, so that the introduction of further remedies does not unintentionally undermine the effectiveness of others. For example, the NRA might have to consider how the availability of wholesale line rental might affect the attractiveness of taking unbundled local loops. This may be important if the business case for using unbundled loops rests on the provision of both narrowband and broadband services, and the availability of a wholesale line rental product puts pressure on narrowband pricing, thus affecting this revenue stream available to the user of unbundled loops. As a general point NRAs should ensure that, where markets are closely related and interdependent, there are consistent price structures for the different access products so as to promote infrastructure and service competition in a balanced way.

Sometimes, within the set of available remedies there will be remedies that require ongoing monitoring to ensure compliance (and perhaps a series of supporting remedies) and others that may bring forward the day that regulation (for a particular issue) may no longer be required. To the extent that both potential remedies would be effective the principle of proportionality would require that the second remedy be preferred to the first.

Remedies will need to be designed to strike the correct balance between generality and specificity. Highly specific remedies provide a greater degree of legal certainty but tend to be inflexible and not well future-proofed. Moreover, careful specification can consume large quantities of time and regulatory resources. If the remedies are not properly designed, they may turn out to be ineffective.

On the other hand, a remedy expressed in general terms may give rise to uncertainty about what it actually means. This may work to the advantage of the SMP player who has incentives to exploit such uncertainty. To resolve this uncertainty will take time but such delays are likely to be contrary to the objectives of the NRA.

4.2.2   Protecting consumers where replication is not considered feasible

As part of the process of arriving at a point where remedies must be selected, the NRA will have undertaken a detailed review of the market. In some areas the NRA will have taken the view that new entry/replication is very unlikely (and there is very little uncertainty surrounding this assessment for the foreseeable future).

In applying remedies under the Access Directive, NRAs are attempting to promote competition[94]. This includes ensuring that users derive the maximum benefit in terms of choice, price and quality and that there is no restriction or distortion of competition. In this regard the promotion of service competition, where replication is not feasible, is an important goal. Service competition increases consumer choice, which is an important end in itself. NRAs will also have to be mindful that they encourage efficient investment in infrastructure and that they promote innovation. However, in the instance of non-replicable infrastructure these concerns are mainly related to ensuring that the network is maintained and necessary upgrades are made.

In general, where entry barriers are structural and competition is (at least in the short run) unlikely to emerge, regulation needs to ensure that the resulting market power is not exploited, focusing in particular on behaviour that distorts or prevents competition in related markets or the SMP market and behaviour that is otherwise to the detriment of end users.

In this situation (non-replicability) the NRA has two concerns. Firstly, to ensure that as much services competition is encouraged as is feasible. Secondly, that there is a sufficient

---

[94]   Directive 2002/19/EC, Article 8 and Directive 2002/ 21/EC, Article 8(2).

return on the existing infrastructure to encourage further investment and to maintain and upgrade existing facilities[95].

The NRA will have to ensure that there is sufficient access to wholesale inputs so that service competition can flourish. Competition at the service level must be undistorted by activities of the upstream infrastructure provider[96]. In those instances where replication is not considered feasible, promoting service competition is an important goal for the NRA as it is only through vigorous competition in services that consumers can enjoy the maximum benefits possible.

However, the incumbent may engage in activities designed to dampen competition. At the retail level, these include familiar practices, when practised by a dominant firm, such as predatory pricing and bundling. At wholesale level, market power can be exercised in a number of different ways by a dominant infrastructure operator. Examples are refusal to supply, discriminatory access prices and quality degradation. These market failures are familiar in the economics and competition law literatures and from regulatory practice[97].

A further type of harmful exercise of market power (when practised by a SMP firm) is a margin squeeze. A vertically integrated firm may choose a combination of upstream and downstream prices, which enable it to foreclose entry into the potentially competitive activity, by denying its competitor an adequate margin to survive. This may be (but need not be) accompanied by charging a price above cost for the product under the firm's dominant control[98]. The Framework Directive explicitly identifies leveraged dominance as a third form of dominance (in addition to single and joint dominance).

The Access Directive contains remedies designed to mandate access, control prices and counter deliberate quality degradation. NRAs will be mindful that tight regulation of interconnection and access charges etc. (e.g. origination and termination charges) may result in attempts to increase the cost of interconnection faced by new entrants through delaying interconnection or degrading the quality of interconnection links or the use of incompatible standards. These incentives are explored in greater detail in Chapter 5.

When replication is not feasible, this fact is likely to affect the upstream supplier's incentive when faced with equally efficient downstream competitors. If competition can only occur at the services layer, a supplier of access to that layer ought to be indifferent between serving equally efficient services competitors and discrimination becomes theoretically less likely. However, for historical reasons and in particular if faced with common ownership between the infrastructure supplier and the services operator, strong incentives to behave in a discriminatory manner may still exist. There is also the consideration that a firm that is operating in both the upstream and downstream market may be concerned that an efficient downstream competitor may try to enter the upstream market once its downstream market position is established. This will reinforce any incentive to discriminate. The regulated firm may also attempt to undermine effective regulation at the wholesale level by extending its market power into the retail level of the value chain. These issues are discussed in greater detail in Chapter 5.

When there is a very limited potential for infrastructure competition, the setting of access prices is critical (as there will be no competitive dynamic to drive upgrades and innovation) and the NRA must ensure that the SMP firm has the incentive (and resources) to maintain

---

[95] Directive 2002/21/EC, Article 8(2) in relation to the promotion of competition in electronic communications services.

[96] Similar considerations apply in markets where infrastructure competition can emerge while the historic supplier retains significant market power.

[97] See in particular Notice on the application of the competition rules to access agreements in the telecommunications sector (98/C 265/02).

[98] See the Annex.

and upgrade its infrastructure. This issue is normally dealt with when considering the cost models that NRAs use in setting access prices and in calculating a reasonable rate of return.

4.2.3 Supporting feasible infrastructure investment

One of the core assessments that the NRA has to make is the degree to which the rolling out of competing infrastructure is feasible in their Member State over the timeframe of the review and over the projectable future[99]. This assessment will depend on national circumstances and on the general sentiment of the market place. The factors that lead to high and non-transitory entry barriers will have been identified at the stage of market definition. There will also have been an examination of the dynamic state of competition behind those barriers. In the circumstances that relate to the subject matter of this chapter, conclusions will also have been made as to the dynamic towards effective competition over the current review period.

However, in forming a view on replicability the NRA must also project beyond the period of the review and make an assessment of how the dynamics of the market will play out over a number of review periods. It could be that, whilst there is no prospect of new investment in the immediate future (and hence SMP exists), this situation may be expected to change in the future.

In a dynamic innovation driven market with the constant potential for disruptive technologies emerging, it is often impossible to predict with any degree of confidence the likely direction the market may take. The possibility that infrastructure may be replicated may have implications for how NRAs design remedies and on access prices for the current review period.

However, this uncertainty itself is an important indicator to consider. In the face of uncertainty the NRA has to consider the risks of not promoting replication where it is, in fact, feasible as opposed to promoting replication where it is not, in fact, feasible.

Consultation amongst NRAs and with industry participants will also help to come to a clearer view as to whether replication is likely.

In coming to a view on feasibility, the NRA will also have to carefully consider the potential of inefficient investment. This concern with inefficient investment will loom larger as new entrants take each additional step on the ladder to infrastructure based competition.

As made clear earlier the NRA has the objective of promoting competition in order to deliver the maximum benefits to end users. However, in the setting where replication is feasible the NRA also has to bear in mind the impact that their actions have on the incentives to invest in alternative infrastructure. This is made explicit in the recitals to the Access Directive where it is stated that "the imposition by national regulatory authorities of mandated access that increases competition in the short-term should not reduce incentives for competitors to invest in alternative facilities that will secure more competition in the long-term[100]." As new entrants roll out more and more investment further down the network hierarchy, both the size of investment and the likely proportion of this that is potentially sunk increases. As a counter-balance to this, however, the benefits that the new entrant obtains from further investment rise as it increases its control of the service offerings. In planning their investment strategy new entrants will, of course, benefit if the NRA has a consistent regulatory access philosophy that gives new entrants the confidence to make the incremental investments.

---

[99] Directive 2002/21/EC, Article 8(2) in relation to promoting competition in electronic communications networks.
[100] Directive 2002/19/EC, Recital 19.

Competition over competing infrastructure has many advantages. The pressure to minimise costs is exerted over the whole value chain. This will induce greater scope for innovation, process innovation etc. which creates a downward dynamic for costs. Consumers also benefit from more diversified offerings, which correspond more closely to their individual needs. There is general agreement that a great potential harm to welfare occurs when replication is feasible but not promoted. This will delay the roll out of new and innovative services and, particularly in relation to broadband, may have large negative consequences on the general economy.

Thus, if the NRA is uncertain as to whether replication is feasible it should maintain a neutral stance and continue to monitor the market (both domestically and internationally) to firm up its view as to the likelihood of replication. Of course, the degree of uncertainty would impact on how vigorously any such policy would be followed. If the level of uncertainty as to replicability is low (i.e. replication that appears efficient has happened elsewhere), then there may be a case for believing replication is feasible in the particular context under consideration. On the other hand, if replication has not occurred elsewhere, then a more cautious approach is warranted. In all of this, the NRA will need to be careful not to second-guess the market place but rather should provide a coherent background against which market developments take place.

If there is no potential for replication (or indeed very little or no uncertainty as to how the market will develop), this will also have implications for the types of remedies selected and on the structure of access prices. Remedies are, thus, the link between reviews. Remedies attempt to overcome the problems identified in the market analysis but may take numerous reviews for their ultimate effect to be fully realised.

Remedies will be designed to deal directly with the basis of the problems identified in the market analysis and to allow competition to emerge. Service competition based on regulated access at cost-oriented prices can be (and in general is) the vehicle for long term infrastructure competition. With this new entrants can decide on their investment in a step-by-step way and can establish a customer base[101] (critical mass) before they go to the next step of deploying their own infrastructure. In those areas where infrastructure based competition is feasible, such interventions have as their long-term objective the emergence of self-sustaining effective competition and the ultimate withdrawal of regulatory obligations which implies a built-in "sunset clause" for the removal of "rungs", i.e. access obligations.

However, if new entrants are to flourish and eventually invest in their own infrastructure, they will need to be supported in this by a dynamic series of supporting remedies that attempt to deal with the SMP firm's on-going efforts to frustrate the process. Without ongoing vigilance in this regard, new entrants may never be able to develop a sufficient market presence to justify making investments and the long-term vision of infrastructure-based competition will never emerge. Of course, the incumbent's incentive to maintain and upgrade their network during the transition process also needs to be considered.

As infrastructure competition will not necessarily develop automatically, it will also be necessary to impose remedies that enable the new entrant to reach a point of the investment ladder which makes commercial sense and which tends to maximize the extent of economically efficient competing infrastructure. This will require a coherent regulatory policy (and in particular a consistent price structure) along the relevant ladder. This is important for three reasons:

---

[101] This assumes a certain degree of customer loyalty or inertia.

- Commercial considerations may mean that the best business plan is to enter the market at a point on the investment ladder lower than the point to which the entrant ultimately aspires

- It may be completely unclear at the outset what would be the economically efficient level of investment. Entrants may make different rational decisions on this point. Such decisions are best taken by the entrants and not by either regulator or SMP player

- Entrants may need access to more than one rung at the same time, for example because of considerations of economies of scale and density.

In the first case in particular, remedies which facilitate climbing of the investment ladder act as a bridge that should enable new entrants to consolidate their market position so that they will undertake the necessary investments. In all three cases, lack of coherence in the set of remedies chosen risks incentivising the new entrants to make investment decisions on the basis of regulatory arbitrage opportunities, rather than economic efficiency. In particular, if rungs are missing, there is a risk that entrants are forced to choose between investment options which are either commercially or economically relatively unattractive. The consequence is that the economically efficient level of investment may not take place.

For broadband services, the following standardized and fit-for-purpose access products are considered to form the "rungs" of the ladder (which may relate to different relevant markets):

> resale;
> bitstream;
> shared / fully unbundled access, the ultimate rung being own infrastructure. Due to the time scales involved, which will differ according to market conditions within each Member State, other remedies may need to be imposed to provide a sufficient number of intermediate steps for new entrants. For example, certain backhaul services (ATM backhaul, ATM broadband conveyance, other backbone transport) may be required, according to national circumstances[102, 103]. Over time, access products may change. More generally, when implementing the ladder NRAs need to adjust ("customise") it in terms of timing, pricing and product design to national circumstances and take into account structural/exogenous factors such as disparity of population density or the existence/non-existence of alternative network infrastructures as well as the development of the market.

For example, in terms of access to the local loop, the fundamental problem is that there are extensive economies of scale and density, from which the incumbent benefits. The availability of a bitstream product on reasonable terms gives entrants access to the incumbent's economies of scale in the local access network, which is the root cause of their market power. Together with appropriate access remedies it allows entrants to build a customer base for their services which in turn may give the critical mass that allows those competitors the chance to invest in their own infrastructure so that competition would become self sustaining. Whilst this addresses the problem directly, it may well be that new entrants will have to be facilitated in progressively rolling out their own infrastructure by a series of other remedies that enable firms to make 'a bridge' between each successive step. Of course, bitstream is a step up from pure re-selling in that some investment has to be made. There is a range of bitstream products available throughout the Community with some Member States having more than one type of bitstream. Each type of bitstream product available will require a different level of investment on the part of the new entrant.

---

[102] Not forgetting the highest rung: own infrastructure.
[103] See Commission comments on case HU/2004/0186.

More generically (and not limited to broadband), the following access products could be distinguished as rungs of a ladder of investment:

> ➤ resale;
> ➤ intermediate wholesale products (typically capacity);
> ➤ access to infrastructure elements,

again the ultimate step rung being own infrastructure.

For example, for corporate multi-site services one could establish the following ladder: leased lines → PPC/core → PPC;[104] for interconnection services it could be: double transit → single transit → local[105].

The setting of access prices is a complex task[106]. If access prices are set too low then there is a risk that the new entrants will not have an incentive to roll out their own infrastructure (nor will the incumbent have sufficient incentives to upgrade and maintain their network). There is also the danger of inefficient firms entering the industry. This factor is especially important where new technologies or networks are being deployed as the NRA tries to encourage efficient investment in infrastructure and promote innovation. On the other hand, if access prices are set too high, otherwise efficient new entrants may be dissuaded from entry and there is also the danger of inefficient investment. Thus, NRAs will have to keep in mind the impact of their decisions on the incentive to build, in instances where replicability is feasible. This will require, for instance, a consistent pricing structure when more than one type of access is offered.

NRAs must still deal with the issue of how to give new entrants the incentive to roll out their own infrastructure. NRAs may have to signal in their reviews that they view some remedies as bridging a gap so that new entrants can more easily make incremental investment but that market players cannot base their long-term business models on the basis of these remedies alone. Thus, the NRA has the ability to change the incentive properties of the regulatory framework over time but must do so in a predictable and transparent manner so that business decisions can be planned accordingly. The principle that regulators must produce reasoned decisions, in a transparent manner, gives the additional benefit that the underlying reasons for imposing a given remedy (series of remedies) will have been made clear. The NRA will also have to show that the remedies are based on the problem identified, proportionate and justified in light of the objectives set them in Article 8 of the Framework Directive.

Consistent relative prices reflect the difference in cost between the products. In other words: the price difference or margin must satisfy the margin squeeze test of covering the incremental costs of providing the "wider" product[107]., Due to incorrect pricing, the new entrant remains sitting on "his" rung without moving up the ladder. Additionally, when rungs are too far away, the move to the next rung becomes too risky, when rungs are too close, it would not pay to move to the next rung. Therefore pricing and distance between rungs should incentivise new entrants to reach the highest point of the ladder at the maximum speed consistent with efficient investment by both incumbent and new entrants.

Complementarity of access products

Regarding the use of access products, the ERG Report[108] recently found that while migration from resale to bitstream and on to shared and full[109] unbundled access is taking

---

[104] Cf. Cave, "Managing the ladder of investment", presentation BNetzA/WIK, NGN Workshop, 5 Dec. 2005.
[105] For the application of the ladder to interconnection Cf. e.g. RTR, notification market 10 (case AT-2004/0090), and Cave et al. (2001).
[106] See paragraph 5.2.2.2.
[107] Cf. Cave, op. cit., p. 22.
[108] ERG Broadband market competition report (ERG (05) 23), pp. 3, 5, 18, 23.

place[110], it also pointed out that in some countries, bitstream access and unbundling are used complementarily ("sitting on 2 rungs"). Depending mainly on population density[111], new entrants use bitstream access in less densely populated areas while turning to unbundling (both shared and full) in big cities in order to get national coverage and to make a complete nationwide offer which is an important marketing aspect. Especially in countries with large differences in population density between the various areas of the national territory, it may be that new entrants would need to serve either the whole country or none of it; they may be limited in their ability to just serve the high density areas. In such cases, it is not a serious option for them to use LLU (say) in urban areas unless bitstream is available in less densely populated (rural/remote) areas. Nevertheless, this does not imply that geographical limitation of the bitstream remedy would be appropriate as different players may be relying on national availability. Regulators in those countries should also bear in mind that in order to get competition across the national territory new entrants will also have to be able to serve low density areas economically, which may necessitate the availability of multiple access products[112].

In the case of services to corporate customers, the removal of one rung may mean that a new entrant may no longer be able to make a multi-site offer based on different access products and would lose the customer seeking a single source supplier. This may have a significant detrimental effect on competition for the supply of services to such customers. For example, while city suburbs are generally thought to be fertile territory for market players which seek to offer broadband services to residential consumers via unbundled local loops, the same may not be the case for providers which address only the corporate market. There may be insufficient density of corporate customers to justify the overheads of using unbundled loops in such areas. In these cases, the competitor would need to rely on bitstream services.

Migration

The other crucial condition besides consistent pricing to maximise efficiency of investment and effectiveness of competition is the availability of well-functioning and cost-effective network migration processes (see below point 5.2.2.3). These will be needed either to allow the entrant to serve its existing customers via its own additional infrastructure (corresponding to a climb of the ladder) or to serve customers who have been attracted from another provider using a different infrastructure configuration. SMP players have commercial incentives to delay and degrade such processes, in order to make it more difficult for entrants to justify infrastructure investments and to win customers from other providers.

For business customers, who are generally extremely sensitive to quality of service, the functioning of migration processes is crucial for the choice of an operator.

4.2.4 Incentive compatible remedies

Remedies are much more likely to be effective if they are designed in such a manner as to give strong incentives for compliance.

At a basic level, incentive compatible regulation is about empowering both parties to engage in commercial negotiation. There should be no restrictions which prevent undertakings negotiating between themselves agreements on access and/or interconnection (other that those restrictions that arise generally from competition law)[113]. Regulation is,

---

[109] This is among other things a result of VoB services replacing traditional voice telephony services.
[110] Especially in those countries where migration processes are running smoothly and at moderate costs.
[111] Number of customers/lines per MDF.
[112] Cf. ARCEP decisions 05-0278 and 05-0280 of 19 May 2005 and 05-0281 of 28 July 2005.
[113] Directive 2002/19/EC, Article 3(1).

however, justified in circumstances where commercial negotiation fails and where there is a large difference in negotiating power and the access seeker relies on infrastructure provided by the other party[114].

However, experience thus far in most circumstances has shown that commercial negotiation is the exception rather than the rule. This is to be regretted but it is nonetheless a fact. In these cases, incentive compatible regulation involves attempting to change the pay-offs to non-compliance. Measures to enforce compliance with a SMP firm's obligations are outlined in the Authorisation Directive[115]. These include the power to obtain information to monitor compliance and the potential to impose penalties.

As was argued earlier, SMP firms are likely to have incentives (and a myriad of means) to attempt to frustrate emerging competition. The NRA can then become locked into a cycle of compliance monitoring and intervention. It would be preferable if the original remedy could be designed in such a way that the advantages to the regulated party of compliance outweigh the benefits of evasion. To be able to achieve this, the NRA must be able to make the penalty from non-compliance (and the probability of action) such that the regulated firm will comply voluntarily. Incentive compatible remedies are likely to be effective and to require a minimum of on-going regulatory intervention.

To achieve incentive compatibility, the NRA needs to be able to adjust the pay-off from non-compliance. This will normally involve giving the SMP firm strong financial incentives to comply. The degree to which this can be achieved in practice will depend largely on the legal powers that NRAs have to apply such administrative measures (against the background of their own legal system). The ability to impose a financial penalty is envisaged (in Article 10 of the Authorisation Directive) if an SMP undertaking fails to comply with an obligation (after such failure has been pointed out to it)[116]. However, such a power has to be given by Member States in accordance with national law. In addition, when there are repeated serious breaches there is the power to prevent an undertaking from supplying communications networks or services or suspend or withdraw rights of use. From an economic perspective, if the NRA has evidence of a breach of an obligation that is so serious so as to create inter alia serious economic or operational problems for other providers or users, the NRA may take immediate interim measures.

In order to illustrate this principle some examples are developed:

4.2.4.1   Private information and the inflation of costs

In circumstances where a cost-orientation obligation is appropriate, the NRA may often choose to specify the appropriate charge or to control it via a price cap. But this is particularly resource-intensive work. For reasons of expediency therefore, the NRA may choose instead simply to specify that the charge should be 'cost-oriented' or 'based on costs which are reasonably and efficiently incurred' or some similar formulation.

One problem with the latter approach is that the SMP player may have an incentive to inflate its estimate of its costs. However, such an incentive can be significantly reduced - if not removed altogether - if the NRA orders that the appropriate charge (once it has been identified) should be levied from the date on which the cost orientation obligation became applicable. The SMP player would therefore be required to repay (preferably with an appropriate commercial rate of interest and at its own expense) any overpayment, which had been made while non-compliant charges were in effect. A provision of 'retrospection' should not, of course prevent an aggrieved party from seeking further redress in Court.

---

[114] Directive 2002/19/EC, Recital 6.
[115] Directive 2002/20/EC, Articles 10 and 11.
[116] Directive 2002/20/EC.

4.2.4.2   Delays in supply

Sometimes the NRA may decide to specify the characteristics of products that an SMP player must supply. On other occasions it may be inappropriate to specify the detail; the NRA could then specify that the SMP player should supply any product within a defined class (for example, interconnection of bitstream access services) which was reasonably requested. That leaves the problem of how to give incentives to the SMP player to deal reasonably with all reasonable requests. The NRA may be able to reduce the size of this problem by issuing guidance on what it would regard as reasonable if it were called upon to resolve a dispute. Although such guidance is not binding, SMP players may prefer to follow it, as a general rule, to avoid adverse publicity from being 'named and shamed'.

Financial incentives can also be created in this area. Where applicable, the NRA may consider imposing a requirement that where a reasonable request is initially refused but subsequently enforced by the NRA, the SMP player is required to pay a set amount per day to the aggrieved party for every day between the date the product should (reasonably) have been delivered and the date it was actually delivered.

Another issue may arise where the SMP player is already selling a retail service but no wholesale equivalent. Where the wholesale equivalent is covered by a general obligation to supply (or where the NRA determines that the SMP player should supply a defined wholesale service) the SMP player needs to be given incentives to supply the wholesale service quickly, once it has been requested. In such circumstances, the NRA may consider imposing a deadline for supply. If the SMP player misses the deadline, it would be liable not only for compensation (as described in the previous paragraph) but also to a prohibition on providing any relevant wholesale input to itself until such time as the requested wholesale service had been made available to others. This would mean that it would not be able to obtain a 'first mover advantage' by supplying its retail product while denying others the ability to compete by withholding the necessary network inputs.

4.2.4.3   Service Level Agreements and Service Level Guarantees

Even where there is an established reference offer for a product, SMP players often prefer not to be committed to supplying that product according to a particular time-scale or quality or to be committed to repairing faults within an agreed time-scale. Commitments of this kind would be normal commercial practice and it is entirely legitimate – and may be necessary for proper functioning of the market – for the NRA to require the SMP player to make reasonable commitments of that nature. What is 'reasonable' will depend on the individual characteristics of the product.

Again, financial incentives can be considered to ensure that the SMP player meets those commitments in practice. The NRA may decide to require the SMP player to compensate an aggrieved party for failing to fulfil an order, at a specified rate. Further discussion is at paragraph 5.2.5.3.

4.3   Conclusions

Under the new regulatory framework regulation will only be imposed where appropriate and will be rolled back once competition becomes effective. In the detailed discussion it is sometimes easy to lose sight of the main goals that remedies are being designed to achieve, which is to promote competition and protect the interests of EU citizens (where this is appropriate). These goals can be simultaneously achieved by structuring remedies (using a harmonised method of analysis, which is able to take account of national circumstances) in such a way as to promote efficient competition and investment in competing infrastructure where appropriate.

The principles outlined above give guidance to NRAs in the consideration of remedies in the new framework. The task of selecting appropriate yet proportionate remedies to achieve the objectives as outlined for NRAs is a complex task. Some Member States have already embarked on this process and we can all expect to learn valuable lessons as the process proceeds.

5. Application of remedies to competition problems

5.1 Introduction

This final chapter will attempt to match the remedies available to NRAs according to Art 9-13 of the Access Directive and Art 17-19 of the Universal Service Directive[117] (see Chapter 3 of this document) to the standard competition problems identified in Chapter 2. Underlying this match are the 'principles to be applied by regulators in choosing appropriate remedies' as discussed in Chapter 4.

In practice, the imposition of remedies will follow the market definition and market analysis stage. The first stage involves a check of the 3 criteria for defining relevant markets as outlined above. After the second stage regulators will have gained detailed knowledge about the market, and will – in case that the market is not effectively competitive – have determined one (or more) SMP undertaking(s), will have investigated the source of market power, and will have identified actual and potential competition problems. All this knowledge is a necessary precondition for the imposition of effective and appropriate remedies. The markets under consideration have passed the 3 criteria test and are therefore characterized by high and non-transitory entry barriers, do not tend towards effective competition over time, and cannot adequately be addressed by competition law alone. As a consequence, the markets qualify for ex ante regulation according to the new regulatory framework.

If markets have the characteristics of natural monopolies (significant economies of scale and/or scope at the relevant level of output) and significant barriers to entry exist

(e.g. because of large sunk costs), effective competition is unlikely to emerge on its own, and regulators will have to deal directly with the adverse effects of market power, such as excessive pricing, price discrimination, lack of investment, inefficiencies, and low quality. In other markets, where no significant economies of scale or scope, and only limited structural (and thus exogenous) barriers to entry exist, concerns about the market power are reduced, however, SMP positions may result from endogenous barriers to entry, i.e., barriers to entry following from the behaviour of the dominant undertaking (foreclosure). In such cases, the NRA is called upon to prevent such behaviour in order to promote market entry and enable competition to develop. The discussion of remedies in this chapter is based on the principles which have been identified in the previous chapter (and which are in turn based on the goals of Art 8 Framework Directive). The chapter takes the following approach to the application of these principles:

Principle 1 (NRAs should produce reasoned decisions in line with their obligations under the Directives): The standard competition problems are described as different kinds of anti-competitive or exploitative behaviour of an SMP undertaking, which may be identified by NRAs in course of the market analysis. The behaviour, in turn, rests on a certain 'strategic variable' like, e.g., price, quality, time, information, or a bundling decision. To be able to address a competition problem, the NRA will have to choose a remedy by which it is possible to – directly or indirectly – address the 'strategic variable' of the SMP undertaking. The ability to address a certain 'strategic variable' will thus be the first criterion applied for selecting an appropriate remedy. This does not only ensure that the remedy is effective but also that it is based on the nature of the underlying problem as stated in principle 1. The

---

[117] When referring to articles of these Directives in this chapter, the abbreviations AD and USD will be used. Other obligations which might be imposed following an Art 8 (3) procedure are not considered in this context.

principle of proportionality is applied by outlining, where possible, factors based on which NRAs should evaluate different regulatory options.

Principle 2 (Protecting consumers where replication is not considered feasible) and Principle 3 (Supporting feasible infrastructure investment): At the core of these principles is the question of replicability, which has technological, economic and time dimensions that will need to be assessed on a case-by-case basis. The issue of access to facilities which are considered to be non-replicable as well as the question how NRAs can influence investment incentives of the SMP undertaking and alternative operators and can support alternative infrastructure investments is particularly relevant for the problem of vertical leveraging and will be discussed extensively in section 5.2.

Principle 4 (Incentive compatible remedies): As the application of principle four crucially depends on NRAs' legal powers and the circumstances of the case at hand, it can be discussed on a general level only to a limited extent.

Once remedies are designed for each standard competition problem, patterns of remedies or competition problems may emerge in two ways: (i) certain competition problems may require the same remedy or set of remedies, (ii) certain remedies have to be imposed together with other (ancillary/accompanying) remedies. Such links will be discussed in a second step following the design of remedies for each competition problem individually. From an economic as well as from a legal point of view, it is important to distinguish between retail and wholesale markets wherever necessary. Reference to particular markets will be made whenever useful.

The analysis of this chapter is made on a general level, abstracting from conditions which NRAs usually will face and will have to take into account when taking decisions about remedies. The conclusions drawn should not be seen as advocating a mechanistic approach or preclude NRAs from coming to different conclusions based on their market analysis.

Where markets meet the 3 criteria test and qualify for ex ante regulation, NRAs do not need to show that an abuse of market power has actually occurred, but may impose remedies based on an SMP undertaking's underlying incentives to exploit its market power. The degree to which such incentives exist, and therefore the likelihood of an SMP undertaking exploiting its market power should be inferred from the NRA's market analysis. Ex ante regulation should aim at eliminating the incentives for incumbents to exercise their market power and, where possible, to create the conditions whereby effective competition can emerge, thereby decreasing the likelihood of anti-competitive or exploitative practices.

Therefore, an incentive-discussion will take place in short introductory sections to each remedies assessment and will provide a summary of the relevant findings in economic literature. The purpose of these introductory sections is not to draw direct conclusions from particular economic models of competition, or to identify mechanisms which are thought to be automatic and tangible. The purpose – in line with the spirit of the new regulatory framework and the use of economic analysis it advocates – rather is to gain an insight into the incentives to dampen the competitive process which exist under specific market structures, thereby informing NRAs on how to best deal with the need to reduce or eliminate such incentives.

5.2   Case 1: Vertical leveraging

Case 1 as set out in Chapter 2 is dealing with leveraging issues which may arise in a situation where a vertically integrated operator has SMP on the wholesale market.

Case 1 may pertain, e.g., to the following communications markets:

- Fixed line telephony, where the access network (or at least parts of the access network) is particularly hard to replicate due to significant economies of scale and large sunk costs in many cases. All retail services making use of the access network could then potentially be foreclosed by the SMP undertaking. This includes voice telephony but is also relevant for narrowband and broadband (e.g. xDSL) internet access.

- Leased lines, where terminating segments and in some cases even trunk segments (e.g. on 'thin routes') may form competitive bottlenecks.

- Terrestrial broadcasting, if the incumbent broadcaster owns the transmission infrastructure.

5.2.1 Relevant concepts: Incentives to anti-competitive behaviour

According to economic literature, a vertically integrated dominant undertaking supplying a necessary input to its downstream competitors has various possibilities to foreclose the potentially competitive retail market[118]. To actually engage in foreclosure, however, the undertaking needs an incentive to do so, i.e., it has to be able to increase its profits by driving its competitors out of the retail market.

In an unregulated environment with perfect competition on the downstream market, an upstream monopolist will in general not have an incentive to foreclose the retail market. Profits can be maximized by granting access to the most efficient downstream firms and setting the access price so as to extract the entire retail profit. This argument became known as the 'Chicago Critique' of foreclosure[119].

This argument, however, only holds under the assumption that the retail stage is perfectly competitive and the monopolist can indeed extract all profits from the retail market solely by setting an appropriate access charge. Beside the problem that the monopolist would earn excess profits and supplies an inefficiently low level of output in this case, these assumptions will usually not be fulfilled in practice for several reasons:

- Where the dominant undertaking is subject to an access obligation with a tightly regulated (i.e., cost-oriented) access price, it is constrained from extracting retail profits by means of its access price. It then has an incentive to raise its rivals' costs by means of non-price parameters like quality or product characteristics. The dominant undertaking in this way can increase its profits by increasing its market share on the retail market as well as the retail price[120] and might even be able to (re-) monopolise the retail market. If the access price is regulated above costs, there is a trade-off between access and retail profits and thus the incentive to raise rivals' costs by means of non-price discrimination may be weaker[121].

- Incentives to foreclose the retail market may also be present without regulation whenever an upstream monopolist faces potential competition on the wholesale market. This might be the case if entry at the retail level facilitates subsequent expansion by entrants into the upstream stage. After having developed a customer base, the risk of sunk-cost investments on the upstream level might be reduced[122].

- An unregulated vertically integrated undertaking with market power on the wholesale market may have an incentive to apply a margin squeeze if there is an alternative supplier of the wholesale product. Independent retail undertakings may buy the access

---

[118] In the following, the upstream market will be referred to as the wholesale market and the downstream market as the retail market. The same considerations apply, however, for any two vertically related markets, i.e., also two wholesale markets.
[119] See, e.g., Armstrong (2002, p. 305) or Rey/Tirole (1997, p. 7).
[120] See Economides (1998) and Beard et al (2001).
[121] Cf. Sibley/Weisman (1998) and Beard et al (2001).
[122] Cf. Beard et al (2003).

service from the alternative supplier, which will reduce the access profits of the incumbent. By setting a retail price which does not allow retail competitors to cover their costs given the access charge, the dominant undertaking is able to foreclose the retail as well as the wholesale market as long as the alternative supplier of the access service cannot undercut the incumbent's access price[123].

- The unregulated monopolist will also deny access to alternative operators less efficient than its own retail business[124]. This may not be a problem from the point of view of static efficiency, however, is likely to be detrimental to customers as in the long run the (dynamic) gains from competition remain unexhausted.

- The unregulated vertically integrated monopolist also is likely to have incentives to foreclose the retail market whenever there is no perfect competition on the downstream level. If alternative operators have (some) market power (e.g. because of product differentiation), they will be able to retain some level of profits. This is also referred to as a double mark-up problem, as both the monopolist upstream as well as the alternative operator downstream set prices above costs. In such situations, the monopolist can increase its profits by foreclosing the retail market as this will allow him to capture the rents, which have been captured by the alternative operator before.

This list is not exhaustive. In general it can be stated that incentives to leverage market power into the retail market exist whenever the dominant undertaking is unable to extract all rents from the retail market and/or wherever downstream competition would lead to an erosion of its upstream market power.

Against this background, the following conclusions can be drawn: A vertically integrated monopolist on the wholesale market may be able to exert its market power by charging an excessive price for the wholesale input. If this is not possible for some reason, which is frequently the case, it is likely to attempt to exploit its market power by leveraging it into the retail market. This can be done either by denial of access or by means of a margin squeeze. Alternatively, and in particular in cases of mandatory access and access price regulation, discrimination on other parameters like quality, time, or product characteristics may be used. Incentives for leveraging will also exist if there is potential competition at the wholesale level, in particular if retail entry facilitates market entry on the upstream market.

It has to be mentioned, finally, that economic literature points out some cases, where exclusionary practices may be economically justified. If, for example, specific investments are necessary for one or both of the vertically related undertakings, a situation of 'bilateral monopoly' may emerge, which is associated with high transaction costs (this is also referred to as a 'hold-up' problem). In such a case, transaction costs can be reduced by vertical integration of the two undertakings[125]. Vertical foreclosure can also be welfare enhancing if it allows the dominant undertaking to enforce price discrimination on the retail market without which the fixed costs of production could not be covered[126]. When – as a consequence of regulatory intervention – price discrimination is rendered impossible, the product fails to cover its costs and will no longer be provided. Thus, although vertical foreclosure will in general have negative effects, welfare is likely to be reduced whenever the production of a particular good is ceased in response to regulatory intervention.

In the remainder of Section 5.2, the competition problems 1.1 to 1.11 (as identified in Chapter 2) will be discussed.

---

[123] Cf. Beard et al (2003).
[124] Cf. Armstrong (2002).
[125] Cf. Rey et al (2001, p. 18).
[126] Cf. Rey et al (2001, pp. 19-21).

5.2.2 Refusal to deal/Denial of access

Refusal to deal/denial of access is referred to as standard competition problem 1.1. in Chapter 2. The strategic variable it is based on is the choice of the 'contractual partner' by the dominant undertaking. If the possibility to bypass the incumbent's wholesale product is limited, a refusal to deal will directly lead to foreclosure of the retail market.

As expressed in the principles 2 and 3 in Chapter 4, NRAs have to ensure sufficient access to wholesale products where replication is not considered feasible, while on the other hand, NRAs have to promote infrastructure investment in those areas where replication is considered to be feasible. In the following, therefore, it will be argued that in case of the competition problem of refusal to deal/denial of access the following measures are appropriate: (i) ensuring access to the necessary input and (ii) setting an appropriate price for the input. These issues will be discussed in turn.

5.2.2.1 Ensuring access

As discussed in the previous section, a vertically integrated operator with market power on the wholesale market will – in absence of access price regulation – deny access to its wholesale product whenever retail entry would – in the short or in the long run – erode its market power on the wholesale market. By denying access, the dominant undertaking can preserve its market power and charge an excessive price on the retail market. In this way it can leverage its market power from the wholesale market into the potentially competitive retail market. The welfare effects of such behaviour are clearly negative.

Competition at the wholesale level of course would solve the problem. In the communications sector, however, market power frequently rests on circumstances exogenous to the NRA like significant economies of scale and large sunk costs which make assets non-replicable. The only way in which competition on the downstream market can be created in such a situation is that the SMP undertaking grants access to the necessary input it produces. If this cannot be secured by commercial negotiation, the provisions of the Access Directive will need to be invoked.

The NRA will need to consider if the obligation of non-discrimination according to Art 10 AD is likely to be appropriate to force the SMP undertaking to grant access to the wholesale input. The NRA would have to ensure that non-discrimination between the own retail business and (potential) retail competitors implied that the same wholesale product is supplied to both companies. If the NRA comes to the conclusion that non-discrimination on its own would not remove the distortion to competition, non-discrimination could be envisaged to be an ancillary remedy.

Transparency as a remedy can help to bolster non-discrimination. Taken together, these remedies, along with regulatory oversight, could be considered. However, whilst transparency would make non-discrimination easier to enforce, it would not tackle the core of the problem. In these circumstances, it is likely that imposing access under Article 12 is the cornerstone of an effective set of remedies.

Establishing the obligation to meet reasonable requests for access, the NRA would also have to consider the potential for commercial negotiation in respect of access prices. If the underlying incentives and experience or evidence gained through the market analysis strongly suggested that there remains a considerable risk of excessive prices (or other pricing practices that can have a negative effect on competition), then the NRA should consider a price control rule.

Where the NRA is considering access to an enduring non-replicable network element, there is an expectation of on-going reliance to a key input. Thus, there is a strong case for setting out a clear and predictable basis for access so that both parties can make long term business plans on a solid platform. In these instances, the difference in negotiation power is likely to be such that on-going regulatory oversight is necessary.

When replication is feasible the NRA should, in line with the Access Directive, use access regulation as a tool to promote competition over competing infrastructure as a long-term goal. This is discussed in section 5.2.2.3 of this Chapter.

5.2.2.2   Setting the wholesale access price

5.2.2.2.1   Introduction

Where an SMP undertaking is vertically integrated, which is typically the case in ECS markets, it is likely to have the incentive and ability to foreclose downstream markets by restricting access to wholesale inputs over which it has SMP, often facilitated in part by excessive pricing at the wholesale level. Whilst the incentive to foreclose downstream markets is not generally present where SMP undertakings are not vertically integrated, the incentive to charge excessive wholesale prices is (as discussed in the sections on single market dominance and termination) still also prevalent. Thus, irrespective of its incentives to foreclose downstream markets, the SMP undertaking will typically have the incentive and ability to supply its input – either voluntarily or because of an Art 12 AD access obligation – at an excessive price, which may ultimately lead to excessive prices at the retail level. To promote downstream competition, and ultimately to protect consumers from the exercise of market power, a price regulation on the wholesale market is likely to be appropriate where the market power cannot be expected to erode within a reasonable period of time.

The only remedy by which a tendency towards excessive prices at the wholesale level can directly be targeted is an Art 13 AD price control and cost accounting obligation. Art 13 AD explicitly refers to access pricing in situations '... where a market analysis indicates that a lack of effective competition means that the operator concerned might sustain prices at an excessively high level, or apply a price squeeze, to the detriment of end users'.

Alternatively to Art 13 AD, a non-discrimination obligation (Art 10 AD) might be considered in order to regulate the access price. Under such an obligation, the SMP undertaking would be required to charge independent retail undertakings the same price it implicitly charges its own retail business or affiliated companies. The internal transfer price may be determined by means of an obligation of accounting separation according to Art 11 AD, and can then be applied as an access price to third parties. A question here from the perspective of proportionality is whether Art 10 in combination with Art 11 AD allows the NRA to arrive at the same access prices as under Art 13 AD. This seems unlikely, however, as Art 11 AD only states that NRAs '... may specify the format and accounting methodology to be used', whereas under Art 13 AD NRAs are also allowed to '... use cost accounting methods independent of those used by the undertaking'. Therefore, certain methodologies to calculate the access price which may be used under Art 13 AD might not be feasible under Art 10.

Relying solely on the combination of non-discrimination and accounting separation remedies as a method of setting access prices also carries a risk that the resultant transfer price will not be meaningful to the SMP undertaking; i.e. it may not reflect the true resource cost to the SMP undertaking of serving its downstream business. Thus in order to ensure that the price cannot be used to distort downstream competition, it should be subject to, and pass, a price squeeze test, for which an Article 13 obligation is a pre-requisite.

Hence an Art 13 AD obligation, which is not only more explicit about the use of cost accounting systems but also about the burden of proof, the requirements on the SMP operator and the goals related to the pricing methodology, may sometimes be more appropriate. In deciding which option to adopt, NRAs have to be aware that the potential costs of regulation may be lower under Art 10 and Art 11 AD obligations compared to Art

13 AD (which may also have to be backed by Art 11 AD). On the other side, the potential benefits from Art 13 AD regulation (for example, more efficient prices) may also be lower under certain circumstances. Thus, the best option can only be selected on a case by case basis.

Art 13 AD requires NRAs to ensure that any cost recovering mechanism or pricing methodology that is mandated serves to promote efficiency and sustainable competition and maximises consumer benefits. There are a range of approaches to determining the appropriate wholesale access price. The selection of the appropriate pricing approach to address a given situation will generally require a balance to be struck between a number of considerations. Whilst this assessment can be made on a case by case basis, this section will examine some considerations to be taken into account. It should also be noted that the price imposed under Art 13AD can take several forms. The NRA can set a specific access price, and/or it may set a glide path, whereby prices must converge from their current levels to a specified level over time, or reduce by a certain percentage as with a price cap. The selection between these methods must again be made on a case by case basis, however the principles of the framework, such as proportionality, must always be taken into account. Another factor to consider is the impact of contract terms (e.g. contract length) between the SMP operator and particular access seekers, which may mean there is no uniquely correct access price.

Current best practice suggests that NRAs use the following main approaches in order to establish the appropriate wholesale access price:

- Cost orientation: Linking prices to cost information derived from cost accounting models/systems, such as, e.g., LRIC (long-run incremental costs) or FDC/FAC (fully distributed/allocated costs);

- The 'retail-minus' approach, in which the "minus" may be calculated on the basis either of the incumbent's efficiently incurred retail costs or alternatively on the basis of an efficient new entrant's retail costs;

- Benchmarking, e.g. against other countries, where the price is arrived at on the basis of comparison with prices of similar services.

5.2.2.2.2 Cost orientation

Cost-oriented prices are most appropriate in situations where market power at the upstream level allows the SMP undertaking to charge prices above costs and where it is unlikely that this market power will be constrained by competition within a reasonable period of time (i.e. particularly in cases where replication is not considered feasible). It is recognised in the Access Directive that cost orientation is the most stringent form of price control.

The cost orientation methodologies most frequently employed by NRAs are LRIC and FDC. The LRIC approach calculates the costs (including a reasonable rate of return) of the increment the SMP undertaking has to produce in order to provide the service to independent retail undertakings (including its own retail arm). This can be understood as broadly reflecting the avoidable costs of providing the service. Given the forward-looking nature of LRIC, the method of asset valuation employed is typically one that reflects current costs, such as with CCA. In practice, the concept of forward-looking costs requires that assets are valued using the cost of replacement with the modern equivalent asset (MEA). The gross MEA value is what it would cost to replace an old asset with a technically up to date new one with the same service capability, allowing for any differences both in quality of output and in operating costs. The MEA will generally incorporate the latest available and proven technology, and will therefore be the asset that a new entrant might be expected to employ. These issues are further explored in the ERG Common Position on Accounting Separation and Cost Accounting[127].

It will also be necessary, particularly with top down LRIC models, to assess what costs are relevant for and appropriate to deriving LRIC data. There may be costs currently incurred that are inconsistent with a forward looking long run view of the business and which should be excluded or adjusted in the modelled cost base. Examples may be restructuring costs or costs of surplus capacity that arise from past decisions contradictory to best management practice

Calculating the LRIC-price, NRAs may use either a 'top-down' model, starting with the undertaking's actual costs and correcting them for inefficiencies, or a 'bottom-up' model, where the costs of an efficient undertaking are reconstructed using economic/engineering models of an efficient network. NRAs may also combine both models in their calculation, or may use one model as a 'sanity check' on the other. When using a cost model, a decision is needed about whether to adopt a "scorched node" or "scorched earth" approach[128].

The LRIC price usually also contains some kind of mark-up allowing for the joint and common costs of the SMP player. Where costs are directly attributable to the provision of a particular service, consistency with the objectives of the framework and considerations such as cost causality would suggest that these costs are allocated to these services. However, to the extent there are indirect costs, there is necessarily a degree of arbitrariness in their allocation amongst the different services served by the common infrastructure. In order to minimise the arbitrariness, the distribution of joint and common costs is usually made by means of distribution keys (e.g. volumes or in proportion to incremental costs) within the LRIC calculation. These types of cost allocation methods have the advantage of being relatively simple to implement, although they do not necessarily represent the most efficient way in which to recover these costs. The notion of Ramsey-Prices refers to a particular method to distribute joints and common costs, whereby these costs are allocated with reference to demand elasticities. Although this allocation method may be more optimal, the requirement for detailed information about total costs, marginal costs and demand elasticities means that Ramsey-Prices can generally be regarded as having low practical feasibility.

With the FDC methodology, access prices are calculated based on the actual cost of the undertaking, which may be evaluated at historic (HCA) or at current (CCA) values. The choice between these two approaches can be largely seen as a trade-off between economic relevance and practicality. Due to the relatively rich availability of historical information, HCA is typically a relatively easy method of asset valuation to implement. However, based on historic costs, an FDC calculation may allow the undertaking to earn returns on inefficient investments, and hence not reflect the economic costs of providing the service consistent with those of a competitive market. This risk is reduced when assets are valued using CCA, since the valuation will tend to be more economically meaningful, and hence send more relevant price signals to current and potential market participants. However, even under this methodology, the undertaking might be compensated for inefficiencies to the extent that the existence of certain cost items is not consistent with the operation of an efficient undertaking. Thus, NRAs may decide to exclude inefficiently accrued costs from the calculation, in which case FDC may come close to a top-down LRIC approach. As Art 13 (2) AD states that NRAs "... shall ensure that any cost recovery mechanism or pricing methodology that is mandated serves to promote efficiency", FDC appears to be in line with Art 13 to the extent that inefficiencies are not allowed for (similar to a top-down LRIC model) or if there is no (or very limited) concern about inefficiencies. In accounting for

---

[127] "Guidelines for implementing the Commission Recommendation C(2005) 3480 on Accounting Separation and Cot Accounting Systems under the regulatory framework for electronic communications" - ERG (05) 29
[128] See paragraph 4.2.3 of the ERG Common Position – ERG (05) 29.

these inefficiencies, NRAs may wish to apply a glide path to prices, whereby prices converge over time to reflect efficient costs, in order not to impose significant shocks on the market and to allow a transitional adjustment period for industry players.

The appropriate costing methodology will tend to reflect the objectives specific to each case[129]. FDC models are useful in providing an indication of access prices. LRIC, whilst typically more resource- and information-intensive, has the advantage, through the use of cost-volume relationships, of better illuminating how costs change in the long-run in response to changes in the relevant volume increment. Due to this close linkage to a notion of forward-looking economic costs, LRIC may better signal the prices that are relevant to decision-making on a forward-looking basis. Where used in preference to LRIC, FDC approaches will require careful analysis and exclusion of inefficiently incurred costs and an assessment of the reasonableness of the allocation of common costs to the services in question.

In order to be able to calculate the access price, an NRA may need information about the dominant undertaking's costs. In the case of a vertically integrated undertaking it might therefore be necessary to impose an Art 11 AD obligation of accounting separation in order to be able to separate parts of the retail business from any or all of the services in the wholesale business and derive the wholesale cost base by specifying the format and accounting methodology to be used. Any further information necessary for the calculation of the access price can be demanded under Art 5 of the Framework Directive (Provision of Information)[130].

Although these methodologies are used by most NRAs, some economists have argued that some costing methodologies may fail to provide the right investment incentives to the entrant and stifle investment incentives of the incumbent[131]. To what extent the allegedly missing incentives are in fact included in the cost calculation is still an open issue. In general it has to be noted that although there is a danger of setting the access price too low, there is also a danger of setting it too high, allowing the incumbent to exploit its market power, resulting in excessive prices for consumers and allowing the SMP undertaking to earn excessive returns, and possibly promoting inefficient entry on the wholesale level.

5.2.2.2.3   Retail-minus access pricing[132]

While "retail minus" prices can be regarded as a special case of an "efficient component pricing rule" (ECPR) price, the more general forms of ECPR are rarely employed in practice, either because of inconsistency with regulatory policy objectives or impracticability or both. They will not be considered further here.

While the label "retail minus" is in universal use, the method can be and is used in practice to derive any upstream price from a price of a service further downstream.

The classical form of retail minus price is calculated on the basis of the incumbent's retail price and its costs of providing the retail service

$$P_A = P_R - C_R$$

---

[129]   For example, the Commission has proposed that in LLU markets characterised by low penetration and prices above the EU average, a forward looking long-run incremental cost ("FL-LRIC") model may be more appropriate in addressing the lack of effective competition than a fully distributed historic costs ("FDHC") methodology, notably in terms of tariffs, potential excessive costs and incumbent's inefficiency. See cases PT/2004/0117, HU/2005/0185.

[130]   This is not an SMP-obligation but a general provision.

[131]   See, e.g., Hausman (1997) and dotecon (2001).

[132]   See also the IRG consultation document IRG(05) 39.

where P_A is the access price, P_R the retail price, and C_R the incumbent's costs at the retail level. This ensures that only undertakings at least as efficient as the incumbent have incentives to enter the market. In some cases, however, 'inefficient' (e.g. small-scale) entry might be desirable, as short-run productive inefficiencies may be more than outweighed by the enhanced allocative efficiencies and long-run (dynamic) advantages provided by competition. In such cases, the 'minus' might be set at the costs of the entrant (including unexhausted economies of scale or scope) to avoid a margin squeeze. This issue is dealt with in depth in the Annex.

The retail-minus approach is - without retail price regulation - not able to immediately bring down excessive access prices to a cost-oriented level. As the wholesale price is calculated as the retail price minus the costs of an efficient undertaking, an excessive retail price will automatically feed into an excessive wholesale price (or vice versa)[133]. It might therefore be applied in cases where the problem of excessive prices is less of a concern to the regulator. This may be the case where circumstances are such that the market power at the wholesale level is likely to erode within a reasonable period of time, such as where replicability of the underlying assets is seen to be a potential future development. Also, there may be a lack of clarity about the evolution of costs, or where flexibility regarding wholesale prices might be appropriate. In these cases, the long-run distortions which result from excessive prices might be negligible such that the remedy of cost-orientation is not appropriate. A retail-minus access price usually also prevents the dominant undertaking from exposing its competitors to a margin squeeze, as it links wholesale and retail prices such that an independent retail undertaking as efficient as the incumbent is able to compete. In the presence of economies of scope or scale on the retail market, however, it will usually be difficult to set the margin such that is allows alternative operators as well as the SMP operator's retail arm to compete on a level playing field. Such issues are considered in greater detail in the Annex.

Under a retail-minus access price, the incentives of the dominant undertaking to discriminate against retail competitors may be reduced, as profits can be made by setting an excessive wholesale price in some cases. As long as the threat of backward integration exists, or if the SMP undertaking cannot extract all rents, the NRA will need to monitor behaviour on the market and ensure that no actions are taken to foreclose the retail market by means of non-price discrimination[134].

5.2.2.2.4 Benchmarking

This section deals with the use of benchmarking for the purpose of setting a wholesale access price. There are of course many other uses and the considerations set out below would not necessarily apply in those cases.

To the extent that it would be considered disproportionate to impose cost-orientation and cost-accounting obligations (e.g. on small operators) or where appropriate cost models do not yet exist, other forms of price-control could be considered for such operators, such as benchmarking against the larger operators who are under a cost-orientation obligation[135]. Benchmarking[136] ties the price in one market to the price in another comparable market (sometimes in the form of an international comparison).

Benchmarking also has a number of other valuable uses. In the context of cost-oriented prices, it may be used as a cross-check on the outputs of a cost model. On the basis of a

---

[133] See Economides (1997) or Armstrong (2002, p. 326).
[134] Sometimes, however, 'inefficient' (e.g. small-scale) entry might be desirable; see discussion above and in the Annex.
[135] See Commission comments on cases FI/2003/0028-0029, FR/2005/0228.
[136] See AD Art 13(2).

suitable comparison, it may also be used to set reasonable prices or as a cross-check on the reasonableness of a retail-minus price derived from the incumbent's financial data.

The relevance of the comparator figures is key to the use of benchmarking for setting an access price. If a NRA decides to impose price regulation on the basis of a comparison with other countries, it needs to have reason to believe that the overseas prices are relevant to its own case. This might not be the case if conditions prevailing on the relevant overseas market(s) were known to be fundamentally different from those which prevailed in its home market. The comparison could also be problematical if different cost standards were used in some of the other countries (e.g. some prices were cost-oriented, others not)[137]. Nevertheless, benchmarking should not be ruled out because a perfect comparison cannot be verified. Other methods also have their disadvantages and the NRA will need to choose the method which strikes the right balance, taking into account the regulatory objectives and the practical considerations of implementing each possible method.

5.2.2.2.5 Conclusion

Selecting a certain methodology for the calculation of the access price, NRAs should also be aware that the obligation to grant access at a cost-oriented price is probably the most intrusive measure an NRA can impose within the new regulatory framework. It is not only demanding to the NRA, which has to set the 'right' access price (in particular with regard to investment incentives) and monitor compliance, but may also create incentives to shift anti-competitive behaviour from price to non-price variables, which are even more difficult to monitor and thus increase monitoring costs. At the same time, the setting of prices on a retail-minus basis can also be a complex and resource-intensive process, particularly where determining the appropriate size of the 'minus' requires considerable work by the NRA. In choosing its methodology, the NRA will need to satisfy itself that the benefits expected from that approach are sufficient to justify the resources which both it and the regulated player will be required to commit. That will sometimes lead the NRA to choose a method which is less resource-intensive, such as benchmarking or an obligation to charge "reasonable" prices, provided that this is consistent with the regulatory policy objectives.

However, the potential benefits from cost-oriented regulation are large. Where market power at the wholesale level is expected to endure (i.e. where replication is not considered feasible), the setting of a cost oriented access price appears to be the only possibility to open the retail market to competitors and bring prices down to a competitive level. Market entry and increased competition is likely to lead to lower prices, efficient production, more innovation and more variety for consumers.

When setting the access price, NRAs are influencing the investment incentives of the incumbent and the alternative operators. This is a crucial point within the new regulatory framework, as only the right investment incentives ensure that alternative infrastructure is built where desirable, leading to the emergence of self-sustained competition.

5.2.2.3 Incentives to invest

As formulated in principle 3 of Chapter 4, NRAs should ensure that investment incentives are such that alternative operators will replicate the incumbent's infrastructure where this is technically possible and economically desirable (undistorted make-or-buy incentive), whereas at the same time they should make sure that the incumbent has incentives to maintain and upgrade its network. In this, NRAs should form, where possible, a view on whether replication can be considered feasible or not on a case-by-case basis, taking into account all the relevant technological, economic and timing dimensions.

---

[137] See Commission comments on case DK/2005/0204.

The concept of the ladder of investment is significant in ensuring coherent access regulation across the value chain. Nevertheless, NRAs should be mindful to avoid "micro-managing" competition. NRAs should not pick the winners or choose winning technologies, but regulation must remove distortions and ensure a level playing field/competitive conditions via consistent pricing giving the right signals for efficient investment in all technologies thereby encouraging sustainable infrastructure competition. Thus NRAs should provide the door of opportunity for investment in a technological neutral manner and not misunderstand the ladder of investment as a form of industry policy. Any regulatory intervention is only justified as long as it fulfils the objective of promoting sustainable competition providing consumers with good choice in quality and price, anything over and above this aim is outside the scope of regulators and must be left to policy makers.

Choosing the access point and the access price are probably the most crucial decisions by which an NRA can influence the investment incentives of the alternative operators as well as of the incumbent(s). The remainder of this section will briefly consider these points.

The setting of the access price has to be considered from a static as well as from a dynamic perspective. From a static point of view[138], NRAs have to ensure productive as well as allocative efficiency. Productive efficiency means that only those undertakings have incentives to produce, which can do so at minimal costs, whereas allocative efficiency refers to a situation where prices reflect costs and no undertaking is able to earn super-normal profits.

If there are no other distortions in the industry, productive and allocative efficiency in a static sense is most likely to be achieved by a cost-oriented access price[139]. Whereas a cost-oriented access price allows the incumbent to cover its costs (allocative efficiency), only those alternative operators will enter the retail market which are at least as efficient as the incumbent (productive efficiency at the retail level). Furthermore, alternative operators will replicate the incumbents' assets only if they can produce the wholesale product at the same or at lower costs than the incumbent (productive efficiency at the wholesale level). An access price above costs is likely to result into inefficient bypass (economically inefficient duplication of the incumbent's assets) and into excessive profits for the incumbent, whereas too low an access price opens the retail market to inefficient entrants whilst at the same time curbing the incumbent's investment incentives to an inefficiently low level.

It follows therefore, that the level of access prices is positively correlated with investment incentives for the incumbent as well as for the entrant in a static framework (although too high an access price is likely to lead to statically inefficient investment decisions). This is not necessarily the case from a dynamic point of view, however[140]. Here, too high access prices may inhibit rather than promote alternative investments. Due to the high risk involved in investments with a high share of sunk costs, alternative operators are likely to follow a step-by-step approach, continuously expanding their customer base and infrastructure investments. The initial availability of the incumbent's infrastructure at low prices will make it easier for alternative operators to enter the market and develop a customer base. Equipped with a customer base, uncertainty is considerably reduced and the operator may then be ready to take further investments (this is sometimes referred to as the 'ladder of investment'). Initially, regulators may even decide to trade static inefficiency for the advantages of dynamic efficiencies resulting from intensified competition by setting the access price at a level allowing for disadvantages in economies of scale and scope of the entrant. In the presence of first mover advantages of the incumbent associated with high

---

[138] For an economic analysis of access pricing in a static environment see, e.g., Armstrong (2002).
[139] See, however, Armstrong (2002) for situations where an access price other than cost-oriented may be desirable, e.g. in situations where retail tariffs are unbalanced or where excess profits on the downstream level exist.
[140] See Cave et al (2001).

switching costs, entry might also be considerably facilitated if the access price is set at a level allowing for these switching costs.

In order to promote investment into alternative infrastructure, NRAs may have to signal in their reviews – as pointed out in Chapter 4 – that they view some remedies as bridging a gap so that new entrants can more easily make incremental investment but that market players cannot base their long-term business models on the basis of these remedies alone. NRAs may decide, for example, to adopt a dynamic access pricing regime, with an access price which is initially low, but rises over time. This allows the alternative operator to develop a customer base without having to make risky investments at the outset, while it also provides incentives to climb up the 'ladder of investment' in order to be able to provide the access service in-house as soon as the (external) access price increases. Pursuing such a strategy, NRAs should also take into account differences in the manner and the point in time of market entry by different alternative operators as well as general investment conditions.

Such an active strategy presupposes, furthermore, that the NRA has sufficient knowledge about which assets of the incumbent can efficiently be replicated, or, more precise, in which segments of the market replication is technically feasible and economically efficient within a reasonable period of time. Whereas this is likely to be the case for some segments, there remains uncertainty of different degree in others. In such situations, regulators have to carefully assess the benefits from increased competition against the danger of eliciting inefficient duplication, stranded costs or excess capacity and the danger of ending up with a new monopoly if replication does not occur and downstream competition is stifled due to high access prices. Wherever an analysis of options indicates that negative aspects are likely to prevail, NRAs may decide to adopt a more 'neutral' approach, set the prices for the relevant access products at some measure of costs (which is consistent with static efficiency), monitor the market outcome, continually reassess their views and keep up discussion with the industry. In these situations NRAs should bear in mind the long term objective of ensuring infrastructure competition where feasible.

Taking such an approach would be justified as alternative operators may also be prepared to climb the ladder of investment without additional incentives (such as a dynamic access price), since market dynamics may create incentives to invest on their own. If an alternative operator starts out at the service level, the risks associated with sunk infrastructure investments will be relatively high, resulting in a high cost of capital. By and by, as the operator develops a customer base, this risk of exit is likely to be reduced, as experience is gained and name recognition is developed. This is likely to result into lower costs of capital as the risk associated with sunk cost investments is linked to the probability of subsequent exit, which clearly declines as soon as a customer base and a 'trademark' have been built up[141]. Therefore, the incentives to invest may increase over time for successful service providers without additional regulatory intervention. However, as more and more of these investments are at lower levels in the network hierarchy, both the size of the investments and the proportion that is potentially sunk increases. Against this, the benefits to the new entrant in terms of controlling more and more of the services that they can deliver to customers are also important in terms of giving incentives to reduce reliance, where feasible, on the access provider. It is then up to the NRA to monitor whether investment incentives are indeed self-propelling or whether additional incentives are needed.

Empirical evidence supporting the 'ladder of investment' idea is provided in Cave et al (2001), who, after an analysis of access policy and investment strategy in the Netherlands, conclude (p. 14):

> 'Our analysis of entrants' strategies in the Netherlands points to the progressive nature of their involvement in infrastructure. Typically, each has a strategic asset,

---

[141] Cf. Beard et al (1998 p. 319).

which might be a cable network, or facilities for the construction of a national network, or a relationship with an international operator, or simply marketing and retailing expertise. Capitalising on these assets, entrants can readily identify areas where they can replicate the incumbent's assets or (in the case of new service) be the first to install them. During this initial period they are heavily reliant upon the incumbent's network services. However, if the signs from the initial investments are favourable, then the entrant will expand the scope of its activities – obviously choosing those areas where the assets are fairly easily replicable.'

In a report for the European Commission, Ovum cited the examples of dynamic pricing for wholesale broadband services by the CRTC in Canada and by OPTA in the Netherlands[142]. Ovum notes that NRAs can justify this measure in that it promotes infrastructure competition on account of the dynamic benefits that this brings.

More recent evidence can be found in the ERG Broadband market competition Report[143] which showed that a number of European NRAs followed – sometimes without explicit reference – the model of the ladder. That Report suggests that in countries with an appropriate range and quality of access products and complementary products such as migration, there tend to be deeper levels of infrastructure investment, leading broadband markets to be more sustainably competitive. Lately, the working of the concept of the ladder was confirmed by data presented in the 11th Implementation Report[144]: "Equally, the data show that market entrants are investing more in infrastructure, thus boding well for the sustainability of competition" and even more explicitly stating that "the framework's concept of the investment ladder is still useful"[145]. "For example the countries with the highest penetration (above 15%) all have high cable penetration but often also well-developed access regimes such as for LLU or bitstream. There have also been some notable successes such as in France, the United Kingdom, Austria and Estonia, where a combination of competing infrastructure and effective regulation have stimulated competition and resulted in relatively high broadband penetration"[146].

The progressive nature of infrastructure investment is in general confirmed by NRAs' experiences, as several cases have been observed already where alternative operators were gradually rolling out their networks making use of different access products (e.g. going from bitstream access to local loop unbundling). The shift[147] from the lower rungs (resale and bitstream) towards higher forms of access (shared and fully unbundled access to the local loop) became more markedly in the period covered by the 11th Implementation Report (October 2004 – October 2005) clearly indicating the process of moving up the ladder is working in practice as the following quotation underlines: "New entrants are gradually shifting from resale and bitstream access towards local loop unbundling in the provision of broadband services"[148]. France is in general the example quoted most often as demonstrating the progression up the ladder. Most recently, this trend (progression up the ladder) has been confirmed with the data collected by the Communications Committee for its latest broadband report[149].

Where new entrants gradually roll-out their own networks, regulators can start removing rungs corresponding to markets shown to have SMP no longer. As new entrants start using their own infrastructure and climb the ladder, the process might also be reinforced by the

---

[142] Cf. Ovum (2003, pp. 52, 53).
[143] Cf. ERG Broadband market competition report (ERG (05) 23), May 2005, Annex A "Country Studies".
[144] Available at:
http://europa.eu.int/information_society/policy/ecomm/implementation_enforcement/index_en.htm.
[145] 11th Implementation Report, Annex I, COM(2006)68, SEC(2006)193, p. 8/9.
[146] 11th Implementation Report, COM(2006)68, p. 6.
[147] Cf. also above 4.2.3, Complementarity of access products", p. 71.
[148] 11th Implementation Report, COM(2006)68, p. 7 and 11th Implementation Report, Annex II, COM(2006)68, SEC(2006)193, p. 57 (Figure 55).
[149] Broadband Data – COCOM 06-12 of 22 March 2006

offering of wholesale products by new entrants. With competition becoming more intense, NRAs may have to regulate only the "higher rungs". For example, in France, the Netherlands and Spain, new entrants offer resale or bitstream access products to third parties on the basis of bitstream access or shared/full unbundled access from the SMP operator. The theoretical model of the ladder of investment foresees that the regulator should not only encourage access, but may actively support the upward move by signalling either through dynamic pricing or sunset clauses that regulation will be removed (thus new entrants should not establish themselves forever on a particular rung, i.e. business models should not be built on the unlimited availability of specific mandated access products). However, at least in the case of broadband markets, it is too early to anticipate when and how these elements can be introduced by NRAs in practice[150] without risking disruption[151].

Wherever the incumbent's network is opened to competitors at more than one level (e.g. local loop unbundling, carrier pre-selection and wholesale line rental), NRAs have to be careful to correctly design the relative prices of the different options in relation to one another and in relation to the retail prices prevailing in the market. Too low a price on one level may inhibit investment on another level, where replication may be desirable. If a new possibility of market entry is opened up by the regulator, therefore, it has to take into account the options which already exist and ensure consistency between them. NRAs should further make sure that frictionless switching from one access service to another, after additional infrastructure investments have been taken (migration), is possible, in particular with regard to the consumer's perception. This could be ensured by obligations attached to an Art 12 AD access obligation and/or to a reference offer according to Art 9 (2) AD.

From a dynamic perspective it is also particularly important to ensure investment incentives for the incumbent to maintain and upgrade its network in those sectors where a replication of assets is unlikely to happen.

In the context of an emerging market there may be the need for regulatory action if a failure to act will lead to the foreclosure of the emerging market. This can occur where the emerging market depends upon inputs that cannot be replicated or substituted within a reasonable period of time. In these circumstances, there may be grounds for early regulatory intervention in the market from which the market power could be leveraged to guarantee access to this input in the normal manner, in order to allow competition to develop in the emerging market. In this way, the distinct nature of the emerging market is maintained whilst at the same time preventing foreclosure by applying regulation only on the necessary input market and not on the emerging market itself.

In these circumstances, the NRA should attempt to leave the incumbent and the new entrant in an equivalent position in terms of investment incentives. In this way, both the new entrant and the incumbent can address the new market opportunities on an equal footing in terms of access to necessary legacy network inputs that are non-replicable. However, if the new investment is being made by a new entrant that necessarily requires an input from an SMP operator, the NRA will have a role to ensure that access to this input is not denied, delayed or otherwise obstructed.

An important issue arises when a new investment by an SMP firm, which is designed to deliver genuinely new services, can also be used to deliver services that are currently subject to regulation. SMP operators, when considering making investments in emerging markets, should bear in mind their on-going obligations in relation to existing markets. Whenever possible, they should configure the new technology such that they continue to accommodate access seekers in existing markets.

---

[150] Until now only OPTA introduced dynamic access pricing.
[151] Speeding up the process too much may create the opposite effect of efficient new entrants "falling down the ladder" (i.e. exiting the market).

In all these cases, NRAs must attempt to strike a balance that maintains competition in current services, whilst at the same time preserving the incentives to invest and innovate both for the SMP operator and the entrants, as these incentives will ensure more competition in the long-term[152]. If it is deemed necessary to set access prices, NRAs should ensure that they bear in mind the initial investment and the risks involved in making the investment[153]. Regulatory controls on retail services are already seen as a last resort[154], and in the case of emerging markets, it is difficult to envisage circumstances where regulation of an emerging retail market could be justified.

Textbox 2: Access regulation

Bitstream-access

If the market review leads to the conclusion that market no. 12 - Wholesale broadband access - is not effectively competitive, because e.g. the dominant voice telephony operator leverages its market power of the local loop into the wholesale broadband access market, the NRA has to decide on the proportionate remedy after having identified that company as being an SMP operator. The reason for the lack of competition may be that the SMP operator is not offering an adequate wholesale access product to new entrants thus preventing competitors to offer a differentiated broadband product, including such services as Voice over IP (VoIP), to the end user. In such a situation, the NRA may choose to impose an access obligation acc. to Art. 12 AD and mandate a bitstream access product as a proportionate remedy.

Bitstream access is defined as follows: 'High speed bit-stream access (provision of DSL services by the incumbent operator) refers to the situation where the incumbent installs a high speed access link to the customer premises (e.g. by installing its preferred ADSL equipment and configuration in its local access network) and then makes this access link available to third parties, to enable them to provide high speed services to customers. The incumbent may also provide transmission services to its competitors, to carry traffic to a 'higher' level in the network hierarchy where new entrants may already have a point of presence (e.g., transit switch location). The bit-stream service may be defined as the provision of transmission capacity (upward/downward channels may be asymmetric) between an end-user connected to a telephone connection and the point of handover to the new entrant. Resale offers are not a substitute for bitstream access because they do not allow new entrants to differentiate their services from those of the incumbent'[155].

As bitstream access can be granted at various points of the network hierarchy (points of handover of traffic), the points in the network at which the wholesale broadband access will need to be supplied will depend on national circumstances such as the network topology and the state of broadband competition, but the following characteristics should be kept in mind: bitstream access is an access product that allows new entrants to differentiate (directly or indirectly) their services by altering (directly or indirectly) technical characteristics and/or the use of their own network, which is definitely more than resale, where the incumbent is in control of the technical parameters and manages the service, whereas the new entrant can only market a commercially similar service. When defining the appropriate point of access, NRAs should take the perspective of market parties. The NRA thus has to assess the reasonableness of the requested points of handover asked for by the new entrants and weigh them in relation to the possibilities of the network hierarchy. Furthermore, the state of competition, i.e., the number of market players, the existence of alternative networks and

---

[152] Directive 2002/19/EC, Recital 19.
[153] Directive, 2002/19/EC, Article 12(2).
[154] Directive 2002/21/EC, recital 26.
[155] ONPCOM01-18Rev1 and ONPCOM02-03, quoted in ERG (03) 33rev2 "Bitstream Access - ERG CP - Adopted on 2nd April 2004 and amended on 25th May 2005.

infrastructure and the long run benefit for the consumer of having more choice have to be taken into account.

Bitstream access allows the competitor to differentiate the end user product by adding specific features such as a better contention rate or a lower overbooking factor (other QoS parameters). As the access to the unbundled local loop, to which it is complementary, it is a means to promote infrastructure competition. By investing more in own infrastructure, the competitor climbs up the value chain or the 'ladder of investment', in other words as it can use more and more of its own infrastructure it is able to add gradually more value to the product offered to the end user. At the same time it reduces the reliance on the wholesale products of the dominant operator. In order to enable a step by step increase of investment, NRAs must regulate prices of the various access products consistently if a price control measure acc. to Art. 13 AD is also in place. As discussed above and in the following sections, other remedies may be required to support the obligations according to Art 12 and 13 AD.

Re-selling Access Lines (Wholesale Line rental)

Wholesale line rental describes the possibility of entrants to get access to a wholesale product that allows them to offer not only voice services (through Carrier Selection or Carrier Pre-Selection) but also to rent (in addition) lines from the dominant operator in the access markets on a wholesale basis[156]. Wholesale line rental may also include ancillary services such as voicemail and call waiting, thus enabling alternative operators to replicate the retail service of the incumbent, making possible for the customer to have access to one-stop shopping and - depending on the circumstances - allowing for greater flexibility in bundling and pricing of services. To the extent that such a product is successful in the market, it may also reduce the need for regulatory intervention on the dominant operator's retail tariffs as it may bring service competition to an area in which competition is currently rather limited.

The main impediment to competition within the access network in fixed line telephony is that it is particularly hard to replicate due to significant economies of scale and large sunk costs, as such characteristics of natural monopolies. This is reflected by the fact that incumbent fixed operators in most Member States still have market shares in the access markets of 90% and more.

According to the principles outlined in Chapter 4 and taking into account the characteristics of access networks, NRAs may come to the conclusion that entry into access networks is rather unlikely as it is hard to replicate. In this case, NRAs will have to ensure that service competition is encouraged, that there is a sufficient return on the existing infrastructure to encourage further investment and that attention is given to likely effects on other markets.

Based on Art 12 (1) AD (or - possibly - Art 10 AD), NRAs may therefore consider to impose a wholesale line rental obligation, if it can promote sustainable competition on the retail market or would be otherwise in the end users' interest. Clearly such an obligation does not contribute to infrastructure competition in the same way as would be the case with rolling out own networks or with unbundling of access lines. However, the positive effects to competition can be broader and faster as it may significantly reduce churn and facilitate entrants to build up a customer basis, which in turn may help them to take another step in the 'ladder of investment'.

If a wholesale charge for line rental is mandated, particular consideration will have to be given to its effects on other markets such as the unbundled local loop, as wrong price

---

[156] See Commission's comments in cases UK/2003/0011-0016 and PT/2004/0091

signals might either frustrate investments of operators (and thus interfere with the long term target of more sustainable competition) or lead to a situation where positive effects to competition will not emerge, as the product may not be competitive. Hence pricing will be central to this decision and NRAs may consider to determine the access price on a cost plus (e.g. LRIC) or - if retail tariffs are balanced and reflect costs due to existing regulation - an ECPR basis (which might be retail minus). Many of those NRAs which have mandated a wholesale charge for line rental so far have followed a retail-minus approach. In applying this methodology NRAs will not only have to decide whether avoided or avoidable costs should be the basis for calculating the minus, but also whether and to what extent set-up and other costs to the entrant will have to be shared and to what extent they should be made variable (reducing entry barriers). NRAs will also have to consider whether in calculating a retail minus rental whether to include or exclude call profits.

NRAs will further need to find a balance between removing existing retail price obligations for access lines and the bundling/pricing possibilities for entrants as otherwise the dominant operator in the access market might be put at a competitive disadvantage. In this context NRAs may need to consider to what extent the obligation of Carrier Selection and Carrier Pre-Selection needs to be re-defined for the dominant operator.

5.2.3 General considerations concerning discrimination between SMP player's own downstream business and third parties

Economists have recognised that, in certain circumstances, variation in the terms of supply can be welfare-enhancing. This can be the case even when the supplier has a position of market power. However, in the case of a vertically integrated SMP operator supplying on more favourable terms to its own downstream business, anti-competitive effects would be expected. In principle therefore, the aim of SMP non-discrimination remedies under the Framework should therefore be to prohibit the negative effects of variations in terms of supply, while permitting those effects which are neutral or (occasionally) beneficial to end-users.

5.2.3.1 Interpretation of discriminatory behaviour

As noted above, when an SMP player makes available services on more favourable terms to its downstream operation than to independent third parties, there is often an anti-competitive effect. Article 10(2) of the Access Directive underlines this point by providing that

> "obligations of non-discriminations shall ensure, in particular, that the operator applies equivalent conditions in equivalent circumstances to other undertakings .... as it provides for its own services, or those of its subsidiaries or partners".

While this appears to be clear in legal terms, there may remain uncertainty about what is meant in practice by "equivalent" conditions or "equivalent" circumstances.

SMP players have commercial incentives to avoid compliance with non-discrimination obligations and, in particular, to take advantage of any uncertainty over the practical effect of such a remedy. Uncertainty has disadvantages for all market players. On balance though, the SMP player can be expected to be a net beneficiary of uncertainty, more often than not. Where entrants believe there is lack of clarity over how remedies operate in practice or where they lack confidence that remedies will be enforced vigorously, this may well create a significant practical barrier to entry.

Clarity of interpretation and vigorous enforcement go hand in hand since the latter is unlikely in the absence of the former. Therefore, NRAs should clarify, as far as possible, how the remedy will be interpreted in practice, via identification of forms of behaviour which will be considered to be discriminatory. Article 10 permits either a general formulation (e.g. "the SMP player must not discriminate") or a formulation of the rule which explicitly identifies specific forms of behaviour considered to be discriminatory. Alternatively, the NRA may prefer to provide clarity about specific forms of behaviour considered to be discriminatory through the issue of guidance to market players.

5.2.3.2 Comparison between non-discrimination remedies under the Framework and competition law obligations

It is significant that Article 10 is drafted so as to permit discretion to NRAs to formulate a fully effective remedy. In particular, where justified, non-discrimination rules compliant with Article 10 may be formulated by NRAs so as to place SMP players under more stringent obligations than they would face if they were considered to be dominant for the purposes of competition law. This is particularly so where the rationale for such variation is that the SMP player is able to benefit from an economy of scope or scale which is not available to independent third parties.

5.2.3.3 Effectiveness of non-discrimination remedies

Clearly, to be effective, non-discrimination remedies must not permit variations in terms of supply by SMP players which could reasonably be expected to give rise to distortions of competition. The test quoted above from Article 10(2) goes some way to achieving this. It is a necessary condition for the avoidance of such distortions but cannot be assumed to be sufficient. NRAs must therefore specify non-discrimination remedies in a suitable manner to avoid such adverse effects. The following sections deal with the formulation of discrimination obligations for non-price and pricing issues.

5.2.4 Non-price issues

Without regulation (i.e., no access obligation and no regulated access price, etc.), a vertically integrated undertaking with SMP on the wholesale market is unlikely to discriminate against retail competitors on non-price parameters like quality, information, or product characteristics. It is likely, instead, to either extract downstream rents by setting an excessive price at the wholesale level, or, if this is – for some (non-regulatory) reason – not possible, to foreclose the retail market by denial of access.

Subject to an access obligation according to Art 12 AD in combination with an obligation to set a cost-oriented price according to Art 13 AD, the vertically integrated undertaking has – deprived of the wholesale price as strategic variable – incentives to discriminate between its own retail affiliate and its retail competitors on other strategic variables[157]. Therefore, NRAs will need to engage in on-going regulatory oversight.

The following standard competition problems have been identified in this context (numbering of Chapter 2):

> 1.2. discriminatory use or withholding of information
> 1.3. delaying tactics
> 1.4. bundling/tying
> 1.5. undue requirements
> 1.6. quality discrimination
> 1.7. strategic design of product
> 1.8. undue use of information about competitors

These potential competition problems will now be discussed in turn. As they are likely to arise under an access obligation and a cost-oriented access price in particular, it will be assumed in the following discussion that these remedies (Art 12 AD and Art 13 AD, possibly backed by 11 AD) are already in place. The discussion is based on principle 2 of

---

[157] See discussion above with reference to Economides (1998), Sibley/Weisman (1998), and Beard et al (2001).

Chapter 4, which states that NRAs should prevent the upstream SMP undertaking from distorting downstream competition where access to non-replicable wholesale inputs is granted. The creation of these incentives and the resources required to police them, should be borne in mind by NRAs in choosing remedies.

5.2.4.1   Discriminatory use or withholding of information

This refers to a situation where the SMP undertaking is not outright denying access to its network, however, it refuses to provide the entrant with information needed in order to be able to provide the retail service.

The strategic variable underlying this particular type of behaviour, information, can be addressed by three different types of obligations:

First, the SMP undertaking might be forced to disclose the information under an Access obligation according to Art 12 AD, which allows the NRA to '... attach to those obligations conditions covering fairness, reasonableness and timeliness'. If the relevant information is essential for the access seeker to take advantage of its rights, it would clearly be unreasonable of the SMP undertaking to withhold it.

Alternatively or additionally (depending on the circumstances), NRAs might impose an obligation of transparency (Art 9 AD) which explicitly relates '... to interconnection and/or access, requiring operators to make public specified information, such as accounting information, technical specifications, network characteristics, terms and conditions of supply and use, and prices'. NRAs might '... specify the precise information to be made available, the level of detail required and the manner of publication', and may oblige the SMP undertaking to publish the relevant information in form of a reference offer.

Finally, the integrated undertaking could be forced to disclose all relevant information which also is available to its retail affiliate under an obligation of non-discrimination according to Art 10 AD. The problem here is that this might provide the downstream competitor either with too little or too much information. Information about collocation, for example, might not be provided to the own retail affiliate, whereas much information provided to the retail branch will not be relevant for competitors in the context of access to network facilities. In the context of this section, the obligation of non-discrimination therefore seems to be suited only in those cases where the SMP undertaking's retail arm and its retail competitor need the same information.

5.2.4.2   Delaying tactics

Delaying tactics refers to situations where the SMP undertaking may have incentives to delay the provision of its (essential) wholesale input to its downstream competitors.

'Time', as the strategic variable on which the anti-competitive behaviour is based in this case, is mentioned in Art 12 AD, which allows NRAs explicitly to attach obligations of '... fairness, reasonableness and timeliness' to an obligation of access. Imposing an access obligation according to Art 12 AD, therefore, NRAs may also specify the time frame within which the network has to be opened to independent retail undertakings. A time frame might also be set through a service level agreement based on Art 9 AD.

Regarding new wholesale products which allow the supply of new retail products, there is the danger that the dominant undertaking will gain a first mover advantage by supplying the wholesale product to its retail competitors at a later point in time as to its retail affiliate. First mover advantages can take the form of network externalities, learning by making cost reductions or customer lock-in effects. Where this may lead to market foreclosure, a non-discrimination obligation (Art 10 AD) might be appropriate in order to ensure that independent retail undertakings are able to compete with the SMP undertaking's retail branch. Art 10 AD may be interpreted such that it also includes time as a parameter the

SMP undertaking is not allowed to use to discriminate. It would then be allowed to offer a new retail product based on a new wholesale product only if the new wholesale product (under Art 12 AD) is also available to independent retail undertakings. The question how to ensure compliance with such an obligation is dealt with in Chapter 4 (Section 4.2.4.2 Delays in supply).

There is the danger, however, that the SMP undertaking offers a wholesale product which is of limited use for its competitors. Such issues are dealt with under Section 5.2.3.6. Although regulatory intervention is possible in such cases, it might be time-consuming and the SMP undertaking may nevertheless be able to achieve a first mover advantage. Furthermore, in some cases, a sensible wholesale product might not even exist or if it existed would not be demanded by other undertakings even at a cost-based price. A solution to these problems could be to ex ante require the SMP undertaking under Art 12 AD to meet all reasonable requests for access within a reasonable period of time. To judge whether a certain wholesale product demanded is reasonable might be – in case of dispute – up to the NRA.

5.2.4.3   Bundling/Tying

A vertically integrated undertaking may attempt to increase its downstream competitors' costs by bundling the wholesale product with other components which are unnecessary for the provision of the retail product.

The strategic variable, i.e., the bundling decision ('components offered together or individually'), is explicitly addressed in Art 9 AD (obligation of transparency). There it says: 'In particular where an operator has obligations of non-discrimination, national regulatory authorities may require that operator to publish a reference offer, which shall be sufficiently unbundled in order to ensure that undertakings are not required to pay for facilities which are not necessary for the service requested'. The wording 'in particular' suggests that a non-discrimination obligation according to Art 10 is not a necessary precondition to oblige an SMP undertaking to publish a sufficiently unbundled reference offer. Undue bundling to raise downstream rivals costs thus could be prevented by requiring the SMP undertaking to publish a sufficiently unbundled reference offer based on Art 9 AD.

Alternatively, the NRA may allow the alternative operator to specify the wholesale product. If an Art 12 AD obligation to meet all reasonable requests is in place, for example, the NRA can assume that a certain access product demanded by an alternative operator is sufficiently unbundled.

Whether an Art 9 AD obligation to publish a sufficiently unbundled reference offer or an Art 12 AD obligation to meet all reasonable requests for access is more suitable (effective and least intrusive), will have to be decided by the NRA according to the circumstances at hand.

5.2.4.4   Undue requirements

Using contract terms as a strategic variable, the dominant undertaking may attempt to foreclose the retail market by requiring a particular behaviour of the downstream competitor, which is unnecessary for the provision of the upstream product but raises rivals' costs.

Contract terms are dealt with in Art 9 AD (obligation of transparency). Paragraph 2 says that the reference offer has to include 'associated terms and conditions', and that NRAs shall be '... able to impose changes to reference offers to give effect to obligations imposed under this Directive'. Thus, as far as undue requirements are included in the reference offer, they can be changed or eliminated by NRAs under Art 9 AD. Alternatively, they can be controlled via a "reasonableness" condition, as discussed below in section 5.2.5.5.

5.2.4.5   Quality discrimination

There are various possibilities to put competitors at a disadvantage by means of quality discrimination. The only way to address the strategic variable 'quality' seems to be an obligation of non-discrimination according to Art 10 AD. Art 10 AD '... shall ensure, in particular, that the operator applies equivalent conditions in equivalent circumstances to other undertakings providing equivalent services, and provides services and information of the same quality as it provides for its own services, or those of its subsidiaries or partners'.

As the quality of a service is particularly difficult to observe for an NRA, an obligation according to Art 10 AD may be backed by an obligation of transparency according to Art 9 AD. This may be done in the form of an obligation to offer service level agreements (SLAs) and periodically report key performance indicators to the NRA and where appropriate to other operators. Such key performance indicators could be reported for services provided to other operators as well as for self-provided services, to monitor compliance with the non-discrimination obligation.

5.2.4.6   Strategic design of product

In case of discrimination between its retail affiliate and downstream competitors, a strategic design of the wholesale product by the SMP undertaking which is targeted at raising rivals' costs or restricting competitors' sales can be addressed – similar to quality-issues – by the obligation of non-discrimination (Art 10 AD).

In case that a non-discrimination obligation does not suffice (the independent undertaking might be at a disadvantage even if it receives exactly the same service as the SMP undertaking's retail branch), an NRA might oblige the dominant undertaking to publish a reference offer according to Art 9(2) AD. It may then impose changes to the reference offer in order to prevent the dominant undertaking from putting its rivals at a disadvantage

Some issues of strategic product design might also be dealt with directly in course of the Art 12 AD access obligation, under which the NRA may attach conditions covering fairness and reasonableness to the access obligation. Where product design is deemed unfair and/or unreasonable, the NRA might intervene.

5.2.4.7   Undue use of information about competitors

The undue use of information about competitors is – independent from an SMP position – prohibited by Art 4 (3) AD: 'Member states shall require that undertakings which acquire information from another undertaking before, during or after the process of negotiating access or interconnection use that information solely for the purpose for which it was supplied and respect as all times the confidentiality of information transmitted or stored. The received information shall not be passed on to any other party, in particular other departments, subsidiaries or partners, for whom such information could provide a competitive advantage.' The task of the NRA thus is to ensure compliance with Art 4 (3) AD.

5.2.4.8   Need for identical treatment in certain circumstances

As noted above in paragraph 5.2.3.4, non-discrimination remedies can be formulated so as to impose additional restrictions on an SMP player over and above those which would apply to a dominant player under competition law. One possible such form of tighter non-discrimination obligation which NRAs should consider is a requirement for identical treatment as between the SMP player's own downstream business and independent third parties ("equivalence of input"). For example, the retail businesses of SMP players might be required to order retail DSL connections using the same operational support systems as third parties, on the basis of exactly the same network information (e.g. line lengths) as the third parties and subject to the same service levels as third parties. Such an obligation provides a much better guarantee of effective downstream competition than a simple obligation "not to discriminate", especially given the attendant difficulties over interpretation of the latter.

On the other hand, this is an especially intrusive form of remedy as it constitutes an instruction to the SMP player not only what is to be achieved but also the means by which it should be achieved. Further, by denying to the SMP player the benefits of any economies of scope, it tends to raise costs. Therefore, in circumstances where an "equivalence of input" remedy is justified, an NRA would need to safeguard against the possibility that the competition benefits may be insufficient to justify the increased costs to the SMP player. One method of achieving this is to permit an exemption from the remedy on a case by case basis, subject to objective justification. This will be addressed in the assessment of proportionality.

More generally, there are circumstances where economies of scope are likely to be minimal. Returning to the above example, where the SMP player's operational support systems needed fundamental redesign for other reasons, it is likely to be economical to design a system which meets the needs of SMP player and third parties equally. In such cases, an equivalence of input remedy may be rather easy to justify.

5.2.5 Non-price issues: Remedies complementary to non-discrimination remedies

5.2.5.1 Possible need for complementary measures

Non-discrimination remedies, however well-formulated and well-understood, may not be fully effective unless they are accompanied by complementary remedies of different types. The NRA may well have found it appropriate to impose an access obligation under Article 12, Access Directive. Where that is the case, the attachment of an obligation dealing with fairness, reasonableness or timeliness of terms of supply may well be essential to avoid negating the value of a non-discrimination remedy. A transparency obligation may similarly be necessary.

As ever, the remedies discussed here need to be justified on the circumstances of the individual case and may well not be the only method of dealing with the relevant problem.

5.2.5.2 Internal reference offers

The purpose of a requirement to publish a third party reference offer is to provide clarity about the terms on which services are to be made available and to permit an early assessment of whether those terms are, in principle, reasonable. It does relatively little to ensure non-discrimination between the SMP player's own downstream business and third parties.

Where the service provided by the SMP player to itself is not identical to that which it supplies to third parties, it may be entirely opaque whether the SMP player is in any sense favouring its own business. Where a third party reference offer obligation and a non-discrimination obligation are both to be imposed, NRAs should consider the merits of a complementary obligation to prepare an internal reference offer. This sets out the terms on which the SMP player makes services available to itself. Comparison of internal and third party reference offers will provide insights as to whether self supply and supply to third parties appear to be envisaged on broadly equivalent terms. This will sometimes allow NRAs to intervene sufficiently early to prevent significant distortion to competition arising from discrimination. Preparation of an internal reference offer in a reasonable timescale is unlikely to be an onerous obligation and may therefore be easy to justify in circumstances where it is reasonable to expect it to be of value.

Ideally, the internal reference offer would be published, since otherwise the insights of competitors as to the practical effect of any differences in internal and external offers would be unavailable to the NRA. However, where national law on business secrets inhibits publication, the NRA may still consider it useful to require presentation of the internal offer to the NRA, for its own analysis.

5.2.5.3 Service level guarantees

Where a service level agreement is in place to underpin an obligation to provide access on reasonable and non-discriminatory terms, NRAs may find it appropriate to oblige the SMP player to make compensation payments to reflect any failure to provide the agreed level of service. This can be justified as a reasonableness condition as it would be common commercial practice in a competitive market. Financial incentives are often an effective means of providing assurance that there will be few discrimination problems in practice.

There are some practical limitations which would need to be considered by an NRA imposing such a remedy. National legal systems may limit the scope of such compensation to damage actually suffered (e.g. revenue foregone) and may not permit the inclusion of an allowance for consequential damage (e.g. damage to reputation) or for exemplary penalties. NRAs will need to consider whether any such limitations undermine the purpose of such a condition.

5.2.5.4 Key performance indicators

One effective means of direct verification of non-discrimination is the formulation and publication of appropriate key performance indicators (KPI), describing parameters such as provisioning times, repair times, percentage of circuits which work on installation and so on. KPIs are in particular likely to be necessary for the verification of service level agreements. As with internal reference offers, publication is preferable to provide confidence to market players in the efficacy of a non-discrimination remedy. A sensible degree of disaggregation will be appropriate, both to guard against subtle forms of discrimination and to allow unforeseen problems to come to light.

Costs will inevitably be incurred by the SMP player in setting up such a monitoring system although typically, the SMP player will need much of the information for its own management purposes. The ongoing maintenance costs are usually fairly low, however. NRAs will need to judge whether the likely benefits of such a system are sufficient to justify the initial and recurring costs[158].

5.2.5.5 Reasonableness conditions – general considerations

Some forms of reasonableness condition may be very effective at preventing certain types of discrimination and can therefore be an invaluable complement to a combination of access obligation and non-discrimination remedy. Article 12 of the Access Directive does not specify how a reasonableness condition should be formulated. Provided there is objective justification and the condition is proportionate, NRAs have considerable discretion to devise an explicit reasonableness condition which is effective in guarding against specific behaviour.

5.2.5.6 Prohibition of unreasonable conditions of supply

Even where the conditions of supply appear to be equivalent, as between the SMP player's downstream business and third parties, they may be very much easier for the SMP player to satisfy than third parties. Such conditions may have the effect of suppressing competition. In the absence of objective justification for such conditions, they can properly be regarded as a form of discrimination.

---

[158] For example, see IRG PIBs on LLU as amended in May 2002, in particular Annex 3 on KPIs.

Nevertheless, where such a practice has no real objective justification, NRAs may find it expedient to formulate a reasonableness condition which prohibits it explicitly. A wide range of possible subtly discriminatory practices can be envisaged but a few examples may nevertheless be helpful.

Textbox 3: Terms of supply which may be discriminatory in effect, even if formulated in a non-discriminatory manner

An SMP player may seek to impose an advance payment obligation, ostensibly to guard against the risk of default. (It might argue that there was no discrimination as it imposed such an obligation on itself. However, given that there was no risk of default to itself, the appropriate advance payment in that case would be zero.) Depending on the scale, this may not be unreasonable policy which would not have the effect of suppressing downstream competition. However, where the scale of the payment would have an anti-competitive effect, the NRA might wish to prohibit such a condition, permitting an allowance for bad debts in the cost base of the products concerned.

An SMP player may seek to impose advance forecasting requirements for access products, offering to fulfil orders in excess of the forecast only on inferior terms and/or imposing a financial penalty in the event of orders failing to meet the forecast. The stated justification for this could be to avoid the incurring of unnecessary costs arising from inaccurate forecasts Even if technically the SMP player itself needs to submit transparent forecasts alongside those of others, it is most unlikely that an over-forecast by the SMP player will cause real costs to be incurred. Objective justification of such a policy requires that the penalties for over- or under-forecasting should be commensurate with additional costs incurred by the SMP player. If not, they should be prohibited. Even where the scale of the penalty is capable of justification, NRAs need to consider whether there are other ways that the SMP player can recover the incremental costs of mis-forecasting which have less adverse effect on downstream competition

An SMP player may seek to require third parties to offer an indemnity against unspecified loss caused to the SMP player in supplying a product due to the fault of the third party. (For example, incumbents have sometimes required such indemnities in order to permit third party access to their exchanges for the purpose of local loop unbundling, ostensibly to guard, against damage caused to the exchange.) in principle, there may be a case for indemnities but they can often be very expensive to provide. NRAs should consider prohibiting such requirements in the absence of objective justification of the scale or if they appear likely to damage completion. It is likely that the identification of reasonable safeguards will in practice minimise the risk of such loss.

5.2.5.7 Network Migration

An end-user's decision to transfer from one retail service provider to another may give rise to a need for an SMP player to intervene at the network level (a "network migration") in order to effect the retail transfer. Equally, a decision by an entrant to move to a different rung of the investment ladder or to acquire from another service provider a customer currently served via different infrastructure (see above) is likely to require a network migration. Competition is likely to be undermined unless the appropriate network migration processes exist in a form suitable to facilitate such decisions by the entrant. While it is obviously in the interests of entrants that such migration processes should work well, retail competition and end-user choice is also likely to be significantly affected by the quality of such processes upstream.

For example, in the case of a retail DSL service, if the two retail service providers are customers of different network operators but both network operators are reliant on the local loop of the SMP player, that SMP player will need to re-route the DSL traffic of that customer for the retail transfer to take place. If the two retail service providers are supplied by the same network operator, no network migration by the SMP player may be necessary. The end-user's choice therefore may or may not give rise to the need for a network migration. In practice, this is likely to be completely hidden from the end-user. Where a network migration is required and the process works badly, the end-user is likely to blame the acquiring service provider whereas the fault may well be that of the SMP player. (Logically, there will always be a migration process to be undertaken between the two service providers, irrespective of the network arrangements. This can also be problematic, causing inconvenience for the end-user. However, it is outside the scope of this discussion as the market concerned is normally not one in which SMP has been designated.)

It is often in the interests of the SMP player that network migration processes work badly as they generally own a much greater number of retail customers than others. Their incentives may be to accept the customer dissatisfaction from the smaller number of customers who find it difficult to transfer to their retail services in the interests of retaining a larger number of customers who would ideally wish to transfer to another service provider.

NRAs may therefore find it necessary to mandate fit-for-purpose and cost-effective network migration processes either to underpin an access obligation, a non-discrimination condition aimed at facilitating effective competition downstream or to facilitate efficient network investment by the entrants. It will usually be helpful to specify in advance what would be "good" or "bad" experiences (both for service providers and end-users) and to ensure that information is collated by the SMP player to allow such experiences to be measured. Verification of performance against measurable targets is likely to be a necessary part of ensuring the fitness-for-purpose of the migration process. To make a migration process fully effective, it may have to be underpinned by an obligation to offer a service level guarantee relating both to the date of introduction of the service and to ongoing service levels.

Practical issues often arise in the pricing of network migration services. SMP players have incentives to understate the demand for such services. Since there are often considerable economies of scale, arising both from set-up costs and from bulk migrations, the understatement may lead to a significant increase in price which (when passed through to the service provider) dampens downstream competition significantly. NRAs should therefore ensure that charges relate to an efficient bulk migration service, unless individual migrations are explicitly requested at an appropriately higher charge.

Moreover, it is appropriate to consider carefully how the set-up costs should be recovered. One method which at first sight appears natural is to apply a percentage "mark-up" to the incremental costs of migration so as to allow the set-up costs to be recovered over a reasonable period. Under such a method, the competitors would bear the bulk of the set-up costs. However, NRAs should consider that even those who choose not to switch service provider benefit from an efficient migration service since it provides them with an increased choice and with the other benefits of a more competitive market. Therefore, it is reasonable that those end-users should ultimately bear a share of the set-up costs. This suggests that the SMP player should recover a significant share (possibly all) of those set-up costs through standard network usage charges (including the transfer charge to the SMP player itself) rather than through explicit migration charges.

In many cases, NRAs will need to pay attention simultaneously to the specification of several different migration processes as any one of them could be undermined by inadequacies in another. Examples include:

- The co-existence of a number of wholesale products with Bitstream such as Carrier Pre Select and Wholesale Line Rental;

- The provision of voice and Broadband by different operators;

- The need for a synchronised Geographic Number Portability (GNP) process to accompany a move to LLU.

Complexity is further increased if the two (or more) access products relevant to a migration are in different relevant markets. NRAs have, in light of an access obligation, the power to require migration processes covering migrations to or from an SMP market even if one of the access products is not within a regulated market. Where the relevant products are in different regulated markets, an SMP migration obligation could in principle be attached to any of them. Where there are multiple migration processes, care will obviously be needed to ensure coherence, especially where there are multiple contracts and bilateral relationships involved. In the absence of such coherence, the experience of end users is likely to be poor and retail competition will be subdued as a consequence.

NRAs have to enforce compliance in this fundamental area and monitor closely the design of the processes as well as the handling. In order to make the ladder operational, it is of great importance that NRAs put the highest emphasis on the design and monitoring of migration processes while not forgetting that migration needs time to work out.

5.2.6 Pricing-issues

In the case of a vertically integrated undertaking with SMP on the wholesale market (case 1), three standard competition problems have been identified in Chapter 2 which are based on the wholesale and/or the retail price as a strategic variable:

> 1.9. price discrimination
> 1.10. cross-subsidisation
> 1.11. predatory pricing

These competition problems have in common that all three lead to a margin squeeze. The incentives for such behaviour and possible remedies against it shall now be discussed for each of the problems in turn. As in the case of non-price issues, this is an application of principle 2 of Chapter 4.

5.2.6.1 Price discrimination

A vertically integrated undertaking with SMP at the wholesale level may subject its downstream competitors to a margin squeeze if it charges them a price which is higher than the price implicitly charged to its own retail affiliate for products or services considered to be within the same relevant market.

Incentives for such behaviour exist whenever the dominant undertaking can increase its profits by foreclosing the retail market and the outright denial of access is for some reason impossible. In such cases the undertaking might simply maintain its price on the retail market and increase the wholesale price charged to its competitors to a level where the retail price is insufficient to cover their costs.

If the access price is regulated at a cost-oriented level, however, the undertaking will only be able to charge a price above costs to its competitors if either the access price has been calculated incorrectly by the NRA or if it transgresses the rules set by the regulator. Thus, if an access obligation according to Art 12 AD together with a cost-oriented price regulation according to Art 13 AD is in place already (possibly backed by Art 9 and 11 AD obligations), the task of the NRA is to ensure compliance with the obligation it has imposed. These monitoring costs need to be considered when choosing cost orientation as a remedy. When calculating a cost-oriented access price, NRAs have to make sure that the access product is sufficiently unbundled (see section 5.2.3.3.), and that the SMP undertaking does not artificially increase the costs at which it is providing the service to the alternative operator ('gold plating'). Inflated costs can be dealt with by the NRA in course of the access price calculation. Further considerations have to be given to economies of scale and scope at the retail level, to allow the alternative operator to compete with the incumbent on a level playing field. These issues are discussed in the Annex.

Under a wholesale price set according to the retail-minus methodology, on the other hand, a dominant undertaking is able to raise the price for its wholesale product. This does not result in a margin squeeze, however, as – according to retail-minus – the retail price has to be increased as well whenever the wholesale price is increased. The task of the NRA thus is to ensure compliance with the retail-minus rule.

5.2.6.2   Unfair cross-subsidisation

A similar reasoning as for price discrimination can be applied to the case of unfair cross-subsidisation. Unfair cross-subsidisation of below-cost retail prices with profits from the access business is only possible when the price on the wholesale market is above costs. This is impossible under a cost-oriented access price regulation.

Unfair cross-subsidisation will also be impossible under a retail-minus regime, as an above-cost access price will automatically feed into an above-cost retail price and a predatory price on the retail market will result into an access price below costs.

Again, the task of the NRA thus is to ensure compliance with the access price it has set or the retail-minus rule. In order to be able to ensure compliance, an obligation of accounting separation (Art 11 AD) may be required.

5.2.6.3   Predatory pricing

When access prices are regulated, the possibility exists for an operator deemed to have SMP on the wholesale market to impose a margin squeeze on its downstream competitors by charging a low retail price. The incentives for such behaviour are similar to the incentives in other cases of predation. If the dominant undertaking is running at a loss during the predation period, predation will only pay if, once competitors have left the market, the retail price can be increased again without immediately attracting entry. This will be the case if barriers to entry exist or the SMP undertaking can build a reputation to resist new entry aggressively. Furthermore, predation is more likely to be successful if there is some asymmetry between the firms, in particular with regard to their access to financial resources[159]. There may also be incentives for dominant undertakings to sell at a retail price that covers short run marginal costs, which may be very small, but makes little or no contribution to joint or common costs, particularly where they are large multi-product firms operating in several markets and where their competitors sell a much more restricted product range. In this case competitors may have to cover a larger proportion of their common costs from the product in question and be unable to compete with the retail prices of the SMP undertaking. In these circumstances, the use of a combinatorial test may be appropriate[160].

If the situation is such that predation can be expected to be profitable for the SMP undertaking, and wholesale remedies are likely to be insufficient, NRAs may want to impose some form of regulation on the undertaking's retail price. The retail price (which is the strategic variable in this case) can be targeted by Art 17 USD (regulatory controls on retail services), which allows NRAs, amongst other things, to impose obligations on the SMP undertaking in order to prevent it from inhibiting market entry or restricting competition by setting predatory prices. A common practice is, for example, to require the SMP undertaking to pre-notify changes in the retail price to the NRA. If the NRA considers the price as predatory, leading to a margin squeeze, and likely to have significant anti-competitive effects, it might prevent the undertaking from changing prices in the intended way. In such cases, NRAs may publish guidelines according to which the effects of a

---

[159] See, for example, Martin (1994, pp. 452-489).
[160] See, for example, OFT (1999b, paras 7.11 and 7.16).

certain price will be assessed. Retail pricing is, however, considered to be a tool of last resort[161].

If the access price is regulated by means of retail-minus, a predatory price at the retail level will lead to a price below costs for the access service and therefore will not result in a margin squeeze.

5.2.6.4 Conclusion on pricing issues

With a cost-oriented access price, the problem of margin squeeze reduces to a problem of compliance with the access regulation at the wholesale level and/or to a potential predation problem at the retail level. If a danger of predation exists, it might be appropriate – after due consideration – to regulate the retail price by means of Art 17 USD (regulatory cost controls on retail services) ex ante.

A retail-minus approach in general should rule out the possibility of a margin squeeze as it links wholesale and retail prices exactly in a way such that all operators that are equally efficient as the dominant undertaking will usually be able to compete.

A margin squeeze thus can also be precluded by linking the retail price to the (cost-oriented) access price in a retail-minus-like fashion. This is sometimes referred to as 'imputation requirement'. Given the variety of retail prices in many communication markets, however, such a rule may be difficult to enforce. Furthermore an imputation requirement might be ineffective under certain circumstances, for example, if new entrants have to bear consumer switching costs which are not born by the SMP undertaking[162]. This could be allowed for by increasing the 'minus' to the level which allows entrants to compete. NRAs should consider taking into account economies of scale and scope when determining the access price to ensure that incumbent and entrant are competing on a level playing field on the retail market (cf. Annex).

5.3 Case 2: Horizontal leveraging

Case 2 as set out in Chapter 2 deals with leveraging issues which may arise in a situation where an undertaking is operating on two or more markets which are not vertically related, and is dominant on one of them, and the links between the two markets are such as to allow the market power held in one market to be leveraged into the other market. Two standard competition problems have been identified in this context:

> 2.1. bundling/tying
> 2.2. cross-subsidisation

Although in most cases only retail markets are involved, there may be cases where market power is leveraged between two wholesale markets or between a wholesale and a (not vertically related) retail market. As a particular remedy of the new regulatory framework can only be applied either to the wholesale or to the retail level, all possible cases will have to be discussed.

By preventing the dominant undertaking from leveraging its market power to horizontally related markets, NRAs promote competition in those markets and protect consumers from the exercise of market power (principle 2 of Chapter 4)

---

[161] Directive 2002/22/EC, Recital 26.
[162] See Beard et al (2003).

5.3.1   Relevant concepts: Incentives to horizontal leveraging

Economic analysis suggests that an undertaking with market power will have an incentive to leverage its market power to an adjacent potentially competitive market whenever it can – in the short or in the long run – increase its profits by doing so. If leveraging is successful, this will usually be the case. Economic literature therefore is dealing with the question if and under which circumstances leveraging between two (not vertically related) markets is possible. The main focus here has been on leveraging by means of bundling and tying.

In general, tying and bundling can be used by monopolists (or, more generally, firms with market power) in order to engage in price discrimination to extract more consumer surplus and increase profits. As such, the welfare implications of tying and bundling are uncertain, i.e., can be either positive or negative depending on the specific conditions of supply and demand. Tying and bundling might also have technological reasons and as such may also be welfare enhancing. If tying and bundling is solely motivated by the intention to leverage market power from a monopolistic to a potentially competitive market, however, it usually is detrimental to overall welfare[163].

Economic theory[164] suggests that it is hardly possible to exactly specify conditions under which leveraging by bundling or tying is possible. It may also be difficult in practice to distinguish cases of anti-competitive bundling or tying from cases where it is used as means of price discrimination or for production efficiency reasons.

Thus, bundling or tying between two not vertically related markets usually should be judged on a case-by-case basis. Particular concern, however, will have to be given to situations where the dominant undertaking is bundling its monopolistically supplied product with a (potentially) competitively supplied product and the bundle cannot be replicated by its competitors.

Besides bundling, a dominant undertaking might also attempt to leverage its market power by means of cross-subsidisation. Basically, predatory pricing cross-subsidized with profits from a monopoly market can be viewed like any other form of predatory pricing: A firm charges a price below (marginal or average) cost in order to drive its competitors out of the market. After the exit of all (or most) of its competitors, it charges an excessive price, covers the losses from predation and makes additional profits. As discussed in Section 5.2.4.3, predation will only be profitable if there are at least some imperfections on the second market (like, e.g., barriers to entry) and/or if there are asymmetries between the SMP undertaking and its competitors, in particular with regard to their access to financial resources.

As prices below (average or marginal) costs are frequently part of business strategies (for example if new products are introduced) and not aimed at driving competitors out of the market, NRAs will have to judge on a case-by-case basis whether such behaviour will lessen competition or not.

5.3.2   Bundling/Tying

Bundling by dominant undertakings which is considered to be detrimental to the development of competition by the NRA can be targeted by two remedies of the new regulatory framework: Art 9 (2) AD requires the undertaking to publish a sufficiently unbundled reference offer, whereas Art 17 (2) USD allows NRAs to impose requirements on the undertaking not to unreasonably bundle services.

---

[163]   As stated in Chapter 2, bundling/tying cannot only be used to leverage market power to a related market but also to inhibit entry to the SMP market. With regard to remedies, however, the same considerations as in the leveraging case apply.

[164]   See, e.g., Nalebuff (2003) or Inderst (2003).

Art 17 (2) USD is a retail obligation and thus can be applied to cases of anti-competitive bundling between two retail products where wholesale obligations are insufficient (Art 17 (1b) USD). As mentioned in the previous section, however, such an obligation should usually not be imposed ex ante to all types of bundles, as this may rule out cases of welfare-enhancing bundling. Rather, the obligation on an SMP undertaking might be to report new bundles to the NRA, which will then judge on a case-by-case basis whether the bundle is likely to have anti-competitive effects. Such a monitoring could be limited, for example, to bundles which are not replicable for competitors. As far as possible, the assessment of the bundle should follow clear guidelines stating when a bundle is likely to be considered to be anti-competitive. NRAs may also prohibit the SMP undertaking ex ante from specific bundling or tying practices which have been found to be anti-competitive in the market analysis.

Alternatively, depending on the circumstances highlighted in the market analysis, NRAs may also decide to make available (additional) wholesale inputs to alternative operators which allow them to replicate a bundle which otherwise is likely to have anticompetitive effects. An example for this could be an obligation for the SMP undertaking to provide flat rate interconnection offers or wholesale line rental (WLR) to allow alternative operators to replicate or at least compete with the bundle of access and a package of call minutes.

Bundling of wholesale services in the communications sector usually does not aim at leveraging market power, but may rather aim at raising rivals' costs by forcing him to buy unnecessary components. This case has been dealt with in section 5.2.3.3 above.

Bundling between wholesale and retail services is seldom observed, however, it may be dealt with by NRAs – depending on the case at hand – either by Art 17 (2) USD or by Art 9 (2) AD.

Although the welfare gains from preventing the dominant undertaking from distorting competition in horizontally related markets are potentially large, NRAs should also take into account in their option assessment the danger of prohibiting bundles which may increase welfare.

5.3.3 Cross-subsidisation

According to economic analysis, cross-subsidisation is based on two strategic variables: the price in market 1 (the SMP market), which is above costs, and the price in market 2 (the potentially competitive market), which is below costs.

To the extent that this strategy hinges on the profits made in the SMP market, to deal with the problem at the source, remedies should first target the SMP market and attempt to eliminate the exploitation of market power there. If competition in the SMP market is unlikely to emerge due to circumstances beyond the control of NRAs, then an ex ante price control may be an appropriate remedy to eliminate the exploitation of market power. Above-cost prices on a retail market can be addressed by Art 17 (2) USD (subject to the conditions for its use being met), whereas excessively high access or interconnection prices may be targeted by Art 13 AD (which usually will be accompanied by an Art 11 AD obligation of accounting separation).

Only if the excess profits on the SMP market cannot be eliminated, or if the predation problem remains after having eliminated excessive profits, the price on the second market may be targeted. This could be done by an Art 17 USD obligation '... not to inhibit market entry or restrict competition by setting predatory prices'. As such cases should be dealt with individually, an ex ante obligation to notify tariff changes to the NRA seems to be most appropriate. Regulatory intervention presupposes, however, that the undertaking is holding an SMP position on the relevant market.

5.4   Case 3: Single market dominance

Whereas cases 1 and 2 were dealing with leveraging issues, where market power is transferred from an SMP-market to a potentially competitive market, case 3 focuses on anti-competitive and exploitative behaviour which may occur within the borders of a single SMP-market. Three different types of problems may arise there: (i) An SMP undertaking might attempt to protect its SMP market by engaging in entry-deterring behaviour; (ii) The dominant undertaking may potentially exploit its customers by charging excessive prices or by means of price discrimination; (iii) Not exposed to (sufficient) competitive pressure, the SMP undertaking may fail to produce efficiently, provide a decent level of quality or to take certain investment decisions.

The following sections will discuss incentives for such behaviour together with the remedies which may be imposed if such behaviour is likely to occur. The cases outlined in this section more closely relate to the concerns that arise when replication is not feasible.

5.4.1   Entry-deterrence

There are several ways in which an SMP operator can behave in order to erect entry barriers, i.e., to either increase the costs of potential entrants or to restrict their sales. Such barriers to entry are sometimes referred to as 'endogenous' entry barriers as opposed to 'exogenous' entry barriers, which do not result from firms' behaviour, such as economies of scale and sunk costs or the limited availability of frequency spectrum.

A number of entry-deterrence strategies have been identified, which are reflected in the following standard competition problems of Chapter 2:

> 3.1. strategic design of product to raise consumers' switching costs
> 3.2. contract terms to raise consumers' switching costs
> 3.3. exclusive dealing
> 3.4. overinvestment
> 3.5. predatory pricing

5.4.1.1   Relevant concepts: Incentives for entry-deterrence

According to economic analysis[165], the conditions under which incentives for a particular type of entry deterring behaviour exist are highly specific and difficult to observe for regulators. Furthermore, there is a large variety of ways in which a dominant undertaking may engage in entry deterrence. Thus it might not be possible to assess ex ante whether incentives for entry deterrence are present and/or which particular type of behaviour is likely to occur. Wherever incentives for such behaviour or a certain behaviour itself is detected in the course of the market analysis, it may be possible to address it by *ex ante* regulation.

A second point is that, in the cases described above, it might be hard for NRAs to distinguish anti-competitive product design, investment, contract terms, contractual relations or pricing behaviour from efficient one. Therefore, some issues might have to be judged on a case-by-case basis.

The problems described may occur on retail as well as on wholesale markets. Wherever a certain competition problem is likely to occur on the retail market, NRAs should, according to the new regulatory framework, first attempt to address it by wholesale remedies, and only if those are insufficient may impose obligations on the relevant retail market.

---

[165] See e.g. Aghion/Bolton (1987) for exclusive contracts or Dixit (1981) and Fudenberg/Tirole (1984) for overinvestment.

5.4.1.2 Strategic design of product to raise consumers' switching costs

The strategic design of products to raise consumers' switching costs can be applied by the SMP operator either on the wholesale or on the retail market.

At the wholesale level, the strategic variable 'product characteristics' can be influenced ex ante by an Art 9 (2) AD obligation to publish a sufficiently unbundled reference offer which might be changed by the NRA. Alternatively (or additionally, depending on the case at hand) product design can be dealt with under Art 12 AD, which allows the NRA to attach conditions covering fairness and reasonableness to an access obligation.

At the retail level, Art 17 (2) USD may be used (if the conditions described in the article are met) to target the SMP operator's product characteristics. This article primarily focuses on pricing issues, however, and thus it is uncertain to which extent properties such as product design, compatibility, norms and standards, etc can be addressed.

Some product characteristic issues might – independent from an SMP position – already be covered by Art 17 Framework Directive. This article is dealing with standardisation and in particular states that Member States shall encourage the use of standards and/or specifications for the provision of services, technical interfaces and/or network functions published by the European Commission to the extent that they are necessary to ensure interoperability of services and to improve freedom of choice for users. Some potentially anti-competitive product designs (in particular with respect to compatibility) might already be ruled out by such standards and specifications.

5.4.1.3 Contract terms to raise consumers' switching costs

The strategic variable on which the anti-competitive behaviour is based in this case is 'contract terms'.

Contract terms at the wholesale level may be influenced via Art 9 (2) AD obligation to publish a reference offer. The NRA might then impose changes with regard to the length of the contract period or penalties in case of premature termination.

At the retail level, switching costs can – given that wholesale obligations are insufficient – be dealt with under Art 17 (2) USD to the extent that switching costs are imposed on customers in forms of charges they have to pay to the SMP operator in case of switching. If, for example, the SMP undertaking charges a certain amount in order to enable customers to make use of carrier pre-selection, the NRA might intervene and limit this charge to the underlying costs.

Other switching costs on the retail market, like lengthy contract durations and high penalties in case of premature termination, are usually not dealt with by the NRA, but by national consumer law.

NRAs should also attempt to reduce exogenous switching costs (switching costs which do not result from the behaviour of an undertaking, but exist due to other circumstances) wherever possible, for example by making prices more transparent (Art 21 USD) or by the introduction of number portability (Art 30 USD)[166].

5.4.1.4 Exclusive dealing

Exclusive dealing is a competition problem, which can arise only at the wholesale level. Two cases can be distinguished: (i) the case where a downstream undertaking is obliged to

---

[166] These are not SMP-obligations but general provisions of the new regulatory framework.

buy its inputs only from the dominant undertaking and (ii) the case in which a supplier is obliged to supply its input only to the dominant undertaking (and not to other undertakings).

In case of an access service, case (i) might be dealt with by imposing changes to a reference offer according to Art 9 (2) AD. An obligation of the downstream undertaking not to buy the input also from other upstream firms could then be eliminated by the NRA.

In case (ii), it does not seem possible for NRAs to address the strategic variable 'contract terms', as Art 9 (2) AD only relates to interconnection and access and Art 17 USD can be applied to retail markets only. Thus, such cases might be dealt with by the national competition authority.

5.4.1.5 Overinvestment

The investment decision (strategic variable 'investment') of an SMP undertaking cannot be targeted by remedies of the new regulatory framework. Such cases should therefore be dealt with by the national competition authority.

Still, when calculating a cost-oriented access or retail price, the NRA has to ensure that an SMP undertaking is not able to earn returns on investments which serve as a device for entry deterrence.

5.4.1.6 Predatory pricing

The case of predatory pricing in one market does not differ – with regard to regulatory consequences – from the case of predatory pricing as described in section 5.2.4.3. Therefore, the same reasoning as above applies.

5.4.2 Exploitative behaviour

An undertaking with market power is able to set prices above costs and earn supernormal profits. It can do this either by simply charging a (uniform) excessive price or by means of price-discrimination, i.e., by setting different prices to different customers which do not reflect differences in underlying costs. This is reflected in the following standard competition problems:

> 3.6. excessive pricing
> 3.7. price discrimination

5.4.2.1 Relevant concepts: Incentives for exploitative behaviour

A dominant undertaking always can increase its profits by setting an excessive price and thus always has a clear incentive to do so. The welfare consequences of an excessive price are clearly negative, as additional supply at lower prices would be beneficial both for the undertaking as well as for the consumer.

Price-discrimination, on the other hand, will only be possible if the undertaking with market power (i) is able to sort customers and (ii) is able to prevent resale. Incentives for price discrimination exist whenever the undertaking is able to extract more consumer surplus compared to a uniform price. The welfare effects of price discrimination are ambiguous. Depending on supply and demand conditions, welfare might either increase or decrease compared to a situation where a uniform price is set. As a general rule, welfare can be expected to increase under price discrimination if total output rises. Nevertheless, as long as market power exists, welfare will usually fall short of its maximum value under competition.

5.4.2.2 Excessive pricing

Excessive pricing on the wholesale market has already been discussed in Section 5.2.2. above. The discussion here therefore will be limited to excessive prices on the retail market.

As a general rule and in the spirit of the new regulatory framework, excessive prices on the retail market should first be addressed at the wholesale level, e.g. by ensuring access at cost-oriented prices. Only if excessive prices on the retail market cannot (or only in the long run) be eliminated by regulation at the wholesale level, a retail price regulation according to Art 17 (2) USD appears appropriate ('... requirements that the identified undertakings do not charge excessive prices'). On most retail communication markets, however, it would be inappropriate to impose a single price or a single two-part tariff. A price cap including several tariff schemes might therefore be reasonable. Such a price cap would allow the undertaking to design its tariffs in response to the peculiarities of retail demand.

If prices are deemed to be in line with costs (due to previous regulation) but are likely to be raised by the SMP undertaking without regulation, another option would be – as for the predatory pricing problem described in Section 5.2.4.3. – an obligation according to Art 17 (2) USD to subject changes in retail prices to approval of the regulator. If a certain tariff change is deemed to lead to excessive prices, it should not be approved by the regulator. If necessary, both instruments (price cap and tariff approval) may be applied together.

5.4.2.3 Price discrimination

Price discrimination on the retail market can – as excessive pricing – be addressed by Art 17 (2) USD ('... requirements that the identified undertakings do not [...] show undue preference to specific end users'), subject to the conditions for its use being met. As price discrimination may also be welfare enhancing, it might be appropriate to deal with it either ex post or ex ante on a case-by-case basis, e.g. in the form of tariff approval, where the SMP undertaking has to pre-notify changes in its tariffs to the NRA. The NRA then has to judge whether the price discrimination is justified in light of the goals of Art 8 Framework Directive. This judgement may be based on guidelines to be set out by the NRA.

5.4.3 Productive inefficiencies

Exposed to competitive pressure, undertakings are forced to minimize costs, provide a decent level of quality and take investments whenever the expected return is above costs of capital. SMP undertakings are not (or only to a limited extent) exposed to such pressure and thus might fail to produce efficiently, provide high quality products or to take efficient investments.

Clearly, there are no 'incentives' for inefficiencies in terms of profit maximization. It rather 'happens' that efficiency is traded off against leisure, fringe benefits, higher wages, etc. where competition is not sufficiently intense.

Three standard competition problems have been identified in this context:

     3.8. lack of investment
     3.9. excessive costs/inefficiency
     3.10. low quality

Productive inefficiencies are particularly likely to occur in sectors which have been monopolies for long periods and are unlikely to see the emergence of effective competition in the near future, such as the fixed network local loop. Wherever possible, NRAs should promote market entry to allow effective competition to emerge, which usually will solve problems of productive inefficiencies. Only where market entry is unlikely to occur and/or where competitive pressure is likely to be limited in the future, NRAs should address these problems directly.

5.4.3.1 Lack of investment

'Investment' as a strategic variable cannot directly be addressed by remedies of the new regulatory framework. Art 13 (3) AD, however, allows NRAs to calculate access prices based on an efficient cost structure, which also include efficient investments. A similar argument can be made about the retail market with reference to the Art 17 (4) USD (although the discretion of the NRA under Art 17 (4) USD with regard to the accounting method applied is unlikely to be equal to that of Art 13 (3) AD).

Regulators will have to set an access price which is low enough to induce the SMP undertaking to take cost-reducing investments, while on the other hand it allows him to earn sufficient returns on such investments and gives incentives to maintain and upgrade infrastructure.

5.4.3.2 Excessive costs/inefficiency

The SMP operator's costs can be targeted by NRAs in course of price regulation on the wholesale as well as on the retail market.

On the wholesale market, NRAs may calculate prices based on '... methods independent of those used by the undertaking' (Art 13 (3) AD). This implies that costs can be calculated based on a (hypothetical) efficient input combination (e.g. an efficient network). This is frequently done in course of the cost calculation by means of a bottom-up model.

A similar method of calculation might – if necessary – be applied on the retail market under Art 17 (4) USD: 'National regulatory authorities shall ensure that, where an undertaking is subject to retail tariff regulation [...], the necessary and appropriate cost accounting systems are implemented. National regulatory authorities may specify the format and accounting methodology to be used'. However, this article does not seem to be as far-reaching as Art 13 (3) AD which allows NRAs to use '... methods independent of those used by the undertaking', such as a bottom-up model. If an RPI-X type[167] of dynamic price cap is imposed, the undertaking has clear incentives to improve efficiency as it can retain the revenues from any efficiency increase beyond the X-factor within the period for which the price cap is set. At the same time, however, NRAs have to ensure that quality is not degraded, as the dominant operator may be able to increase its profits by saving costs on quality[168]. Benchmarking may be used as a way of measuring inefficiency and the incentive properties of price caps as a way of encouraging efficiency.

5.4.3.3 Low quality

If an access obligation is in force, the variable 'quality' can be dealt with at the wholesale level by an Art 9 (2) AD obligation to publish a reference offer, to which the NRA might impose changes which may also concern the quality of service. Some quality issues might be dealt with directly under Art 12 AD which allows NRAs to attach conditions covering fairness and reasonableness to the access obligation.

At the wholesale level, quality of service can to some extent also be dealt with by a non-discrimination obligation (Art 10 AD) as described in section 5.2.3.5. Such an obligation will only be useful however, if the wholesale service is also provided internally, and even in this case the SMP undertaking cannot be obliged to provide a quality better than the one it provides to its retail affiliate. The obligation of non-discrimination therefore cannot be used to address degraded quality resulting from the lack of competitive pressure.

---

[167] Under such a regime, the change of the maximum price (the price cap) per period is equal to the change of an inflation factor (e.g. the retail price index RPI) minus a productivity factor X.
[168] See, e.g., Intven (2000, Module 4 – price regulation, p. 4-30).

On the retail market, quality of service remedies could be imposed by NRAs if they met all the usual tests. Quality is indirectly addressed in Art 22 USD (quality of service): NRAs may '... require undertakings that provide publicly available electronic communications services to publish comparable, adequate and up-to-date information for end-users on the quality of their services'. Making transparent differences in quality may increase pressure on the SMP undertaking and induce it to supply better quality at the retail level. Indirectly, quality on the retail market can be influenced by setting quality requirements at the wholesale level as discussed above.

With regard to fixed line telephony, according to Art 11 USD, NRAs may set performance targets for the provider of universal service according to the USD and for the provider of the minimum set of leased lines if an Art 18 USD obligation has been imposed.

5.5 Case 4: Termination

Case 4 (termination) refers to a situation of two-way access (as opposed to one-way access dealt with in case 1) in which two or several networks in a first step negotiate interconnection agreements and in a second step set their prices on the retail market where they may or may not be in competition with other networks. Given the nature of fixed networks and the current state of technology and conventions in the mobile sector, it is not possible for the firm seeking access to replicate the service being provided by the access provider that "owns" the access to the customer. Thus, the considerations that arise in relation to non-replicable situations also apply in relation to termination.

Four standard competition problems have been identified in such a setting (see Chapter 2):

        4.1. tacit collusion
        4.2. excessive pricing
        4.3. price discrimination
        4.4. refusal to deal/denial to interconnect

In the following sections, incentives for such behaviour and possible remedies for each of the four problems are discussed. Wherever useful, a distinction between mobile to mobile (M2M) and fixed to mobile (F2M) telephony will be made (although the termination service itself is the same in both cases). The main differences between the two are that mobile networks compete for customers, whereas the competition between fixed and mobile networks for the same customers is limited[169].

5.5.1 Tacit collusion

Tacit collusion is a competition problem pertaining to M2M (and possibly to F2F) interconnection. Tacit collusion may take different forms, among other things some form of reciprocal rate setting. Any type of collusion related to termination rates would be an inter-market collusion, however, where operators use their market power in the termination market (in which they are likely to be individually dominant) in a coordinated fashion. As discussed in Chapter 2, the setting of reciprocal termination charges will result in excessive retail prices only under specific circumstances and is unlikely to emerge in practice where networks of different size with different cost structures exist. Tacit collusion may occur, however, where market conditions are stable, networks are of similar size, have similar cost structures, and traffic between networks is symmetric. Depending on the price-setting mechanism on the retail market, a collusive outcome might be maintained either by setting above- or below-cost reciprocal termination charges.

---

[169] The actual extent of competition between fixed and mobile telephony is considered in the course of the market definition / market analysis.

In such cases, welfare can potentially be increased by bringing access charges back to a cost-oriented level. The termination charge of individual networks can directly be targeted by an Art 13 AD price control and cost accounting obligation. In order to be able to calculate a cost-oriented termination charge, an NRA may have to impose an obligation of accounting separation according to Art 11 AD.

Other remedies like an Art 10 AD obligation of non-discrimination and/or an Art 9 AD obligation of transparency are unlikely to solve the problem on their own. The collusive access charge between symmetric networks may already be non-discriminatory, and transparency on the wholesale-level is likely to further collusion rather than prevent it, as it allows the operators to observe each other's charges and thus makes cooperation easier.

5.5.2 Excessive pricing

Market power on individual termination markets is likely to result in excessive pricing of the termination service which will lead in turn to allocative inefficiencies and a distorted pricing structure. This holds even true if the profits made are competed away on the retail market. As outlined in section 2.3.4, this problem may, in particular, arise in the F2M and F2F situations.

The remedies to be considered in this context are those which can – directly or indirectly – influence individual network's termination charges, i.e., Art 9 AD (transparency), Art 10 AD (non-discrimination) and Art 13 AD (price control and cost accounting).

Economic theory[170] suggests that transparency of retail prices may mitigate the excessive pricing problem to the extent that customers aware of prices of calls to individual networks can better adjust their demand in response to price increases following from the increase of termination rates. However, given the situation of fragmented numbering areas for mobile, number portability and customer ignorance this might not be easy to achieve. But even under perfect transparency, the termination-monopoly continues to exist, and prices may still be set at the (inefficiently high) monopoly level, (without transparency, prices are likely to be even above that level). Furthermore, an Art 9 AD obligation of transparency at the wholesale level does not lead by itself to increased transparency of retail prices. The obligation of transparency therefore would in most cases be inappropriate to solve the problem at hand.

An Art 10 AD obligation of non-discrimination (possibly backed by an Art 11 AD obligation of accounting separation) is also unlikely to sufficiently restrict the SMP undertaking in its power to raise prices above costs. Although such an obligation would make the costs of terminating on-net calls visible, the SMP undertaking can still set an excessive termination charge externally and have at the same time low (on-net) retail tariffs that do not take into account the full costs of the service. The operator may claim that it is charging the same (high) price he is charging externally also to its own retail business, but that he is ready to take a loss on his retail service.

An obligation by which the termination charge can be targeted directly is by setting a cost-oriented price based on an Art 13 AD price control and cost accounting obligation. This may have to be backed by an Art 11 obligation of accounting separation. With a cost-oriented access price, excessive pricing is made impossible and allocative inefficiencies are reduced.

When determining the level of the termination charge for mobile networks, it should be taken into account that cross-subsidisation from the fixed to the mobile sector may increase penetration rates on the mobile retail market and thus may – to some extent – increase total welfare (as long as high levels of penetration have not already been reached). Both effects,

---

[170] See Gans/King (1999).

the distortions from cross-subsidisation as well as the welfare-effects from increased penetration (which may now be exhausted in relation to 2G services in most of the EU countries) should be taken into account when the access price is determined.

In cases where an immediate implementation of charge control that sets charges at the competitive level could cause disproportionate problems for mobile operators, NRAs may apply a price cap system or a glide path to achieve a competitive level over a reasonable period of years.

For example NRAs may consider that, in the short term, new entrants into the mobile sector, where high initial investments are required, do not benefit from economies of scale (and possibly scope) to the same extent as the incumbents such that an immediate implementation of charge control that sets charges at the competitive level could cause disproportionate problems for operators. In such circumstances NRAs may apply a price cap system or a glide path to achieve a competitive level over a reasonable period of years. The period of the glide path must be strictly limited in time to that appropriate to the particular market conditions. Where price regulation is appropriate some Member States already use long-range dynamic cost models.

Economic analyses point to the fact, however, that, if only the termination market is considered, smaller operators might even have a greater, and not smaller, degree of market power due the limited consequences of an increase in their termination rates on the consumers perception of tariffs for calls to mobiles[171]. NRAs will have to formulate expectations about a reasonable period of time until when the price of the entrant may become regulated according to the general regulatory approach to the sector, taking into account the competitive situation in the markets. Otherwise more efficient operators in the market might be put at a competitive disadvantage, as they have to subsidize less efficient operators. Although it might be justified in the light of the goal of sustainable competition that new entrants are treated differently, the long run goal is to ensure that all operators are producing efficiently.

Similar considerations apply to new entrants into the fixed sector. Although entry into the fixed market usually does not require as much initial investment as in the mobile sector (investments can usually be made – at least to some extent – in a step-by-step manner), there may still be significant economies of scale, which are likely to remain un-exhausted in the early stages of market entry. This may justify higher termination rates at the outset, which may then be reduced along a glide path down to a level where scale economies can be considered to be exhausted. When setting the initial termination charge, NRAs may also take into account differences in network topologies, and the geographic dimension of network coverage. However, similar to the reasoning above for the mobile sector, in the long run all operators have to be treated equally in a way that ensures efficient production. While in principle the same considerations apply in the case of both fixed and mobile termination, the nature of the market dynamic and the ability to reach minimum efficient scale may in practice lead to different outcomes with regard to the appropriate period of any possible glide path. Nevertheless, where glide paths are to be used, NRAs should construct glide paths which encourages greater efficiency over time. A further factor, which has to be considered by NRAs compared to the mobile sector is the larger number of operators in the fixed sector, which may lead to complex retail tariff structures if operators charge prices which reflect the differences in termination charges.

---

[171] This effect is also referred to as horizontal externality or horizontal separation, see e.g. Gans/King (1999, p. 7).

5.5.3   Price discrimination

There are various types of price discrimination relevant to a termination market context that under certain circumstances have the potential to distort competition. For example, a mobile operator might charge different termination prices i) between different MNOs, ii) between different FNOs, or iii) between FNOs and MNOs. Another type of price discrimination is where SMP players may attempt to leverage market power from the relevant call termination market with the effect of dampening competition in the retail market by charging a high (above-cost) termination charge to other operators while (implicitly) charging a low price for on-net termination internally. This is likely to result in high off-net and low on-net tariffs on the retail market which may put entrants with a small customer base at a disadvantage.

An obligation of non-discrimination (Art 10 AD) prohibiting the SMP operator from charging a higher termination charge to other operators than it is charging internally (on-net) is unlikely to be necessary to prevent foreclosure of the retail calls market. Very large market shares are needed in order to tip a market to one supplier and such market shares happen infrequently. Therefore prices at cost-oriented levels are likely to resolve any residual leverage problem that might be created by on/off-net price differentials. High termination charges can be addressed by an Art 13 AD price control and cost accounting obligation (possibly together with an Art 11 AD obligation of accounting separation). The alternative approach of a non-discrimination obligation, even in combination with an obligation of accounting separation, is unlikely to be sufficient to achieve the intended aim of regulation, i.e., termination tariffs at an efficient level.

There may however be a case for a non-discrimination requirement where there is a concern about leverage of a position of SMP in termination so as to suppress competition for bundles of services to certain customer segments. For example, fixed operators sometimes express concern about their inability to compete for contracts to supply packages of services (for example voice and VPNs) to corporate customers, where on-net discounting is practised, arguing that MNOs are unfairly cross-subsidising. There is no presumption that any such on-net discounting will inevitably distort competition in this way even if it prevented particular competitors from offering the relevant package. Each case would need examination on its merits. Nevertheless, where this was a legitimate concern, a non-discrimination obligation would be an ineffective means of dealing with it, unless complementary obligations were applied in the relevant retail market. Otherwise, the MNO could avoid the intent of the obligation by charging itself the same termination rate as charged to third parties and taking a loss (or reduced margin) on on-net voice calls in the retail market. In the absence of a dominant position in the retail market, such behaviour would offend no rule.

5.5.4   Refusal to deal/Denial to interconnect

Without an obligation to interconnect, the incumbent operator(s) might be able to foreclose the market by refusing to interconnect with new entrants. Without interconnection, the service of the new entrant will be of limited use to customers, as they cannot reach a large share of mobile subscribers.

The interconnection decision of an operator can be addressed by Art 12 AD: 'Operators may be required [...] to interconnect networks or network facilities'. Independent from an SMP position, interconnection can also be imposed based on Art 5 AD. Therefore, where an Art 5 AD obligation is already in place, it will not be necessary to impose an Art 12 AD obligation in addition. Where Art 5 is not in place and only the SMP undertakings are to be addressed, an Art 12 obligation appears appropriate.

As soon as an obligation to interconnect is in place, however, an interconnection charge may have to be determined. With regard to the competition problems reviewed above, a cost-oriented regulation of the termination charge according to Art 13 AD appears appropriate.

5.6 Other issues

5.6.1 Variations in remedies

In circumstances where it is likely that the market failure identified will be the same in all markets (for example, very high market share, high barriers to entry and the economic viability of installing a competing local access infrastructure), where it is intended to impose different remedies on different operators within similarly defined markets, such differential treatment (i.e. variations in remedies across markets) should be adequately reasoned[172].

However, variations may be appropriate within a market for various reasons including geographical variations and variations arising from differences in demand and supply factors. Such reasons do not imply that the market should be segmented by geography or demand or supply factor, because of the presence of a common pricing constraint or an atypically responsive supply function.

NRAs have the ability to vary remedies within SMP markets according to the problems identified and the proposed resolution. The varying of remedies within an SMP market may be required in order to achieve the objectives set out in Article 8 of Framework Directive.

Single geographic markets are capable of supporting geographical variations within them which are not insignificant and which may warrant specific adjustments to the remedies proposed. It is often the case that geographical markets are national in character due to a common pricing constraint. The origin of such a common downstream pricing constraint may in fact be regulatory or the result of normal economic forces. However the national pricing system may not reflect inherent differences in the underlying demand or supply conditions in certain geographic areas within the national market.

The economics of density which are so important to the viability of infrastructural deployments are markedly different in urban rather than rural areas. In this context the long-term prospects for competition development, due to the presence of potentially non-replicable assets in less densely populated areas, may mean that the basis on which competition develops may differ within a single geographic market. The phenomenon of variations across geographic markets may not be stable over time such that any remedies reflecting geographic variations will need to be sensitive to developments that affect those variations.

It is also true that market definition normally places far greater emphasis on demand conditions than on supply conditions. However the supply function in communication markets is atypically responsive such that what might at first have been considered as separate markets are sometimes brought into one as a result.

Within such product markets variation in either demand or supply condition may warrant the use of asymmetrical remedies. In some markets products such as partial private circuits[173], LLU backhaul and Radio Base Station backhaul were all placed in the same market since from a supply perspective all three products are essentially the same product and can be used to provide service to any of the customer segments. It is also the case that these customer segments have the capacity to exert differing levels of buyer power, especially in the case of the radio base station operators who often have self supply as a

---

[172] See Commission comments on cases FI/2003/0028-0029, FI/2003/0030, FI/2003/0031, HU/2005/0152, DK/2005/0204, FR/2005/0228.

[173] For example, see Commission comments in case DK/2005/0245

backstop in negotiations with backhaul suppliers. The result is that certain product users may need less regulatory intervention to protect their interests from the exertion of SMP than others, justifying such asymmetrical remedies. From this perspective variations in remedies to reflect the variations within the market can be justified.

While any of the above arguments may provide a prima facie justification for variation in remedies in particular circumstances, consideration of the principle of incentive-compatibility of remedies tends to lead to uniformity. Introduction of variations is bound to complicate the task of enforcement and, consequently, the practical opportunities for avoidance of compliance. NRAs will need to strike the right balance between these considerations before concluding that variations are appropriate.

Textbox 4: Variations in remedies associated with new or upgraded infrastructure

Existing services delivered via new infrastructure

New infrastructure investments that provide existing services would not a priori warrant any different treatment from existing infrastructure. This is in line with the principle of technological neutrality. The delivery of existing services through networks using new technology may enhance total welfare as a result of cost reductions. These welfare gains may not be achieved if there is room for re-monopolization of the downstream markets through foreclosure or leveraging.

Substitute products delivered via new technology

For some time substitute products may be delivered through different technologies with different economies of scale and cost conditions, leading to different supply functions. This may facilitate leveraging of market power based on the old technology into the market segment served through innovative technology, for instance where services delivered through both technologies should be interconnected or need to be interoperable. In such situations ex-ante regulation should intervene on the SMP market to prevent leveraging while ensuring that migration to the innovative technology is not inhibited and end users profit from the introduction of innovative technology, by ensuring interoperability (e.g. via standardisation and/or interconnection). To achieve this balance, a (temporary) differentiation of remedies, where innovative services delivered through the new technology are regulated less stringently, can be justified. Whether a differentiation of remedies is justified and proportionate depends on the nature and cause of the competition problems in the relevant market. Where the competition problem is such that it can be solved by applying a remedy only to the products delivered through the old technology, proportionality requires leaving alone the innovative part and vice versa.

For example, the non-imposition of remedies on Voice over Broadband (VoB) services, where SMP has been found on a retail market comprising both PSTN calls and VoB services, may be justified if wholesale access regulation is sufficient to prevent leveraging. If the SMP player offers a retail bundle of VoB and internet access, this can in principle be replicated by any competitor able to gain wholesale access on non-discriminatory terms or to provide its own broadband connection on a competitive basis.

However, each case must be treated on its merits and monitoring of market development is necessary to ensure timely reaction of the regulator if the SMP operator engages in anti-competitive behaviour[174]. For example:

- where bundling of traditional voice and data services is prohibited (or subject to an advance notification requirement) because it would risk distorting competition, it may

---

[174] See Commission comments in case FR/2005/0221-0226.

equally be necessary to apply the same remedy to bundling of those data services with VoB;

- where no regulation has been applied to the service supplied using new technology on the grounds that regulation of the traditional service offering is sufficient to protect end-user interests, care needs to be taken that the remedy remains effective and the SMP operator is prevented from undermining regulation by offering the unregulated service only.

New services delivered via new infrastructure

The question of regulation - or avoidance of regulation - of new services delivered via new or upgraded infrastructure is a particularly difficult one. Services of this nature may not fall in a market which would be considered to be susceptible to ex-ante regulation (see discussion in Textbox 1 on "emerging markets") taking into account the Commission's guidance on the subject. But in practice, such infrastructure will often be used partly in substitution for existing infrastructure and partly (probably to a limited extent initially) for delivery of new services. In such a case, the access services are in practice quite likely to fall within an existing SMP market. The following general remarks therefore apply only to the case where the services fall inside a market which is considered to be susceptible to ex-ante regulation and a position of SMP is established.

The challenge for NRAs is therefore to assess the likelihood of replicability of such facilities. Where early replication seems probable, "traditional" forms of regulation may be unjustified; where it is unlikely, the justification is greater.

In assessing the appropriate regulatory approach, NRAs will certainly wish to avoid deterring investments which facilitate the introduction of innovative services. Badly-designed access regulation could have such an effect. But provided that regulation is well-designed so as to permit the investor a return on its investment which properly reflects the levels of risk borne, such deterrence may be avoidable.

NRAs will also need to consider the negative effects which could result if access to non-replicable bottleneck facilities is not guaranteed, resulting in foreclosure of the downstream markets. Consumers would not of course derive the benefits of the competitive downstream markets which would result from innovation and investment by other market players in those downstream markets. Moreover, foreclosure could ultimately leave the NRA with the most unattractive prospect of long-term regulation of an enduring downstream monopoly.

It is undoubtedly the case that the investors require a reasonable opportunity to make a fair return on their investments, which properly reflects the risks undertaken. However, a guaranteed monopoly over access is by no means a pre-requisite for such a return. Given the major disadvantages outlined above, ERG considers that it will not be justifiable to grant such access holidays, implicitly or explicitly, to infrastructure where the access services fall within an existing SMP market. This does not imply that any regulated access to new and old infrastructure should be on precisely the same terms. ERG is currently developing its thinking on appropriate ways of ensuring that access remedies properly reflect investment risks.

5.6.2 Removal or replacement of remedies

When considering the removal of an obligation, it is of course necessary to take into account whether removal would cause a material adverse effect on competition in the relevant market. It is equally necessary to consider the effect of that obligation in related markets, especially downstream. It would not be appropriate to remove obligations which were a pre-requisite for effective competition in the related markets.

Before concluding that an existing SMP remedy should be removed or replaced by a different one, NRAs should consider the disruptive effects on the market players of changing remedies and the consequential risk to achievement of the objectives of the framework. As above, NRAs should consider not only the effects in the market in which SMP has been established but in all related markets.

When an NRA removes an obligation or replaces one obligation with another, it should give an appropriate period of notice before the change takes effect, in order to avoid undue disruption to the market players.

Where the effects of removal or replacement are not fully predictable, a period of monitoring of such effects would be appropriate to ensure the validity of the assumptions made by the NRA which led to the removal or replacement.

5.6.3   Remedies in linked markets

In dealing with lack of effective competition arising from a position of SMP in an identified market, it may be necessary to impose several obligations to remedy the competition problem relating to services both inside and outside the market. In principle, an NRA may impose obligations in an area outside but closely related to the relevant market under review[175], provided such imposition constitutes

(i)   an essential element in support of obligation(s) imposed on the relevant SMP market without which these obligations would be ineffective and

(ii)   in combination the most appropriate, proportionate and efficient means of remedying the lack of effective competition found on the relevant market.

- In such cases, it is not necessary to consider whether the area outside the identified market forms a coherent economic market itself; nor

- to notify it separately under Article 7, Framework Directive; nor

- to notify the remedy as an exceptional measure under Article 8(3), Access Directive. Any such remedies should be notified under Article 7, Framework Directive alongside remedies which apply to services within the identified SMP market

For example, as a consequence of SMP in the local loop unbundling market, NRAs may need to impose an obligation to provide a tie-cable to link the main distribution frame to the entrant's premises

---

Textbox 5: Price squeeze

It is frequently the case that the regulatory objective of imposition of an access obligation in a wholesale market is to enhance or protect competition in an adjacent market, usually downstream. In imposing such an obligation, NRAs will be concerned that it will be ineffective if the SMP player conducts a price squeeze by using the flexibility available to them to set either the wholesale access price or the price of downstream services. To guard against such an outcome, it will usually be appropriate to impose a non-discrimination obligation, as discussed earlier. Even assuming effective formulation of such an obligation, there will remain an opportunity for the SMP player to squeeze margins and foreclose competition by lowering the retail price. It cannot be assumed that obligations under

---

[175] Cf. Commission Recommendation on Relevant Product and Service Markets
Cf. Commission comments of 4 August 2004 in case EL/2004/0078 (Voice call termination on individual mobile networks in Greece).

competition law will be sufficient to prevent a price squeeze in a regulatory environment. This is because a competition authority, in assessing whether or not a dominant position has been abused, would tend to base its calculations on the costs actually incurred by the dominant undertaking. In particular, this would allow the dominant player to take credit for economies of scope or scale and consequently to be able to operate a profitable downstream service on thinner margins than would be possible for an entrant. Any such action will tend however to foreclose the downstream market, contrary to the intentions of the regulator. These issues are explored in more depth in the Annex. To prevent this, the NRA should consider the need to specify (for regulatory purposes) a price squeeze test with treatment of common costs which is appropriate to the regulatory objectives. The test for the price squeeze should be determined in advance and made transparent when making the decision to apply wholesale price controls.

To ensure effective operation of the price squeeze test, NRAs should also consider the need for either or both of the following:

(a) an accounting separation obligation which provides effective separation of costs between the SMP and downstream markets;

(b) an obligation to provide advance notification of downstream price changes.

It is apparent that these remedies apply, partly or wholly to the linked market(s), In their absence, effective regulation may be impossible and consequently foreclosure of the downstream market may take place. Since, in a regulatory environment, price squeeze tests need to be applied ex-ante, a requirement to provide information on retail prices may be imposed as part of the price control obligation (Art 13 AD).

Annex: Margin squeeze – dealing with economies of scope and scale

This annex focuses on three questions that arise when considering whether there is or has been a margin squeeze: (i) how to assess the costs of an efficient competitor, (ii) how to deal with economies of scale, and (iii) how to deal with economies of scope.

A margin squeeze occurs when:

- a dominant provider supplies an "upstream" product A which is itself (or is closely related to) a component of a "downstream" product A+B (product B is supplied by the dominant provider only to itself: those who compete against A+B will supply their own alternative to B).

- the implicit charge by the dominant provider to itself for B (i.e. the difference between the prices at which it supplies A+B and A only) is so low that a reasonably efficient competitor cannot profitably compete against A+B[176].

With regard to the issue of how to assess the costs of an efficient operator, it is assumed to be impractical to obtain the actual costs of an efficient competitor[177]. Competitors may not naturally have prepared their accounting records on a basis, or to a standard necessary to support a margin squeeze calculation. Furthermore, it will be difficult for NRAs to assess whether or not a particular competitor is efficient, at least without a major time-consuming exercise involving all of them.

Therefore, the natural course is to take the incumbent's costs as a proxy for efficient entrant costs, although some adjustments may be necessary. To the extent that the incumbent is inefficient, the margin squeeze calculation favours the entrants.

Economies of scope may arise because there are things which a dominant provider does not need to do in order to provide the equivalent product A* to itself[178]. One possible approach is to recalculate the incumbent's unit costs, disallowing the economies of scope. This amounts to assuming that the dominant provider supplies precisely the same product on precisely the same terms to itself as to others. There are dynamic efficiency arguments for this, along the lines of those discussed below under economies of scale. But this amounts to raising the dominant provider's own charges above the minimum level they need to be. The NRA needs to be clear that the dynamic efficiency gains from competition will outweigh the short-term consumer disadvantages.

Upstream economies of scale in the provision of A or A* are irrelevant to the margin squeeze investigation as both the dominant provider and those to which it supplies A are entitled to benefit equally. But there is an issue to be resolved on how to treat the economies of scale in the self-provision of B.

If the dominant provider assumes that it will achieve a significant share of the downstream market, then it will be able to be profitable with a relatively low margin for

B. But those who do not expect to achieve that scale cannot be profitable on such a margin. Accordingly, they would exit the market, thus fulfilling the dominant provider's prophecy. On the other hand, if the dominant provider assumed that it would achieve only a small share of the market, it would not benefit from economies of scale and would need to set a higher margin for B. This would allow others to compete successfully once again fulfilling

---

[176] In the event that the price paid for A is not transparent, accounting separation will be needed to establish the price paid by the incumbent's retail arm.

[177] In some circumstances it may be appropriate and practical to use new entrants' costs.

[178] For example, whereas a competing operator will have to interconnect with the incumbent's network, the incumbent does not have to bear this cost because the network connection already exists to supply other services.

the dominant provider's prophecy. Unless otherwise constrained, the dominant provider is therefore in a strong position to dictate how much competition will emerge in the downstream market. There is a circularity in the margin squeeze test which can be broken only by the regulator.

The dilemma is this: If there are genuine economies of scale in the provision of B, it will at first sight be less efficient for B to be provided by multiple suppliers. The product may be a natural monopoly. On the other hand, multiple supply will often give rise to dynamic efficiency gains which benefit consumers in the long run. And where the competitors each have scale which is above the level at which economies of scale are substantially exhausted, there should be considerable benefits from competition. The ideal outcome would therefore be a sufficient number of competitors to generate substantial dynamic efficiency benefits but not too many so that none can benefit from economies of scale. The NRA cannot possibly hope to 'manage' competition to achieve some theoretical ideal. If it has decided that the product does not have the characteristics of natural monopoly, an adequate policy would be to take steps to ensure that a number of competitors can enter the market, each with reasonable prospect of being profitable. The market itself will sort out which of them survive.

The conclusion is that when imposing a wholesale supply obligation on a retail basis, the NRA should conduct the margin squeeze test on the assumption that the downstream market will be reasonably competitive. While there can be no hard and fast rules and it will always be necessary to examine the dynamics of the market in question, it might be reasonable to assume that the incumbent will attract, e.g., 20 or 25% of the downstream market and to use that assumption in the calculation of the minimum margin. This should in principle allow several competitors to enter and compete vigorously against the dominant provider for downstream business.

The same approach might be considered independent of whether the test is being defined ex ante (i.e., how to set a price for A which prevents squeezing the margin for B) or whether an investigation into an alleged past or existing margin squeeze is being carried out (i.e., is the margin between A and A+B sufficient to permit competitors to enter the market?). In the latter case, it may be inappropriate to use the actual market share of the dominant provider for the calculation of unit costs to avoid the self-fulfilling prophecy discussed above. The more justifiable approach may be to recalculate the unit costs on the basis of a market share for the dominant provider consistent with a competitive market.

Finally, one potential downside of this approach is that it cannot guarantee that the long-term outcome will be a competitive market. It may well be monopoly or oligopoly. But that result will at least have been determined by market dynamics, not by the dominant provider or by the NRA.

List of Abbreviations

AD	Access Directive
ECPR	efficient component pricing rule
ERG	European Regulators Group
F2F	fixed to fixed
F2M	fixed to mobile
FAC	fully allocated costs
FDC	fully distributed costs
GSMA	GSM Association
IRG	Independent Regulators Group
IOT	Inter Operator Tariffs
LRIC	long-run incremental costs
M2F	mobile to fixed
M2M	mobile to mobile
MNO	mobile network operator
NRA	National Regulatory Authority
ONP	Open Network Provision
SMP	significant market power
USD	Universal Service Directive

Glossary

Accounting separation: the preparation of separate accounts to reflect the performance of markets as though they were separate businesses. In particular, transactions across the boundaries of these markets are identified and treated as if the transactions were between separate companies. These are called transfer charges.

Allocative efficiency: the extent to which the economy's finite resources are deployed in a fashion so as to derive maximum benefit. An important condition is that prices reflect underlying costs.

Barrier to entry: an additional cost which must be borne by entrants but not by undertakings already in the industry; or other factors, which enable an undertaking with significant market power to maintain prices above the competitive level without inducing entry.

Bitstream: a wholesale product provided by an incumbent that consists of bidirectional high speed transmission capacity between an end user connected to a telephone connection and the point of handover to the new entrant. It is essentially the corresponding wholesale product for DSL services.

Bundling: where services are only sold together and not available for individual purchase (pure bundle) or services sold as a package at a discount to their individual prices (mixed bundle).

Calling party pays principle: where the person who initiates a call pays the full retail price for the call (the standard arrangement In Europe).

Carrier pre-selection/Carrier selection: carrier pre-selection is the facility offered to customers which allows them to opt for certain defined classes of calls to be carried by an operator selected in advance (and having a contract with the customer), without having to dial a routing prefix or follow any other different procedure to invoke such routing. Carrier selection is the facility whereby customers can opt to use an alternative operator on a call by call basis by dialling a routing prefix.

Charge control: in the context of termination charges, a control on the level of charges operators can make to another operator for connecting calls to its network.

Collocation: the ability for other operators to install equipment in the incumbent's local exchanges in order to supply services over the access network (local loop).

Combinatorial test: a test to be applied on a combination of services where there are common costs between services. The revenue from any combination of services would need to cover the common costs between the services as well as the incremental cost of each service.

Cost accounting: the preparation and presentation of financial information including the attribution of costs, revenues, assets and liabilities to regulatory "objects" such as product/service markets, activities or cost components. It enables prices to be demonstrated to be transparently and reasonably derived from costs.

Common costs: costs that are incurred in the supply of all or a group of products provided by an undertaking and that do not arise directly from the production of a single good or service.

Common Position: an ERG Common Position is a document expressing the position of the Group on any given topic within the ERG's domain. A Common Position is published at the initiative of the Group itself.

Deadweight loss: a measure of allocative inefficiency. It is equal to the loss in total surplus (consumer surplus plus producer surplus) that results from producing less than the efficient level of output.

Demand: the relationship between the quantity of a good or service that consumers plan to buy and its price with all other factors remaining the same.

Downstream market: a market one step down the supply chain. In the context of this document downstream market frequently refers to the retail market.

Efficient component pricing rule (ECPR): a price for a good or service calculated as the costs of the provision of the service plus the opportunity costs the undertaking incurs from providing the service to a retail competitor.

Endogenous barrier to entry: a barrier to entry caused by the behaviour of the SMP undertaking.

Exogenous barrier to entry: a barrier to entry which arises for factors outside the control of market players.

Foreclosure: any behaviour by a SMP undertaking which aims at excluding competitors from the market.

Fully allocated costs (FAC): the fully allocated cost or fully distributed cost of a service, is where all reasonably incurred costs are attributed to all the services of the regulated entity.

Fully distributed costs (FDC): see "fully allocated costs".

Internalisation (of negative external effects): refers to actions which account for (internalise) the possible negative consequences of other agents' (e.g. firms, consumers) actions. For example, exclusive vertical relations can allow an upstream firm to better control the behaviour of a firm in the downstream market, and thus force the downstream firm to take into account any external effects (on the upstream firm) in its decisions.

Joint costs: see "common costs".

Leveraging: transfer of market power from one market in which an undertaking has SMP into an adjacent vertically or horizontally related market.

LRIC (Long Run Incremental Costs): the costs caused by the provision of a defined increment of output, taking a long run perspective, assuming that some output is already produced. The 'long run' means the time horizon over which all costs (including capital investment) are avoidable.

Margin squeeze: a margin squeeze occurs when the prices set by a vertically integrated company have anticompetitive effects in a downstream market. A margin-squeeze results in a reduction of the profitability of rivals in the downstream market or forecloses the downstream market altogether.

NRAs (National Regulatory Authorities): the body or bodies, legally distinct and functionally independent of the telecommunications organisations, charged by a Member State with the elaboration of, and supervision of compliance with, telecoms authorisations.

Network externality: the effect which existing subscribers enjoy as additional subscribers join the network which is not taken into account when this decision is made.

Price cap: a control on prices which specifies the maximum price which can be charged for a product/service or for a set of products/services included in the cap.

Productive efficiency: a situation where it is not possible to produce more of one good or service without producing less of some other good or service.

Predatory pricing: a strategy where an undertaking deliberately incurs short term losses so as to eliminate a competitor and be able to charge excessive prices in the future.

Remedy: a specific regulatory obligation or a set of obligations imposed on an undertaking which is found to have significant market power in a specified market.

Rent: monopoly rents is another way of expressing the profits a monopoly can make; that is consumer surplus plus producer surplus (surplus being the difference between value of a good and its price).

Super normal profits: a level of profits greater than those would be typically earned by an undertaking facing competition

Service provider: a provider of electronic communications services to third parties whether over its own network or otherwise.

SMP: Significant Market Power in the new regulatory framework is equivalent to the competition law concept of dominance.

Structural barrier: structural barriers to entry are market characteristics which cannot be influenced by firms' decisions (such as technology and the level of demand) and which make it difficult for new entrants to enter profitably.

Sunk costs: costs which, once incurred, cannot be recouped, e.g. when exiting the market. Examples for sunk costs are transaction costs, advertising expenses or investment in infrastructure for which there is no or little alternative use.

Upstream market: a market one step up the supply chain. In the context of this document upstream market frequently refers to the wholesale market.

Vertically integrated: a situation where a firm owns operations at different levels in a supply chain, e.g. owning both a retail and a wholesale operation.

Welfare: a measure of total well-being achieved by all agents in a market, e.g. by firms via making profits and by consumers via consuming goods at a price at or below their valuation of that good.

xDSL: a family of technologies capable of transforming ordinary phone lines (also known as copper pairs/the access network/local loop) into high speed digital lines capable of supporting fast internet access. Individual variants include ADSL, SDSL, HSDL and VDSL.

References

Aghion, P./Bolton, P., 1987: 'Contracts as a barrier to entry', *American Economic Review*, Vol. 77 No. 3, pp. 388-401.

Armstrong, M., 2002: 'The Theory of Access Pricing and Interconnection', in: Cave, M./Majumdar, S. K./Vogelsang, I. (Eds.): *Handbook of Telecommunications Economics*, Elsevier, Amsterdam, pp. 295-384.

Beard, T.R./Kaserman, D.L./Mayo, J.W., 2003: 'On the impotence of imputation', *Telecommunications Policy* 27, pp. 585-595.

Beard, T.R./Kaserman, D.L./Mayo, J.W., 1998: 'The role of resale entry in promoting local exchange competition', *Telecommunications Policy* 22, No. 4/5, pp. 315-326.

Beard, T.R./Kaserman, D.L./Mayo, J.W., 2001: 'Regulation, vertical integration and sabotage', *The Journal of Industrial Economics*, vol. XLIX, no. 3, pp. 319-333.

Canoy, M./de Bijl, P./Kemp, R., 2002: 'Access to telecommunications networks', Paper prepared for the European Commission, DG Competition.

Cave, M., 2003: 'Remedies for Broadband Services', paper prepared for the European Commission.

Cave, M., 2002; 'Remedies in Network Industries: Competition Lay and Sector-Specific Legislation. An Economic Analysis of remedies in network industries', Brussels, 26 September 2002.

Cave, M./Majumdar, S./Rood, H./Valetti, T./Vogelsang, I, 2001: 'The Relationship between Access Pricing and Infrastructure Competition', Report to OPTA and DG Telecommunications and Post, Brunel University.

Dixit, A., 1981: 'The role of investment in entry deterrence', *Economic Journal*, 90, pp. 95-106.

dotecon (.econ), 2001: 'Network Charge Controls and Infrastructure Investments', Paper prepared on behalf of BT, www.dotecon.com.

Economides, N., 1998: 'The Incentive for Non-Price Discrimination by an Input Monopolist', *International Journal of Industrial Organization* vol. 16 (May 1998), pp. 271-284.

Economides, N., 1997: 'The Tragic Inefficiency Of The M-ECPR', mimeo.

Fudenberg, D./Tirole, J., 1984: 'The fat-cat effect, the puppy-dog ploy, and the lean and hungry look', *American Economic Review Papers and Proceedings*, 74, pp. 361-366.

Gans, J. S./King, S. P., 2000: 'Using 'Bill and Keep' Interconnect Arrangements to Soften Network Competition', *Economics Letters*,.71, pp. 413-420.

Gans, J. S./King, S. P., 1999: 'Termination Charges for Mobile Phone Networks. Competitive Analysis and Regulatory Options', University of Melbourne, mimeo.

Gilbert, R. J., 1989: 'Mobility barriers and the value of incumbency', in: Schmalensee, R./Willig, R. D. (eds.): *Handbook of Industrial Organization*, vol. I, pp. 475-535.

Hausman, J.A., 1997: 'Valuing the Effects of Regulation on new Services in Telecommunications', Brookings Papers on Economic Activity: Microeconomics, pp. 1-38.

Hicks, J.R., 1935: 'Annual Survey of Economic Theory: The Theory of Monopoly', Econometrica, 3, pp. 1-20.

Inderst, Roman, 2003: 'Bundling', Lecture material for the workshop at: Centre for Management under Regulation, Warwick Business School, http://econ.lse.ac.uk/staff/rinderst/personal/OFTEL_lecture_notes.pdf.

Intven, H. (ed.), 2000: *Telecommunications Regulation Handbook*, http://www.infodev.org/projects/314regulationhandbook/.

Koboldt, C., 2003: 'Regulatory obligations to be imposed on operators with significant market power: narrowband services', paper prepared for the European Commission.

Laffont, J.J./Tirole, J., 2000: *Competition in Telecommunications*, MIT Press, Cambridge, MA.

Martin, S., 1994: *Industrial Economics. Economic Analysis and Public Policy*. 2nd Ed., Prentice-Hall.

Nalebuff, B., 2003: 'Bundling, Tying, and Portfolio Effects. Part 1 – Conceptual Issues', DTI Economics Paper No. 1.

OFT (Office of Fair Trading), 1999a: 'Assessment of Individual Agreements and Conduct', OFT 141.

OFT (Office of Fair Trading), 1999b: 'Competition Act 1998 – The Application in the Telecommunications Sector', OFT 417.

Ovum, 2003: 'Barriers to competition in the supply of electronic communications networks and services', A final report to the European Commission.

Oxera, 2003: 'Analysis of Competition Problems and *ex ante* Regulatory Instruments under the EC Electronic Communications Directives', Report prepared for OPTA.

Rey, P./Seabright, P./Tirole, J., 2001: 'The Activities of a Monopoly firm in adjacent competitive markets: Economic Consequences and Implications for competition policy', Institut d'Economie Industrielle, Université de Toulouse-1, mimeo.

Rey, P./Tirole, J., 1997: 'A Primer on Foreclosure', IDEI, Toulouse, mimeo.

Sibley, David S./Weisman, Dennis L.: 'Raising rivals' costs: The entry of an upstream monopolist into downstream markets', *Information Economics and Policy*, 10, pp. 451-470.

Varian, H. R., 1989: 'Price Discrimination', in: Schmalensee, R./Willig, R.D. (eds.): *Handbook of Industrial Organization*, vol. I, pp. 597-654.

Wright, J., 2000: 'Competition and Termination in Cellular Networks', University of Auckland, mimeo.

Valletti, T., 2003: 'Obligations that can be imposed on operators with significant market power under the new regulatory framework for electronic communications', paper prepared for the European Commission.

COMMISSION RECOMMENDATION

of 21 January 2005[a]

on the provision of leased lines in the European Union (Part 1 - Major supply conditions for wholesale leased lines)

C(2005)103

THE COMMISSION OF THE EUROPEAN COMMUNITIES,

Having regard to Directive 2002/21/EC of the European Parliament and of the Council of 7 March 2002 on a common regulatory framework for electronic communications networks and services[1] (Framework Directive), and in particular Article 19(1) thereof,

Whereas:

(1) Users in the Community require the competitive provision of leased lines, and access to high-speed transmission data services so that in particular Europe's small and medium-sized enterprises can benefit from the opportunities offered by the rapid development of the Internet and electronic commerce.

(2) Competitive provision of leased lines has begun to emerge since liberalisation of telecommunications infrastructure on 1 January 1996, but has been largely confined to long distance high capacity routes; leased line markets will be reviewed as explained below.

(3) Certain organisations operating leased lines services had the obligation to provide these services under the principles of non-discrimination in accordance with Directive 97/33/EC of the European Parliament and of the Council of 30 June 1997 on interconnection in Telecommunications with regard to ensuring universal service and interoperability through application of the principles of Open Network Provision (ONP)[2] and Council Directive 92/44/EEC of 5 June 1992 on the application of Open Network Provision to leased lines[3]; these Directives were repealed by Article 26 of the Framework Directive with effect on 24 July 2003.

(4) However, the obligations will remain in place according to Article 27 of the Framework Directive and Article 16 of Directive 2002/22/EC of the European Parliament and of the Council of 7 March 2002 on universal service and users' rights relating to electronic communications networks and services (Universal Service Directive)[4]. In accordance with Article 16(1) of the Universal Service Directive and Article 7 of Directive 2002/19/EC of the European Parliament and of the Council of 7 March 2002 on access to, and interconnection of, electronic communications networks and associated facilities (Access Directive)[5], the former obligations are maintained until such time as the relevant markets have been reviewed in accordance with Article 16 of the Framework Directive and Article 16(3) of the Universal Service Directive.

(5) In accordance with Article 16(4) of the Framework Directive, where a national regulatory authority (NRA) determines that a relevant market is not effectively competitive, it shall identify undertakings with significant market power and shall on

---

[1] OJ L 108, 24.4.2002, p. 33.
[2] OJ L 199, 26.7.1997, p. 32. Directive as last amended by Directive 98/61/EC (OJ L 268, 3.10.1998, p. 37).
[3] OJ L 165, 19.6.1992, p. 27. Directive as last amended by Commission Decision 98/80/EC (OJ L 14, 20.1.1998), p. 27).
[4] OJ L 108, 24.4.2002, p. 51.
[5] OJ L 108, 24.4.2002, p. 7.

such undertakings impose appropriate specific regulatory obligations or maintain or amend such obligations where they already exist. In accordance with Article 18(1) of the Universal Service Directive, where an NRA determines that the market for the minimum set of leased lines is not effectively competitive, it shall identify undertakings with significant market power and impose obligations regarding the provision of the minimum set and the conditions for such provision. In accordance with Article 5(1) of the Access Directive, NRAs shall encourage and where appropriate ensure adequate access and interconnection and shall be able to impose obligations to that effect.

(6) On 11 February 2003 the Commission adopted Recommendation 2003/311/EC[6] on relevant product and service markets, defining the relevant markets within the electronic communications sector that NRAs should analyse. The list includes wholesale terminating segments of leased lines and wholesale trunk segments of leased lines. The supply of the services addressed in this recommendation, namely the supply of wholesale leased lines and leased line part circuits, is included in these markets.

(7) The supply of wholesale leased lines and leased line part circuits is included in the market of wholesale terminating segments of leased lines and for sufficient line lengths also in the market for wholesale trunk segments of leased lines referred to in Recommendation 2003/311/EC; the NRA will decide what constitutes a terminating segment depending on the network topology specific to their national market.

(8) The supply of 64 kbit/s, 2 Mbit/s unstructured and 2 Mbit/s structured leased lines is included in the minimum set of leased lines services referred to in the Recommendation on relevant markets. The minimum set of leased lines is defined in Commission Decision 2003/548/EC of 24 July 2003 on the minimum set of leased lines with harmonised characteristics and associated standards referred to in Article 18 of the Universal Service Directive[7].

(9) Information provided by Member States reveals problems with the length and the variation of delivery times for retail and wholesale leased lines and leased line part circuits. This is without prejudice to the review by NRAs of relevant markets in accordance with Article 16 of the Framework Directive and Article 16(3) of the Universal Service Directive.

(10) Where, in accordance with Article 10 of the Access Directive and Article 18 of and Annex VII to the Universal Service Directive, NRAs impose obligations of non-discrimination for the provision of certain leased line services, the principle of non-discrimination applies to all relevant aspects of the services provided such as ordering, migration, delivery, quality, repair time, reporting and penalties; in leased line contracts it is most appropriate to cover these aspects by a service level agreement; instead of penalties, compensation for failure to meet contractual requirements could be included into the agreement where this would be more appropriate with regard to the legal context in a Member State.

(11) In particular, contractual delivery times should be included in the service level agreement so as to ensure that delivery times for wholesale leased lines by such operators are the same as those provided for their own services and thus sufficiently below delivery times observed on retail markets.

(12) The publication of best current practice figures for overall delivery times of leased lines will help NRAs to ensure that contractual delivery times applied to wholesale

---

[6] OJ L 114, 8.5.2003, p. 45.
[7] OJ L 186, 25.7.2003, p. 43.

leased lines and leased line part circuits in particular provided by operators with an obligation for non-discrimination do not prevent other operators competing in leased lines retail markets from providing similar delivery time figures to their customers. Contractual delivery times for wholesale leased lines should therefore at least permit competing operators in retail markets to meet best current practice delivery times of designated operators providing leased lines in these retail markets. Retail delivery times longer than best current practice delivery times could result in obstacles to the development of the internal market for electronic communication networks and services; in accordance with Article 8(3)(a) of the Framework Directive, it is an objective for NRAs to remove such obstacles. Best current practice delivery times of designated operators in retail markets include the retail delivery processes of designated operators; thus corresponding wholesale delivery times would be shorter.

(13) According to Article 18 of and Annex VII to the Universal Service Directive, NRAs are to ensure that the typical delivery period for the minimum set of leased lines provided by identified undertakings is published; in order to review this Recommendation the Commission may need to have also available data on leased lines not covered by the minimum set.

(14) The Commission will review this Recommendation no later than 31 December 2005 in order to take account of changing technologies and of markets.

(15) The Communications Committee has delivered its opinion in accordance with Article 22(2) of the Framework Directive,

HEREBY RECOMMENDS:

1.　When imposing or maintaining an obligation for non-discrimination under Article 10 of the Access Directive or Article 18 of and Annex VII to Directive 2002/22/EC (the Universal Service Directive) with regard to operators providing leased line services (hereinafter referred to as designated operators), national regulatory authorities should:

　　(a)　ensure that contracts include enforceable agreements (hereinafter referred to as service level agreements) which cover all relevant aspects of the wholesale leased line services provided such as ordering, migration, delivery, quality, repair time, reporting and dissuasive financial penalties;

　　(b)　ensure that the contractual delivery times for wholesale leased lines in these service level agreements are as short as possible for each category of lines. Contractual delivery times at the wholesale level should be in any case shorter than best current practice delivery times of designated operators in retail markets. Best current practice delivery times of designated operators in the retail markets for 64 kbit/s, 2 Mbit/s unstructured, 2 Mbit/s structured and 34 Mbit/s unstructured are given in the Annex.

　　　　The methodology used to calculate the best current practice figures given in the Annex is considered to be appropriate to cover recognised differences of network structures and delivery procedures between different designated operators in different Member States;

　　(c)　ensure in particular that financial penalties included into the contracts as referred to in paragraph (a) apply in cases of delayed delivery of lines and consist of a specified amount for each day of delay for each line ordered; the contract shall provide also that the amount shall not be due where and insofar as the designated operator provides proof that the reason for the delay does not lie on him;

(d) ensure that the information necessary to prepare any review of this Recommendation is provided in accordance with Article 5(1) of Directive 2002/21/EC (the Framework Directive) and report this information to the Commission in accordance with Article 5(2) of the Framework Directive.

2. This Recommendation is addressed to the Member States.

Editors' Notes:

[a] OJ L 268, 27.1. 2005, p. 24

ANNEX

METHODOLOGY AND DATA FOR LEASED LINES IN MEMBER STATES

Methodology

The methodology for recommended ceilings for contractual delivery times is based on the third lowest value observed in the Member States in order to accommodate justified differences in network structures and delivery procedures in the different Member States. Based on this methodology and the data given below, the following best current practice delivery time figures have been derived for leased lines provided by designated operators:

1. for **64 kbit/s** leased lines: **18** calendar days

2. for **2 Mbit/s** leased lines unstructured: **30** calendar days

3. for **2 Mbit/s** leased lines structured: **33** calendar days

4. for **34 Mbit/s** leased lines unstructured: **52** calendar days

Delivery time data for leased lines in Member States

The Commission has obtained data from Member States on delivery times for leased lines of operators notified by the NRA as having significant market power according to Article 11(1)(a) of Directive 92/44/EEC[1] in response to the questionnaire for the Leased Lines Report 2002[2]. The data was received by September 2003. Delivery times reported are defined as the periods, counted from the date when the user has made a firm request for a leased line, in which 95% of all leased lines of the same type have been put through to the customers[3, 4].

---

[1]   Directive 92/44/EEC of 5 June 1992 on the application of Open Network Provisions to leased lines (OJ L 165, 19.6. 1992, p. 2), as last amended by Directive 97/51/EC (OJ L 295, 29.10.1997, p. 23) and Commission Decision N°98/80/EC (OJ L 14, 20.1.1998, p. 27).

[2]   2001 Report available at: http://europa.eu.int/information_society/topics/telecoms/implementation/leasedlines/doc/COCOM02-10%20final.pdf

[3]   See Article 2(3) of Directive 97/51/EC, OJ L 295, 29.10.1997, p. 23.

[4]   Luxembourg provided only half year figures for 2002. Here the figures for both half year periods are displayed. In relevant cases the higher of the two half year figures has been taken into account as an upper bound for full year figures in order to derive best current practice figures.
      Data given for Austria: data concern retail and wholesale lines; statistics correspond to the Directive (95 % of delivery times), data include also orders in locations where infrastructure has to be built; for 2 Mbit/s no distinction between structured and unstructured lines; for 34 Mbit/s and 155 Mbit/s the sample is too small for reliable statistics; specific customer delay, customer-requested changes on the target-delivery date (no 'best effort deliveries') and on project orders are excluded; delivery times are calculated from time of acceptance of a signed contract, if no other date (see customers' delays) is agreed.

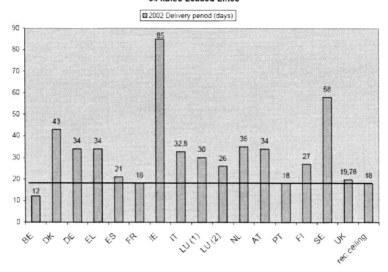

64 kbit/s Leased Lines

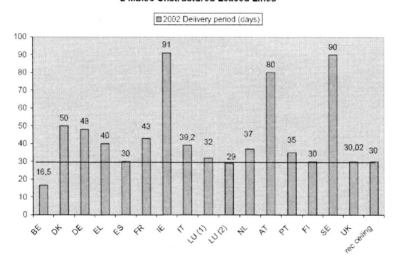

2 Mbit/s Unstructured Leased Lines

2 Mbit/s Structured Leased Lines

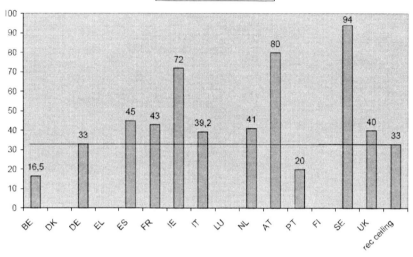

34 Mbit/s Unstructured Leased Lines

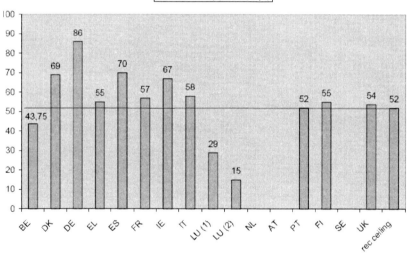

COMMISSION RECOMMENDATION

of 29 March 2005[a]

on the provision of leased lines in the European Union — Part 2 — pricing aspects of wholesale leased lines part circuits

C(2005)951

THE COMMISSION OF THE EUROPEAN COMMUNITIES,

Having regard to Directive 2002/21/EC of the European Parliament and of the Council of 7 March 2002 on a common regulatory framework for electronic communications networks and services[1] (the framework Directive), and in particular Article 19(1) thereof,

Whereas:

(1) New entrants (or other authorised operators) often have to rely on the incumbent to provide a short-distance leased circuit to link the customer's premises to the new entrant's network (a leased line part circuit).

(2) (Under Directive 97/33/EC of the European Parliament and of the Council of 30 June 1997 on interconnection in telecommunications with regard to ensuring universal service and interoperability through application of the principles of open network provision (ONP)[2] and Council Directive 92/44/EEC of 5 June 1992 on the application of Open Network Provision to leased lines[3], that have now been repealed[4], certain organisations operating leased lines services were obliged to provide their leased line services (including leased lines part circuits) under the principles of non-discrimination and cost orientation.

(3) In accordance with Article 27 of the Framework Directive and Article 16(1) of Directive 2002/22/EC of the European Parliament and of the Council of 7 March 2002 on universal service and user's rights relating to electronic communications networks and services[5] (the universal service Directive) and Article 7 of Directive 2002/19/EC of the European Parliament and of the Council of 7 March 2002 on access to, and interconnection of, electronic communications networks and associated facilities[6] (the access Directive), the former obligations are therefore maintained until such time as the relevant markets have been reviewed in accordance with Article 16 of the framework Directive and Article 16(3) of the universal service Directive.

(4) In accordance with Article 16(4) of the framework Directive, where a national regulatory authority (NRA) determines that a relevant market is not effectively competitive, it shall identify undertakings with significant market power and shall impose appropriate specific regulatory obligations on such undertakings, or maintain or amend such obligations where they already exist. In accordance with Article 18(1) of the universal service Directive, where an NRA determines that the market for the minimum set of leased lines is not effectively competitive, it shall identify undertakings with significant market power and impose obligations regarding the provision of the minimum set and the conditions for such provision. Hereinafter

---

[1] OJ L 108, 24.4.2002, p. 33.
[2] OJ L 199, 26.7.1997, p. 32. Directive as amended by Directive 98/61/EC, OJ L 268, 3.10.1998, p. 37).
[3] OJ L 165, 19.6.1992, p.27. Directive as last amended by Commission Decision 98/80/EC, OJ L 14, 20.1.1998, p. 27).
[4] These Directives were repealed by Article 26 of the framework Directive with effect on 24 July 2003.
[5] OJ L 108, 24.4.2002, p. 51.
[6] OJ L 108, 24.4.2002, p. 7.

undertakings with obligations under any of the abovementioned directives are referred to as "notified operators".

(5) On 11 February 2003, the Commission adopted a recommendation on relevant product and service markets[7] defining the relevant markets within the electronic communications sector that NRAs must analyse under the provisions of Article 15 of the framework Directive. The list includes wholesale terminating segments of leased lines and wholesale trunk segments of leased lines.

(6) The supply of leased lines part circuits is included in the market of wholesale terminating segments of leased lines and for sufficient line lengths also in the market for wholesale trunk segments of leased lines referred to in the Recommendation of the Commission of 11 February 2003. It is a matter for the NRA to decide what constitutes a terminating segment depending on the network topology specific to their national market.

(7) Without prejudice to the market reviews and market power assessments by NRAs in accordance with Articles 15 and 16 of the framework Directive and Article 16(3) of the universal service Directive, information provided by Member States reveals a persistent pattern of worsening problems with the level of prices for leased line part circuits given by notified operators and confirms problems with the variation of such prices.

(8) Where, in accordance with Article 13 of the Access Directive or Article 18 of the universal service Directive, a national regulatory authority imposes obligations for cost orientation with regard to leased line part circuits, it may take into account the fact that the cost information received from the operator concerned may not fully reflect the costs of an efficient operator deploying modern technologies. It may also take into account prices available in comparable competitive markets with regard to mandated cost recovery mechanisms or pricing methodologies.

(9) In these circumstances, the publication of recommended price ceilings for leased line part circuits should inform and guide NRAs as to how to apply the best current practices in leased line provision, when devising regulatory remedies for leased line markets that are not effectively competitive in their territory. In so doing, it would contribute to the development of an internal market by improving EU-wide consistency in application of the regulatory framework and thereby underpin the creation of a more competitive and cost-efficient market for leased lines.

(10) The derivation of price ceilings in this recommendation takes account of average prices in those Member States that allow notified operators price flexibility in different geographical areas.

(11) As provided in Article 13(3) of the access Directive, NRAs may require a SMP-designated undertaking to provide full justification for its prices, and may, where appropriate, require prices to be adjusted.

(12) The Commission shall consider the need to review this recommendation no later than 31 July 2006 in order to take account of changing technologies and of markets.

(13) The Communications Committee has been consulted in accordance with the procedure referred to in Article 22(2) of the framework Directive,

---

[7] C(2003) 497, OJ L 114, 8.5.2003, p. 45.

HEREBY RECOMMENDS:

1. For the purpose of this recommendation, the following definitions shall apply:

(a) a "leased line part circuit" (LLPC) means the dedicated link between the customer premises and the point of interconnection of the other authorised operator at (or close to) the network node of the notified operator, and should be regarded as a particular type of a wholesale leased line which can be used by the other authorised operator to provide services to retail users, other operators or for its own use such as, but not limited to, leased lines, connections to the switched telephone network, data services or broadband access;

(b) "line length" means the radial distance between the locations of the two ends of the line, i.e. from the point of interconnection to the customer premises;

(c) "customer" means customer of the other authorised operator.

2. When imposing or maintaining an obligation for cost orientation of prices under Article 13(1) of Directive 2002/19/EC (the access Directive) with regard to operators providing leased line part circuits, national regulatory authorities should:

(a) ensure that the prices associated with the provision of a leased line part circuit reflect only the costs of the underlying network elements and the services being requested including a reasonable rate of return. In particular, the tariff structure may include one-off connection prices covering the justified initial implementation costs of the service being requested (e.g. specific equipment, line conditioning, testing and human resources), and monthly prices covering the on-going cost for maintenance and use of equipment and resources provided;

(b) ensure that any of the price ceilings listed in Annex I for leased line part circuits based on the price data and methodology given in the Commission services working document are respected unless there is reliable evidence from cost accounting analysis as approved by the national regulatory authority that the recommended ceiling would result in a price level below the efficient costs of the underlying network elements and the services being requested including a reasonable rate of return.

The methodology used to calculate recommended price ceilings, as described in the associated Commission Staff working document[8], is considered to be appropriate to cover recognised cost differences between different operators in different Member States;

(c) use their rights under Article 13 of the access Directive to request full justification of the proposed charges, and if appropriate, to require these charges to be adjusted.

3. This Recommendation is addressed to the Member States.

---

[8] "Commission staff working document — Methodology, reference configuration and data of leased lines in Member States related to the Commission recommendation on the provision of leased lines in the European Union — Part 2 — Pricing aspects of wholesale leased line part circuits" - http://europa.eu.int/information_society/topics/ecomm/useful_information/library/commiss_serv_doc/index_en.htm

Editors' Notes:

[a] OJ L 83, 1.4. 2005, p. 52.

EUR

Capacity	Ceiling for the sum of the monthly price and 1/24 of the one-off connection price for a circuit length of up to 2 km	Ceiling for the sum of the monthly price and 1/24 of the one-off connection price for a circuit length of up to 5 km	Ceiling for the sum of the monthly price and 1/24 of the one-off connection price for a circuit length of up to 15 km	Ceiling for the sum of the monthly price and 1/24 of the one-off connection price for a circuit length of up to 50 km	Ceiling for the One-off connection price
64 kbit/s	61	78	82	99	542
2 Mbit/s	186	248	333	539	1112
34 Mbit/s	892	963	1597	2539	2831
155 Mbit/s	1206	1332	1991	4144	3144

COMMISSION RECOMMENDATION 98/195/EC

of 8 January 1998

on interconnection in a liberalised telecommunications market

(Part 1 – Interconnection pricing)

[as amended]ᵃ

THE COMMISSION OF THE EUROPEAN COMMUNITIES,

Having regard to the Treaty establishing the European Community,

Having regard to Directive 97/33/EC of the European Parliament and of the Council of 30 June 1997 on interconnection in telecommunications with regard to ensuring universal service and interoperability through the application of the principles of open network provision (ONP)[1], and in particular Article 7(5) thereof,

Whereas Commission Directive 96/19/EC of 13 March 1996 amending Directive 90/388/EEC with regard to the implementation of full competition in telecommunications markets[2], abolishes special and exclusive rights as regards the provision of telecommunications networks and services;

Whereas it is Community policy to create an open and competitive market in the telecommunications sector; whereas for new entrants in the telecommunications market seeking to compete with the incumbent operators, interconnection to the existing public switched telecommunications networks is essential, and interconnection charges represent one of the biggest items of expenditure for new market entrants; whereas the Community has agreed a regulatory framework for interconnection as set out in Directive 97/33/EC;

Whereas Directive 97/33/EC gives national regulatory authorities for telecommunications (NRAs) an important role in securing adequate interconnection of networks, in accordance with Community law, taking into account recommendations defined by the Commission so as to facilitate the development of a genuine European home market (recital 12); whereas, in particular, Article 7(5) of Directive 97/33/EC calls upon the Commission to draw up recommendations on cost accounting systems and accounting separation; whereas, in accordance with the principle of subsidiarity, the setting of tariffs for interconnection is a responsibility of the Member States;

Whereas Article 7(2) of Directive 97/33/EC requires that certain organisations notified by their NRA as having significant market power (hereinafter referred to as 'notified operators') follow the principles of transparency and cost orientation for interconnection charges, and states that the burden of proof that charges are cost-oriented lies with the organisation providing interconnection to its network;

Whereas the Commission considers that that most appropriate approach to interconnection pricing is one based on forward-looking long-run average incremental costs, since this is most compatible with a competitive market; whereas this approach does not preclude the use of justified 'mark-ups' as a means of recovering the forward-looking joint and common costs of an efficient operator as would arise under competitive conditions;

Whereas until interconnection charges based on forward-looking long-run average incremental costs are put in place, it is appropriate to publish international comparisons of

---

[1] OJ L 199, 26.7.1997, p. 32.
[2] OJ L 74, 22.3.1996, p.13.

interconnection charges as a means of assisting national regulatory authorities in ensuring the implementation of cost-oriented interconnection to the networks of notified operators;

Whereas Article 7(5) of Directive 97/33/EC calls for NRAs to ensure that the cost accounting systems used by the organisations concerned are suitable to ensure transparency and cost orientation, but does not specify a particular cost accounting system; whereas an approach to interconnection pricing based on forward-looking long-run average incremental costs implies an accounting system based on current costs rather than historic costs; whereas activity based accounts can be used to build a 'top-down' model of the long-run average incremental cost of interconnection;

Whereas the cost of terminating a call from an interconnected network should not depend on the type of network on which the call originated; whereas the principle of non-discrimination means that the interconnection tariffs for call termination services provided by notified operators should not in general discriminate between calls originating from fixed networks and calls originating from mobile networks, nor between calls originating from networks in the same Member State and calls originating from networks in other Member States;

Whereas Member State may make the provision of telecommunications services, including the establishment and/or operation of telecommunications networks required for the provision of such services, subject to authorisations in accordance with Directive 97/13/EC of the European Parliament and of the Council of 10 April 1997 on a common framework for general authorisations and individual licences in the field of telecommunications services[3]; whereas the general principles of the Treaty and the particular requirements of the Directive 97/33/EC, mean that all points of interconnection open to national operators should also be open to authorised operators in other Member States who wish to deliver cross-border traffic; whereas the established practice that existing network operators can deliver traffic to other Member States without needing authorisations in the destination Member State, or needing to be established in the destination Member State, is consistent with the principle that delivery of traffic to a Member State does not constitute the offering of a service in that Member State;

Whereas Directive 97/33/EC allows Member States to establish mechanisms for sharing the net cost of universal service obligations between organisations operating public telecommunications networks and/or publicly available voice telephony services;

Whereas Article 12(1) of Directive 95/62/EC of the European Parliament and the Council of 13 December 1995 on the application of open network provision to voice telephony[4] requires tariffs for use of the fixed public telephone network and the voice telephony service to follow the basic principles of cost orientation and transparency; whereas contributions by interconnected parties to 'access deficit' type schemes are only permissible when tariff constraints are imposed by NRAs on the grounds of affordability and accessibility of telephone service in accordance with Article 12(2) of Directive 95/62/EC; whereas the Commission has indicated that it believes such schemes should disappear by 1 January 2000[5];

Whereas the application of the principles set out in this recommendation is without prejudice to the duty of the Member States and of undertakings to fully comply with the EU competition rules, taking account of the specific positions set out in the communication

---

[3]   OJ L 117, 7.5.1997, p. 15.
[4]   OJ L 321, 30.12.1995, p. 6.
[5]   COM(96) 608, 27.11.1996, Commission communication on assessment criteria for national schemes for the costing and financing of universal service in telecommunications and guidelines for the Member States on operation of such schemes.

from the Commission on the application of the competition rules to access agreements in the telecommunications sector[6];

Whereas the advisory committee set up by Article 9(1) of Directive 90/387/EEC on the establishment of the internal market for telecommunications services through the implementation of open network provision[7] ('the ONP Committee') has given broad support to the principles contained in this recommendation, and the Commission has taken utmost account of the views expressed,

MAKES THE FOLLOWING RECOMMENDATION:

1.   This recommendation concerns the interconnection of telecommunications networks, and in particular the pricing of call termination on the networks of operators designated by their national regulatory authority as having significant market power (hereinafter referred to as 'notified operators') in accordance with Directive 97/33/EC.

2.   Article 7(2) of Directive 97/33/EC requires the interconnection charges of notified operators to follow the principles of cost orientation and transparency. The principle of cost orientation when applied to interconnection means that interconnection charges should reflect the way in which the costs of interconnection are actually incurred. Notified operators should be able to recover the one-off incremental cost required to connect the networks, and the incremental capacity costs imposed by the interconnecting traffic.

      Annex I of this recommendation provides further details on the type of costs associated with call termination.

3.   Interconnection costs should be calculated on the basis of forward-looking long run average incremental costs, since these costs closely approximate those of an efficient operator employing modern technology. Interconnection charges which are based on such costs may include justified 'mark-ups' to cover a portion of the forward-looking joint and common costs of an efficient operator, as would arise under competitive conditions.

4.   [Deleted][b]

4a.   [Deleted][b]

5.   [Deleted][b]

6.   The use of forward-looking, long-run average incremental costs implies a cost accounting system using activity-based allocations of current costs, rather than historic costs. It is recommended that national regulatory authorities (NRAs) set deadlines for their notified operators for the implementation of new costs accounting systems based on current costs, where such systems are not already in place. Activity-based costing systems, in which costs are allocated to each product and/or service on the basis of the underlying cost drivers and activities of an efficient operator, are recommended in order to minimise the joint and common costs that cannot be directly allocated.

7.   In keeping with current practice for cross-border interconnection between operators of established networks, and the principle of non-discrimination, operators authorised in one Member State that merely interconnect to deliver traffic to another Member State,

---

[6]   OJ C 76, 11.3.1997, p. 9.
[7]   OJ L 192, 24.7.1990, p. 1.

and that do not offer services or operate infrastructure in that other Member State, should not need to be authorised or established in that other Member State.

It is recommended that the reference interconnection offer of notified organisations should include - as a discrete unbundled element of the interconnection offer - terms and conditions and tariffs for the transmission link between the actual point of interconnection and the border of the Member State.

8.   Without prejudice to the principle of non-discrimination, any contributions to access deficits or universal service paid by organisations operating public telecommunications networks and/or voice telephony services operators in a Member State (which in accordance with Community law must be separated from interconnection charges), should not be imposed on organisations which merely interconnect to deliver traffic to a Member State and do not actually offer telecommunications services in that Member State, nor be imposed indirectly on consumers in other Member States.

9.   [Deleted][b]

10.   This recommendation is addressed to the Member States.

Editors' Notes:

[a] Commission Recommendation 98/195/EC (OJ L 73, 12.03.1998, p. 42) is reproduced in this book as amended by Commission Recommendation 98/511/EC (OJ L 228, 15.8.1998, p. 30); Commission Recommendation 2000/263/EC (OJ L 83, 4.4.2000, p. 30); and Commission Recommendation 2002/175/EC (OJ L 58, 28.2.2002, p. 56). See also Commission Communication on interconnection pricing in a liberalised telecommunications market (98/C 84/03) (not reproduced in this book).

A second Recommendation on the same subject, Commission Recommendation of 8 April 1998 on interconnection in a liberalised telecommunications environment (Part 2 - accounting separation and cost accounting), OJ L 141, 13.5.1998, p. 6. has been superseded by a Commission Recommendation of 19 September 2005 on the same subject (reproduced below) and has accordingly been omitted.

[b] Points 4, 4a, 5 and 9 were deleted by Commission Recommendation 2002/175/EC. The deleted points were concerned with "best current practice" interconnection charges. The preamble to Commission Recommendation 2002/175/EC states inter alia (some editorial changes and omissions made):

       (1)   Point 9 of Commission Recommendation 98/195/EC on Inter-
              connection in a liberalised telecommunications market (Part 1 -
              Interconnection Pricing), as last amended by Recommendation
              2000/263/EC, states that the Recommendation will be reviewed by
              the Commission by 31 December 2000. In particular it was also
              indicated in the Recommendation that an assessment should be
              made on the need to continue with publication of "best current
              practice" charges.

       (2)   The sixth and seventh Commission reports on the implementation
              of the telecommunications regulatory package (COM(2000) 814 of
              7.12.2000 and COM(2001) 706 of 26.11.2001) note the progressive
              reduction of interconnection charges in the Community to the levels
              published by the Commission's best practice price

Editors' Notes (continued)

recommendations, and the increasing availability of cost accounting systems for operators with obligations to interconnect, and therefore, from 1 January 2002 onwards it is considered no longer necessary to refer to the "best current practice" approach and update of price recommendation as originally included in Recommendation 98/195/EC.

(3)   Other elements of the Recommendation continue to provide guidance to national regulatory authorities and should be retained.

The last best practice price range recommendations published by the Commission for call termination interconnection to fixed networks were (at peak time, in EUR, exclusive of VAT):

— local interconnection: 0,5-0,9 cent per minute,

— single transit: 0,8-1,5 cent per minute,

— double transit (>200 km): 1,5-1,8 cent per minute.

ANNEX I

Components of Interconnection Charges for Call Termination

Directive 97/33/EC requires the interconnection charges of notified operators to follow the principles of cost orientation. This Annex considers the implications of this requirement for the components of an interconnection charge for call termination.

1.   Pricing the local loop for interconnection purposes

The local loop refers to the final links between the customer and the local exchange. In a fixed network using wired or wireless local loops, the cost of an unswitched local loop is largely a one-off cost, with periodic maintenance costs. Where call termination is being purchased, the 'lowest' place in the network where this can occur is on the main network side of the local switch[1]. Interconnection at this point may impose additional switch capacity costs, but there is no additional capacity cost or investment requirement relating to those components of the local loop which are dedicated to a particular customer (i.e. the pair of copper wires in a traditional network).

It follows from the principle of cost orientation that since the provision of interconnection does not lead to any increase of costs in the dedicated components of the local loop of the terminating network, the calculation of interconnection charges should not include any component relating to the direct cost of the subscriber-dedicated components of the local loop. The cost of those components in the unswitched local loop that are dedicated to a particular customer should therefore be recovered from that customer through a subscriber line charge, or as a combination of this and revenues from other services, to the extent that competition permits.

A difficulty arises if the incumbent is prevented from rebalancing its tariffs by regulatory measures and thus cannot charge an economic price to its own customers to cover the cost of the local loop. This gives rise to the so-called 'access deficit'. In a monopoly environment the operator compensates for the deficit in the 'access network' (i.e. the local loop) by charging prices in excess of economic cost for other services, such as international calls. With cost-oriented interconnection, competitors are able to capture some of this long distance and international traffic, and the incumbent's ability to compensate for the access deficit is reduced. An access deficit scheme involves contributions being imposed on other operators to compensate the incumbent for the loss of revenues that would have been used to fund this deficit.

Access deficit contribution schemes always provide inefficient investment signals, and raise overall industry costs. They are also administratively cumbersome, and lack transparency. As mentioned in the 'Guidelines on costing and pricing of universal service' published by the Commission in November 1996[2] it is expected that access deficit type schemes will only be applied on a temporary basis, up to the year 2000, by which time a sufficient level of re-balancing should have been completed in all Member States.

In accordance with the Interconnection Directive, any contribution to 'access deficits' paid by interconnecting parties must be clearly separated from the interconnection charges. Payment of 'access deficit contributions' by interconnected parties is only permissible under Community law where Member States impose regulatory constraints on the retail tariffs of notified operators. Where an operator is not prevented by regulatory measures from rebalancing its tariffs, and 'access deficit' charge is not justified.

---

[1]   The provision of 'unbundled' local loop, whereby a new entrant takes over and has exclusive use of a local loop installed by an incumbent, for an appropriate fee, is not strictly 'interconnection' in EU terms.
[2]   COM(96) 608, 27.11.1996.

2.   Pricing uncompleted calls for interconnection purposes

Uncompleted busy hour calls that originate from interconnected networks may impose additional capacity costs on a terminating network. In some cases, however, the reason for call failure could be lack of performance of the incumbent's own network. The Interconnection Directive places the onus of proof regarding costs on the network operator, so any operator seeking to include in its interconnection tariffs a fee for uncompleted calls would have to demonstrate that lack of performance of its own network had not been a reason for call failure.

3.   Call set-up charges for interconnection purposes

In a fixed network, switch costs are mainly driven by two factors - call duration and call events (i.e. signalling and call set-up). A great deal of information is required to determine the proper balance in terms of cost causation between these two types of costs. Partly because of this, it is common for regulatory authorities to allow recovery of switching costs only on the basis of duration of completed calls. A charge for call set-up could only be considered to be a valid component of an interconnection tariff if the operator could demonstrate the extent to which calls originating from interconnected networks imposed incremental costs on the terminating network in terms of additional processing power required to handle the additional call set-up attempts occurring during the peak period. If a call set-up charge is used, the corresponding call duration charges should be lower than when there is no call set-up charge.

4.   Interconnection charges and retail pricing

Some countries have in the past calculated interconnection charges on the basis of discounted retail tariffs. However, current retail tariffs are not necessarily cost-oriented, and this approach would in most cases be incompatible with the requirements of Community law.

Even if retail tariffs were cost-oriented, the approach is not desirable because it tends to lock new entrants into the same retail tariff structure as that of the incumbent, thus preventing the development by new entrants of innovative retail tariff schemes targeted at different types of user. The variety and choice of retail tariff schemes currently available on mobile networks in Member States shows there is considerable scope for innovative retail tariffing as a means of providing consumer choice and increasing the market demand for telecommunications services.

Where interconnection charges include time of day and day of week variations, they should be applied in a non-discriminatory manner to new entrants and to the incumbent's own traffic.

COMMISSION RECOMMENDATION

of 19 September 2005[a]

on accounting separation and cost accounting systems under the regulatory framework for electronic communications

(2005/698/EC)

THE COMMISSION OF THE EUROPEAN COMMUNITIES,

Having regard to Directive 2002/21/EC of the European Parliament and of the Council of 7 March 2002 on a common regulatory framework for electronic communications networks and services (Framework Directive)[1], and in particular to Article I 9(1) thereof,

After consulting the Communications Committee,

Whereas:

(1) Certain provisions of the regulatory framework for electronic communications networks and services require necessary and appropriate cost accounting mechanisms to be implemented, namely Articles 9, 11, 13 and 6(1) in connection with Annex I, of Directive 2002/19/EC of the European Parliament and of the Council of 7 March 2002 on access to, and interconnection of, electronic communications networks and associated facilities (Access Directive)[2]; Articles 17 and 18(1) of and Annex VII(2) to Directive 2002/22/EC of the European Parliament and of the Council of 7 March 2002 on universal service and users' rights relating to electronic communications networks and services (Universal Service Directive)[3]; and Article 13 of Directive 2002/21/EC.

(2) Operators designated as having significant market power (SMP) on a relevant market (hereinafter referred to as notified operators), as a result of a market analysis carried out in accordance with Article 16 of Directive 2002/21/EC, may be subject, inter alia, to obligations concerning the preparation of separated accounts and/or implementation of a cost accounting system. The purpose of imposing such obligations is to make transactions between operators more transparent and/or to determine the actual cost of services provided. Furthermore, accounting separation and the implementation of cost accounting systems may be used by national regulatory authorities to complement the application of other regulatory measures (e.g. transparency, non discrimination, cost orientation) on notified operators.

(3) This Recommendation updates Commission Recommendation 98/322/EC of 8 April 1998 on interconnection in a liberalised telecommunications market (Part 2 - Accounting separation and cost accounting)[4], following the application of the regulatory framework for electronic communications (25 July 2003). This revision is necessary since the regulatory framework of 2002 brought about some important changes to the regulatory package of 1998 such as the enlarged scope of application of the framework; a different approach to the imposition of ex ante obligations; a different scope of application of the specific provisions concerning cost accounting and accounting separation; and the application of the principle of technology neutrality.

---

[1]   OJ L 108, 24.4.2002, p. 33.
[2]   OJ L 108, 24.4.2002, p. 7.
[3]   OJ L 108, 24.4.2002, p. 51.
[4]   OJ L 141, 13.5.1998, p. 6.

(4)　The overall objectives of this Recommendation are to foster the application of consistent accounting principles and methodologies at EU level, taking into account the experience gained by the national regulatory authorities in the domain of cost accounting and accounting separation; improve the transparency of the accounting systems, the methodologies, the data elaborated, the auditing and reporting process to the benefit of all involved parties.

(5)　Operators may operate in markets in which they have been designated as having significant market power, as well as in competitive markets where they are not so designated. In order to carry out its regulatory tasks, a national regulatory authority may need information about markets where operators do not have SMP. When an obligation for accounting separation is imposed on a notified operator with SMP on one or more markets, the imposition of accounting separation may cover markets where the operator does not have SMP, e.g. to ensure the coherence of data.

(6)　Any mandated cost accounting or accounting separation methodology used in particular as a basis for price control decisions should be specified in a way that encourages efficient investment, identifies potential anti- competitive behaviour, notably margin squeezes, and should be in accordance with the national regulatory authority's policy objectives as set out in Article 8 of Directive 2002/21/EC.

(7)　The implementation of a new or revised costing methodology may indicate that current levels of regulated charges and/or price mechanisms are inappropriate or misaligned in some way. If a national regulatory authority believed corrective action is required then due regard should be taken of the commercial and economic environment to minimise risk and uncertainty in the relevant markets. This action could include, for example, spreading any price adjustment over a reasonable period of time.

(8)　When implementing an accounting system that uses a forward-looking approach (such as long run incremental cost) based not on historic costs but on current costs, e.g. where assets are revalued based on the cost of using a modern equivalent infrastructure built with the most efficient technology available, national regulatory authorities may need to adjust the parameters of the cost methodology in order to achieve these objectives. The coordinated use of top-down and bottom-up approaches should be envisaged, where applicable. Accounting systems should be based on the principle of cost causation, such as activity based costing.

(9)　When current cost accounting (CCA) is applied to network assets, such as the local loop which is considered to be less replicable in the medium term, consistent application of costing methodologies requires parameters (such as cost of capital, depreciation profiles, mark-ups, time varying components) to be adjusted by the national regulatory authorities accordingly.

(10)　When the implementation of a cost accounting system is mandated in accordance with Article 13(4) of Directive 2002/1 9/EC, rules used for the allocation of costs should be displayed at a level of detail that makes clear the relationship between costs and charges of networks components and services; the basis on which directly and indirectly attributable costs have been allocated between different accounts also needs to be provided.

(11)　This Recommendation provides guidance on how to implement cost accounting and accounting separation under the new regulatory framework of 2002. Recommendation 98/322/EC provides guidance on the implementation of cost accounting and accounting separation under the regulatory framework of 1998. The Recommendation of 1998 continues to apply in situations where Member States have not completed the review of existing obligations concerning cost accounting and accounting separation in accordance with Article 16 of Directive 2002/21 /EC.

(12) Where a compensation mechanism which involves financial transfers is implemented by Member States, Annex IV, part B to the Universal Service Directive requires that these transfers are undertaken in an objective, transparent, non-discriminatory and proportionate manner. In order to meet these purposes, any compensation received for the provision of universal service obligations should be duly reported in the systems for accounting separation.

(13) As regards the funding of universal service obligations, the Recommendation does not prejudice Commission Directive 80/723/EEC of 25 June 1980 on transparency of financial relations between Member States and public undertakings as well as on financial transparency within certain undertakings[5].

(14) The application of the principles of this Recommendation is without prejudice to the duty of the Member States and of undertakings to comply fully with the Community competition rules.

(15) Commission Recommendation 2002/590/EC of 16 May 2002 on 'Statutory Auditor's Independence in the EU: A Set of Fundamental Principles'[6], establishes a sound framework against which the auditor's independence can be tested, where relevant.

(16) The European Regulators Group (ERG)[7] has provided an opinion on the revision of Commission Recommendation on accounting separation and cost accounting of 1998 which includes a detailed annex on aspects of cost accounting and accounting separation.

HEREBY RECOMMENDS:

1. This Recommendation concerns the implementation of accounting separation and cost accounting systems by operators designated by their national regulatory authority as having significant market power on relevant markets as a result of a market analysis carried out in accordance with Article 16 of Directive 2002/21/EC. Operators with such obligations are hereinafter referred to as 'notified operators'.

   The purpose of imposing an obligation to implement a cost accounting system is to ensure that fair, objective and transparent criteria are followed by notified operators in allocating their costs to services in situations where they are subject to obligations for price controls or cost-oriented prices.

   The purpose of imposing an obligation regarding accounting separation is to provide a higher level of detail of information than that derived from the statutory financial statements of the notified operator, to reflect as closely as possible the performance of parts of the notified operator's business as if they had operated as separate businesses, and in the case of vertically integrated undertakings, to prevent discrimination in favour of their own activities and to prevent unfair cross-subsidy.

2. It is recommended that national regulatory authorities require from the notified operators the disaggregation of their operating costs, capital employed and revenues to the level required to be consistent with the principles of proportionality, transparency and regulatory objectives mandated by national or Community law.

---

[5] OJ l. 195, 29.7.1980, p. 35. Directive as last amended by Directive 2000/52/EC (OJ L 193, 29.7.2000, p. 75).

[6] OJ l. 191, 19.7.2002, p. 22.

[7] The ERG was established by Commission Decision 2002/627/EC (OJ l. 200, 30.7.2002, p. 38) as amended by Decision 2004/641/EC (0) L 293, 16.9.2004, p. 30).

It is recommended that the allocation of costs, capital employed and revenue be undertaken in accordance with the principle of cost causation (such as activity-based costing, 'ABC').

The cost accounting and accounting separation systems of the notified operators need to be capable of reporting regulatory financial information to demonstrate full compliance with regulatory obligations. It is recommended that this capability be measured against the qualitative criteria of relevance, reliability, comparability and materiality.

It is recommended that national regulatory authorities satisfy themselves as to the adequacy and effectiveness of the cost accounting and accounting separation systems; such systems may be subject to public consultation.

3.   It is recommended that a national regulatory authority, when assessing the features and specification of the cost accounting system, reviews the capability of the notified operator's cost accounting system to analyse and present cost data in a way that supports regulatory objectives. In particular, the cost accounting system of the notified operator should be capable of differentiating between direct costs[8], and indirect costs[9].

It is recommended that national regulatory authorities, having adopted a decision on a cost accounting system based on current costs set clear deadlines and a base year for their notified operators' implementation of new cost accounting systems based on current costs.

Evaluation of network assets at forward-looking or current value of an efficient operator, that is, estimating the costs faced by equivalent operators if the market were vigorously competitive, is a key element of the 'current cost accounting' (CCA) methodology. This requires that the depreciation charges included in the operating costs be calculated on the basis of current valuations of modem equivalent assets. Consequently, reporting on the capital employed also needs to be on a current cost basis. Other cost adjustments may be required to reflect the current purchase cost of an asset and its operating cost base. Evaluation of network assets at forward-looking or current value may be complemented by the use of a cost accounting methodology such as long run incremental costs (LRIC), where appropriate.

It is recommended that national regulatory authorities have due regard to price and competition issues that might be raised when implementing CCA, such as in the case of local loop unbundling.

It is recommended that national regulatory authorities take due regard to further adjustments to financial information in respect of efficiency factors, particularly when using cost data to inform pricing decisions since the use of cost accounting systems (even applying CCA) may not fully reflect efficiently incurred or relevant costs[10]. Efficiency factors may consist of evaluations of different network topology and architecture, of depreciation techniques, of technology used or planned for use in the network.

---

[8] Direct costs are those costs wholly and unambiguously incurred against specified activities.
[9] Indirect costs are those costs that require apportionment using a fair and objective attribution methodology.
[10] Some of the assets may be in excess of requirements or network architecture may be suboptimal. Implementation of a bottom-up economic/engineering model helps providing information about inefficient and unnecessary incurred costs, which should be removed.

4. It is recommended that notified operators required to report accounting separation provide a profit and loss statement and statement of capital employed for each of the regulatory reporting entities (based on the relevant markets and services). Transfer charges or purchases between markets and services need to be clearly identified in sufficient detail to justify compliance with non discrimination obligations. These accounting separation reporting obligations may require the preparation and disclosure of information for markets where an operator does not have SMP.

    For consistency and data integrity, it is recommended that the financial reports of the regulatory accounts be consolidated into a profit and loss statement and a statement of capital employed for the undertaking as a whole. A reconciliation of the separate regulatory accounts to the statutory accounts of the operator is also required. These statements should be subject to an independent audit opinion or a national regulatory authority compliance audit (subject to the availability of suitably qualified staff).

5. It is recommended that national regulatory authorities make relevant accounting information from notified operators available to interested parties at a sufficient level of detail. The detail of information provided should serve to ensure that there has been no undue discrimination between the provision of services internally and those provided externally and allow identification of the average cost of services and the method by which costs have been calculated. In providing information for these purposes, national regulatory authorities should have due regard for commercial confidentiality.

    In this respect, the publication by the notified operator of sufficiently detailed cost statements showing, for example, the average cost of network components will increase transparency and raise confidence on the part of competitors that there are no anti-competitive cross-subsidies. This is considered to be particularly important for wholesale services. Implementing guidelines on reporting requirements and publication of information are set out in the Annex.

6. Certain undertakings may be designated as universal service providers in accordance with Article 8 of the Universal Service Directive and may be subject to regulatory control on retail tariffs in accordance with the provisions of Article 17 of the universal service Directive. For those Member States that operate schemes to finance universal service obligations, it is recommended that any contribution that designated undertaking(s) receive as part of a compensation mechanism is identified in the systems for accounting separation.

7. These accounting guidelines are concerned with regulatory reporting and they are not intended as a replacement for any statutory financial reporting that may be required in the Member State.

8. This Recommendation will be reviewed not later than three years after the date of application.

9. This Recommendation is addressed to the Member States.

Editors' Notes:

a OJ L 266, 11.10.2005, p. 64

GUIDELINES ON REPORTING REQUIREMENTS AND PUBLICATION OF INFORMATION

This Annex outlines the periodic reporting framework, publication issues and the statement of compliance.

Pursuant to the principles recommended at point 2 of the Recommendation, cost accounting and accounting separation systems must produce financial information at a level of detail which demonstrates compliance with the principles of non-discrimination and transparency, adequately identifying and attributing revenues, costs, capital employed and volumes for the various activities performed by the operator. Such accounting information should be made available promptly to the national regulatory authority.

Good presentation of regulatory accounts ensures that the essential messages of the financial statements are communicated clearly and effectively and in as simple and straightforward a manner as possible. The presentation of information in financial statements involves some degree of abstraction and aggregation. if this process is carried out in an orderly manner, greater knowledge will result because such a presentation will satisfy the various regulatory objectives such as demonstrating that charges are cost-orientated or that there is no undue discrimination.

Accounting reports comprise supporting notes and supplementary schedules that amplify and explain the financial statements. Both the financial statements and the supporting notes form an integrated whole.

Regulatory accounting information serves national regulatory authorities and other parties that may be affected by regulatory decisions based on that information, such as competitors, investors and consumers. In this context, publication of information may contribute to an open and competitive market and also add credibility to the regulatory accounting system.

However, full disclosure may be restricted by national and Community rules regarding business confidentially. Therefore, it is recommended that national regulatory authorities, having taken the opinion of operators, define what information can be considered as confidential and should not be made available.

1. **Preparation and publication of information**

   The following financial information should be prepared and published (subject to confidentiality and national law obligations) for the relevant market/service:

   – profit and loss statements,

   – capital employed statement (detailed calculation methodology and value of parameters used),

   – consolidation and reconciliation with statutory accounts or other source of costing information,

   – a description of the costing methodologies including reference to cost base and standards, allocation and valuation methodologies, identification and treatment of indirect costs,

   – non-discrimination notes (detailed transfer charges),

   – audit opinion (if required by the national regulatory authority),

- a description of accounting policies and regulatory accounting principles,

- a statement of compliance with Community and national rules,

- other supplementary schedules as required.

Reporting formats, which may follow standard statutory accounting design. should be defined in advance by the national regulatory authority, in consultation with operators. The statement of compliance with Community and national legislation, audit opinion and description of accounting principles, policies, methodologies and procedures used, namely the cost allocation methodologies, cannot be considered confidential. Without prejudice to national and Community laws on business confidentiality, the audit results should be made publicly available.

2.   The statement of compliance

The annual statement of compliance should at least include:

- the conclusions of the auditor,

- all identified irregularities,

- recommendations made by the auditor (with a description of the corresponding effects),

- the full description of the verification methodology followed, and

- some aggregate financial and accounting data (such as CCA adjustments, main assumptions made on attribution methodologies, level of costs allocated and the level of granularity of the model).

Publication of the statement of compliance and of the audit results should be presented in a form easily accessible by interested parties, such as a paper or electronic version, or published on the operator's or national regulatory authority's website.

3.   **Reporting period**

Publication of regulatory accounts should take place annually and as soon as possible after the end of the accounting (reporting) year. Publication of the statement must take place no later than two months after the completion of the regulatory audit or no later than the current practice as specified by regulatory obligations.

COMMISSION RECOMMENDATION 2003/558/EC

of 25 July 2003[a]

on the processing of caller location information in electronic communication networks for the purpose of location-enhanced emergency call services

THE COMMISSION OF THE EUROPEAN COMMUNITIES,

Having regard to the Directive 2002/21/EC on a common regulatory framework for electronic communications and services (the "Framework Directive")[1], and in particular Article 19 thereof,

Whereas:

(1) Decision 91/396/EEC on the introduction of a single European emergency call number[2] required Member States to ensure that the number 112 was introduced in public telephone networks as the single European emergency call number by 31 December 1992, with under certain conditions, a possibility for derogation until 31 December 1996.

(2) Directive 2002/22/EC on universal service and users' rights relating to electronic communications networks and services (the "Universal Service Directive")[3], requires public telephone network operators (hereafter "operators") to make caller location information available to authorities handling emergencies, to the extent technically feasible, for all calls made to the single European emergency call number 112. Directive 2002/58/EC concerning the processing of personal data and the protection of privacy in the electronic communications sector (the "Directive on privacy and electronic communications")[4] establishes that providers of public communications networks and services may override the elimination of the presentation of calling line identification and the temporary denial or absence of consent of a subscriber or user for the processing of location data, on a per-line basis for organisations dealing with emergency calls and recognised as such by a Member State, including law enforcement agencies, ambulance services and fire brigades, for the purpose of responding to such calls.

(3) Although this Recommendation is concerned with location-enhanced 112, it is understood that parallel national emergency call numbers will be enhanced with the same functionality and following the same principles. Organisations operating private telecommunication installations are not affected by this Recommendation.

(4) For the successful implementation of E112 services throughout the Community, implementation issues must be addressed and timescales for the introduction of new systems coordinated. The Coordination Group on Access to Location Information by Emergency Services (CGALIES) established by the Commission in May 2000 as a partnership of public service and private sector players has allowed players of different sectors to discuss and find agreement on the principles for harmonised and timely implementation.

(5) Following on from the recommendation by CGALIES, providers of the public telephone network or service should use their best effort to determine and forward the

---

[1] OJ L 108, 24.4.2002, p. 33.
[2] OJ L 217, 6.8.1991, p. 31.
[3] OJ L 108, 24.4.2002, p. 31.
[4] OJ L 201, 31.7.2002, p. 37.

most reliable caller location information available for all calls to the single European emergency call number 112.

(6)   During the introductory phase of E112 services, application of the best efforts principle is considered preferable to mandating specific performance characteristics for location determination. However, as public safety answering points and emergency services gain practical experiences with location information, their requirements will become more defined. Moreover, location technology will continue to evolve, both within mobile cellular networks and satellite location systems. Therefore, the best effort approach will need to be reviewed after the initial phase.

(7)   It is important for all Member States to develop common technical solutions and practices for the provision of E112. The elaboration of common technical solutions should be pursued through the European standardisation organisations, in order to facilitate the introduction of E112, create interoperable solutions and decrease the costs of implementation to the European Union.

(8)   A harmonised solution across Europe would serve interoperability for advanced safety applications, such as calls which can be originated manually or automatically by an in-vehicle telematics terminal. These calls can provide additional information, for instance on the number of passengers in a car or bus, on compass-direction, on crash-sensor indicators, on the type of load of dangerous goods or on health records of drivers and passengers. With the high volume of cross-border traffic in Europe, there is a growing need for a common data transfer protocol for passing such information to public safety answering points and emergency services in order to avoid the risk of confusion or a wrong interpretation of data passed.

(9)   The arrangements for forwarding location information by operators to public safety answering points should be established in a transparent and non-discriminatory way including, where appropriate, any cost aspects.

(10)   The effective implementation of location-enhanced emergency call services requires that the caller's location as determined by the provider of the public telephone network or service is transmitted automatically to any appropriate public safety answering point that can receive and use the location data provided.

(11)   Directive 2002/58/EC concerning the processing of personal data and the protection of privacy in the electronic communications sector (the "Directive on privacy and electronic communications") generally requires that privacy and data protection rights of individuals should be fully respected and adequate technical and organisational security measures should be implemented for that purpose. However, it allows the use of location data by emergency services without consent of the user concerned. In particular, Member States should ensure that there are transparent procedures governing the way in which a provider of a public telecommunications network and/or service may override the temporary denial or absence of consent of a user for the processing of location data, on a per-line basis for organisations dealing with emergency calls and that are recognised as such by a Member State.

(12)   Actions conducted in the context of the Community action programme in the field of Civil Protection (hereinafter "Civil Protection Action Programme")[5] should aim to contribute to the integration of civil protection objectives in other Community policies and actions as well as to the consistency of the programme with other Community actions. This entitles the Commission to implement actions aiming at increasing the degree of preparedness of organisations involved in civil protection in the Member

---

[5]   OJ L 327, 21.12.1999, p. 53.

States, by enhancing their ability to respond to emergencies and improving the techniques and methods of response and immediate aftercare. This may include the handling and use of location information associated to E112 emergency calls by public safety answering points and emergency services.

(13) To achieve the objectives of this Recommendation, the need for a continued dialogue between public network operators and service providers and public authorities including emergency services becomes even stronger.

(14) When reporting on the situation of E112 implementation, national authorities should address any relevant technical feasibility issue that hinders the introduction of E112 for specific categories of end-users, as well as the technical requirements for handling emergency calls that may originate from SMS and telematic data services.

(15) The measures set out in this Recommendation are in accordance with the advisory opinion of the Communications Committee set up by Article 22 of Directive 2002/21/EC,

HEREBY RECOMMENDS THAT:

1. Member States should apply the following harmonised conditions and principles to the provision of caller location information to emergency services for all calls to the single European emergency call number 112.

2. For the purposes of this Recommendation, the following definitions should apply:

    (a) "emergency service" means a service, recognised as such by the Member State, that provides immediate and rapid assistance in situations where there is a direct risk to life or limb, individual or public health or safety, to private or public property, or the environment but not necessarily limited to these situations.

    (b) "location information" means in a public mobile network the data processed indicating the geographic position of a user's mobile terminal and in a public fixed network the data about the physical address of the termination point.

    (c) "E112" means an emergency communications service using the single European emergency call number, 112, which is enhanced with location information of the calling user.

    (d) "public safety answering point" means a physical location where emergency calls are received under the responsibility of a public authority.

3. Member States should draw up detailed rules for public network operators, to include, inter alia, the provisions in points 4 to 9 below.

4. For every emergency call made to the European emergency call number 112, public telephone network operators should, initiated by the network, forward (push) to public safety answering points the best information available as to the location of the caller, to the extent technically feasible. For the intermediate period up to the conclusion of the review as referred to in point 13 below, it is acceptable that operators make available location information on request only (pull).

5. Fixed public telephone network operators should make available the installation address of the line from which the emergency call is made.

6. Public telephone network operators should provide location information in a non-discriminatory way, and in particular should not discriminate between the quality of information provided concerning their own subscribers and other users. In the case of

the fixed networks, other users include users of public pay phones; in the case of mobile networks or mobility applications, other users include roamers or visiting users, or, where appropriate, users of mobile terminals which can not be identified by the subscriber or user number.

7. All location information provided should be accompanied by an identification of the network on which the call originates.

8. Public telephone network operators should keep sources of location information, including address information, accurate and up-to-date.

9. For each emergency call for which the subscriber or user number has been identified, public telephone network operators should provide the capability to public safety answering points and emergency services of renewing the location information through a call back functionality (pulling) for the purpose of handling the emergency.

10. In order to facilitate data transfer between operators and public safety answering points, Member States should encourage the use of a common open interface standard, and in particular for a common data transfer protocol, adopted by the European Telecommunications Standards Institute (ETSI), where available. Such a standard should include the necessary flexibility to accommodate future requirements as they may arise, for instance from in-vehicle telematics terminals. Member States should ensure that the interface is best suited to the effective handling of emergencies.

11. In the context of the obligation for E112 services prescribed by the Universal Service Directive, Member States should provide adequate information to their citizens about the existence, use and benefits of E112 services. Citizens should be informed that 112 connects them to emergency services all across the European Union and that their location will be forwarded. They should also be informed about the identity of the emergency services that will receive their location information and of other necessary details to guarantee fair processing of their personal data.

12. In the context of the continuous evolution of concepts and technologies, Member States are encouraged to foster and support the development of services for emergency assistance, for instance to tourists and travellers and for the transport of dangerous goods by road or rail, including handling procedures for forwarding location and other emergency or accident related information to public safety answering points; to support the development and implementation of common interface specifications in ensuring Europe-wide interoperability of such services; and to encourage the use of location technologies with high precision such as third generation cellular network location technologies and Global Navigation Satellite Systems.

13. Member States should require their national authorities to report to the Commission on the situation of E112 implementation by the end of 2004 so that the Commission can undertake a review taking into account the emerging requirements from public safety answering points and emergency services and the evolutions and availability of technological capabilities for location determination.

14. This Recommendation is addressed to the Member States.

Editors' Notes:

[a] OJ L 189, 29.7.2003, p. 49. Notified under document number C(2003) 2657.

COMMISSION DECISION 2003/548/EC

of 24 July 2003[a]

on the minimum set of leased lines with harmonised characteristics
and associated standards referred to in Article 18 of the Universal Service Directive

THE COMMISSION OF THE EUROPEAN COMMUNITIES,

Having regard to the Treaty establishing the European Community,

Having regard to Directive 2002/22/EC of the European Parliament and of the Council of 7 March 2002 on universal service and users' rights relating to electronic communications networks and services (Universal Service Directive)[1] and in particular Article 18(3) thereof,

Whereas:

(1)   Article 18(3) of the Universal Service Directive provides for the publication of the minimum set of leased lines with harmonised characteristics and associated standards to be published in the Official Journal of the European Union as part of the list of standards referred to in Article 17 of Directive 2002/21/EC of the European Parliament and of the Council of 7 March 2002 on a common regulatory framework for electronic communications networks and services (Framework Directive)[2].

(2)   The minimum set of leased lines was defined in Annex II to Council Directive 92/44/EEC of 5 June 1992 on the application of open network provision (ONP) to leased lines[3], as last amended by Commission Decision 98/80/EC[4]. That Directive was repealed with effect from 25 July 2003 by the Framework Directive.

(3)   This Decision provides continuity of the legal basis for the minimum set of leased lines, for the purpose of implementation of the relevant provisions in the Framework Directive and the Universal Service Directive. The minimum set of leased lines in this Decision is the same as that in Directive 92/44/EEC, except that the references to European Telecommunications Standards (ETSs) have been replaced by references to European Standards (EN), as agreed by the European Telecommunications Standards Institute in 2001. However, leased lines that comply with the previous ETS standards should continue to be deemed in accordance with the requirements for the minimum set of leased lines.

(4)   This Decision identifies the minimum set of leased lines with harmonised characteristics and associated standards and forms an integral part of the list of standards published in accordance with Article 17 of the Framework Directive 2002/21/EC. The current version of the list of standards, only containing voluntary provisions, was published in the Official Journal of the European Union in December 2002[5]. For reasons of differences in procedure and in legal effect, it is appropriate to distinguish the chapters of the list of standards that include mandatory provisions in this Decision from those chapters that only include voluntary provisions.

(5)   The measures provided for in this Decision are in accordance with the opinion of the Communications Committee,

---

[1]   OJ L 108, 24.4.2002, p. 51.
[2]   OJ L 108, 24.4.2002, p. 33.
[3]   OJ L 165, 19.6.1992, p. 27.
[4]   OJ L 14, 20.1.1998, p. 27.
[5]   OJ C 331, 31.12.2002, p. 32.

HAS DECIDED AS FOLLOWS:

Sole Article

The minimum set of leased lines with harmonised characteristics and associated standards are set out in the Annex.

––––––––––––––––

Editors' Notes:

[a] OJ L 186, 25.7.2003, p. 43.

In March 2004, the European Commission launched a public consultation on a possible revision of this Decision. The consultation document is available at:

http://europa.eu.int/information_society/topics/ecomm/doc/useful_information/library/publi c_consult/leased_lines/documents/publiccallforinput_min_set_ll.pdf

The Editors have been advised by European Commission that, following the consultation, it was decided not to change this Decision.

ANNEX

LIST OF STANDARDS AND/OR SPECIFICATIONS FOR ELECTRONIC
COMMUNICATIONS NETWORKS, SERVICES AND ASSOCIATED FACILITIES
AND SERVICES

Mandatory part

Identification of the minimum set of leased lines

1. *Purpose*

    This publication identifies the minimum set of leased lines with harmonised
    characteristics and associated standards referred to in Article 18 of Directive
    2002/22/EC (Universal Service Directive).

    This list forms part of the list of standards referred to in Article 17 of Directive
    2002/21/EC (the Framework Directive).

    This publication is in addition to the list of standards and/or specifications for
    electronic communications networks, services and associated facilities and services
    published in the Official Journal of the European Communities in December 2002[1].

2. *Technical Standards*

    The standards mentioned in this publication are ETSI deliverables under the current
    ETSI nomenclature. According to the "ETSI Directives"[2], these deliverables are
    defined as follows:

    European Standard (telecommunications series), EN: An ETSI deliverable containing
    normative provisions, approved for publication in a process involving the National
    Standards Organisations and/or ETSI National Delegations with implications
    concerning standstill and national transposition.

    Harmonised Standard: An EN (telecommunications series) the drafting of which has
    been entrusted to ETSI by a mandate from the European Commission pursuant to
    Directive 98/48/EC (latest amendment to Council Directive 83/189/EEC) and has
    been drafted taking into account the applicable essential requirements of the "New
    Approach" Directive and whose reference has subsequently been announced in the
    Official Journal of the European Communities.

    The version of the standards referred to in this list is the version valid at the time that
    the list is published.

3. Addresses where documents referenced can be obtained

    ETSI Publications Office[3]

Postal address:	F-06921 Sophia Antipolis Cedex France		
Telephone	(0033) 4 9294 4241	E-mail:	publication@etsi.fr
	(0033) 4 9294 4258		
Fax:	(0033) 4 9395 8133	Web site:	http://www.etsi.fr

---

[1] OJ C 331, 31.12.2002, p. 32.
[2] Available at http://portal.etsi.org/directives/.
[3] ETSI documents can be downloaded from the ETSI Publications Download Area
     (http://pda.etsi.org/pda/queryform.asp).

4. References to EU legislation

The list refers to the following legislative documents which may be found at http://europa.eu.int/ information_society/topics/ telecoms/regulatory/index_en.htm

- Directive 2002/21/EC of the European Parliament and of the Council of 7 March 2002 on a common regulatory framework for electronic communications networks and services (Framework Directive) (OJ L 108, 24.4.2002, p. 33).

- Directive 2002/22/EC of the European Parliament and of the Council of 7 March 2002 on Universal service and users' rights relating to electronic communications networks and services (Universal Service Directive) (OJ L 108, 24.4.2002, p. 51).

Identification of the minimum set of leased lines
with harmonised characteristics and associated standards

ANALOGUE LEASED LINES

Leased line type	Reference	Notes
Ordinary quality voice bandwith[a]	- 2 wire: ETSI EN 300 448 or - 4 wire: ETSI EN 300 451	Connection characteristics and network interface presentation
Special quality voice bandwith[b]	- 2 wire: ETSI EN 300 449 or - 4 wire: ETSI EN 300 452	Connection characteristics and network interface presentation

[a] Leased lines meeting the requirements of ETS 300 448 (2 wire) or ETS 300 451 (4 wire) are deemed to comply with the requirements for this type of leased line.
[b] Leased lines meeting the requirements of ETS 300 449 (2 wire) or ETS 300 452 (4 wire) are deemed to comply with the requirements for this type of leased line.

DIGITAL LEASED LINES

Leased line type	Reference	Notes
64 kbit/s[c]	- ETSI EN 300 288 - ETSI EN 300 289	Network interface presentation Connection characteristics
2048 kbit/s – E1 (unstructured)[d]	- ETSI EN 300 418 - ETSI EN 300 247	Network interface presentation Connection characteristics
2048 kbit/s – E1 (structured)[e]	- ETSI EN 300 418 - ETSI EN 300 419	Network interface presentation Connection characteristics

[c] Leased lines meeting the requirements of ETS 300 288, ETS 300 288/A1 and ETS 300 289 are deemed to comply with the requirements for this type of leased line.
[d] Leased lines meeting the requirements of ETS 300 418, ETS 300 247 and ETS 300 247/A1 are deemed to comply with the requirements for this type of leased line.
[e] Leased lines meeting the requirements of ETS 300 418 and ETS 300 419 are deemed to comply with the requirements for this type of leased line.

COMMUNICATION FROM THE COMMISSION

of 30 July 2004

on interoperability of digital interactive television services

COM(2004)541 final

EXECUTIVE SUMMARY

This Communication sets out the Commission's position on interoperability of digital interactive television services pursuant to Art. 18(3) of Directive 2002/21/EC on a common regulatory framework for electronic communications networks and services (the Framework directive).

The Commission has undertaken this review in two stages. Stage 1 entailed publication for comment of a Commission Staff Working Paper on the interoperability of digital interactive television services SEC (2004) 346 in March 2004.

This Communication thaws upon the public consultation inputs. Underlying analysis for this Communication is contained in the accompanying Extended Impact Assessment (ETA) issued as SEC (2004) 1028.

Art. 18(3) of the Framework directive requires the Commission to examine the effects of Art. 18, concerning interactive television services. If interoperability and freedom of choice for users have not been adequately achieved in one or more Member States, the Commission may act with the aim of making certain standards mandatory.

Responses to the public consultation paint a conflicting picture as to whether adequate interoperability has been effectively achieved. The Commission considers that in view of the complexity of the technological and market environment, the very different perceptions of interoperability held by market players, and late implementation of the Framework Directive in many Member States, the aim of the review is essentially to determine whether there is a case to propose making one or more standards mandatory.

The Commission concludes that there is no clear case for mandating standards at present; the issue should be reviewed in 2005. Meanwhile, a range of promotional actions are proposed to promote the deployment of interactive digital services using the Multimedia Home Platform (MHP) standard, currently the only open standard for APIs adopted by EU standards bodies. These include the creation of a Member State group on MHP implementation, confirmation that Member States can offer consumer subsidies for interactive television receiver equipment, subject to conformity with state aid rules, and monitoring of access to proprietary technologies.

The Commission seeks to ensure that European citizens benefit from a growing range of interactive television services, and considers that the market is best served at the present time by continuing to apply the provisions already agreed by the European Parliament and the Council in the Framework Directive.

1. Background

Interactive TV adds another layer of functionality to digital television (DTV) beyond video. It consists of applications sent in the transmission alongside the video, processed by a software stack in the receiver called an applications program interface (API). Today there are over 32m digital receivers in use in Europe,[1] of which at least 25m have interactive capability.[2]

The market for interactive television developed without a European API standard. Initially there were five significant APIs in Europe, none of which was standardised by a European standards body. Content or applications authored for one API could not be used by a receiver containing a different API.[3]

This triggered concerns about lack of interoperability (covering both technical interoperability and access issues) and possible constraints on consumer choice, which could affect the free flow of information, media pluralism, and cultural diversity. These concerns could be summarised as follows. Consumers would be unable to buy a standardised, universal receiver able to receive all free-to-air and pay television interactive services and could be locked into using more costly receivers containing proprietary APIs. Broadcasters would face obstacles in developing and delivering interactive services because they would have to negotiate with vertically-integrated network operators, in control of proprietary API technologies.

These concerns were led to Art. 18 of Directive 2002/21/EC (the 'Framework Directive') entitled 'Interoperability of digital interactive television services'.

Art. 18(1) requires Member States to encourage providers of digital interactive television services and equipment providers to use an open API.

Art. 18(2) requires Member States to encourage proprietors of APIs to make available all such information as is necessary to enable providers of digital interactive television to provide all services supported by their APIs in fully functional form.

Art. 18(1) is consistent with general EU policy of encouraging open standards for the single market. Art. 18(2) accepts the market reality that proprietary API standards exist, and seeks to ensure transparency of technical specifications so that content providers can build interactive applications that function with these proprietary standards.

Art. 18(3) requires the Commission to examine the effects of Art. 18 by 24 July 2004, following which the Commission may take action to impose a standard using the powers contained in Art. 17 of the Framework Directive.

At the European Parliament Plenary of December 2001, the Commission gave an oral undertaking to include the MHP standards on the list of standards published in the Official Journal of the EU to be encouraged by the Member States, as foreseen in Art. 17 of the Framework Directive.

Process

The Commission began preparing for this review as soon as the Framework Directive was adopted, by undertaking a study through an independent consultancy on possible policy options and by issuing a mandate to the European standardisation bodies in order to investigate how further standardisation could help interoperability.[4] The MHP standards

---

[1]   ETSI TR 102 282, February 2004, p.11.
[2]   Standardisation in digital interactive television, Contest consultancy for CENELEC, April 2003, p.13.
[3]   Delivery of conventional DTV does not require an API to be included in the receiver. An API is an optional extra. Moreover, DTV transmission is fully standardised, with only ETSI standards used in Europe.
[4]   Referenced in SEC(2004) 346 at footnotes 31, 32, 40.

were included in the published list.[5] The Commission also stated that the obvious way to achieve interoperability would be widespread adoption of MHP.[6]

In March 2004, the Commission Services launched a public consultation, based on a Commission Staff Working Paper SEC (2004)346 (the Working Paper). The consultation included a public hearing, and an informal seminar organised by Members of the European Parliament.

2.   The Views of the Players

A wide range of players responded to the consultation, notably manufacturers, network operators, broadcasters and API providers; also consumer associations and others dedicated to particular viewpoints. In total, 51 entities contributed over 350 pages of closely-argued views, strong testimony to the importance of the debate for industry. Responses fall into two main groups.

2.1. Those in favour of the imposition of standards

For those who support mandatory imposition of open standards - including MHP - interoperability at the level of the consumer has not been achieved. They argue this is the most empowering form of interoperability as it maximises the choice of services and equipment for consumers. Currently, the market is fragmented and unable to attain the benefits linked to a single standard.

Market forces are unlikely to deliver adequate interoperability without public authority intervention. Attaining a critical mass of sales at European level is still an important objective for manufacturers in order to achieve economies of scale. Solutions like the proposed Portable Content Format (PCF) - which enables content to be written once and to operate on multiple API platforms — are helpful, but are not a solution for free-to-air broadcasters. For these broadcasters, access rules are a compromise solution in respect of pluralism and freedom of choice. Broadcasters still depend on network operators acting as gatekeepers in order to deliver their services to viewers. Public authorities should take a more interventionist role, following the GSM example.

The benefits of mandating open standards including MHP would include increased consumer choice and legal certainty, leading to lower prices for receivers and acceleration of the switchover from analogue to digital television. If broadcasters did not have to confront the unnecessary obstacle of proprietary APIs, this would improve the flow of information and therefore help pluralism. Service innovation should no longer depend on API proprietors. Sub-segments argue either that Member States should have the possibility to require use of a single API within their territory or that across the EU, only open standard APIs should be legal. Imposition of open standards should not be limited just to free-to-air terrestrial TV, as this would not solve the gatekeeping problem caused by proprietary APIs on cable and satellite. Other standards should be listed if they do not overlap with already listed standards.

General remarks focused on the potential for interactive television to contribute to the Lisbon agenda as underlined by the Seville Council, and criticised the Working Paper for neglecting the social role of free-to-air television. Market players supporting this position were predominantly free-to-air broadcasters from Member States where digital television is less well-developed, and a major manufacturer.

---

[5]   OJ C 331, 31. 12.2002, p. 32.
[6]   EP Oral question 0/2002/40

2.2. Those against imposition of standards

This group argued that interoperability had already been achieved. Their view of interoperability is different: it means the availability of the same interactive services on different distribution platforms. Head-end and network technologies enable content to be ported between different API systems. These include authoring systems able to generate applications for several APIs - multiple authoring - or the proposed PCF.

For this group, interoperability is sensitive to market demand. Where there is demand, interactive applications become available on several different platforms. Examples include gambling, video games and weather forecasting. A one box universal receiver is unlikely because of high costs, and unnecessary because of simulcasting on different networks; however there are no technical barriers. Regarding public authority intervention, they argue that the European DTV market is more dynamic than in the USA because of regulatory forbearance by public authorities. Within the remit of communications regulation, access rules are largely sufficient for preserving pluralism and user choice. Ex post imposition of standards to the detriment of substantial investments in earlier, proprietary systems would deter future investments in subsequent generations of innovative technologies.

These players' general remarks supported the line taken in the working paper, that the greater complexity of DTV alters many factors compared with the simpler analogue model. They favour the possibility to innovate on top of a standardised layer of transmission technologies, as in the internet model. No single technology is appropriate for the diverse market situations to be found across the Member States. When assessing adequacy of implementation, the Commission should take into account the current level of market acceptance and interoperability across the whole value chain. No defmitive future decision on adequacy of implementation should be reached before the passage of 3-5 years.

For this group, the costs of imposing open standards would outweigh the benefits. Imposition of MHP would provide a strong incentive for the market to promote receivers without interactive capability, given the additional costs of MHP receivers and the lack of strong demand for interactive television services.

The players supporting these views were predominantly satellite pay TV and cable operators, frequently from Member States where DTV is well-developed, containing substantial populations of receivers with proprietary APIs. Other members of this constituency were software and IT companies, including owners of proprietary APIs, and a major manufacturer.

2.3. Other views

Public authority inputs reflected whether their DTV markets are well-developed — and therefore contain a substantial population of receivers using proprietary APIs — or less well-developed. Respondents from countries where interactive television is most advanced were in general satisfied that there was an adequate level of interoperability.

Consumer organisations at national and European level favoured imposition of open standards in order to achieve interoperability.

At the public hearing, several major Italian players strongly supported MHP, but were sceptical about imposing it. Government subsidies to Italian consumers for the purchase of an MHP receiver with return channel functionality reduce the additional cost of MHP. Such receivers sell for the same price as in other markets using cheaper API technologies.

3.   The Commission's Analysis and Position

3.1.   The impact to date of Art. 18

Delays in the transposition of the Framework Directive[7] mean that it is premature to reach an overall assessment of the effects of Art. 18(3). Discussions in the broadcasting sub-group of the Communications Committee (COCOM) have revealed a rich seam of activity regarding interoperability at working level in many Member States, frequently linked to implementation of digital terrestrial television.

Regarding Art. 18(2), relatively few Member States have API providers based or represented in their territory; so this provision has limited application for the majority. The Commission is unaware of any regulator having received a fonnal complaint regarding failure by an API owner to make available all information necessary to enable providers of interactive television services to provide all services supported by the API in a fully-functional form. Owners of proprietary APIs argue that they have incentives to ensure that all users obtain maximum benefit from a particular system, on fair, reasonable non-discriminatory terms — notably because there are competing APIs.

In the Commission's view, the provision of Art. 18 that has had the most impact is the requirement to review interoperability and its impact on user choice by July 2004. This has galvanised the market players to debate interoperability in considerable depth. The standards bodies received significant support from market players on both sides in developing their two reports on interoperability. Market players have given high priority to the issue, even if their views on the nature of the legal requirement and how best to fulfil it may differ.

The consultation revealed no significant, substantiated threats to the free flow of information, media pluralism and cultural diversity. The Commission notes recent political concerns however expressed in the European Parliament[8].

3.2.   Central issues

Responses to the consultation are sharply divided. Free-to-air broadcasters are ranged against satellite and cable TV operators and IT players. Both sides claim support from a major consumer electronics manufacturer.

The crux of the dispute is the relationship between general interests and market forces. Free-to-air broadcasters — notably public service broadcasters — are charged with fulfilling important general interest objectives such as media pluralism and cultural diversity, achieved through programming and distribution obligations. Network operators play a key role in achieving the Lisbon agenda through the investment needed to roll out advanced communications networks. Each side seeks to champion their particular role in these policies when it finds some aspect of the other side's behaviour constraining.

Vertical integration of the delivery of broadcasting services with digital infrastructures is a particular source of concern among free-to-air public service broadcasters. Vertical integration can for instance create the potential for proprietary technologies to lock consumers into a particular digital platform or leverage market power. Use of proprietary technologies needs to be kept under competition law review. In some instances, vertical integration can lead to higher economic efficiency[9].

---

[7]   On the date of application, 24 July 2003, 5 of the 15 Member States had transposed the Directive into national law. By the end of May 2004, 9 of the 25 Member States had not completed transposition.

[8]   Resolution P5_TA(2004)0373

[9]   e.g by eliminating double margins.

General interests like cultural diversity and media pluralism are central to the European social model, while economic success is essential to ensure that the Union retains competitiveness and the resources necessary to fund the achievement of general interest objectives and digital switchover. In the EU, these dual policy objectives are implemented by separating content regulation - which targets the achievement of general interests - from communications regulation, aiming to promote a competitive market as the means of generating innovation and new investment. These two policies meet at the API, which is why this debate is so intense.

3.3. Interoperabiity and Art. 18(3) of the Framework Directive

Art. 18(3) of the Framework Directive requires the Commission to assess the effects of Art. 18. If adequate interoperability has not been achieved, the Commission may invoke the procedure in Art. 17 by which certain standards can be made mandatory.

Interoperability is not defined in the Framework Directive or in the associated directives. In addition to its use in Art. 17 and 18 of the Framework Directive, interoperability is used in Art. 24 of the Universal Service directive[10], where the term covers provision of an open interface socket for the connection of peripherals.

Recital 31 - motivating Art. 18 - reflects different aspects of interoperability, stating:

(1)   interoperability of digital interactive television services, at the level of the consumer, should be encouraged in order to ensure the free flow of information, media pluralism and cultural diversity;

(2)   open APIs facilitate interoperability, i.e portability of interactive content between delivery mechanisms with full functionality of the content intact.

The Commission concludes that, in view of the complex environment described in the Working Paper, and differing perceptions revealed by the public consultation, the review's aim is to determine whether there is now a case to propose making one or more API standards mandatory for one or more segments of the market.

The consequences of different scenarios under which standards could be made mandatory, have been examined in the accompanying EIA. Proposals that individual Member States should be able to make one or more open API standards mandatory are incompatible with the single market. Such a policy would erect barriers to trade between Member States.

Making the MHP standard mandatory by a certain date at EU level could ensure technical interoperability of equipment and services, but content providers would still have to negotiate access to the networks and associated services, as mentioned above. Most commentators recognise the problems this policy would create for the estimated 25m set top boxes with API functionality already in the market, and in fact no major contributor proposes this level of intervention. In the light of the negotiating history of the Framework Directive, it is unlikely that such a proposal would find the necessary support from Member States.

The Commission concludes that there is no clear case to mandate EU wide standards generally at the present stage of market evolution, and that more time will allow the provisions of Art. 18 of the Framework Directive to take full effect. It will also be necessary to see whether the concerns related to the "gatekeeping" role of operators using proprietary APIs materialise in the form of formal complaints to regulatory authorities.

---

[10]   Directive 2002/22/EC, OJ L 108, 24.4.2002, p.51.

The limited commercial success of interactive television so far has not provided much incentive for market players to ensure that all services can be made available to all receivers, however this might be achieved. As the market grows, interoperability of services can be expected to develop in parallel. The possibility to develop interactive content so that it can be adapted to different API platforms is the minimum requirement for service interoperability in a growing market. PCF and improved authoring techniques can facilitate portability of content between APIs.[11] This does not rule out other forms of interoperability, including migration to open standards from proprietary standards where there is a business case. Uncertainty regarding demand suggests that simpler, cheaper presentation engines should continue to be available alongside the more sophisticated and more costly execution engine, in order to provide consumer choice.

The Commission will review this issue in the second half of 2005. Meanwhile, further promotion of the MHP standard could benefit European consumers.

3.4. Promotional measures

3.4.1. Improved co-ordination of Member States' implementation of MHP

The Commission will constitute a working group of Member States in order to achieve a clustering effect. Fragmentation caused inter alia by widely varying rates of market development in different Member States makes it hard for manufacturers to achieve economies of scale. The aim would be to identify actions that would help MHP achieve critical mass and exploit economies of scale, leading to price reductions and improved prospects of market take-up. Currently, the additional costs of MHP are a barrier to widespread take up. This measure is intended to help smaller Member States in particular.

3.4.2. Consumer subsidies

One way of reducing the additional costs to consumers of equipment incorporating standard execution engines such as MHP is to subsidise purchases at the level of the consumer. Consumer subsidies are already available in Italy, and MHP receivers with the subsidy now retail for the same price as a digital receiver using an earlier, cheaper API in other, more mature national markets. The conditions imposed also provide the public with an incentive to acquire a receiver with both interactivity and a return channel, rather than a simple receiver without these functionalities. Member States may therefore offer consumer subsidies. Such consumer subsidies need to be technologically neutral and must be notified and conform to State Aid rules. They should be temporary and reduce in proportion to the falling cost of receivers, in order to avoid over compensation. Subsidies to undertakings are not included in this initiative and would need to be notified to the Commission in accordance with the normal procedure.

3.4.3. List of standards published in the Official Journal

The Commission signals its intention to add two presentation engines, MHEG 5 and WTVML, when the list is next updated, conditional upon their adoption by ETSI. The revised list would be submitted for opinion to COCOM as foreseen in Art. 17 of the Framework Directive.

Other standards emerging from the standardisation work programme defined in phase 1 of mandate M331, will be considered for inclusion in the List of Standards when they become available. These deliverables have the potential to improve interoperability as described in the Working Paper.

---

[11] PCF could cover 80% of the interactive television application, but not the most complex ones, e.g Electronic Programme guides.

3.4.4. Monitoring access to proprietary technologies

The Commission — assisted by the Member States as appropriate — will continue to monitor the availability of proprietary technologies for licensing by manufacturers. Combining multiple complementary technologies into receivers is one way of achieving a "one box" universal receiver. Where these functions are standardised — tuners for instance — the only barrier is cost; but there could be greater clarity regarding the availability of proprietary technologies such as APIs. Art. 6, Annex I of the Access and Interconnection Directive[12] already imposes a requirement on providers of conditional access systems to ensure that these are made available on fair, reasonable and non-discriminatory terms, when granting licences to manufacturers of consumer equipment.

The Commission will follow up through its regular implementation reports on the eCommunications package.

4. Conclusion

The Commission seeks to ensure that European citizens benefit from a growing range of interactive DTV services, available on an increasing number of transmission platforms, and considers that the market is best served at the present time by continuing to apply the provisions already agreed by the European Parliament and the Council in the Framework Directive. Moreover, use of proprietary technologies will remain subject to competition law review.

The Commission will take additional measure to promote the voluntary implementation of the MHP standard, which is currently the most advanced open API standard in Europe.

The Commission will continue to pursue the aim of full and effective transposition of Art. 18 by all Member States, but in view of the complexity of the environment, the different perceptions held by market players, and late implementation of the Framework Directive in many Member States concludes it is inappropriate to determine that interoperability has or has not been adequately achieved in the context of Art. 18(3). However, this review has not substantiated the view that concerns related to cultural diversity and media pluralism could only be overcome by imposition of a single standard for APIs. More significant elements in the media pluralism debate lie within the competence of Member States, notably media ownership and control.

The Commission will review the situation in the second half of 2005[a].

Editors' Notes:

[a] In a Communication reviewing the interoperability of digital interactive television services pursuant to Communication COM(2004) 541 of 30 July 2004, COM(2006) 37 final, the Commission concluded that "mandating EU-wide standards under Article 18(3) of the Framework Directive would not contribute significantly to the growth of interactive digital television in Europe, and could have significant negative effects."

---

[12] Directive 2002/19/EC, OJ L 108, 24.4.2002, p.12

DECISION NO 1336/97/EC OF THE EUROPEAN PARLIAMENT AND OF THE COUNCIL

of 17 June 1997

[as amended]^a

on a series of guidelines for trans-European telecommunications networks

THE EUROPEAN PARLIAMENT AND THE COUNCIL OF THE EUROPEAN UNION,

Having regard to the Treaty establishing the European Community, and in particular the first paragraph of Article 129d thereof,

Having regard to the proposal from the Commission[1],

Having regard to the opinion of the Economic and Social Committee[2],

Having regard to the opinion of the Committee of the Regions[3],

Acting in accordance with the procedure laid down in Article 189b of the Treaty[4] in the light of the joint text approved on 16 April 1997 by the Conciliation Committee,

(1)	Whereas the establishment and development of trans-European telecommunications networks aim at ensuring the circulation and exchange of information across the Community; whereas this outlay in equipment is a precondition to enable citizens and industry - especially SMEs - in the Community to derive full benefit from the potential of telecommunications so as to make possible the establishment of the 'information society', in which the development of applications, services and telecommunications networks will be of crucial importance with a view to ensuring the availability for each citizen, company or public authority, including in the less developed or peripheral regions, of any type or quantity of information they may need;

(2)	Whereas, in its White Paper on 'Growth, Competitiveness and Employment', the Commission stressed the importance of establishing the information society, which, by introducing new forms of economic, political and social relations, will help the Union to face the new challenges of the next century, including the challenge of employment creation; whereas this was recognized by the Brussels European Council of December 1993;

(3)	Whereas the internal market constitutes an area without borders, within which the free movement of goods, persons, capital and services has to be ensured, and where Community measures already adopted or in the process of being adopted require significant exchange of information between individuals, economic operators and administrations; whereas the fact of possessing efficient means of exchanging information is of vital importance for improving the competitiveness of undertakings; whereas these exchanges of information can be ensured by trans-European telecommunications networks; whereas the availability of trans-European networks will strengthen social and economic cohesion in the Community;

---

[1]	OJ No C 302, 14.11.1995, p. 23 and OJ No C 175, 18.6.1996, p. 4.
[2]	OJ No C 39, 12.2.1996, p. 20.
[3]	OJ No C 129, 2.5.1996, p. 32.
[4]	Opinion of the European Parliament of 1 February 1996 (OJ No C 47, 19.2.1996, p. 15), Council Common Position of 21 March 1996 (OJ No C 134, 6.5.1996, p. 18) and Decision of the European Parliament of 17 July 1996 (OJ No C 261, 9.9.1996, p. 59). Decision of the European Parliament of 14 May 1997 and Council Decision of 26 May 1997.

(4)   Whereas establishment and development of trans-European telecommunications networks must enable information to be freely exchanged between individuals, economic operators and administrations, while respecting individuals' rights to privacy and intellectual and industrial property rights;

(5)   Whereas, in June 1994, in their report on 'Europe and the global information society`, which they prepared for the Corfu European Council of 24 and 25 June 1994, the members of a group of prominent representatives of industry recommended the implementation of trans-European telecommunications networks and the securing of their interconnectivity with all European networks; whereas the report identified mobile communications as a pillar of the information society whose potential should be strengthened; whereas the Corfu European Council gave its general approval to that recommendation;

(6)   Whereas those recommendations were followed by the Commission in its communication to the European Parliament and the Council entitled 'Europe's way to the information society: an action plan`; whereas the conclusions of the Council meeting on 28 September 1994 on this action plan stressed the fact that the fast development of high-performance information infrastructures is essential for the Community on the basis of a global, coherent and balanced approach;

(7)   Whereas Article 129c of the Treaty requires the Community to establish a series of guidelines covering the objectives, priorities and broad lines of measures envisaged in the sphere of trans-European networks; whereas these guidelines must identify projects of common interest; whereas trans-European networks in the area of telecommunications infrastructure cover the three layers constituting these networks: applications, generic services and basic networks;

(8)   Whereas the information society cannot develop without the existence of accessible applications, and especially applications of collective interest, addressing user needs as well as possible, and taking into account, where appropriate, the needs of the elderly and disabled; whereas applications will thus form an important part of the projects of common interest; whereas the applications relevant to teleworking must take account in particular of legal provisions concerning workers' rights applying in the Member States concerned;

(9)   Whereas projects of common interest can, in many cases, already be implemented in the present telecommunications networks, especially the Euro-ISDN, and thereby offer trans-European applications; whereas guidelines have to be drawn up to identify these projects of common interest;

(10)   Whereas there should be coordination between the implementation of the proposals chosen and similar initiatives adopted at national or regional level in the Community;

(11)   Whereas in the selection and implementation of such projects account should be taken of all infrastructures offered by incumbent and new providers;

(12)   Whereas on 9 November 1995 the European Parliament and the Council adopted Decision No 2717/95/EC on a set of guidelines for the development of the EURO-ISDN (Integrated Services Digital Network) as a trans-European network[5];

(13)   Whereas the present networks, which include existing ISDN, are evolving towards becoming advanced networks offering a variable data flow rate up to broadband capabilities, adaptable to different needs, in particular to the provision of multimedia services and applications; whereas implementation of Integrated Broadband

---

[5]   OJ No L 282, 24.11.1995, p. 16.

Communication Networks (IBC networks) will be the outcome of this evolution; whereas IBC networks will constitute the optimum platform for information society applications;

(14) Whereas the work of the RACE Programme (specific research and technological development programme in the field of communication technologies (1990 to 1994)) laid down in Decision 91/352/EEC[6] has prepared the ground and provided the technology base for the introduction of IBC networks in Europe;

(15) Whereas the work of the Esprit Programme (specific programme for research and technological development, including demonstration, in the field of information technologies (1994 to 1998)), laid down in Decision 94/802/EC[7], has prepared the ground and provided the technology base for the introduction of information technology applications;

(16) Whereas the results of the work of the specific research and technological development programmes in the field of telematic systems of general interest (1991 to 1994) laid down by Decision 91/353/EEC[8] and of the specific programme for research and technological development, including demonstration, in the field of telematic applications of common interest (1994 to 1998) laid down by Decision 94/801/EEC[9] prepare the ground for the introduction of interoperable applications of common interest across Europe;

(17) Whereas effective coordination needs to be ensured between the development of the trans-European telecommunications networks, which must address real-world concerns, without attempting to carry out purely experimental projects, and the different Community programmes, in particular the specific programmes of the fourth framework programme for research, technological development and demonstration, programmes in favour of SMEs, information-content-oriented programmes (such as INFO 2000 and MEDIA II) and other information society activities; whereas such coordination must also be ensured with the projects provided for by Decisions of the European Parliament and of the Council applying to trans-European networks;

(18) Whereas the measures aimed at ensuring the interoperability of telematic networks between administrations fall within the framework of priorities adopted in relation to the present guidelines for trans-European telecommunications networks;

(19) Whereas in its communication of 24 July 1993 on preparatory actions in the field of trans-European networks in respect of integrated broadband communications, the Commission recognized the need to carry out preparatory actions with the sector actors to draw up appropriate guidelines; whereas the result of these actions forms the basis for the guidelines relating to IBC networks in this Decision;

(20) Whereas the telecommunications sector is being progressively liberalized; whereas the development of trans-European applications, generic services and basic networks will increasingly rely on private initiative; whereas these trans-European developments must respond on a European scale to market needs or to actual and sizeable needs of society which are not covered by market forces alone; whereas, taking this into account, the interested sector actors will be requested to submit, through the application of appropriate procedures giving everyone equal opportunities, specific proposals; whereas these procedures have to be defined;

---

[6]   OJ No L 192, 16.7.1991, p. 8.
[7]   OJ No L 334, 22.12.1994, p. 24.
[8]   OJ No L 192, 16.7.1991, p. 18.
[9]   OJ No L 334, 22.12.1994, p. 1.

whereas a Committee will assist the Commission for specification of projects of common interest;

(21) Whereas a modus vivendi between the European Parliament, the Council and the Commission concerning the implementing measures for acts adopted in accordance with the procedure laid down in Article 189b of the Treaty was concluded on 20 December 1994[10];

(22) Whereas projects of common interest which relate to the territory of a Member State require the approval of the Member State concerned;

(23) Whereas the Commission and the Member States will have to act to ensure interoperability of the networks and coordinate, on the one hand, the activities of the Member States aimed at implementation of trans-European telecommunications networks and, on the other, comparable national projects, only to the extent necessary to ensure overall coherence;

(24) Whereas it is important, for the optimum development of the information society, to ensure an efficient exchange of information between the Community and third countries, in particular the States parties to the Agreement on the European Economic Area or countries having concluded an Association Agreement with the Community;

(25) Whereas, however, activities undertaken in the context of these guidelines are subject to the full application of the competition rules laid down in the Treaty and implementing legislation,

HAVE ADOPTED THIS DECISION:

Article 1

This Decision establishes guidelines covering the objectives, priorities and broad lines of measures envisaged in the sphere of trans-European networks in the area of telecommunications infrastructure. These guidelines identify projects of common interest by listing those projects in Annex I and by laying down the procedure and criteria for the specification thereof.

For the purpose of this Decision, 'telecommunications infrastructure' shall refer to the electronic data transmission networks and the services which make use of them.

Article 2

The Community shall support the interconnection of networks in the sphere of telecommunications infrastructure, the establishment and development of interoperable services and applications as well as access to them, with the objectives of:

- facilitating the transition towards the information society, as well as providing experience on the effects of the deployment of new networks and applications on social activities and promoting the satisfaction of social and cultural needs and improving the quality of life,

- improving the competitiveness of Community firms, in particular SMEs, and strengthening the internal market,

---

[10] OJ No C 102, 4.4.1996, p. 1.

-   strengthening economic and social cohesion, taking account in particular of the need to link island, land-locked and peripheral regions to the central regions of the Community,

-   accelerating the development of new growth-area activities leading to job creation.

Article 3

The priorities for the realization of the objectives referred to in Article 2 shall be:

-   study and validation of the technical and commercial feasibility, followed by the deployment of applications supporting the development of a European information society, in particular applications of collective interest,

-   study and validation of feasibility, followed by the deployment of applications contributing to economic and social cohesion, by improving access to information throughout the Community and building on European cultural diversity,

-   stimulation of trans-boundary interregional initiatives and of initiatives involving regions, in particular the less-favoured ones, for the launch of trans-European telecommunications services and applications,

-   study and validation of feasibility, followed by the deployment of applications and services contributing to the strengthening of the internal market and job creation, in particular those offering to SMEs means to improve their competitiveness in the Community and at world level,

-   identification, study and validation of the technical and commercial feasibility, followed by the deployment of trans-European generic services providing seamless access to all kinds of information, including in rural and peripheral regions, and interoperable with equivalent services at world level,

-   study and validation of the feasibility of new integrated broadband communication (IBC) networks, where required for such applications and services, and promotion of the interconnectivity of such networks,

-   identification and removal of gaps and missing links for effective interconnection and interoperability of all the components of telecommunications networks in the Community and at world level, with particular emphasis on basic telecommunications networks as defined in Annex I.

Article 4

The broad lines of measures to be implemented for achieving the objectives defined in Article 2 shall cover:

-   specification of projects of common interest by the establishment of a work programme,

-   actions aimed at increasing the awareness of individuals, economic operators and administrations of the benefits they can derive from the new advanced trans-European telecommunications services and applications,

-   actions aimed at the stimulation of combined initiatives by users and providers to launch projects in the sphere of trans-European telecommunications networks, in particular IBC networks,

- support, within the framework of the methods laid down in the Treaty, for actions to study and validate the feasibility, followed by the deployment, of applications, in particular applications of collective interest, and encouragement of the establishment of public/private collaboration, in particular through partnerships,

- stimulation of the supply and use of services and applications for SMEs and professional users, which constitute a source of employment and growth,

- promotion of interconnectivity of networks, of interoperability of broadband services and applications and of the infrastructure they require, in particular for multimedia applications, and of interoperability between existing and broadband services and applications.

Article 5

The development of trans-European networks in the sphere of telecommunications infrastructure shall be undertaken under this Decision through the implementation of projects of common interest. The projects of common interest are listed in Annex I.

Article 6

In accordance with Articles 7, 8 and 9, projects of common interest listed in Annex I shall be specified, using the criteria listed in Annex II. The projects identified are eligible for Community support in compliance with Council Regulation (EC) No 2236/95 of 18 September 1995 laying down general rules for the granting of Community financial aid in the field of trans-European networks[11].

Article 7

1. On the basis of Annex I the Commission, following consultation of the sector operators and taking the other trans-European network policies into account, shall prepare a work programme, adopted in accordance with the procedure laid down in Article 8, and subsequently proceed with calls for proposals.

2. The Commission shall verify that the projects relating to the territory of a Member State are approved by the Member State concerned.

Article 8

1. The Commission shall be assisted by a Committee (hereinafter referred to as 'the Committee').

2. Where reference is made to this paragraph, Articles 5 and 7 of Decision 1999/468/EC shall apply, having regard to the provisions of Article 8 thereof.

   The period laid down in Article 5(6) of Decision 1999/468/EC shall be set at three months.

3. The Committee shall adopt its rules of procedure.

Article 9

1. The procedure laid down in Article 8 shall apply to:

---

[11] OJ No L 228, 23.9.1995, p. 1.

- the preparation and updating of the work programme referred to in Article 7,

- the determination of the content of calls for proposals,

- the specification of projects of common interest using the criteria set out in Annex II,

- the determination of supplementary support and coordination actions,

- the measures to be taken to evaluate the implementation of the work programme on a financial and technical level.

2. The Commission shall inform the committee, at each of its meetings, of the progress made in implementing the work programme.

Article 10

This Decision shall apply to the Integrated Services Digital Network (ISDN) without prejudice to Decision No 2717/95/EC of the European Parliament and of the Council.

Article 11

Member States shall take all the measures necessary to facilitate the implementation of the projects of common interest in conformity with Community rules. The authorization procedures which may be necessary shall be completed as quickly as possible in conformity with Community legislation.

Article 12

This Decision shall not prejudice any financial commitment by a Member State or the Community.

Article 13

The participation of third countries, in particular countries party to the Agreement on the European Economic Area or having concluded an Association Agreement with the Community, may be authorized by the Council on a case-by-case basis, in accordance with the procedure laid down in Article 228 of the Treaty, in order to allow them to contribute to the implementation of projects of common interest, and to promote the interconnection and interoperability of telecommunications networks, provided that it does not entail an increase in Community aid.

Article 14

1. Before 31 January 2005, the Commission shall submit a report on the implementation of this Decision during the period July 2000 to June 2004, to the European Parliament, the Council, the Economic and Social Committee and the Committee of the Regions.

2. The report shall contain an evaluation of the results achieved with Community support in the various project fields in relation to the overall objectives and shall contain an assessment of the social and societal impact of the introduction of the applications after they are deployed.

3. Together with that report, the Commission shall submit appropriate proposals for revision of Annex I to this Decision on the basis of technical developments and experience gained.

4.   In the absence of a decision by 31 December 2006, Annex I shall be deemed to have lapsed except in respect of calls for proposals which have already been published in the Official Journal of the European Communities before that date.

Article 15

This Decision is addressed to the Member States.

———————

Editors' Notes:

[a] Decision No 1336/97/EC (OJ L 183, 11.7.1997, p. 12) is reproduced in this book as amended by Decision No. 1376/2002/EC of the European Parliament and of the Council of 12 July 2002 (OJ L 200, 30.07.2002. p 1).

<u>Identification of projects of common interest</u>

1. Trans-European telecommunications networks will contribute to the introduction of innovative trans-European services in the general interest. The services will contribute to the development of the information society in terms of growth, employment, social cohesion and participation for all in the knowledge-based economy.

2. TEN-Telecom supports the technical and economic feasibility, validation and deployment of services. Services must be innovative, trans-European and based on proven technology:

    –   a service may be launched in separate Member States with appropriate adaptation in each State,

    –   a service that has already been deployed in a single Member State without support under this programme may be extended to other Member States,

    –   a service of demonstrably trans-European interest may be implemented in a single Member State.

3. As services should be considered to be trans-European, the participation of organisations from more than one Member State and implementation in more than one Member State, though not required, will be encouraged.

4. In this context, projects of common interest shall be identified on the basis of their operational capability to support the objectives laid down in this Decision.

5. The projects of common interest described below shall be on three levels, forming a coherent structure.

(i) **Applications**

Applications serve user needs, taking into account cultural and linguistic differences and the requirements for accessibility, in particular for disabled people. Where it is applicable, they shall accommodate the specific needs of less developed or less populated regions. They shall use the potential of broadband, mobile and other communications networks as appropriate.

(ii) **Generic Services**

Generic Services shall support applications' common requirements by providing common tools for the development and implementation of new applications based on interoperable standards. They shall provide services for the transfer and integrity of data across networks, including broadband and mobile communication networks.

(iii) **Interconnection and interoperability of networks**

Support will be provided for the interconnection, interoperability and security of networks underpinning the operation of specific public interest applications and services.

The following sections identify at each level of the trans-European networks the projects of common interest that must be specified in accordance with Article 9 and under the procedure laid down in Article 8.

I.   Applications

–   e-Government and e-Administration: more efficient, interactive, and integrated governmental services benefiting citizens and SME's constitute a major opportunity for the information society. On-line services including those in the field of electronic procurement, secured access to on-line public services for citizens and SME's, personal security, environment and tourism, business support for SME's (including information services and electronic commerce), and services aimed at broadening participation in the democratic decision-making process will be supported at all levels: European, national, regional and local. Services may be provided by, or with the support of, public authorities as a service in the public interest benefiting citizens and SME's.

–   Health: health telematics networks and services offer significant opportunities for the improvement of access and quality of care, as well as handling the impacts of medical advances and demographic changes. Innovative services will be supported linking health care institutions and other points of care, and providing health services directly to the public, in particular supporting actions on disease prevention and health promotion.

–   Disabled and elderly: developments in network communications offer significant opportunities for the participation of older people and people with disabilities in the information society. Network applications and services addressing their specific needs are able to contribute to the overcoming of socio-economic, geographical and cultural barriers. Services will be supported catering for the requirements of older people and people with disabilities with the purpose of promoting their full integration and participation in the information society.

–   Learning and culture: high levels of education, training and cultural awareness are crucial to economic development and social cohesion. Their importance will continue to be underlined in future with the increasing influence of technology in the information society. Services will be supported providing new innovative ways of presenting educational and cultural information, including services for lifelong learning.

II.   Generic services

-    Advanced mobile services: trials are under way on the interoperability aspects of innovative applications for 2,5 to 3G mobile networks. They will establish the basis for advanced end-to-end solutions in the mobile environment providing location-based, personalised, and context-sensitive services. Support will be provided for the launch of advanced mobile applications and services in the general interest including those for navigation and guidance, traffic and travel information, network security and billing, m-commerce, m-business and mobile work, learning and culture, emergency services and health.

-    Trust and confidence services: the active involvement of businesses and citizens in the information society is dependent on their trust and confidence in the available services. Security is therefore a priority issue presenting a major challenge for the future. Support will be provided for services in the public interest aimed at all aspects of security including cooperation for effective networking within the European Union on national CERT systems.

III. Interconnection and interoperability of networks

–   Interconnection and interoperability: the interconnection and interoperability of networks is a pre-requisite for effective trans-European services. Support will be provided for the interconnection, interoperability and security of networks necessary for the operation of specific public interest services. Projects concerning the development and enhancement of telecommunications networks will receive particular scrutiny to ensure that there is no interference with free market conditions.

IV. Supplementary support and coordination actions

In addition to its support for projects of common interest, the Community shall initiate actions aimed at providing the appropriate environment for the realisation of the projects. The financing of these actions should not take away in any significant manner from the amounts allocated to the rest of the programme. The actions will contribute to programme awareness, consensus development and concerted efforts concerning European, national, regional and local activities for stimulation and promotion of new applications and services, in conformity with the implementation of programmes in other areas, as well as the development of broadband networks. They will involve consultation with European standardisation and strategic planning bodies and coordination with actions funded by the different Community financial instruments, including:

— strategic studies toward target specifications, and transition towards these targets. These specifications will help sector actors to make sound economic investment decisions,

— definition of means of accessing broadband networks,

— establishment of common specifications based on European and world standards,

— furthering cooperation among sector actors, including public and private partnerships (PPP),

— coordination of the activities undertaken under this Decision with related Community and national programmes.

Criteria for the specification of projects of common interest

Projects of common interest will be specified from among the projects submitted by interested sector actors in response to a call for proposals, as provided for in Article 7, on the basis of their compliance with the objectives and priorities laid down in Articles 2 and 3 respectively. These projects must be transnational in the sense that they shall be conceived to satisfy needs existing in several Member States. As a general rule, they shall be implemented in several Member States but implementation in a single Member State shall be allowed if it contributes to a broader trans-European interest.

In addition, account will be taken of the economic and financial criteria set out in Regulation (EC) No 2236/95. These criteria, which will be used in the framework of the said Regulation for deciding on the granting of financial support to a specific project, are:

-       the potential economic viability of the project, which should be assured,

-       the maturity of the project,

-       the stimulative effect of Community intervention on public and private financing,

-       the soundness of the financial package,

-       the direct or indirect socio-economic effects, in particular on employment,

-       the consequences for the environment,

-       for cross-border projects in particular, coordination of the timing of the different parts of a project.

COMMISSION OF THE EUROPEAN COMMUNITIES

Brussels, 06/IV/2005
C(2005)1031 final

COMMISSION RECOMMENDATION

of 06/I V12005

on broadband electronic communications through powerlines

(Text with EEA relevance)

THE COMMISSION OF THE EUROPEAN COMMUNITIES,

Having regard to Directive 2002/21/EC of the European Parliament and of the Council of 7 March 2002 on a common regulatory framework for electronic communications networks and services (Framework Directive)[1], and in particular Article 19(1) thereof,

Whereas:

(1) The present Recommendation seeks to ensure transparent, proportionate and non-discriminatory conditions for the deployment of powerline communications systems, and removal of any inappropriate regulatory barriers. Powerline communications systems include both equipment and networks.

(2) The EU regulatory framework for electronic communications aims to create conditions for the competitive provision of electronic communications networks and services and ensure that users obtain the maximum benefit in terms of choice, price and quality. National authorities have an objective to promote competition in the provision of electronic communications networks, which include powerline communications networks. They should thus remove any unjustified regulatory obstacles, in particular on utility companies, to deploy and operate electronic communications networks over their powerlines.

(3) Deployment of powerline communication systems is subject only to a general authorisation pursuant to Directive 2002/20/EC of the European Parliament and of the Council of 7 March 2002 on the authorisation of electronic communications networks and services (the Authorisation Directive)[2]. This may include, where appropriate, obligations provided for in Directive 89/336/EEC of the Council of 3 May 1989 on the approximation of laws of the Member States relating to electromagnetic compatibility (the EMC Directive)[3], Directive 1999/5/EC of the European Parliament and of the Council of 9 March 1999 on radio equipment and telecommunications terminal equipment and the mutual recognition of their conformity (the Terminal Directive)[4], the Framework Directive, Directive 2002/22/EC of the European Parliament and of the Council of 7 March 2002 on universal service and users' rights relating to electronic communication networks and services (the Universal Service Directive)[5] such as for emergency communications and the integrity of the network. With a view to avoiding discrimination, crosssubsidisation and distortion of competition, there may also be obligations on certain undertakings in accordance with Directive 2003/54/EC of the European Parliament and of the Council of 26 June 2003 concerning common rules for

---

[1] OJ L 108, 24.4.2002, p.33.
[2] OJ L 108, 2442002, p.21.
[3] OJ L139, 23.5.1989, p.19, as last amended by Directive 93/68/EEC, OJ L 220, 30.8.1993, p.1.
[4] OJ L 91, 7.4.1999, p.10.
[5] OJ L 108, 24.4.2002, p.51.

the internal market in electricity and repealing Directive 96/92/EC[6], to keep separate consolidated accounts for the non-electricity activities, such as powerline communications.

(4) Powerline communication networks are cable networks and as such they are guided media. They do not use radio frequencies for transmission within the meaning of Annex B of the Authonsation Directive or Decision 676/2002/EC of the European Parliament and of the Council of 7 March 2002 on a regulatory framework for radio spectrum policy in the European Community[7].

(5) Powerline communications systems fall within the scope of the EMC Directive. The term 'apparatus' as defined in the EMC Directive means all electrical and electronic appliances together with equipment and installations containing electrical and/or electronic components. Powerline communications systems are considered as fixed installations and can only be put into service if they comply with the Directive.

(6) In powerline communications systems, the cabling involved may already be in service for other uses, and networks may be subject to constant alteration. These characteristics, together with the specific nature of unwanted radiated emissions along wireline systems, means that is impractical to carry out measurements on a complete system, and an ex-post model for interference management of wireline systems with radio systems is appropriate, in accordance with the EMC Directive. Therefore, a network made up of equipment compliant with the EMC Directive and used for its intended purpose, which is installed and operated according to good engineering practices designed to meet the essential requirements of the EMC Directive, should be considered compliant with the requirements of the EMC Directive. The documented good engineering practices should include targeted in-situ measurements, demonstrating that the objectives of the EMC Directive are met in respect of unwanted radiated emissions, especially in situations where interference is more likely to occur.

(7) This approach shall not prevent Member States from taking special measures for safety reasons concerning the putting into service or use of equipment to protect public telecommunication networks or receiving or transmitting stations used for safety purposes in well-defined spectrum situations, in accordance with Article 6 of the EMC Directive.

(8) If the interference caused by a powerline communications system can not be resolved by the parties concerned, the competent authorities should request evidence of compliance of the system concerned and, where appropriate, initiate a further assessment. That assessment should include a verification of compliance of the system under the EMC Directive. If non-compliance is identified, the competent authorities should impose proportionate, non-discriminatory and transparent enforcement measures to bring the system into compliance.

(9) If a system is deemed compliant but is nevertheless creating harmful interference, the competent authorities of the Member States should take special measures according to Article 6 of the EMC Directive, with a view to resolve such interference. Measures taken should be proportionate, non-discriminatory and transparent. In examining the proportionality of measures, Member States should take into account economic and social aspects of the services involved. Member States may also take into account the technical capability of modern powerline communications equipment to allow for a timely resolution of interference problems by reducing emissions at the specific interfering frequencies and places by so called 'notching'.

---

[6] OJ L 176, 15.7.2003, p.37.
[7] OJ L 108, 24.4.2002, p.1.

(10) In order to achieve a consistent application of either enforcement measures or of special measures under Article 6 of the EMC Directive, the competent authorities should exchange information between themselves and the Commission.

(11) This approach, combined with regular and detailed interference reporting, will allow for further test results and experiences to be gathered on the roll-out of powerline communications networks, in particular in view of the protection of the use of the radio spectrum. The frequency of reporting should be semi-annually initially, but may be varied depending on the results obtained.

(12) In 2001 the Commission called upon the European Standardisation Organisations (ESOs) to draft harmonised European standards for wireline networks to include digital subscriber line (DSL), coaxial cable, Ethernet and powerline communications networks[8]. However, the work of the ESOs has not yet been completed. In order to facilitate the development of a harmonised European standard for wireline networks and apparatus, national authorities should monitor developments in close cooperation with market players.

(13) The Communications Committee has been consulted in accordance with the procedure referred to in Article 22(2) of the Framework Directive,

HEREBY RECOMMENDS:

1. Member States should apply the following conditions and principles to the provision of publicly available broadband powerline communications systems.

2. Without prejudice to the provisions of points 3 to 5, Member States should remove any unjustified regulatory obstacles, in particular from utility companies, on the deployment of broadband powerline communications systems and the provision of electronic communications services over such systems.

3. Until standards to be used for gaining presumption of conformity for powerline communications systems have been harmonised under Directive 89/336/EEC, Member States should consider as compliant with that Directive a powerline communications system which is:

    - made up of equipment compliant with the Directive and used for its intended purpose;

    - installed and operated according to good engineering practices designed to meet the essential requirements of the Directive.

    The documentation on good engineering practices should be held at the disposal of the relevant national authorities for inspection purposes as long as the system is in operation.

4. Where it is found that a powerline communications system is causing harmful interference that can not be resolved by the parties concerned, the competent authorities of the Member State should request evidence of compliance of the system and, where appropriate, initiate an assessment.

---

[8] Standardisation mandate addressed to CEN, CENELEC and ETSI concerning electromagnetic compatibility (EMC) on EMC harmonised standards for telecommunications networks, Mandate M/313, 7 August 2001.

5. If the assessment leads to an identification of non-compliance of the powerline communications system, the competent authorities should impose proportionate, non-discriminatory and transparent enforcement measures to ensure compliance.

6. If there is compliance of the powerline communications system but nevertheless the interference remains, the competent authorities of the Member State should consider taking special measures in accordance with Article 6 of the Directive 89/336/EEC in a proportionate, non-discriminatory and transparent manner.

7. Member States should report to the Communications Committee on a regular basis on the deployment and operations of powerline communications systems in their territory. Such reports should include any relevant data about disturbance levels (including measurement data, related injected signal levels and other data useful for the drafting of a harmonised European standard), interference problems and any enforcement measures related to powerline communications systems. The first such report is due on 31/XII/2005.

8. This Recommendation is addressed to the Member States.

DIRECTIVE 2002/58/EC OF THE EUROPEAN PARLIAMENT AND OF THE COUNCIL

of 12 July 2002

concerning the processing of personal data and the protection of privacy in the electronic communications sector

[as amended][a]

THE EUROPEAN PARLIAMENT AND THE COUNCIL OF THE EUROPEAN UNION,

Having regard to the Treaty establishing the European Community, and in particular Article 95 thereof,

Having regard to the proposal from the Commission[1],

Having regard to the opinion of the Economic and Social Committee[2],

Having consulted the Committee of the Regions,

Acting in accordance with the procedure laid down in Article 251 of the Treaty[3],

Whereas:

(1)   Directive 95/46/EC of the European Parliament and of the Council of 24 October 1995 on the protection of individuals with regard to the processing of personal data and on the free movement of such data[4] requires Member States to ensure the rights and freedoms of natural persons with regard to the processing of personal data, and in particular their right to privacy, in order to ensure the free flow of personal data in the Community.

(2)   This Directive seeks to respect the fundamental rights and observes the principles recognised in particular by the Charter of fundamental rights of the European Union. In particular, this Directive seeks to ensure full respect for the rights set out in Articles 7 and 8 of that Charter.

(3)   Confidentiality of communications is guaranteed in accordance with the international instruments relating to human rights, in particular the European Convention for the Protection of Human Rights and Fundamental Freedoms, and the constitutions of the Member States.

(4)   Directive 97/66/EC of the European Parliament and of the Council of 15 December 1997 concerning the processing of personal data and the protection of privacy in the telecommunications sector[5] translated the principles set out in Directive 95/46/EC into specific rules for the telecommunications sector. Directive 97/66/EC has to be adapted to developments in the markets and technologies for electronic communications services in order to provide an equal level of protection of personal data and privacy for users of publicly available electronic communications services, regardless of the

---

[1]   OJ C 365 E, 19.12.2000, p. 223.
[2]   OJ C 123, 25.4.2001, p. 53.
[3]   Opinion of the European Parliament of 13 November 2001 [OJ C 140 E, 13.06.2002, p. 132], Council Common Position of 28 January 2002 [OJ C 113 E, 14.5.2002, p. 39] and Decision of the European Parliament of 30 May 2002, OJ C 187E, 7.8.2003, p.103. Council Decision of 25 June 2002.
[4]   OJ L 281, 23.11.1995, p. 31.
[5]   OJ L 24, 30.1.1998, p. 1.

technologies used. That Directive should therefore be repealed and replaced by this Directive.

(5) New advanced digital technologies are currently being introduced in public communications networks in the Community, which give rise to specific requirements concerning the protection of personal data and privacy of the user. The development of the information society is characterised by the introduction of new electronic communications services. Access to digital mobile networks has become available and affordable for a large public. These digital networks have large capacities and possibilities for processing personal data. The successful cross-border development of these services is partly dependent on the confidence of users that their privacy will not be at risk.

(6) The Internet is overturning traditional market structures by providing a common, global infrastructure for the delivery of a wide range of electronic communications services. Publicly available electronic communications services over the Internet open new possibilities for users but also new risks for their personal data and privacy.

(7) In the case of public communications networks, specific legal, regulatory and technical provisions should be made in order to protect fundamental rights and freedoms of natural persons and legitimate interests of legal persons, in particular with regard to the increasing capacity for automated storage and processing of data relating to subscribers and users.

(8) Legal, regulatory and technical provisions adopted by the Member States concerning the protection of personal data, privacy and the legitimate interest of legal persons, in the electronic communication sector, should be harmonised in order to avoid obstacles to the internal market for electronic communication in accordance with Article 14 of the Treaty. Harmonisation should be limited to requirements necessary to guarantee that the promotion and development of new electronic communications services and networks between Member States are not hindered.

(9) The Member States, providers and users concerned, together with the competent Community bodies, should cooperate in introducing and developing the relevant technologies where this is necessary to apply the guarantees provided for by this Directive and taking particular account of the objectives of minimising the processing of personal data and of using anonymous or pseudonymous data where possible.

(10) In the electronic communications sector, Directive 95/46/EC applies in particular to all matters concerning protection of fundamental rights and freedoms, which are not specifically covered by the provisions of this Directive, including the obligations on the controller and the rights of individuals. Directive 95/46/EC applies to non-public communications services.

(11) Like Directive 95/46/EC, this Directive does not address issues of protection of fundamental rights and freedoms related to activities which are not governed by Community law. Therefore it does not alter the existing balance between the individual's right to privacy and the possibility for Member States to take the measures referred to in Article 15(1) of this Directive, necessary for the protection of public security, defence, State security (including the economic well-being of the State when the activities relate to State security matters) and the enforcement of criminal law. Consequently, this Directive does not affect the ability of Member States to carry out lawful interception of electronic communications, or take other measures, if necessary for any of these purposes and in accordance with the European Convention for the Protection of Human Rights and Fundamental Freedoms, as interpreted by the rulings of the European Court of Human Rights. Such measures must be appropriate, strictly proportionate to the intended purpose and necessary within a democratic society and should be subject to adequate safeguards in

accordance with the European Convention for the Protection of Human Rights and Fundamental Freedoms.

(12) Subscribers to a publicly available electronic communications service may be natural or legal persons. By supplementing Directive 95/46/EC, this Directive is aimed at protecting the fundamental rights of natural persons and particularly their right to privacy, as well as the legitimate interests of legal persons. This Directive does not entail an obligation for Member States to extend the application of Directive 95/46/EC to the protection of the legitimate interests of legal persons, which is ensured within the framework of the applicable Community and national legislation.

(13) The contractual relation between a subscriber and a service provider may entail a periodic or a one-off payment for the service provided or to be provided. Prepaid cards are also considered as a contract.

(14) Location data may refer to the latitude, longitude and altitude of the user's terminal equipment, to the direction of travel, to the level of accuracy of the location information, to the identification of the network cell in which the terminal equipment is located at a certain point in time and to the time the location information was recorded.

(15) A communication may include any naming, numbering or addressing information provided by the sender of a communication or the user of a connection to carry out the communication. Traffic data may include any translation of this information by the network over which the communication is transmitted for the purpose of carrying out the transmission. Traffic data may, inter alia, consist of data referring to the routing, duration, time or volume of a communication, to the protocol used, to the location of the terminal equipment of the sender or recipient, to the network on which the communication originates or terminates, to the beginning, end or duration of a connection. They may also consist of the format in which the communication is conveyed by the network.

(16) Information that is part of a broadcasting service provided over a public communications network is intended for a potentially unlimited audience and does not constitute a communication in the sense of this Directive. However, in cases where the individual subscriber or user receiving such information can be identified, for example with video-on-demand services, the information conveyed is covered within the meaning of a communication for the purposes of this Directive.

(17) For the purposes of this Directive, consent of a user or subscriber, regardless of whether the latter is a natural or a legal person, should have the same meaning as the data subject's consent as defined and further specified in Directive 95/46/EC. Consent may be given by any appropriate method enabling a freely given specific and informed indication of the user's wishes, including by ticking a box when visiting an Internet website.

(18) Value added services may, for example, consist of advice on least expensive tariff packages, route guidance, traffic information, weather forecasts and tourist information.

(19) The application of certain requirements relating to presentation and restriction of calling and connected line identification and to automatic call forwarding to subscriber lines connected to analogue exchanges should not be made mandatory in specific cases where such application would prove to be technically impossible or would require a disproportionate economic effort. It is important for interested parties to be informed of such cases and the Member States should therefore notify them to the Commission.

(20) Service providers should take appropriate measures to safeguard the security of their services, if necessary in conjunction with the provider of the network, and inform subscribers of any special risks of a breach of the security of the network. Such risks may especially occur for electronic communications services over an open network such as the Internet or analogue mobile telephony. It is particularly important for subscribers and users of such services to be fully informed by their service provider of the existing security risks which lie outside the scope of possible remedies by the service provider. Service providers who offer publicly available electronic communications services over the Internet should inform users and subscribers of measures they can take to protect the security of their communications for instance by using specific types of software or encryption technologies. The requirement to inform subscribers of particular security risks does not discharge a service provider from the obligation to take, at its own costs, appropriate and immediate measures to remedy any new, unforeseen security risks and restore the normal security level of the service. The provision of information about security risks to the subscriber should be free of charge except for any nominal costs which the subscriber may incur while receiving or collecting the information, for instance by downloading an electronic mail message. Security is appraised in the light of Article 17 of Directive 95/46/EC.

(21) Measures should be taken to prevent unauthorised access to communications in order to protect the confidentiality of communications, including both the contents and any data related to such communications, by means of public communications networks and publicly available electronic communications services. National legislation in some Member States only prohibits intentional unauthorised access to communications.

(22) The prohibition of storage of communications and the related traffic data by persons other than the users or without their consent is not intended to prohibit any automatic, intermediate and transient storage of this information in so far as this takes place for the sole purpose of carrying out the transmission in the electronic communications network and provided that the information is not stored for any period longer than is necessary for the transmission and for traffic management purposes, and that during the period of storage the confidentiality remains guaranteed. Where this is necessary for making more efficient the onward transmission of any publicly accessible information to other recipients of the service upon their request, this Directive should not prevent such information from being further stored, provided that this information would in any case be accessible to the public without restriction and that any data referring to the individual subscribers or users requesting such information are erased.

(23) Confidentiality of communications should also be ensured in the course of lawful business practice. Where necessary and legally authorised, communications can be recorded for the purpose of providing evidence of a commercial transaction. Directive 95/46/EC applies to such processing. Parties to the communications should be informed prior to the recording about the recording, its purpose and the duration of its storage. The recorded communication should be erased as soon as possible and in any case at the latest by the end of the period during which the transaction can be lawfully challenged.

(24) Terminal equipment of users of electronic communications networks and any information stored on such equipment are part of the private sphere of the users requiring protection under the European Convention for the Protection of Human Rights and Fundamental Freedoms. So-called spyware, web bugs, hidden identifiers and other similar devices can enter the user's terminal without their knowledge in order to gain access to information, to store hidden information or to trace the activities of the user and may seriously intrude upon the privacy of these users. The use of such devices should be allowed only for legitimate purposes, with the knowledge of the users concerned.

(25) However, such devices, for instance so-called "cookies", can be a legitimate and useful tool, for example, in analysing the effectiveness of website design and advertising, and in verifying the identity of users engaged in on-line transactions. Where such devices, for instance cookies, are intended for a legitimate purpose, such as to facilitate the provision of information society services, their use should be allowed on condition that users are provided with clear and precise information in accordance with Directive 95/46/EC about the purposes of cookies or similar devices so as to ensure that users are made aware of information being placed on the terminal equipment they are using. Users should have the opportunity to refuse to have a cookie or similar device stored on their terminal equipment. This is particularly important where users other than the original user have access to the terminal equipment and thereby to any data containing privacy-sensitive information stored on such equipment. Information and the right to refuse may be offered once for the use of various devices to be installed on the user's terminal equipment during the same connection and also covering any further use that may be made of those devices during subsequent connections. The methods for giving information, offering a right to refuse or requesting consent should be made as user-friendly as possible. Access to specific website content may still be made conditional on the well-informed acceptance of a cookie or similar device, if it is used for a legitimate purpose.

(26) The data relating to subscribers processed within electronic communications networks to establish connections and to transmit information contain information on the private life of natural persons and concern the right to respect for their correspondence or concern the legitimate interests of legal persons. Such data may only be stored to the extent that is necessary for the provision of the service for the purpose of billing and for interconnection payments, and for a limited time. Any further processing of such data which the provider of the publicly available electronic communications services may want to perform, for the marketing of electronic communications services or for the provision of value added services, may only be allowed if the subscriber has agreed to this on the basis of accurate and full information given by the provider of the publicly available electronic communications services about the types of further processing it intends to perform and about the subscriber's right not to give or to withdraw his/her consent to such processing. Traffic data used for marketing communications services or for the provision of value added services should also be erased or made anonymous after the provision of the service. Service providers should always keep subscribers informed of the types of data they are processing and the purposes and duration for which this is done.

(27) The exact moment of the completion of the transmission of a communication, after which traffic data should be erased except for billing purposes, may depend on the type of electronic communications service that is provided. For instance for a voice telephony call the transmission will be completed as soon as either of the users terminates the connection. For electronic mail the transmission is completed as soon as the addressee collects the message, typically from the server of his service provider.

(28) The obligation to erase traffic data or to make such data anonymous when it is no longer needed for the purpose of the transmission of a communication does not conflict with such procedures on the Internet as the caching in the domain name system of IP addresses or the caching of IP addresses to physical address bindings or the use of log-in information to control the right of access to networks or services.

(29) The service provider may process traffic data relating to subscribers and users where necessary in individual cases in order to detect technical failure or errors in the transmission of communications. Traffic data necessary for billing purposes may also be processed by the provider in order to detect and stop fraud consisting of unpaid use of the electronic communications service.

(30) Systems for the provision of electronic communications networks and services should be designed to limit the amount of personal data necessary to a strict minimum. Any activities related to the provision of the electronic communications service that go beyond the transmission of a communication and the billing thereof should be based on aggregated, traffic data that cannot be related to subscribers or users. Where such activities cannot be based on aggregated data, they should be considered as value added services for which the consent of the subscriber is required.

(31) Whether the consent to be obtained for the processing of personal data with a view to providing a particular value added service should be that of the user or of the subscriber, will depend on the data to be processed and on the type of service to be provided and on whether it is technically, procedurally and contractually possible to distinguish the individual using an electronic communications service from the legal or natural person having subscribed to it.

(32) Where the provider of an electronic communications service or of a value added service subcontracts the processing of personal data necessary for the provision of these services to another entity, such subcontracting and subsequent data processing should be in full compliance with the requirements regarding controllers and processors of personal data as set out in Directive 95/46/EC. Where the provision of a value added service requires that traffic or location data are forwarded from an electronic communications service provider to a provider of value added services, the subscribers or users to whom the data are related should also be fully informed of this forwarding before giving their consent for the processing of the data.

(33) The introduction of itemised bills has improved the possibilities for the subscriber to check the accuracy of the fees charged by the service provider but, at the same time, it may jeopardise the privacy of the users of publicly available electronic communications services. Therefore, in order to preserve the privacy of the user, Member States should encourage the development of electronic communication service options such as alternative payment facilities which allow anonymous or strictly private access to publicly available electronic communications services, for example calling cards and facilities for payment by credit card. To the same end, Member States may ask the operators to offer their subscribers a different type of detailed bill in which a certain number of digits of the called number have been deleted.

(34) It is necessary, as regards calling line identification, to protect the right of the calling party to withhold the presentation of the identification of the line from which the call is being made and the right of the called party to reject calls from unidentified lines. There is justification for overriding the elimination of calling line identification presentation in specific cases. Certain subscribers, in particular help lines and similar organisations, have an interest in guaranteeing the anonymity of their callers. It is necessary, as regards connected line identification, to protect the right and the legitimate interest of the called party to withhold the presentation of the identification of the line to which the calling party is actually connected, in particular in the case of forwarded calls. The providers of publicly available electronic communications services should inform their subscribers of the existence of calling and connected line identification in the network and of all services which are offered on the basis of calling and connected line identification as well as the privacy options which are available. This will allow the subscribers to make an informed choice about the privacy facilities they may want to use. The privacy options which are offered on a per-line basis do not necessarily have to be available as an automatic network service but may be obtainable through a simple request to the provider of the publicly available electronic communications service.

(35) In digital mobile networks, location data giving the geographic position of the terminal equipment of the mobile user are processed to enable the transmission of

communications. Such data are traffic data covered by Article 6 of this Directive. However, in addition, digital mobile networks may have the capacity to process location data which are more precise than is necessary for the transmission of communications and which are used for the provision of value added services such as services providing individualised traffic information and guidance to drivers. The processing of such data for value added services should only be allowed where subscribers have given their consent. Even in cases where subscribers have given their consent, they should have a simple means to temporarily deny the processing of location data, free of charge.

(36) Member States may restrict the users' and subscribers' rights to privacy with regard to calling line identification where this is necessary to trace nuisance calls and with regard to calling line identification and location data where this is necessary to allow emergency services to carry out their tasks as effectively as possible. For these purposes, Member States may adopt specific provisions to entitle providers of electronic communications services to provide access to calling line identification and location data without the prior consent of the users or subscribers concerned.

(37) Safeguards should be provided for subscribers against the nuisance which may be caused by automatic call forwarding by others. Moreover, in such cases, it must be possible for subscribers to stop the forwarded calls being passed on to their terminals by simple request to the provider of the publicly available electronic communications service.

(38) Directories of subscribers to electronic communications services are widely distributed and public. The right to privacy of natural persons and the legitimate interest of legal persons require that subscribers are able to determine whether their personal data are published in a directory and if so, which. Providers of public directories should inform the subscribers to be included in such directories of the purposes of the directory and of any particular usage which may be made of electronic versions of public directories especially through search functions embedded in the software, such as reverse search functions enabling users of the directory to discover the name and address of the subscriber on the basis of a telephone number only.

(39) The obligation to inform subscribers of the purpose(s) of public directories in which their personal data are to be included should be imposed on the party collecting the data for such inclusion. Where the data may be transmitted to one or more third parties, the subscriber should be informed of this possibility and of the recipient or the categories of possible recipients. Any transmission should be subject to the condition that the data may not be used for other purposes than those for which they were collected. If the party collecting the data from the subscriber or any third party to whom the data have been transmitted wishes to use the data for an additional purpose, the renewed consent of the subscriber is to be obtained either by the initial party collecting the data or by the third party to whom the data have been transmitted.

(40) Safeguards should be provided for subscribers against intrusion of their privacy by unsolicited communications for direct marketing purposes in particular by means of automated calling machines, telefaxes, and e-mails, including SMS messages. These forms of unsolicited commercial communications may on the one hand be relatively easy and cheap to send and on the other may impose a burden and/or cost on the recipient. Moreover, in some cases their volume may also cause difficulties for electronic communications networks and terminal equipment. For such forms of unsolicited communications for direct marketing, it is justified to require that prior explicit consent of the recipients is obtained before such communications are addressed to them. The single market requires a harmonised approach to ensure simple, Community-wide rules for businesses and users.

(41) Within the context of an existing customer relationship, it is reasonable to allow the use of electronic contact details for the offering of similar products or services, but only by the same company that has obtained the electronic contact details in accordance with Directive 95/46/EC. When electronic contact details are obtained, the customer should be informed about their further use for direct marketing in a clear and distinct manner, and be given the opportunity to refuse such usage. This opportunity should continue to be offered with each subsequent direct marketing message, free of charge, except for any costs for the transmission of this refusal.

(42) Other forms of direct marketing that are more costly for the sender and impose no financial costs on subscribers and users, such as person-to-person voice telephony calls, may justify the maintenance of a system giving subscribers or users the possibility to indicate that they do not want to receive such calls. Nevertheless, in order not to decrease existing levels of privacy protection, Member States should be entitled to uphold national systems, only allowing such calls to subscribers and users who have given their prior consent.

(43) To facilitate effective enforcement of Community rules on unsolicited messages for direct marketing, it is necessary to prohibit the use of false identities or false return addresses or numbers while sending unsolicited messages for direct marketing purposes.

(44) Certain electronic mail systems allow subscribers to view the sender and subject line of an electronic mail, and also to delete the message, without having to download the rest of the electronic mail's content or any attachments, thereby reducing costs which could arise from downloading unsolicited electronic mails or attachments. These arrangements may continue to be useful in certain cases as an additional tool to the general obligations established in this Directive.

(45) This Directive is without prejudice to the arrangements which Member States make to protect the legitimate interests of legal persons with regard to unsolicited communications for direct marketing purposes. Where Member States establish an opt-out register for such communications to legal persons, mostly business users, the provisions of Article 7 of Directive 2000/31/EC of the European Parliament and of the Council of 8 June 2000 on certain legal aspects of information society services, in particular electronic commerce, in the internal market (Directive on electronic commerce)[6] are fully applicable.

(46) The functionalities for the provision of electronic communications services may be integrated in the network or in any part of the terminal equipment of the user, including the software. The protection of the personal data and the privacy of the user of publicly available electronic communications services should be independent of the configuration of the various components necessary to provide the service and of the distribution of the necessary functionalities between these components. Directive 95/46/EC covers any form of processing of personal data regardless of the technology used. The existence of specific rules for electronic communications services alongside general rules for other components necessary for the provision of such services may not facilitate the protection of personal data and privacy in a technologically neutral way. It may therefore be necessary to adopt measures requiring manufacturers of certain types of equipment used for electronic communications services to construct their product in such a way as to incorporate safeguards to ensure that the personal data and privacy of the user and subscriber are protected. The adoption of such measures in accordance with Directive 1999/5/EC of the European Parliament and of the Council of 9 March 1999 on radio equipment and telecommunications terminal

---

[6] OJ L 178, 17.7.2000, p. 1.

equipment and the mutual recognition of their conformity[7] will ensure that the introduction of technical features of electronic communication equipment including software for data protection purposes is harmonised in order to be compatible with the implementation of the internal market.

(47) Where the rights of the users and subscribers are not respected, national legislation should provide for judicial remedies. Penalties should be imposed on any person, whether governed by private or public law, who fails to comply with the national measures taken under this Directive.

(48) It is useful, in the field of application of this Directive, to draw on the experience of the Working Party on the Protection of Individuals with regard to the Processing of Personal Data composed of representatives of the supervisory authorities of the Member States, set up by Article 29 of Directive 95/46/EC.

(49) To facilitate compliance with the provisions of this Directive, certain specific arrangements are needed for processing of data already under way on the date that national implementing legislation pursuant to this Directive enters into force,

HAVE ADOPTED THIS DIRECTIVE:

Article 1

Scope and aim

1. This Directive harmonises the provisions of the Member States required to ensure an equivalent level of protection of fundamental rights and freedoms, and in particular the right to privacy, with respect to the processing of personal data in the electronic communication sector and to ensure the free movement of such data and of electronic communication equipment and services in the Community.

2. The provisions of this Directive particularise and complement Directive 95/46/EC for the purposes mentioned in paragraph 1. Moreover, they provide for protection of the legitimate interests of subscribers who are legal persons.

3. This Directive shall not apply to activities which fall outside the scope of the Treaty establishing the European Community, such as those covered by Titles V and VI of the Treaty on European Union, and in any case to activities concerning public security, defence, State security (including the economic well-being of the State when the activities relate to State security matters) and the activities of the State in areas of criminal law.

Article 2

Definitions

Save as otherwise provided, the definitions in Directive 95/46/EC and in Directive 2002/21/EC of the European Parliament and of the Council of 7 March 2002 on a common regulatory framework for electronic communications networks and services (Framework Directive)[8] shall apply.

The following definitions shall also apply:

---

[7] OJ L 91, 7.4.1999, p. 10.
[8] OJ L 108, 24.4.2002, p. 33.

(a) "user" means any natural person using a publicly available electronic communications service, for private or business purposes, without necessarily having subscribed to this service;

(b) "traffic data" means any data processed for the purpose of the conveyance of a communication on an electronic communications network or for the billing thereof;

(c) "location data" means any data processed in an electronic communications network, indicating the geographic position of the terminal equipment of a user of a publicly available electronic communications service;

(d) "communication" means any information exchanged or conveyed between a finite number of parties by means of a publicly available electronic communications service. This does not include any information conveyed as part of a broadcasting service to the public over an electronic communications network except to the extent that the information can be related to the identifiable subscriber or user receiving the information;

(e) "call" means a connection established by means of a publicly available telephone service allowing two-way communication in real time;

(f) "consent" by a user or subscriber corresponds to the data subject's consent in Directive 95/46/EC;

(g) "value added service" means any service which requires the processing of traffic data or location data other than traffic data beyond what is necessary for the transmission of a communication or the billing thereof;

(h) "electronic mail" means any text, voice, sound or image message sent over a public communications network which can be stored in the network or in the recipient's terminal equipment until it is collected by the recipient.

Article 3

Services concerned

1. This Directive shall apply to the processing of personal data in connection with the provision of publicly available electronic communications services in public communications networks in the Community.

2. Articles 8, 10 and 11 shall apply to subscriber lines connected to digital exchanges and, where technically possible and if it does not require a disproportionate economic effort, to subscriber lines connected to analogue exchanges.

3. Cases where it would be technically impossible or require a disproportionate economic effort to fulfil the requirements of Articles 8, 10 and 11 shall be notified to the Commission by the Member States.

Article 4

Security

1. The provider of a publicly available electronic communications service must take appropriate technical and organisational measures to safeguard security of its services, if necessary in conjunction with the provider of the public communications network with respect to network security. Having regard to the state of the art and the cost of their implementation, these measures shall ensure a level of security appropriate to the risk presented.

2.   In case of a particular risk of a breach of the security of the network, the provider of a publicly available electronic communications service must inform the subscribers concerning such risk and, where the risk lies outside the scope of the measures to be taken by the service provider, of any possible remedies, including an indication of the likely costs involved.

Article 5

Confidentiality of the communications

1.   Member States shall ensure the confidentiality of communications and the related traffic data by means of a public communications network and publicly available electronic communications services, through national legislation. In particular, they shall prohibit listening, tapping, storage or other kinds of interception or surveillance of communications and the related traffic data by persons other than users, without the consent of the users concerned, except when legally authorised to do so in accordance with Article 15(1). This paragraph shall not prevent technical storage which is necessary for the conveyance of a communication without prejudice to the principle of confidentiality.

2.   Paragraph 1 shall not affect any legally authorised recording of communications and the related traffic data when carried out in the course of lawful business practice for the purpose of providing evidence of a commercial transaction or of any other business communication.

3.   Member States shall ensure that the use of electronic communications networks to store information or to gain access to information stored in the terminal equipment of a subscriber or user is only allowed on condition that the subscriber or user concerned is provided with clear and comprehensive information in accordance with Directive 95/46/EC, inter alia about the purposes of the processing, and is offered the right to refuse such processing by the data controller. This shall not prevent any technical storage or access for the sole purpose of carrying out or facilitating the transmission of a communication over an electronic communications network, or as strictly necessary in order to provide an information society service explicitly requested by the subscriber or user.

Article 6

Traffic data

1.   Traffic data relating to subscribers and users processed and stored by the provider of a public communications network or publicly available electronic communications service must be erased or made anonymous when it is no longer needed for the purpose of the transmission of a communication without prejudice to paragraphs 2, 3 and 5 of this Article and Article 15(1).

2.   Traffic data necessary for the purposes of subscriber billing and interconnection payments may be processed. Such processing is permissible only up to the end of the period during which the bill may lawfully be challenged or payment pursued.

3.   For the purpose of marketing electronic communications services or for the provision of value added services, the provider of a publicly available electronic communications service may process the data referred to in paragraph 1 to the extent and for the duration necessary for such services or marketing, if the subscriber or user to whom the data relate has given his/her consent. Users or subscribers shall be given the possibility to withdraw their consent for the processing of traffic data at any time.

4. The service provider must inform the subscriber or user of the types of traffic data which are processed and of the duration of such processing for the purposes mentioned in paragraph 2 and, prior to obtaining consent, for the purposes mentioned in paragraph 3.

5. Processing of traffic data, in accordance with paragraphs 1, 2, 3 and 4, must be restricted to persons acting under the authority of providers of the public communications networks and publicly available electronic communications services handling billing or traffic management, customer enquiries, fraud detection, marketing electronic communications services or providing a value added service, and must be restricted to what is necessary for the purposes of such activities.

6. Paragraphs 1, 2, 3 and 5 shall apply without prejudice to the possibility for competent bodies to be informed of traffic data in conformity with applicable legislation with a view to settling disputes, in particular interconnection or billing disputes.

Article 7

Itemised billing

1. Subscribers shall have the right to receive non-itemised bills.

2. Member States shall apply national provisions in order to reconcile the rights of subscribers receiving itemised bills with the right to privacy of calling users and called subscribers, for example by ensuring that sufficient alternative privacy enhancing methods of communications or payments are available to such users and subscribers.

Article 8

Presentation and restriction of calling and connected line identification

1. Where presentation of calling line identification is offered, the service provider must offer the calling user the possibility, using a simple means and free of charge, of preventing the presentation of the calling line identification on a per-call basis. The calling subscriber must have this possibility on a per-line basis.

2. Where presentation of calling line identification is offered, the service provider must offer the called subscriber the possibility, using a simple means and free of charge for reasonable use of this function, of preventing the presentation of the calling line identification of incoming calls.

3. Where presentation of calling line identification is offered and where the calling line identification is presented prior to the call being established, the service provider must offer the called subscriber the possibility, using a simple means, of rejecting incoming calls where the presentation of the calling line identification has been prevented by the calling user or subscriber.

4. Where presentation of connected line identification is offered, the service provider must offer the called subscriber the possibility, using a simple means and free of charge, of preventing the presentation of the connected line identification to the calling user.

5. Paragraph 1 shall also apply with regard to calls to third countries originating in the Community. Paragraphs 2, 3 and 4 shall also apply to incoming calls originating in third countries.

6. Member States shall ensure that where presentation of calling and/or connected line identification is offered, the providers of publicly available electronic communications services inform the public thereof and of the possibilities set out in paragraphs 1, 2, 3 and 4.

Article 9

Location data other than traffic data

1. Where location data other than traffic data, relating to users or subscribers of public communications networks or publicly available electronic communications services, can be processed, such data may only be processed when they are made anonymous, or with the consent of the users or subscribers to the extent and for the duration necessary for the provision of a value added service. The service provider must inform the users or subscribers, prior to obtaining their consent, of the type of location data other than traffic data which will be processed, of the purposes and duration of the processing and whether the data will be transmitted to a third party for the purpose of providing the value added service. Users or subscribers shall be given the possibility to withdraw their consent for the processing of location data other than traffic data at any time.

2. Where consent of the users or subscribers has been obtained for the processing of location data other than traffic data, the user or subscriber must continue to have the possibility, using a simple means and free of charge, of temporarily refusing the processing of such data for each connection to the network or for each transmission of a communication.

3. Processing of location data other than traffic data in accordance with paragraphs 1 and 2 must be restricted to persons acting under the authority of the provider of the public communications network or publicly available communications service or of the third party providing the value added service, and must be restricted to what is necessary for the purposes of providing the value added service.

Article 10

Exceptions

Member States shall ensure that there are transparent procedures governing the way in which a provider of a public communications network and/or a publicly available electronic communications service may override:

(a) the elimination of the presentation of calling line identification, on a temporary basis, upon application of a subscriber requesting the tracing of malicious or nuisance calls. In this case, in accordance with national law, the data containing the identification of the calling subscriber will be stored and be made available by the provider of a public communications network and/or publicly available electronic communications service;

(b) the elimination of the presentation of calling line identification and the temporary denial or absence of consent of a subscriber or user for the processing of location data, on a per-line basis for organisations dealing with emergency calls and recognised as such by a Member State, including law enforcement agencies, ambulance services and fire brigades, for the purpose of responding to such calls.

Article 11

Automatic call forwarding

Member States shall ensure that any subscriber has the possibility, using a simple means and free of charge, of stopping automatic call forwarding by a third party to the subscriber's terminal.

Article 12

Directories of subscribers

1. Member States shall ensure that subscribers are informed, free of charge and before they are included in the directory, about the purpose(s) of a printed or electronic directory of subscribers available to the public or obtainable through directory enquiry services, in which their personal data can be included and of any further usage possibilities based on search functions embedded in electronic versions of the directory.

2. Member States shall ensure that subscribers are given the opportunity to determine whether their personal data are included in a public directory, and if so, which, to the extent that such data are relevant for the purpose of the directory as determined by the provider of the directory, and to verify, correct or withdraw such data. Not being included in a public subscriber directory, verifying, correcting or withdrawing personal data from it shall be free of charge.

3. Member States may require that for any purpose of a public directory other than the search of contact details of persons on the basis of their name and, where necessary, a minimum of other identifiers, additional consent be asked of the subscribers.

4. Paragraphs 1 and 2 shall apply to subscribers who are natural persons. Member States shall also ensure, in the framework of Community law and applicable national legislation, that the legitimate interests of subscribers other than natural persons with regard to their entry in public directories are sufficiently protected.

Article 13

Unsolicited communications

1. The use of automated calling systems without human intervention (automatic calling machines), facsimile machines (fax) or electronic mail for the purposes of direct marketing may only be allowed in respect of subscribers who have given their prior consent.

2. Notwithstanding paragraph 1, where a natural or legal person obtains from its customers their electronic contact details for electronic mail, in the context of the sale of a product or a service, in accordance with Directive 95/46/EC, the same natural or legal person may use these electronic contact details for direct marketing of its own similar products or services provided that customers clearly and distinctly are given the opportunity to object, free of charge and in an easy manner, to such use of electronic contact details when they are collected and on the occasion of each message in case the customer has not initially refused such use.

3. Member States shall take appropriate measures to ensure that, free of charge, unsolicited communications for purposes of direct marketing, in cases other than those referred to in paragraphs 1 and 2, are not allowed either without the consent of the subscribers concerned or in respect of subscribers who do not wish to receive these

communications, the choice between these options to be determined by national legislation.

4.   In any event, the practice of sending electronic mail for purposes of direct marketing disguising or concealing the identity of the sender on whose behalf the communication is made, or without a valid address to which the recipient may send a request that such communications cease, shall be prohibited.

5.   Paragraphs 1 and 3 shall apply to subscribers who are natural persons. Member States shall also ensure, in the framework of Community law and applicable national legislation, that the legitimate interests of subscribers other than natural persons with regard to unsolicited communications are sufficiently protected.

Article 14

Technical features and standardisation

1.   In implementing the provisions of this Directive, Member States shall ensure, subject to paragraphs 2 and 3, that no mandatory requirements for specific technical features are imposed on terminal or other electronic communication equipment which could impede the placing of equipment on the market and the free circulation of such equipment in and between Member States.

2.   Where provisions of this Directive can be implemented only by requiring specific technical features in electronic communications networks, Member States shall inform the Commission in accordance with the procedure provided for by Directive 98/34/EC of the European Parliament and of the Council of 22 June 1998 laying down a procedure for the provision of information in the field of technical standards and regulations and of rules on information society services[9].

3.   Where required, measures may be adopted to ensure that terminal equipment is constructed in a way that is compatible with the right of users to protect and control the use of their personal data, in accordance with Directive 1999/5/EC and Council Decision 87/95/EEC of 22 December 1986 on standardisation in the field of information technology and communications[10].

Article 15

Application of certain provisions of Directive 95/46/EC

1.   Member States may adopt legislative measures to restrict the scope of the rights and obligations provided for in Article 5, Article 6, Article 8(1), (2), (3) and (4), and Article 9 of this Directive when such restriction constitutes a necessary, appropriate and proportionate measure within a democratic society to safeguard national security (i.e. State security), defence, public security, and the prevention, investigation, detection and prosecution of criminal offences or of unauthorised use of the electronic communication system, as referred to in Article 13(1) of Directive 95/46/EC. To this end, Member States may, inter alia, adopt legislative measures providing for the retention of data for a limited period justified on the grounds laid down in this paragraph. All the measures referred to in this paragraph shall be in accordance with the general principles of Community law, including those referred to in Article 6(1) and (2) of the Treaty on European Union.

---

[9]   OJ L 204, 21.7.1998, p. 37. Directive as amended by Directive 98/48/EC (OJ L 217, 5.8.1998, p. 18).
[10] OJ L 36, 7.2.1987, p. 31. Decision as last amended by the 1994 Act of Accession.

1a.   Paragraph 1 shall not apply to data specifically required by Directive 2006/24/EC of the European Parliament and of the Council of 15 March 2006 on the retention of data generated or processed in connection with the provision of publicly available electronic communications services or of public communications networks [OJ L 105, 13.4.2006, p. 54] to be retained for the purposes referred to in Article 1(1) of that Directive.

2.   The provisions of Chapter III on judicial remedies, liability and sanctions of Directive 95/46/EC shall apply with regard to national provisions adopted pursuant to this Directive and with regard to the individual rights derived from this Directive.

3.   The Working Party on the Protection of Individuals with regard to the Processing of Personal Data instituted by Article 29 of Directive 95/46/EC shall also carry out the tasks laid down in Article 30 of that Directive with regard to matters covered by this Directive, namely the protection of fundamental rights and freedoms and of legitimate interests in the electronic communications sector.

Article 16

Transitional arrangements

1.   Article 12 shall not apply to editions of directories already produced or placed on the market in printed or off-line electronic form before the national provisions adopted pursuant to this Directive enter into force.

2.   Where the personal data of subscribers to fixed or mobile public voice telephony services have been included in a public subscriber directory in conformity with the provisions of Directive 95/46/EC and of Article 11 of Directive 97/66/EC before the national provisions adopted in pursuance of this Directive enter into force, the personal data of such subscribers may remain included in this public directory in its printed or electronic versions, including versions with reverse search functions, unless subscribers indicate otherwise, after having received complete information about purposes and options in accordance with Article 12 of this Directive.

Article 17

Transposition

1.   Before 31 October 2003 Member States shall bring into force the provisions necessary to comply with this Directive. They shall forthwith inform the Commission thereof.

        When Member States adopt those provisions, they shall contain a reference to this Directive or be accompanied by such a reference on the occasion of their official publication. The methods of making such reference shall be laid down by the Member States.

2.   Member States shall communicate to the Commission the text of the provisions of national law which they adopt in the field governed by this Directive and of any subsequent amendments to those provisions.

Article 18

Review

The Commission shall submit to the European Parliament and the Council, not later than three years after the date referred to in Article 17(1), a report on the application of this Directive and its impact on economic operators and consumers, in particular as regards the provisions on unsolicited communications, taking into account the international environment. For this purpose, the Commission may request information from the Member States, which shall be supplied without undue delay. Where appropriate, the Commission shall submit proposals to amend this Directive, taking account of the results of that report, any changes in the sector and any other proposal it may deem necessary in order to improve the effectiveness of this Directive.

Article 19

Repeal

Directive 97/66/EC is hereby repealed with effect from the date referred to in Article 17(1).

References made to the repealed Directive shall be construed as being made to this Directive.

Article 20

Entry into force

This Directive shall enter into force on the day of its publication in the Official Journal of the European Communities.

Article 21

Addressees

This Directive is addressed to the Member States.

———————

Editors' Notes:

[a] OJ L 201, 31.07.2002, p. 37, as amended by directive 2006/24/EC. Some citations in the original text have been updated to the current and complete Official Journal citation.

OPINION 5/2004 OF THE WORKING PARTY ON THE PROTECTION OF INDIVIDUALS WITH REGARD TO THE PROCESSING OF PERSONAL DATA

of 17 February 2004

on unsolicited communications for marketing purposes
under Article 13 of Directive 2002/58/EC

THE WORKING PARTY ON THE PROTECTION OF INDIVIDUALS WITH REGARD TO THE PROCESSING OF PERSONAL DATA

set up by Directive 95146/EC of the European Parliament and of the Council of 24 October 1995[1],

having regard to Articles 29 and 30 paragraphs 1 (a) and 3 of that Directive,

having regard to its Rules of Procedure and in particular to articles 12 and 14 thereof,

HAS ADOPTED THE PRESENT OPINION:

1. INTRODUCTION

Directive 2002/58/EC on Privacy and Electronic Communications notably harmonised the conditions under which electronic communications (e.g. e-mail, SMS, fax, telephone) can be used for marketing purposes[1]. While the present document focuses on these conditions, the Working Party notes that other provisions in the Directive may require attention in the future.

Building on the existing opt-in rules in place in certain Member States, Article 13 of Directive 2002/58/EC has introduced a harmonised regime for electronic communications to natural persons for direct marketing purposes.

There is a general understanding that, despite this hannonisation, some concepts used in Article 13 of Directive 2002/58/EC on unsolicited communications appear to be subject to differences of interpretation.

In accordance with Article 15 (3) of Directive 2002/58/EC in conjunction with Article 30 of Directive 95/46/EC, the Working Party has examined these concepts more closely and adopted the present opinion in order to contribute to a uniform application of national measures under Directive 2002/58/EC. Note that communications for direct marketing purposes have been addressed in previous documents of the Working Party[2].

2. OVERVIEW OF ISSUES RAISED IN THE PRESENT OPINION

The opt-in rule requires that consent be given by subscribers prior to the use of automated calling machines, faxes or electronic mails, including SMS, for the purpose of direct marketing.

---

[1] The Directive has to be transposed by the 31st of October 2003.
[2] See for instance Opinion 7/2000 On the European Commission Proposal for a Directive of the European Parliament and of the Council concerning the processing of personal data and the protection of privacy in the electronic communications sector of 12 July 2000; Recommendation 2/2001 on certain minimum requirements for collecting personal data on-line in the European Union.

There is an exception for communications sent to existing customers, subject to certain conditions (see below). For (fixed and mobile) voice telephony marketing calls, other than via automated calling machines, Member States may choose between an opt-in and an opt-out system[3].

In addition, the sender on whose behalf the communication is made may not disguise or conceal its identity. There must also be a valid address to which the recipient may send a request that such communications cease.[4]

The Working Party had decided to provide an opinion on the following elements of this new regime:

— the concept of electronic mail;

— the concept of prior consent of subscribers;

— the concept of direct marketing;

— the exception to the opt-in rule;

— the regime for communications to legal persons.

3.   **ISSUES RAISED**

3.1. The concept of electronic mail

While the concepts of facsimile machines (fax) or automated calling systems without human intervention (automated calling machines) were present in Directive 97/66/EC, the predecessor of Directive 2002/58/EC, the concept of "electronic mail" is new and deserves specific attention.

The definition of electronic mail is as follows (see Article 2 (h) of Directive 2002/58/EC): "*any text, voice, sound or image message sent over a public communications network which can be stored in the network or in the recipient's terminal equipment until it is collected by the recipient.*"

In short, any message by electronic communications where the simultaneous participation of the sender and the recipient is not required is covered by this concept of electronic mail.

This definition is broad and intended to be technology neutral. The objective was to adapt the predecessor of Directive 2002/58/EC[5] to "*developments in the markets and the technologies for electronic communications services in order to provide an equal level of protection of personal data and privacy for users of publicly available electronic communications services, regardless of the technologies used.*" (Recital 4 of Directive 2002/58/EC)

As an illustration, services currently covered by the definition of electronic mail include: Simple Mail Transport Protocol or 'SMTP'-based mail, i.e. the classic 'e-mail'; Short Message Service or 'SMS'-based mail (Recital 40 of Directive 2002/58/EC indeed clarifies that electronic mail also includes SMS); Multimedia Messaging Service or 'MMS'-based mail; messages left on answering machines[6]; voice mail service systems including on

---

[3]   Paragraph 3 of Article 13: [Editors' Note: quotation omitted, see footnote 4 below]
[4]   Paragraph 4 of Directive 2002/58/EC reads as follows: [Editors' Note: quotation omitted, please see page 442 of this book for the text of Article 13 of Directive 2002/58/EC]
[5]   Directive 97/66EC, OJ L 24, 30 January 1998.
[6]   Note that some service providers offer the translation of SMS into voice messages. If the message results from a manually assisted call and is not further stored as an electronic message, Article 13(3) applies.

mobile services; 'net send' communications addressed directly to an IP-address. Newsletters sent by email also fall under the scope of this definition. Such a list cannot be considered as exhaustive and might have to be revised in view of market and technology developments.

3.2. Prior consent

The opt-in rule is based on prior consent as indicated in Paragraph 1 of Article 13 of Directive 2002/58/EC: *"1. The use of automated calling systems without human intervention (automatic calling machines), facsimile machines (fax) or electronic mail for the purposes of direct marketing may only be allowed in respect of subscribers who have given their prior consent."*

However, according to Article 2 (f) and Recital 17, *"consent of a user or subscriber, regardless of whether the latter is a natural or a legal person, should have the same meaning as the data subject's consent as defined and further specified in Directive 95/46/EC. (...)"*

Directive 95/46/BC defines the data subject's consent as *"any freely given spec j/Ic and informed indication of his wishes by which the data subject sign ffies his agreement to personal data related to him being processed."* (Article 2 (h) of Directive 95/46/EC).

Consent in this context is not specific to communications for direct marketing purposes. Reference can be made to Recommendation 2/2001 of the Working Party on certain minimum requirements for collecting personal data on-line in the European Union[7].

There may be various ways by which consent may be provided in accordance with Community law. The actual method to collect that consent has not been specifically provided for in Directive 2002/58/EC.

Recital 17 re-affirms this: *"(...) Consent may be given by any appropriate method enabling a freely given spec jf Ic and informed indication of the user's wishes, including by ticking a box when visiting an Internet website."*

Without prejudice to other applicable requirements on e.g. information, methods whereby a subscriber gives prior consent by registering on a website and is later asked to confirm that he was the person who registered and to confirm his consent seem to be compatible with the Directive. Other methods may also be compatible with legal requirements.

In contrast, it would not be compatible with Article 13 of Directive 2002/58/EC simply to ask, by a general email sent to recipients, theft consent to receive marketing c-mails, because of the requirement that the purpose be legitimate, explicit and specific.

Moreover, consent given on the occasion of the general acceptance of the terms and conditions governing the possible main contract (e.g., a subscription contract, in which consent is also sought to send communications for direct marketing purposes) must respect the requirements in Directive 95/46/EC, that is, be informed, specific and freely given. Provided that these latter conditions are met, consent might be given by the data subject for instance, through the ticking of a box.

Implied consent to receive such mails is not compatible with the definition of consent of Directive 95/46/EC and in particular with the requirement of consent being the indication of someone's wishes, including where this would be done 'unless opposition is made' (opt-

---

[7] Document WP 43, adopted on 17 May 2001. Reference could also be made to the first report on the implementation of the Data Protection Directive (95/46/EC (COM(2003) 265 final, p. 18).

out). Similarly, pre-ticked boxes, e.g., on websites are not compatible with the definition of the Directive either.

The purpose(s) should also be clearly indicated. This implies that the goods and services, or the categories of goods and services, for which marketing emails may be sent should be clearly indicated to the subscriber. Consent to pass on the personal data to third parties should also be asked where applicable. The information provided to the data subject should then indicate the purpose(s), the goods and services (or categories of goods and services) for which those third parties would send c-mails.

The Working Party would invite industry (e.g. via industry associations such as the Federation of European Direct Marketing (FEDMA)) to incorporate into their codes of conduct, and promote, specific methods to collect consent in accordance with Community law. The Working Party would ask industry to pay attention in particular to 'systems likely to offer better guarantees that consent has truly and effectively been given by the subscriber.

Moreover, such codes should include an obligation to effectively deal with complaints addressed to them by recipients of emails. In accordance with Article 30 of Directive 95/46/EC, the Working Party also recalls that it can give an opinion on codes of conduct drawn up at European level.

Practical elements such as specific indications in headers could also be envisaged in those codes of conduct, so that code-compliant e-mails can be identified easily by users (and possible filters)[8].

Lists of email addresses

Lists which have not been established according to the prior consent requirement may in principle not be used anymore under the opt-in regime, at least until they have been adapted to the new requirements. Selling such incompatible lists to third parties is not legal either. Companies wishing to buy lists of e-mail addresses should be cautious that those lists are in accordance with applicable requirements, and in particular that prior consent was given in accordance with those requirements.

Other conditions

While there may be no specific method provided to give consent to opt-in - to receiving e-mails, conditions laid down in Community law have to be respected. The Working Party wishes to recall that the conditions in the general 95/46/EC Directive for processing personal data must be respected. These notably include, in accordance with Article 10 of Directive 95/46/EC, the requirement to inform, at the moment of collection, at least about:

— the identity of the controller or his/her representative if any,
— the purposes of the collection of data.

There is also a requirement to provide information to individuals on the recipients or categories of recipients of the data, whether replies to questions are obligatory or voluntary, as well as the possible consequences of failure to reply, and about the existence of the right of access to and the right to rectify the data in so far as such information is necessary, having regard to the specific circumstances in which the data are collected, to guarantee fair processing in respect of the data subject (see Article 10 of Directive 95/46/EC).

---

[8]   Reference can be made in this regard to the requirement in the c-Commerce Directive that 'commercial communications' be clearly identifiable as such (see Article 6 (a) of Directive 2000/31/EC)

Note also that Article 13 also provides for the obligation to offer an opt-out possibility on each and every message sent. Such an opt-out should at least be possible using the same communications service (e.g., by sending an SMS to opt-out of an SMS-based marketing list).

Moreover, the Working Party also recalls that e-mail harvesting, i.e., the automatic collection of personal data on public Internet places, e.g. the web, chatrooms, etc, is unlawful under the general 95/46/EC Directive. Notably, it constitutes unfair processing of personal data and does respect neither the purpose limitation principle (finality) nor the obligation of information mentioned above. This is also the case when automatic collection is performed by software. These issues have been discussed in the Working document entitled "Privacy on the Internet" - An integrated EU Approach to On-line Data Protection"[9].

This is without prejudice to additional requirement stemming from any other legislation related to the marketing or selling of (specific) products or services (e.g. financial products and services, health products and services, distant selling).

3.3. The concept of direct marketing

There is no definition of direct marketing in either the specific or general data protection Directives. There is however a description of marketing purposes in Recital 30 of Directive 95/46/EC, which states that: *"(...) whereas Member States may similarly specify the conditions under which personal data may be disclosed to a third party for the purposes of marketing whether carried out commercially or by a charitable organisation or by any other association or foundation, of a political nature for example, subject to the provisions allowing a data subject to object to the processing of data regarding him, at no cost and without having to state his reasons".*

The Working Party's opinion is that Article 13 of Directive 2002/58/EC consequently covers any form of sales promotion, including direct marketing by charities and political organisations (e.g. fund raising, etc.).

Note that a broad definition has been used in the Federation of European Direct Marketing (FEDMA) code of practice for the use of personal data in direct marketing, which has been approved by the Working Party on 13 June 2003[10].

3.4. Communication to legal persons

Paragraph 5 of Article 13 of Directive 2002/58/EC reads as follows:

"5. Paragraphs 1 and 3 shall apply to subscribers who are natural persons. Member States shall also ensure, in the framework of Community law and applicable national legislation, that the legitimate interests of subscribers other than natural persons with regard to unsolicited communications are sufficiently protected."

---

[9]   Document No WP 37, adopted on 21 November 2000, in particular on p 77
[10] See Working Party Opinion 3/2003 on the European Code of conduct of FEDMA for the use of personal data in direct marketing, available at:
      http://europa.eu.int/comm/internal_market/privacy/docs/wpdocs/2003/wp77_en.pdf. The FEDMA Code is available at the following URL address:
      http://europa.eu.int/comm/internal_market/privacy/docs/wpdocs/2003/wp77-annex_en.pdf. This Code defines direct marketing as 'The communication by whatever means (including but not limited to mail, fax, telephone, on-line services etc.) of any advertising or marketing material, which is carried out by the Direct Marketer itself or on its behalf and which is directed to particular individuals.'

In other words, while Member States must also ensure that the legitimate interests of legal persons are sufficiently protected, they remain free to determine the appropriate safeguards to do so.

In 2002, a number of Member States - five out of eight - with an opt-in regime for e-mails had chosen to apply the same regime to legal persons as well[11]. While the distinction between natural and legal persons seems relatively straightforward, it may not always be easy to make in practice.

An easy situation would be where electronic contact details have been disclosed by a potential addressee e.g. on a website or otherwise. It may then be fairly easy to ask for the nature of the person e.g. by a simple question, or for the capacity in which the person left those details.

Still, this is an important element since it is for the sender to make sure that the rules are respected. In particular in those Member States that would distinguish between communications to legal and to natural persons, the Working Party is of the opinion that practical rules should be developed.

While it may become necessary to devote further attention to this specific issue on the basis of Member States' implementation of Article 13, the Working Party wishes to raise the following issues at this point in time:

-   Such practical rules should take account of cross-border effects. One question raised in this regard is what rule to apply to c-mails originating in a Member State not affording safeguards for legal persons received in a Member State offering the same level of protection for legal and natural persons.

-   One question remains how the sender can determine whether a recipient is a natural or a legal person. In other words, what efforts will a sender be required to make to verify whether the number /address really belongs to a legal person? Great caution would be needed as long as the sender would not be sure that the e-mail address belongs to a legal person ('secretariat@company.com). Often, natural persons use e-mail addresses with pseudonyms or generic terms without being deprived of the protection provided by the Directive.

-   Another issue is related to persons who are not directly subscribers to electronic communications services. This can be the case for the members of a single family or for employees working for a given company. In cases where a family member or a company would provide other family members or their employees with e-mail addresses containing their name (*e.g.*, name.surname@company.com), those persons would in principle not be 'subscribers'[12]. Some EU Member States have decided to apply the opt-in regime to such email addresses.

Member States are invited to pay attention to the fact that personal data are included in such addresses and must be protected as such.

---

[11] 8th Implementation Report of the European Commission, December 2002.

[12] The concept of subscriber is defined in the Directive 2002/21/EC on a common regulatory framework for electronic communications networks and services (Framework Directive). This is the notion to be used except as otherwise provided, in accordance with Article 2 of Directive 2002/58/EC.
     The concept of subscriber is defined in the Framework Directive as "any natural person or legal entity who or which is party to a contract with the provider of publicly available electronic communications services for the supply of such services" (see Article 2 (k) of Directive 2002/2 1/EC).
     Recital 12 of Directive 2002/58/EC clarifies this concept, by stating that: [Editors' Note: quotation omitted, please see page 430 of this book for the text of Recital 12 of Directive 2002/58/EC]

In the Working Party's opinion, such protection implies that sending marketing electronic mail, related or unrelated to business purposes, to a'personal' e-mail address should be considered as marketing to natural persons. In any case, the provisions of Directive 95/46/BC have to be taken into account.

3.5 The exception for similar products and services

Paragraph 2 of Article 13 provides for a harmonised exception to the opt-in rule which applies for existing customers, subject to certain conditions.

"2. Notwithstanding paragraph 1, where a natural or legal person obtains from its customers their electronic contact details for electronic mail, in the context of the sale of a product or a service, in accordance with Directive 95/46/EC, the same natural or legal person may use these electronic contact details for direct marketing of its own similar products or services provided that customers clearly and distinctly are given the opportunity to object, free of charge and in an easy manner, to such use of electronic contact details when they are collected and on the occasion of each message in case the customer has not initially refused such use."

Recital 41 provides useful elements to help understand Article 13 (2):

(41) Within the context of an existing customer relationship, it is reasonable to allow the use of electronic contact details for the offering of similar products or services, but only by the same company that has obtained the electronic contact details in accordance with Directive 95/46/EC. When electronic contact details are obtained, the customer should be informed about their further use for direct marketing in a clear and distinct manner, and be given the opportunity to refuse such usage. This opportunity should continue to be offered with each subsequent direct marketing message, free of charge, except for any costs for the transmission of this refusal.

While the description leaves some room for interpretation, the Working Party would emphasise that this exception is limited in several ways and must be interpreted restrictively

Firstly, this exception is limited to customers in accordance with the first sentence of Article 13(2). In addition, emails may only be sent to customers from whom electronic contact details for electronic mail have been obtained, in the context of the sale of a product or a service, and in accordance with Directive 95/46/EC. This latter requirement for instance includes information about the purposes of the collection (see above). The purpose principle (compatible use, fair processing) should help in this regard. In that context, attention should also be paid to the period of time during which consent might reasonably be considered as valid, and hence emails can be sent.

Secondly, only the same natural or legal person that collected the data may send marketing e-mails. For instance, subsidiaries or mother companies are not the same company.

Thirdly, this is limited to the marketing of similar products and services. The opinion of the Working Party is that, while this concept of 'similar products and services' is not an easy concept to apply in practice and justify further attention, similarity could be judged in particular from the objective perspective (reasonable expectations) of the recipient, rather than from the perspective of the sender.

The Working Party recalls that there is an obligation, including under the exception, to continue to offer an opt-out in each marketing message.

DIRECTIVE 2006/24/EC OF THE EUROPEAN PARLIAMENT AND OF THE COUNCIL

of 15 March 2006[a]

on the retention of data generated or processed in connection with the provision of publicly available electronic communications services or of public communications networks and amending Directive 2002/58/EC

THE EUROPEAN PARLIAMENT AND THE COUNCIL OF THE EUROPEAN UNION,

Having regard to the Treaty establishing the European Community, and in particular Article 95 thereof,

Having regard to the proposal from the Commission,

Having regard to the Opinion of the European Economic and Social Committee[1],

Acting in accordance with the procedure laid down in Article 251 of the Treaty[2],

Whereas:

(1) Directive 95/46/EC of the European Parliament and of the Council of 24 October 1995 on the protection of individuals with regard to the processing of personal data and on the free movement of such data[3] requires Member States to protect the rights and freedoms of natural persons with regard to the processing of personal data, and in particular their right to privacy, in order to ensure the free flow of personal data in the Community.

(2) Directive 2002/58/EC of the European Parliament and of the Council of 12 July 2002 concerning the processing of personal data and the protection of privacy in the electronic communications sector (Directive on privacy and electronic communications)[4] translates the principles set out in Directive 95/46/EC into specific rules for the electronic communications sector.

(3) Articles 5, 6 and 9 of Directive 2002/58/EC lay down the rules applicable to the processing by network and service providers of traffic and location data generated by using electronic communications services. Such data must be erased or made anonymous when no longer needed for the purpose of the transmission of a communication, except for the data necessary for billing or interconnection payments. Subject to consent, certain data may also be processed for marketing purposes and the provision of value added services.

(4) Article 15(1) of Directive 2002/58/EC sets out the conditions under which Member States may restrict the scope of the rights and obligations provided for in Article 5, Article 6, Article 8(1), (2), (3) and (4), and Article 9 of that Directive. Any such restrictions must be necessary, appropriate and proportionate within a democratic society for specific public order purposes, i.e. to safeguard national security (i.e. State security), defence, public security or the prevention, investigation, detection and prosecution of criminal offences or of unauthorised use of the electronic communications systems.

---

[1] Opinion delivered on 19 January 2006 (not yet published in the official journal).
[2] Opinion of the European Parliament of 14 December 2005 (not yet published in the Official Journal) and Council Decision of 21 February 2006.
[3] OJ L 281, 23.11.1995, p. 31. Directive as amended by Regulation (EC) No 18822003 (OJ L 284, 31.10.2003, p. 1).
[4] OJ L 201, 31.7.2002, p. 37.

(5) Several Member States have adopted legislation providing for the retention of data by service providers for the prevention, investigation, detection, and prosecution of criminal offences. Those national provisions vary considerably.

(6) The legal and technical differences between national provisions concerning the retention of data for the purpose of prevention, investigation, detection and prosecution of criminal offences present obstacles to the internal market for electronic communications, since service providers are faced with different requirements regarding the types of traffic and location data to be retained and the conditions and periods of retention.

(7) The Conclusions of the Justice and Home Affairs Council of 19 December 2002 underline that, because of the significant growth in the possibilities afforded by electronic communications, data relating to the use of electronic communications are particularly important and therefore a valuable tool in the prevention, investigation, detection and prosecution of criminal offences, in particular organised crime.

(8) The Declaration on Combating Terrorism adopted by the European Council on 25 March 2004 instructed the Council to examine measures for establishing rules on the retention of communications traffic data by service providers.

(9) Under Article 8 of the European Convention for the Protection of Human Rights and Fundamental Freedoms (ECHR), everyone has the right to respect for his private life and his correspondence. Public authorities may interfere with the exercise of that right only in accordance with the law and where necessary in a democratic society, inter alia, in the interests of national security or public safety, for the prevention of disorder or crime, or for the protection of the rights and freedoms of others. Because retention of data has proved to be such a necessary and effective investigative tool for law enforcement in several Member States, and in particular concerning serious matters such as organised crime and terrorism, it is necessary to ensure that retained data are made available to law enforcement authorities for a certain period, subject to the conditions provided for in this Directive. The adoption of an instrument on data retention that complies with the requirements of Article 8 of the ECHR is therefore a necessary measure.

(10) On 13 July 2005, the Council reaffirmed in its declaration condemning the terrorist attacks on London the need to adopt common measures on the retention of telecommunications data as soon as possible.

(11) Given the importance of traffic and location data for the investigation, detection, and prosecution of criminal offences, as demonstrated by research and the practical experience of several Member States, there is a need to ensure at European level that data that are generated or processed, in the course of the supply of communications services, by providers of publicly available electronic communications services or of a public communications network arc retained for a certain period, subject to the conditions provided for in this Directive.

(12) Article 15(1) of Directive 2002/58/EC continues to apply to data, including data relating to unsuccessful call attempts, the retention of which is not specifically required under this Directive and which therefore fall outside the scope thereof, and to retention for purposes, including judicial purposes, other than those covered by this Directive.

(13) This Directive relates only to data generated or processed as a consequence of a communication or a communication service and does not relate to data that are the content of the information communicated. Data should be retained in such a way as to avoid their being retained more than once. Data generated or processed when supplying the communications services concerned refers to data which are accessible.

In particular, as regards the retention of data relating to Internet e-mail and Internet telephony, the obligation to retain data may apply only in respect of data from the providers' or the network providers' own services.

(14) Technologies relating to electronic communications are changing rapidly and the legitimate requirements of the competent authorities may evolve. In order to obtain advice and encourage the sharing of experience of best practice in these matters, the Commission intends to establish a group composed of Member States' law enforcement authorities, associations of the electronic communications industry, representatives of the European Parliament and data protection authorities, including the European Data Protection Supervisor.

(15) Directive 95/46/EC and Directive 2002/58JEC are fully applicable to the data retained in accordance with this Directive. Article 30(1)(c) of Directive 95/46/EC requires the consultation of the Working Party on the Protection of individuals with regard to the Processing of Personal Data established under Article 29 of that Directive.

(16) The obligations incumbent on service providers concerning measures to ensure data quality, which derive from Article 6 of Directive 95/46/EC, and their obligations concerning measures to ensure confidentiality and security of processing of data, which derive from Articles 16 and 17 of that Directive, apply in full to data being retained within the meaning of this Directive.

(17) It is essential that Member States adopt legislative measures to ensure that data retained under this Directive are provided to the competent national authorities only in accordance with national legislation in full respect of the fundamental rights of the persons concerned.

(18) In this context, Article 24 of Directive 95/46/EC imposes an obligation on Member States to lay down sanctions for infringements of the provisions adopted pursuant to that Directive. Article 15(2) of Directive 2002/58/EC imposes the same requirement in relation to national provisions adopted pursuant to Directive 2002/58/EC. Council Framework Decision 2005/222/JHA of 24 February 2005 on attacks against information systems[5] provides that the intentional illegal access to information systems, including to data retained therein, is to be made punishable as a criminal offence.

(19) The right of any person who has suffered damage as a result of an unlawful processing operation or of any act incompatible with national provisions adopted pursuant to Directive 95/46/EC to receive compensation, which derives from Article 2 3 of that Directive, applies also in relation to the unlawful processing of any personal data pursuant to this Directive.

(20) The 2001 Council of Europe Convention on Cybercrime and the 1981 Council of Europe Convention for the Protection of Individuals with Regard to Automatic Processing of Personal Data also cover data being retained within the meaning of this Directive.

(21) Since the objectives of this Directive, namely to harmonise the obligations on providers to retain certain data and to ensure that those data are available for the purpose of the investigation, detection and prosecution of serious crime, as defined by each Member State in its national law, cannot be sufficiently achieved by the Member States and can therefore, by reason of the scale and effects of this Directive, be better achieved at Community level, the Community may adopt measures, in accordance with the principle of subsidiary as set out in Article 5 of the Treaty. In accordance with

---

[5] OJ L 69, 16.3.2005, p. 67.

the principle of proportionality, as set out in that Article, this Directive does not go beyond what is necessary in order to achieve those objectives.

(22) This Directive respects the fundamental rights and observes the principles recognised, in particular, by the Charter of Fundamental Rights of the European Union. In particular, this Directive, together with Directive 2002/58/EC, seeks to ensure full compliance with citizens' fundamental rights to respect for private life and communications and to the protection of their personal data, as enshrined in Articles 7 and 8 of the Charter.

(23) Given that the obligations on providers of electronic communications services should be proportionate, this Directive requires that they retain only such data as are generated or processed in the process of supplying their communications services. To the extent that such data are not generated or processed by those providers, there is no obligation to retain them. This Directive is not intended to harmonise the technology for retaining data, the choice of which is a matter to be resolved at national level.

(24) In accordance with paragraph 34 of the Interinstitutional agreement on better law-making[6], Member States are encouraged to draw up, for themselves and in the interests of the Community, their own tables illustrating, as far as possible, the correlation between this Directive and the transposition measures, and to make them public.

(25) This Directive is without prejudice to the power of Member States to adopt legislative measures concerning the right of access to, and use of, data by national authorities, as designated by them. Issues of access to data retained pursuant to this Directive by national authorities for such activities as are referred to in the first indent of Article 3(2) of Directive 95/46/EC fall outside the scope of Community law. However, they may be subject to national law or action pursuant to Title VI of the Treaty on European Union. Such laws or action must fully respect fundamental rights as they result from the common constitutional traditions of the Member States and as guaranteed by the ECHR. Under Article 8 of the ECHR, as interpreted by the European Court of Human Rights, interference by public authorities with privacy rights must meet the requirements of necessity and proportionality and must therefore serve specified, explicit and legitimate purposes and be exercised in a manner that is adequate, relevant and not excessive in relation to the purpose of the interference,

HAVE ADOPTED THIS DIRECTIVE:

Article 1

Subject matter and scope

1. This Directive aims to harmonise Member States' provisions concerning the obligations of the providers of publicly available electronic communications services or of public communications networks with respect to the retention of certain data which are generated or processed by them, in order to ensure that the data are available for the purpose of the investigation, detection and prosecution of serious crime, as defined by each Member State in its national law.

2. This Directive shall apply to traffic and location data on both legal entities and natural persons and to the related data necessary to identify the subscriber or registered user. It shall not apply to the content of electronic communications, including information consulted using an electronic communications network.

---

[6] OJ C 321, 31.12.2003, p. 1.

Article 2

Definitions

1. For the purpose of this Directive, the definitions in Directive 95/46/EC, in Directive 2002/21/EC of the European Parliament and of the Council of 7 March 2002 on a common regulatory framework for electronic communications networks and services (Framework Directive)[7], and in Directive 2002/58/EC shall apply.

2. For the purpose of this Directive:

(a) 'data' means traffic data and location data and the related data necessary to identify the subscriber or user;

(b) 'user' means any legal entity or natural person using a publicly available electronic communications service, for private or business purposes, without necessarily having subscribed to that service;

(c) 'telephone service' means calls (including voice, voicemail and conference and data calls), supplementary services (including call forwarding and call transfer) and messaging and multi-media services (including short message services, enhanced media services and multi-media services);

(d) 'user ID' means a unique identifier allocated to persons when they subscribe to or register with an Internet access service or Internet communications service;

(e) 'cell ID' means the identity of the cell from which a mobile telephony call originated or in which it terminated;

(f) 'unsuccessful call attempt' means a communication where a telephone call has been successfully connected but not answered or there has been a network management intervention.

Article 3

Obligation to retain data

1. By way of derogation from Articles 5, 6 and 9 of Directive 2002/58/EC, Member States shall adopt measures to ensure that the data specified in Article 5 of this Directive are retained in accordance with the provisions thereof, to the extent that those data are generated or processed by providers of publicly available electronic communications services or of a public communications network within their jurisdiction in the process of supplying the communications services concerned.

2. The obligation to retain data provided for in paragraph 1 shall include the retention of the data specified in Article 5 relating to unsuccessful call attempts where those data are generated or processed, and stored (as regards telephony data) or logged (as regards Internet data), by providers of publicly available electronic communications services or of a public communications network within the jurisdiction of the Member State concerned in the process of supplying the communication services concerned. This Directive shall not require data relating to unconnected calls to be retained.

---

[7] OJ L 108, 24.4.2002, p. 33.

Article 4

Access to data

Member States shall adopt measures to ensure that data retained in accordance with this Directive are provided only to the competent national authorities in specific cases and in accordance with national law. The procedures to be followed and the conditions to be fulfilled in order to gain access to retained data in accordance with necessity and proportionality requirements shall be defined by each Member State in its national law, subject to the relevant provisions of European Union law or public international law, and in particular the ECHR as interpreted by the European Court of Human Rights.

Article 5

Categories of data to be retained

1. Member States shall ensure that the following categories of data are retained under this Directive:

(a) data necessary to trace and identify the source of a communication:

    (1) concerning fixed network telephony and mobile telephony:

        (i) the calling telephone number;

        (ii) the name and address of the subscriber or registered user:

    (2) concerning Internet access, Internet e-mail and Internet telephony:

        (i) the user ID(s) allocated;

        (ii) the user ID and telephone number allocated to any communication entering the public telephone network;

        (iii) the name and address of the subscriber or registered user to whom an Internet Protocol (IP) address, user ID or telephone number was allocated at the time of the communication;

(b) data necessary to identify the destination of a communication:

    (1) concerning fixed network telephony and mobile telephony:

        (i) the number(s) dialled (the telephone number(s) called), and, in cases involving supplementary services such as call forwarding or call transfer, the number or numbers to which the call is routed;

        (ii) the name(s) and address(es) of the subscriber(s) or registered user(s);

    (2) concerning Internet e-mail and Internet telephony:

        (i) the user ID or telephone number of the intended recipient(s) of an Internet telephony call;

        (ii) the name(s) and address(es) of the subscriber(s) or registered user(s) and user ID of the intended recipient of the communication;

(c) data necessary to identify the date, time and duration of a communication:

    (1) concerning fixed network telephony and mobile telephony, the date and time of the start and end of the communication;

    (2)   concerning Internet access, Internet e-mail and Internet telephony:

        (i)   the date and time of the log-in and log-off of the Internet access service, based on a certain time zone, together with the IP address, whether dynamic or static, allocated by the Internet access service provider to a communication, and the user ID of the subscriber or registered user;

        (ii) the date and time of the log-in and log-off of the Internet e-mail service or Internet telephony service, based on a certain time zone;

(d)   data necessary to identify the type of communication:

    (1)   concerning fixed network telephony and mobile telephony: the telephone service used;

    (2)   concerning Internet e-mail and Internet telephony: the Internet service used;

(e)   data necessary to identify users' communication equipment or what purports to be their equipment:

    (1)   concerning fixed network telephony, the calling and called telephone numbers;

    (2)   concerning mobile telephony:

        (i)   the calling and called telephone numbers;

        (ii)   the International Mobile Subscriber Identity (IMSI) of the calling party;

        (iii) the International Mobile Equipment Identity (IMEI) of the calling party;

        (iv) the IMSI of the called party;

        (v)   the IMEI of the called party;

        (vi) in the case of pre-paid anonymous services, the date and time of the initial activation of the service and the location label (Cell ID) from which the service was activated;

    (3)   concerning Internet access, Internet e-mail and Internet telephony:

        (i)   the calling telephone number for dial-up access;

        (ii)   the digital subscriber line (DSL) or other end point of the originator of the communication;

(f)   data necessary to identify the location of mobile communication equipment:

    (1)   the location label (Cell ID) at the start of the communication;

    (2)   data identifying the geographic location of cells by reference to their location labels (Cell ID) during the period for which communications data are retained.

2.   No data revealing the content of the communication may be retained pursuant to this Directive.

Article 6

Periods of retention

Member States shall ensure that the categories of data specified in Article 5 are retained for periods of not less than six months and not more than two years from the date of the communication.

Article 7

Data protection and data security

Without prejudice to the provisions adopted pursuant to Directive 95/46/EC and Directive 2002/58/EC, each Member State shall ensure that providers of publicly available electronic communications services or of a public communications network respect, as a minimum, the following data security principles with respect to data retained in accordance with this Directive:

(a) the retained data shall be of the same quality and subject to the same security and protection as those data on the network;

(b) the data shall be subject to appropriate technical and organisational measures to protect the data against accidental or unlawful destruction, accidental loss or alteration, or unauthorised or unlawful storage, processing, access or disclosure;

(c) the data shall be subject to appropriate technical and organisational measures to ensure that they can be accessed by specially authorised personnel only;

and

(d) the data, except those that have been accessed and preserved, shall be destroyed at the end of the period of retention.

Article 8

Storage requirements for retained data

Member States shall ensure that the data specified in Article 5 are retained in accordance with this Directive in such a way that the data retained and any other necessary information relating to such data can be transmitted upon request to the competent authorities without undue delay.

Article 9

Supervisory authority

1. Each Member State shall designate one or more public authorities to be responsible for monitoring the application within its territory of the provisions adopted by the Member States pursuant to Article 7 regarding the security of the stored data. Those authorities may be the same authorities as those referred to in Article 28 of Directive 95/46/EC.

2. The authorities referred to in paragraph 1 shall act with complete independence in carrying out the monitoring referred to in that paragraph.

Article 10

Statistics

1.   Member States shall ensure that the Commission is provided on a yearly basis with statistics on the retention of data generated or processed in connection with the provision of publicly available electronic communications services or a public communications network. Such statistics shall include:

-    the cases in which information was provided to the competent authorities in accordance with applicable national law, the time elapsed between the date on which the data were retained and the date on which the competent authority requested the transmission of the data,

-    the cases where requests for data could not be met.

2.   Such statistics shall not contain personal data.

Article 11

Amendment of Directive 2002/58/EC

The following paragraph shall be inserted in Article 15 of Directive 2002/58/EC:

'1 a. Paragraph 1 shall not apply to data specifically required by Directive 2006/24/EC of the European Parliament and of the Council of 15 March 2006 on the retention of data generated or processed in connection with the provision of publicly available electronic communications services or of public communications networks(*) to be retained for the purposes referred to in Article 1(1) of that Directive.

_____

(*)   OJ L 105, 13.4.2006, p. 54.'

Article 12

Future measures

1.   A Member State facing particular circumstances that warrant an extension for a limited period of the maximum retention period referred to in Article 6 may take the necessary measures. That Member State shall immediately notify the Commission and inform the other Member States of the measures taken under this Article and shall state the grounds for introducing them.

2.   The Commission shall, within a period of six months after the notification referred to in paragraph 1, approve or reject the national measures concerned, after having examined whether they are a means of arbitrary discrimination or a disguised restriction of trade between Member States and whether they constitute an obstacle to the functioning of the internal market. In the absence of a decision by the Commission within that period the national measures shall be deemed to have been approved.

3.   Where, pursuant to paragraph 2, the national measures of a Member State derogating from the provisions of this Directive are approved, the Commission may consider whether to propose an amendment to this Directive.

Article 13

Remedies, liability and penalties

1.   Each Member State shall take the necessary measures to ensure that the national measures implementing Chapter III of Directive 95/46/EC providing for judicial remedies, liability and sanctions are fully implemented with respect to the processing of data under this Directive.

2.   Each Member State shall, in particular, take the necessary measures to ensure that any intentional access to, or transfer of, data retained in accordance with this Directive that is not permitted under national law adopted pursuant to this Directive is punishable by penalties, including administrative or criminal penalties, that are effective, proportionate and dissuasive.

Article 14

Evaluation

1.   No later than 15 September 2010, the Commission shall submit to the European Parliament and the Council an evaluation of the application of this Directive and its impact on economic operators and consumers, taking into account further developments in electronic communications technology and the statistics provided to the Commission pursuant to Article 10 with a view to determining whether it is necessary to amend the provisions of this Directive, in particular with regard to the list of data in Article 5 and the periods of retention provided for in Article 6. The results of the evaluation shall be made public.

2.   To that end, the Commission shall examine all observations communicated to it by the Member States or by the Working Party established under Article 29 of Directive 95/46/EC.

Article 15

Transposition

1.   Member States shall bring into force the laws, regulations and administrative provisions necessary to comply with this Directive by no later than 15 September 2007. They shall forthwith inform the Commission thereof. When Member States adopt those measures, they shall contain a reference to this Directive or shall be accompanied by such reference on the occasion of their official publication. The methods of making such reference shall be laid down by Member States.

2.   Member States shall communicate to the Commission the text of the main provisions of national law which they adopt in the field covered by this Directive.

3.   Until 15 March 2009, each Member State may postpone application of this Directive to the retention of communications data relating to Internet Access, Internet telephony and Internet e-mail. Any Member State that intends to make use of this paragraph shall, upon adoption of this Directive, notify the Council and the Commission to that effect by way of a declaration. The declaration shall be published in the Official Journal of the European Union.

Article 16

Entry into force

This Directive shall enter into force on the twentieth day following that of its publication in the official Journal of the European Union.

Article 17

Addressees

This Directive is addressed to the Member States.

_____

Declaration by the Netherlands

pursuant to Article 15(3) of Directive 2006/24/EC

Regarding the Directive of the European Parliament and of the Council on the retention of data processed in connection with the provision of publicly available electronic communications services and amending Directive 2002/58/EC, the Netherlands will be making use of the option of postponing application of the Directive to the retention of communications data relating to Internet access, Internet telephony and Internet e-mail, for a period not exceeding 18 months following the date of entry into force of the Directive.

Declaration by Austria

pursuant to Article 15(3) of Directive 2006/24/EC

Austria declares that it will be postponing application of this Directive to the retention of communications data relating to Internet access, Internet telephony and Internet e-mail, for a period of 18 months following the date specified in Article 15(1).

Declaration by Estonia

pursuant to Article 15(3) of Directive 2006/24/EC

In accordance with Article 15(3) of the Directive of the European Parliament and of the Council on the retention of data generated or processed in connection with the provision of publicly available electronic communications services or of public communications networks and amending Directive 2002/58/EC, Estonia hereby states its intention to make use of use that paragraph and to postpone application of the Directive to retention of communications data relating to Internet access, Internet telephony and Internet e-mail until 36 months after the date of adoption of the Directive.

Declaration by the United Kingdom

pursuant to Article 15(3) of Directive 2006/24/EC

The United Kingdom declares in accordance with Article 15(3) of the Directive on the retention of data generated or processed in connection with the provision of publicly available electronic communications services or of public communications networks and amending Directive 2002/58/EC that it will postpone application of that Directive to the retention of communications data relating to Internet access, Internet telephony and Internet e-mail.

Declaration by the Republic of Cyprus

pursuant to Article 15(3) of Directive 2006/24/EC

The Republic of Cyprus declares that it is postponing application of the Directive in respect of the retention of communications data relating to Internet access, Internet telephony and Internet e-mail until the date fixed in Article 15(3).

Declaration by the Hellenic Republic

pursuant to Article 15(3) of Directive 2006/24/EC

Greece declares that, pursuant to Article 15(3), it will postpone application of this Directive in respect of the retention of communications data relating to Internet access, Internet telephony and Internet e-mail until 18 months after expiry of the period provided for in Article 15(1).

Declaration by the Grand Duchy of Luxembourg

pursuant to Article 15(3) of Directive 2006124/EC

Pursuant to Article 15(3) of the Directive of the European Parliament and of the Council on the retention of data generated or processed in connection with the provision of publicly available electronic communications services or of public communications networks and amending Directive 2002/58/EC, the Government of the Grand Duchy of Luxembourg declares that it intends to make use of Article 15(3) of the Directive in order to have the option of postponing application of the Directive to the retention of communications data relating to Internet access, Internet telephony and Internet e-mail.

Declaration by Slovenia

pursuant to Article 15(3) of Directive 2006/24/EC

Slovenia is joining the group of Member States which have made a declaration under Article 15(3) of the Directive of the European Parliament and the Council on the retention of data generated or processed in connection with the provision of publicly available electronic communications services or of public communications networks, for the 18 months postponement of the application of the Directive to the retention of communication data relating to Internet, Internet telephony and Internet e-mail.

Declaration by Sweden

pursuant to Article 15(3) of Directive 2006/24/EC

Pursuant to Article 15(3), Sweden wishes to have the option of postponing application of this Directive to the retention of communications data relating to Internet access, Internet telephony and Internet e-mail.

Declaration by the Republic of Lithuania

pursuant to Article 15(3) of Directive 2006/24/EC

Pursuant to Article 15(3) of the draft Directive of the European Parliament and of the Council on the retention of data generated or processed in connection with the provision of publicly available electronic communications services or public communications networks and amending Directive 2002158/EC (hereafter the 'Directive'), the Republic of Lithuania declares that once the Directive has been adopted it will postpone the application thereof to the retention of communications data relating to Internet access, Internet telephony and Internet e-mail for the period provided for in Article 15(3).

Declaration by the Republic of Latvia

pursuant to Article 15(3) of Directive 2006/24/EC

Latvia states in accordance with Article 15(3) of Directive 2006/24/EC of 15 March 2006 on the retention of data generated or processed in connection with the provision of publicly available electronic communications services or of public communications networks and amending Directive 2002/58/EC that it is postponing application of the Directive to the retention of communications data relating to Internet access, Internet telephony and Internet e-mail until 15 March 2009.

Declaration by the Czech Republic

pursuant to Article 15(3) of Directive 2006/24/EC

Pursuant to Article 15(3), the Czech Republic hereby declares that it is postponing application of this Directive to the retention of communications data relating to Internet access, Internet telephony and Internet e-mail until 36 months after the date of adoption thereof.

Declaration by Belgium

pursuant to Article 15(3) of Directive 2006/24/EC

Belgium declares that, taking up the option available under Article 15(3), it will postpone application of this Directive, for a period of 36 months after its adoption, to the retention of communications data relating to Internet access, Internet telephony and Internet e-mail.

Declaration by the Republic of Poland

pursuant to Article 15(3) of Directive 2006/24/EC

Poland hereby declares that it intends to make use of the option provided for under Article 15(3) of the Directive of the European Parliament and of the Council on the retention of data processed in connection with the provision of publicly available electronic communications services and amending Directive 2002/58/EC and postpone application of the Directive to the retention of communications data relating to Internet access, Internet telephony and Internet e-mail for a period of 18 months following the date specified in Article 15(1).

Declaration by Finland

pursuant to Article 15(3) of Directive 2006/24/EC

Finland declares in accordance with Article 15(3) of the Directive on the retention of data generated or processed in connection with the provision of publicly available electronic communications services or of public communications networks and amending Directive 2002/58/EC that it will postpone application of that Directive to the retention of communications data relating to Internet access, Internet telephony and Internet e-mail.

Declaration by Germany

pursuant to Article 15(3) of Directive 2006/24/EC

Germany reserves the right to postpone application of this Directive to the retention of communications data relating to Internet access, Internet telephony and Internet e-mail for a period of 18 months following the date specified in the first sentence of Article 15(1).

Editors' Notes:

[a] OJ L 105, 13.4.06, p.62.

LIST OF STANDARDS AND/OR SPECIFICATIONS FOR ELECTRONIC COMMUNICATIONS NETWORKS, SERVICES AND ASSOCIATED FACILITIES AND SERVICES

(interim issue)

(2002/C 331/04)[a]

EXPLANATORY NOTE CONCERNING THE INTERIM ISSUE OF THE LIST OF STANDARDS AND/OR SPECIFICATIONS FOR ELECTRONIC COMMUNICATIONS NETWORKS, SERVICES AND ASSOCIATED FACILITIES AND SERVICES

In accordance with Article 5(1)of Directive 90/387/EEC[1], as amended by Directive 97/51/EC and Article 17 of the Framework Directive 2002/21/EC[2], the Commission shall publish in the Official Journal of the European Communities a list of standards and/or specifications which serve as a basis for encouraging the harmonised provision of electronic communications networks, electronic communications services and associated facilities and services (first paragraph of Article 17), to ensure interoperability of services and to improve freedom of choice for users. (second paragraph of Article 17)[3].

This publication replaces the former ONP list of standards (the sixth issue)published on 7 November 1998[4] under the ONP Directive. The obligations under the current regulatory framework remain applicable until the new regulatory framework is applied from 25 July 2003, in accordance with Article 28 of the Framework Directive.

The new regulatory framework implies a number of changes. All electronic communications networks, services and associated services are now covered. The list of standards needed to be changed accordingly.

Major changes in this issue compared with the sixth issue of the ONP list of standards from 1998 are:

— a number of standards have been withdrawn from the ONP list of standards. Most standards associated with the PSDS Recommendation 92/382/EEC and ISDN Recommendation 92/383/EEC have been withdrawn,

— a number of additional standards have been added to the list, in particular in a new broadcasting chapter.

This is a selective list of standards in the areas concerned. In accordance with Art 17(2)of the Framework Directive, in the absence of standards and/or specifications in this list, Member States must encourage the implementation of standards and/or specifications adopted by European standards organisations and, in the absence of such standards and/or specifications, encourage the implementation of international standards or recommendations adopted by the International Telecommunication Union (ITU), the International Organisation for Standardisation (ISO)or the International Electrotechnical Commission (IEC)[5].

---

[1] Council Directive 90/387/EEC of 28 June 1990 on the establishment of the internal market for telecommunications services through the implementation of open network provision (OJ L 192, 24.7.1990), as amended by Directive 97/51/EC of the European Parliament and of the Council of 6 October 1997 (OJ L 295, 29.10.1997).
[2] OJ L 108, 24.4.2002,p.33.
[3] Equivalent wording is found in Article 5(1) of Directive 90/387/EEC, as amended by Directive 97/51/EC.
[4] OJ C 339, 7.11.1998,p.6.
[5] Equivalent wording is found in Article 5(2) of Directive 90/387/EEC, as amended by Directive 97/51/EC.

PREFACE

1. General

Pursuant to Article 5(1) of Directive 90/387/EEC, as amended by Directive 97/51/EC the Commission publishes a list of standards for harmonised technical interfaces and/or service features in the context of open network provision.

Pursuant to Article 17(1) of the Framework Directive the Commission shall draw up and publish in the *Official Journal of the European Communities* a list of standards and/or specifications for encouraging the harmonised provision of electronic communications networks, electronic communications services and associated facilities and services.

The obligations under the current regulatory framework remain applicable until the new regulatory framework is applied from 25 July 2003, in accordance with Article 28 of the Framework Directive.

The list of standards will be revised on a regular basis to take account of requirements resulting from new technologies and market changes. Interested parties are encouraged to comment on this interim issue.

The Communications Committee has been consulted in so far as the list relates to Article 17 of the Framework Directive[6].

2. Structure of the list of standards

— Chapter I: Reference list for leased lines beyond the minimum set defined in chapter I of the Annex.

— Chapter II: Access and interconnection. Number portability, carrier selection and carrier pre-selection.

— Chapter III: Unbundled access to the local loop.

— Chapter IV: Standards for implementing various user services.

— Chapter V: Standards for implementing data protection requirements.

— Chapter VI: Standards for electronic communications networks established for the distribution of digital broadcasting services including their associated facilities.

Annex

The annex includes, for information purposes only, a list of standards and/or specifications the implementation of which is made mandatory under the current Directives.

— Chapter I: Reference list for the minimum set of leased lines listed in Annex II of Directive 92/44/EEC[7] as amended by Directive 97/51/EC[8], and in future by Directive 2002/22/EC (Universal Service Directive)[9].

---

[6] Established under Article 22 of the Framework Directive.
[7] OJ L 165, 19.6.1992.
[8] OJ L 295, 29.10.1997, p. 23.
[9] Article 18(1): 'Where (...) a national regulatory authority determines that the market for the provision of part or all of the minimum set of leased lines is not effectively competitive, it (...) shall impose obligations regarding the provision of the minimum set of leased lines, as identified in the list of standards published in

— Chapter II: Quality of service parameters, as established in Annex III of Directive 98/10/EC[10] as amended by Commission Decision 2001/22/EC[11], and in future by Directive 2002/22/EC (Universal Service Directive), for operators with universal service obligations.

When no version number of the standard is quoted, the version referred to in this list is the version valid at the time that the list is published.

See section 7 of this preface for full references to the abovementioned Directives.

3. Status of the standards in the list

The use of standards listed in Chapters I to VI is encouraged but there is no legal obligation to implement them.

According to Article 17(2)of the Framework Directive, 'Member States shall encourage the use of the standards and/or specifications referred to (. . .) for the provision of services, technical interfaces and/or network functions, to the extent strictly necessary to ensure interoperability of services and to improve freedom of choice for users.'[12].

In accordance with Article 17 of the framework Directive, the purpose of this list is 'to serve as a basis for encouraging the harmonised provision of electronic communications networks, electronic communications services and associated facilities and services' (first paragraph), 'to ensure interoperability of services and to improve freedom of choice for users.' (second paragraph). This should be borne in mind when implementing standards which contain alternatives or optional clauses.

According to Article 17(5)and (6)of the Framework Directive, 'where the Commission considers that standards and/or specifications (. . .) no longer contribute to the provision of harmonised electronic communications services, or that they no longer meet consumers' needs or are hampering technological development, it shall (. . .) remove them from the list of standards and/or specifications (. . .).'.

4. Technical standards and/or specifications

Most of the standards and specifications mentioned in this list are ETSI deliverables under both the previous and current ETSI nomenclature. According to the 'ETSI Directives'[13], these deliverables are defined as follows:

Deliverables under the current ETSI nomenclature:

ETSI guide, EG: An ETSI deliverable, containing mainly informative elements, approved for publication by application of the membership approval procedure.

ETSI standard, ES: An ETSI deliverable, containing normative provisions, approved for publication by application of the membership approval procedure.

ETSI technical specification, TS: An ETSI deliverable, containing normative provisions, approved for publication by a technical body.

---

the *Official Journal of the European Communities* in accordance with Article 17 of Directive 2002/21/EC (Framework Directive), and the conditions for such provision set out in (Annex VII to this Directive (...).'.
[10] OJ L 101. 1.4.1998, p. 24.
[11] OJ L 5, 10.1.2001, p. 12.
[12] Equivalent wording is found in Article 5(1) of Directive 90/387/EEC, as amended by Directive 97/51/EC.
[13] Available at http://portal.etsi.org/directives/

ETSI technical report, TR: An ETSI deliverable, containing mainly informative elements, approved for publication by a technical body.

European Standard (telecommunications series), EN: An ETSI deliverable containing normative provisions, approved for publication in a process involving the national standards organisations and/or ETSI national delegations with implications concerning standstill and national transposition.

Harmonised standard: An EN (telecommunications series) the drafting of which has been entrusted to ETSI by a mandate from the European Commission under European Directive 98/48/EC (latest amendment to Directive 83/189/EEC)and has been drafted taking into account the applicable essential requirements of the 'New Approach' Directive and whose reference has subsequently been announced in the *Official Journal of the European Communities* .

Special report, SR: An ETSI deliverable, which contains information made publicly available for reference purposes.

Deliverables under the previous ETSI nomenclature to which reference is made in the list:

European telecommunication standard (ETS): An ETSI deliverable, containing normative, provisions approved for publication in a process involving the national standards organisations and/or ETSI national delegations with implications concerning standstill and national transposition.

ETSI technical report, (ETR): An ETSI deliverable, containing informative elements, approved for publication by a technical committee.

5. The three-stage specification methodology used by ETSI

In the list stage 1, 2 and 3 standards are included where appropriate. These refer to the three-stage specification methodology used by ETSI (see ETR-010).

Stage 1 is an overall service description from the user's standpoint. Stage 2 is a description of the functional capabilities and the information flows needed to support the service described in stage 1. Stage 3 is the specification of the signalling protocol at the user-network access interface or at the gateway between two public networks.

6. Addresses where documents referenced can be obtained

ETSI Publications Office[14] postal address:

F-06921 Sophia Antipolis Cedex
tel.(33-4)92 94 42 41 or (33-4)92 94 42 58
fax (33-4)93 95 81 33
e-mail:publications@etsi.fr
website:http://www.etsi.fr

ITU Sales and Marketing Service (For ITU-T documents) postal address:

Place des Nations
CH-1211 Geneva 20
tel.(41-22)730 61 41 (English)

---

[14] ETSI documents can be downloaded from the ETSI publications download area:
http://pda.etsi.org/pda/queryform.asp

(41-22)730 61 42 (French)
(41-22)730 61 43 (Spanish)
fax (41-22)730 51 94
e-mail:sales@itu.int
website:http://www.itu.int

7. References to EU legislation

The list refers to the following legislative documents which may be found at http://europa.eu.int/information_society/ topics/telecoms/regulatory/index_en.htm.

[list of legislation omitted]

The present list deals with standards on telecommunication networks and broadcasting networks and associated facilities. It is without prejudice to the Directive 1999/5/EC of the European Parliament and of the Council on radio equipment and telecommunications terminal equipment and the mutual recognition of their conformity[15], and any list of standards published pursuant to that Directive.

LIST OF STANDARDS AND/OR SPECIFICATIONS FOR ELECTRONIC NETWORKS, SERVICES AND ASSOCIATED FACILITIES AND SERVICES

The purpose of publishing standards in the list is to encourage the provision of harmonised electronic communications services to the benefit of users throughout the Community, to ensure interoperability and to support the implementation of the current and future regulatory framework. The main guiding principle to include standards is to focus on standards related closely to the provisions in the Directives.

[list omitted]

Editors' Notes:

[a] Due to space limitations, the list of standards attached to this instrument has been omitted. The list is available at
http://europa.eu.int/eur-lex/pri/en/oj/dat/2002/c_331/c_33120021231en00320049.pdf
and has been further updated by "Amendment to the List of Standards and/or specifications for electronic communications networks, associated services and associated facilities and services", which may be found at:
http://eur-lex.europa.eu/LexUriServ/site/en/oj/2006/c_071/c_07120060323en00090009.pdf

---

[15] OJ L 91, 7.4.1999, p. 10.

COMMISSION DIRECTIVE 88/301/EEC

of 16 May 1988

on competition in the markets in telecommunications terminal equipment

[as amended]ᵃ

THE COMMISSION OF THE EUROPEAN COMMUNITIES,

Having regard to the Treaty establishing the European Economic Community, and in particular Article 90 (3) thereof,

Whereas:

(1)   In all the Member States, telecommunications are, either wholly or partly, a State monopoly generally granted in the form of special or exclusive rights to one or more bodies responsible for providing and operating the network infrastructure and related services. Those rights, however, often go beyond the provision of network utilization services and extend to the supply of user terminal equipment for connection to the network. The last decades have seen considerable technical developments in networks, and the pace of development has been especially striking in the area of terminal equipment.

(2)   Several Member States have, in response to technical and economic developments, reviewed their grant of special or exclusive rights in the telecommunications sector. The proliferation of types of terminal equipment and the possibility of the multiple use of terminals means that users must be allowed a free choice between the various types of equipment available if they are to benefit fully from the technological advances made in the sector.

(3)   Article 30 of the Treaty prohibits quantitative restrictions on imports from other Member States and all measures having equivalent effect. The grant of special or exclusive rights to import and market goods to one organization can, and often does, lead to restrictions on imports from other Member States.

(4)   Article 37 of the Treaty states that 'Member States shall progressively adjust any State monopolies of a commercial character so as to ensure that when the transitional period has ended no discrimination regarding the conditions under which goods are procured and marketed exists between nationals of Member States.

The provisions of this Article shall apply to any body through which a Member State, in law or in fact, either directly or indirectly supervises, determines or appreciably influences imports or exports between Member States. These provisions shall likewise apply to monopolies delegated by the State to others.' Paragraph 2 of Article 37 prohibits Member States from introducing any new measure contrary to the principles laid down in Article 37 (1).

(5)   The special or exclusive rights relating to terminal equipment enjoyed by national telecommunications monopolies are exercised in such a way as, in practice, to disadvantage equipment from other Member States, notably by preventing users from freely choosing the equipment that best suits their needs in terms of price and quality, regardless of its origin. The exercise of these rights is therefore not compatible with Article 37 in all the Member States except Spain and Portugal, where the national monopolies are to be adjusted progressively before the end of the transitional period provided for by the Act of Accession.

(6)   The provision of installation and maintenance services is a key factor in the purchasing or rental of terminal equipment. The retention of exclusive rights in this field would be tantamount to retention of exclusive marketing rights. Such rights must therefore also be abolished if the abolition of exclusive importing and marketing rights is to have any practical effect.

(7)   Article 59 of the Treaty provides that 'restrictions on freedom to provide services within the Community shall be progressively abolished during the transitional period in respect of nationals of Member States who are established in a State of the Community other than that of the person for whom the services are intended.' Maintenance of terminals is a service within the meaning of Article 60 of the Treaty. As the transitional period has ended, the service in question, which cannot from a commercial point of view be dissociated from the marketing of the terminals, must be provided freely and in particular when provided by qualified operators.

(8)   Article 90 (1) of the Treaty provides that 'in the case of public undertakings and undertakings to which Member States grant special or exclusive rights, Member States shall neither enact nor maintain in force any measure contrary to the rules contained in this Treaty, in particular to those rules provided for in Article 7 and Articles 85 to 94.'

(9)   The market in terminal equipment is still as a rule governed by a system which allows competition in the common market to be distorted; this situation continues to produce infringements of the competition rules laid down by the Treaty and to affect adversely the development of trade to such an extent as would be contrary to the interests of the Community. Stronger competition in the terminal equipment market requires the introduction of transparent technical specifications and type-approval procedures which meet the essential requirements mentioned in Council Directive 86/361/EEC[1] and allow the free movement of terminal equipment. In turn, such transparency necessarily entails the publication of technical specifications and type-approval procedures. To ensure that the latter are applied transparently, objectively and without discrimination, the drawing-up and application of such rules should be entrusted to bodies independent of competitors in the market in question. It is essential that the specifications and type-approval procedures are published simultaneously and in an orderly fashion. Simultaneous publication will also ensure that behaviour contrary to the Treaty is avoided. Such simultaneous, orderly publication can be achieved only by means of a legal instrument that is binding on all the Member States. The most appropriate instrument to this end is a directive.

(10)   The Treaty entrusts the Commission with very clear tasks and gives it specific powers with regard to the monitoring of relations between the Member States and their public undertakings and enterprises to which they have delegated special or exclusive rights, in particular as regards the elimination of quantitative restrictions and measures having equivalent effect, discrimination between nationals of Member States, and competition. The only instrument, therefore, by which the Commission can efficiently carry out the tasks and powers assigned to it, is a Directive based on Article 90 (3).

(11)   Telecommunications bodies or enterprises are undertakings within the meaning of Article 90 (1) because they carry on an organized business activity involving the production of goods or services. They are either public undertakings or private enterprises to which the Member States have granted special or exclusive rights for the importation, marketing, connection, bringing into service of telecommunications terminal equipment and/or maintenance of such equipment. The grant and maintenance of special and exclusive rights for terminal equipment constitute measures within the meaning of that Article. The conditions for applying the

---

[1]   OJ L 217, 5.8.1986, p. 21.

exception of Article 90 (2) are not fulfilled. Even if the provision of a telecommunications network for the use of the general public is a service of general economic interest entrusted by the State to the telecommunications bodies, the abolition of their special or exclusive rights to import and market terminal equipment would not obstruct, in law or in fact, the performance of that service. This is all the more true given that Member States are entitled to subject terminal equipment to type-approval procedures to ensure that they conform to the essential requirements.

(12) Article 86 of the Treaty prohibits as incompatible with the common market any conduct by one or more undertakings that involves an abuse of a dominant position within the common market or a substantial part of it.

(13) The telecommunications bodies hold individually or jointly a monopoly on their national telecommunications network. The national networks are markets. Therefore, the bodies each individually or jointly hold a dominant position in a substantial part of the market in question within the meaning of Article 86.

The effect of the special or exclusive rights granted to such bodies by the State to import and market terminal equipment is to:

- restrict users to renting such equipment, when it would often be cheaper for them, at least in the long term, to purchase this equipment. This effectively makes contracts for the use of networks subject to acceptance by the user of additional services which have no connection with the subject of the contracts,

- limit outlets and impede technical progress since the range of equipment offered by the telecommunications bodies is necessarily limited and will not be the best available to meet the requirements of a significant proportion of users.

Such conduct is expressly prohibited by Article 86 (d) and (b), and is likely significantly to affect trade between Member States.

At all events, such special or exclusive rights in regard to the terminal equipment market give rise to a situation which is contrary to the objective of Article 3 (f) of the Treaty, which provides for the institution of a system ensuring that competition in the common market is not distorted, and requires a fortiori that competition must not be eliminated. Member States have an obligation under Article 5 of the Treaty to abstain from any measure which could jeopardize the attainment of the objectives of the Treaty, including Article 3 (f).

The exclusive rights to import and market terminal equipment must therefore be regarded as incompatible with Article 86 in conjunction with Article 3, and the grant or maintenance of such rights by a Member State is prohibited under Article 90 (1).

(14) To enable users to have access to the terminal equipment of their choice, it is necessary to know and make transparent the characteristics of the termination points of the network to which the terminal equipment is to be connected. Member States must therefore ensure that the characteristics are published and that users have access to termination points.

(15) To be able to market their products, manufacturers of terminal equipment must know what technical specifications they must satisfy. Member States should therefore formalize and publish the specifications and type-approval rules, which they must notify to the Commission in draft form, in accordance with Council Directive 83/189/EEC[2]. The specifications may be extended to products imported from other

---

[2] OJ L 109, 28.3.1932, p. 8.

Member States only insofar as they are necessary to ensure conformity with the essential requirements specified in Article 2 (17) of Directive 86/361/EEC that can legitimately be required under Community law. Member States must, in any event, comply with Articles 30 and 36 of the Treaty, under which an importing Member State must allow terminal equipment legally manufactured and marketed in another Member State to be imported on to its territory, and may only subject it to such type-approval and possibly refuse approval for reasons concerning conformity with the abovementioned essential requirements.

(16)   The immediate publication of these specifications and procedures cannot be considered in view of their complexity. On the other hand, effective competition is not possible without such publication, since potential competitors of the bodies or enterprises with special or exclusive rights are unaware of the precise specifications with which their terminal equipment must comply and of the terms of the type-approval procedures and hence their cost and duration. A deadline should therefore be set for the publication of specifications and the type-approval procedures. A period of two-and-a-half years will also enable the telecommunications bodies with special or exclusive rights to adjust to the new market conditions and will enable economic operators, especially small and medium-sized enterprises, to adapt to the new competitive environment.

(17)   Monitoring of type-approval specifications and rules cannot be entrusted to a competitor in the terminal equipment market in view of the obvious conflict of interest. Member States should therefore ensure that the responsibility for drawing up type-approval specifications and rules is assigned to a body independent of the operator of the network and of any other competitor in the market for terminals.

(18)   The holders of special or exclusive rights in the terminal equipment in question have been able to impose on their customers long-term contracts preventing the introduction of free competition from having a practical effect within a reasonable period. Users must therefore be given the right to obtain a revision of the duration of their contracts,

HAS ADOPTED THIS DIRECTIVE:

Article 1

For the purposes of this Directive:

-    "terminal equipment" means equipment directly or indirectly connected to the termination of a public telecommunications network to send, process or receive information. A connection is indirect if equipment is placed between the terminal and the termination of the network. In either case (direct or indirect), the connection may be made by wire, optical fibre or electromagnetically.

     Terminal equipment also means satellite earth station equipment.

-    "undertaking" means a public or private body, to which a Member State grants special or exclusive rights for the importation, marketing, connection, bringing into service of telecommunications terminal equipment and/or maintenance of such equipment,

-    "special rights" means rights that are granted by a Member State to a limited number of undertakings, through any legislative, regulatory or administrative instrument, which, within a given geographical area,

     -    limits to two or more the number of such undertakings, otherwise than according t objective, proportional and non-discriminatory criteria, or

- designates, otherwise than according to such criteria, several competing undertakings, or

- confers on any undertaking or undertakings, otherwise than according to such criteria, any legal or regulatory advantages which substantially affect the ability of any other undertaking to import, market, connect, bring into service and/or maintain telecommunication terminal equipment in the same geographical area under substantially equivalent conditions;

- "satellite earth station equipment" means equipment which is capable of being used for the transmission only, or for the transmission and reception ("transmit/receive"), or for the reception only ("receive-only") of radiocommunication signals by means of satellites or other space-based systems.

Article 2^b

Member States which have granted special or exclusive rights to undertakings shall ensure that all exclusive rights are withdrawn, as well as those special rights which

(a) limit two or more the number of undertakings within the meaning of Article 1, otherwise than according to objective, proportional and non-discriminatory criteria, or

(b) designate, otherwise than according to such criteria, several competing undertakings within the meaning of Article 1.

They shall, not later than three months following the notification of this Directive, inform the Commission of the measures taken or draft legislation introduced to that end.

Article 3

Member States shall ensure that economic operators have the right to import, market, connect, bring into service and maintain terminal equipment. However, Member States may:

- in the case of satellite earth station equipment, refuse to allow such equipment to be connected to the public telecommunications network and/or to be brought into service where it does not satisfy the relevant common technical regulations adopted in pursuance of Council Directive 93/97/EEC[3] or, in the absence thereof, the essential requirements laid down in Article 4 of that Directive. In the absence of common technical rules of harmonized regulatory conditions, national rules shall be proportionate to those essential requirements and shall be notified to the Commission in pursuance of Directive 83/189/EEC where that Directive so requires,

- in the case of other terminal equipment, refuse to allow such equipment to be connected to the public telecommunications network where it does not satisfy the relevant common technical regulations adopted in pursuance of Council Directive 91/263/EEC[4] or, in the absence thereof, the essential requirements laid down in Article 4 of that Directive,

- require economic operators to possess the technical qualifications needed to connect, bring into service and maintain terminal equipment on the basis of objective, non-discriminatory and publicly available criteria.

---

[3] OJ L 290, 24.11.1993, p. 1.
[4] OJ L 128, 23.5.1991, p. 1.

Article 4

Member States shall ensure that users have access to new public network termination points and that the physical characteristics of these points are published not later than 31 December 1988.

Access to public network termination points existing at 31 December 1988 shall be given within a reasonable period to any user who so requests.

Article 5

1. Member States shall, not later than the date mentioned in Article 2, communicate to the Commission a list of all technical specifications and type-approval procedures which are used for terminal equipment, and shall provide the publication references.

    Where they have not as yet been published in a Member State, the latter shall ensure that they are published not later than the dates referred to in Article 8.

2. Member States shall ensure that all other specifications and type-approval procedures for terminal equipment are formalized and published. Member States shall communicate the technical specifications and type-approval procedures in draft form to the Commission in accordance with Directive 83/189/EEC and according to the timetable set out in Article 8.

Article 6^c

Member States shall ensure that, from 1 July 1989, responsibility for drawing up the specifications referred to in Article 5, monitoring their application and granting type-approval is entrusted to a body independent of public or private undertakings offering goods and/or services in the telecommunications sector.

Article 7

Member States shall take the necessary steps to ensure that undertakings within the meaning of Article 1 make it possible for their customers to terminate, with maximum notice of one year, leasing or maintenance contracts which concern terminal equipment subject to exclusive or special rights at the time of the conclusion of the contracts.

For terminal equipment requiring type-approval, Member States shall ensure that this possibility of termination is afforded by the undertakings in question no later than the dates provided for in Article 8. For terminal equipment not requiring type-approval, Member States shall introduce this possibility no later than the date provided for in Article 2.

Article 8

Member States shall inform the Commission of the draft technical specifications and type-approval procedures referred to in Article 5 (2);

-   not later than 31 December 1988 in respect of equipment in category A of the list in Annex I,

-   not later than 30 September 1989 in respect of equipment in category B of the list in Annex I,

-   not later than 30 June 1990 in respect of other terminal equipment in category C of the list in Annex I.

Member States shall bring these specifications and type-approval procedures into force after expiry of the procedure provided for by Directive 83/189/EEC.

Article 9

Member States shall provide the Commission at the end of each year with a report allowing it to monitor compliance with the provisions of Articles 2, 3, 4, 6 and 7.

An outline of the report is attached as Annex II.

Article 10

The provisions of this Directive shall be without prejudice to the provisions of the instruments of accession of Spain and Portugal, and in particular Articles 48 and 208 of the Act of Accession.

Article 11

This Directive is addressed to the Member States.

———————

Editors' Notes:

[a] Directive 88/301/EEC (OJ L 131, 27.5.1998, p. 73) is reproduced in this book as amended by Directive 94/46/EC of 13 October 1994 (OJ L 268, 19.10.1994, p. 15).

[b] The Court of Justice of the European Communities in Case C-202/88, France v. Commission ([1991] ECR I-1223) declared void Article 2 of the Directive in so far as it requires Member States which grant undertakings special rights regarding the importation, marketing, connection or bringing into service of terminal equipment and/or maintenance of such equipment to withdraw such rights and to inform the Commission of the measures taken or draft legislation introduced to that end; declared void Article 7 of the Directive; and declared void Article 9 of the Directive in so far as it refers to the provisions of Article 2 which are concerned with special rights and to Article 7 of the directive. See also Recitals 6 and 7 of Directive 94/46/EC, which read as follows:

"(6) In its judgement in Case C-202/88, France v. Commission, the Court of Justice of the European Communities upheld Commission Directive 88/301/EEC. However, in so far as it relates to special rights, the Directive was declared void on the grounds that neither the provisions of the Directive nor the preamble thereto specify the type of rights which are actually involved and in what respect the existence of such rights is contrary to the various provisions of the Treaty. As far as importation, marketing, connection, bringing into service and maintenance of telecommunications equipment are concerned, special rights are in practice rights that are granted by a Member State to a limited number of undertakings, through any legislative, regulatory or administrative instrument which, within a given geographical area,

- limits to two or more the number of such undertaking, otherwise than according to objective, proportional and non-discriminatory criteria, or

- designates, otherwise than according to such criteria, several competing undertakings, or

- confers on any undertaking or undertakings, otherwise than according to such criteria, legal or regulatory advantages which substantially affect the ability of any other undertaking to engage in any of the abovementioned activities in the same geographical area under substantially equivalent conditions.

This definition is without prejudice to the application of Article 92 of the EC Treaty.

(7) The existence of exclusive rights has the effect of restricting the free movement of such equipment either as regards the importation and marketing of telecommunications equipment (including satellite equipment), because certain products are not marketed, or as regards the connection, bringing into service or maintenance because, taking into account the characteristics of the market and in particular the diversity and technical nature of the products, a monopoly has no incentive to provide these services in relation to products which it has not marketed or imported, nor to align its prices on costs, since there is no threat of competition from new entrants. Taking into account the fact that in most equipment markets there is typically a large range of telecommunication equipment, and the likely development of the markets in which there are as yet a limited number of manufacturers, any special right which directly or indirectly - for example by not providing for an open and non-discriminatory authorization procedure - limits the number of the undertakings authorized to import, market, connect, bring into service and maintain such equipment, is liable to have the same kind of effect as the grant of exclusive rights.

Such exclusive or special rights constitute measures having equivalent effect to quantitative restrictions incompatible with Article 30 of the EC Treaty. None of the specific features of satellite earth stations or of the market for their sale or maintenance is such as to justify their being treated differently in law from other telecommunications terminal equipment. Thus it is necessary to abolish all existing exclusive rights in the importation, marketing, connection, bringing into service and maintenance of satellite earth station equipment, as well as those rights having comparable effects - that is to say, all special rights except those consisting in legal or regulatory advantages conferred on one or more undertakings and affecting only the ability of other undertakings to engage in any of the abovementioned activities in the same geographical area under substantially equivalent conditions."

On interpretation of the scope of the Directive, see also Case C-314/93 ([1994] ECR I-3257).

[c] See the following decisions of the Court of Justice of the European Communities on the interpretation of Article 6: Joined Cases C-46/90 and C-93/91 ([1993] ECR I-05267); Case C-92/91 ([1993] ECR I-05383); C-91/94 ([1995] ECR I-03911).

List of terminal equipment referred to in Article 8

	Category
Additional telephone set; private automatic branch exchanges (PABXs):	A
Modems:	A
Telex terminals:	B
Data-transmission terminals:	B
Mobile telephones:	B
Receive-only satellite stations not reconnected to the public network of a Member State:	B
First telephone set:	C
Other terminal equipment:	C

Outline of the report provided for in Article 9

Implementation of Article 2

1. Terminal equipment for which legislation is being or has been modified.

    By category of terminal equipment:

    -   date of adoption of the measure or,

    -   date of introduction of the bill or,

    -   date of entry into force of the measure.

2. Terminal equipment still subject to special or exclusive rights:

    -   type of terminal equipment and rights concerned.

Implementation of Article 3

-   terminal equipment, the connection and/or commissioning of which has been restricted,

-   technical qualifications required, giving reference of their publication.

Implementation of Article 4

-   references of publications in which the physical characteristics are specified,

-   number of existing network termination points,

-   number of network termination points now accessible.

Implementation of Article 6

-   independent body or bodies appointed.

Implementation of Article 7

-   measures put into force, and

-   number of terminated contracts.

DIRECTIVE 1999/5/EC OF THE EUROPEAN PARLIAMENT AND OF THE COUNCIL

of 9 March 1999

on radio equipment and telecommunications terminal equipment and the mutual recognition of their conformity

[as amended]ª

THE EUROPEAN PARLIAMENT AND THE COUNCIL OF THE EUROPEAN UNION,

Having regard to the Treaty establishing the European Community, and in particular Article 100a,

Having regard to the proposal from the Commission[1],

Having regard to the opinion of the Economic and Social Committee[2],

Acting in accordance with the procedure laid down in Article 189b of the Treaty[3], in the light of the joint text approved by the Conciliation Committee on 8 December 1998,

(1)   Whereas the radio equipment and telecommunications terminal equipment sector is an essential part of the telecommunications market, which is a key element of the economy in the Community; whereas the directives applicable to the telecommunications terminal equipment sector are no longer capable of accommodating the expected changes in the sector caused by new technology, market developments and network legislation;

(2)   Whereas in accordance with the principles of subsidiarity and proportionality referred to in Article 3b of the Treaty, the objective of creating an open competitive single market for telecommunications equipment cannot be sufficiently achieved by the Member States and can therefore be better achieved by the Community; whereas this Directive does not go beyond what is necessary to achieve this aim;

(3)   Whereas Member States may rely upon Article 36 of the Treaty to exclude certain classes of equipment from this Directive;

(4)   Whereas Directive 98/13/EC[4] consolidated the provisions relating to telecommunications terminal equipment and satellite earth station equipment, including measures for the mutual recognition of their conformity;

(5)   Whereas that Directive does not cover a substantial proportion of the radio equipment market;

(6)   Whereas dual-use goods are subject to the Community regime of export controls introduced by Council Regulation (EC) No 3381/94[5];

---

[1]   OJ C 248, 14.8.1997, p. 4.
[2]   OJ C 73, 9.3.1998, p. 10.
[3]   Opinion of the European Parliament of 29 January 1998 (OJ C 56, 23.2.1998, p. 27), Council common position of 8 June 1998 (OJ C 227, 20.7.1998, p. 37) and Decision of the European Parliament of 6 October 1998 (OJ C 328, 26.10.1998, p. 32). Decision of the Council of 25 January 1999 and Decision of the European Parliament of 10 February 1999.
[4]   OJ L 74, 12.3.1998, p. 1.
[5]   OJ L 367, 31.12.1994, p. 1.

(7) Whereas the broad scope of this Directive requires new definitions of the expressions "radio equipment" and "telecommunications terminal equipment"; whereas a regulatory regime aimed at the development of a single market for radio equipment and telecommunications terminal equipment should permit investment, manufacture and sale to take place at the pace of technology and market developments;

(8) Whereas, given the increasing importance of telecommunications terminal equipment and networks using radio transmission besides equipment connected through wired links, any rules governing the manufacturing, marketing and use of radio equipment and telecommunications terminal equipment should cover both classes of such equipment;

(9) Whereas Directive 98/10/EC of the European Parliament and of the Council of 26 February 1998 on the application of open network provision (ONP) to voice telephony and on universal service for telecommunications in a competitive environment[6] calls on national regulatory authorities to ensure the publication of details of technical interface specifications for network access for the purpose of ensuring a competitive market for the supply of terminal equipment;

(10) Whereas the objectives of Council Directive 73/23/EEC of 19 February 1973 on the harmonisation of the laws of the Member States relating to electrical equipment designed for use within certain voltage limits[7] are sufficient to cover radio equipment and telecommunications terminal equipment, but with no lower voltage limit applying;

(11) Whereas the electromagnetic compatibility related protection requirements laid down by Council Directive 89/336/EEC of 3 May 1989 on the approximation of the laws of Member States relating to electromagnetic compatibility[8] are sufficient to cover radio equipment and telecommunications terminal equipment;

(12) Whereas Community law provides that obstacles to the free movement of goods within the Community, resulting from disparities in national legislation relating to the marketing of products, can only be justified where any national requirements are necessary and proportionate; whereas, therefore, the harmonisation of laws must be limited to those requirements necessary to satisfy the essential requirements relating to radio equipment and telecommunications terminal equipment;

(13) Whereas the essential requirements relevant to a class of radio equipment and telecommunications terminal equipment should depend on the nature and the needs of that class of equipment; whereas these requirements must be applied with discernment in order not to inhibit technological innovation or the meeting of the needs of a free-market economy;

(14) Whereas care should be taken that radio equipment and telecommunications terminal equipment should not represent an avoidable hazard to health;

(15) Whereas telecommunications are important to the well-being and employment of people with disabilities who represent a substantial and growing proportion of the population of Europe; whereas radio equipment and telecommunications terminal equipment should therefore in appropriate cases be designed in such a way that disabled people may use it without or with only minimal adaptation;

---

[6] OJ L 101, 1.4.1998, p. 24.
[7] OJ L 77, 26.3.1973, p. 29. Directive as amended by Directive 93/68/EEC (OJ L 220, 30.8.1993, p. 1).
[8] OJ L 139, 23.5.1989, p. 19. Directive as last amended by Directive 93/68/EEC.

(16) Whereas radio equipment and telecommunications terminal equipment can provide certain functions required by emergency services;

(17) Whereas some features may have to be introduced on the radio equipment and telecommunications terminal equipment in order to prevent the infringement of personal data and privacy of the user and of the subscriber and/or the avoidance of fraud;

(18) Whereas in some cases interworking via networks with other apparatus within the meaning of this Directive and connection with interfaces of the appropriate type throughout the Community may be necessary;

(19) Whereas it should therefore be possible to identify and add specific essential requirements on user privacy, features for users with a disability, features for emergency services and/or features for avoidance of fraud;

(20) Whereas it is recognised that in a competitive market, voluntary certification and marking schemes developed by consumer organisations, manufacturers, operators and other industry actors contribute to quality and are a useful means of improving consumers' confidence in telecommunications products and services; whereas Member States may support such schemes; whereas such schemes should be compatible with the competition rules of the Treaty;

(21) Whereas unacceptable degradation of service to persons other than the user of radio equipment and telecommunications terminal equipment should be prevented; whereas manufacturers of terminals should construct equipment in a way which prevents networks from suffering harm which results in such degradation when used under normal operating conditions; whereas network operators should construct their networks in a way that does not oblige manufacturers of terminal equipment to take disproportionate measures to prevent networks from being harmed; whereas the European Telecommunications Standards Institute (ETSI) should take due account of this objective when developing standards concerning access to public networks;

(22) Whereas effective use of the radio spectrum should be ensured so as to avoid harmful interference; whereas the most efficient possible use, according to the state of the art, of limited resources such as the radio frequency spectrum should be encouraged;

(23) Whereas harmonised interfaces between terminal equipment and telecommunications networks contribute to promoting competitive markets both for terminal equipment and network services;

(24) Whereas, however, operators of public telecommunications networks should be able to define the technical characteristics of their interfaces, subject to the competition rules of the Treaty; whereas, accordingly, they should publish accurate and adequate technical specifications of such interfaces so as to enable manufacturers to design telecommunications terminal equipment which satisfies the requirements of this Directive;

(25) Whereas, nevertheless, the competition rules of the Treaty and Commission Directive 88/301/EEC of 16 May 1988 on competition in the markets in telecommunications terminal equipment[9] establish the principle of equal, transparent and non-discriminatory treatment of all technical specifications having regulatory implications; whereas therefore it is the task of the Community and the Member States, in consultation with the economic players, to ensure that the regulatory framework created by this Directive is fair;

---

[9] OJ L 131, 27.5.1988, p. 73. Directive as amended by Directive 94/46/EC (OJ L 268, 19.10.1994, p. 15).

(26) Whereas it is the task of the European standardisation organisations, notably ETSI, to ensure that harmonised standards are appropriately updated and drafted in a way which allows for unambiguous interpretation; whereas maintenance, interpretation and implementation of harmonised standards constitute very specialised areas of increasing technical complexity; whereas those tasks require the active participation of experts drawn from amongst the economic players; whereas in some circumstances it may be necessary to provide more urgent interpretation of or corrections to harmonised standards than is possible through the normal procedures of the European standardisation organisations operating in conformity with Directive 98/34/EC of 22 June 1998 of the European Parliament and of the Council laying down a procedure for the provision of information in the field of technical standards and regulations and of rules on information society services[10];

(27) Whereas it is in the public interest to have harmonised standards at European level in connection with the design and manufacture of radio equipment and telecommunications terminal equipment; whereas compliance with such harmonised standards gives rise to a presumption of conformity to the essential requirements; whereas other means of demonstrating conformity to the essential requirements are permitted;

(28) Whereas the assignment of equipment class identifiers should draw on the expertise of CEPT/ERC and of the relevant European standards bodies in radio matters; whereas other forms of cooperation with those bodies is to be encouraged where possible;

(29) Whereas, in order to enable the Commission to monitor market control effectively, the Member States should provide the relevant information concerning types of interfaces, inadequate or incorrectly applied harmonised standards, notified bodies and surveillance authorities;

(30) Whereas notified bodies and surveillance authorities should exchange information on radio equipment and telecommunications terminal equipment with a view to efficient surveillance of the market; whereas such cooperation should make the utmost use of electronic means; whereas, in particular, such cooperation should enable national authorities to be informed about radio equipment placed on their market operating in frequency bands not harmonised in the Community;

(31) Whereas manufacturers should notify Member States of their intention to place radio equipment on the market using frequency bands whose use is not harmonised throughout the Community; whereas Member States therefore need to put in place procedures for such notification; whereas such procedures should be proportionate and should not constitute a conformity assessment procedure additional to those provided for in Annexes IV or V; whereas it is desirable that those notification procedures should be harmonised and preferably implemented by electronic means and one-stop-shopping;

(32) Whereas radio equipment and telecommunications terminal equipment which complies with the relevant essential requirements should be permitted to circulate freely; whereas such equipment should be permitted to be put into service for its intended purpose; whereas the putting into service may be subject to authorisations on the use of the radio spectrum and the provision of the service concerned;

(33) Whereas, for trade fairs, exhibitions, etc., it must be possible to exhibit radio equipment and telecommunications terminal equipment which does not conform to this Directive; whereas, however, interested parties should be properly informed that

---

[10] OJ L 204, 21.7.1998, p. 37. Directive as amended by Directive 98/48/EC (OJ L 217, 5.8.1998, p. 18).

such equipment does not conform and cannot be purchased in that condition; whereas Member States may restrict the putting into service, including the switching on, of such exhibited radio equipment for reasons related to the effective and appropriate use of the radio spectrum, avoidance of harmful interference or matters relating to public health;

(34) Whereas radio frequencies are allocated nationally and, to the extent that they have not been harmonised, remain within the exclusive competence of the Member States; whereas it is necessary to include a safeguard provision permitting Member States, in conformity with Article 36 of the Treaty, to prohibit, restrict or require the withdrawal from its market of radio equipment which has caused, or which it reasonably considers will cause, harmful interference; whereas interference with nationally allocated radio frequencies constitutes a valid ground for Member States to take safeguard measures;

(35) Whereas manufacturers are liable for damage caused by defective apparatus according to the provisions of Council Directive 85/374/EEC[11]; whereas without prejudice to any liability on the part of the manufacturer, any person who imports apparatus into the Community for sale in the course of his business is liable according to that Directive; whereas the manufacturer, his authorised representative or the person responsible for placing the apparatus on the Community market is liable according to the rules of the law of contractual or non-contractual liability in the Member States;

(36) Whereas the measures which are appropriate to be taken by the Member States or the Commission where apparatus declared to be compliant with the provisions of this Directive causes serious damage to a network or harmful radio interference shall be determined in accordance with the general principles of Community law, in particular, the principles of objectivity, proportionality and non-discrimination;

(37) Whereas on 22 July 1993 the Council adopted Decision 93/465/EEC concerning the modules for the various phases of the conformity assessment procedures and the rules for the affixing and the use of EC conformity marking which are intended to be used in the technical harmonisation directives[12]; whereas the applicable conformity assessment procedures should preferably be chosen from among the available modules laid down by that Decision;

(38) Whereas Member States may request that notified bodies they designate and their surveillance authorities be accredited according to appropriate European standards;

(39) Whereas it is appropriate that compliance of radio equipment and telecommunications terminal equipment with the requirements of Directives 73/23/EEC and 89/336/EEC may be demonstrated using the procedures specified in those Directives where the apparatus is within their scope; whereas, as a result, the procedure provided for in Article 10(1) of Directive 89/336/EEC may be used where the application of harmonised standards gives rise to a presumption of conformity with the protection requirements; whereas the procedure provided for in Article 10[13] may be used where the manufacturer has not applied harmonised standards or where no such standards exist;

(40) Whereas Community undertakings should have effective and comparable access to third countries' markets and enjoy treatment in third countries similar to that offered in the Community to undertakings owned wholly, controlled through majority ownership or effectively controlled by nationals of the third countries concerned;

---

[11] OJ L 210, 7.8.1985, p. 29.
[12] OJ L 220, 30.8.1993, p. 23.
[13] OJ L 220, 30.8.1993, p. 23.

(41) Whereas it is desirable to establish a committee bringing together parties directly involved in the implementation of regulation of radio equipment and telecommunications terminal equipment, in particular the national conformity assessment bodies and national bodies responsible for market surveillance, in order to assist the Commission in achieving a harmonised and proportionate application of the provisions so as to meet the needs of the market and the public at large; whereas representatives of telecommunications operators, users, consumers, manufacturers and service providers should be consulted where appropriate;

(42) Whereas a modus vivendi between the European Parliament, the Council and the Commission concerning the implementing measures for acts adopted in accordance with the procedure laid down in Article 189b of the Treaty was concluded on 20 December 1994[14];

(43) Whereas the Commission should keep under review the implementation and practical application of this and other relevant directives and take steps to ensure coordination of the application of all relevant directives in order to avoid disturbance to telecommunications equipment which affects the health of humans or is harmful to property;

(44) Whereas the functioning of this Directive should be reviewed in due course in the light of the development of the telecommunications sector and of experience gained from application of the essential requirements and the conformity assessment procedures provided for in this Directive;

(45) Whereas it is necessary to ensure that with the introduction of changes to the regulatory regime there is a smooth transition from the previous regime in order to avoid disruption to the market and legal uncertainty;

(46) Whereas this Directive replaces Directive 98/13/EC, which should accordingly be repealed; whereas Directives 73/23/EEC and 89/336/EEC will no longer apply to apparatus within the scope of this Directive, with the exception of protection and safety requirements and certain conformity assessment procedures,

HAVE ADOPTED THIS DIRECTIVE:

CHAPTER I

GENERAL ASPECTS

Article 1[b]

Scope and aim

1. This Directive establishes a regulatory framework for the placing on the market, free movement and putting into service in the Community of radio equipment and telecommunications terminal equipment.

2. Where apparatus as defined in Article 2(a) incorporates, as an integral part, or as an accessory:

---

[14] OJ C 102, 4.4.1996, p. 1.

(a)   a medical device within the meaning of Article 1 of Council Directive 93/42/EEC of 14 June 1993 concerning medical devices[15], or

(b)   an active implantable medical device within the meaning of Article 1 of Council Directive 90/385/EEC of 20 June 1990 on the approximation of the laws of the Member States relating to active implantable medical devices[16],

the apparatus shall be governed by this Directive, without prejudice to the application of Directives 93/42/EEC and 90/385/EEC to medical devices and active implantable medical devices, respectively.

3.   Where apparatus constitutes a component or a separate technical unit of a vehicle within the meaning of Council Directive 72/245/EEC[17] relating to the radio interference (electromagnetic compatibility) of vehicles or a component or a separate technical unit of a vehicle within the meaning of Article 1 of Council Directive 92/61/EEC[18] of 30 June 1992 relating to the type-approval of two or three-wheel motor vehicles, the apparatus shall be governed by this Directive without prejudice to the application of Directive 72/245/EEC or of Directive 92/61/EEC respectively.

4.   This Directive shall not apply to equipment listed in Annex I.

5.   This Directive shall not apply to apparatus exclusively used for activities concerning public security, defence, State security (including the economic well-being of the State in the case of activities pertaining to State security matters) and the activities of the State in the area of criminal law.

Article 2

Definitions

For the purpose of this Directive the following definitions shall apply:

(a)   "apparatus" means any equipment that is either radio equipment or telecommunications terminal equipment or both;

(b)   "telecommunications terminal equipment" means a product enabling communication or a relevant component thereof which is intended to be connected directly or indirectly by any means whatsoever to interfaces of public telecommunications networks (that is to say, telecommunications networks used wholly or partly for the provision of publicly available telecommunications services);

(c)   "radio equipment" means a product, or relevant component thereof, capable of communication by means of the emission and/or reception of radio waves utilising the spectrum allocated to terrestrial/space radiocommunication;

(d)   "radio waves" means electromagnetic waves of frequencies from 9 kHz to 3000 GHz, propagated in space without artificial guide;

(e)   "interface" means

(i)   a network termination point, which is a physical connection point at which a user is provided with access to public telecommunications network, and/or

---

[15]   OJ L 169, 12.7.1993, p. 1.
[16]   [OJ L 189, 20.7.1990, p. 17.]
[17]   OJ L 152, 6.7.1972, p. 15. Directive as last amended by Commission Directive 95/54/EC (OJ L 266, 8.11.1995, p. 1).
[18]   OJ L 225, 10.8.1992, p. 72. Directive as amended by the 1994 Act of Accession.

(ii)   an air interface specifying the radio path between radio equipment

and their technical specifications;

(f)   "equipment class" means a class identifying particular types of apparatus which under this Directive are considered similar and those interfaces for which the apparatus is designed. Apparatus may belong to more than one equipment class;

(g)   "technical construction file" means a file describing the apparatus and providing information and explanations as to how the applicable essential requirements have been implemented;

(h)   "harmonised standard" means a technical specification adopted by a recognised standards body under a mandate from the Commission in conformity with the procedures laid down in Directive 98/34/EC for the purpose of establishing a European requirement, compliance with which is not compulsory.

(i)   "harmful interference" means interference which endangers the functioning of a radionavigation service or of other safety services or which otherwise seriously degrades, obstructs or repeatedly interrupts a radiocommunications service operating in accordance with the applicable Community or national regulations.

Article 3

Essential requirements

1.   The following essential requirements are applicable to all apparatus:

(a)   the protection of the health and the safety of the user and any other person, including the objectives with respect to safety requirements contained in Directive 73/23/EEC, but with no voltage limit applying;

(b)   the protection requirements with respect to electromagnetic compatibility contained in Directive 89/336/EEC.

2.   In addition, radio equipment shall be so constructed that it effectively uses the spectrum allocated to terrestrial/space radio communication and orbital resources so as to avoid harmful interference.

3.   In accordance with the procedure laid down in Article 15, the Commission may decide that apparatus within certain equipment classes or apparatus of particular types shall be so constructed that:

(a)   it interworks via networks with other apparatus and that it can be connected to interfaces of the appropriate type throughout the Community; and/or that

(b)   it does not harm the network or its functioning nor misuse network resources, thereby causing an unacceptable degradation of service; and/or that

(c)   it incorporates safeguards to ensure that the personal data and privacy of the user and of the subscriber are protected; and/or that

(d)   it supports certain features ensuring avoidance of fraud; and/or that

(e)   it supports certain features ensuring access to emergency services[c]; and/or that

(f)   it supports certain features in order to facilitate its use by users with a disability.

Article 4

Notification and publication of interface specifications

1. Member States shall notify the interfaces which they have regulated to the Commission insofar as the said interfaces have not been notified under the provisions of Directive 98/34/EC. After consulting the committee in accordance with the procedure set out in Article 15, the Commission shall establish the equivalence between notified interfaces and assign an equipment class identifier, details of which shall be published in the *Official Journal of the European Communities.*[d]

2. Each Member State shall notify to the Commission the types of interface offered in that State by operators of public telecommunications networks. Member States shall ensure that such operators publish accurate and adequate technical specifications of such interfaces before services provided through those interfaces are made publicly available, and regularly publish any updated specifications. The specifications shall be in sufficient detail to permit the design of telecommunications terminal equipment capable of utilising all services provided through the corresponding interface. The specifications shall include, *inter alia*, all the information necessary to allow manufacturers to carry out, at their choice, the relevant tests for the essential requirements applicable to the telecommunications terminal equipment. Member States shall ensure that those specifications are made readily available by the operators.

Article 5

Harmonised standards

1. Where apparatus meets the relevant harmonised standards or parts thereof whose reference numbers have been published in the *Official Journal of the European Communities*, Member States shall presume compliance with those of the essential requirements referred to in Article 3 as are covered by the said harmonised standards or parts thereof.[e]

2. Where a Member State or the Commission considers that conformity with a harmonised standard does not ensure compliance with the essential requirements referred to in Article 3 which the said standard is intended to cover, the Commission or the Member State concerned shall bring the matter before the committee.

3. In the case of shortcomings of harmonised standards with respect to the essential requirements, the Commission may, after consulting the committee and in accordance with the procedure laid down in Article 14, publish in the *Official Journal of the European Communities* guidelines on the interpretation of harmonised standards or the conditions under which compliance with that standard raises a presumption of conformity. After consultation of the committee and in accordance with the procedure laid down in Article 14, the Commission may withdraw harmonised standards by publication of a notice in the *Official Journal of the European Communities*.

Article 6[f]

Placing on the market

1. Member States shall ensure that apparatus is placed on the market only if it complies with the appropriate essential requirements identified in Article 3 and the other relevant provisions of this Directive when it is properly installed and maintained and used for its intended purpose. It shall not be subject to further national provisions in respect of placing on the market.

2.   In taking a decision regarding the application of essential requirements under Article 3(3), the Commission shall determine the date of application of the requirements. If it is determined that an equipment class needs to comply with particular essential requirements under Article 3(3), any apparatus of the equipment class in question which is first placed on the market before the date of application of the Commission's determination can continue to be placed on the market for a reasonable period. Both the date of application and the period shall be determined by the Commission in accordance with the procedure laid down in Article 14.

3.   Member States shall ensure that the manufacturer or the person responsible for placing the apparatus on the market provides information for the user on the intended use of the apparatus, together with the declaration of conformity to the essential requirements. Where it concerns radio equipment, such information shall be sufficient to identify on the packaging and the instructions for use of the apparatus the Member States or the geographical area within a Member State where the equipment is intended to be used and shall alert the user by the marking on the apparatus referred to in Annex VII, paragraph 5, to potential restrictions or requirements for authorisation of use of the radio equipment in certain Member States. Where it concerns telecommunications terminal equipment, such information shall be sufficient to identify interfaces of the public telecommunications networks to which the equipment is intended to be connected. For all apparatus such information shall be prominently displayed.

4.   In the case of radio equipment using frequency bands whose use is not harmonised throughout the Community, the manufacturer or his authorised representative established within the Community or the person responsible for placing the equipment on the market shall notify the national authority responsible in the relevant Member State for spectrum management of the intention to place such equipment on its national market.

      This notification shall be given no less than four weeks in advance of the start of placing on the market and shall provide information about the radio characteristics of the equipment (in particular frequency bands, channel spacing, type of modulation and RF-power) and the identification number of the notified body referred to in Annex IV or V.

Article 7

Putting into service and right to connect

1.   Member States shall allow the putting into service of apparatus for its intended purpose where it complies with the appropriate essential requirements identified in Article 3 and the other relevant provisions of this Directive.

2.   Not withstanding paragraph 1, and without prejudice to conditions attached to authorisations for the provision of the service concerned in conformity with Community law, Member States may restrict the putting into service of radio equipment only for reasons related to the effective and appropriate use of the radio spectrum, avoidance of harmful interference or matters relating to public health.

3.   Without prejudice to paragraph 4, Member States shall ensure that operators of public telecommunications networks do not refuse to connect telecommunications terminal equipment to appropriate interfaces on technical grounds where that equipment complies with the applicable requirements of Article 3.

4.   Where a Member State considers that apparatus declared to be compliant with the provisions of this Directive causes serious damage to a network or harmful radio interference or harm to the network or its functioning, the operator may be authorized

to refuse connection, to disconnect such apparatus or to withdraw it from service. The Member States shall notify each such authorisation to the Commission, which shall convene a meeting of the committee for the purpose of giving its opinion on the matter. After the committee has been consulted, the Commission may initiate the procedures referred to in Article 5(2) and (3). The Commission and the Member States may also take other appropriate measures.

5.　In case of emergency, an operator may disconnect apparatus if the protection of the network requires the equipment to be disconnected without delay and if the user can be offered, without delay and without costs for him, an alternative solution. The operator shall immediately inform the national authority responsible for the implementation of paragraph 4 and Article 9.

Article 8

Free movement of apparatus

1.　Member States shall not prohibit, restrict or impede the placing on the market and putting into service in their territory of apparatus bearing the CE marking referred to in Annex VII, which indicates its conformity with all provisions of this Directive, including the conformity assessment procedures set out in Chapter II. This shall be without prejudice to Articles 6(4), 7(2) and 9(5).

2.　At trade fairs, exhibitions, demonstrations, etc., Member States shall not create any obstacles to the display of apparatus which does not comply with this Directive, provided that a visible sign clearly indicates that such apparatus may not be marketed or put into service until it has been made to comply.

3.　Where the apparatus is subject to other directives which concern other aspects and also provide for the affixing of the CE marking, the latter shall indicate that such apparatus also fulfils the provisions of those other directives. However, should one or more of those directives allow the manufacturer, during a transitional period, to choose which arrangements to apply, the CE marking shall indicate that the apparatus fulfils the provisions only of those directives applied by the manufacturer. In this case, the particulars of those directives, as published in the *Official Journal of the European Communities*, must be given in the documents, notices or instructions required by those directives and accompanying such products.

Article 9

Safeguards

1.　Where a Member State ascertains that apparatus within the scope of this Directive does not comply with the requirements of this Directive, it shall take all appropriate measures in its territory to withdraw the apparatus from the market or from service, prohibit its placing on the market or putting into service or restrict its free movement.

2.　The Member State concerned shall immediately notify the Commission of any such measures indicating the reasons for its decision and whether non-compliance is due to:

(a)　incorrect application of the harmonised standards referred to in Article 5(1);

(b)　shortcomings in the harmonised standards referred to in Article 5(1);

(c)　failure to satisfy the requirements referred to in Article 3 where the apparatus does not meet the harmonised standards referred to in Article 5(1).

3.   If the measures referred to in paragraph 1 are attributed to incorrect application of the harmonised standards referred to in Article 5(1) or to a failure to satisfy the requirements referred to in Article 3 where the apparatus does not meet the harmonised standards referred to in Article 5(1), the Commission shall consult the parties concerned as soon as possible. The Commission shall forthwith inform the Member States of its findings and of its opinion as to whether the measures are justified, within two months of notification of the said measures to the Commission.

4.   Where the decision referred to in paragraph 1 is attributed to shortcomings in the harmonised standards referred to in Article 5(1), the Commission shall bring the matter before the committee within two months. The committee shall deliver an opinion in accordance with the procedure laid down in Article 14. After such consultation, the Commission shall inform the Member States of its findings and of its opinion as to whether the action by the Member State is justified. If it finds that the action is justified it shall forthwith initiate the procedure referred to in Article 5(2).

5.   (a) Notwithstanding the provisions of Article 6, a Member State may, acting in conformity with the Treaty, and in particular Articles 30 and 36 thereof, adopt any appropriate measures with a view to:

     (i)   prohibiting or restricting the placing on its market, and/or

     (ii) requiring the withdrawal from its market,

     of radio equipment, including types of radio equipment, which has caused or which it reasonably considers will cause harmful interference, including interference with existing or planned services on nationally allocated frequency bands.

     (b) Where a Member State takes measures in accordance with subparagraph (a) it shall immediately inform the Commission of the said measures, specifying the reasons for adopting them.

6.   When a Member State notifies the Commission of a measure referred to in paragraph 1 or 5 the Commission shall in turn inform other Member States and consult the committee on the matter.

     Where, after such consultation, the Commission considers that:

     -   the measure is justified, it shall immediately so inform the Member State which took the initiative and the other Member States,

     -   the measure is unjustified, it shall immediately so inform the Member State and request it to withdraw the measure.

7.   The Commission shall maintain a record of the cases notified by Member States, which shall be made available to them on request.

CHAPTER II

CONFORMITY ASSESSMENT

Article 10

Conformity assessment procedures

1. The conformity assessment procedures identified in this Article shall be used to demonstrate the compliance of the apparatus with all the relevant essential requirements identified in Article 3.

2. At the choice of the manufacturer, compliance of the apparatus with the essential requirements identified in Article 3(1)(a) and (b) may be demonstrated using the procedures specified in Directive 73/23/EEC and Directive 89/336/EEC respectively, where the apparatus is within the scope of those Directives, as an alternative to the procedures laid out below.

3. Telecommunications terminal equipment which does not make use of the spectrum allocated to terrestrial/space radio communication and receiving parts of radio equipment shall be subject to the procedures described in any one of Annexes II, IV or V at the choice of the manufacturer.

4. Where a manufacturer has applied the harmonised standards referred to in Article 5(1), radio equipment not within the scope of paragraph 3 shall be subject to the procedures described in any one of Annexes III, IV or V at the choice of the manufacturer.

5. Where a manufacturer has not applied or has only applied in part the harmonised standards referred to in Article 5(1), radio equipment not within the scope of paragraph 3 of this Article shall be subject to the procedures described in either of Annexes IV or V at the choice of the manufacturer.

6. Records and correspondence relating to the conformity assessment procedures referred to in paragraphs 2 to 5 shall be in an official language of the Member State where the procedure will be carried out, or in a language accepted by the notified body involved.

Article 11

Notified bodies and surveillance authorities

1. Member States shall notify the Commission of the bodies which they have designated to carry out the relevant tasks referred to in Article 10. Member States shall apply the criteria laid down in Annex VI in determining the bodies to be designated.

2. Member States shall notify the Commission of the authorities established within their territory which are to carry out the surveillance tasks related to the operation of this Directive.

3. The Commission shall publish a list of the notified bodies, together with their identification numbers and the tasks for which they have been notified, in the *Official Journal of the European Communities*. The Commission shall also publish a list of surveillance authorities in the *Official Journal of the European Communities*. Member States shall provide the Commission with all information necessary to keep these lists up to date.[g]

CHAPTER III

CE CONFORMITY MARKING AND INSCRIPTIONS

Article 12

CE marking

1. Apparatus complying with all relevant essential requirements shall bear the EC conformity marking referred to in Annex VII. It shall be affixed under the responsibility of the manufacturer, his authorized representative within the Community or the person responsible for placing the apparatus on the market.

    Where the procedures identified in Annex III, IV or V are used, the marking shall be accompanied by the identification number of the notified body referred to in Article 11(1). Radio equipment shall in addition be accompanied by the equipment class identifier where such identifier has been assigned. Any other marking may be affixed to the equipment provided that the visibility and legibility of the EC marking is not thereby reduced.

2. No apparatus, whether or not it complies with the relevant essential requirements, may bear any other marking which is likely to deceive third parties as to the meaning and form of the EC marking specified in Annex VII.

3. The competent Member State shall take appropriate action against any person who has affixed a marking not in conformity with paragraphs 1 and 2. If the person who affixed the marking is not identifiable, appropriate action may be taken against the holder of the apparatus at the time when non-compliance was discovered.

4. Apparatus shall be identified by the manufacturer by means of type, batch and/or serial numbers and by the name of the manufacturer or the person responsible for placing the apparatus on the market.

CHAPTER IV

THE COMMITTEE

Article 13

Constitution of the committee

1. The Commission shall be assisted by the Telecommunication Conformity Assessment and Market Surveillance Committee (TCAM), hereinafter referred to as "the Committee".

2. The Committee shall adopt its rules of procedure.

Article 14

Advisory committee procedure

1. The Committee shall be consulted on the matters covered by Articles 5, 6(2), 7(4), 9(4) and Annex VII(5).

2. The Commission shall consult the Committee periodically on the surveillance tasks relating to the application of this Directive, and, where appropriate, issue guidelines on this matter.

3. Articles 3 and 7 of Decision 1999/468/EC[19] shall apply, having regard to the provisions of Article 8 thereof.

4. The Commission shall periodically consult the representatives of the telecommunications networks providers, the consumers and the manufacturers. It shall keep the Committee regularly informed of the outcome of such consultations.

Article 15

Regulatory committee procedure

1. The procedure laid down in paragraph 2 shall apply in respect of the matters covered by Articles 3(3) and 4(1).

2. Where reference is made to this Article, Articles 5 and 7 of Decision 1999/468/EC[19] shall apply, having regard to the provisions of Article 8 thereof.

    The period laid down in Article 5(6) of Decision 1999/468/EC shall be set at three months.

3. The Committee shall adopt its rules of procedure.

CHAPTER V

FINAL AND TRANSITIONAL PROVISIONS

Article 16

Third countries

1. Member States may inform the Commission of any general difficulties encountered, *de jure* or *de facto*, by Community undertakings with respect to placing on the market in third countries, which have been brought to their attention.

2. Whenever the Commission is informed of such difficulties, it may, if necessary, submit proposals to the Council for an appropriate mandate for negotiation of comparable rights for Community undertakings in these third countries. The Council shall decide by qualified majority.

3. Measures taken pursuant to paragraph 2 shall be without prejudice to the obligations of the Community and of the Member States under relevant international agreements.

Article 17[h]

Review and reporting

The Commission shall review the operation of this Directive and report thereon to the European Parliament and to the Council, on the first occasion not later than 7 October 2000 18 months after the entry into force of this Directive and every third year thereafter. The report shall cover progress on drawing up the relevant standards, as well as any problems that have arisen in the course of implementation. The report shall also outline the activities of the committee, assess progress in achieving an open competitive market for apparatus at

---

[19] Council Decision 1999/468/EC of 28 June 1999 laying down the procedures for the exercise of implementing powers conferred on the Commission (OJ L 184, 17.7.1999, p. 23).

Community level and examine how the regulatory framework for the placing on the market and putting into service of apparatus should be developed to:

(a)   ensure that a coherent system is achieved at Community level for all apparatus;

(b)   allow for convergence of the telecommunications, audiovisual and information technology sectors;

(c)   enable harmonisation of regulatory measures at international level.

It shall in particular examine whether essential requirements are still necessary for all categories of apparatus covered and whether the procedures contained in Annex IV, third paragraph, are proportionate to the aim of ensuring that the essential requirements are met for apparatus covered by that Annex. Where necessary, further measures may be proposed in the report for full implementation of the aim of the Directive.

Article 18

Transitional provisions

1.   Standards under Directive 73/23/EEC or 89/336/EEC whose references have been published in the *Official Journal of the European Communities* may be used as the basis for a presumption of conformity with the essential requirements referred to in Article 3(1)(a) and Article 3(1)(b). Common technical regulations under Directive 98/13/EC whose references have been published in the *Official Journal of the European Communities* may be used as the basis for a presumption of conformity with the other relevant essential requirements referred to in Article 3. The Commission shall publish a list of references to those standards in the Official *Journal of the European Communities* immediately after this Directive enters into force.

2.   Member States shall not impede the placing on the market and putting into service of apparatus which is in accordance with the provisions in Directive 98/13/EC or rules in force in their territory and was placed on the market for the first time before this Directive entered into force or at the latest two years after this Directive entered into force.

3.   Apart from the essential requirements referred to in Article 3(1), the Member States may request to continue, for a period of up to 30 months following the date referred to in the first sentence of Article 19(1), and in conformity with the provisions of the Treaty, to require telecommunications terminal equipment not to be capable of causing unacceptable deterioration of a voice telephony service accessible within the framework of the universal service as defined in Directive 98/10/EC.

The Member State shall inform the Commission of the reasons for requesting a continuation of such a requirement, the date by which the service concerned will no longer need the requirement, and the measures envisaged in order to meet this deadline. The Commission shall consider the request taking into account the particular situation in the Member State and the need to ensure a coherent regulatory environment at Community level, and shall inform the Member State whether it deems that the particular situation in that Member State justifies a continuation and, if so, until which date such continuation is justified.[1]

Article 19

Transposition

1.   Member States shall not later than 7 April 2000 adopt and publish the laws, regulations and administrative provisions necessary to comply with this Directive.

They shall forthwith inform the Commission thereof. They shall apply these provisions as from 8 April 2000.

When Member States adopt these measures, they shall contain a reference to this Directive or shall be accompanied by such reference on the occasion of their official publication. The methods of making such a reference shall be laid down by Member States.

2.   Member States shall inform the Commission of the main provisions of domestic law which they adopt in the field covered by this Directive.

Article 20

Repeal

1.   Directive 98/13/EC is hereby repealed as from 8 April 2000.

2.   This Directive is not a specific directive within the meaning of Article 2(2) of Directive 89/336/EEC. The provisions of Directive 89/336/EEC shall not apply to apparatus falling within the scope of this Directive, with the exception of the protection requirements in Article 4 and Annex III and the conformity assessment procedure in Article 10(1) and (2) of, and Annex I to, Directive 89/336/EEC, as from 8 April 2000.

3.   The provisions of Directive 73/23/EEC shall not apply to apparatus falling within the scope of this Directive, with the exceptions of the objectives with respect to safety requirements in Article 2 and Annex I and the conformity assessment procedure in Annex III, Section B, and Annex IV to Directive 73/23/EEC, as from 8 April 2000.

Article 21

Entry into force

This Directive shall enter into force on the day of its publication in the Official Journal of the European Communities.

Article 22

Addressees

This Directive is addressed to the Member States.

Editors' Notes:

[a] Directive 1999/5/EC (OJ L 91, 7.4.1999, p. 10) is reproduced in this book as amended by Regulation (EC) No 1882/2003 of the European Parliament and of the Council of 29 September 2003 (OJ L 284, 31.10.2003, p. 1).

[b] Footnoting errors appearing in the Official Journal have been corrected in this reproduction.

[c] The following decisions have been issued by the Commission pursuant to Article 3(3)(e):

–   Commission Decision 2000/637/EC of 22 September 2000 on the application of Article (3)(e) of Directive 1999/5/EC to radio equipment covered by the regional

<u>Editors' Notes (continued)</u>

arrangement concerning the radiotelephone service on inland waterways, OJ L 269, 21.10.2000, p. 50.

– Commission Decision 2001/148/EC of 21 February 2001 on the application of Article 3(3)(e) of Directive 1999/5/EC to avalanche beacons, OJ L 55, 24.2.2001, p. 65.

– Commission Decision 2003/213/EC of 25 March 2003 on the application of Article 3(3)(e) of Directive 1999/5/EC to radio equipment intended to be used on non-SOLAS vessels and which is intended to participate in the Automatic Identification System (AIS), OJ L 81, 28.03.2003, p. 46.

– Commission Decision 2004/71/EC of 4 September 2003 on essential requirements relating to marine radio communication equipment which is intended to be used on non-SOLAS vessels and to participate in the Global Maritime Distress and Safety System (GMDSS), OJ L 016, 23.01.2004, p. 54.

[d] See Commission Decision 2000/299/EC of 6 April 2000 establishing the initial classification of radio equipment and telecommunications terminal equipment and associated identifiers, OJ L 97, 19.4.2000. p. 13.

[e] The latest publication of titles and references of harmonised standards is contained in the Commission communication in the framework of the implementation of Directive 1999/5/EC, OJ C 104, 30.04.2004, p. 22.

[f] See Judgment of the Court (Sixth Chamber) of 20 June 2002, *Radiosistemi Srl v Prefetto di Genova*, joined cases C-388/00 and C-429/00, [2002] ECR I-5845, on the interpretation and application of Articles 6, 7 and 8 of the Directive.

[g] The latest list of bodies notified under Directive 1999/5/EC is contained in the List of notified bodies designated by the Member States and the EFTA Countries (EEA Members) under the new approach Directives, OJ C 302, 12.12.2003, p. 361.

[h] See Report from the Commission to the Council and the European Parliament - First Progress Report Directive 1999/5/EC (the R&TTE Directive), COM(2004) 288 final.

[i] See Commission Decision 2000/373/EC of 26 May 2000 concerning the request by France to maintain pursuant to Article 18(3) of Directive 1999/5/EC of the European Parliament and of the Council (the 'R&TTE Directive') a requirement for telecommunications terminal equipment intended for connection to the analogue public switched telephone network of France Telecom, OJ L 135, 8.6.2000, p.25.

ANNEX I

Equipment not covered by this Directive as referred to in Article 1(4)

1. Radio equipment used by radio amateurs within Article 1, definition 53, of the International Telecommunications Union (ITU) radio regulations unless the equipment is available commercially.

   Kits of components to be assembled by radio amateurs and commercial equipment modified by and for the use of radio amateurs are not regarded as commercially available equipment.

2. Equipment falling within the scope of Council Directive 96/98/EC of 20 December 1996 on marine equipment[1].

3. Cabling and wiring.

4. Receive only radio equipment intended to be used solely for the reception of sound and TV broadcasting services.

5. Products, appliances and components within the meaning of Article 2 of Council Regulation (EEC) No 3922/91 of 16 December 1991 on the harmonisation of technical requirements and administrative procedures in the field of civil aviation[2].

6. Air-traffic-management equipment and systems within the meaning of Article 1 of Council Directive 93/65/EEC of 19 July 1993 on the definition and use of compatible technical specifications for the procurement of air-traffic-management equipment and systems[3].

---

[1] OJ L 46, 17.2.1997, p. 25.
[2] OJ L 373, 31.12.1991, p. 4. Regulation as amended by Commission Regulation (EC) No 2176/96 (OJ L 291, 14.11.1996, p. 15).
[3] OJ L 187, 29.7.1993, p. 52. Directive as last amended by Commission Directive 97/15/EC (OJ L 95, 10.4.1997, p. 16).

Conformity Assessment Procedure referred to in Article 10(3)

Module A (internal production control)

1. This module describes the procedure whereby the manufacturer or his authorised representative established within the Community, who carries out the obligations laid down in point 2, ensures and declares that the products concerned satisfy the requirements of this Directive that apply to them. The manufacturer or his authorised representative established within the Community must affix the CE marking to each product and draw up a written declaration of conformity.

2. The manufacturer must establish the technical documentation described in point 4 and he or his authorised representative established within the Community must keep it for a period ending at least 10 years after the last product has been manufactured at the disposal of the relevant national authorities of any Member State for inspection purposes.

3. Where neither the manufacturer nor his authorised representative is established within the Community, the obligation to keep the technical documentation available is the responsibility of the person who places the product on the Community market.

4. The technical documentation must enable the conformity of the product with the essential requirements to be assessed. It must cover the design, manufacture and operation of the product, in particular:

    -   a general description of the product,

    -   conceptual design and manufacturing drawings and schemes of components, sub-assemblies, circuits, etc.,

    -   descriptions and explanations necessary for the understanding of said drawings and schemes and the operation of the product,

    -   a list of the standards referred to in Article 5, applied in full or in part, and descriptions and explanations of the solutions adopted to meet the essential requirements of the Directive where such standards referred to in Article 5 have not been applied or do not exist,

    -   results of design calculations made, examinations carried out, etc.,

    -   test reports.

5. The manufacturer or his authorised representative must keep a copy of the declaration of conformity with the technical documentation.

6. The manufacturer must take all measures necessary in order that the manufacturing process ensures compliance of the manufactured products with the technical documentation referred to in point 2 and with the requirements of this Directive that apply to them.

Conformity Assessment Procedure referred to in Article 10(4)

(Internal production control plus specific apparatus tests)[1]

This Annex consists of Annex II, plus the following supplementary requirements:

For each type of apparatus, all essential radio test suites must be carried out by the manufacturer or on his behalf. The identification of the test suites that are considered to be essential is the responsibility of a notified body chosen by the manufacturer except where the test suites are defined in the harmonised standards. The notified body must take due account of previous decisions made by notified bodies acting together.

The manufacturer or his authorised representative established within the Community or the person responsible for placing the apparatus on the market must declare that these tests have been carried out and that the apparatus complies with the essential requirements and must affix the notified body's identification number during the manufacturing process.

---

[1] Annex based on Module A with additional requirements appropriate to the sector.

Conformity Assessment Procedure Referred To In Article 10(5)

(Technical construction file)

This Annex consists of Annex III plus the following supplementary requirements:

The technical documentation described in point 4 of Annex II and the declaration of conformity to specific radio test suites described in Annex III must form a technical construction file.

The manufacturer, his authorised representative established within the Community or the person responsible for placing the apparatus on the market, must present the file to one or more notified bodies, each of the notified bodies must be informed of others who have received the file.

The notified body must review the file and if it is considered that it has not been properly demonstrated that the requirements of the Directive have been met, the notified body may issue an opinion to the manufacturer, his representative or the person responsible for placing the apparatus on the market and must inform the other notified bodies who have received the file accordingly. Such an opinion must be given within four weeks of receipt of the file by the notified body. On receipt of this opinion, or after the end of the four-week period, the apparatus may be placed on the market, without prejudice to Articles 6(4) and 9(5).

The manufacturer or his authorised representative established within the Community or the person responsible for placing the apparatus on the market must keep the file for a period ending at least 10 years after the last apparatus has been manufactured at the disposal of the relevant national authorities of any Member States for inspection.

Conformity Assessment Procedure referred to in Article 10

Full quality assurance

1. Full quality assurance is the procedure whereby the manufacturer who satisfies the obligations of point 2 ensures and declares that the products concerned satisfy the requirements of the Directive that apply to them. The manufacturer must affix the marks referred to in Article 12(1) to each product and draw up a written declaration of conformity.

2. The manufacturer must operate an approved quality system for design, manufacture and final product inspection and testing as specified in point 3 and must be subject to surveillance as specified in point 4.

3. Quality system

3.1. The manufacturer must lodge an application for assessment of his quality system with a notified body.

The application must include:

-   all relevant information for the products envisaged,

-   the quality system's documentation.

3.2. The quality system must ensure compliance of the products with the requirements of the Directive that apply to them. All the elements, requirements and provisions adopted by the manufacturer must be documented in a systematic and orderly manner in the form of written policies, procedures and instructions. This quality system documentation must ensure a common understanding of the quality policies and procedures such as quality programmes, plans, manuals and records.

It must contain in particular an adequate description of:

-   the quality objectives and the organisational structure, responsibilities and powers of the management with regard to design and product quality,

-   the technical specifications, including the harmonised standards and technical regulations as well as relevant test specifications that will be applied and, where the standards referred to in Article 5(1) will not be applied in full, the means that will be used to ensure that the essential requirements of the Directive that apply to the products will be met,

-   the design control and design verification techniques, processes and systematic actions that will be used when designing the products pertaining to the product category covered,

-   the corresponding manufacturing, quality control and quality assurance techniques, processes and systematic actions that will be used,

-   the examinations and tests that will be carried out before, during and after manufacture, and the frequency with which they will be carried out, as well as the results of the tests carried out before manufacture where appropriate,

-   the means by which it is ensured that the test and examination facilities respect the appropriate requirements for the performance of the necessary test,

- the quality records, such as inspection reports and test data, calibration data, qualification reports of the personnel concerned, etc.,

- the means to monitor the achievement of the required design and product quality and the effective operation of the quality system.

3.3. The notified body must assess the quality system to determine whether it satisfies the requirements referred to in point 3.2. It must presume compliance with these requirements in respect of quality systems that implement the relevant harmonised standard.

The notified body must assess in particular whether the quality control system ensures conformity of the products with the requirements of the Directive in the light of the relevant documentation supplied in respect of points 3.1 and 3.2 including, where relevant, test results supplied by the manufacturer.

The auditing team must have at least one member experienced as an assessor in the product technology concerned. The evaluation procedure must include an assessment visit to the manufacturer's premises.

The decision must be notified to the manufacturer. The notification must contain the conclusions of the examination and the reasoned assessment decision.

3.4. The manufacturer must undertake to fulfil the obligations arising out of the quality system as approved and to uphold it so that it remains adequate and efficient.

The manufacturer or his authorised representative must keep the notified body that has approved the quality system informed of any intended updating of the quality system.

The notified body must evaluate the modifications proposed and decide whether the amended quality system will still satisfy the requirements referred to in point 3.2 or whether a reassessment is required.

It must notify its decision to the manufacturer. The notification must contain the conclusions of the examination and the reasoned assessment decision.

4. EC surveillance under the responsibility of the notified body

4.1. The purpose of surveillance is to make sure that the manufacturer duly fulfils the obligations arising out of the approved quality system.

4.2. The manufacturer must allow the notified body access for inspection purposes to the locations of design, manufacture, inspection and testing, and storage and must provide it with all necessary information, in particular:

- the quality system documentation,

- the quality records as foreseen by the design part of the quality system, such as results of analyses, calculations, tests, etc.,

- the quality records as foreseen by the manufacturing part of the quality system, such as inspection reports and test data, calibration data, qualification reports of the personnel concerned, etc.

4.3. The notified body must carry out audits at reasonable intervals to make sure that the manufacturer maintains and applies the quality system and must provide an audit report to the manufacturer.

4.4. Additionally, the notified body may pay unexpected visits to the manufacturer. At the time of such visits, the notified body may carry out tests or have them carried out in order to check the proper functioning of the quality system where necessary; it must provide the manufacturer with a visit report and, if a test has been carried out, with a test report.

5. The manufacturer must, for a period ending at least 10 years after the last product has been manufactured, keep at the disposal of the national authorities:

- the documentation referred to in the second indent of point 3.1,

- the updating referred to in the second paragraph of point 3.4,

- the decisions and reports from the notified body which are referred to in the final paragraph of point 3.4 and in points 4.3 and 4.4.

6. Each notified body must make available to the other notified bodies the relevant information concerning quality system approvals including references to the product(s) concerned, issued and withdrawn.

Minimum criteria to be taken into account by Member States when designating notified bodies in accordance with article 11(1)

1. The notified body, its director and the staff responsible for carrying out the tasks for which the notified body has been designated must not be a designer, manufacturer, supplier or installer of radio equipment or telecommunications terminal equipment, or a network operator or a service provider, nor the authorised representative of any of such parties. They must be independent and not become directly involved in the design, construction, marketing or maintenance of radio equipment or telecommunications terminal equipment, nor represent the parties engaged in these activities. This does not preclude the possibility of exchanges of technical information between the manufacturer and the notified body.

2. The notified body and its staff must carry out the tasks for which the notified body has been designated with the highest degree of professional integrity and technical competence and must be free from all pressures and inducements, particularly financial, which might influence their judgement or the results of any inspection, especially from persons or groups of persons with an interest in such results.

3. The notified body must have at its disposal the necessary staff and facilities to enable it to perform properly the administrative and technical work associated with the tasks for which it has been designated.

4. The staff responsible for inspections must have:

    -   sound technical and professional training,

    -   satisfactory knowledge of the requirements of the tests or inspections that are carried out and adequate experience of such tests or inspections,

    -   the ability to draw up the certificates, records and reports required to authenticate the performance of the inspections.

5. The impartiality of inspection staff must be guaranteed. Their remuneration must not depend on the number of tests or inspections carried out nor on the results of such inspections.

6. The notified body must take out liability insurance unless its liability is assumed by the Member State in accordance with national law, or the Member State itself is directly responsible.

7. The staff of the notified body is bound to observe professional secrecy with regard to all information gained in carrying out its tasks (except vis-à-vis the competent administrative authorities of the Member State in which its activities are carried out) under this Directive or any provision of national law giving effect thereto.

ANNEX VII

Marking of equipment referred to in Article 12(1)

1. The CE conformity marking must consist of the initials "CE" taking the following form:

If the CE marking is reduced or enlarged, the proportions given in the above graduated drawing must be respected.

2. The CE marking must have a height of at least 5 mm except where this is not possible on account of the nature of the apparatus.

3. The CE marking must be affixed to the product or to its data plate. Additionally it must be affixed to the packaging, if any, and to the accompanying documents.

4. The CE marking must be affixed visibly, legibly and indelibly.

5. The equipment class identifier must take a form to be decided by the Commission in accordance with the procedure laid down in Article 14.

   Where appropriate it must include an element intended to provide information to the user that the apparatus makes use of radio frequency bands where their use is not harmonised throughout the Community.

   It must have the same height as the initials "CE".

JOINT DECLARATION OF THE EUROPEAN PARLIAMENT, THE COUNCIL AND THE COMMISSION

The European Parliament, the Council and the Commission recognise the importance of the requirement relating to the prevention of harm to the network or its functioning which causes an unacceptable degradation of service taking into account in particular the need to safeguard the interests of the consumer.

Therefore, they note that the Commission will carry out a continuous assessment of the situation in order to evaluate whether that risk occurs frequently and, in such a case, to find an appropriate solution in the framework of the Committee acting in accordance with the procedure laid down in Article 15.

Such a solution will, where appropriate, consist of the systematic application of the essential requirement provided for in Article 3(3)(b).

Furthermore, the European Parliament, the Council and the Commission state that the procedure described above applies without prejudice to the possibilities foreseen in Article 7(5) and to the development of voluntary certification and marking schemes to prevent either the degradation of service or any harm to the network.

DIRECTIVE 98/34/EC OF THE EUROPEAN PARLIAMENT AND OF THE COUNCIL

of 22 June 1998

laying down a procedure for the provision of information in the field of technical standards and regulations and of rules on Information Society services

[as amended][a]

THE EUROPEAN PARLIAMENT AND THE COUNCIL OF THE EUROPEAN UNION,

Having regard to the Treaty establishing the European Community, and in particular Articles 100a, 213 and 43 thereof,

Having regard to the proposal from the Commission[1],

Having regard to the opinion of the Economic and Social Committee[2],

Acting in accordance with the procedure laid down in Article 189b of the Treaty[3],

(1) Whereas Council Directive 83/189/EEC of 28 March 1983 laying down a procedure for the provision of information in the field of technical standards and regulations[4] has been variously and substantially amended; whereas for reasons of clarity and rationality the said Directive should be consolidated;

(2) Whereas the internal market comprises an area without internal frontiers in which the free movement of goods, persons, services and capital is ensured; whereas, therefore, the prohibition of quantitative restrictions on the movement of goods and of measures having an equivalent effect is one of the basic principles of the Community;

(3) Whereas in order to promote the smooth functioning of the internal market, as much transparency as possible should be ensured as regards national initiatives for the establishment of technical standards or regulations;

(4) Whereas barriers to trade resulting from technical regulations relating to products may be allowed only where they are necessary in order to meet essential requirements and have an objective in the public interest of which they constitute the main guarantee;

(5) Whereas it is essential for the Commission to have the necessary information at its disposal before the adoption of technical provisions; whereas, consequently, the Member States which are required to facilitate the achievement of its task pursuant to Article 5 of the Treaty must notify it of their projects in the field of technical regulations;

(6) Whereas all the Member States must also be informed of the technical regulations contemplated by any one Member State;

(7) Whereas the aim of the internal market is to create an environment that is conducive to the competitiveness of undertakings; whereas increased provision of information is

---

[1] OJ C 78, 12.3.1997, p. 4.
[2] OJ C 133, 28.4.1997, p. 5.
[3] Opinion of the European Parliament of 17 September 1997 (OJ C 304, 6.10.1997, p. 79), Council Common Position of 23 February 1998 (OJ C 110, 8.4.1998, p. 1) and Decision of the European Parliament of 30 April 1998 (OJ C 152, 18.5.1998). Decision of the Council of 28 May 1998.
[4] OJ L 109, 26.4.1983, p. 8. Directive as last amended by Commission Decision 96/139/EC (OJ L 32, 10.2.1996, p. 31).

one way of helping undertakings to make more of the advantages inherent in this market; whereas it is therefore necessary to enable economic operators to give their assessment of the impact of the national technical regulations proposed by other Member States, by providing for the regular publication of the titles of notified drafts and by means of the provisions relating to the confidentiality of such drafts;

(8) Whereas it is appropriate, in the interests of legal certainty, that Member States publicly announce that a national technical regulation has been adopted in accordance with the formalities laid down in this Directive;

(9) Whereas, as far as technical regulations for products are concerned, the measures designed to ensure the proper functioning or the continued development of the market include greater transparency of national intentions and a broadening of the criteria and conditions for assessing the potential effect of the proposed regulations on the market;

(10) Whereas it is therefore necessary to assess all the requirements laid down in respect of a product and to take account of developments in national practices for the regulation of products;

(11) Whereas requirements, other than technical specifications, referring to the life cycle of a product after it has been placed on the market are liable to affect the free movement of that product or to create obstacles to the proper functioning of the internal market;

(12) Whereas it is necessary to clarify the concept of a *de facto* technical regulation; whereas, in particular, the provisions by which the public authority refers to technical specifications or other requirements, or encourages the observance thereof, and the provisions referring to products with which the public authority is associated, in the public interest, have the effect of conferring on such requirements or specifications a more binding value than they would otherwise have by virtue of their private origin;

(13) Whereas the Commission and the Member States must also be allowed sufficient time in which to propose amendments to a contemplated measure, in order to remove or reduce any barriers which it might create to the free movement of goods;

(14) Whereas the Member State concerned must take account of these amendments when formulating the definitive text of the measure envisaged;

(15) Whereas it is inherent in the internal market that, in particular where the principle of mutual recognition cannot be implemented by the Member States, the Commission adopts or proposes the adoption of binding Community acts; whereas a specific temporary standstill period has been established in order to prevent the introduction of national measures from compromising the adoption of binding Community acts by the Council or the Commission in the same field;

(16) Whereas the Member State in question must, pursuant to the general obligations laid down in Article 5 of the Treaty, defer implementation of the contemplated measure for a period sufficient to allow either a joint examination of the proposed amendments or the preparation of a proposal for a binding act of the Council or the adoption of a binding act of the Commission; whereas the time limits laid down in the Agreement of the representatives of the Governments of the Member States meeting within the Council of 28 May 1969 providing for standstill and notification to the Commission[5], as amended by the Agreement of 5 March 1973[6], have proved inadequate in the cases concerned and should accordingly be extended;

---

[5] OJ C 76, 17.6.1969, p. 9.
[6] OJ C 9, 15.3.1973, p. 3.

(17) Whereas the procedure concerning the standstill arrangement and notification of the Commission contained in the abovementioned agreement of 28 May 1969 remains applicable to products subject to that procedure which are not covered by this Directive;

(18) Whereas, with a view to facilitating the adoption of Community measures by the Council, Member States should refrain from adopting technical regulations once the Council has adopted a common position on a Commission proposal concerning that sector;

(19) Whereas, in practice, national technical standards may have the same effects on the free movement of goods as technical regulations;

(20) Whereas it would therefore appear necessary to inform the Commission of draft standards under similar conditions to those which apply to technical regulations; whereas, pursuant to Article 213 of the Treaty, the Commission may, within the limits and under the conditions laid down by the Council in accordance with the provisions of the Treaty, collect any information and carry out any checks required for the performance of the tasks entrusted to it;

(21) Whereas it is also necessary for the Member States and the standards institutions to be informed of standards contemplated by standards institutions in the other Member States;

(22) Whereas systematic notification is actually necessary only in the case of new subjects for standardisation and in so far as the treatment of these subjects at national level may give rise to differences in national standards which are liable to disturb the functioning of the market as a result; whereas any subsequent notification or communication relating to the progress of national activities must depend on the interest in such activities expressed by those to whom this new subject has already been communicated;

(23) Whereas the Commission must nevertheless be able to request the communication of all or part of the national standardisation programmes so that it can review the development of standardisation activity in particular economic sectors;

(24) Whereas the European standardisation system must be organised by and for the parties concerned, on a basis of coherence, transparency, openness, consensus, independence of special interests, efficiency and decision-making based on national representation;

(25) Whereas the functioning of standardisation in the Community must be based on fundamental rights for the national standardisation bodies, such as the possibility of obtaining draft standards, being informed of the action taken in response to comments submitted, being associated with national standardisation activities or requesting the preparation of European standards in place of national standards; whereas it is for the Member States to take the appropriate measures in their power to ensure that their standardisation bodies observe these rights;

(26) Whereas the provisions concerning the standstill arrangements applicable to national standardisation bodies when a European standard is in preparation must be brought into line with the relevant provisions adopted by the standardisation bodies within the framework of the European standardisation bodies;

(27) Whereas it is necessary to set up a Standing Committee, the members of which will be appointed by the Member States with the task of helping the Commission to examine draft national standards and cooperating in its efforts to lessen any adverse effects thereof on the free movement of goods;

(28) Whereas the Standing Committee should be consulted on the draft standardisation requests referred to in this Directive;

(29) Whereas this Directive must not affect the obligations of the Member States concerning the deadlines for transposition of the Directives set out in Annex III, Part B,

HAVE ADOPTED THIS DIRECTIVE:

Article 1

For the purposes of this Directive, the following meanings shall apply:

1. "product", any industrially manufactured product and any agricultural product, including fish products;

2. "service", any Information Society service, that is to say, any service normally provided for remuneration, at a distance, by electronic means and at the individual request of a recipient of services.

    For the purposes of this definition:

    -   "at a distance" means that the service is provided without the parties being simultaneously present,

    -   "by electronic means" means that the service is sent initially and received at its destination by means of electronic equipment for the processing (including digital compression) and storage of data, and entirely transmitted, conveyed and received by wire, by radio, by optical means or by other electromagnetic means,

    -   "at the individual request of a recipient of services" means that the service is provided through the transmission of data on individual request.

    An indicative list of services not covered by this definition is set out in Annex V.

    This Directive shall not apply to:

    -   radio broadcasting services,

    -   television broadcasting services covered by point (a) of Article 1 of Directive 89/552/EC[7]

3. "technical specification", a specification contained in a document which lays down the characteristics required of a product such as levels of quality, performance, safety or dimensions, including the requirements applicable to the product as regards the name under which the product is sold, terminology, symbols, testing and test methods, packaging, marking or labelling and conformity assessment procedures.

    The term "technical specification" also covers production methods and processes used in respect of agricultural products as referred to Article 38(1) of the Treaty, products intended for human and animal consumption, and medicinal products as defined in

---

[7] OJ L 298, 17.10.1989, p. 23. Directive as last amended by Directive 97/36/EC (OJ L 202, 30.7.1997, p. 1).

Article 1 of Directive 65/65/EEC[8], as well as production methods and processes relating to other products, where these have an effect on their characteristics;

4.   "other requirements", a requirement, other than a technical specification, imposed on a product for the purpose of protecting, in particular, consumers or the environment, and which affects its life cycle after it has been placed on the market, such as conditions of use, recycling, reuse or disposal, where such conditions can significantly influence the composition or nature of the product or its marketing;

5.   "rule on services", requirement of a general nature relating to the taking-up and pursuit of service activities within the meaning of point 2, in particular provisions concerning the service provider, the services and the recipient of services, excluding any rules which are not specifically aimed at the services defined in that point.

This Directive shall not apply to rules relating to matters which are covered by Community legislation in the field of telecommunications services, as defined by Directive 90/387/EEC[9].

This Directive shall not apply to rules relating to matters which are covered by Community legislation in the field of financial services, as listed non-exhaustively in Annex VI to this Directive.

With the exception of Article 8(3), this Directive shall not apply to rules enacted by or for regulated markets within the meaning of Directive 93/22/EEC or by or for other markets or bodies carrying out clearing or settlement functions for those markets.

For the purposes of this definition:

-    a rule shall be considered to be specifically aimed at Information Society services where, having regard to its statement of reasons and its operative part, the specific aim and object of all or some of its individual provisions is to regulate such services in an explicit and targeted manner,

-    a rule shall not be considered to be specifically aimed at Information Society services if it affects such services only in an implicit or incidental manner.

6.   "standard", a technical specification approved by a recognised standardisation body for repeated or continuous application, with which compliance is not compulsory and which is one of the following:

-    international standard: a standard adopted by an international standardisation organisation and made available to the public,

-    European standard: a standard adopted by a European standardisation body and made available to the public,

-    national standard: a standard adopted by a national standardisation body and made available to the public;

7.   "standards programme", a work programme of a recognised standardisation body listing the subjects on which standardisation work is being carried out;

---

[8]   Council Directive 65/65/EEC of 26 January 1965 on the approximation of provisions laid down by law, regulation or administrative action relating to medicinal products (OJ 22, 9.2.1965, p. 369/65), Directive as last amended by Directive 93/39/EEC (OJ L 214, 24.8.1993, p. 22).
[9]   OJ L 192, 24. 7. 1990, p. 1. Directive as amended by Directive 97/51/EC (OJ L 295, 29.10.1997, p. 23.

8.   "draft standard", document containing the text of the technical specifications concerning a given subject, which is being considered for adoption in accordance with the national standards procedure, as that document stands after the preparatory work and as circulated for public comment or scrutiny;

9.   "European standardisation body", a body referred to in Annex I;

10.   "national standardisation body", a body referred to in Annex II;

11.   "technical regulation", technical specifications and other requirements or rules on services, including the relevant administrative provisions, the observance of which is compulsory, *de jure* or *de facto*, in the case of marketing, provision of a service, establishment of a service operator or use in a Member State or a major part thereof, as well as laws, regulations or administrative provisions of Member States, except those provided for in Article 10, prohibiting the manufacture, importation, marketing or use of a product or prohibiting the provision or use of a service, or establishment as a service provider.

   De facto technical regulations include:

   -   laws, regulations or administrative provisions of a Member State which refer either to technical specifications or to other requirements or to rules on services, or to professional codes or codes of practice which in turn refer to technical specifications or to other requirements or to rules on services, compliance with which confers a presumption of conformity with the obligations imposed by the aforementioned laws, regulations or administrative provisions,

   -   voluntary agreements to which a public authority is a contracting party and which provide, in the general interest, for compliance with technical specifications or other requirements or rules on services, excluding public procurement tender specifications,

   -   technical specifications or other requirements or rules on services which are linked to fiscal or financial measures affecting the consumption of products or services by encouraging compliance with such technical specifications or other requirements or rules on services; technical specifications or other requirements or rules on services linked to national social security systems are not included.

   This comprises technical regulations imposed by the authorities designated by the Member States and appearing on a list to be drawn up by the Commission before 5 August 1999, in the framework of the Committee referred to in Article 5.

   The same procedure shall be used for amending this list;

12.   "draft technical regulation", the text of a technical specification or other requirement or of a rule on services, including administrative provisions, formulated with the aim of enacting it or of ultimately having it enacted as a technical regulation, the text being at a stage of preparation at which substantial amendments can still be made.

This Directive shall not apply to those measures Member States consider necessary under the Treaty for the protection of persons, in particular workers, when products are used, provided that such measures do not affect the products.

Article 2

1.   The Commission and the standardisation bodies referred to in Annexes I and II shall be informed of the new subjects for which the national bodies referred to in Annex II

have decided, by including them in their standards programme, to prepare or amend a standard, unless it is an identical or equivalent transposition of an international or European standard.

2. The information referred to in paragraph 1 shall indicate, in particular, whether the standard concerned:

    - will transpose an international standard without being the equivalent,

    - will be a new national standard, or

    - will amend a national standard.

    After consulting the Committee referred to in Article 5, the Commission may draw up rules for the consolidated presentation of this information and a plan and criteria governing the presentation of this information in order to facilitate its evaluation.

3. The Commission may ask for all or part of the standards programmes to be communicated to it.

    It shall make this information available to the Member States in a form which allows the different programmes to be assessed and compared.

4. Where appropriate, the Commission shall amend Annex II on the basis of communications from the Member States.

5. The Council shall decide, on the basis of a proposal from the Commission, on any amendment to Annex I.

Article 3

The standardisation bodies referred to in Annexes I and II, and the Commission, shall be sent all draft standards on request; they shall be kept informed by the body concerned of the action taken on any comments they have made relating to drafts.

Article 4

1. Member States shall take all necessary steps to ensure that their standardisation bodies:

    - communicate information in accordance with Articles 2 and 3,

    - publish the draft standards in such a way that comments may also be obtained from parties established in other Member States,

    - grant the other bodies referred to in Annex II the right to be involved passively or actively (by sending an observer) in the planned activities,

    - do not object to a subject for standardisation in their work programme being discussed at European level in accordance with the rules laid down by the European standardisation bodies and undertake no action which may prejudice a decision in this regard.

2. Member States shall refrain in particular from any act of recognition, approval or use by reference to a national standard adopted in breach of Articles 2 and 3 and of paragraph 1 of this Article.

Article 5

A Standing Committee shall be set up consisting of representatives appointed by the Member States who may call on the assistance of experts or advisers; its chairman shall be a representative of the Commission.

The Committee shall draw up its own rules of procedure.

Article 6

1. The Committee shall meet at least twice a year with the representatives of the standards institutions referred to in Annexes I and II.

   The Committee shall meet in a specific composition to examine questions concerning Information Society services.

2. The Commission shall submit to the Committee a report on the implementation and application of the procedures set out in this Directive, and shall present proposals aimed at eliminating existing or foreseeable barriers to trade.

3. The Committee shall express its opinion on the communications and proposals referred to in paragraph 2 and may in this connection propose, in particular, that the Commission:

   - request the European standards institutions to draw up a European standard within a given time limit,

   - ensure where necessary, in order to avoid the risk of barriers to trade, that initially the Member States concerned decide amongst themselves on appropriate measures,

   - take all appropriate measures,

   - identify the areas where harmonisation appears necessary, and, should the case arise, undertake appropriate harmonisation in a given sector.

4. The Committee must be consulted by the Commission:

   (a) before any amendment is made to the lists in Annexes I and II (Article 2(1));

   (b) when drawing up the rules for the consolidated presentation of information and the plan and criteria for the presentation of standards programmes (Article 2(2));

   (c) when deciding on the actual system whereby the exchange of information provided for in this Directive is to be effected and on any change to it;

   (d) when reviewing the operation of the system set up by this Directive;

   (e) on the requests to the standards institutions referred to in the first indent of paragraph 3.

5. The Committee may be consulted by the Commission on any preliminary draft technical regulation received by the latter.

6. Any question regarding the implementation of this Directive may be submitted to the Committee at the request of its chairman or of a Member State.

7. The proceedings of the Committee and the information to be submitted to it shall be confidential.

However, the Committee and the national authorities may, provided that the necessary precautions are taken, consult, for an expert opinion, natural or legal persons, including persons in the private sector.

8. With respect to rules on services, the Commission and the Committee may consult natural or legal persons from industry or academia, and where possible representative bodies, capable of delivering an expert opinion on the social and societal aims and consequences of any draft rule on services, and take notice of their advice whenever requested to do so.

Article 7

1. Member States shall take all appropriate measures to ensure that, during the preparation of a European standard referred to in the first indent of Article 6(3) or after its approval, their standardisation bodies do not take any action which could prejudice the harmonisation intended and, in particular, that they do not publish in the field in question a new or revised national standard which is not completely in line with an existing European standard.

2. Paragraph 1 shall not apply to the work of standards institutions undertaken at the request of the public authorities to draw up technical specifications or a standard for specific products for the purpose of enacting a technical regulation for such products.

    Member States shall communicate all requests of the kind referred to in the preceding subparagraph to the Commission as draft technical regulations, in accordance with Article 8(1), and shall state the grounds for their enactment.

Article 8

1. Subject to Article 10, Member States shall immediately communicate to the Commission any draft technical regulation, except where it merely transposes the full text of an international or European standard, in which case information regarding the relevant standard shall suffice; they shall also let the Commission have a statement of the grounds which make the enactment of such a technical regulation necessary, where these have not already been made clear in the draft.

    Where appropriate, and unless it has already been sent with a prior communication, Member States shall simultaneously communicate the text of the basic legislative or regulatory provisions principally and directly concerned, should knowledge of such text be necessary to assess the implications of the draft technical regulation.

    Member States shall communicate the draft again under the above conditions if they make changes to the draft that have the effect of significantly altering its scope, shortening the timetable originally envisaged for implementation, adding specifications or requirements, or making the latter more restrictive.

    Where, in particular, the draft seeks to limit the marketing or use of a chemical substance, preparation or product on grounds of public health or of the protection of consumers or the environment, Member States shall also forward either a summary or the references of all relevant data relating to the substance, preparation or product concerned and to known and available substitutes, where such information may be available, and communicate the anticipated effects of the measure on public health and the protection of the consumer and the environment, together with an analysis of the risk carried out as appropriate in accordance with the general principles for the risk evaluation of chemical substances as referred to in Article 10(4) of Regulation

(EEC) No 793/93[10] in the case of an existing substance or in Article 3(2) of Directive 67/548/EEC[11], in the case of a new substance.

The Commission shall immediately notify the other Member States of the draft and all documents which have been forwarded to it; it may also refer this draft, for an opinion, to the Committee referred to in Article 5 and, where appropriate, to the committee responsible for the field in question.

With respect to the technical specifications or other requirements or rules on services referred to in the third indent of the second subparagraph of point 11 of Article 1, the comments or detailed opinions of the Commission or the Member States may concern only aspects which may hinder trade or, in respect of rules on services, the free movement of services or the freedom of establishment of service operators and not the fiscal or financial aspects of the measure.

2.   The Commission and the Member States may make comments to the Member State which has forwarded a draft technical regulation; that Member State shall take such comments into account as far as possible in the subsequent preparation of the technical regulation.

3.   Member States shall communicate the definitive text of a technical regulation to the Commission without delay.

4.   Information supplied under this Article shall not be confidential except at the express request of the notifying Member State. Any such request shall be supported by reasons.

In cases of this kind, if necessary precautions are taken, the Committee referred to in Article 5 and the national authorities may seek expert advice from physical or legal persons in the private sector.

5.   When draft technical regulations form part of measures which are required to be communicated to the Commission at the draft stage under another Community act, Member States may make a communication within the meaning of paragraph 1 under that other act, provided that they formally indicate that the said communication also constitutes a communication for the purposes of this Directive.

The absence of a reaction from the Commission under this Directive to a draft technical regulation shall not prejudice any decision which might be taken under other Community acts.

Article 9

1.   Member States shall postpone the adoption of a draft technical regulation for three months from the date of receipt by the Commission of the communication referred to in Article 8(1).

2.   Member States shall postpone:

---

[10] Council Regulation (EEC) No 793/93 of 23 March 1993 on the evaluation and control of the risks of existing substances (OJ L 84, 5.4.1993, p. 1).

[11] Council Directive 67/548/EEC of 27 June 1967 on the approximation of the laws, regulations and administrative provisions relating to the classification, packaging and labelling of dangerous substances (OJ L 196, 16.8.1967, p. 1). Directive, as amended by Directive 92/32/EEC, (OJ L 154, 5.6.1992, p. 1).

-       for four months the adoption of a draft technical regulation in the form of a voluntary agreement within the meaning of the second indent of the second subparagraph of point 11 of Article 1,

-       without prejudice to paragraphs 3, 4 and 5, for six months the adoption of any other draft technical regulation (except for draft rules on services),

from the date of receipt by the Commission of the communication referred to in Article 8(1) if the Commission or another Member State delivers a detailed opinion, within three months of that date, to the effect that the measure envisaged may create obstacles to the free movement of goods within the internal market;

-       without prejudice to paragraphs 4 and 5, for four months the adoption of any draft rule on services, from the date of receipt by the Commission of the communication referred to in Article 8(1) if the Commission or another Member State delivers a detailed opinion, within three months of that date, to the effect that the measure envisaged may create obstacles to the free movement of services or to the freedom of establishment of service operators within the internal market.

With regard to draft rules on services, detailed opinions from the Commission or Member States may not affect any cultural policy measures, in particular in the audiovisual sphere, which Member States might adopt in accordance with Community law, taking account of their linguistic diversity, their specific national and regional characteristics and their cultural heritage.

The Member State concerned shall report to the Commission on the action it proposes to take on such detailed opinions. The Commission shall comment on this reaction.

With respect to rules on services, the Member State concerned shall indicate, where appropriate, the reasons why the detailed opinions cannot be taken into account.

3.   With the exclusion of draft rules relating to services, Member States shall postpone the adoption of a draft technical regulation for twelve months from the date of receipt by the Commission of the communication referred to in Article 8(1) if, within three months of that date, the Commission announces its intention of proposing or adopting a directive, regulation or decision on the matter in accordance with Article 189 of the Treaty.

4.   Member States shall postpone the adoption of a draft technical regulation for 12 months from the date of receipt by the Commission of the communication referred to in Article 8(1) if, within the three months following that date, the Commission announces its finding that the draft technical regulation concerns a matter which is covered by a proposal for a directive, regulation or decision presented to the Council in accordance with Article 189 of the Treaty.

5.   If the Council adopts a common position during the standstill period referred to in paragraphs 3 and 4, that period shall, subject to paragraph 6, be extended to 18 months.

6.   The obligations referred to in paragraphs 3, 4 and 5 shall lapse:

-       when the Commission informs the Member States that it no longer intends to propose or adopt a binding Community act,

-       when the Commission informs the Member States of the withdrawal of its draft or proposal,

-       when the Commission or the Council has adopted a binding Community act.

7. Paragraphs 1 to 5 shall not apply in cases where:

- for urgent reasons, occasioned by serious and unforeseeable circumstances relating to the protection of public health or safety, the protection of animals or the preservation of plants, and for rules on services, also for public policy, notably the protection of minors, a Member State is obliged to prepare technical regulations in a very short space of time in order to enact and introduce them immediately without any consultations being possible or

- for urgent reasons occasioned by serious circumstances relating to the protection of the security and the integrity of the financial system, notably the protection of depositors, investors and insured persons, a Member State is obliged to enact and implement rules on financial services immediately.

In the communication referred to in Article 8, the Member State shall give reasons for the urgency of the measures taken. The Commission shall give its views on the communication as soon as possible. It shall take appropriate action in cases where improper use is made of this procedure. The European Parliament shall be kept informed by the Commission.

Article 10

1. Articles 8 and 9 shall not apply to those laws, regulations and administrative provisions of the Member States or voluntary agreements by means of which Member States:

- comply with binding Community acts which result in the adoption of technical specifications or rules on services,

- fulfil the obligations arising out of international agreements which result in the adoption of common technical specifications or rules on services in the Community,

- make use of safeguard clauses provided for in binding Community acts,

- apply Article 8(1) of Directive 92/59/EEC[12],

- restrict themselves to implementing a judgment of the Court of Justice of the European Communities,

- restrict themselves to amending a technical regulation within the meaning of point 11 of Article 1, in accordance with a Commission request, with a view to removing an obstacle to trade or, in the case of rules on services, to the free movement of services or the freedom of establishment of service operators.

2. Article 9 shall not apply to the laws, regulations and administrative provisions of the Member States prohibiting manufacture insofar as they do not impede the free movement of products.

3. Paragraphs 3 to 6 of Article 9 shall not apply to the voluntary agreements referred to in the second indent of the second subparagraph of point 11 of Article 1.

4. Article 9 shall not apply to the technical specifications or other requirements or the rules on services referred to in the third indent of the second subparagraph of point 11 of Article 1.

---

[12] Council Directive 92/59/EEC of 29 June 1992 on general product safety (OJ L 228, 11.8.1992, p. 24).

Article 11

The Commission shall report every two years to the European Parliament, the Council and the Economic and Social Committee on the results of the application of this Directive. Lists of standardisation work entrusted to the European standardisation organisations pursuant to this Directive, as well as statistics on the notifications received, shall be published on an annual basis in the *Official Journal of the European Communities*.

Article 12

When Member States adopt a technical regulation, it shall contain a reference to this Directive or shall be accompanied by such reference on the occasion of its official publication. The methods of making such reference shall be laid down by Member States.

Article 13

1.   The Directives and Decisions listed in Annex III, Part A are hereby repealed without prejudice to the obligations of the Member States concerning the deadlines for transposition of the said Directives, set out in Annex III, Part B.

2.   References to the repealed directives and decisions shall be construed as references to this Directive and shall be read in accordance with the correlation table set out in Annex IV.

Article 14

This Directive shall enter into force on the 20th day following that of its publication in the *Official Journal of the European Communities*.

Article 15

This Directive is addressed to the Member States.

———————

Editors' Notes:

[a] Directive 98/34/EEC (OJ L 204, 21.7.1998, p. 37) is reproduced in this book as amended by Directive 98/48/EEC of 20 July 1998 (OJ L 217, 5.8.1997, p. 18) and the Act concerning the conditions of accession of the Czech Republic, the Republic of Estonia, the Republic of Cyprus, the Republic of Latvia, the Republic of Lithuania, the Republic of Hungary, the Republic of Malta, the Republic of Poland, the Republic of Slovenia and the Slovak Republic and the adjustments to the Treaties on which the European Union is founded.

<u>European Standardisation Bodies</u>

CEN

European Committee for Standardisation

Cenelec

European Committee for Electrotechnical Standardisation

ETSI

European Telecommunications Standards Institute

<u>National Standardisation Bodies</u>

1. BELGIUM

    IBN/BIN
    Institut belge de normalisation
    Belgisch Instituut voor Normalisatie

    CEB/BEC
    Comité électrotechnique belge
    Belgisch Elektrotechnisch Comité

2. CZECH REPUBLIC

    ČSNI
    Český normalizační institut

3. DENMARK

    DS
    Dansk Standard

    NTA
    Telestyrelsen, National Telecom Agency

4. GERMANY

    DIN
    Deutsches Institut für Normung e.V.

    DKE
    Deutsche Elektrotechnische Kommission im DIN und VDE

5. ESTONIA

    EVS
    Eesti Standardikeskus

    Sideamet

6. GREECE

    ΕΛΟΤ
    Ελληνικός Οργανισμός Τυποποίησης

7. SPAIN

    AENOR
    Asociación Española de Normalización y Certificación

8. FRANCE

    AFNOR
    Association française de normalisation

    UTE
    Union technique de l'électricité - Bureau de normalisation auprès de l'AFNOR

9. IRELAND

    NSAI
    National Standards Authority of Ireland

    ETCI
    Electrotechnical Council of Ireland

10. ITALY

    UNI[1]
    Ente nazionale italiano di unificazione

    CEI[1]
    Comitato elettrotecnico italiano

11. CYPRUS

    ΚΟΠΠ
    Κυπριακός Οργανισμός Προώθησης Ποιότητας
    (The Cyprus Organisation for Quality Promotion)

12. LATVIA

    LVS
    Latvijas Standarts

13. LITHUANIA

    LST
    Lietuvos standartizacijos departamentas

14. LUXEMBOURG

    ITM
    Inspection du travail et des mines

    SEE
    Service de l'énergie de l'État

---

[1] UNI and CEI, in cooperation with the Istituto superiore delle Poste e Telecommunicazioni and the ministero dell'Industria, have allocated the work within ETSI to CONCIT, Comitato nazionale di coordinamento per le tecnologie dell'informazione.

15. HUNGARY

    MSZT
    Magyar Szabványügyi Testület

16. MALTA

    MSA
    L-Awtorita' ta' Malta dwar l-Istandards (Malta Standards Authority)

17. NETHERLANDS

    NNI
    Nederlands Normalisatie Instituut

    NEC
    Nederlands Elektrotechnisch Comité

18. AUSTRIA

    ÖN
    Österreichisches Normungsinstitut

    ÖVE
    Österreichischer Verband für Elektrotechnik

19. POLAND

    PKN
    Polski Komitet Normalizacyjny

20. PORTUGAL

    IPQ
    Instituto Português da Qualidade

21. SLOVENIA

    SIST
    Slovenski inštitut za standardizacijo

22. SLOVAKIA

    SÚTN
    Slovenský ústav technickej normalizácie

23. FINLAND

    SFS
    Suomen Standardisoimisliitto SFS ry
    Finlands Standardiseringsförbund SFS rf

THK/TFC
Telehallintokeskus
Teleförvaltningscentralen

SESKO
Suomen Sähköteknillinen Standardisoimisyhdistys SESKO ry
Finlands Elektrotekniska Standardiseringsförening SESKO rf

24. SWEDEN

SIS
Standardiseringen i Sverige

SEK
Svenska elektriska kommissionen

ITS
Informationstekniska standardiseringen

25. UNITED KINGDOM

BSI
British Standards Institution

BEC
British Electrotechnical Committee

ANNEX III

Part A

Repealed Directives and Decisions

(referred to by Article 13)

Directive 83/189/EEC and its following amendments

Council Directive 88/182/EEC

Commission Decision 90/230/EEC

Commission Decision 92/400/EEC

Directive 94/10/EC of the European Parliament and Council

Commission Decision 96/139/EC

Part B

List of deadlines for transposition into national law

(referred to in Article 13)

Directive	Deadline for transposition
83/189/EEC (OJ L 109, 26.4.1983, p. 8)	31.3.1984
88/182/EEC (OJ L 81, 26.3.1988, p. 75)	1.1.1989
94/10/EC (OJ L 100, 19.4.1994 p. 30)	1.7.1995

Correlation Table

Directive 83/189/EEC	This Directive
Article 1	Article 1
Article 2	Article 2
Article 3	Article 3
Article 4	Article 4
Article 5	Article 5
Article 6	Article 6
Article 7	Article 7
Article 8	Article 8
Article 9	Article 9
Article 10	Article 10
Article 11	Article 11
Article 12	Article 12
-	Article 13
-	Article 14
-	Article 15
Annex I	Annex I
Annex II	Annex II
-	Annex III
-	Annex IV

ANNEX V

<u>Indicative list of services not covered by the
second sub-paragraph of point 2 of Article 1</u>

1.   Services not provided "at a distance"

Services provided in the physical presence of the provider and the recipient, even if they involve the use of electronic devices

    (a)   medical examinations or treatment at a doctor's surgery using electronic equipment where the patient is physically present;

    (b)   consultation of an electronic catalogue in a shop with the customer on site;

    (c)   plane ticket reservation at a travel agency in the physical presence of the customer by means of a network of computers;

    (d)   electronic games made available in a video-arcade where the customer is physically present.

2.   Services not provided "by electronic means"

    -    Services having material content even though provided via electronic devices:

       (a)   automatic cash or ticket dispensing machines (banknotes, rail tickets);

       (b)   access to road networks, car parks, etc., charging for use, even if there are electronic devices at the entrance/exit controlling access and/or ensuring correct payment is made,

    -    Off-line services: distribution of CD roms or software on diskettes,

    -    Services which are not provided via electronic processing/inventory systems:

       (a)   voice telephony services;

       (b)   telefax/telex services;

       (c)   services provided via voice telephony or fax;

       (d)   telephone/telefax consultation of a doctor;

       (e)   telephone/telefax consultation of a lawyer;

       (f)   telephone/telefax direct marketing.

3.   Services not supplied "at the individual request of a recipient of services"

Services provided by transmitting data without individual demand for simultaneous reception by an unlimited number of individual receivers (point to multipoint transmission):

(a)   television broadcasting services (including near-video on-demand services), covered by point (a) of Article 1 of Directive 89/552/EEC;

(b)   radio broadcasting services;

(c)   (televised) teletext.

ANNEX VI

<u>Indicative list of the financial services covered by the third
sub-paragraph of point 5 of Article 1</u>

-     Investment services

-     Insurance and reinsurance operations

-     Banking services

-     Operations relating to pension funds

-     Services relating to dealings in futures or options

Such services include in particular:

(a)   investment services referred to in the Annex to Directive 93/22/EEC[1]; services of collective investment undertakings,

(b)   services covered by the activities subject to mutual recognition referred to in the Annex to Directive 89/646/EEC[2],

(c)   operations covered by the insurance and reinsurance activities referred to in:

-     Article 1 of Directive 73/239/EEC[3],

-     the Annex to Directive 79/267/EEC[4],

-     Directive 64/225/EEC[5],

-     Directives 92/49/EEC[6],

-     Directives 92/49/EEC[7] and 92/96/EEC[8].

----

[1]   OJ L 141, 11.6.1993, p. 27.
[2]   OJ L 386, 30.12.1989, p. 1. Directive as amended by Directive 92/30/EEC (OJ L 110, 28.4.1992, p. 52).
[3]   OJ L 228, 16.8.1973, p. 3. Directive as last amended by Directive 92/49/EEC (OJ L 228, 11.8.1992, p. 1).
[4]   OJ L 63, 13.3.1979, p. 1. Directive as last amended by Directive 90/619/EEC (OJ L 330, 29.11.1990, p. 50).
[5]   OJ 56, 4.4.1964, p. 878/64. Directive as amended by the 1973 Act of Accession.
[6]   OJ L 228, 11.8.1992, p. 1.
[7]   OJ L 228, 11.8.1992, p. 1.
[8]   OJ L 360, 9.12.1992, p. 1.

DECISION NO 676/2002/EC OF THE EUROPEAN PARLIAMENT AND OF THE COUNCIL

of 7 March 2002[a]

on a regulatory framework for radio spectrum policy in the European Community

(Radio Spectrum Decision)

THE EUROPEAN PARLIAMENT AND THE COUNCIL OF THE EUROPEAN UNION,

Having regard to the Treaty establishing the European Community, and in particular Article 95 thereof,

Having regard to the proposal from the Commission[1],

Having regard to the opinion of the Economic and Social Committee[2],

Acting in accordance with the procedure laid down in Article 251 of the Treaty[3].

Whereas:

(1) On 10 November 1999 the Commission presented a communication to the European Parliament, the Council, the Economic and Social Committee and the Committee of the Regions proposing the next steps in radio spectrum policy on the basis of the results of the public consultation on the Green Paper on radio spectrum policy in the context of European Community policies such as telecommunications, broadcasting, transport and research and development (R & D). This Communication was welcomed by the European Parliament in a Resolution of 18 May 2000[4]. It should be emphasised that a certain degree of further harmonisation of Community policy on the radio spectrum is desirable for services and applications, in particular for services and applications with Community or European coverage, and that it is necessary to ensure that the Member States make applicable in the required manner certain decisions of the European Conference of Postal and Telecommunications Administrations (CEPT).

(2) A policy and legal framework therefore needs to be created in the Community in order to ensure coordination of policy approaches and, where appropriate, harmonised conditions with regard to the availability and efficient use of radio spectrum necessary for the establishment and functioning of the internal market in Community policy areas, such as electronic communications, transport and R & D. The policy approach with regard to the use of radio spectrum should be coordinated and, where appropriate, harmonised at Community level, in order to fulfil Community policy objectives efficiently. Community coordination and harmonisation may also help achieving harmonisation and coordination of the use of the radio spectrum at global level in certain cases. At the same time, appropriate technical support can be provided at national level.

(3) Radio spectrum policy in the Community should contribute to freedom of expression, including freedom of opinion and freedom to receive and disseminate information and ideas, irrespective of borders, as well as freedom and plurality of the media.

---

[1] OJ C 365 E, 19.12.2000, p. 256 and OJ C 25 E, 29.1.2002, p. 468.
[2] OJ C 123, 25.4.2001, p. 61.
[3] Opinion of the European Parliament of 5 July 2001 [OJ C 65 E, 14.03.2002, p. 301], Council Common Position of 16 October 2001 (OJ C 9, 11.1.2002, p. 7) and Decision of the European Parliament of 12 December 2001 [OJ C 177 E, 25.07.2002, p. 164]. Council Decision of 14 February 2002.
[4] OJ C 59, 23.2.2001, p. 245.
[5] OJ L 184, 17.7.1999, p. 23.

(4)   This Decision is based on the principle that, where the European Parliament and the Council have agreed on a Community policy which depends on radio spectrum, committee procedures should be used for the adoption of accompanying technical implementing measures.   Technical implementing measures should specifically address harmonised conditions with regard to the availability and efficient use of radio spectrum, as well as the availability of information related to the use of radio spectrum. The measures necessary for the implementation of this Decision should be adopted in accordance with Council Decision 1999/468/EC of 28 June 1999 laying down the procedures for the exercise of implementing powers conferred on the Commission[5].

(5)   Any new Community policy initiative depending on radio spectrum should be agreed by the European Parliament and the Council as appropriate, on the basis of a proposal from the Commission. Without prejudice to the right of initiative of the Commission, this proposal should include, inter alia, information on the impact of the envisaged policy on existing spectrum user communities as well as indications regarding any general radio frequency reallocation that this new policy would require.

(6)   For the development and adoption of technical implementing measures and with a view to contributing to the formulation, preparation and implementation of Community radio spectrum policy, the Commission should be assisted by a committee, to be called the Radio Spectrum Committee, composed of representatives of the Member States and chaired by a representative of the Commission.   The Committee should consider proposals for technical implementing measures related to radio spectrum. These may be drafted on the basis of discussions in the Committee and may in specific cases require technical preparatory work by national authorities responsible for radio spectrum management. Where committee procedures are used for the adoption of technical implementing measures, the Committee should also take into account the views of the industry and of all users involved, both commercial and non-commercial, as well as of other interested parties, on technological, market and regulatory developments which may affect the use of radio spectrum. Radio spectrum users should be free to provide all input they believe is necessary. The Committee may decide to hear representatives of radio spectrum user communities at its meetings where necessary to illustrate the situation in a particular sector.

(7)   Where it is necessary to adopt harmonisation measures for the implementation of Community policies which go beyond technical implementing measures, the Commission may submit to the European Parliament and to the Council a proposal on the basis of the Treaty.

(8)   Radio spectrum policy cannot be based only on technical parameters but also needs to take into account economic, political, cultural, health and social considerations. Moreover, the ever increasing demand for the finite supply of available radio spectrum will lead to conflicting pressures to accommodate the various groups of radio spectrum users in sectors such as telecommunications, broadcasting, transport, law enforcement, military and the scientific community. Therefore, radio spectrum policy should take into account all sectors and balance the respective needs.

(9)   This Decision should not affect the right of Member States to impose restrictions necessary for public order and public security purposes and defence.   Where a technical implementing measure would affect *inter alia* radio frequency bands used by a Member State exclusively and directly for its public security and defence purposes, the Commission may, if the Member State requests it on the basis of justified reasons, agree to transitional periods and/or sharing mechanisms, in order to facilitate the full implementation of that measure. In this regard, Member States may also notify the Commission of their national radio frequency bands used exclusively and directly to pursue public security and defence purposes.

(10) In order to take into account the views of Member States, Community institutions, industry and of all users involved, both commercial and non-commercial, as well as of other interested parties on technological, market and regulatory developments which may affect the use of radio spectrum, the Commission may organise consultations outside the framework of this Decision.

(11) Radio spectrum technical management includes the harmonisation and allocation of radio spectrum. Such harmonisation should reflect the requirements of general policy principles identified at Community level. However, radio spectrum technical management does not cover assignment and licensing procedures, nor the decision whether to use competitive selection procedures for the assignment of radio frequencies.

(12) With a view to the adoption of technical implementing measures addressing the harmonisation of radio frequency allocation and of information availability, the Committee should cooperate with radio spectrum experts from national authorities responsible for radio spectrum management. Building on the experience of mandating procedures gained in specific sectors, for example as a result of the application of Decision No 710/97/EC of the European Parliament and of the Council of 24 March 1997 on a coordinated authorisation approach in the field of satellite personal-communication services in the Community[6] and Decision No 128/1999/EC of the European Parliament and of the Council of 14 December 1998 on the coordinated introduction of a third generation mobile and wireless communications system (UMTS) in the Community[7], technical implementing measures should be adopted as a result of mandates to the CEPT. Where it is necessary to adopt harmonised measures for the implementation of Community policies which do not fall within the remit of CEPT, the Commission could adopt implementation measures with the assistance of the Radio Spectrum Committee.

(13) The CEPT comprises 44 European countries. It drafts technical harmonisation measures with the objective of harmonising the use of radio spectrum beyond the Community borders, which is particularly important for those Member States where the use of radio spectrum may be affected by that of the non-EU members of CEPT. Decisions and measures taken in accordance with this Decision should take account of the specific situation of Member States with external frontiers. Where necessary, the Commission should be able to make the results of mandates issued to CEPT compulsory for Member States, and where the results of such mandates are not available or deemed not acceptable, to take appropriate alternative action. This will in particular provide for the harmonisation of use of radio frequencies across the Community, in line with Directive 2002/21/EC of the European Parliament and of the Council of 7 March 2002 on a common regulatory framework for electronic communications networks and services (Framework Directive)[8] and taking into account the provisions of Directive 2002/20/EC of the European Parliament and the Council of 7 March 2002 on the authorisation of electronic communications networks and services (Authorisation Directive)[9].

(14) The coordinated and timely provision to the public of appropriate information concerning the allocation, availability and use of radio spectrum in the Community is an essential element for investments and policy making. So are technological developments which will give rise to new radio spectrum allocation and management techniques and radio frequency assignment methods. Development of long-term strategic aspects require proper understanding of the implications of how technology

---

[6] OJ L 105, 23.4.1997, p. 4. Decision as amended by Decision No 1215/2000/EC (OJ L 139, 10.6.2000, p. 1).
[7] OJ L 17, 22.1.1999, p. 1.
[8] [OJ L 108, 24.4.2002, p. 33].
[9] [OJ L 108, 24.4.2002, p. 21].

evolves. Such information should therefore be made accessible in the Community, without prejudice to confidential business and personal information protection under Directive 97/66/EC of the European Parliament and of the Council of 15 December 1997 concerning the processing of personal data and the protection of privacy in the telecommunications sector[10]. The implementation of a cross-sectoral radio spectrum policy makes the availability of information on the whole radio spectrum necessary. In view of the general purpose of harmonising radio spectrum use in the Community and elsewhere in Europe, the availability of such information needs to be harmonised at European level in a user-friendly manner.

(15) It is therefore necessary to complement existing Community and international requirements for publication of information on use of radio spectrum. At international level, the reference paper on regulatory principles negotiated in the context of the World Trade Organisation by the Group on Basic Telecommunications also requires that the existing state of allocated radio frequency bands be made publicly available. Commission Directive 96/2/EC of 16 January 1996 amending Directive 90/388/EEC with regard to mobile and personal communications[11] required Member States to publish every year or make available on request the allocation scheme of radio frequencies, including plans for future extension of such frequencies, but covered only mobile and personal communications services. Moreover, Directive 1999/5/EC of the European Parliament and of the Council of 9 March 1999 on radio equipment and telecommunications terminal equipment and the mutual recognition of their conformity[12], as well as Directive 98/34/EC of the European Parliament and of the Council of 22 June 1998 laying down a procedure for the provision of information in the field of technical standards and regulations and of rules on information society services[13], require Member States to notify the Commission of the interfaces which they have regulated so as to assess their compatibility with Community law.

(16) Directive 96/2/EC was at the origin of the adoption of a first set of measures by CEPT such as European Radiocommunications Committee Decision (ERC/DEC/(97)01) on the publication of national tables of radio spectrum allocations. It is necessary to ensure that CEPT solutions reflect the needs of Community policy and are given the appropriate legal basis so as to be implemented in the Community. For that purpose, specific measures have to be adopted in the Community both on procedure and substance.

(17) Community undertakings should obtain fair and non-discriminatory treatment on access to radio spectrum in third countries. As access to radio spectrum is a key factor for business development and public interest activities, it is also necessary to ensure that Community requirements for radio spectrum are reflected in international planning.

(18) Implementation of Community policies may require coordination of radio spectrum use, in particular with regard to the provision of communications services including Community-wide roaming facilities. Moreover, certain types of radio spectrum use entail a geographical coverage which goes beyond the borders of a Member State and allow for transborder services without requiring the movement of persons, such as satellite communications services. The Community should therefore be adequately represented in the activities of all relevant international organisations and conferences related to radio spectrum management matters, such as within the International Telecommunication Union (ITU) and its World Radiocommunications Conferences.

---

[10] OJ L 24, 30.1.1998, p. 1.
[11] OJ L 20, 26.1.1996, p. 59.
[12] OJ L 91, 7.4.1999, p. 10.
[13] OJ L 204, 21.7.1998, p. 37. Directive as amended by Directive 98/48/EC (OJ L 217, 5.8.1998, p. 18).

(19) The existing preparation and negotiation mechanisms for ITU World Radiocommunication Conferences have generated excellent results due to willing cooperation within the CEPT, and the Community's interests have been taken into account in the preparations. In international negotiations, Member States and the Community should develop a common action and closely cooperate during the whole negotiations process so as to safeguard the unity of the international representation of the Community in line with the procedures which had been agreed in the Council conclusions of 3 February 1992 for the World Administrative Radio Conference and as confirmed by the Council conclusions of 22 September 1997 and 2 May 2000. For such international negotiations, the Commission should inform the European Parliament and the Council whether Community policies are affected, with a view to obtaining endorsement by the Council on the Community policy objectives to be achieved and on the positions to be taken by Member States at international level. In order to ensure that such positions also appropriately address the technical dimension related to radio spectrum management, the Commission may issue mandates to the CEPT for this purpose. Member States should accompany any act of acceptance of any agreement or regulation within international fora in charge of, or concerned with, radio spectrum management by a joint declaration stating that they will apply such agreement or regulation in accordance with their obligations under the Treaty.

(20) In addition to international negotiations specifically addressing radio spectrum, there are other international agreements involving the Community and third countries which may affect radio frequency bands usage and sharing plans and which may address issues such as trade and market access, including in the World Trade Organisation framework, free circulation and use of equipment, communications systems of regional or global coverage such as satellites, safety and distress operations, transportation systems, broadcasting technologies, and research applications such as radio astronomy and earth observation. It is therefore important to ensure compatibility between the Community's arrangements for negotiating trade and market access issues with the radio spectrum policy objectives to be pursued under this Decision.

(21) It is necessary, due to the potential commercial sensitivity of information which may be obtained by national authorities in the course of their action relating to radio spectrum policy and management, that the national authorities apply common principles in the field of confidentiality laid down in this Decision.

(22) Since the objective of the proposed action, namely to establish a common framework for radio spectrum policy, cannot be sufficiently achieved by the Member States and can therefore, by reason of the scale and effects of the action, be better achieved at Community level, the Community may adopt measures, in accordance with the principle of subsidiarity as set out in Article 5 of the Treaty. In accordance with the principle of proportionality as set out in that Article, this Decision does not go beyond what is necessary in order to achieve that objective.

(23) Member States should implement this common framework for radio spectrum policy in particular through their national authorities and provide the Commission with the relevant information required to assess its proper implementation throughout the Community, taking into account international trade obligations of the Community and its Member States.

(24) Decisions No 710/97/EC and No 128/1999/EC remain in force.

(25) The Commission should report annually to the European Parliament and the Council on the results achieved under this Decision, as well as on planned future actions. This may allow the European Parliament and the Council to express their political support, where appropriate,

HAVE ADOPTED THIS DECISION:

Article 1

Aim and scope

1. The aim of this Decision is to establish a policy and legal framework in the Community in order to ensure the coordination of policy approaches and, where appropriate, harmonised conditions with regard to the availability and efficient use of the radio spectrum necessary for the establishment and functioning of the internal market in Community policy areas such as electronic communications, transport and research and development (R & D).

2. In order to meet this aim, this Decision establishes procedures in order to:

 (a) facilitate policy making with regard to the strategic planning and harmonisation of the use of radio spectrum in the Community taking into consideration inter alia economic, safety, health, public interest, freedom of expression, cultural, scientific, social and technical aspects of Community policies as well as the various interests of radio spectrum user communities with the aim of optimising the use of radio spectrum and of avoiding harmful interference;

 (b) ensure the effective implementation of radio spectrum policy in the Community, and in particular establish a general methodology to ensure harmonised conditions for the availability and efficient use of radio spectrum;

 (c) ensure the coordinated and timely provision of information concerning the allocation, availability and use of radio spectrum in the Community;

 (d) ensure the effective coordination of Community interests in international negotiations where radio spectrum use affects Community policies.

3. Activities pursued under this Decision shall take due account of the work of international organisations related to radio spectrum management, e.g. the International Telecommunication Union (ITU) and the European Conference of Postal and Telecommunications Administrations (CEPT).

4. This Decision is without prejudice to measures taken at Community or national level, in compliance with Community law, to pursue general interest objectives, in particular relating to content regulation and audio-visual policy, to the provisions of Directive 1999/5/EC and to the right of Member States to organise and use their radio spectrum for public order and public security purposes and defence.

Article 2

Definition

For the purposes of this Decision, "radio spectrum" includes radio waves in frequencies between 9 kHz and 3000 GHz; radio waves are electromagnetic waves propagated in space without artificial guide.

Article 3

Committee procedure

1. The Commission shall be assisted by a committee ("the Radio Spectrum Committee").

2. Where reference is made to this paragraph, Articles 3 and 7 of Decision 1999/468/EC shall apply, having regard to the provisions of Article 8 thereof.

3. Where reference is made to this paragraph, Articles 5 and 7 of Decision 1999/468/EC shall apply, having regard to the provisions of Article 8 thereof.

    The period provided for in Article 5(6) of Decision 1999/468/EC shall be set at three months.

4. The Committee shall adopt its rules of procedure.

Article 4

Function of the Radio Spectrum Committee

1. In order to meet the aim set out in Article 1, the Commission shall submit to the Radio Spectrum Committee, in accordance with the procedures set out in this Article, appropriate technical implementing measures with a view to ensuring harmonised conditions for the availability and efficient use of radio spectrum, as well as the availability of information related to the use of radio spectrum, as referred to in Article 5.

2. For the development of technical implementing measures referred to in paragraph 1 which fall within the remit of the CEPT, such as the harmonisation of radio frequency allocation and of information availability, the Commission shall issue mandates to the CEPT, setting out the tasks to be performed and the timetable therefor. The Commission shall act in accordance with the procedure referred to in Article 3(2).

3. On the basis of the work completed pursuant to paragraph 2, the Commission shall decide whether the results of the work carried out pursuant to the mandates shall apply in the Community and on the deadline for their implementation by the Member States. These decisions shall be published in the Official Journal of the European Communities. For the purpose of this paragraph, the Commission shall act in accordance with the procedure referred to in Article 3(3).

4. Notwithstanding paragraph 3, if the Commission or any Member State considers that the work carried out on the basis of a mandate issued pursuant to paragraph 2 is not progressing satisfactorily having regard to the set timetable or if the results of the mandate are not acceptable, the Commission may adopt, acting in accordance with the procedure referred to in Article 3(3), measures to achieve the objectives of the mandate.

5. The measures referred to in paragraphs 3 and 4 may, where appropriate, provide the possibility for transitional periods and/or radio spectrum sharing arrangements in a Member State to be approved by the Commission, where justified, taking into account the specific situation in the Member State, on the basis of a reasoned request by the Member State concerned and provided such exception would not unduly defer implementation or create undue differences in the competitive or regulatory situations between Member States.

6. To achieve the aim set out in Article 1, the Commission may also adopt technical implementing measures referred to in paragraph 1 which are not covered by paragraph 2, acting in accordance with the procedure referred to in Article 3(3).

7. With a view to contributing to the formulation, preparation and implementation of Community radio spectrum policy, and without prejudice to the procedures set out in this Article, the Commission shall consult the Radio Spectrum Committee periodically on the matters covered by Article 1.

Article 5

Availability of information

Member States shall ensure that their national radio frequency allocation table and information on rights, conditions, procedures, charges and fees concerning the use of radio spectrum, shall be published if relevant in order to meet the aim set out in Article 1. They shall keep this information up to date and shall take measures to develop appropriate databases in order to make such information available to the public, where applicable in accordance with the relevant harmonisation measures taken under Article 4.

Article 6

Relations with third countries and international organisations

1.   The Commission shall monitor developments regarding radio spectrum in third countries and in international organisations, which may have implications for the implementation of this Decision.

2.   Member States shall inform the Commission of any difficulties created, *de jure* or *de facto*, by third countries or international organisations for the implementation of this Decision.

3.   The Commission shall report regularly on the results of the application of paragraphs 1 and 2 to the European Parliament and the Council and may propose measures with the aim of securing the implementation of the principles and objectives of this Decision, where appropriate. When necessary to meet the aim set out in Article 1, common policy objectives shall be agreed to ensure Community coordination among Member States.

4.   Measures taken pursuant to this Article shall be without prejudice to the Community's and Member States' rights and obligations under relevant international agreements.

Article 7

Notification

Member States shall give the Commission all information necessary for the purpose of verifying the implementation of this Decision. In particular, Member States shall immediately inform the Commission of the implementation of the results of the mandates pursuant to Article 4(3).

Article 8

Confidentiality

1.   Member States shall not disclose information covered by the obligation of business confidentiality, in particular information about undertakings, their business relations or their cost components.

2.   Paragraph 1 shall be without prejudice to the right of relevant authorities to undertake disclosure where it is essential for the purposes of fulfilling their duties, in which case such disclosure shall be proportionate and shall have regard to the legitimate interests of undertakings in the protection of their business secrets.

3.   Paragraph 1 shall not preclude publication of information on conditions linked to the granting of rights to use radio spectrum which does not include information of a confidential nature.

Article 9

Report

The Commission shall report on an annual basis to the European Parliament and the Council on the activities developed and the measures adopted pursuant to this Decision, as well as on future actions envisaged pursuant to this Decision.

Article 10

Implementation

Member States shall take all measures necessary, by laws, regulations and administrative provisions, for the implementation of this Decision and all resulting measures.

Article 11

Entry into force

This Decision shall enter into force on the day of its publication in the Official Journal of the European Communities.

Article 12

Addressees

This Decision is addressed to the Member States.

———————————

Editors' Notes:

[a] OJ L 108, 24.4.2002, p. 1. Some citations in the original text have been updated to the current and complete Official Journal citation.

COMMISSION DECISION 2002/622/EC

of 26 July 2002[a]

establishing a Radio Spectrum Policy Group

THE COMMISSION OF THE EUROPEAN COMMUNITIES,

Having regard to the Treaty establishing the European Community,

Whereas:

(1) Decision No 676/2002/EC of the European Parliament and of the Council of 7 March 2002 on a regulatory framework for radio spectrum policy in the European Community[1] (hereinafter the Radio Spectrum Decision) establishes a policy and legal framework in the Community for radio spectrum policy so as to ensure the coordination of policy approaches and, where appropriate, harmonised conditions with regard to the availability and efficient use of the radio spectrum necessary for the establishment and functioning of the internal market in Community policy areas such as electronic communications, transport and Research and Development.

(2) The Radio Spectrum Decision recalls that the Commission may organise consultations in order to take into account the views of Member States, Community institutions, industry and of all radio spectrum users involved, both commercial and non-commercial, as well as of other interested parties on technological, market and regulatory developments which may relate to the use of radio spectrum.

(3) A consultative group to be called the Radio Spectrum Policy Group (hereinafter the Group) should be established. The Group should assist and advise the Commission on radio spectrum policy issues such as radio spectrum availability, harmonisation and allocation of radio spectrum, provision of information concerning allocation, availability and use of radio spectrum, methods for granting rights to use spectrum, refarming, relocation, valuation and efficient use of radio spectrum as well as protection of human health.

(4) The Group should contribute to the development of a radio spectrum policy in the Community that takes into account not only technical parameters but also economic, political, cultural, strategic, health and social considerations, as well as the various potentially conflicting needs of radio spectrum users with a view to ensuring that a fair, non-discriminatory and proportionate balance is achieved.

(5) The Group should gather high-level governmental experts from the Member States and a high level representative of the Commission. The Group could also include observers and invite other persons to attend meetings as appropriate, including regulators, competition authorities, market participants, user or consumer groups. The Group should therefore allow cooperation between Member States and the Commission in such a way as to contribute to the development of the internal market.

(6) As the focal point for addressing radio spectrum policy issues in the context of all relevant Community policies, close operational links should be maintained between the Group and specific groups or committees established for the implementation of sectoral Community policies including transport policy, internal market policy for radio equipment, audiovisual policy, space policy, and communications.

---

[1] OJ L 108,. 24.4..2002, p. 1.

(7) The Radio Spectrum Decision has created a Radio Spectrum Committee to assist the Commission in the elaboration of binding implementing measures addressing harmonised conditions for the availability and efficient use of radio spectrum. The work of the Group should not interfere with the work of the Committee.

(8) In order to guarantee effective discussions, each national delegation attending the Group should have a consolidated and coordinated national view of all policies which affect the use of radio spectrum in that Member State in relation not only to the internal market but also to public order, public security, civil protection and defence policies as the use of radio spectrum for such policies may influence the organisation of radio spectrum as a whole. At present, different national government departments have responsibility over different parts of the radio spectrum.

(9) The Group should consult extensively and in a forward-looking manner on technological, market and regulatory developments relating to the use of radio spectrum with all radio spectrum users involved, both commercial and non-commercial, as well as with any other interested parties.

(10) The use of radio spectrum does not stop at borders and given the forthcoming accession of additional Member States, the Group may be opened to these countries and to countries which are members of the European Economic Area.

(11) CEPT (European Conference of Postal and Telecommunications administrations, comprising 44 European countries) should be invited as observer with the work of the Group considering the impact of the activities of the Group on radio spectrum at a pan-European level and considering the technical expertise gained by CEPT and its affiliate bodies in radio spectrum management. It is also appropriate to draw on such expertise on the basis of mandates to be granted pursuant to the Radio Spectrum Decision in view to the development of technical implementing measures in the areas of radio spectrum allocation and information availability. In view of the importance of European standardisation for the development of equipment using radio spectrum, it is likewise important to associate as observer the European Telecommunications Standardisation Institute (ETSI),

HAS DECIDED AS FOLLOWS:

Article 1

Subject matter

An advisory group on radio spectrum policy, called the Radio Spectrum Policy Group (hereinafter referred to as the Group), is hereby established.

Article 2

Aims

The Group shall assist and advise the Commission on radio spectrum policy issues, on coordination of policy approaches and, where appropriate, on harmonised conditions with regard to the availability and efficient use of radio spectrum necessary for the establishment and functioning of the internal market.

Article 3

Membership

The Group shall be composed of one high level governmental expert from each Member State as well as of a high-level representative from the Commission.

The Commission shall provide the secretariat to the Group.

Article 4

Operational arrangements

At the Commission's request or at its own initiative, the Group shall adopt opinions to be addressed to the Commission, upon consensus or, if not possible, on the basis of a simple majority, each member having one vote except the Commission which shall not vote. Dissenting opinions shall be attached to the adopted opinions. Observers may participate in the deliberation but shall not vote.

The Group shall elect a chairperson from among its members. The Commission may organise the work of the Group into subgroups and expert working groups as appropriate.

The Commission shall convene the meetings of the Group through the secretariat in agreement with the chairperson. The Group shall adopt its rules of procedure upon a proposal from the Commission, by consensus or, in the absence of consensus, by a two-thirds majority vote, one vote being expressed per Member State, subject to the approval of the Commission.

The Group may invite observers, including those from EEA States and those States that are candidates for accession to the European Union, as well as from the European Parliament, CEPT and ETSI, to attend its meetings and it may hear experts and interested parties.

Article 5

Consultation

The Group shall consult extensively and at an early stage with market participants, consumers and end-users in an open and transparent manner.

Article 6

Confidentiality

Without prejudice to the provisions of Article 287 of the Treaty, where the Commission informs them that the opinion requested or the question raised is on a matter of a confidential nature, members of the Group as well as observers and any other person attending shall be under an obligation not to disclose information which has come to their knowledge through the work of the Group, its subgroups or expert working groups. The Commission may decide in such cases that only members of the Group may be present at meetings.

Article 7

Entry into force

This Decision shall enter into force on the day of its publication in the Official Journal of the European Communities.

The Group shall take up its duties on the date of entry into force of this Decision.

_____

Editors' Notes:

[a] OJ L 198, 27.07.2002, p. 49.

COMMISSION RECOMMENDATION 2003/203/EC

of 20 March 2003[a]

on the harmonisation of the provision of public R-LAN access to public electronic
communications networks and services in the Community

THE COMMISSION OF THE EUROPEAN COMMUNITIES,

Having regard to the Treaty establishing the European Community,

Having regard to Directive 2002/21/EC of the European Parliament and of the Council of 7
March 2002 on a common regulatory framework for electronic communications networks
and services (Framework Directive)[1], hereinafter referred to as "the Framework Directive",
and in particular Article 19 thereof,

Whereas:

(1)　　The European Council on 15 and 16 March 2002 in Barcelona advocated fostering
multiple broadband access platforms to the Information Society and stressed the need
to complete the internal market for electronic communications services.

(2)　　In accordance with Article 19(1) of the Framework Directive, the Communications
Committee delivered its favourable opinion on 24 January 2003.

(3)　　As the least onerous authorisation system possible should be used to allow the
provision of electronic communications networks and services, pursuant to Article
3(2) of Directive 2002/20/EC of the European Parliament and of the Council of 7
March 2002 on the authorisation of electronic communications networks and services
(Authorisation Directive)[2], hereinafter referred to as "the Authorisation Directive", the
provision of electronic communications networks or services may, without prejudice
to specific obligations referred to in Article 6(2) or rights of use referred to in Article
5 of that Directive, only be subject to a general authorisation.

(4)　　Pursuant to Article 5(1) of the Authorisation Directive, Member States are required,
where possible, and in particular where the risk of harmful interference is negligible,
not to make the use of radio frequencies subject to the grant of individual rights of
use; furthermore, pursuant to Article 2(1) and Article 4 of Directive 2002/77/EC[3] of
the Commission, Member States shall not adopt or maintain measures limiting the
number of undertakings authorised to provide services or to use radio frequencies
unless they are objective, proportional and non-discriminatory.

(5)　　Pursuant to policy objectives and regulatory principles defined by Article 8 of the
Framework Directive, the national regulatory authorities should take all reasonable
measures to promote competition in the provision of electronic communications
networks, electronic communications services and associated facilities and services by
promoting innovation and by encouraging efficient use and ensuring the effective
management of radio frequencies; national regulatory authorities should also remove
obstacles to the provision of electronic communications networks, associated facilities
and services and electronic communications services at European level.

---

[1]　　OJ L 108, 24.4.2002, p. 33.
[2]　　OJ L 108, 24.4.2002, p. 21.
[3]　　Commission Directive 2002/77/EC of 16 September 2002 on competition in the markets for electronic
communications networks and services (OJ L 249, 17.9.2002, p. 21).

(6) Radio Local Area Networks (R-LAN) are an innovative means for the provision of broadband wireless access to the Internet and to corporate intranet networks not only for private uses but also for the public in general in areas such as airports, train stations and shopping malls.

(7) A majority of Member States already allow R-LAN access to public electronic communications networks and services on a commercial or non-commercial basis; considering the importance of R-LAN as an alternative platform for broadband access to Information Society services, it is now desirable to promote a harmonised approach for the provision of such public R-LAN access throughout the Community; a distinction is to be drawn between the provision of services and the use of radio spectrum; the provision of R-LAN access to public electronic communications networks and services on a commercial basis should be allowed under the least onerous system, i.e. to the extent possible without any sector specific conditions.

(8) R-LAN may use all or part of either the 2400,0 - 2483,5 MHz (hereinafter the 2,4 GHz band) or the 5150-5350 MHz or 5470-5725 MHz bands (hereinafter the 5 GHz bands); part of these bands may currently not be available to R-LAN in certain Member States; further harmonisation of these bands may therefore be necessary in the framework of Decision 676/2002/EC of the European Parliament and of the Council of 7 March 2002 on a regulatory framework for radio spectrum policy in the European Community (Radio Spectrum Decision)[4].

(9) The risk of interference between the various different users who may share the 2,4 GHz band and between coexisting R-LAN systems is accepted by the parties involved; as long as R-LAN users do not create harmful interference to possible protected users in the same bands, the use of the 2,4 and 5 GHz bands should not be subject to individual rights nor, to the extent possible, to general authorisation conditions other than as allowed under point 17 of the Annex to the Authorisation Directive; opening the 5 GHz band to public R-LAN access services would also reduce the pressure on the 2,4 GHz band.

(10) In order to minimise the risk of harmful interference, general authorisation conditions might be imposed where justified and in a proportionate manner; such general authorisation may refer to appropriate requirements, in conformity with Directive 1999/5/EC of the European Parliament and of the Council of 9 March 1999 on radio equipment and telecommunications terminal equipment and the mutual recognition of their conformity (R& TTE Directive)[5], the harmonisation of which may be achieved pursuant to the Radio Spectrum Decision and the R& TTE Directive.

(11) In line with Community competition rules, Article 8(1) of the Framework Directive lays down the principle of technologically neutral regulation, so that there should be no discrimination between the various R-LAN and other technologies giving access to communications networks and services.

(12) The terms on which access may be allowed to public and private property for providers of public R-LAN access services are subject to competition rules of the Treaty, as well as, where relevant, to the Framework Directive.

(13) Security and confidentiality are regulated at present by Articles 4 and 5 of Directive 97/66/EC of the European Parliament and of the Council of 15 December 1997 concerning the processing of personal data and the protection of privacy in the telecommunications sector[6]; on the forthcoming repeal of that Directive, those

---

[4] OJ L 108, 24.4.2002, p. 1.
[5] OJ L 91, 7.4.1999, p. 10.
[6] OJ L 24, 30.1.1998, p. 1.

provisions will be replaced by Articles 4 and 5 of Directive 2002/58/EC of the European Parliament and of the Council of 12 July 2002 concerning the processing of personal data and the protection of privacy in the electronic communications sector[7] as from 1 November 2003,

HEREBY RECOMMENDS:

1. That, in applying the measures necessary to comply with Directives 2002/20/EC and 2002/21/EC, Member States should allow the provision of public R-LAN access to public electronic communications networks and services in the available 2,4 GHz and 5 GHz bands to the extent possible without sector specific conditions and in any case subject only to general authorisation.

2. That Member States should not make the use of the available 2,4 GHz or 5 GHz bands for the operation of R-LAN systems subject to the grant of any individual right.

3. That Member States should not restrict the choice of R-LAN equipment to be used by service providers where these meet the requirements laid down under Directive 1999/5/EC.

4. That Member States should pay special attention to the requirements of Articles 4 and 5 of Directive 97/66/EC and the equivalent provisions in Directive 2002/58/EC, which regulate security and confidentiality of public communications networks and services.

Editors' Notes:

[a] OJ L 78, 25.02.2003, p. 12.

---

[7]   OJ L 201, 31.7.2002, p. 37.

COMMISSION DECISION

of 11 July 2005[a]

on the harmonised use of radio spectrum in the 5 GHz frequency band for the implementation of
wireless access systems including radio local area networks (WAS/RLANs)

(2005/513/EC)

THE COMMISSION OF THE EUROPEAN COMMUNITIES,

Having regard to the Treaty establishing the European Community,

Having regard to Decision No 676/2002/EC of the European Parliament and of the Council of 7 March 2002 on a regulatory framework for radio spectrum policy in the European Community (radio spectrum Decision)[1], and in particular Article 4(3) thereof,

Whereas:

(1) Commission recommendation 2003/203/EC of 20 March 2003 on the harmonisation of the provision of public R-LAN access to public electronic communications networks and services in the Community[2] recommended Member States to allow the provision of public R-LAN access to public electronic communications networks and services in the available 5 GHz band.

(2) It also considered that further harmonisation in particular of the 5 GHz band would be necessary in the framework of Decision No 676/2002/EC to ensure that the band be available for R-LAN in all Member States and to alleviate the growing overloading of the 2,4 GHz band designated for R-LAN by Decision (01)07 of the European Radio-communications Committee[3].

(3) The relevant parts of the 5 GHz band have been allocated to the mobile service, except aeronautical mobile service, on a primary basis, in all three Regions of the International Telecommunication Union (ITU) by the World Radiocommunication Conference 2003 (WRC-03), taking into account the need to protect other primary services in these frequency bands.

(4) WRC-03 adopted ITU-R Resolution 229 on the Use of the bands 5 150-5 250, 5 250-5 350 MHz and 5 470- 5 725 MHz by the mobile service for the implementation of wireless access systems including radio local area networks' which was an incentive for further European harmonisation to allow R-LAN systems to rapidly access the European Union.

(5) With a view to such harmonisation, a mandate[4] was issued on 23 December 2003 by the Commission to the European Conference of Postal and Telecommunications Administrations (CEPT), pursuant to Article 4(2) of Decision No 676/2002/EC, to harmonise radio spectrum in the 5 GHz band for use by RLANs.

---

[1] OJ L 108, 24.4.2002, P. 1.
[2] OJ L 78, 25.3.2003, p. 12.
[3] ERC Decision (01)07 of 12 March 2001 on harmonised frequencies, technical characteristics and exemption from individual licensing of short range devices used for radio local area networks (RLANs) operating in the frequency band 2 400-2 483,5 MHz.
[4] Mandate to CEPT to harmonise technical and, in particular, operational conditions aiming at efficient spectrum use by RLANs in the bands 5 150-5 350 MHz and 5 470-5 725 MHz.

(6) As a result of that mandate, the CEPT, through its Electronic Communications Committee, has defined in its report[5] of 12 November 2004 and in its Decision ECC/DEC(04)08 of 12 November 2004 specific technical and operational conditions for the use of specific frequencies in the 5 GHz band, which are acceptable to the Commission and the Radio Spectrum Committee and should be made applicable in the Community in order to ensure the development of WAS/RLANs on a harmonised basis in the Community.

(7) WAS/RLAN equipment must fulfil the requirements of Directive 1999/5/EC of the European Parliament and of the Council of 9 March 1999 on radio equipment and telecommunications terminal equipment and the mutual recognition of their conformity[6]. Article 3.2 of this Directive obliges manufacturers to ensure that equipment does not cause harmful interference to other users of the spectrum.

(8) In several Member States, there is an essential need for the operation of military and meteorological radars in the bands between 5 250 and 5 850 MHz which requires specific protection against harmful interference by WAS/RLAN.

(9) There also is a need to specify appropriate equivalent isotropic radiated power limits and operational restrictions, such as indoor use restrictions, for WAS/RLANs in particular in the frequency band 5 150- 5 350 MHz in order to protect systems in the Earth exploration-satellite service (active), space research service (active) and mobile-satellite service feeder links.

(10) As specified in the CEPT report sharing between the radars in the radiodetermination service and WAS/RLANs in the frequency bands 5 250-5 350 MHz and 5 470-5 725 MHz is only feasible with the application of power limits and mitigation techniques that ensure that WAS/RLANs do not interfere with radar applications/systems. Transmitter Power Control (TPC) and Dynamic Frequency Selection (DFS) have therefore been included in the harmonised standard EN 301 893[7] developed by the European Telecommunications Standards Institute (ETSI) to provide presumption of conformity for WAS/RLAN equipment with Directive 1999/5/EC. Transmitter power control (TPC) in WAS/RLANs in the bands 5 250-5 350 MHz and 5 470-5 725 MHz would facilitate sharing with satellite services by significantly reducing the aggregate interference. DFS, which complies with the detection, operational and response requirements set out in Annex I to Recommendation ITU-RM. 1652[8] avoids that WAS/RLANs use frequencies that are in use by radars. The effectiveness of the mitigation techniques in EN 301 893 to protect fixed frequency radars will be monitored. It is subject to review so as to take account of new developments, based on the study by Member States of suitable test methods and procedures for mitigation techniques.

(11) It is recognised at Community and ITU level that there is a need for further studies and the possibility of development of alternative technical/operational conditions for

---

[5] CEPT response to the EC mandate to harmonise technical and, in particular, operational conditions aiming at efficient spectrum use by RLANs in the bands 5 150-5 350 MHz and 5 470-5 725 MHz.

[6] OJ L 91, 7.4.1999, p. 10.

[7] EN 301 893 is a harmonised standard developed by ETSI (European Telecommunications Standards Institute), ETSI Secretariat, entitled Broadband Radio Access Networks (BRAN); 5 GHz high performance RLAN; Harmonised EN covering essential requirements of Article 3.2 of the R&TTE Directive. The ETSI is recognised according to European Parliament and Council Directive 98/34/EC. This harmonised standard has been produced according to a mandate issued in accordance with relevant procedures of European Parliament and Council Directive 98/34/EC. The full text of EN 301 893 can be obtained from ETSI 650 Route des Eucioles F-06921 Sophia Antipolis Cedex.

[8] Recommendation ITU-R M. 1 652 Dynamic frequency selection (DFS) in wireless access systems including radio local area networks for the purpose of protecting the radiodetermination service in the 5 GHz band (Questions ITU-R 212/8 and ITU-R 142/9).

WAS/RLANs, whilst still providing appropriate protection of other primary services in particular radiolocation. Furthermore, it is appropriate for national administrations to perform measurement campaigns and testing to facilitate coexistence between various services. Such studies and development will be taken into account in the future review of this Decision.

(12) The measures provided for in this Decision are in accordance with the opinion of the Radio Spectrum Committee,

HAS ADOPTED THIS DECISION:

Article 1

The purpose of this Decision is to harmonise the conditions for the availability and efficient use of the frequency bands 5 150- 5 350 MHz and 5 470-5 725 MHz for wireless access systems including radio local area networks (WAS/RLANs).

Article 2

For the purposes of this Decision the following definitions shall apply:

(a) 'wireless access systems including radio local area networks (WAS/RLANs)' shall mean broadband radio systems that allow wireless access for public and private applications disregarding the underlying network topology.

(b) 'indoor use' shall mean use inside a building, including places assimilated thereto such as an aircraft, in which the shielding will typically provide the necessary attenuation to facilitate sharing with other services.

(c) 'mean equivalent isotropically radiated power (e.i.r.p.)' shall mean e.i.r.p. during the transmission burst which corresponds to the highest power, if power control is implemented.

Article 3

Member States shall designate by 31 October 2005 at the latest the frequency bands 5150-5 350 MHz and 5 470-5 725 MHz and take all appropriate means relating thereto for the implementation of WAS/RLANs, subject to the specific conditions laid down in Article 4.

Article 4

1. In the frequency band 5 150-5 350 MHz, WAS/RLANs shall be restricted to indoor use with a maximum mean e.i.r.p. of 200 mW.

Furthermore, the maximum mean e.i.r.p. density shall be limited:

(a) to 0,25 mW/25 kHz in any 25 kHz band, in the band 5 150-5 250 MHz and

(b) to 10 mW/MHz in any 1 MHz band, in the band 5 250- 5 350 MHz.

2. In the frequency band 5 470-5 725 MHz, the indoor and outdoor use of WAS/RLANs shall be restricted to a maximum mean e.i.r.p. of 1 W and a maximum mean e.i.r.p. density of 50 mW/MHz in any 1 MHz band.

3. WAS/RLANs operating in the bands 5 250-5 350 MHz and 5 470-5 725 MHz shall employ transmitter power control, which provides, on average, a mitigation factor of at least 3 dB on the maximum permitted output power of the systems.

If transmitter power control is not in use, the maximum permitted mean e.i.r.p. and the corresponding mean e.i.r.p. density limits for the 5 250-5 350 MHz and 5 470-5 725 MHz bands shall be reduced by 3 dB.

4.   WAS/RLANs operating in the bands 5 250-5 350 MHz and 5 470-5 725 MHz shall use mitigation techniques that give at least the same protection as the detection, operational and response requirements described in EN 301 893 to ensure compatible operation with radiodetermination systems. Such mitigation techniques shall equalise the probability of selecting a specific channel for all available channels so as to ensure, on average, a near-uniform spread of spectrum loading.

5.   Member States shall keep mitigation techniques under regular review and report to the Commission thereupon.

Article 5

This Decision is addressed to the Member States.

Editors' Notes:

[a] Notified under document number C(2005) 2467.

COUNCIL DIRECTIVE 87/372/EEC

of 25 June 1987[a]

on the frequency bands to be reserved for the coordinated introduction of public
pan-European cellular digital land-based mobile communications in the Community[b]

THE COUNCIL OF THE EUROPEAN COMMUNITIES,

Having regard to the Treaty establishing the European Economic Community, and in particular Article 100 thereof,

Having regard to the proposal from the Commission[1],

Having regard to the opinion of the European Parliament[2],

Whereas recommendation 84/549/EEC[3] calls for the introduction of services on the basis of a common harmonized approach in the field of telecommunications;

Whereas the resources offered by modern telecommunications networks should be utilized to the full for the economic development of the Community;

Whereas mobile radio services are the only means of contacting users on the move and the most efficient means for those users to be connected to public telecommunications networks;

Whereas mobile communications depend on the allocation and availability of frequency bands in order to transmit and receive between fixed-base stations and mobile stations;

Whereas the frequencies and land-based mobile communications systems currently in use in the Community vary widely and do not allow all users on the move in vehicles, boats, trains, or on foot throughout the Community, including on inland or coastal waters, to reap the benefits of European-wide services and European-wide markets;

Whereas the change-over to the second generation cellular digital mobile communications system will provide a unique opportunity of establishing truly pan-European mobile communications;

Whereas the European Conference of Postal and Telecommunications Administrations (CEPT) has recommended that frequencies 890-915 and 935-960 MHz be allocated to such a system, in accordance with the International Telecommunications Union (ITU) Radio Regulations allocating such frequencies to mobile radio services use as well;

Whereas parts of these frequency bands are being used or are intended for use by certain Member States for interim systems and other radio services;

Whereas the progressive availability of the full range of the frequency bands set out above will be indispensable for the establishment of truly pan-European mobile communications;

Whereas the implementation of Council recommendation 87/371/EEC of 25 June 1987 on the coordinated introduction of public pan-European cellular digital land-based mobile

---

[1]   OJ No C 69, 17.3.1987, p. 9.
[2]   OJ No C 125, 11.5.1987, p. 159.
[3]   OJ No C 298, 16.11.1984, p. 49.

communications in the Community[4], aiming at starting a pan-European system by 1991 at the latest, will allow the speedy specification of the radio transmission path;

Whereas on the basis of present technological and market trends it would appear to be realistic to envisage the exclusive occupation of the 890-915 and 935-960 MHz frequency bands by the pan-European system within 10 years of 1 January 1991;

Whereas Council Directive 86/361/EEC of 24 July 1986 on the initial stage of the mutual recognition of type approval for telecommunications terminal equipment[5] will allow the rapid establishment of common conformity specifications for the pan-European cellular digital mobile communications system;

Whereas the report on public mobile communications drawn up by the Analysis and Forecasting Group (GAP) for the Senior Officials Group on Telecommunications (SOG-T) has drawn attention to the necessity for the availability of adequate frequencies as a vital pre-condition for pan-European cellular digital mobile communications;

Whereas favourable opinions on this report have been delivered by the telecommunications administrations, by the European Conference of Postal and Telecommunications Administrations (CEPT) and the telecommunications equipment manufacturers in the Member States,

HAS ADOPTED THIS DIRECTIVE:

Article 1

1. Member States shall ensure that the 905-914 and 950-959 MHz frequency bands or equivalent parts of the bands mentioned in paragraph 2 are reserved exclusively[6] for a public pan-European cellular digital mobile communications service by 1 January 1991.

2. Member States shall ensure that the necessary plans are prepared for the public pan-European cellular digital mobile communications service to be able to occupy the whole of the 890-915 and 935-960 Mhz bands according to commercial demand as quickly as possible.

Article 2

The Commission shall report to the Council on the implementation of the Directive not later than the end of 1996.

Article 3

For the purposes of this Directive, a public pan-European cellular digital land-based mobile communications service shall mean a public cellular radio service provided in each of the Member States to a common specification, which includes the feature that all voice signals are encoded into binary digits prior to radio transmission, and where users provided with a service in one Member State can also gain access to the service in any other Member State.

---

[4] [OJ No L 196, 17.7.1987, p. 81].
[5] OJ No L 217, 5.8.1986, p. 21.
[6] With the exception of the use of these frequencies for point-to-point connections existing when the Directive enters into force provided they do not interfere with the public pan-European cellular digital mobile communications service and do not prevent its establishment or extension.

Article 4

1.   Member States shall bring into force the provisions necessary to comply with this Directive within 18 months of its notification[7]. They shall forthwith inform the Commission thereof.

2.   Member States shall communicate to the Commission the text of the provisions of national law which they adopt in the field governed by this Directive.

Article 5

This Directive is addressed to the Member States.

Editors' Notes:

[a] OJ L 196, 17.7.1987, p. 85.   Account has been taken of the Corrigendum printed in OJ L 265, 16.09.1987, p. 15. Some citations in the original text have been updated to the current and complete Official Journal citation.

[b] See also Communication from the Commission on the coordinated introduction of the pan-European digital cellular mobile communications system (COM/90/565 final), and Council Resolution of 14 December 1990 on the final stage of the coordinated introduction of pan-European land-based public digital mobile cellular communications in the Community (GSM), OJ C 329, 31.12.1990, p. 25.

---

[7]   This Directive was notified to the Member States on 26 June 1987.

COUNCIL DIRECTIVE 90/544/EEC

of 9 October 1990[a]

on the frequency bands designated for the coordinated introduction
of pan-European land-based public radio paging in the Community

THE COUNCIL OF THE EUROPEAN COMMUNITIES,

Having regard to the Treaty establishing the European Economic Community, and in particular Article 100a thereof,

Having regard to the proposal from the Commission[1],

In cooperation with the European Parliament[2],

Having regard to the opinion of the Economic and Social Committee[3],

Whereas, by Recommendation 84/549/EEC[4], the Council calls for the introduction of services on the basis of a common harmonized approach in the field of telecommunications;

Whereas the resources offered by modern telecommunications networks should be utilized to the full for the economic development of the Community;

Whereas radio paging services depend on the allocation and availability of appropriate frequencies in order to transmit and receive between fixed-base stations and radio paging receivers respectively;

Whereas the frequencies and land-based public radio paging systems currently in use in the Community vary widely and do not allow all users on the move to reap the benefits of European-wide services and European-wide-markets;

Whereas the introduction of the more advanced radio paging system codenamed European Radio Messaging System (Ermes) being specified by the European Telecommunications Standards Institute (ETSI) will provide a unique opportunity of establishing a truly pan-European radio paging service;

Whereas the European Conference of Postal and Telecommunications Administrations (CEPT) has identified the unpaired frequency band 169,4-169,8 MHz as the most suitable band for public radio paging; whereas that choice is in accordance with the provisions of the International Telecommunications Union (ITU) Radio Regulations;

Whereas CEPT Recommendation T/R 25-07 on the coordination of frequencies for the European Radio Messaging System has designated the European channels for the ERMES system;

Whereas parts of the frequency band are being used or are intended for use by certain Member States for other radio services;

Whereas the progressive availability of the requisite part of the frequency band set out above will be indispensable for the establishment of a truly pan-European radio paging service;

---

[1]   OJ No C 43, 23.2.1990, p. 6.
[2]   OJ No C 15, 22.1.1990, p. 84 and OJ No C 231, 17.9.1990, p. 86.
[3]   OJ No C 298, 27.11.1989, p. 27.
[4]   OJ No L 298, 16.11.1984, p. 49.

Whereas some flexibility will be needed in order to take account of different frequency requirements in different Member States; whereas it will be necessary to ensure that such flexibility does not slow down the expansion of a pan-European system;

Whereas coordination procedures will have to be established between neighbouring countries as required;

Whereas the implementation of Council Recommendation 90/543/EEC of 9 October 1990 on the coordinated introduction of pan-European land-based public radio paging in the Community[5] will ensure the start of a pan-European system by 31 December 1992 at the latest;

Whereas on the basis of present technological and market trends, it appears realistic to envisage the designation of the 169,4 - 169,8 MHz frequency band as the band from which frequencies are selected in accordance with commercial requirements for the implementation and expansion of a pan-European radio paging system;

Whereas Council Directive 86/361/EEC of 24 July 1986 on the initial stage of the mutual recognition of type approval for telecommunications terminal equipment[6] will allow the rapid establishment of common conformity specifications for the pan-European land-based public radio paging system;

Whereas the report on public mobile communication drawn up by the Analysis and Forecasting Group (GAP) for the Senior Officials Group for Telecommunications (SOG-T) strongly recommends that telecommunications administrations reach an agreement to use the same radio frequencies for radio paging;

Whereas favourable opinions on this report have been delivered by the telecommunications administrations, by CEPT and by telecommunications equipment manufacturers in the Member States;

Whereas radio paging is a particularly spectrum-efficient communications method for alerting and/or sending messages to users on the move,

HAS ADOPTED THIS DIRECTIVE:

Article 1

For the purposes of this Directive, "pan-European land-based public radio paging service" shall mean a public radio paging service based on a terrestrial infrastructure in the Member States in accordance with a common specification which allows persons wishing to do so to send and/or to receive alert and/or numeric or alphanumeric messages anywhere within the coverage of the service in the Community.

Article 2

1.   Member States shall, in accordance with CEPT Recommendation T/R 25-07 designate in the 169,4 to 169,8 MHz waveband four channels which shall have priority and be protected, and preferably be:

-     169,6 MHz,

-     169,65 MHz,

---

[5]   [OJ L 310, 9.11.1990, p. 23].
[6]   OJ No L 217, 5.8.1986, p. 21.

- 169,7 MHz,

- 169,75 MHz,

for the pan-European land-based public radio paging service by 31 December 1992 at the latest.

2. Member States shall ensure that plans are prepared as quickly as possible to enable the pan-European public radio paging service to occupy the whole of the band 169,4 to 169,8 MHz according to commercial demand.

Article 3

1. Member States shall bring into force the laws, regulations and administrative provisions necessary to comply with this Directive no later than 18 October 1991. They shall forthwith inform the Commission thereof.

2. Member States shall communicate to the Commission the texts of the provisions of national law which they adopt in the field governed by this Directive.

Article 4

The Commission shall report to the Council on the implementation of this Directive not later than the end of 1996.

Article 5

This Directive is addressed to the Member States.

Editors' Notes:

[a] OJ L 310, 9.11.1990, p. 28. Some citations in the original text have been updated to the current and complete Official Journal citation.

COUNCIL DIRECTIVE 91/287/EEC

of 3 June 1991[a]

on the frequency band to be designated for the coordinated introduction
of digital European cordless telecommunications (DECT) into the Community

THE COUNCIL OF THE EUROPEAN COMMUNITIES,

Having regard to the Treaty establishing the European Economic Community, and in particular Article 100a thereof,

Having regard to the proposal from the Commission[1],

In cooperation with the European Parliament[2],

Having regard to the opinion of the Economic and Social Committee[3],

Whereas recommendation 84/549/EEC[4] calls for the introduction of services on the basis of a common harmonized approach in the field of telecommunications;

Whereas the Council in its resolution of 30 June 1988[5] on the development of the common market for telecommunications services and equipment calls for the promotion of Europe-wide services according to market requirements;

Whereas the resources offered by modern telecommunications networks should be utilized to the full for the economic development of the Community;

Whereas Council Directive 89/336/EEC of 3 May 1989 on the approximation of the laws of Member States relating to electromagnetic compatibility[6] is applicable, and particular attention should be taken to avoid harmful electromagnetic interference;

Whereas current cordless telephone systems in use in the Community, and the frequency bands they operate in, vary widely and may not allow the benefits of Europe-wide services or benefit from the economies of scale associated with a truly European market;

Whereas the European Telecommunications Standard Institute (ETSI) is currently developing the European Telecommunications Standard (ETS) or digital European cordless telecommunications (DECT);

Whereas the development of the European Telecommunications Standard (ETS) must take account of the safety of users, and the need for Europe-wide interoperability and enable users provided with a service based on DECT technology in one Member State to gain access to the service in any other Member State, where appropriate;

Whereas the European implementation of DECT will provide an important opportunity to establish truly European digital cordless telephone facilities;

Whereas ETSI has estimated that DECT will require 20 MHz in high density areas;

---

[1] OJ No C 187, 27.7.1990, p. 5.
[2] OJ No C 19, 28.1.1991, p. 97 and OJ No C 106, 22.4.1991, p. 78.
[3] OJ No C 332, 31.12.1990, p. 172.
[4] OJ No L 298, 16.11.1984, p. 49.
[5] OJ No C 257, 4.10.1988, p. 1
[6] OJ No L 139, 23.5.1989, p. 19.

Whereas the European Conference of Postal and Telecommunications Administrations (CEPT) has recommended the common European frequency band 1880-1900 MHz for DECT, recognizing that, subject to the system, development of DECT additional frequency spectrum may be required;

Whereas this should be taken into account in the preparation for the 1992 World Administrative Radio Conference (WARC);

Whereas after the date of designation of the frequency band for DECT, existing services may continue in the band, providing that they do not interfere with DECT systems that may be established according to commercial demand;

Whereas the implementation of Council recommendation 91/288/EEC of 3 June 1991 on the coordinated introduction of DECT into the Community[7], will ensure the implementation of DECT by 31 December 1992 at the latest;

Whereas Council Directive 91/263/EEC of 29 April 1991 on the approximation of the laws of the Member States concerning telecommunications terminal equipment, including the mutual recognition of their conformity[8] will allow the rapid establishment of common conformity specifications for DECT;

Whereas the establishment of DECT depends on the allocation and availability of a frequency band in order to transmit and receive between fixed-base stations and mobile stations;

Whereas some flexibility will be needed in order to take account of different frequency requirements in different Member States;

Whereas it will be necessary to ensure that such flexibility does not slow down the implementation of DECT technology according to commercial demand across the Community;

Whereas the progressive availability of the full range of the frequency band set out above will be indispensable for the establishment of DECT on a Europe-wide basis,

HAS ADOPTED THIS DIRECTIVE:

Article 1

For the purposes of this Directive, the digital European cordless telecommunications (DECT) system shall mean technology conforming to the European Telecommunications Standard (ETS) for digital cordless telecommunications referred to in recommendation 91/288/EEC, and the telecommunications systems, both public and private, which directly utilize such technology.

Article 2

Member States shall, in accordance with CEPT Recommendation T/R 22-02 of the European Conference of Postal and Telecommunications Administration designate the frequency band 1880-1900 MHz for digital European cordless telecommunications (DECT) by 1 January 1992.

---

[7]   [OJ No L 144, 8.6.1991, p.47].
[8]   OJ No L 128, 23.5.1991, p. 1.

In accordance with the CEPT Recommendation, DECT shall have priority over other services in the same band, and be protected in the designated band.

Article 3

1. Member States shall bring into force the laws, regulations and administrative provisions necessary to comply with this Directive by 31 December 1991. They shall forthwith inform the Commission thereof.

2. When Member States adopt these measures, they shall contain a reference to this Directive or shall be accompanied by such reference on the occasion of their official publication. The methods of making such a reference shall be laid down by the Member States.

Article 4

The Commission shall report to the Council on the implementation of this Directive not later than the end of 1995.

Article 5

This Directive is addressed to the Member States.

Editors' Notes:

^a OJ L 144, 8.6.1991, p.45. Some citations in the original text have been updated to the current and complete Official Journal citation.

THE TREATY ESTABLISHING THE EUROPEAN COMMUNITY

ARTICLES 81 AND 82
(Annotated)

Article 81 (ex 85)

1. The following shall be prohibited as incompatible with the common market: all agreements between undertakings, decisions by associations of undertakings and concerted practices which may affect trade between Member States and which have as their object or effect the prevention, restriction or distortion of competition within the common market, and in particular those which:

    (a) directly or indirectly fix purchase or selling prices or any other trading conditions;

    (b) limit or control production, markets, technical development, or investment;

    (c) share markets or sources of supply;

    (d) apply dissimilar conditions to equivalent transactions with other trading parties, thereby placing them at a competitive disadvantage;

    (e) make the conclusion of contracts subject to acceptance by the other parties of supplementary obligations which, by their nature or according to commercial usage, have no connection with the subject of such contracts.

2. Any agreements or decisions prohibited pursuant to this Article shall be automatically void.

3. The provisions of paragraph 1 may, however, be declared inapplicable in the case of:

    -   any agreement or category of agreements between undertakings;

    -   any decision or category of decisions by associations of undertakings;

    -   any concerted practice or category of concerted practices;

    which contributes to improving the production or distribution of goods or to promoting technical or economic progress, while allowing consumers a fair share of the resulting benefit, and which does not:

    (a) impose on the undertakings concerned restrictions which are not indispensable to the attainment of these objectives;

    (b) afford such undertakings the possibility of eliminating competition in respect of a substantial part of the products in question.

Editors' Notes:

The Commission has published general *Guidelines on the application of EEC competition rules in the telecommunications sector* (91/C 233/02) (not reproduced in this book) as well as a *Notice on the application of the competition rules to access agreements in the telecommunications sector* (reproduced at page 565).

See generally *Council Regulation (EC) No 1/2003 of 16 December 2002 on the implementation of the rules of competition laid down in Articles 81 and 82 of the Treaty*, 2003/L 1/1 (not reproduced in this book).

The following is a list of selected Commission decisions under Article 81, annotated by the Editors.

1.   Operator "Alliances"

Uniworld, 1997/L 318/24 (exemption under Art 81(3) of agreement creating AT&T-Unisource JV ("Uniworld") for the provision of pan-European telecommunications services with global connectivity to the European business market, subject to undertakings by Unisource shareholders regarding non-preferential access by Uniworld to Unisource shareholders' domestic networks, cross-subsidisation of Uniworld services from revenues earned by Unisource shareholders in markets where they are dominant, tying, bundling of Uniworld services with services of Unisource shareholders, etc.).

*Unisource,*1997/L 318/1 (exemption under Art 81(3) of agreement between Dutch, Swiss and Swedish incumbents creating JV ("Unisource") for the provision of pan-European data services etc., subject to conditions regarding non- discriminatory access by third parties to Unisource shareholders' networks, cross-subsidisation of Unisource services from revenues earned by Unisource shareholders in markets where they are dominant, tying of Unisource services to services of Unisource shareholders, etc.).   See also *Unisource/Telefónica,* 1995/C 13/3 (addition of Telefonica as fourth Unisource shareholder); and 2001/L 52/30 (1997 exemption repealed on application of Unisource shareholders in light of abandonment of JV).

Phoenix/GlobalOne, 1996/L 239/57 (exemption under Art 81(3) of agreement creating Atlas-Sprint JV ("GlobalOne") for the provision of "non-reserved" services to corporate customers and carriers outside France, Germany and US, subject to conditions regarding non-preferential access by GlobalOne or Sprint to FT's and DT's leased line and PSTN/ISDN services, correspondent services and domestic networks, provision of interconnection to FT's and DT's networks on non-discriminatory terms, structural separation of GlobalOne, cross-subsidisation of GlobalOne by FT and DT, bundling of GlobalOne services with services of FT and DT, etc.).

Atlas, 1996/L 239/23 (negative clearance of appointment of DT-FT JV ("Atlas") as exclusive distributor of "non-reserved" services to corporate customers outside France and Germany, subject to divestiture of Info AG by FT and conditions regarding non-preferential access by Atlas to FT's and DT's leased line and PSTN/ISDN services, provision of interconnection to FT's DT's networks on non-discriminatory terms, etc.; exemption under Art 81(3)).

Concert, 1994/L 223/36 (negative clearance of (i) the acquisition by BT of a 20% equity stake in MCI and (ii) appointment of BT and MCI as exclusive distributors of global value-added and enhanced services to be provided by BT-MCI JV ("Concert"); exemption under Art 81(3)).

2.   Site Sharing

O2 UK/ T-Mobile UK, 2003/L 200/59 ((i) negative clearance of agreement providing for sharing of basic network infrastructure (masts, power supply, racking, etc.) at 3G sites in the UK, and (ii) exemption under Art 81(3) for agreement providing for temporary supply of 3G national roaming by each party to the other party where the latter has a coverage gap in the UK.

T-Mobile Deutschland/O2 Germany, 2004/L 75/32 (negative clearance of agreement for site sharing in Germany and restrictions on resale to voice MVNOs; exemption for agreement for temporary supply of 3G national roaming by T-Mobile to O2 in Germany; exemption of restrictions on resale to voice MVNOs). The latter decision was annulled in part by the Court of First Instance in *O2 (Germany) GmbH & Co. OHG v. Commission, Case T328/03,*

2 May 2006. The Court said that "the [Commission's] Decision, in so far as it concerns the application of Article 81(1) EC and Article 53(1) of the EEA Agreement, suffers from insufficient analysis, first, in that it contains no objective discussion of what the competition situation would have been in the absence of the agreement, which distorts the assessment of the actual and potential effects of the agreement on competition and, second, in that it does not demonstrate, in concrete terms, in the context of the relevant emerging market, that the provisions of the agreement on roaming have restrictive effects on competition, but is confined, in this respect, to a petitio principii and to broad and general statements.

3.   Other

Télécom Développement, 1999/L 218/24 (negative clearance of agreement between Cégétel-SNCF for creation of JV ("TD") to develop and run a national long-distance telecommunications network along the French national railway network, including terms providing for exclusive use by the JV of SNCF optical fibre cable network capacity, the priority use of railway land, exclusive distribution of TD's voice-telephony services to the general public by a Cégétel-TD JV, etc., where these provisions were found to be "directly related and necessary to the successful implementation of the network and operation of TD").

4.   Merger Decisions under Regulation No. 1/2003 and predecessor legislation

T-mobile Austria/Tele.ring, IP/06/535 (declaration that acquisition of Tele.ring by T-mobile compatible with common market, subject to divestiture of UMTS frequencies and mobile telephony sites of Tele.ring to operators with lower market shares than T-Mobile Austria; T-mobile to sell two 5MHz 3G/UMTS frequency blocks licensed to Tele.ring (at least one to be taken by Hutchinson 3G).

O2/Telefónica 2006/C 29/11 (declaration that acquisition of O2 by Telefónica compatible with common market, subject to undertakings by Telefónica that it leave the FreeMove alliance as soon as possible and in any event no later than 30 September 2006 and not re-enter the alliance before 1 January 2011 without the Commission's prior approval).

Telia/Telenor, 2001/L 40/1 (declaration that merger of Telia and Telenor compatible with common market, subject to undertaking by parties to divest voice-telephony services, Internet and data communication services, and cable TV networks and certain other businesses, and unbundle local loops).

Vodafone AirTouch/Mannesmann, 2000/C 141/19 (declaration that merger compatible with common market, subject to undertakings to divest Orange plc, to maintain separate accounts for different entities, not to enter into exclusive roaming agreements within the Group, not to discriminate in retail roaming tariffs and wholesale services vis-á-vis third party operators, etc.).

Vodafone/AirTouch, 1999/C 295/2 (declaration that acquisition of AirTouch by Vodafone compatible with common market, subject to undertaking to divest Vodafone stake in German mobile operator E-Plus).

Worldcom/MCI, 1999/L 116/1 (declaration that merger of Worldcom and MCI compatible with common market, subject to undertaking to divest MCI's Internet and certain related businesses, and enter into collocation, local access and network service agreements with purchaser of divested assets).

BT/MCI II, 1997/L 336/1 (declaration that merger of BT and MCI compatible with common market, subject to undertakings, including commitment that "overlapping" capacity on TAT12/13 will be made available for sale to other international operators on an IRU basis, and divestiture of UK audio-conferencing business).

Article 82 (ex. 86)

Any abuse by one or more undertakings of a dominant position within the common market or in a substantial part of it shall be prohibited as incompatible with the common market in so far as it may affect trade between Member States.

Such abuse may, in particular, consist in:

(a)   directly or indirectly imposing unfair purchase or selling prices or other unfair trading conditions;

(b)   limiting production, markets or technical development to the prejudice of consumers;

(c)   applying dissimilar conditions to equivalent transactions with other trading parties, thereby placing them at a competitive disadvantage;

(d)   making the conclusion of contracts subject to acceptance by the other parties of supplementary obligations which, by their nature or according to commercial usage, have no connection with the subject of such contracts.

Editors' Notes:

See generally *Council Regulation (EC) No 1/2003 of 16 December 2002 on the implementation of the rules of competition laid down in Articles 81 and 82 of the Treaty* 2003/L 1/1 [not reproduced in this volume].

The following is a list of decisions under Article 82, selected and annotated by the Editors.

1.   ECJ Decisions under Article 82

Gibtelecom Limited v. Commission, Case T-244/05, 2005/C 205/65 (action to annul a Commission decision dated 26 April 2005 rejecting a complaint by Gibtelecom alleging that the Spanish telecommunications operator, Telefonica SA, had committed a series of abuses of dominant position contrary to Article 82 (later converted into one under Article 86 , in conjunction with Article 82) by refusing to recognise Gibraltar's International Dialling Code and insisting on acceptance of restrictive conditions for the exchange of automatic direct dial traffic between Spain and Gibraltar).
Italy v. Commission, Case 41/83, [1985] ECR 873 (restrictions imposed by British Telecommunications on the transmission of international messages telex and telephone on behalf of third parties violated Article 82 (b), (c) and (d)).

2.   Commission Decisions under Article 82

Deutsche Telekom, 2003/L 263/9 (DT engaged in abuse of dominant position by pricing access to local loops in a predatory manner).

Wanadoo, Press Release IP/03/1025 (Wanadoo engaged in abuse of dominant position by pricing access to its retail xDSL services in a predatory manner). [Note: An application for annulment of this decision has been commenced: see *France Telecom (Wanadoo Interactive S.A.) v. Commission,* Case T-340/03.]

Omnitel, 1995/L 280/49 (Italy violated art. 82 and art 86 by requiring the second mobile operator to pay a licence fee when no similar fee had been imposed on the incumbent operator). See also *Second Operator of GSM Services in Spain,* 1997/L 76/19, which is to similar effect.

The Commission has issued "statements of objection" in the following matters:

T-Mobile/Vodafone, Press Release IP/05/161 (statement of objections alleging abuses of dominant position in the German market for the provision of international roaming services at wholesale level on each of their networks by charging unfair and excessive prices under inter-operator tariffs to European MNOs).

O2/Vodafone, Press Release IP/04/994 (statement of objections alleging abuses of dominant position in the UK market for the provision of international roaming services at wholesale level on each of their networks by charging unfair and excessive prices under inter operator tariffs to European MNOs).

NOTICE ON THE APPLICATION OF THE COMPETITION RULES TO ACCESS AGREEMENTS IN THE TELECOMMUNICATIONS SECTOR

FRAMEWORK, RELEVANT MARKETS AND PRINCIPLES

(98/C 265/02)

PREFACE

In the telecommunications industry, access agreements are central in allowing market participants the benefits of liberalisation.

The purpose of this notice is threefold:

-   to set out access principles stemming from Community competition law as shown in a large number of Commission decisions in order to create greater market certainty and more stable conditions for investment and commercial initiative in the telecoms and multimedia sectors;

-   to define and clarify the relationship between competition law and sector specific legislation under the Article 100a framework (in particular this relates to the relationship between competition rules and open network provision legislation);

-   to explain how competition rules will be applied in a consistent way across the sectors involved in the provision of new services, and in particular to access issues and gateways in this context.

INTRODUCTION

(1)   The timetable for full liberalisation in the telecommunications sector has now been established, and most Member States had to remove the last barriers to the provision of telecommunications networks and services in a competitive environment to consumers by 1 January 1998[1]. As a result of this liberalisation a second set of related products or services will emerge as well as the need for access to facilities necessary to provide these services. In this sector, interconnection to the public switched telecommunications network is a typical, but not the only, example of such access. The Commission has stated that it will define the treatment of access agreements in the telecommunications sector under the competition rules[2]. This notice, therefore, addresses the issue of how competition rules and procedures apply to access agreements in the context of harmonised EC and national regulation in the telecommunications sector.

(2)   The regulatory framework for the liberalisation of telecommunications consists of the liberalisation directives issued under Article 90 of the Treaty and the harmonisation Directives under Article 100a, including in particular the open network provision (ONP) framework. The ONP framework provides harmonised rules for access and interconnection to the telecommunications networks and the voice telephony services. The legal framework provided by the liberalisation and harmonisation legislation is the background to any action taken by the Commission in its application of the competition rules. Both the liberalisation legislation (the Article 90 Directives)[3] and the harmonisation legislation (the ONP Directives)[4] are aimed at ensuring the attainment of the objectives of the Community as laid out in Article 3 of the Treaty, and specifically, the establishment of 'a system ensuring that competition in the internal market is not distorted' and 'an internal market characterised by the abolition, as between Member States, of obstacles to the free movement of goods, persons, services and capital'.

(3)   The Commission has published Guidelines on the application of EEC competition rules in the telecommunications sector[5]. The present notice is intended to build on those Guidelines, which do not deal explicitly with access issues.

(4)   In the telecommunications sector, liberalisation and harmonisation legislation permit and simplify the task of Community firms in embarking on new activities in new markets and consequently allow users to benefit from increased competition. These advantages must not be jeopardised by restrictive or abusive practices of undertakings: the Community's competition rules are therefore essential to ensure the completion of this development. New entrants must in the initial stages be guaranteed the right to have access to the networks of incumbent telecommunications operators (TOs). Several authorities, at the regional, national and Community levels, have a role in regulating this sector. If the competition process is to work well in the internal market, effective coordination between these institutions must be ensured.

(5)   Part I of the notice sets out the legal framework and details how the Commission intends to avoid unnecessary duplication of procedures while safeguarding the rights of undertakings and users under the competition rules. In this context, the Commission's efforts to encourage decentralised application of the competition rules by national courts and national authorities aim at achieving remedies at a national level, unless a significant Community interest is involved in a particular case. In the telecommunications sector, specific procedures in the ONP framework likewise aim at resolving access problems in the first place at a decentralised, national level, with a further possibility for conciliation at Community level in certain circumstances. Part II defines the Commission's approach to market definition in this sector. Part III details the principles that the Commission will follow in the application of the competition rules: it aims to help telecommunications market participants shape their access agreements by explaining the competition law requirements. The principles set out in this Notice apply not only to traditional fixed line telecommunications, but also to all telecommunications, including areas such as satellite communications and mobile communications.

(6)   The notice is based on the Commission's experience in several cases[6], and certain studies into this area carried out on behalf of the Commission[7]. As this notice is based on the generally applicable competition rules, the principles set out in this Notice will, to extent that comparable problems arise, be equally applicable in other areas, such as access issues in digital communications sectors generally. Similarly, several of the principles contained in the Treaty - will be of relevance to any company occupying a dominant position including those in fields other than telecommunications.

(7)   The present notice is based on issues which have arisen during the initial stages of transition from monopolies to competitive markets. Given the convergence of the telecommunications, broadcasting and information technology sectors[8], and the increased competition on these markets, other issues will emerge. This may make it necessary to adapt the scope and principles set out in this notice to these new sectors.

(8)   The principles set out in this document will apply to practices outside the Community to the extent that such practices have an effect on competition within the Community and affect trade between Member States. In applying the competition rules, the Commission is obliged to comply with the Community's obligations under the WTO telecommunications agreement[9]. The Commission also notes that there are continuing discussions with regard to the international accounting rates system in the context of the ITU. The present notice is without prejudice to the Commission's position in these discussions.

(9)   This notice does not in any way restrict the rights conferred on individuals or undertakings by Community law, and is without prejudice to any interpretation of the Community competition rules that may be given by the Court of Justice or the Court of First Instance of the European Communities. This notice does not purport to be a comprehensive

analysis of all possible competition problems in this sector: other problems already exist and more are likely to arise in the future.

(10)   The Commission will consider whether the present notice should be amended or added to in the light of experience gained during the first period of a liberalised telecommunications environment.

PART I - FRAMEWORK

1.   Competition rules and sector specific regulation

(11)   Access problems in the broadest sense of the word can be dealt with at different levels and on the basis of a range of legislative provisions, of both national and Community origin. A service provider faced with an access problem such as a TO's unjustified refusal to supply (or on reasonable terms) a leased line needed by the applicant to provide services to its customers could therefore contemplate a number of routes to seek a remedy. Generally speaking, aggrieved parties will experience a number of benefits, at least in an initial stage, in seeking redress at a national level. At a national level, the applicant has two main choices, namely (1) specific national regulatory procedures now established in accordance with Community law and harmonised under Open Network Provision (see footnote 4), and (2) an action under national and/or Community law before a national court or national competition authority[10].

(12)   Complaints made to the Commission under the competition rules in the place of or in addition to national courts, national competition authorities and/or to national regulatory authorities under ONP procedures will be dealt with according to the priority which they deserve in view of the urgency, novelty and transnational nature of the problem involved and taking into account the need to avoid duplicate proceedings (see points 23 et seq.).

(13)   The Commission recognises that national regulatory authorities (NRAs)[11] have different tasks, and operate in a different legal framework from the Commission when the latter is applying the competition rules. First, the NRAs operate under national law, albeit often implementing European law. Secondly, that law, based as it is on considerations of telecommunications policy, may have objectives different to, but consistent with, the objectives of Community competition policy. The Commission cooperates as far as possible with the NRAs, and NRAs also have to cooperate between themselves in particular when dealing with cross-border issues[12]. Under Community law, national authorities, including regulatory authorities and competition authorities, have a duty not to approve any practice or agreement contrary to Community competition law.

(14)   Community competition rules are not sufficient to remedy all of the various problems in the telecommunications sector. NRAs therefore have a significantly wider ambit and a significant and far-reaching role in the regulation of the sector. It should also be noted that as a matter of Community law, the NRAs must be independent[13].

(15)   It is also important to note that the ONP Directives impose on TOs having significant market power certain obligations of transparency and non-discrimination that go beyond those that would normally be imposed under Article 86 of the Treaty. ONP Directives lay down obligations relating to transparency, obligations to supply and pricing practices. These obligations are enforced by the NRAs, which also have jurisdiction to take steps to ensure effective competition[14].

(16)   In relation to Article 86, this notice is written, for convenience, in most respects as if there was one telecommunications operator occupying a dominant position. This will not necessarily be the case in all Member States: for example new telecommunications networks offering increasingly wide coverage will develop

progressively. These alternative telecommunications networks may, or may ultimately, be large and extensive enough to be partly or even wholly substitutable for the existing national networks, and this should be kept in mind. The existence and the position on the market of competing operators will be relevant in determining whether sole or joint dominant positions exist: references to the existence of a dominant position in this notice should be read with this in mind.

(17)   Given the Commission's responsibility for the Community's competition policy, the Commission must serve the Community's general interest. The administrative resources at the Commission's disposal to perform its task are necessarily limited and cannot be used to deal with all the cases brought to its attention. The Commission is therefore obliged, in general, to take all organisational measures necessary for the performance of its task and, in particular, to establish priorities[15].

(18)   The Commission has therefore indicated that it intends, in using its decision-making powers, to concentrate on notifications, complaints and own-initiative proceedings having particular political, economic or legal significance for the Community[16]. Where these features are absent in a particular case, notifications will not normally be dealt with by means of a formal decision, but rather a comfort letter (subject to the consent of the parties), and complaints should, as a rule, be handled by national courts or other relevant authorities. In this context, it should be noted that the competition rules are directly effective[17] so that Community competition law is enforceable in the national courts. Even where other Community legislation has been respected, this does not remove the need to comply with the Community competition rules[18].

(19)   Other national authorities, in particular NRAs acting within the ONP framework, have jurisdiction over certain access agreements (which must be notified to them). However, notification of an agreement to an NRA does not make notification of an agreement to the Commission unnecessary. The NRAs must ensure that actions taken by them are consistent with Community competition law[19]. This duty requires them to refrain from action that would undermine the effective protection of Community law rights under the competition rules[20]. Therefore, they may not approve arrangements which are contrary to the competition rules[21]. If the national authorities act so as to undermine those rights, the Member State may itself be liable for damages to those harmed by this action[22]. In addition, NRAs have jurisdiction under the ONP directives to take steps to ensure effective competition[23].

(20)   Access agreements in principle regulate the provision of certain services between independent undertakings and do not result in the creation of an autonomous entity which would be distinct from the parties to the agreements. Access agreements are thus generally outside the scope of the Merger Regulation[24].

(21)   Under Regulation No 17[25], the Commission could be seised of an issue relating to access agreements by way of a notification of an access agreement by one or more of the parties involved[26], by way of a complaint against a restrictive access agreement or against the behaviour of a dominant company in granting or refusing access[27], by way of a Commission own-initiative procedure into such a grant or refusal, or by way of a sector inquiry[28]. In addition, a complainant may request that the Commission take interim measures in circumstances where there is an urgent risk of serious and irreparable harm to the complainant or to the public interest[29]. It should however, be noted in cases of great urgency that procedures before national courts can usually result more quickly in an order to end the infringements than procedures before the Commission[30].

(22)   There are a number of areas where agreements will be subject to both the competition rules and national or European sector specific measures, most notably Internal Market measures. In the telecommunications sector, the ONP Directives aim at establishing a regulatory regime for access agreements. Given the detailed nature of ONP rules and the fact that they may go beyond the requirements of Article 86, undertakings operating in the

telecommunications sector should be aware that compliance with the Community competition rules does not absolve them of their duty to abide by obligations imposed in the ONP context, and vice versa.

2. Commission action in relation to access agreements[31]

(23) Access agreements taken as a whole are of great significance, and it is therefore appropriate for the Commission to spell out as clearly as possible the Community legal framework within which these agreements should be concluded. Access agreements having restrictive clauses will involve issues under Article 85. Agreements which involve dominant, or monopolist, undertakings involve Article 86 issues: concerns arising from the dominance of one or more of the parties will generally be of greater significance in the context of a particular agreement than those under Article 85.

Notifications

(24) In applying the competition rules, the Commission will build on the ONP Directives which set a framework for action at the national level by the NRAs. Where agreements fall within Article 85(1), they must be notified to the Commission if they are to benefit from an exemption under Article 85(3). Where agreements are notified, the Commission intends to deal with some notifications by way of formal decisions, following appropriate publicity in the Official Journal of the European Communities, and in accordance with the principles set out below. Once the legal principles have been clearly established, the Commission then proposes to deal by way of comfort letter with other notifications raising the same issues.

3. Complaints

(25) Natural or legal persons with a legitimate interest may, under certain circumstances, submit a complaint to the Commission, requesting that the Commission by decision require that an infringement of Article 85 or Article 86 of the Treaty be brought to an end. A complainant may additionally request that the Commission take interim measures where there is an urgent risk of serious and irreparable harm[32]. A prospective complainant has other equally or even more effective options, such as an action before a national court. In this context, it should be noted that procedures before the national courts can offer considerable advantages for individuals and companies, such as in particular[33]:

- national courts can deal with and award a claim for damages resulting from an infringement of the competition rules,

- national courts can usually adopt interim measures and order the termination of an infringement more quickly than the Commission is able to do,

- before national courts, it is possible to combine a claim under Community law with a claim under national law,

- legal costs can be awarded to the successful applicant before a national court.

Furthermore, the specific national regulatory principles as harmonised under ONP Directives can offer recourse both at the national level and, if necessary, at the Community level.

3.1. Use of national and ONP procedures

(26) As referred to above[34] the Commission will take into account the Community interest of each case brought to its attention. In evaluating the Community interest, the Commission examines '... the significance of the alleged infringement as regards the functioning of the common market, the probability of establishing the existence of the

infringement and the scope of the investigation required in order to fulfil, under the best possible conditions, its task of ensuring that Articles 85 and 86 are complied with ...'[35].

Another essential element in this evaluation is the extent to which a national judge is in a position to provide an effective remedy for an infringement of Article 85 or 86. This may prove difficult, for example, in cases involving extra-territorial elements.

(27)   Article 85(1) and Article 86 of the Treaty produce direct effects in relations between individuals which must be safeguarded by national courts[36]. As regards actions before the NRA, the ONP Interconnection Directive provides that such an authority has power to intervene and order changes in relation to both the existence and content of access agreements. NRAs must take into account 'the need to stimulate a competitive market' and may impose conditions on one or more parties, inter alia, 'to ensure effective competition'[37].

(28)   The Commission may itself be seised of a dispute either pursuant to the competition rules, or pursuant to an ONP conciliation procedure. Multiple proceedings might lead to unnecessary duplication of investigative efforts by the Commission and the national authorities. Where complaints are lodged with the Commission under Article 3 of Regulation No 17 while there are related actions before a relevant national or European authority or court, the Directorate-General for Competition will generally not initially pursue any investigation as to the existence of an infringement under Article 85 or 86 of the Treaty. This is subject, however, to the following points.

3.2.   Safeguarding complainant's rights

(29)   Undertakings are entitled to effective protection of their Community law rights[38]. Those rights would be undermined if national proceedings were allowed to lead to an excessive delay of the Commission's action, without a satisfactory resolution of the matter at a national level. In the telecommunications sector, innovation cycles are relatively short, and any substantial delay in resolving an access dispute might in practice be equivalent to a refusal of access, thus prejudging the proper determination of the case.

(30)   The Commission therefore takes the view that an access dispute before an NRA should be resolved within a reasonable period of time, normally speaking not extending beyond six months of the matter first being drawn to the attention of that authority. This resolution could take the form of either a final determination of the action or another form of relief which would safeguard the rights of the complainant. If the matter has not reached such a resolution then, prima facie, the rights of the parties are not being effectively protected, and the Commission would in principle, upon request by the complainant, begin its investigations into the case in accordance with its normal procedures, after consultation and in cooperation with the national authority in question. In general, the Commission will not begin such investigations where there is already an ongoing action under ONP conciliation procedures.

(31)   In addition, the Commission must always look at each case on its merits: it will take action if it feels that in a particular case, there is a substantial Community interest affecting, or likely to affect, competition in a number of Member States.

3.3.   Interim measures

(32)   As regards any request for interim measures, the existence or possibility of national proceedings is relevant to the question of whether there is a risk of serious and irreparable harm. Such proceedings should, prima facie, remove the risk of such harm and it would therefore not be appropriate for the Commission to grant interim measures in the absence of evidence that the risk would nevertheless remain.

(33)   The availability of and criteria for interim injunctive relief is an important factor which the Commission must take into account in reaching this prima facie conclusion. If interim injunctive relief were not available, or if such relief was not likely adequately to protect the complainant's rights under Community law, the Commission would consider that the national proceedings did not remove the risk of harm, and could therefore commence its examination of the case.

4.   Own-initiative investigation and sector inquiries

(34)   If it appears necessary, the Commission will open an own-initiative investigation. It can also launch a sector inquiry, subject to consultation of the Advisory Committee of Member State competition authorities.

5.   Fines

(35)   The Commission may impose fines of up to 10 % of the annual worldwide turnover of undertakings which intentionally or negligently breach Article 85(1) or Article 86[39]. Where agreements have been notified pursuant to Regulation No 17 for an exemption under Article 85(3), no fine may be levied by the Commission in respect of activities described in the notification[40] for the period following notification. However, the Commission may withdraw the immunity from fines by informing the undertakings concerned that, after preliminary examination, it is of the opinion that Article 85(1) of the Treaty applies and that application of Article 85(3) is not justified[41].

(36)   The ONP Interconnection Directive has two particular provisions which are relevant to fines under the competition rules. First, it provides that interconnection agreements must be communicated to the relevant NRAs and made available to interested third parties, with the exception of those parts which deal with the commercial strategy of the parties[42]. Secondly, it provides that the NRA must have a number of powers which it can use to influence or amend the interconnection agreements[43]. These provisions ensure that appropriate publicity is given to the agreements, and provide the NRA with the opportunity to take steps, where appropriate, to ensure effective competition on the market.

(37)   Where an agreement has been notified to an NRA, but has not been notified to the Commission, the Commission does not consider it would be generally appropriate as a matter of policy to impose a fine in respect of the agreement, even if the agreement ultimately proves to contain conditions in breach of Article 85. A fine would, however, be appropriate in some cases, for example where:

(a)   the agreement proves to contain provisions in breach of Article 86; and/or

(b)   the breach of Article 85 is particularly serious.

The Commission has recently published Guidelines on how fines will be calculated[44].

(38)   Notification to the NRA is not a substitute for a notification to the Commission and does not limit the possibility for interested parties to submit a complaint to the Commission, or for the Commission to begin an own-initiative investigation into access agreements. Nor does such notification limit the rights of a party to seek damages before a national court for harm caused by anti-competitive agreements[45].

PART II - RELEVANT MARKETS

(39)   In the course of investigating cases within the framework set out in Part I above, the Commission will base itself on the approach to the definition of relevant markets set out in the Commission's Notice on the definition of the relevant market for the purposes of Community competition law[46].

(40)　　Firms are subject to three main sources of competitive constraints; demand substitutability, supply substitutability and potential competition, with the first constituting the most immediate and effective disciplinary force on the suppliers of a given product or service. Demand substitutability is therefore the main tool used to define the relevant product market on which restrictions of competition for the purposes of Article 85(1) and Article 86 can be identified.

(41)　　Supply substitutability may in appropriate circumstances be used as a complementary element to define relevant markets. In practice it cannot be clearly distinguished from potential competition. Supply side substitutability and potential competition are used for the purpose of determining whether the undertaking has a dominant position or whether the restriction of competition is significant within the meaning of Article 85, or whether there is elimination of competition.

(42)　　In assessing relevant markets it is necessary to look at developments in the market in the short term.

The following sections set out some basic principles of particular relevance to the telecommunications sector.

1.　Relevant product market

(43)　　Section 6 of Form A/B defines the relevant product market as follows:

'A relevant product market comprises all those products and/or services which are regarded as interchangeable or substitutable by the consumer, by reason of the products' characteristics, their prices and their intended use'.

(44)　　Liberalisation of the telecommunications sector will lead to the emergence of a second type of market, that of access to facilities which are currently necessary to provide these liberalised services. Interconnection to the public switched telecommunications network would be a typical example of such access. Without interconnection, it will not be commercially possible for third parties to provide, for example, comprehensive voice telephony services.

(45)　　It is clear, therefore, that in the telecommunications sector there are at least two types of relevant markets to consider - that of a service to be provided to end users and that of access to those facilities necessary to provide that service to end users (information, physical network, etc.). In the context of any particular case, it will be necessary to define the relevant access and services markets, such as interconnection to the public telecommunications network, and provision of public voice telephony services, respectively.

(46)　　When appropriate, the Commission will use the test of a relevant market which is made by asking whether, if all the suppliers of the services in question raised their prices by 5 to 10 %, their collective profits would rise. According to this test, if their profits would rise, the market considered is a separate relevant market.

(47)　　The Commission considers that the principles under competition law governing these markets remain the same regardless of the particular market in question. Given the pace of technological change in this sector, any attempt to define particular product markets in this notice would run the risk of rapidly becoming inaccurate or irrelevant. The definition of particular product markets - for example, the determination of whether call origination and call termination facilities are part of the same facilities market - is best done in the light of a detailed examination of an individual case.

1.1. Services market

(48)   This can be broadly defined as the provision of any telecommunications service to users. Different telecommunications services will be considered substitutable if they show a sufficient degree of interchangeability for the end-user, which would mean that effective competition can take place between the different providers of these services.

1.2. Access to facilities

(49)   For a service provider to provide services to end-users it will often require access to one or more (upstream or downstream) facilities. For example, to deliver physically the service to end-users, it needs access to the termination points of the telecommunications network to which these end-users are connected. This access can be achieved at the physical level through dedicated or shared local infrastructure, either self provided or leased from a local infrastructure provider. It can also be achieved either through a service provider who already has these end-users as subscribers, or through an interconnection provider who has access directly or indirectly to the relevant termination points.

(50)   In addition to physical access, a service provider may need access to other facilities to enable it to market its service to end users: for example, a service provider must be able to make end-users aware of its services. Where one organisation has a dominant position in the supply of services such as directory information, similar concerns arise as with physical access issues.

(51)   In many cases, the Commission will be concerned with physical access issues, where what is necessary is access to the network facilities of the dominant TO[47].

(52)   Some incumbent TOs may be tempted to resist providing access to third party service providers or other network operators, particularly in areas where the proposed service will be in competition with a service provided by the TO itself. This resistance will often manifest itself as unjustified delay in giving access, a reluctance to allow access or a willingness to allow it only under disadvantageous conditions. It is the role of the competition rules to ensure that these prospective access markets are allowed to develop, and that incumbent TOs are not permitted to use their control over access to stifle developments on the services markets.

(53)   It should be stressed that in the telecommunications sector, liberalisation can be expected to lead to the development of new, alternative networks which will ultimately have an impact on access market definition involving the incumbent telecommunications operator.

2.   Relevant geographic market

(54)   Relevant geographic markets are defined in Form A/B as follows:

'The relevant geographic market comprises the area in which the undertakings concerned are involved in the supply and demand of products or services, in which the conditions of competition are sufficiently homogeneous and which can be distinguished from neighbouring areas because the conditions of competition are appreciably different in those areas.'

(55)   As regards the provision of telecommunication services and access markets, the relevant geographic market will be the area in which the objective conditions of competition applying to service providers are similar, and competitors are able to offer their services. It will therefore be necessary to examine the possibility for these service providers to access an end-user in any part of this area, under similar and economically viable

conditions. Regulatory conditions such as the terms of licences, and any exclusive or special rights owned by competing local access providers are particularly relevant[48].

PART III - PRINCIPLES

(56)　　The Commission will apply the following principles in cases before it.

(57)　　The Commission has recognised that 'Articles 85 and 86 ... constitute law in force and enforceable throughout the Community. Conflicts should not arise with other Community rules because Community law forms a coherent regulatory framework ... it is obvious that Community acts adopted in the telecommunications sector are to be interpreted in a way consistent with competition rules, so as to ensure the best possible implementation of all aspects of the Community telecommunications policy ... This applies, inter alia, to the relationship between competition rules applicable to undertakings and the ONP rules'[49].

(58)　　Thus, competition rules continue to apply in circumstances where other Treaty provisions or secondary legislation are applicable. In the context of access agreements, the internal market and competition provisions of Community law are both important and mutually reinforcing for the proper functioning of the sector. Therefore in making an assessment under the competition rules, the Commission will seek to build as far as possible on the principles established in the harmonisation legislation. It should also be borne in mind that a number of the competition law principles set out below are also covered by specific rules in the context of the ONP framework. Proper application of these rules should often avoid the need for the application of the competition rules.

(59)　　As regards the telecommunications sector, attention should be paid to the cost of universal service obligations. Article 90(2) of the Treaty may justify exceptions to the principles of Articles 85 and 86. The details of universal service obligations are a regulatory matter. The field of application of Article 90(2) has been specified in the Article 90 Directives in the telecommunications sector, and the Commission will apply the competition rules in this context.

(60)　　Articles 85 and 86 of the Treaty apply in the normal manner to agreements or practices which have been approved or authorised by a national authority[50], or where the national authority has required the inclusion of terms in an agreement at the request of one or more of the parties involved.

(61)　　However, if a NRA were to require terms which were contrary to the competition rules, the undertakings involved would in practice not be fined, although the Member State itself would be in breach of Article 3(g) and Article 5 of the Treaty[51] and therefore subject to challenge by the Commission under Article 169. Additionally, if an undertaking having special or exclusive rights within the meaning of Article 90, or a State-owned undertaking, were required or authorised by a national regulator to engage in behaviour constituting an abuse of its dominant position, the Member State would also be in breach of Article 90(1) and the Commission could adopt a decision requiring termination of the infringement[52].

(62)　　NRAs may require strict standards of transparency, obligations to supply and pricing practices on the market, particularly where this is necessary in the early stages of liberalisation. When appropriate, legislation such as the ONP framework will be used as an aid in the interpretation of the competition rules[53]. Given the duty resting on NRAs to ensure that effective competition is possible, application of the competition rules is likewise required for an appropriate interpretation of the ONP principles. It should also be noted that many of the issues set out below are also covered by rules under the Full Competition Directive and the ONP Licensing and Data protection Directives: effective enforcement of this regulatory framework should prevent many of the competition issues set out below from arising.

1.   Dominance (Article 86)

(63)   In order for an undertaking to provide services in the telecommunications services market, it may need to obtain access to various facilities. For the provision of telecommunications services, for example, interconnection to the public switched telecommunications network will usually be necessary. Access to this network will almost always be in the hands of a dominant TO. As regards access agreements, dominance stemming from control of facilities will be the most relevant to the Commission's appraisal.

(64)   Whether or not a company is dominant does not depend only on the legal rights granted to that company. The mere ending of legal monopolies does not put an end to dominance. Indeed, notwithstanding the liberalisation Directives, the development of effective competition from alternative network providers with adequate capacity and geographic reach will take time.

(65)   The judgment of the Court of Justice in Tetra Pak[54] is also likely to prove important in the telecommunications sector. The Court held that given the extremely close links between the dominated and non-dominated market, and given the extremely high market share on the dominated market, Tetra Pak was 'in a situation comparable to that of holding a dominant position on the markets in question as a whole'.

The Tetra Pak case concerned closely related horizontal markets: the analysis is equally applicable, however, to closely related vertical markets which will be common in the telecommunications sector. In the telecommunications sector, it is often the case that a particular operator has an extremely strong position on infrastructure markets, and on markets downstream of that infrastructure. Infrastructure costs also typically constitute the single largest cost of the downstream operations. Further, operators will often face the same competitors on both the infrastructure and downstream markets.

(66)   It is therefore possible to envisage a number of situations where there will be closely related markets, together with an operator having a very high degree of market power on at least one of those markets.

(67)   It these circumstances are present, it may be appropriate for the Commission to find that the particular operator was in a situation comparable to that of holding a dominant position on the markets in question as a whole.

(68)   In the telecommunications sector, the concept of 'essential facilities' will in many cases be of relevance in determining the duties of dominant TOs. The expression essential facility is used to describe a facility or infrastructure which is essential for reaching customers and/or enabling competitors to carry on their business, and which cannot be replicated by any reasonable means[55].

(69)   A company controlling the access to an essential facility enjoys a dominant position within the meaning of Article 86. Conversely, a company may enjoy a dominant position pursuant to Article 86 without controlling an essential facility.

1.1.   Services market

(70)   One of the factors used to measure the market power of an undertaking is the sales attributable to that undertaking, expressed as a percentage of total sales in the market for substitutable services in the relevant geographic area. As regards the services market, the Commission will assess, inter alia, the turnover generated by the sale of substitutable services, excluding the sale or internal usage of interconnection services and the sale or internal usage of local infrastructure[56], taking into consideration the competitive conditions and the structure of supply and demand on the market.

1.2. Access to facilities

(71)   The concept of 'access' as referred to in point 45 can relate to a range of situations, including the availability of leased lines enabling a service provider to build up its own network, and interconnection in the strict sense, that is interconnecting two telecommunication networks, for example mobile and fixed. In relation to access it is probable that the incumbent operator will remain dominant for some time after the legal liberalisation has taken place. The incumbent operator, which controls the facilities, is often also the largest service provider, and it has in the past not needed to distinguish between the conveyance of telecommunications services and the provision of these services to end-users. Traditionally, an operator who is also a service provider has not required its downstream operating arm to pay for access, and therefore it has not been easy to calculate the revenue to be allocated to the facility. In a case where an operator is providing both access and services it is necessary to separate so far as possible the revenues as the basis for the calculation of the company's share of whichever market is involved. Article 8(2) of the Interconnection Directive addresses this issue by introducing a requirement for separate accounting for 'activities related to interconnection - covering both interconnection services provided internally and interconnection services provided to others - and other activities'. The proposed Commission Recommendation on Accounting Separation in the context of Interconnection will also be helpful in this regard.

(72)   The economic significance of obtaining access also depends on the coverage of the network with which interconnection is sought. Therefore, in addition to using turnover figures, the Commission will, where possible, also take into account the number of customers who have subscribed to services offered by the dominant company comparable with those which the service provider requesting access intends to provide. Accordingly, market power for a given undertaking will be measured partly by the number of subscribers who are connected to termination points of the telecommunications network of that undertaking expressed as a percentage of the total number of subscribers connected to termination points in the relevant geographic area.

Supply-side substitutability

(73)   As stated in point 41, supply-side substitutability is also relevant to the question of dominance. A market share of over 50 %[57] is usually sufficient to demonstrate dominance although other factors will be examined. For example, the Commission will examine the existence of other network providers, if any, in the relevant geographic area to determine whether such alternative infrastructures are sufficiently dense to provide competition to the incumbent's network and the extent to which it would be possible for new access providers to enter the market.

Other relevant factors

(74)   In addition to market share data, and supply-side substitutability, in determining whether an operator is dominant the Commission will also examine whether the operator has privileged access to facilities which cannot reasonably be duplicated within an appropriate time frame, either for legal reasons or because it would cost too much.

(75)   As competing access providers appear and challenge the dominance of the incumbent, the scope of the rights they receive from Member States' authorities, and notably their territorial reach, will play an important part in the determination of market power. The Commission will closely follow market evolution in relation to these issues and will take account of any altered market conditions in its assessment of access issues under the competition rules.

1.3. Joint dominance

(76)   The wording of Article 86 makes it clear that the Article also applies when more than one company shares a dominant position. The circumstances in which a joint dominant position exists, and in which it is abused, have not yet been fully clarified by the case law of the Community judicature or the practice of the Commission, and the law is still developing.

(77)   The words of Article 86 ('abuse by one or more undertakings`) describe something different from the prohibition of anti-competitive agreements or concerted practices in Article 85. To hold otherwise would be contrary to the usual principles of interpretation of the Treaty, and would render the words pointless and without practical effect. This does not, however, exclude the parallel application of Articles 85 and 86 to the same agreement or practice, which has been upheld by the Commission and the Court in a number of cases[58], nor is there anything to prevent the Commission from taking action only under one of the provisions, when both apply.

(78)   Two companies, each dominant in a separate national market, are not the same as two jointly dominant companies. For two or more companies to be in a joint dominant position, they must together have substantially the same position vis-à-vis their customers and competitors as a single company has if it is in a dominant position. With specific reference to the telecommunications sector, joint dominance could be attained by two telecommunications infrastructure operators covering the same geographic market.

(79)   In addition, for two or more companies to be jointly dominant it is necessary, though not sufficient, for there to be no effective competition between the companies on the relevant market. This lack of competition may in practice be due to the fact that the companies have links such as agreements for cooperation, or interconnection agreements. The Commission does not, however, consider that either economic theory or Community law implies that such links are legally necessary for a joint dominant position to exist[59]. It is a sufficient economic link if there is the kind of interdependence which often comes about in oligopolistic situations. There does not seem to be any reason in law or in economic theory to require any other economic link between jointly dominant companies. This having been said, in practice such links will often exist in the telecommunications sector where national TOs nearly inevitably have links of various kinds with one another.

(80)   To take as an example access to the local loop, in some Member States this could well be controlled in the near future by two operators - the incumbent TO and a cable operator. In order to provide particular services to consumers, access to the local loop of either the TO or the cable television operator is necessary. Depending on the circumstances of the case and in particular on the relationship between them, it is possible that neither operator holds a dominant position: together, however, they may hold a joint monopoly of access to these facilities. In the longer term, technological developments may lead to other local loop access mechanisms being viable, such as energy networks: the existence of such mechanisms will be taken into account in determining whether dominant positions or joint dominant positions exist.

2.   Abuse of dominance

(81)   Application of Article 86 presupposes the existence of a dominant position and some link between the dominant position and the alleged abusive conduct. It will often be necessary in the telecommunications sector to examine a number of associated markets, one or more of which may be dominated by a particular operator. In these circumstances, there are a number of possible situations where abuses could arise:

-      conduct on the dominated market having effects on the dominated market[60],

- conduct on the dominated market having effects on markets other than the dominated market[61],

- conduct on a market other than the dominated market and having effects on the dominated market[62],

- conduct on a market other than the dominated market and having effects on a market other than the dominated market[63].

(82)   Although the factual and economic circumstances of the telecommunications sector are often novel, in many cases it is possible to apply established competition law principles. When looking at competition problems in this sector, it is important to bear in mind existing case law and Commission decisional practice on, for example, leveraging market power, discrimination and bundling.

2.1.   Refusal to grant access to facilities and application of unfavourable terms

(83)   A refusal to give access may be prohibited under Article 86 if the refusal is made by a company which is dominant because of its control of facilities, as incumbent TOs will usually be for the foreseeable future. A refusal may have 'the effect of hindering the maintenance of the degree of competition still existing in the market or the growth of that competition[64].

A refusal will only be abusive if it has exploitative or anti-competitive effects. Service markets in the telecommunications sector will initially have few competitive players and refusals will therefore generally affect competition on those markets. In all cases of refusal, any justification will be closely examined to determine whether it is objective.

(84)   Broadly there are three relevant scenarios:

(a)   a refusal to grant access for the purposes of a service where another operator has been given access by the access provider to operate on that services market;

(b)   a refusal to grant access for the purposes of a service where no other operator has been given access by the access provider to operate on that services market;

(c)   a withdrawal of access from an existing customer.

Discrimination

(85)   As to the first of the above scenarios, it is clear that a refusal to supply a new customer in circumstances where a dominant facilities owner is already supplying one or more customers operating in the same downstream market would constitute discriminatory treatment which, if it would restrict competition on that downstream market, would be an abuse. Where network operators offer the same, or similar, retail services as the party requesting access, they may have both the incentive and the opportunity to restrict competition and abuse their dominant position in this way. There may, of course, be justifications for such refusal - for example, vis-à-vis applicants which represent a potential credit risk. In the absence of any objective justifications, a refusal would usually be an abuse of the dominant position on the access market.

(86)   In general terms, the dominant company's duty is to provide access in such a way that the goods and services offered to downstream companies are available on terms no less favourable than those given to other parties, including its own corresponding downstream operations.

Essential facilities

(87)   As to the second of the above situations, the question arises as to whether the access provider should be obliged to contract with the service provider in order to allow the service provider to operate on a new service market. Where capacity constraints are not an issue and where the company refusing to provide access to its facility has not provided access to that facility, either to its downstream arm or to any other company operating on that services market, then it is not clear what other objective justification there could be.

(88)   In the transport field[65], the Commission has ruled that a firm controlling an essential facility must give access in certain circumstances[66]. The same principles apply to the telecommunications sector. If there were no commercially feasible alternatives to the access being requested, then unless access is granted, the party requesting access would not be able to operate on the service market. Refusal in this case would therefore limit the development of new markets, or new products on those markets, contrary to Article 86(b), or impede the development of competition on existing markets. A refusal having these effects is likely to have abusive effects.

(89)   The principle obliging dominant companies to contract in certain circumstances will often be relevant in the telecommunications sector. Currently, there are monopolies or virtual monopolies in the provision of network infrastructure for most telecom services in the Community. Even where restrictions have already been, or will soon be, lifted, competition in downstream markets will continue to depend upon the pricing and conditions of access to upstream network services that will only gradually reflect competitive market forces. Given the pace of technological change in the telecommunications sector, it is possible to envisage situations where companies would seek to offer new products or services which are not in competition with products or services already offered by the dominant access operator, but for which this operator is reluctant to provide access.

(90)   The Commission must ensure that the control over facilities enjoyed by incumbent operators is not used to hamper the development of a competitive telecommunications environment. A company which is dominant on a market for services and which commits an abuse contrary to Article 86 on that market may be required, in order to put an end to the abuse, to supply access to its facility to one or more competitors on that market. In particular, a company may abuse its dominant position if by its actions it prevents the emergence of a new product or service.

(91)   The starting point for the Commission's analysis will be the identification of an existing or potential market for which access is being requested. In order to determine whether access should be ordered under the competition rules, account will be taken of a breach by the dominant company of its duty not to discriminate (see below) or of the following elements, taken cumulatively:

(a)   access to the facility in question is generally essential in order for companies to compete on that related market[67].

The key issue here is therefore what is essential. It will not be sufficient that the position of the company requesting access would be more advantageous if access were granted - but refusal of access must lead to the proposed activities being made either impossible or seriously and unavoidably uneconomic.

Although, for example, alternative infrastructure may as from 1 July 1996 be used for liberalised services, it will be some time before this is in many cases a satisfactory alternative to the facilities of the incumbent operator. Such alternative infrastructure does not at present offer the same dense geographic coverage as that of the incumbent TO's network;

(b)   there is sufficient capacity available to provide access;

(c)   the facility owner fails to satisfy demand on an existing service or product market, blocks the emergence of a potential new service or product, or impedes competition on an existing or potential service or product market;

(d)   the company seeking access is prepared to pay the reasonable and non-discriminatory price and will otherwise in all respects accept non-discriminatory access terms and conditions;

(e)   there is no objective justification for refusing to provide access.

Relevant justifications in this context could include an overriding difficulty of providing access to the requesting company, or the need for a facility owner which has undertaken investment aimed at the introduction of a new product or service to have sufficient time and opportunity to use the facility in order to place that new product or service on the market. However, although any justification will have to be examined carefully on a case-by-case basis, it is particularly important in the telecommunications sector that the benefits to end-users which will arise from a competitive environment are not undermined by the actions of the former State monopolists in preventing competition from emerging and developing.

(92)   In determining whether an infringement of Article 86 has been committed, account will be taken both of the factual situation in that and other geographic areas, and, where relevant, the relationship between the access requested and the technical configuration of the facility.

(93)   The question of objective justification will require particularly close analysis in this area. In addition to determining whether difficulties cited in any particular case are serious enough to justify the refusal to grant access, the relevant authorities must also decide whether these difficulties are sufficient to outweigh the damage done to competition if access is refused or made more difficult and the downstream service markets are thus limited.

(94)   Three important elements relating to access which could be manipulated by the access provider in order, in effect, to refuse to provide access are timing, technical configuration and price.

(95)   Dominant TOs have a duty to deal with requests for access efficiently: undue and inexplicable or unjustified delays in responding to a request for access may constitute an abuse. In particular, however, the Commission will seek to compare the response to a request for access with:

(a)   the usual time frame and conditions applicable when the responding party grants access to its facilities to its own subsidiary or operating branch;

(b)   responses to requests for access to similar facilities in other Member States;

(c)   the explanations given for any delay in dealing with requests for access.

(96)   Issues of technical configuration will similarly be closely examined in order to determine whether they are genuine. In principle, competition rules require that the party requesting access must be granted access at the most suitable point for the requesting party, provided that this point is technically feasible for the access provider. Questions of technical feasibility may be objective justifications for refusing to supply - for example, the traffic for which access is sought must satisfy the relevant technical standards for the infrastructure - or there may be questions of capacity restraints, where questions of rationing may arise[68].

(97)   Excessive pricing for access, as well as being abusive in itself[69], may also amount to an effective refusal to grant access.

(98)   There are a number of elements of these tests which require careful assessment. Pricing questions in the telecommunications sector will be facilitated by the obligations under ONP Directives to have transparent cost-accounting systems.

Withdrawal of supply

(99)   As to the third of the situations referred to in point 84, some previous Commission decisions and the case law of the Court have been concerned with the withdrawal of supply from downstream competitors. In Commercial Solvents, the Court held that 'an undertaking which has a dominant position on the market in raw materials and which, with the object of reserving such raw material for manufacturing its own derivatives, refuses to supply a customer, which is itself a manufacturer of these derivatives, and therefore risks eliminating all competition on the part of this customer, is abusing its dominant position within the meaning of Article 86[70]

(100)   Although this case dealt with the withdrawal of a product, there is no difference in principle between this case and the withdrawal of access. The unilateral termination of access agreements raises substantially similar issues to those examined in relation to refusals. Withdrawal of access from an existing customer will usually be abusive. Again, objective reasons may be provided to justify the termination. Any such reasons must be proportionate to the effects on competition of the withdrawal.

2.2.   Other forms of abuse

(101)   Refusals to provide access are only one form of possible abuse in this area. Abuses may also arise in the context of access having been granted. An abuse may occur inter alia where the operator is behaving in a discriminatory manner or the operator's actions otherwise limit markets or technical development. The following are non-exhaustive examples of abuse which can take place.

Network configuration

(102)   Network configuration by a dominant network operator which makes access objectively more difficult for service providers[71] could constitute an abuse unless it were objectively justifiable. One objective justification would be where the network configuration improves the efficiency of the network generally.

Tying

(103)   This is of particular concern where it involves the tying of services for which the TO is dominant with those for which it is not[72]. Where the vertically integrated dominant network operator obliges the party requesting access to purchase one or more services[73] without adequate justification, this may exclude rivals of the dominant access provider from offering those elements of the package independently. This requirement could thus constitute an abuse under Article 86.

The Court has further held that '... even where tied sales of two products are in accordance with commercial usage or there is a natural link between the two products in question, such sales may still constitute abuse within the meaning of Article 86 unless they are objectively justified ...'[74].

Pricing

(104)   In determining whether there is a pricing problem under the competition rules, it will be necessary to demonstrate that costs and revenues are allocated in an appropriate

way. Improper allocation of costs and interference with transfer pricing could be used as mechanisms for disguising excessive pricing, predatory pricing or a price squeeze.

Excessive Pricing

(105) Pricing problems in connection with access for service providers to a dominant operator's facilities will often revolve around excessively high prices[75]: In the absence of another viable alternative to the facility to which access is being sought by service providers, the dominant or monopolistic operator may be inclined to charge excessive prices.

(106) An excessive price has been defined by the Court of Justice as being 'excessive in relation to the economic value of the service provided'[76]. In addition the Court has made it clear that one of the ways this could be calculated is as follows:

'This excess could, inter alia, be determined objectively if it were possible for it to be calculated by making a comparison between the selling price of the product in question and its cost of production'[77].

(107) It is necessary for the Commission to determine what the actual costs for the relevant product are. Appropriate cost allocation is therefore fundamental to determining whether a price is excessive. For example, where a company is engaged in a number of activities, it will be necessary to allocate relevant costs to the various activities, together with an appropriate contribution towards common costs. It may also be appropriate for the Commission to determine the proper cost allocation methodology where this is a subject of dispute.

(108) The Court has also indicated that in determining what constitutes an excessive price, account may be taken of Community legislation setting out pricing principles for the particular sector[78].

(109) Further, comparison with other geographic areas can also be used as an indicator of an excessive price: the Court has held that if possible a comparison could be made between the prices charged by a dominant company, and those charged on markets which are open to competition[79]. Such a comparison could provide a basis for assessing whether or not the prices charged by the dominant company were fair[80]. In certain circumstances, where comparative data are not available, regulatory authorities have sought to determine what would have been the competitive price were a competitive market to exist[81]. In an appropriate case, such an analysis may be taken into account by the Commission in its determination of an excessive price.

Predatory pricing

(110) Predatory pricing occurs, inter alia, where a dominant firm sells a good or service below cost for a sustained period of time, with the intention of deterring entry, or putting a rival out of business, enabling the dominant firm to further increase its market power and later its accumulated profits. Such unfairly low prices are in breach of Article 86(a). Such a problem could, for example, arise in the context of competition between different telecommunications infrastructure networks, where a dominant operator may tend to charge unfairly low prices for access in order to eliminate competition from other (emerging) infrastructure providers. In general a price is abusive if it is below the dominant company's average variable costs or if it is below average total costs and part of an anti-competitive plan[82]. In network industries a simple application of the above rule would not reflect the economic reality of network industries.

(111) This rule was established in the AKZO case where the Court of Justice defined average variable costs as 'those which vary depending on the quantities produced'[83] and explained the reasoning behind the rule as follows:

'A dominant undertaking has no interest in applying such prices except that of eliminating competitors so as to enable it subsequently to raise its prices by taking advantage of its monopolistic position, since each sale generates a loss, namely the total amount of the fixed costs (that is to say, those which remain constant regardless of the quantities produced) and, at least, part of the variable costs relating to the unit produced.`

(112) In order to trade a service or group of services profitably, an operator must adopt a pricing strategy whereby its total additional costs in providing that service or group of services are covered by the additional revenues earned as a result of the provision of that service or group of services. Where a dominant operator sets a price for a particular product or service which is below its average total costs of providing that service, the operator should justify this price in commercial terms: a dominant operator which would benefit from such a pricing policy only if one or more of its competitors was weakened would be committing an abuse.

(113) As indicated by the Court of Justice in AKZO, the Commission must determine the price below which a company could only make a profit by weakening or eliminating one or more competitors. Cost structures in network industries tend to be quite different to most other industries since the former have much larger common and joint costs.

(114) For example, in the case of the provision of telecommunications services, a price which equates to the variable cost of a service may be substantially lower than the price the operator needs in order to cover the cost of providing the service. To apply the AKZO test to prices which are to be applied over time by an operator, and which will form the basis of that operator's decisions to invest, the costs considered should include the total costs which are incremental to the provision of the service. In analysing the situation, consideration will have to be given to the appropriate time frame over which costs should be analysed. In most cases, there is reason to believe that neither the very short nor very long run are appropriate.

(115) In these circumstances, the Commission will often need to examine the average incremental costs of providing a service, and may need to examine average incremental costs over a longer period than one year.

(116) If a case arises, the ONP rules and Commission recommendations concerning accounting requirements and transparency will help to ensure the effective application of Article 86 in this context.

Price Squeeze

(117) Where the operator is dominant in the product or services market, a price squeeze could constitute an abuse. A price squeeze could be demonstrated by showing that the dominant company's own downstream operations could not trade profitably on the basis of the upstream price charged to its competitors by the upstream operating arm of the dominant company. A loss-making downstream arm could be hidden if the dominant operator has allocated costs to its access operations which should properly be allocated to the downstream operations, or has otherwise improperly determined the transfer prices within the organisation. The Commission Recommendation on Accounting Separation in the context of Interconnection addresses this issue by recommending separate accounting for different business areas within a vertically integrated dominant operator. The Commission may, in an appropriate case, require the dominant company to produce audited separated accounts dealing with all necessary aspects of the dominant company's business. However, the existence of separated accounts does not guarantee that no abuse exists: the Commission will, where appropriate, examine the facts on a case-by-case basis.

(118) In appropriate circumstances, a price squeeze could also be demonstrated by showing that the margin between the price charged to competitors on the downstream

market (including the dominant company's own downstream operations, if any) for access and the price which the network operator charges in the downstream market is insufficient to allow a reasonably efficient service provider in the downstream market to obtain a normal profit (unless the dominant company can show that its downstream operation is exceptionally efficient)[84].

(119) If either of these scenarios were to arise, competitors on the downstream market would be faced with a price squeeze which could force them out of the market.

Discrimination

(120) A dominant access provider may not discriminate between the parties to different access agreements where such discrimination would restrict competition. Any differentiation based on the use which is to be made of the access rather than differences between the transactions for the access provider itself, if the discrimination is sufficiently likely to restrict or distort actual or potential competition, would be contrary to Article 86. This discrimination could take the form of imposing different conditions, including the charging of different prices, or otherwise differentiating between access agreements, except where such discrimination would be objectively justified, for example on the basis of cost or technical considerations or the fact that the users are operating at different levels. Such discrimination could be likely to restrict competition in the downstream market on which the company requesting access was seeking to operate, in that it might limit the possibility for that operator to enter the market or expand its operations on that market[85].

(121) Such discrimination could similarly have an effect an competition where the discrimination was between operators on closely related downstream markets. Where two distinct downstream product markets exist, but one product would be regarded as substitutable for another save for the fact that there was a price difference between the two products, discriminating in the price charged to the providers of these two products could decrease existing or potential competition. For example, although fixed and mobile voice telephony services at present probably constitute separate product markets, the markets are likely to converge. Charging higher interconnection prices to mobile operators as compared to fixed operators would tend to hamper this convergence, and would therefore have an effect on competition. Similar effects on competition are likely in other telecommunications markets.

Such discrimination would in any event be difficult to justify given the obligation to set cost-related prices.

(122) With regard to price discrimination, Article 86(c) prohibits unfair discrimination by a dominant firm between customers of that firm[86] including discriminating between customers on the basis of whether or not they agree to deal exclusively with that dominant firm.

(123) Article 7 of the Interconnection Directive provides that 'different tariffs, terms and conditions for interconnection may be set for different categories of organisations which are authorised to provide networks and services, where such differences can be objectively justified on the basis of the type of interconnection provided and/or the relevant national licensing conditions ...` (provided that such differences do not result in distortions of competition).

(124) A determination of whether such differences result in distortions of competition must be made in the particular case. It is important to remember that Articles 85 and 86 deal with competition and not regulatory matters. Article 86 cannot require a dominant company to treat different categories of customers differently, except where this is the result of market conditions and the principles of Article 86. On the contrary, Article 86 prohibits dominant companies from discriminating between similar transactions where such a discrimination would have an effect on competition.

(125) Discrimination without objective justification as regards any aspects or conditions of an access agreement may constitute an abuse. Discrimination may relate to elements such as pricing, delays, technical access, routing[87], numbering, restrictions on network use exceeding essential requirements and use of customer network data. However, the existence of discrimination can only be determined on a case-by-case basis. Discrimination is contrary to Article 86 whether or not it results from or is apparent from the terms of a particular access agreement.

(126) There is, in this context, a general duty on the network operator to treat independent customers in the same way as its own subsidiary or downstream service arm. The nature of the customer and its demands may play a significant role in determining whether transactions are comparable. Different prices for customers at different levels (for example, wholesale and retail) do not necessarily constitute discrimination.

(127) Discrimination issues may arise in respect of the technical configuration of the access, given its importance in the context of access.

The degree of technical sophistication of the access: restrictions on the type or 'level` in the network hierarchy of exchange involved in the access or the technical capabilities of this exchange are of direct competitive significance. These could be the facilities available to support a connection or the type of interface and signalling system used to determine the type of service available to the party requesting access (for example, intelligent network facilities).

The number and/or location of connection points: the requirement to collect and distribute traffic for particular areas at the switch which directly serves that area rather than at a higher level of the network hierarchy may be important. The party requesting access incurs additional expense by either providing links at a greater distance from its own switching centre or being liable to pay higher conveyance charges.

Equal access: the possibility for customers of the party requesting access to obtain the services provided by the access provider using the same number of dialled digits as are used by the customers of the latter is a crucial feature of competitive telecommunications.

Objective justification

(128) Justifications could include factors relating to the actual operation of the network owned by the access provider, or licensing restrictions consistent with, for example, the subject matter of intellectual property rights.

2.3. Abuses of joint dominant positions

(129) In the case of joint dominance (see points 76 et seq.) behaviour by one of several jointly dominant companies may be abusive even if others are not behaving in the same way.

(130) In addition to remedies under the competition rules, if no operator was willing to grant access, and if there was no technical or commercial justification for the refusal, one would expect that the NRA would resolve the problem by ordering one or more of the companies to offer access, under the terms of the relevant ONP Directive or under national law.

3. Access agreements (Article 85)

(131) Restrictions of competition included in or resulting from access agreements may have two distinct effects: restriction of competition between the two parties to the access agreement, or restriction of competition from third parties, for example through exclusivity for one or both of the parties to the agreement. In addition, where one party is

dominant, conditions of the access agreement may lead to a strengthening of that dominant position, or to an extension of that dominant position to a related market, or may constitute an unlawful exploitation of the dominant position through the imposition of unfair terms.

(132) Access agreements where access is in principle unlimited are not likely to be restrictive of competition within the meaning of Article 85(1). Exclusivity obligations in contracts providing access to one company are likely to restrict competition because they limit access to infrastructure for other companies. Since most networks have more capacity than any single user is likely to need, this will normally be the case in the telecommunications sector.

(133) Access agreements can have significant pro-competitive effects as they can improve access to the downstream market. Access agreements in the context of interconnection are essential to interoperability of services and infrastructure, thus increasing competition in the downstream market for services, which is likely to involve higher added value than local infrastructure.

(134) There is, however, obvious potential for anti-competitive effects of certain access agreements or clauses therein. Access agreements may, for example:

(a)   serve as a means of coordinating prices;

(b)   serve as a means of market sharing;

(c)   have exclusionary effects on third parties[88];

(d)   lead to an exchange of commercially sensitive information between the parties.

(135) The risk of price coordination is particularly acute in the telecommunications sector since interconnection charges often amount to 50 % or more of the total cost of the services provided, and where interconnection with a dominant operator will usually be necessary. In these circumstances, the scope for price competition is limited and the risk (and the seriousness) of price coordination correspondingly greater.

(136) Furthermore, interconnection agreements between network operators may under certain circumstances be an instrument of market sharing between the network operator providing access and the network operator seeking access, instead of the emergence of network competition between them.

(137) In a liberalised telecommunications environment, the above types of restrictions of competition will be monitored by the national authorities and the Commission under the competition rules. The right of parties who suffer from any type of anti-competitive behaviour to complain to the Commission is unaffected by national regulation.

Clauses falling within Article 85(1)

(138) The Commission has identified certain types of restriction which would potentially infringe Article 85(1) of the Treaty and therefore require individual exemption. These clauses will most commonly relate to the commercial framework of the access.

(139) In the telecommunications sector, it is inherent in interconnection that parties will obtain certain customer and traffic information about their competitors. This information exchange could in certain cases influence the competitive behaviour of the undertakings concerned, and could easily be used by the parties for collusive practices, such as market sharing[89]. The Interconnection Directive requires that information received from an organisation seeking interconnection be used only for the purposes for which it was supplied. In order to comply with the competition rules and the Interconnection Directives, operators will have to introduce safeguards to ensure that confidential information is only

disclosed to those parts of the companies involved in making the interconnection agreements, and to ensure that the information is not used for anti-competitive purposes. Provided that these safeguards are complete and function correctly, there should be no reason in principle why simple interconnection agreements should be caught by Article 85(1).

(140) Exclusivity arrangements, for example where traffic would be conveyed exclusively through the telecommunications network of one or both parties rather than to the network of other parties with whom access agreements have been concluded will similarly require analysis under Article 85(3). If no justification is provided for such routing, such clauses will be prohibited. Such exclusivity clauses are not, however, an inherent part of interconnection agreements.

(141) Access agreements that have been concluded with an anti-competitive object are extremely unlikely to fulfil the criteria for an individual exemption under Article 85(3).

(142) Furthermore, access agreements may have an impact on the competitive structure of the market. Local access charges will often account for a considerable portion of the total cost of the services provided to end-users by the party requesting access, thus leaving limited scope for price competition. Because of the need to safeguard this limited degree of competition, the Commission will therefore pay particular attention to scrutinising access agreements in the context of their likely effects on the relevant markets in order to ensure that such agreements do not serve as a hidden and indirect means for fixing or coordinating end-prices for end-users, which constitutes one of the most serious infringements of Article 85 of the Treaty[90]. This would be of particular concern in oligopolistic markets.

(143) In addition, clauses involving discrimination leading to the exclusion of third parties are similarly restrictive of competition. The most important is discrimination with regard to price, quality or other commercially significant aspects of the access to the detriment of the party requesting access, which will generally aim at unfairly favouring the operations of the access provider.

4.   Effect on trade between Member States

(144) The application of both Article 85 and Article 86 presupposes an effect on trade between Member States.

(145) In order for an agreement to have an effect on trade between Member States, it must be possible for the Commission to 'foresee with a sufficient degree of probability on the basis of a set of objective factors of law or of fact that the agreement in question may have an influence, direct or indirect, actual or potential, on the pattern of trade between Member States'[91].

It is not necessary for each of the restrictions of competition within the agreement to be capable of affecting trade[92], provided the agreement as a whole does so.

(146) As regards access agreements in the telecommunications sector, the Commission will consider not only the direct effect of restrictions of competition on inter-state trade in access markets, but also the effects on inter-State trade in downstream telecommunications services. The Commission will also consider the potential of these agreements to foreclose a given geographic market which could prevent undertakings already established in other Member States from competing in this geographic market.

(147) Telecommunications access agreements will normally affect trade between Member States as services provided over a network are traded throughout the Community and access agreements may govern the ability of a service provider or an operator to provide any given service. Even where markets are mainly national, as is generally the case

at present given the stage of development of liberalisation, abuses of dominance will normally speaking affect market structure, leading to repercussions on trade between Member States.

(148)   Cases in this area involving issues under Article 86 are likely to relate either to abusive clauses in access agreements, or a refusal to conclude an access agreement on appropriate terms or at all. As such, the criteria listed above for determining whether an access agreement is capable of affecting trade between Member States would be equally relevant here.

CONCLUSIONS

(149)   The Commission considers that competition rules and sector specific regulation form a coherent set of measures to ensure a liberalised and competitive market environment for telecommunications markets in the Community.

(150)   In taking action in this sector, the Commission will aim to avoid unnecessary duplication of procedures, in particular competition procedures and national/Community regulatory procedures as set out under the ONP framework.

(151)   Where competition rules are invoked, the Commission will consider which markets are relevant and will apply Articles 85 and 86 in accordance with the principles set out above.

---

[1]   According to Commission Directives 96/19/EC and 96/2/EC (cited in footnote 3), certain Member States may request a derogation from full liberalisation for certain limited periods. This notice is without prejudice to such derogations, and the Commission will take account of the existence of any such derogation when applying the competition rules to access agreements, as described in this notice. See:
Commission Decision 97/114/EC of 27 November 1996 concerning the additional implementation periods requested by Ireland for the implementation of Commission Directives 90/388/EEC and 96/2/EC as regards full competition in the telecommunications markets (OJ L 41, 12.2.1997, p. 8);
Commission Decision 97/310/EC of 12 February 1997 concerning the granting of additional implementation periods to the Portuguese Republic for the implementation of Commission Directives 90/388/EEC and 96/2/EC as regards full competition in the telecommunications markets (OJ L 133, 24.5.1997, p. 19);
Commission Decision 97/568/EC of 14 May 1997 on the granting of additional implementation periods to Luxembourg for the implementation of Directive 90/388/EEC as regards full competition in the telecommunications markets (OJ L 234, 26.8.1997, p. 7);
Commission Decision 97/603/EC of 10 June 1997 concerning the granting of additional implementation periods to Spain for the implementation of Commission Directive 90/388/EEC as regards full competition in the telecommunications markets (OJ L 243, 5.9.1997, p. 48).
Commission Decision 97/607/EC of 18 June 1997 concerning the granting of additional implementation periods to Greece for the implementation of Directive 90/388/EEC as regards full competition in the telecommunications markets (OJ L 245, 9.9.1997, p. 6).

[2]   Communication by the Commission of 3 May 1995 to the European Parliament and the Council, Consultation on the Green Paper on the liberalisation of telecommunications infrastructure and cable television networks, COM(95) 158 final.

[3]   Commission Directive 88/301/EEC of 16 May 1988, on competition in the markets in telecommunications terminal equipment (OJ L 131, 27.5.1988, p. 73);
Commission Directive 90/388/EEC of 28 June 1990 on competition in the markets for telecommunications services (OJ L 192, 24.7.1990, p. 10) (the 'Services Directive');
Commission Directive 94/46/EC of 13 October 1994, amending Directive 88/301/EEC and Directive 90/388/EEC in particular with regard to satellite communications (OJ L 268, 19.10.1994, p. 15);
Commission Directive 95/51/EC of 18 October 1995 amending Directive 90/388/EEC with regard to the abolition of the restrictions on the use of cable television networks for the provision of already liberalised telecommunications services (OJ L 256, 26.10.1995, p. 49);
Commission Directive 96/2/EC of 16 January 1996 amending Directive 90/388/EEC with regard to mobile and personal communications (OJ L 20, 26.1.1996, p. 59);

Commission Directive 96/19/EC of 13 March 1996 amending Directive 90/388/EEC with regard to the implementation of full competition in the telecommunications markets (OJ L 74, 22.3.1996, p. 13) (the 'Full Competition Directive').

[4] Interconnection agreements are the most significant form of access agreement in the telecommunications sector. A basic framework for interconnection agreements is set up by the rules on open network provision (ONP), and the application of competition rules must be seen against this background:
Directive 97/13/EC of the European Parliament and of the Council of 10 April 1997 on a common framework for authorisations and individual licences in the field of telecommunications services (OJ L 117, 7.5.1997, p. 15) (the 'Licensing Directive');
Directive 97/33/EC of the European Parliament and of the Council of 30 June 1997 on interconnection in Telecommunications with regard to ensuring universal service and interoperability through application of the principles of open network provision (ONP) (OJ L 199, 26.7.1997, p. 32) (the 'Interconnection Directive');
Council Directive 90/387/EEC of 28 June 1990 on the establishment of the internal market for telecommunications services through the implementation of open network provision (OJ L 192, 24.7.1990, p. 1) (the 'Framework Directive');
Council Directive 92/44/EEC of 5 June 1992 on the application of open network provision to leased lines (OJ L 165, 19.6.1992, p. 27) (the 'Leased Lines Directive');
Directive 95/62/EEC of the European Parliament and of the Council of 13 December 1995 on the application of open network provision to voice telephony (OJ L 321, 30.12.1995, p. 6) replaced by Directive 98/10/EC of the European Parliament and of the Council of 26 February 1998 on the application of open network provision (ONP) to voice telephony and on universal service for telecommunications in a competitive environment (OJ L 101, 1.4.1998, p. 24) (the 'Voice Telephony Directive');
Directive 97/66/EC of the European Parliament and of the Council of 15 December 1997 concerning the processing of personal data and the protection of privacy in the telecommunications sector (OJ L 24, 30.1.1998, p. 1) (the 'Data Protection Directive').

[5] OJ C 233, 6.9.1991, p. 2.

[6] In the telecommunications area, notably:
Commission Decision 91/562/EEC of 18 October 1991, Eirpage (OJ L 306, 7.11.1991, p. 22);
Commission Decisions 96/546/EC and 96/547/EC of 17 July 1996, Atlas and Phoenix (OJ L 239, 19.9.1996, p. 23 and p. 57); and
Commission Decision 97/780/EC of 29 October 1997, Unisource (OJ L 318, 20.11.1997, p. 1).
There are also a number of pending cases involving access issues.

[7] Competition aspects of interconnection agreements in the telecommunications sector, June 1995;
Competition aspects of access by service providers to the resources of telecommunications operators, December 1995. See also Competition Aspects of Access Pricing, December 1995.

[8] See the Commission's Green Paper of 3 December 1997 on the Convergence of the Telecommunications, Media and Information Technology sectors and the implications for Regulation - Towards an information society approach (COM(97) 623).

[9] See Council Decision 97/838/EC of 28 November 1997 concerning the conclusion on behalf of the European Community, as regards matters within its competence, of the results of the WTO negotiations on basic telecommunications services (OJ L 347, 18.12.1997, p. 45).

[10] In the case of the ONP Leased Lines Directive, a first stage is foreseen which allows the aggrieved user to appeal to the National Regulatory Authority. This can offer a number of advantages. In the telecommunications areas where experience has shown that companies are often hesitant to be seen as complainants against the TO on which they heavily depend not only with respect to the specific point of conflict but also much broader and far-reaching sense, the procedures foreseen under ONP are an attractive option. ONP procedures furthermore can cover a broader range of access problems than could be approached on the basis of the competition rules. Finally, these procedures can offer users the advantage of proximity and familiarity with national administrative procedures; language is also a factor to be taken into account.
Under the ONP Leased Lines Directive, if a solution cannot be found at the national level, a second stage is organised at the European level (conciliation procedure). An agreement between the parties involved must then be reached within two months, with a possible extension of one month if the parties agree.

[11] An NRA is a national telecommunications regulatory body created by a Member State in the context of the services directive as amended, and the ONP framework. The list of NRAs is published regularly in the Official Journal of the European Communities, and a copy of the latest list can be found at http://www.ispo.cec.be.

[12] Articles 9 and 17 of the Interconnection Directive.

[13] Article 7 of the Services Directive (see footnote 3), and Article 5a of the ONP Framework Directive (see footnote 4). See also Communication by the Commission to the European Parliament and the Council on the status and implementation of Directive 90/388/EEC on competition in the markets for telecommunications services (OJ C 275, 20.10.1995, p. 2).

See also the judgment of the Court of Justice of the European Communities in Case C-91/94, Thierry Tranchant and Telephones Stores [1995] ECR I-3911.

[14] The Interconnection Directive cited in footnote 4, Article 9(3).

[15] Judgments of the Court of First Instance of the European Communities: Case T-24/90, Automec v. Commission [1992] ECR II-2223, at paragraph 77 and Case T-114/92 BEMIM [1995] ECR II-147.

[16] Notice on cooperation between national courts and the Commission in applying Articles 85 and 86 of the EC Treaty (OJ C 39, 13.2.1993, p. 6, at paragraph 14).
Notice on cooperation between national competition authorities and the Commission (OJ C 313, 15.10.1997, p. 3).

[17] Case 127/73, BRT v. SABAM [1974] ECR 51.

[18] Case 66/86, Ahmed Saeed [1989] ECR 838.

[19] They must not, for example, encourage or reinforce or approve the results of anti-competitive behaviour:
- Ahmed Saeed, see footnote 18;
- Case 153/93, Federal Republic of Germany v. Delta Schiffahrtsges. [1994] ECR I-2517,
- Case 267/86, Van Eycke [1988] ECR 4769.

[20] Case 13/77, GB-Inno-BM/ATAB [1977] ECR 2115, at paragraph 33:
- 'while it is true that Article 86 is directed at undertakings, nonetheless it is also true that the Treaty imposes a duty on Member States not to adopt or maintain in force any measure which could deprive the provision of its effectiveness.'

[21] For further duties of national authorities see:
Case 103/88, Fratelli Costanzo [1989] ECR 1839.
See Ahmed Saeed, cited in footnote 18:
- 'Articles 5 and 90 of the EEC Treaty must be interpreted as (i) prohibiting the national authorities from encouraging the conclusion of agreements on tariffs contrary to Article 85(1) or Article 86 of the Treaty, as the case may be; (ii) precluding the approval by those authorities of tariffs resulting from such agreements'.

[22] Joined Cases C-6/90, and C-9/90 Francovich [1991] ECR I-5357;
Joined Cases C-46/93, Brasserie de Pêcheur v. Germany and Case C-48/93, R v. Secretary of State for Transport ex parte Factortame and others [1996] ECR I-1029.

[23] For example, recital 18 of the Leased Lines Directive and Article 9(3) of the ONP Interconnection Directive, see footnote 4.

[24] Council Regulation (EEC) No 4064/89 of 21 December 1989 on the control of concentrations between undertakings (OJ L 395, 30.12.1989, p. 1); corrected version (OJ L 257, 21.9.1990, p. 13).

[25] Council Regulation No 17 of 6 February 1962, First Regulation implementing Articles 85 and 86 of the Treaty (OJ 13, 21.2.1962, p. 204).

[26] Articles 2 and 4(1) of Regulation No 17.

[27] Article 3 of Regulation No 17.

[28] Articles 3 and 12 of Regulation No 17.

[29] Case 792/79R, Camera Care v. Commission [1980] ECR 119.
See also Case T-44/90, La Cinq v. Commission [1992] ECR II-1.

[30] See point 16 of the Notice cited in footnote 16.

[31] Article 2 or Article 4(1) of Regulation No 17.

[32] Camera Care and La Cinq, referred to at footnote 29.

[33] See point 16 of the Notice cited in footnote 16.

[34] See point 18.

[35] See Automec, cited in footnote 15, at paragraph 86.

[36] BRT v. SABAM, cited in footnote 17.

[37] Article 9(1) and (3) of the ONP Interconnection Directive.

[38] Case 14/83, Von Colson [1984] ECR 1891.

[39] Article 15(2) of Regulation No 17.

[40] Article 15(5) of Regulation No 17.

[41] Article 15(6) of Regulation No 17.

[42] Article 6(c) of the ONP Interconnection Directive.

[43] Inter alia, at Article 9 of the ONP Interconnection Directive.

[44] Guidelines on the method of setting fines imposed pursuant to Article 15(2) of Regulation No 17 and Article 65(5) of the ECSC Treaty (OJ C 9, 14.1.1998, p. 3).

[45] See footnote 22.

[46] OJ C 372, 9.12.1997, p. 5.

[47] Interconnection is defined in the Full Competition Directive as '... the physical and logical linking of the telecommunications facilities of organisations providing telecommunications networks and/or telecommunications services, in order to allow the users of one organisation to communicate with the users of the same or another organisation or to access services provided by third organisations.'
In the Full Competition Directive and ONP Directives, telecommunications services are defined as 'services, whose provision consists wholly or partly in the transmission and/or routing of signals on a telecommunications network.'
It therefore includes the transmission of broadcasting signals and CATV networks.
A telecommunications network is itself defined as '... the transmission equipment and, where applicable, switching equipment and other resources which permit the conveyance of signals between defined termination points by wire, by radio, by optical or by other electromagnetic means'.

[48] Commission Decision 94/894/EC of 13 December 1994, Eurotunnel (OJ L 354, 21.12.1994, p. 66).

[49] See Guidelines cited in footnote 5, at paragraphs 15 and 16.

[50] Commission Decision 82/896/EEC of 15 December 1982, AROW/BNIC (OJ L 379, 31.12.1982, p. 19).

[51] See footnote 18.

[52] Joined Cases C-48 and 66/90 Netherlands and others v. Commission, [1992] ECR I-565.

[53] See Ahmed Saeed, cited in footnote 18, where internal market legislation relating to pricing was used as an aid in determining what level of prices should be regarded as unfair for the purposes of Article 86.

[54] On each market, Tetra Pak was faced with the same potential customers and actual competitors. Case C-333/94 P, Tetra Pak International SA v. Commission [1996] ECR I-5951.

[55] See also the definition included in the 'Additional commitment on regulatory principles by the European Communities and their Member States' used by the Group on basic telecommunications in the context of the World Trade Organisation (WTO) negotiations:
'Essential facilities mean facilities of a public telecommunications transport network and service that:
(a) are exclusively or predominantly provided by a single or limited number of suppliers;
and(b) cannot feasibly be economically or technically substituted in order to provide a service.'

[56] Case 6/72 Continental Can [1973] ECR 215.

[57] It should be noted in this context that under the ONP framework an organisation may be notified as having significant market power. The determination of whether an organisation does or does not have significant market power depends on a number of factors, but the starting presumption is that an organisation with a market share of more than 25 % will normally be considered to have significant market power. The Commission will take account of whether an undertaking has been notified as having significant market power under the ONP rules in its appraisal under the competition rules. It is clear, however, that the notion of significant market power generally describes a position of economic power on a market less than that of dominance: the fact that an undertaking has significant market power under the ONP rules will generally therefore not lead to a presumption of dominance, although in a particular situation, this may prove to be the case. One important factor to be taken into consideration, however, will be whether the market definition used in the ONP procedures is appropriate for use in applying the competition rules.

[58] Case 85/76 Hoffmann-La Roche [1979] ECR 461.
Commission Decision 89/113/EEC of 21 December 1988, Decca Navigator System (OJ L 43, 15.2.1989, p. 27).

[59] Commission Decision 92/553/EEC of 22 July 1992, Nestlé/Perrier (OJ L 356, 5.12.1992, p. 1).

[60] The most common situation.

[61] Joined Cases 6/73 and 7/73 Commercial Solvents v. Commission [1974] ECR 223 and Case 311/84 CBEM v. CLT and IPB [1985] ECR 3261.

[62] Case C-62/86, AKZO v. Commission [1991] ECR I-3359 and Case T-65/89 BPB Industries and British Gypsum v. Commission [1993] ECR II-389.

[63] Case C-333/94 P, Tetra Pak International v. Commission [1996] ECR I-5951. In this fourth case, application of Article 86 can only be justified by special circumstances (Tetra Pak, at paragraphs 29 and 30).

64   Case 85/76, Hoffmann-La Roche [1979] ECR 461.

65   Commission Decision 94/19/EC of 21 December 1993, Sea Containers v. Stena Sealink - Interim measure (OJ L 15, 18.1.1994, p. 8).
Commission Decision 94/119/EEC of 21 December 1993, Port of Rødby (Denmark) (OJ L 55, 26.2.1994, p. 52).

66   See also (among others):
Judgments of the Court of Justice and the Court of First Instance:
Cases 6 and 7/73 Commercial Solvents v. Commission [1974] ECR 223;
Case 311/84, Télémarketing [1985] ECR 3261;
Case C-18/88 RTT v. GB-Inno [1991] ECR I-5941;
Case C-260/89, Elliniki Radiophonia Teleorassi [1991] ECR I-2925;
Cases T-69, T-70 and T-76/89, RTE, BBC and ITP v. Commission [1991] ECR II-485, 535, 575;
Case C-271/90, Spain v. Commission [1992] ECR I-5833;
Cases C-241 and 242/91 P, RTE and ITP Ltd v. Commission (Magill), [1995] ECR I-743.
Commission Decisions:
Commission Decision 76/185/ECSC of 29 October 1975, National Carbonising Company (OJ L 35, 10.2.1976, p. 6).
Commission Decision 88/589/EEC of 4 November 1988, London European/Sabena (OJ L 317, 24.11.1988, p. 47).
Commission Decision 92/213/EEC of 26 February 1992, British Midland v. Aer Lingus (OJ L 96, 10.4.1992, p. 34); B& I v. Sealink (1992) 5 CMLR 255; EC Bulletin, No 6 - 1992, point 1.3.30.

67   It would be insufficient to demonstrate that one competitor needed access to a facility in order to compete in the downstream market. It would be necessary to demonstrate that access is necessary for all except exceptional competitors in order for access to be made compulsory.

68   As noted in point 91.

69   See point 105.

70   Cases 6 and 7/73, Commercial Solvents [1974] ECR 223.

71   That is to say, to use the network to reach their own customers.

72   This is also dealt with under the ONP framework: see Article 7(4) of the Interconnection Directive, Article 12(4) of the Voice telephony Directive and Annex II to the ONP Framework Directive.

73   Including those which are superfluous to the party requesting access, or indeed those which may constitute services which that party itself would like to provide for its customers.

74   Tetra Pak International, cited in footnote 63.

75   The Commission Communication of 27 November 1996 on Assessment Criteria for National Schemes for the Costing and Financing of Universal Service and Guidelines for the Operation of such Schemes will be relevant for the determination of the extent to which the universal service obligation can be used to justify additional charges related to the sharing of the net cost in the provision of universal service (COM(96) 608). See also the reference to the universal service obligation in point 59.

76   Case 26/75, General Motors Continental v. Commission [1975] ECR 1367, at paragraph 12.

77   Case 27/76, United Brands Company and United Brands Continental BV v. Commission [1978] ECR 207.

78   Ahmed Saeed, cited in footnote 18, at paragraph 43.

79   Case 30-87, Corinne Bodson v. Pompes funèbres des régions libérées [1988] ECR 2479.
See also:
Joined cases 110/88, 241/88 and 242/88 François Lucazeau and others v. Société des Auteurs, Compositeurs et Editeurs de Musique (SACEM) and others [1989] ECR 2811, at paragraph 25: 'When an undertaking holding a dominant position imposes scales of fees for its services which are appreciably higher than those charged in other Member States and where a comparison of the fee levels has been made on a consistent basis, that difference must be regarded as indicative of an abuse of a dominant position. In such a case it is for the undertaking in question to justify the difference by reference to objective dissimilarities between the situation in the Member State concerned and the situation prevailing in all the other Member States.'

80   See ONP rules and Commission Recommendation on Interconnection in a liberalised telecommunications market (OJ L 73, 12.3.1998, p. 42 (Text of Recommendation) and OJ C 84, 19.3.1998, p. 3 (Communication on Recommendation)).

81   For example, in their calculation of interconnection tariffs.

82   AKZO, cited in footnote 62.

83   AKZO, paragraph 71.

84   Commission Decision 88/518/EEC of 18 July 1988, Napier Brown/British Sugar (OJ L 284, 19.10.1988, p. 41): the margin between industrial and retail prices was reduced to the point where the wholesale purchaser with packaging operations as efficient as those of the wholesale supplier could not profitably serve the retail market. See also National Carbonising Company, cited in footnote 66.

85   However, when infrastructure capacity is under-utilised, charging a different price for access depending on the demand in the different downstream markets may be justified to the extent that such differentiation permits a better development of certain markets, and where such differentiation does not restrict or distort competition. In such a case, the Commission will analyse the global effects of such price differentiation on all of the downstream markets.

86   Case C-310/93 P, BPB Industries und British Gypsum v. Commission [1995] ECR I-865, at p. 904, applying to discrimination by BPB among customers in the related market for dry plaster.

87   That is to say, to a preferred list of correspondent network operators.

88   Commission Decision 94/663/EC of 21 September 1994, Night Services (OJ L 259, 7.10.1994, p. 20); Commission Decision 94/894/EC, see footnote 48.

89   Case T-34/92, Fiatagri UK and New Holland Ford v. Commission [1994] ECR II-905;
      Case C-8/95 P, New Holland Ford v. Commission, judgment of 28 May 1988, not yet reported;
      Case T-35/92, John Deere v. Commission [1994] ECR II-957;
      Case C-7/95 P, John Deere v. Commission, judgment of 28 May 1988, not yet reported.
      (Cases involving applications brought against Commission Decision 92/157/EEC of 17 February 1992, UK Agricultural Tractor Registration Exchange) (OJ L 68, 13.3.1992, p. 19).

90   Case 8/72, Vereniging van Cementhandelaaren v. Commission [1972] ECR 977;
      Case 123/85, Bureau National Interprofessionnel du Cognac v. Clair [1985] ECR 391.

91   Case 56/65, STM [1966] ECR 235, p. 249.

92   Case 193/83, Windsurfing International v. Commission [1986] ECR 611.

THE TREATY ESTABLISHING THE EUROPEAN COMMUNITY

ARTICLES 87 - 89
(Annotated)

Article 87

1. Save as otherwise provided in this Treaty, any aid granted by a Member State or through State resources in any form whatsoever which distorts or threatens to distort competition by favouring certain undertakings or the production of certain goods shall, in so far as it affects trade between Member States, be incompatible with the common market.

2. The following shall be compatible with the common market:

    (a) aid having a social character, granted to individual consumers, provided that such aid is granted without discrimination related to the origin of the products concerned;

    (b) aid to make good the damage caused by natural disasters or exceptional occurrences;

    (c) aid granted to the economy of certain areas of the Federal Republic of Germany affected by the division of Germany, in so far as such aid is required in order to compensate for the economic disadvantages caused by that division.

3. The following may be considered to be compatible with the common market:

    (a) aid to promote the economic development of areas where the standard of living is abnormally low or where there is serious underemployment;

    (b) aid to promote the execution of an important project of common European interest or to remedy a serious disturbance in the economy of a Member State;

    (c) aid to facilitate the development of certain economic activities or of certain economic areas, where such aid does not adversely affect trading conditions to an extent contrary to the common interest;

    (d) aid to promote culture and heritage conservation where such aid does not affect trading conditions and competition in the Community to an extent that is contrary to the common interest;

    (e) such other categories of aid as may be specified by decision of the Council acting by a qualified majority on a proposal from the Commission.

Article 88

1. The Commission shall, in cooperation with Member States, keep under constant review all systems of aid existing in those States. It shall propose to the latter any appropriate measures required by the progressive development or by the functioning of the common market.

2. If, after giving notice to the parties concerned to submit their comments, the Commission finds that aid granted by a State or through State resources is not compatible with the common market having regard to Article 87, or that such aid is being misused, it shall decide that the State concerned shall abolish or alter such aid within a period of time to be determined by the Commission.

If the State concerned does not comply with this decision within the prescribed time, the Commission or any other interested State may, in derogation from the provisions of Articles 226 and 227, refer the matter to the Court of Justice direct.

On application by a Member State, the Council may, acting unanimously, decide that aid which that State is granting or intends to grant shall be considered to be compatible with the common market, in derogation from the provisions of Article 87 or from the regulations provided for in Article 89, if such a decision is justified by exceptional circumstances.

If, as regards the aid in question, the Commission has already initiated the procedure provided for in the first subparagraph of this paragraph, the fact that the State concerned has made its application to the Council shall have the effect of suspending that procedure until the Council has made its attitude known.

If, however, the Council has not made its attitude known within three months of the said application being made, the Commission shall give its decision on the case.

3.   The Commission shall be informed, in sufficient time to enable it to submit its comments, of any plans to grant or alter aid. If it considers that any such plan is not compatible with the common market having regard to Article 87, it shall without delay initiate the procedure provided for in paragraph 2. The Member State concerned shall not put its proposed measures into effect until this procedure has resulted in a final decision.

Article 89

The Council, acting by a qualified majority on a proposal from the Commission and after consulting the European Parliament, may make any appropriate regulations for the application of Articles 87 and 88 and may in particular determine the conditions in which Article 88(3) shall apply and the categories of aid exempted from this procedure.

Editors' Notes:

The Commission has published *Guidelines on criteria and modalities of implementation of structural funds in support of electronic communications* SEC(2003) 895 (reproduced below).

The following is a list of selected Commission decisions under Articles 87 and 88 annotated by the Editors.

1.   Broadband Cases

Project Atlas, 2005/C 131/10, (investment of funds by Scottish Enterprises, a State agency, in creation of broadband infrastructure in business parks for leasing as dark fibre to commercial enterprises on non-discriminatory terms and at prices which would yield a positive return, albeit one lower than normally required by the market, found to be compatible with Article 87(3) and "not [to] distort competition to an extent contrary to the public interest" where the following factors were present: (i) design and construction of project was to be solicited from open market, thereby minimising cost of investment and need for public funding; (ii) the original plan to include regional backhaul infrastructure, which would overlap with existing commercial facilities, had been abandoned; (iii) the asset management would be outsourced to an "asset manager" pursuant to a public tender; (iv) the project and the activities of the asset manager would be limited to maintenance and lease of "passive infrastructure" (ducts, dark fibre, etc.) and the asset manager would not compete with service providers; (v) capacity would be leased on wholesale operators on transparent and non-discriminatory terms; (vi) pricing afforded favourable terms to SME's; (vi) existing fibre would be used wherever practicable and owners of fibre already in place in business parks would be given an opportunity to supply fibre; and (viii) the rate of return, "while rather low, is not entirely inappropriate," and the amount of aid is limited).

Commission prohibits public funding for additional broadband network in Appingedam, Netherlands, IP/06/1013 (see OJ 2005/C 321/07) (public funding of a fibre access network in the Dutch town of Appingedam neither justified nor proportionate to remedy either a market failure or unaffordable prices for broadband services where area already served by broadband networks and the proposed funding would distort competition and harm private investment).

The Commission has authorised the use of state aid to fund the extension of broadband in the following instances:

Commission endorses public funding to bridge broadband communications gap in Wales, IP/05/646 (see OJ 2004/C 16/03).

Commission approves public funding of broadband projects in Pyrenees-Atlantiques, Scotland and East Midlands, IP/04/1371 (see OJ 2005/C 126/05).

Commission endorses public funding for broadband network in Limousin, France, IP/05/530 (see OJ 2005/C 230/04).

Commission endorses public funding for broadband communications in rural and remote areas of Spain, IP/05/398 (see OJ 2005/C 252/05).

Commission endorses public funding for broadband communications in Midlands and South West of England, IP/05/1231 (see OJ 2005/C 323/05).

Commission endorses public funding to bridge broadband communications gap in Ireland, IP/06/284 (see N 284/2005).

Commission endorses public funding to bridge broadband communications gap in Greece, IP/06/949 (see N 201/2006).

2.   Other Cases

MobilCom AG, 2005/L 116/55 (provision, by Germany and the Land of Schleswig-Holstein, of an 80% "deficiency guarantee" for a loan of EUR 112 million to MobilCom, a mobile operator threatened with insolvency, was "restructuring aid" not "rescue aid" within the meaning of the Community guidelines on State aid for rescuing and restructuring firms in difficulty (1999/C 288/2) that conferred a selective advantage on MobilCom which it would not have received under normal market conditions and that could have an adverse effect on competition; measure found not to meet the conditions for such aid laid down in the guidelines and, accordingly, incompatible with Article 87(3); aid approved subject to conditions which included cessation of the supply of online direct sales of mobile telephony contracts by MobilCom for a period of 7 months.) *Note:* The Commission approved, in an earlier decision referenced in this decision, the provision of a State guarantee for a loan of EUR 50 million to MobilCom as "rescue aid."

France Télécom, 2005/L 269/30 (adoption of a special business tax scheme applicable to FT for the period from 1 January 1994 to 31 December 2002 was a state aid that gave FT an advantage which distorted or threatened to distort competition and that infringed Article 88(3); France directed to recover the money without delay inform the Commission of the measures it proposed to take in that regard). *Note:* On 19 July 2006, the Commission referred France to the Court of Justice over its alleged failure to comply with this decision.

France Télécom, 2006 L 257/11 (the granting of a shareholder loan in December 2002 in the form of EUR 9 billion credit line was a state aid incompatible with the common market, however, the aid referred does not have to be recovered).

See also:

Commission considers revision of past licence fee liabilities for Polish Telecom operators not to be aid, IP/06/83 (see N 305/2005) (changes in Polish law that revised the outstanding payment obligations of telecoms companies, including the prolongation of deadlines for license fee payments, debt write offs and the conversion of outstanding debt into companies' shares does not constitute state aid as the measures do not entail any economic advantage to the companies concerned and do not distort competition as they aim to restore equal conditions for all telecoms operators).

Commission opens formal investigation into UK property tax on telecommunications, IP/05/63 (see OJ 2005/C 62/08) (announcing opening of a formal investigation to assess the way in which a property tax is applied to British Telecommunications and Kingston Communications in the United Kingdom, noting that a certain asset valuation method is applied to assets of BT and Kingston than to assets of their competitors which may favour those operators vis-à-vis their competitors).

GUIDELINES ON CRITERIA AND MODALITIES OF IMPLEMENTATION OF STRUCTURAL FUNDS IN SUPPORT OF ELECTRONIC COMMUNICATIONS

of 28 July 2003

SEC(2003) 895[a]

1. Aims of the Document

These guidelines are intended to help those regions who wish to co-finance investments through structural funds in the electronic communications sector. Under structural funds, the selection of projects within EU regional programmes is driven by decentralised management where the decisions on projects to be co-financed are taken by the programme partnership, i.e. a range of public and private bodies which contribute to the realisation of programme goals. The European Regional Development Fund (ERDF) is the main financial instrument in support of EU cohesion and regional policy.

The guidelines are similar to a range of guidance provided to programme managers and investors under the aegis of the Directorate General for Regional Policy. In particular, they update and complement the Commission's Staff Working paper[1] prepared in 1999 for the current programming period to reflect recent developments in the sector.

Following a Commission proposal[2] endorsed by the Spring European Council, the guidelines set out the '*criteria and modalities of implementation of Structural funds in support of the electronic communications sector, especially for broadband, in particular in rural and remote areas of geographic isolation and low population density*'[3].

The main focus of the present guidelines is on communications infrastructure, whilst maintaining the relevance of demand and content related measures. . They also address the issue of second generation mobile telephony, which may arise in particular contexts over the period 2004-2006.

The guidelines are meant to be indicative[4]. They are complementary to the broad guidelines for the Mid-term review of Structural Funds interventions, which is due to take place in 2003. They also take account of the specific situation of the new Member States.

2. Background

Since 1999, the information society has undergone substantial changes as regards both the policy context (e-Europe) and the new regulatory framework on electronic communication networks and services (new set of directives). These changes may have a significant impact on structural fund support for the development of the information society in the less favoured regions.

---

[1] European Commission, *Information society and regional development- ERDF interventions 2000-2006-* criteria for programme assessment, SEC/1999/1217.

[2] In 2003, the Commission Communication on Electronic Communications: the Road to the Knowledge Economy (COM(2003)65Final), states that: "*As the mid term review of structural Funds programmes will take place in 2003, this would provide an opportunity for Member States to give greater emphasis to this priority on the basis of an assessment of the regional needs By Spring 2003, the Commission will provide Member States with guidelines on criteria and modalities of implementation of structural Funds in support of the electronic communications sector, notably broadband fixed and wireless infrastructure*" (p7).

[3] Conclusions of Spring European Council, Corfu, 21 March 2003.

[4] These guidelines are without prejudice to any guidelines or Communication that the Commission could adopt concerning the applicability of the State aid rules to Services of General Economic Interest.

Policy developments

The e-Europe 2002 Action Plan[5], agreed by Heads of State and Government in the Feira Council in June 2000 established that a priority for the Union is to ensure that less favoured regions can fully participate in the Information Society. It also recommends that new infrastructure and services across Europe may be supported with European funding, provided that public aid does not distort competition and respects technology neutrality.

In 2002, the Seville European Council endorsed the e-Europe 2005 Action Plan that sets out a strategy to make broadband infrastructure widely available to businesses and citizens throughout the European territory at affordable prices. It also outlines the need to develop adequate content and services, with particular emphasis on public administrations (e-government), a dynamic business environment (e-business), health services (e-health) and education (c-learning). Subsequently, the Spring European Council of March 2003 called upon Member States to put their national broadband strategies in place by the end of 2003.

Regulatory framework for electronic communications

In response to the conclusions of the special European Council of Lisbon of 2 3-24 March 2000, and building on the Communication on the results of the public consultation on the 1999 Review of the Electronic Communications Sector and the principles and orientations for the new Regulatory Framework (COM (2000)239), a package of measures for a new regulatory framework for electronic communication services and networks was adopted during 2002.

The new regulatory framework is intended to provide a coherent, reliable and flexible approach to the regulation of electronic communication networks and services in liberalising markets while ensuring that a minimum of services are available to all users at an affordable price and that the basic rights of consumers are protected.

Rationale for structural funds intervention

Community action through the structural funds has among its main objectives to promote the development and structural adjustment of regions which are lagging behind (Objective 1) or the economic and social restructuring of regions (Objective 2)[6]. The operations financed by the Funds must also be in conformity with other Community policies, including competition rules.

In its guidelines for the 2000-2006 programmes[7], the Commission identified Information society as a key priority for structural funds interventions, with a strong emphasis on demand for services and applications.

Information Society has considerable potential for strengthening economic and social cohesion, i.e. bridging economic and social disparities in Europe. However, the success of regional development strategies will depend on the ability of regions to integrate the Information and Communication Technologies (ICT) made available.

Major changes in the electronic communications sector — e.g. the rapid pace of technological change, slow take up of broadband services, changes in the regulatory framework- make it necessary to rethink the role of public funding taking into account its strategic nature for economic development. After years of market liberalisation, there is also

---

[5] e-Europe 2002- An Information Society for all- Action Plan, p6.
[6] General regulation on structural finds- Reg. 1260/99.
[7] European Commission, *The structural funds and their coordination with the Cohesion Fund-Guidelines for programmes in the period 2000-2006*, COM 1999 (344).

clear evidence of inadequate geographical coverage even for mature technologies such as the GSM network.

In the new Member States, the implementation of the '*acquis*' in the area of Information Society may have significant financial implications, as the roll out of basic electronic communications infrastructure is far from being completed. This includes the financing of universal service obligations[8].

The risk of a widening 'digital divide' and its economic consequences, e.g. the delocalisation of economic activities, has led many governments to explore new solutions to encourage the deployment of broadband infrastructure in less favoured areas. In such areas, geographical isolation and low density of population can make the cost of upgrading the existing infrastructure unsustainable. In rural areas, the unavailability of adequate infrastructure is an important obstacle for the development of certain economic activities such as tourism as well as a source of social disparities.

The investment costs to meet present and future requirements for the development of the Information Society are often difficult to justify on purely commercial grounds. There is a risk, that because the investment is potentially unprofitable, the underlying cohesion objective which underpins e-Europe 2000, i.e. "ensuring access for all to Information Society" is put into question.

Investments through structural funds need to go beyond commercial considerations and must take into account wider issues of public policy. Their role is to enable less favoured areas to come to the forefront of information society development by accelerating broadband deployment as well as ensuring greater territorial cohesion. It is also particularly important with regard to possible future funding of communication infrastructure and services for the new member States within their own development plans and programmes.

3.   Demand and Content

The existence of high quality communications infrastructure is a key condition to enable citizens, businesses and administrations to exploit the opportunities offered by the Information society.

However, the availability of such infrastructure may be irrelevant if adequate services and applications are not provided to the end users or if these lack the knowledge or ability to use them properly. A relatively weak content base, a generally low level of awareness about the benefits and opportunities of the IS, relatively high prices as well as a scarcity of ICT skills are often common barriers in less favoured regions.

Though infrastructure is important, there is a need for businesses and regions to have a clear vision of the demand for the new services it will generate.

Structural funds should support regions in strengthening the demand side of the IS, especially the capacity of firms and institutions to effectively use ICT. Several approaches may be taken to boost demand:

---

[8]   Under the new regulatory framework (Directive 2002/22/EC on Universal service and users rights), universal service is <<provided to all end users throughout the territory, regardless of their geographical location, at a specified level of quality, and taking account of particular national circumstances, at an affordable price >>. The scope of the universal service is defined as covering, inter alia, access to the fixed public telephone network based on voice and data communications as well as narrow band Internet access. It does not include mobile telephony or broadband access to the Internet.

Modernising the public sector

> Demand aggregation for broadband services should be encouraged in order to ensure critical mass of users in public administrations whilst avoiding dependence on one single operator

Stimulating demand in the private sector:

> Stimulation of demand for types or 'clusters' of SMEs allows to increase awareness and use of ICT

Developing content:

> Financing content, including e-government, in particular local and regional services in order to boost demand for broadband on a sufficiently focused basis to develop supply.

Raising digital skills

> Equipping the population with the necessary skills to use broadband connections

Public authorities, and particularly regional and local authorities, have a key role to play in the development of the information society by (1) using information society applications and services in the process of modemisation of services provided to citizens and companies, (2) promoting the information society in the region and (3) monitoring the evolution of the communications networks and services provision on the region in order to avoid exclusion and contribute to the balanced development of regional activities.

In this latter respect, accessibility[9] is especially important because it promotes demand by increasing interest and giving citizens, firms and institutions a chance to become aware of generic services and ICT applications and the practical benefits of their use. This, in turn, will bring about the critical mass or sufficient level of demand needed to strengthen the regional information society development.

> Public funding for the above initiatives must comply with the Treaty rules on State aid. Depending on the particular case, such funding may be found compatible under the rules governing e.g. aid to small and medium-sized enterprises[10], regional aid[11] or "de minimis" aid.[12]

4. Financing of Electronic Communications Infrastructure: Criteria For ERDF Intervention

The e-Europe 2005 Action Plan indicates that new infrastructure and services may be supported through structural funds in eligible regions, especially in rural and remote areas. It is, however, conditional upon certain criteria, which must be taken into consideration for the appraisal of Information society investments. These are outlined below.

---

[9]   In particular, the ERDF could support local and regional governments in their effort to introduce on-line administration and telematic services and provide people with easy access to this system. For example, the ERDF should help to establish tailored access points in municipalities or local communities.

[10] Commission Regulation (EC) No 70/2001 of 12 January 2001 on the application of Articles 87 and 88 of the EC Treaty to State aid to small and medium-sized enterprises, OJ L 10 of 13.1.2001, p.33.

[11] Guidelines on national regional aid, OJ C 74 of 10.3.1998, p. 9.

[12] Commission Regulation (EC) No 69/2001 of 12 January 2001 on the application of Articles 87 and 88 of the EC Treaty to *de minimis* aid, OJ L 10 of 13.1.2001, p.30.

Need for a strategic framework

ERDF support should be linked and determined by the information society development strategy of the region. More specifically, infrastructure projects must be connected with the objectives of regional economic development, i.e. economic growth, regional competitiveness as well as balanced distribution of economic activities. Isolated projects should not receive support. They should be articulated with other actions aiming at developing new applications and services.

As part of the strategy, infrastructure projects should be based on an analysis of regional needs and opportunities identified in consultation with economic and social partners, taking into account specific economic and institutional conditions as well as the pre-existing infrastructure (i.e. an inventory of existing infrastructure endowment before planning any new investment)

Accordingly, public authorities, especially at sub-national level (regions, local authorities) will propose information society measures within national or regional programmes. They also have the responsibility to ensure that the investment measures are relevant to the regional objectives and needs and that these measures are coherent with the overall economic development strategy as well as guaranteeing their economic sustainability.

> In view of future adjustments to be made to Objective 1 and 2 programmes, the Commission should be informed of the content of the strategies, in the form of a simplified framework (Annex I)

Geographical targeting

ERDF support take into account regional specificities, such as geographic factors that may vary greatly across eligible regions. In principle, investments must be targeted towards areas that would otherwise be neglected under free market conditions. The main focus should be on rural and remote areas, which are not covered by adequate infrastructure. ERDF support is also justified in areas where there are insufficient commercial incentives to provide adequate infrastructure allowing for advanced applications and services of general interest.

Although regional aid is, in principle, strictly concerned with eligible areas under Objective 1 or 2, investments can be financed outside these areas to the extent that they are realised in contiguous areas (NUTS III) and comply with eligibility rules laid down in Reg. (EC) n°1685/2000[13].

Technological neutrality

Selection criteria for investments in electronic communications infrastructure must adhere to the principle of 'technology neutrality'. ERDF support should not a priori favour any particular technology, nor limit the technology choice of the regions.

When a project involves the financing of a specific technology — in the case of broadband, e.g. DSL, cable, satellite, wireless, etc. — or a specialised infrastructure, the choice must be

---

[13] "The maximum eligible expenditure of the operation is determined pro rata to the proportion of the benefits from the operation which it is foreseen will accrue to the region and shall be based on an evaluation by a body independent of the managing authority. The benefits shall be assessed taking account of the specific targets of the assistance and its expected impact. The operation cannot be accepted for co-financing where the proportion of benefits is less than 50 %. For each measure of the assistance, the eligible expenditure of the operations accepted under point 2.1 should not exceed 10 % of the total eligible expenditure of the measure. In addition, the eligible expenditure of all operations in the assistance accepted under point 2.1 should not exceed 5 % of the total eligible expenditure of the assistance".

clearly justified on the basis of a cost-benefit analysis, taking into account possible alternatives for the provision of the service.

Open access

Financial support will be granted to projects which are consistent and in accordance with the new regulatory framework on communications networks and services as well as competition rules (state aids and antitrust). Compliance with these rules is a key condition of eligibility for ERDF support, which needs to be accompanied by clear open access obligations.

ERDF support should be limited, in principle, to infrastructure, i.e. installations (dark fibre, ducts, masts,...) and equipment which is open to all operators and service providers.

The local area concerned may be subject to unbundling of access to the local loop. Location and technical requirements of the points of access to the new infrastructure should not favour dominant operators on the local access nor give rise to distortions on other markets.

The case of non-open infrastructure projects

Direct financing of installations and equipment which are not open to all, but are dedicated to one or more operators, does not qualify as funding of an 'open infrastructure' project, e.g. the case of installations reserved to a specific operator as a result of an agreement with the regulatory authority.

Funding of installations and equipment dedicated to a specific final user may constitute State aid whenever such user is an undertaking. Depending on particular cases, such funding may not constitute State aid when it is necessary for the provision of a 'service of general economic interest' (SGEI). When it constitutes a State aid, it may be compatible under rules governing aid to small and medium size enterprises, regional aid or '*de minimis*'.

The provision of the service should respect the principles of transparency, non-discrimination, proportionality and least market distortion. If the service is not awarded as a result of an open, transparent and non-discriminatory procedure, the operator is required to hold a separate accounting system for the service in question, which would allow to establish the amount of public compensation or tariffs applicable for the use of the service and subject to annual revision.

---

5. Modalities of Implementation

Once infrastructure projects are considered as being consistent with the above criteria, they should follow a number of key implementation rules. With respect to competition rules, it should be noted that EDRF support does not represent a state aid in the meaning of Article 87(1), but must follow the same rules and, where is the case, concurs with Member States' funding to determine the compatible amount of aid.

Tendering process

Contracts should be awarded through open calls for tender. As a general rule, this should be organised at the appropriate level (national, regional, local) under the supervision of the competent authority, which should ensure compliance with relevant legislation and coherence with national IS policies.

Competitors should be invited to submit their technical and financial offers. The contract should be awarded to the operator who will provide the service with the specific characteristics of the required solution at the lowest cost.

Financing

ERDF support should be limited to the necessary amounts of resources for the provision of the service. In principle, it covers both the financing of installations and equipment that are open to all operators and service providers.

Projects should contain sufficient and detailed information in order to ensure a proper assessment —on the part of the managing authorities- of whether or not they are coherent with economic development objectives as well as compatible with competition rules.

Ownership

The subsidised infrastructure can remain owned by a public authority, a private entity which provides co-funding, or by a public-private entity. In all cases, access for all operators to the infrastructure at non-discriminatory conditions must be granted. In principle, Community support should not strengthen a dominant position by any operator, or distort competition rules.

The modalities of renting of the infrastructure to private undertakings will have to be accurately defined on a case by case basis. In some countries, national regulatory frameworks are being modified, e.g. local authorities having the right under certain conditions to become operators.

With a view to determining compliance with the regulatory frameworks, it is useful to distinguish the funding of an infrastructure which is owned by a public authority from the funding of an infrastructure which is owned by an undertaking.

Infrastructure owned by the public authority

The funding of an infrastructure owned by the public authority does not constitute granting of State aid in the meaning of Article 87(1). The procurement of the works for the creation of such infrastructure must follow the appropriate community legislation in the matter.

However, when the infrastructure is made available to undertakings, this should be done on non-discriminatory terms and upon payment of appropriate fees. Such fees are not expected to cover the entire cost of investment —in cases when the market is not capable of providing equivalent services — and should also not allow the users of the infrastructure to make extra profits in excess of a fair return

When a service equivalent to that provided by the infrastructure is already supplied by the market, then the infrastructure should be rented out at fees allowing coverage of costs and a fair return on investment.

If the management of the facility is entrusted to a third party, it should be awarded for a limited amount of time as a result of an open, transparent and non-discriminatory procedure, preferably determined through a competitive process and leading to a market compensation paid by the concession holder. As a general rule, this should be organised at the appropriate level (national, regional, local) under the supervision of the competent authority, which should ensure compliance with relevant legislation and coherence with national and regional IS policies.

The manager of the infrastructure is submitted to operating requirements that preserve the nature of the infrastructure as a facility open to all operators providing electronic communication networks and services at non-discriminatory conditions.

Infrastructure owned by undertaking(s)

In the case of (co-)funding of a facility which is owned by an undertaking, the State financial contribution would have to be made conditional on the acceptance of operating requirements which would preserve the nature of the infrastructure as a facility open to all operators providing electronic communication networks and services at non discriminatory conditions.

There should be evidence that the amount of state funding was the minimum necessary to allow the project to proceed, so to ensure that the operator using the facility does not receive more than a normal market return for its activity. To this end, State funding should be awarded through open call for tender. As a general rule, this should be organised at the appropriate level (national, regional, local) under the supervision of the competent authority, which should ensure compliance with relevant legislation and coherence with national and regional IS policies. Competitors would be invited to submit their technical and financial offer. The contract will need to be awarded to the operator/s providing electronic communication networks which fulfil the minimum specified requirements for the service (in terms of quality of service, future improvements, etc) at the lowest cost

Transparency

Infrastructure operators will have to develop a cost accounting system, which allows the calculation and justification of any compensation or subsidy in accordance with competition legislation. Only on the basis of such a system, will it be possible to establish tariffs in a transparent and efficient way and to charge cost elements to the relevant parts of the network.

The regulatory framework for electronic communications requires inter alia that regulatory authorities are legally distinct and functionally independent from the organisations — which are in charge of the provision of networks, equipment or communication services. In cases where local authorities have regulatory functions, notably with regard to passage and building permits, the Member States will respect the principles of transparency and non-discrimination and ensure that such rights are obtained under similar conditions by applicants which do not benefit from the assistance.

Determination of co-financing rates

The responsibility for the appraisal and selection of the projects lies in the regions. ERDF aid rates apply to the projects co-financed, according to economic and financial profitability of projects, in accordance with the provisions laid down in article 29 (4) of Reg. 1260/99[14].

When communications infrastructure projects are considered as investments generating substantial net revenues, co-financed rates should be justified and modulated on the basis of

---

[14] EC Regulation on structural funds 1260/99, art. 29.4 "...Where the assistance concerned entails the financing of revenue-generating investments, the contribution from the funds to these investments shall be determined in the light of their intrinsic characteristics, including the size of the gross self-financing margin which would normally be expected for the class of investments concerned in the light of the macro-economic circumstances in which the investments are to be implemented, and without there being any increase in the national budget effort as a result of the contribution by the funds. In any event, the contribution of the funds shall be subject to the following ceilings:
(a) in the case of investment in infrastructure generating substantial net revenue, the contribution may not exceed:
(i) 40% of the total eligible cost in the regions covered by Objective 1, which may be increased by not more than an extra 10% in the Member States covered by the cohesion fund;
(ii) 25% of the total eligible cost in the areas covered by Objective 2;
(iii) these rates may be increased by an amount for forms of finance other than direct assistance, provided that this increase does not exceed 10% of the total eligible cost; ...".

a full cost-benefit analysis. As a general indication, these projects are those which generate at least 25% of net revenues in relation to the actual cost of investment using an appropriate discount rate (i.e.6%).

Evaluation, monitoring and benchmarking

Judging the effectiveness of structural funds assistance to the regions is an essential part of accountability, achieving value for money and appraising future investment decisions.

In terms of the prior appraisal of information society related projects, and especially communications infrastructure projects, criteria could include:

– Electronic communication networks penetration (per 100 residence households and, if this is not available, lines per 100 inhabitants)

– Electronic communication networks revenue per inhabitant;

– Active operators (services and networks) in the regional area;

– Market evolution (share and market growth);

– Penetration, revenue and diffusion of any other communication means (satellite, wireless, mobile communications, etc).

– Improvement in affordability of services

Furthermore, detailed information on the project and on the promoter should be provided. This should include: total cost, expected return on capital investment, estimated (direct) employment creation, diversification of the local economy into knowledge related activities

A checklist of indicators should be used to monitor over time outputs and impacts generated by ERDF-supported IS projects. Regional indicators should be developed, where appropriate, with due regard to e-Europe 2005 indicators. Targets would have to reflect particular local conditions.

6. The Case Of Second Generation Mobile Telephony

As a general rule, investment in 2nd generation mobile telephony is profitable and therefore ERDF support is not justifiable on economic grounds. Although coverage of certain areas might not be entirely profitable, wide coverage of a significant proportion of the territory is normally required and this includes the use of cross-subsidisation. However, there might be a case of a member State that wishes to extend coverage to the remaining part of the population living in uncovered areas in order to ensure economic viability of these investments. Under these circumstances, ERDF support could be granted to 'uncovered areas' where investments are not financially viable.

Competition issues

Investments limited to open infrastructure i.e. installations and equipment ensuring non-discriminatory access to all operators do not raise particular problems in terms of competition policy. Local roaming must be provided at fair tariffs to other operators when this is necessary to avoid discrimination between operators. This involves the set up of a local itinerant service to ensure the sharing of active infrastructures, to be carried out in accordance with competition rules.

Direct aid for a service or equipment which is dedicated to one or more operators does not qualify as an 'infrastructure' project, e.g. the case of installations reserved to a specific operator as a result of an agreement with the regulatory authority. In such cases, State intervention might be justified by the need to provide a 'service of general economic interest' (in accordance with art.86.2 of the Treaty) insofar as operators are not granted a financial advantage which exceeds the funding of the net additional cost of the service.

The provision of the service should respect the principles of transparency, non-discrimination, proportionality and least market distortion. If the service is not awarded as a result of an open, transparent and non-discriminatory procedure, the operator is required to hold a separate accounting system for the service in question, which would allow the amount of public compensation or tariffs applicable for the use of the service to be established and which would be subject to annual revision.

Editors' Notes:

[a] Reproduced with minor changes and omissions.

ANNEX 1

REGIONAL INFORMATION SOCIETY STRATEGY

Indicative schema

I. State of play

– Existing strategic documents (to be sent to DG REGIO)

– Existing projects: census of network infrastructure (mobile / broadband), applications / services and content

– Economic development needs

II. Challenges and medium-long term objectives

– Coherence of IS regional strategy with the overall development strategy of the region

– Relevance of IS objectives and their contribution to the programme's objectives

– Main challenges for economic development

III. Main projects to be funded

In relation to point I, it would be necessary to provide relevant information with regard to:

– Nature of actions

– Content of projects

– Location of investments

– Financial incidence

– Economic viability

IV. Estimated costs

– The region will have to provide an estimation of the overall investment costs, for both co-financed and non co-financed projects.

Annexes: Maps on broadband / mobile telephony coverage

<u>SCHEMA I: CRITERIA FOR FINANCING INFRASTRUCTURE UNDER
STRUCTURAL FUNDS</u>

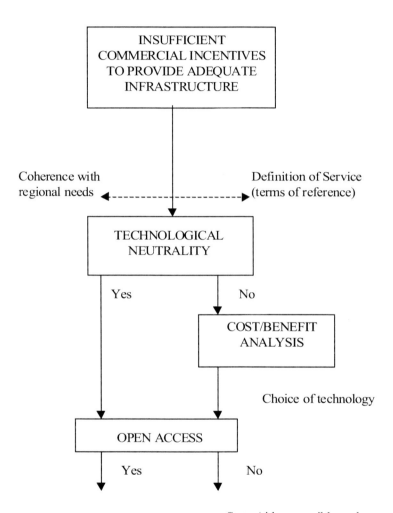

SCHEMA II: MODALITIES OF IMPLEMENTATION

OWNER	PUBLIC	Public –Private Partnership	PRIVATE
ACTION			
Choice of private undertaking		Tender	Tender
Choice of supplier of equipment + services	Public procurement application rules	Tender	Free
Choice of infrastructure manager	Concession or Direct management without conflict with regulation	Without conflict with regulation	Free
Access to infrastructure	Open to all → no problem Not open → possible notification	Open to all → no problem Not open → possible notification	Open to all → no problem Not open → possible notification

COUNCIL DECISION 1999/468/EC

of 28 June 1999[a]

laying down the procedures for the exercise of
implementing powers conferred on the Commission[1]

THE COUNCIL OF THE EUROPEAN UNION,

Having regard to the Treaty establishing the European Community, and in particular the third indent of Article 202 thereof,

Having regard to the proposal from the Commission[2],

Having regard to the opinion of the European Parliament[3],

Whereas:

(1)   in the instruments which it adopts, the Council has to confer on the Commission powers for the implementation of the rules which the Council lays down; the Council may impose certain requirements in respect of the exercise of these powers; it may also reserve to itself the right, in specific and substantiated cases, to exercise directly implementing powers;

(2)   the Council adopted Decision 87/373/EEC of 13 July 1987 laying down the procedures for the exercise of implementing powers conferred on the Commission[4]; that Decision has provided for a limited number of procedures for the exercise of such powers;

(3)   declaration No 31 annexed to the Final Act of the Intergovernmental Conference which adopted the Amsterdam Treaty calls on the Commission to submit to the Council a proposal amending Decision 87/373/EEC;

(4)   for reasons of clarity, rather than amending Decision 87/373/EEC, it has been considered more appropriate to replace that Decision by a new Decision and, therefore, to repeal Decision 87/373/EEC;

(5)   the first purpose of this Decision is, with a view to achieving greater consistency and predictability in the choice of type of committee, to provide for criteria relating to the choice of committee procedures, it being understood that such criteria are of a non-binding nature;

(6)   in this regard, the management procedure should be followed as regards management measures such as those relating to the application of the common agricultural and common fisheries policies or to the implementation of programmes with substantial budgetary implications; such management measures should be taken by the Commission by a procedure ensuring decision-making within suitable periods; however, where non-urgent measures are referred to the Council, the Commission should exercise its discretion to defer application of the measures;

(7)   the regulatory procedure should be followed as regards measures of general scope designed to apply essential provisions of basic instruments, including measures

---

[1]   Three statements in the Council minutes relating to this Decision are set out in OJ C 203 of 17 June, page 1.
[2]   OJ C 279, 8.9.1998, p. 5.
[3]   Opinion delivered on 6 May 1999 (not yet published in the Official Journal).
[4]   OJ L 197, 18.7.1987, p. 33.

concerning the protection of the health or safety of humans, animals or plants, as well as measures designed to adapt or update certain non-essential provisions of a basic instrument; such implementing measures should be adopted by an effective procedure which complies in full with the Commission's right of initiative in legislative matters;

(8)   the advisory procedure should be followed in any case in which it is considered to be the most appropriate; the advisory procedure will continue to be used in those cases where it currently applies;

(9)   the second purpose of this Decision is to simplify the requirements for the exercise of implementing powers conferred on the Commission as well as to improve the involvement of the European Parliament in those cases where the basic instrument conferring implementation powers on the Commission was adopted in accordance with the procedure laid down in Article 251 of the Treaty; it has been accordingly considered appropriate to reduce the number of procedures as well as to adjust them in line with the respective powers of the institutions involved and notably to give the European Parliament an opportunity to have its views taken into consideration by, respectively, the Commission or the Council in cases where it considers that, respectively, a draft measure submitted to a committee or a proposal submitted to the Council under the regulatory procedure exceeds the implementing powers provided for in the basic instrument;

(10)   the third purpose of this Decision is to improve information to the European Parliament by providing that the Commission should inform it on a regular basis of committee proceedings, that the Commission should transmit to it documents related to activities of committees and inform it whenever the Commission transmits to the Council measures or proposals for measures to be taken;

(11)   the fourth purpose of this Decision is to improve information to the public concerning committee procedures and therefore to make applicable to committees the principles and conditions on public access to documents applicable to the Commission, to provide for a list of all committees which assist the Commission in the exercise of implementing powers and for an annual report on the working of committees to be published as well as to provide for all references to documents related to committees which have been transmitted to the European Parliament to be made public in a register;

(12)   the specific committee procedures created for the implementation of the common commercial policy and the competition rules laid down by the Treaties that are not currently based upon Decision 87/373/EEC are not in any way affected by this Decision,

HAS DECIDED AS FOLLOWS:

Article 1

Other than in specific and substantiated cases where the basic instrument reserves to the Council the right to exercise directly certain implementing powers itself, such powers shall be conferred on the Commission in accordance with the relevant provisions in the basic instrument. These provisions shall stipulate the essential elements of the powers thus conferred.

Where the basic instrument imposes specific procedural requirements for the adoption of implementing measures, such requirements shall be in conformity with the procedures provided for by Articles 3, 4, 5 and 6.

Article 2

The choice of procedural methods for the adoption of implementing measures shall be guided by the following criteria:

(a) management measures, such as those relating to the application of the common agricultural and common fisheries policies, or to the implementation of programmes with substantial budgetary implications, should be adopted by use of the management procedure;

(b) measures of general scope designed to apply essential provisions of basic instruments, including measures concerning the protection of the health or safety of humans, animals or plants, should be adopted by use of the regulatory procedure; where a basic instrument stipulates that certain non-essential provisions of the instrument may be adapted or updated by way of implementing procedures, such measures should be adopted by use of the regulatory procedure;

(c) without prejudice to points (a) and (b), the advisory procedure shall be used in any case in which it is considered to be the most appropriate.

Article 3

Advisory procedure

1. The Commission shall be assisted by an advisory committee composed of the representatives of the Member States and chaired by the representative of the Commission.

2. The representative of the Commission shall submit to the Committee a draft of the measures to be taken. The committee shall deliver its opinion on the draft, within a time-limit which the chairman may lay down according to the urgency of the matter, if necessary by taking a vote.

3. The opinion shall be recorded in the minutes; in addition, each Member State shall have the right to ask to have its position recorded in the minutes.

4. The Commission shall take the utmost account of the opinion delivered by the committee. It shall inform the committee of the manner in which the opinion has been taken into account.

Article 4

Management procedure

1. The Commission shall be assisted by a management committee composed of the representatives of the Member States and chaired by the representative of the Commission.

2. The representative of the Commission shall submit to the committee a draft of the measures to be taken. The committee shall deliver its opinion on the draft within a time-limit which the chairman may lay down according to the urgency of the matter. The opinion shall be delivered by the majority laid down in Article 205(2) of the Treaty, in the case of decisions which the Council is required to adopt on a proposal from the Commission. The votes of the representatives of the Member States within the committee shall be weighted in the manner set out in that Article. The chairman shall not vote.

3.   The Commission shall, without prejudice to Article 8, adopt measures which shall apply immediately. However, if these measures are not in accordance with the opinion of the committee, they shall be communicated by the Commission to the Council forthwith. In that event, the Commission may defer application of the measures which it has decided on for a period to be laid down in each basic instrument but which shall in no case exceed three months from the date of such communication.

4.   The Council, acting by qualified majority, may take a different decision within the period provided for by paragraph 3.

Article 5

Regulatory procedure

1.   The Commission shall be assisted by a regulatory committee composed of the representatives of the Member States and chaired by the representative of the Commission.

2.   The representative of the Commission shall submit to the committee a draft of the measures to be taken. The committee shall deliver its opinion on the draft within a time-limit which the chairman may lay down according to the urgency of the matter. The opinion shall be delivered by the majority laid down in Article 205(2) of the Treaty in the case of decisions which the Council is required to adopt on a proposal from the Commission. The votes of the representatives of the Member States within the Committee shall be weighted in the manner set out in that Article. The chairman shall not vote.

3.   The Commission shall, without prejudice to Article 8, adopt the measures envisaged if they are in accordance with the opinion of the committee.

4.   If the measures envisaged are not in accordance with the opinion of the committee, or if no opinion is delivered, the Commission shall, without delay, submit to the Council a proposal relating to the measures to be taken and shall inform the European Parliament.

5.   If the European Parliament considers that a proposal submitted by the Commission pursuant to a basic instrument adopted in accordance with the procedure laid down in Article 251 of the Treaty exceeds the implementing powers provided for in that basic instrument, it shall inform the Council of its position.

6.   The Council may, where appropriate in view of any such position, act by qualified majority on the proposal, within a period to be laid down in each basic instrument but which shall in no case exceed three months from the date of referral to the Council.

    If within that period the Council has indicated by qualified majority that it opposes the proposal, the Commission shall re-examine it. It may submit an amended proposal to the Council, re-submit its proposal or present a legislative proposal on the basis of the Treaty.

    If on the expiry of that period the Council has neither adopted the proposed implementing act nor indicated its opposition to the proposal for implementing measures, the proposed implementing act shall be adopted by the Commission.

Article 6

Safeguard procedure

The following procedure may be applied where the basic instrument confers on the Commission the power to decide on safeguard measures:

(a) the Commission shall notify the Council and the Member States of any decision regarding safeguard measures. It may be stipulated that before adopting its decision, the Commission shall consult the Member States in accordance with procedures to be determined in each case;

(b) Any Member State may refer the Commission's decision to the Council within a time-limit to be determined within the basic instrument in question;

(c) the Council, acting by a qualified majority, may take a different decision within a time-limit to be determined in the basic instrument in question. Alternatively, it may be stipulated in the basic instrument that the Council, acting by qualified majority, may confirm, amend or revoke the decision adopted by the Commission and that, if the Council has not taken a decision within the abovementioned time-limit, the decision of the Commission is deemed to be revoked.

Article 7

1. Each committee shall adopt its own rules of procedure on the proposal of its chairman, on the basis of standard rules of procedure which shall be published in the Official Journal of the European Communities.

   Insofar as necessary existing committees shall adapt their rules of procedure to the standard rules of procedure.

2. The principles and conditions on public access to documents applicable to the Commission shall apply to the committees.

3. The European Parliament shall be informed by the Commission of committee proceedings on a regular basis. To that end, it shall receive agendas for committee meetings, draft measures submitted to the committees for the implementation of instruments adopted by the procedure provided for by Article 251 of the Treaty, and the results of voting and summary records of the meetings and lists of the authorities and organisations to which the persons designated by the Member States to represent them belong. The European Parliament shall also be kept informed whenever the Commission transmits to the Council measures or proposals for measures to be taken.

4. The Commission shall, within six months of the date on which this Decision takes effect, publish in the Official Journal of the European Communities, a list of all committees which assist the Commission in the exercise of implementing powers. This list shall specify, in relation to each committee, the basic instrument(s) under which the committee is established. From 2000 onwards, the Commission shall also publish an annual report on the working of committees.

5. The references of all documents sent to the European Parliament pursuant to paragraph 3 shall be made public in a register to be set up by the Commission in 2001.

Article 8

If the European Parliament indicates, in a Resolution setting out the grounds on which it is based, that draft implementing measures, the adoption of which is contemplated and which have been submitted to a committee pursuant to a basic instrument adopted under Article

251 of the Treaty, would exceed the implementing powers provided for in the basic instrument, the Commission shall re-examine the draft measures. Taking the Resolution into account and within the time-limits of the procedure under way, the Commission may submit new draft measures to the committee, continue with the procedure or submit a proposal to the European Parliament and the Council on the basis of the Treaty.

The Commission shall inform the European Parliament and the committee of the action which it intends to take on the Resolution of the European Parliament and of its reasons for doing so.

Article 9

Decision 87/373/EEC shall be repealed.

Article 10

This Decision shall take effect on the day following that of its publication in the Official Journal of the European Communities.

Editors' Notes:

[a] OJ L 184, 17.7.1999, p. 23.

See also:

Agreement between the European Parliament and the Commission on procedures for implementing Council Decision 1999/468/EC of 28 June 1999 laying down the procedures for the exercise of implementing powers conferred on the Commission, Official Journal L 256, 10/10/2000, pp 19-20;

Information from the Commission - List of committees which assist the Commission in the exercise of its implementing powers, Official Journal C 225, 08/08/2000 pp 2-18;

Declarations on Council Decision 1999/468/EC of 28 June 1999 laying down the procedures for the exercise of implementing powers conferred on the Commission Official Journal C 203, 17/07/1999, p1; and

Proposal for a Council Decision amending Decision 1999/468/EC laying down the procedures for the exercise of implementing powers conferred on the Commission, COM/2002/0719 final - CNS 2002/0298.

COMMISSION DECISION 2002/627/EC

of 29 July 2002

establishing the European Regulators Group for
Electronic Communications Networks and Services

[as amended][a]

THE COMMISSION OF THE EUROPEAN COMMUNITIES,

Having regard to the Treaty establishing the European Community,

Whereas:

(1) A new regulatory framework for electronic communications networks and services has been established in accordance with European Parliament and Council Directives 2002/21/EC of 7 March 2002 on a common regulatory framework for electronic communications networks and services (Framework Directive)[1], 2002/19/EC of 7 March 2002 on access to, and interconnection of, electronic communications networks and associated facilities (Access Directive)[2], 2002/20/EC of 7 March 2002 on the authorisation of electronic communications networks and services (Authorisation Directive)[3] and 2002/22/EC of 7 March 2002 on the universal services and users' rights related to electronic communications networks and services (Universal Service Directive)[4].

(2) National regulatory authorities have been set up in all Member States to carry out the regulatory tasks specified in these Directives and as to be notified to the Commission in accordance with Article 3(6) of the Framework Directive. In accordance with the Framework Directive, Member States must guarantee the independence of national regulatory authorities by ensuring that they are legally distinct from and functionally independent of all organisations providing electronic communications networks, equipment or services. Member States that retain ownership or control of undertakings providing electronic communications networks and/or services must also ensure effective structural separation of the regulatory function from activities associated with ownership or control.

(3) Detailed responsibilities and tasks of the national regulatory authorities differ among the various Member States, but all of them have at least one national regulatory authority who is charged with application of the rules once they have been transposed into national law, in particular the rules concerning day-to-day supervision of the market.

(4) The need for the relevant rules to be consistently applied in all Member States is essential for the successful development of an internal market for electronic communications networks and services. The new regulatory framework sets out objectives to be achieved and provides a framework for action by national regulatory authorities, whilst granting them flexibility in certain areas to apply the rules in the light of national conditions.

---

[1]   OJ L 108, 24.4.2002, p. 33.
[2]   OJ L 108, 24.4.2002, p. 7.
[3]   OJ L 108, 24.4.2002, p. 21.
[4]   OJ L 108, 24.4.2002, p. 51.

(5)   A European Regulators Group for Electronic Communications Networks and Services (hereinafter referred to as the Group) should be established to provide an interface for advising and assisting the Commission in the electronic communications field.

(6)   The Group should provide an interface between national regulatory authorities and the Commission in such a way as to contribute to the development of the internal market. It should also allow cooperation between national regulatory authorities and the Commission in a transparent manner so as to ensure the consistent application in all Member States of the regulatory framework for electronic communications networks and services.

(7)   The Group should serve as a body for reflection, debate and advice for the Commission in the electronic communications field, including on matters related to the implementation and revision of Recommendation on Relevant Product and Service Markets and in drawing up the Decision on transnational markets.

(8)   Close cooperation should be maintained between the Group and the Communications Committee established under the Framework Directive. The work of the Group should not interfere with the work of the Committee.

(9)   Coordination should be ensured with the Radio Spectrum Committee established under a Decision No 676/2002/EC of the European Parliament and Council of 7 March 2002 on a regulatory framework for radio spectrum policy in the European Community (Radio Spectrum Decision)[5], the Radio Spectrum Policy Group established under the Commission Decision 2002/622/EC of 26 July 2002 establishing a Radio Spectrum Policy Group[6] and the Television Without frontiers Contact Committee, created pursuant to Directive 97/36/EC of the European Parliament and of the Council[7] on the coordination of certain provisions laid down by law, regulation or administrative action in Member States concerning the pursuit of television broadcasting activities,

HAS DECIDED AS FOLLOWS:

Article 1

Subject matter

An advisory group of the independent national regulatory authorities on electronic communications networks and services, called the European Regulators Group for Electronic Communications Networks and Services (hereinafter referred to as the Group), is hereby established.

Article 2

[deleted]^b

---

[5]   OJ L 108, 24.4.2002, p. 1.
[6]   OJ L 198, 27.7.2002, p. 49.
[7]   OJ L 202, 30.7.1997, p. 60.

Article 3

Aims

The role of the Group shall be to advise and assist the Commission in consolidating the internal market for electronic communications networks and services.

The Group shall provide an interface between national regulatory authorities and the Commission in such a way as to contribute to the development of the internal market and to the consistent application in all Member States of the regulatory framework for electronic communications networks and services.

The Group shall advise and assist the Commission on any matter related to electronic communications networks and services within its competence, either at its own initiative or at the Commission's request.

Article 4

Membership

1. The Group shall be composed of the heads of the independent national regulatory authority established in each Member State with primary responsibility for overseeing the day-to-day operation of the market for electronic communications networks and services, or their representatives.

   There shall be one member per Member State. The Commission shall be represented at an appropriate level and shall provide the secretariat to the Group.

2. The relevant national authorities referred to in paragraph 1 are listed in the Annex. The Commission shall keep this list under review in the light of any changes introduced by Member States to the names or responsibilities of these authorities.

Article 5

Operational arrangements

The Group shall elect a chairperson from among its members. The work of the group may be organised into subgroups and expert working groups as appropriate.

The chairperson shall convene the meetings of the Group in agreement with the Commission.

The Group shall adopt its rules of procedure by consensus or, in the absence of consensus, by a two-thirds majority vote, one vote being expressed per Member State, subject to the approval of the Commission.

The Commission shall be represented at all meetings of the Group and be able to attend all meetings of its subgroups and expert working groups.

Experts from EEA States that are not members of the European Union and those States that are candidates for accession to the European Union may participate as observers in the Group. The Group may invite other experts and observers to attend its meetings.

Article 6

Consultation

The Group shall consult extensively and at an early stage with market participants, consumers and end-users in an open and transparent manner.

Article 7

Confidentiality

Without prejudice to the provisions of Article 287 of the Treaty, where the Commission informs them that the advice requested or the question raised is of a confidential nature, members of the Group as well as observers and any other person shall be under an obligation not to disclose information which has come to their knowledge through the work of the Group, its subgroups or expert groups. The Commission may decide in such cases that only members of the Group may be present at meetings.

Article 8

Annual report

The Group shall submit an annual report of its activities to the Commission. The Commission shall transmit the report to the European Parliament and to the Council, where appropriate with comments.

Article 9

Entry into force

This Decision shall enter into force the day of its publication in the Official Journal of the European Communities.

The Group shall take up its duties on the date of entry into force of this Decision.

Editors' Notes:

[a] Commission Decision 2002/627/EC (OJ L 200, 30.07.2002, p. 38) is reproduced in this book as amended by Commission Decision 2004/641/EC of 14 September 2004 (OJ L 293, 16.09.2004, p. 30).

[b] Article 2 deleted by Commission Decision 2004/641/EC.

List of Members of the ERG

Country	National Regulatory Authority
Belgique/België	Institut belge des services postaux et des télécommunications (IBPT)
	Belgisch Instituut voor postdiensten en telecommunicatie (BIPT)
Česká republika	Český telekomunikační úřad (ČTÚ)
Danmark	IT- og Telestyrelsen — National IT and Telecom Agency (NITA)
Deutschland	Regulierungsbehörde für Telekommunikation und Post (Reg TP)
Eesti	Sideamet (SIDEAMET)
Ελλάδα Elláda	Εθνική Επιτροπή Τηλεπικοινωνιών και Ταχυδρομείων National Telecommunications and Post Commission (EETT)
España	Comisión del Mercado de las Telecomunicaciones (CMT)
France	Autorité de Régulation des Télécommunications (ART)
Ireland	Commission for Communications Regulation (ComReg)
Italia	Autorità per le garanzie nelle comunicazioni (AGCOM)
Kypros	Office of the Commissioner of Telecommunications and Postal Regulation (OCTPR)
Latvija	Sabiedrisko pakalpojumu regulēšanas komisija (SPRK)
Lietuva	Ryšių reguliavimo tarnyba (RRT)
Luxembourg	Institut Luxembourgeois de Régulation (ILR)
Magyarország	Nemzeti Hírközlési Hatóság (NHH)
Malta	Malta Communications Authority (MCA)
Nederland	Onafhankelijke Post en Telecommunicatie Autoriteit (OPTA)
Österreich	Rundfunk und Telekom Regulierungs-GmbH (RTR)
Polska	Urząd Regulacji Telekomunikacji i Poczty (URTiP)
Portugal	ICP — Autoridade Nacional de Comunicações (ICP-ANACOM)
Slovenija	Agencija za telekomunikacije, radiodifuzijo in pošto Republike Slovenije (ATRP)
Slovensko	Telekomunikačný úrad Slovenskej republiky (TU SR)
Suomi Finland	Viestintävirasto Kommunikationsverket (FICORA)
Sverige	Post- och telestyrelsen (PTS)
United Kingdom	Office of Communications (Ofcom)

REGULATION (EC) NO 460/2004
OF THE EUROPEAN PARLIAMENT AND OF THE COUNCIL

of 10 March 2004[a]

establishing the European Network and Information Security Agency

THE EUROPEAN PARLIAMENT AND THE COUNCIL OF THE EUROPEAN UNION,

Having regard to the Treaty establishing the European Community, and in particular Article 95 thereof,

Having regard to the proposal from the Commission,

Having regard to the opinion of the European Economic and Social Committee[1],

After consulting the Committee of the Regions,

Acting in accordance with the procedure laid down in Article 251 of the Treaty[2],

Whereas:

(1) Communication networks and information systems have become an essential factor in economic and societal development. Computing and networking are now becoming ubiquitous utilities in the same way as electricity or water supply already are. The security of communication networks and information systems, in particular their availability, is therefore of increasing concern to society not least because of the possibility of problems in key information systems, due to system complexity, accidents, mistakes and attacks, that may have consequences for the physical infrastructures which deliver services critical to the well-being of EU citizens.

(2) The growing number of security breaches has already generated substantial financial damage, has undermined user confidence and has been detrimental to the development of e-commerce. Individuals, public administrations and businesses have reacted by deploying security technologies and security management procedures. Member States have taken several supporting measures, such as information campaigns and research projects, to enhance network and information security throughout society.

(3) The technical complexity of networks and information systems, the variety of products and services that are interconnected, and the huge number of private and public actors that bear their own responsibility risk undermining the smooth functioning of the Internal Market.

(4) Directive 2002/21/EC of the European Parliament and of the Council of 7 March 2002 on a common regulatory framework for electronic communications networks and services (the Framework Directive)[3] lays down the tasks of national regulatory authorities, which include cooperating with each other and the Commission in a transparent manner to ensure the development of consistent regulatory practice, contributing to ensuring a high level of protection of personal data and privacy, and ensuring that the integrity and security of public communications networks are ensured.

---

[1] OJ C 220, 16.9.2003, p. 33.
[2] Opinion of the European Parliament of 19 November 2003 (not yet published in the Official Journal) and Council Decision of 19 February 2004.
[3] OJ L 108, 24.4.2002, p. 33.

(5)   Present Community legislation also includes Directive 2002/20/EC[4], Directive 2002/22/EC[5], Directive 2002/19/EC[6], Directive 2002/58/EC[7], Directive 1999/93/EC[8], Directive 2000/31/EC[9], as well as the Council Resolution of 18 February 2003 on the implementation of the *e*Europe 2005 Action Plan[10].

(6)   Directive 2002/20/EC entitles Member States to attach to the general authorisation, conditions regarding the security of public networks against unauthorised access in accordance with Directive 97/66/EC[11].

(7)   Directive 2002/22/EC requires that Member States take necessary steps to ensure the integrity and availability of the public telephone networks at fixed locations and that undertakings providing publicly available telephone services at fixed locations take all reasonable steps to ensure uninterrupted access to emergency services.

(8)   Directive 2002/58/EC requires a provider of a publicly available electronic communications service to take appropriate technical and organisational measures to safeguard security of its services and also requires the confidentiality of the communications and related traffic data. Directive 95/46/EC of the European Parliament and of the Council of 24 October 1995 on the protection of individuals with regard to the processing of personal data and on the free movement of such data[12], requires Member States to provide that the controller must implement appropriate technical and organisational measures to protect personal data against accidental or unlawful destruction or accidental loss, alteration, unauthorised disclosure or access, in particular where the processing involves the transmission of data over a network and against all other unlawful forms of processing.

(9)   Directive 2002/21/EC and Directive 1999/93/EC contain provisions on standards that are to be published in the *Official Journal of the European Union*. Member States also use standards from international bodies as well as de facto standards developed by the global industry. It is necessary for the Commission and the Member States to be able to track those standards which meet the requirements of Community legislation.

(10)   These internal market measures require different forms of technical and organisational applications by the Member States and the Commission. These are technically complex tasks with no single, self-evident solutions. The heterogeneous application of these requirements can lead to inefficient solutions and create obstacles to the internal market. This calls for the creation of a centre of expertise at European level providing

---

[4]   Directive 2002/20/EC of the European Parliament and of the Council of 7 March 2002 on the authorisation of electronic communications networks and services (Authorisation Directive) (OJ L 108, 24.4.2002, p. 21).

[5]   Directive 2002/22/EC of the European Parliament and of the Council of 7 March 2002 on universal service and users' rights relating to electronic communications networks and services (Universal Service Directive) (OJ L 108, 24.4.2002, p. 51).

[6]   Directive 2002/19/EC of the European Parliament and of the Council of 7 March 2002 on access to, and interconnection of, electronic communications networks and associated facilities (Access Directive) (OJ L 108, 24.4.2002, p. 7).

[7]   Directive 2002/58/EC of the European Parliament and of the Council of 12 July 2002 concerning the processing of personal data and the protection of privacy in the electronic communications sector (Directive on privacy and electronic communications) (OJ L 201, 31.7.2002, p. 37).

[8]   Directive 1999/93/EC of the European Parliament and of the Council of 13 December 1999 on a Community framework for electronic signatures (OJ L 13, 19.1.2000, p. 12).

[9]   Directive 2000/31/EC of the European Parliament and of the Council of 8 June 2000 on certain legal aspects of information society services, in particular electronic commerce, in the Internal Market (Directive on electronic commerce) (OJ L 178, 17.7.2000, p. 1).

[10]   OJ C 48, 28.2.2003, p. 2.

[11]   Directive 97/66/EC of the European Parliament and of the Council of 15 December 1997 concerning the processing of personal data and the protection of privacy in the telecommunications sector (OJ L 24, 30.1.1998, p. 1). Directive repealed and replaced by Directive 2002/58/EC.

[12]   OJ L 281, 23.11.1995, p. 31. Directive as amended by Regulation (EC) No 1882/2003 (OJ L 284, 31.10.2003, p. 1).

guidance, advice, and when called upon, with assistance within its objectives, which may be relied upon by the European Parliament, the Commission or competent bodies appointed by the Member States. National Regulatory Authorities, designated under Directive 2002/21/EC, can be appointed by a Member State as a competent body.

(11) The establishment of a European agency, the European Network and Information Security Agency, hereinafter referred to as "the Agency", operating as a point of reference and establishing confidence by virtue of its independence, the quality of the advice it delivers and the information it disseminates, the transparency of its procedures and methods of operation, and its diligence in performing the tasks assigned to it, would respond to these needs. The Agency should build on national and Community efforts and therefore perform its tasks in full cooperation with the Member States and be open to contacts with industry and other relevant stakeholders. As electronic networks, to a large extent, are privately owned, the Agency should build on the input from and cooperation with the private sector.

(12) The exercise of the Agency's tasks should not interfere with the competencies and should not pre-empt, impede or overlap with the relevant powers and tasks conferred on:

- the national regulatory authorities as set out in the Directives relating to the electronic communications networks and services, as well as on the European Regulators Group for Electronic Communications Networks and Services established by Commission Decision 2002/627/EC[13] and the Communications Committee referred to in Directive 2002/21/EC,

- the European standardisation bodies, the national standardisation bodies and the Standing Committee as set out in Directive 98/34/EC of the European Parliament and of the Council of 22 June 1998 laying down a procedure for the provision of information in the field of technical standards and regulations and of rules on Information Society Services[14],

- the supervisory authorities of the Member States relating to the protection of individuals with the regard to the processing of personal data and on the free movement of such data.

(13) To understand better the challenges in the network and information security field, there is a need for the Agency to analyse current and emerging risks and for that purpose the Agency may collect appropriate information, in particular through questionnaires, without imposing new obligations on the private sector or the Member States to generate data. Emerging risks should be understood as issues already visible as possible future risks to network and information security.

(14) Ensuring confidence in networks and information systems requires that individuals, businesses and public administrations are sufficiently informed, educated and trained in the field of network and information security. Public authorities have a role in increasing awareness by informing the general public, small and medium-sized enterprises, corporate companies, public administrations, schools and universities. These measures need to be further developed. An increased information exchange between Member States will facilitate such awareness raising actions. The Agency should provide advice on best practices in awareness-raising, training and courses.

(15) The Agency should have the task of contributing to a high level of network and information security within the Community and of developing a culture of network

[13] OJ L 200, 30.7.2002, p. 38.
[14] OJ L 204, 21.7.1998, p. 37. Directive as amended by Directive 98/48/EC (OJ L 217, 5.8.1998, p. 18).

and information security for the benefit of citizens, consumers, businesses and public sector organisations in the European Union, thus contributing to the smooth functioning of the internal market.

(16) Efficient security policies should be based on well-developed risk assessment methods, both in the public and private sector. Risk assessment methods and procedures are used at different levels with no common practice on their efficient application. The promotion and development of best practices for risk assessment and for interoperable risk management solutions within public and private sector organisations will increase the security level of networks and information systems in Europe.

(17) The work of the Agency should utilise ongoing research, development and technological assessment activities, in particular those carried out by the different Community research initiatives.

(18) Where appropriate and useful for fulfilling its scope, objectives and tasks, the Agency could share experience and general information with bodies and agencies created under European Union law and dealing with network and information security.

(19) Network and information security problems are global issues. There is a need for closer cooperation at global level to improve security standards, improve information, and promote a common global approach to network and information security issues, thereby contributing to the development of a culture of network and information security. Efficient cooperation with third countries and the global community has become a task also at European level. To this end, the Agency should contribute to Community efforts to cooperate with third countries and, where appropriate, with international organisations.

(20) In its activities the Agency should pay attention to small and medium-sized enterprises.

(21) In order effectively to ensure the accomplishment of the tasks of the Agency, the Member States and the Commission should be represented on a Management Board entrusted with the necessary powers to establish the budget, verify its execution, adopt the appropriate financial rules, establish transparent working procedures for decision making by the Agency, approve the Agency's work programme, adopt its own rules of procedure and the Agency's internal rules of operation, appoint and remove the Executive Director. The Management Board should ensure that the Agency carries out its tasks under conditions which enable it to serve in accordance with this Regulation.

(22) A Permanent Stakeholders' Group would be helpful, in order to maintain a regular dialogue with the private sector, consumers organisations and other relevant stakeholders. The Permanent Stakeholders' Group, established and chaired by the Executive Director, should focus on issues relevant to all stakeholders and bring them to the attention of the Executive Director. The Executive Director may, where appropriate and according to the agenda of the meetings, invite representatives of the European Parliament and from other relevant bodies to take part in the meetings of the Group.

(23) The smooth functioning of the Agency requires that its Executive Director is appointed on the grounds of merit and documented administrative and managerial skills, as well as competence and experience relevant for network and information security and that he/she performs his/her duties with complete independence and flexibility as to the organisation of the internal functioning of the Agency. To this end, the Executive Director should prepare a proposal for the Agency's work programme, after prior consultation of the Commission and of the Permanent Stakeholders' Group, and take all necessary steps to ensure the proper accomplishment of the working

programme of the Agency, should prepare each year a draft general report to be submitted to the Management Board, should draw up a draft statement of estimates of revenue and expenditure of the Agency and should implement the budget.

(24) The Executive Director should have the possibility to set up ad hoc Working Groups to address in particular scientific and technical matters. In establishing the ad hoc Working Groups the Executive Director should seek input from and mobilise the relevant expertise of private sector. The ad hoc Working Groups should enable the Agency to have access to the most updated information available in order to be able to respond to the security challenges posed by the developing information society. The Agency should ensure that its ad hoc Working Groups are competent and representative and that they include, as appropriate according to the specific issues, representation of the public administrations of the Member States, of the private sector including industry, of the users and of academic experts in network and information security. The Agency may, if necessary, add to the Working Groups independent experts recognised as competent in the field concerned. The experts who participate in the ad hoc Working Groups organised by the Agency should not belong to the Agency's staff. Their expenses should be met by the Agency in accordance with its internal rules and in conformity with the existing Financial Regulations.

(25) The Agency should apply the relevant Community legislation concerning public access to documents as set out in Regulation (EC) No 1049/2001[15] of the European Parliament and of the Council and the protection of individuals with regard to the processing of personal data as set out in Regulation (EC) No 45/2001[16] of the European Parliament and of the Council.

(26) Within its scope, its objectives and in the performance of its tasks, the Agency should comply in particular with the provisions applicable to the Community institutions, as well as the national legislation regarding the treatment of sensitive documents.

(27) In order to guarantee the full autonomy and independence of the Agency, it is considered necessary to grant it an autonomous budget whose revenue comes essentially from a contribution from the Community. The Community budgetary procedure remains applicable as far as any subsidies chargeable to the general budget of the European Union are concerned. Moreover, the Court of Auditors should undertake the auditing of accounts.

(28) Where necessary and on the basis of arrangements to be concluded, the Agency may have access to the interpretation services provided by the Directorate General for Interpretation (DGI) of the Commission, or by Interpretation Services of other Community institutions.

(29) The Agency should be initially established for a limited period and its operations evaluated in order to determine whether the duration of its operations should be extended,

---

[15] Regulation (EC) No 1049/2001 of the European Parliament and of the Council of 30 May 2001 regarding public access to European Parliament, Council and Commission documents (OJ L 145, 31.5.2001, p. 43).

[16] Regulation (EC) No 45/2001 of the European Parliament and of the Council of 18 December 2000 on the protection of individuals with regard to the processing of personal data by the Community institutions and bodies and on the free movement of such data (OJ L 8, 12.1.2001, p. 1).

HAVE ADOPTED THIS REGULATION:

SECTION 1

SCOPE, OBJECTIVES AND TASKS

Article 1

Scope

1. For the purpose of ensuring a high and effective level of network and information security within the Community and in order to develop a culture of network and information security for the benefit of the citizens, consumers, enterprises and public sector organisations of the European Union, thus contributing to the smooth functioning of the internal market, a European Network and Information Security Agency is hereby established, hereinafter referred to as "the Agency".

2. The Agency shall assist the Commission and the Member States, and in consequence cooperate with the business community, in order to help them to meet the requirements of network and information security, thereby ensuring the smooth functioning of the internal market, including those set out in present and future Community legislation, such as in the Directive 2002/21/EC.

3. The objectives and the tasks of the Agency shall be without prejudice to the competencies of the Member States regarding network and information security which fall outside the scope of the EC Treaty, such as those covered by Titles V and VI of the Treaty on European Union, and in any case to activities concerning public security, defence, State security (including the economic well-being of the State when the issues relate to State security matters) and the activities of the State in areas of criminal law.

Article 2

Objectives

1. The Agency shall enhance the capability of the Community, the Member States and, as a consequence, the business community to prevent, address and to respond to network and information security problems.

2. The Agency shall provide assistance and deliver advice to the Commission and the Member States on issues related to network and information security falling within its competencies as set out in this Regulation.

3. Building on national and Community efforts, the Agency shall develop a high level of expertise. The Agency shall use this expertise to stimulate broad cooperation between actors from the public and private sectors.

4. The Agency shall assist the Commission, where called upon, in the technical preparatory work for updating and developing Community legislation in the field of network and information security.

Article 3

Tasks

In order to ensure that the scope and objectives set out in Articles 1 and 2 are complied with and met, the Agency shall perform the following tasks:

(a)   collect appropriate information to analyse current and emerging risks and, in particular at the European level, those which could produce an impact on the resilience and the availability of electronic communications networks and on the authenticity, integrity and confidentiality of the information accessed and transmitted through them, and provide the results of the analysis to the Member States and the Commission;

(b)   provide the European Parliament, the Commission, European bodies or competent national bodies appointed by the Member States with advice, and when called upon, with assistance within its objectives;

(c)   enhance cooperation between different actors operating in the field of network and information security, inter alia, by organising, on a regular basis, consultation with industry, universities, as well as other sectors concerned and by establishing networks of contacts for Community bodies, public sector bodies appointed by the Member States, private sector and consumer bodies;

(d)   facilitate cooperation between the Commission and the Member States in the development of common methodologies to prevent, address and respond to network and information security issues;

(e)   contribute to awareness raising and the availability of timely, objective and comprehensive information on network and information security issues for all users by, inter alia, promoting exchanges of current best practices, including on methods of alerting users, and seeking synergy between public and private sector initiatives;

(f)   assist the Commission and the Member States in their dialogue with industry to address security-related problems in the hardware and software products;

(g)   track the development of standards for products and services on network and information security;

(h)   advise the Commission on research in the area of network and information security as well as on the effective use of risk prevention technologies;

(i)   promote risk assessment activities, interoperable risk management solutions and studies on prevention management solutions within public and private sector organisations;

(j)   contribute to Community efforts to cooperate with third countries and, where appropriate, with international organisations to promote a common global approach to network and information security issues, thereby contributing to the development of a culture of network and information security;

(k)   express independently its own conclusions, orientations and give advice on matters within its scope and objectives.

Article 4

Definitions

For the purposes of this Regulation the following definitions shall apply:

(a)   "network" means transmission systems and, where applicable, switching or routing equipment and other resources which permit the conveyance of signals by wire, by radio, by optical or by other electromagnetic means, including satellite networks, fixed (circuit- and packet-switched, including Internet) and mobile terrestrial networks, electricity cable systems, to the extent that they are used for the purpose of transmitting signals, networks used for radio and television broadcasting, and cable TV networks, irrespective of the type of information conveyed;

(b) "information system" means computers and electronic communication networks, as well as electronic data stored, processed, retrieved or transmitted by them for the purposes of their operation, use, protection and maintenance;

(c) "network and information security" means the ability of a network or an information system to resist, at a given level of confidence, accidental events or unlawful or malicious actions that compromise the availability, authenticity, integrity and confidentiality of stored or transmitted data and the related services offered by or accessible via these networks and systems;

(d) "availability" means that data is accessible and services are operational;

(e) "authentication" means the confirmation of an asserted identity of entities or users;

(f) "data integrity" means the confirmation that data which has been sent, received, or stored are complete and unchanged;

(g) "data confidentiality" means the protection of communications or stored data against interception and reading by unauthorised persons;

(h) "risk" means a function of the probability that a vulnerability in the system affects authentication or the availability, authenticity, integrity or confidentiality of the data processed or transferred and the severity of that effect, consequential to the intentional or non-intentional use of such a vulnerability;

(i) "risk assessment" means a scientific and technologically based process consisting of four steps, threats identification, threat characterisation, exposure assessment and risk characterisation;

(j) "risk management" means the process, distinct from risk assessment, of weighing policy alternatives in consultation with interested parties, considering risk assessment and other legitimate factors, and, if need be, selecting appropriate prevention and control options;

(k) "culture of network and information security" has the same meaning as that set out in the OECD Guidelines for the security of Information Systems and Networks of 25 July 2002 and the Council Resolution of 18 February 2003 on a European approach towards a culture of network and information security[17].

SECTION 2

ORGANISATION

Article 5

Bodies of the Agency

The Agency shall comprise:

(a) a Management Board;

---

[17] OJ C 48, 28.2.2003, p. 1.

(b) an Executive Director, and

(c) a Permanent Stakeholders' Group.

Article 6

Management Board

1. The Management Board shall be composed of one representative of each Member State, three representatives appointed by the Commission, as well as three representatives, proposed by the Commission and appointed by the Council, without the right to vote, each of whom represents one of the following groups:

    (a) information and communication technologies industry;

    (b) consumer groups;

    (c) academic experts in network and information security.

2. Board members shall be appointed on the basis of their degree of relevant experience and expertise in the field of network and information security. Representatives may be replaced by alternates, appointed at the same time.

3. The Management Board shall elect its Chairperson and a Deputy Chairperson from among its members for a two-and-a-half-year period, which shall be renewable. The Deputy Chairperson shall ex-officio replace the Chairperson in the event of the Chairperson being unable to attend to his/her duties.

4. The Management Board shall adopt its rules of procedure, on the basis of a proposal by the Commission. Unless otherwise provided, the Management Board shall take its decisions by a majority of its members with the right to vote.

    A two-thirds majority of all members with the right to vote is required for the adoption of its rules of procedure, the Agency's internal rules of operation, the budget, the annual work programme, as well as the appointment and the removal of the Executive Director.

5. Meetings of the Management Board shall be convened by its Chairperson. The Management Board shall hold an ordinary meeting twice a year. It shall also hold extraordinary meetings at the instance of the Chairperson or at the request of at least a third of its members with the right to vote. The Executive Director shall take part in the meetings of the Management Board, without voting rights, and shall provide the Secretariat.

6. The Management Board shall adopt the Agency's internal rules of operation on the basis of a proposal by the Commission. These rules shall be made public.

7. The Management Board shall define the general orientations for the operation of the Agency. The Management Board shall ensure that the Agency works in accordance with the principles laid down in Articles 12 to 14 and 23. It shall also ensure consistency of the Agency's work with activities conducted by Member States as well as at Community level.

8. Before 30 November each year, the Management Board, having received the Commission's opinion shall adopt the Agency's work programme for the following year. The Management Board shall ensure that the work programme is consistent with the Agency's scope, objectives and tasks as well as with the Community's legislative and policy priorities in the area of network and information security.

9. Before 31 March each year, the Management Board shall adopt the general report on the Agency's activities for the previous year.

10. The financial rules applicable to the Agency shall be adopted by the Management Board after the Commission has been consulted. They may not depart from Commission Regulation (EC, Euratom) No 2343/2002 of 19 November 2002 on the framework Financial Regulation for the bodies referred to in Article 185 of the Council Regulation (EC, Euratom) No 1605/2002 on the Financial Regulation applicable to the general budget of the European Communities[18], unless such departure is specifically required for the Agency's operation and the Commission has given its prior consent.

Article 7

Executive Director

1. The Agency shall be managed by its Executive Director, who shall be independent in the performance of his/her duties.

2. The Executive Director shall be appointed by the Management Board on the basis of a list of candidates proposed by the Commission after an open competition following publication in the Official Journal of the European Union and elsewhere of a call for expressions of interest. The Executive Director shall be appointed on the grounds of merit and documented administrative and managerial skills, as well as competence and experience relevant for network and information security. Before appointment the candidate nominated by the Management Board shall be invited without delay to make a statement before the European Parliament and to answer questions put by members of that institution. The European Parliament or the Council may also ask at any time for a hearing with the Executive Director on any subject related to the Agency's activities. The Executive Director may be removed from office by the Management Board.

3. The term of office of the Executive Director shall be up to five years.

4. The Executive Director shall be responsible for:

    (a) the day-to-day administration of the Agency;

    (b) drawing up a proposal for the Agency's work programmes after prior consultation of the Commission and of the Permanent Stakeholders Group;

    (c) implementing the work programmes and the decisions adopted by the Management Board;

    (d) ensuring that the Agency carries out its tasks in accordance with the requirements of those using its services, in particular with regard to the adequacy of the services provided;

    (e) the preparation of the Agency's draft statement of estimates of revenue and expenditure and the execution of its budget;

    (f) all staff matters;

    (g) developing and maintaining contact with the European Parliament and for ensuring a regular dialogue with its relevant committees;

---

[18] OJ L 357, 31.12.2002, p. 72.

(h)   developing and maintaining contact with the business community and consumers organisations for ensuring a regular dialogue with relevant stakeholders;

(i)   chairing the Permanent Stakeholders' Group.

5.   Each year, the Executive Director shall submit to the Management Board for approval:

(a)   a draft general report covering all the activities of the Agency in the previous year;

(b)   a draft work programme.

6.   The Executive Director shall, following adoption by the Management Board, forward the work programme to the European Parliament, the Council, the Commission and the Member States and shall have it published.

7.   The Executive Director shall, following adoption by the Management Board, transmit the Agency's general report to the European Parliament, the Council, the Commission, the Court of Auditors, the European Economic and Social Committee and the Committee of the Regions and shall have it published.

8.   Where necessary and within the Agency's scope, objectives and tasks, the Executive Director may establish, in consultation with the Permanent Stakeholders' Group, ad hoc Working Groups composed of experts. The Management Board shall be duly informed. The procedures regarding in particular the composition, the appointment of the experts by the Executive Director and the operation of the ad hoc Working Groups shall be specified in the Agency's internal rules of operation.

Where established, the ad hoc Working Groups shall address in particular technical and scientific matters.

Members of the Management Board may not be members of the ad hoc Working Groups. Representatives of the Commission shall be entitled to be present in their meetings.

Article 8

Permanent Stakeholders' Group

1.   The Executive Director shall establish a Permanent Stakeholders' Group composed of experts representing the relevant stakeholders, such as information and communication technologies industry, consumer groups and academic experts in network and information security.

2.   The procedures regarding in particular the number, the composition, the appointment of the members by the Executive Director and the operation of the Group shall be specified in the Agency's internal rules of operation and shall be made public.

3.   The Group shall be chaired by the Executive Director. The term of office of its members shall be two-and-a-half years. Members of the Group may not be members of the Management Board.

4.   Representatives of the Commission shall be entitled to be present in the meetings and participate in the work of the Group.

5.   The Group may advise the Executive Director in the performance of his/her duties under this Regulation, in drawing up a proposal for the Agency's work programme, as

well as in ensuring communication with the relevant stakeholders on all issues related to the work programme.

SECTION 3

OPERATION

Article 9

Work programme

The Agency shall base its operations on carrying out the work programme adopted in accordance with Article 6(8). The work programme shall not prevent the Agency from taking up unforeseen activities that fall within its scope and objectives and within the given budget limitations.

Article 10

Requests to the Agency

1. Requests for advice and assistance falling within the Agency's scope, objectives and tasks shall be addressed to the Executive Director and accompanied by background information explaining the issue to be addressed. The Executive Director shall inform the Commission of the received requests. If the Agency refuses a request, justification shall be given.

2. Requests referred to in paragraph 1 may be made by:

    (a) the European Parliament;

    (b) the Commission;

    (c) any competent body appointed by a Member State, such as a national regulatory authority as defined in Article 2 of Directive 2002/21/EC.

3. The practical arrangements for the application of paragraphs 1 and 2, regarding in particular the submission, the prioritisation, the follow up as well as the information of the Management Board on the requests to the Agency shall be laid down by the Management Board in the Agency's internal rules of operation.

Article 11

Declaration of interests

1. The Executive Director, as well as officials seconded by Member States on a temporary basis shall make a declaration of commitments and a declaration of interests indicating the absence of any direct or indirect interests, which might be considered prejudicial to their independence. Such declarations shall be made in writing.

2. External experts participating in ad hoc Working Groups, shall declare at each meeting any interests, which might be considered prejudicial to their independence in relation to the items on the agenda.

Article 12

Transparency

1. The Agency shall ensure that it carries out its activities with a high level of transparency and in accordance with Article 13 and 14.

2. The Agency shall ensure that the public and any interested parties are given objective, reliable and easily accessible information, in particular with regard to the results of its work, where appropriate. It shall also make public the declarations of interest made by the Executive Director and by officials seconded by Member States on a temporary basis, as well as the declarations of interest made by experts in relation to items on the agendas of meetings of the ad hoc Working Groups.

3. The Management Board, acting on a proposal from the Executive Director, may authorise interested parties to observe the proceedings of some of the Agency's activities.

4. The Agency shall lay down in its internal rules of operation the practical arrangements for implementing the transparency rules referred to in paragraphs 1 and 2.

Article 13

Confidentiality

1. Without prejudice to Article 14, the Agency shall not divulge to third parties information that it processes or receives for which confidential treatment has been requested.

2. Members of the Management Board, the Executive Director, the members of the Permanent Stakeholders Group, external experts participating in ad hoc Working Groups, and members of the staff of the Agency including officials seconded by Member States on a temporary basis, even after their duties have ceased, are subject to the requirements of confidentiality pursuant to Article 287 of the Treaty.

3. The Agency shall lay down in its internal rules of operation the practical arrangements for implementing the confidentiality rules referred to in paragraphs 1 and 2.

Article 14

Access to documents

1. Regulation (EC) No 1049/2001 shall apply to documents held by the Agency.

2. The Management Board shall adopt arrangements for implementing the Regulation (EC) No 1049/2001 within six months of the establishment of the Agency.

3. Decisions taken by the Agency pursuant to Article 8 of Regulation (EC) No 1049/2001 may form the subject of a complaint to the Ombudsman or of an action before the Court of Justice of the European Communities, under Articles 195 and 230 of the Treaty respectively.

SECTION 4

FINANCIAL PROVISIONS

Article 15

Adoption of the budget

1. The revenues of the Agency shall consist of a contribution from the Community and any contribution from third countries participating in the work of the Agency as provided for by Article 24.

2. The expenditure of the Agency shall include the staff, administrative and technical support, infrastructure and operational expenses, and expenses resulting from contracts entered into with third parties.

3. By 1 March each year at the latest, the Executive Director shall draw up a draft statement of estimates of the Agency's revenue and expenditure for the following financial year, and shall forward it to the Management Board, together with a draft establishment plan.

4. Revenue and expenditure shall be in balance.

5. Each year, the Management Board, on the basis of a draft statement of estimates of revenue and expenditure drawn up by the Executive Director, shall produce a statement of estimates of revenue and expenditure for the Agency for the following financial year.

6. This statement of estimates, which shall include a draft establishment plan together with the provisional work programme, shall by 31 March at the latest, be transmitted by the Management Board to the Commission and the States with which the Community has concluded agreements in accordance with Article 24.

7. This statement of estimates shall be forwarded by the Commission to the European Parliament and the Council (both hereinafter referred to as the "budgetary authority") together with the preliminary draft general budget of the European Union.

8. On the basis of this statement of estimates, the Commission shall enter in the preliminary draft general budget of the European Union the estimates it deems necessary for the establishment plan and the amount of the subsidy to be charged to the general budget, which it shall submit to the budgetary authority in accordance with Article 272 of the Treaty.

9. The budgetary authority shall authorise the appropriations for the subsidy to the Agency.

    The budgetary authority shall adopt the establishment plan for the Agency.

10. The Management Board shall adopt the Agency's budget. It shall become final following final adoption of the general budget of the European Union. Where appropriate, the Agency's budget shall be adjusted accordingly. The Management Board shall forward it without delay to the Commission and the budgetary authority.

11. The Management Board shall, as soon as possible, notify the budgetary authority of its intention to implement any project which may have significant financial implications for the funding of the budget, in particular any projects relating to property such as the rental or purchase of buildings. It shall inform the Commission thereof.

Where a branch of the budgetary authority has notified its intention to deliver an opinion, it shall forward its opinion to the Management Board within a period of six weeks from the date of notification of the project.

Article 16

Combating fraud

1. In order to combat fraud, corruption and other unlawful activities the provisions of Regulation (EC) No 1073/1999 of the European Parliament and of the Council of 25 May 1999 concerning investigations conducted by the European Anti-fraud Office (OLAF)[19] shall apply without restriction.

2. The Agency shall accede to the Interinstitutional Agreement of 25 May 1999 between the European Parliament and the Council of the European Union and the Commission of the European Communities concerning internal investigations by the European Anti-fraud Office (OLAF)[20] and shall issue, without delay, the appropriate provisions applicable to all the employees of the Agency.

Article 17

Implementation of the budget

1. The Executive Director shall implement the Agency's budget.

2. The Commission's internal auditor shall exercise the same powers over the Agency as over Commission departments.

3. By 1 March at the latest following each financial year, the Agency's accounting officer shall communicate the provisional accounts to the Commission's accounting officer together with a report on the budgetary and financial management for that financial year. The Commission's accounting officer shall consolidate the provisional accounts of the institutions and decentralised bodies in accordance with Article 128 of Council Regulation (EC, Euratom) No 1605/2002 of 25 June 2002 on the Financial Regulation applicable to the general budget of the European Communities[21] (hereinafter referred to as the general Financial Regulation).

4. By 31 March at the latest following each financial year, the Commission's accounting officer shall transmit the Agency's provisional accounts to the Court of Auditors, together with a report on the budgetary and financial management for that financial year. The report on the budgetary and financial management for the financial year shall also be transmitted to the budgetary authority.

5. On receipt of the Court of Auditor's observations on the Agency's provisional accounts, pursuant to Article 129 of the general Financial Regulation, the Executive Director shall draw up the Agency's final accounts under his/her own responsibility and transmit them to the Management Board for an opinion.

6. The Management Board shall deliver an opinion on the Agency's final accounts.

7. The Executive Director shall, by 1 July at the latest following each financial year, transmit the final accounts to the European Parliament, the Council, the Commission and the Court of Auditors, together with the Management Board's opinion.

---

[19] OJ L 136, 31.5.1999, p. 1.
[20] OJ L 136, 31.5.1999, p. 15.
[21] OJ L 248, 16.9.2002, p. 1.

8.   The final accounts shall be published.

9.   The Executive Director shall send the Court of Auditors a reply to its observations by 30 September at the latest. He/she shall also send this reply to the Management Board.

10.   The Executive Director shall submit to the European Parliament, at the latter's request, all information necessary for the smooth application of the discharge procedure for the financial year in question, as laid down in Article 146(3) of the general Financial Regulation.

11.   The European Parliament, on a recommendation from the Council acting by a qualified majority, shall, before 30 April of year N+2 give a discharge to the Executive Director in respect of the implementation of the budget for the year N.

SECTION 5

GENERAL PROVISIONS

Article 18

Legal status

1.   The Agency shall be a body of the Community. It shall have legal personality.

2.   In each of the Member States the Agency shall enjoy the most extensive legal capacity accorded to legal persons under their laws. It may in particular, acquire and dispose of movable and immovable property and be a party to legal proceedings.

3.   The Agency shall be represented by its Executive Director.

Article 19

Staff

1.   The staff of the Agency, including its Executive Director, shall be subject to the rules and regulations applicable to officials and other staff of the European Communities.

2.   Without prejudice to Article 6, the powers conferred on the appointing authority by the Staff Regulations and on the authority authorised to conclude contracts by the Conditions of employment of other servants, shall be exercised by the Agency in respect of its own staff.

The Agency may also employ officials seconded by Member States on a temporary basis and for a maximum of five years.

Article 20

Privileges and immunities

The Protocol on the Privileges and Immunities of the European Communities shall apply to the Agency and its staff.

Article 21

Liability

1. The contractual liability of the Agency shall be governed by the law applicable to the contract in question.

    The Court of Justice of the European Communities shall have jurisdiction to give judgment pursuant to any arbitration clause contained in a contract concluded by the Agency.

2. In the case of non-contractual liability, the Agency shall, in accordance with the general principles common to the laws of the Member States, make good any damage caused by it or its servants in the performance of their duties.

    The Court of Justice shall have jurisdiction in any dispute relating to compensation for such damage.

3. The personal liability of its servants towards the Agency shall be governed by the relevant conditions applying to the staff of the Agency.

Article 22

Languages

1. The provisions laid down in Regulation No 1 of 15 April 1958 determining the languages to be used in the European Economic Community[22] shall apply to the Agency. The Member States and the other bodies appointed by them may address the Agency and receive a reply in the Community language of their choice.

2. The translation services required for the functioning of the Agency shall be provided by the Translation Centre for the Bodies of the European Union[23].

Article 23

Protection of personal data

When processing data relating to individuals, the Agency shall be subject to the provisions of Regulation (EC) No 45/2001.

Article 24

Participation of third countries

1. The Agency shall be open to the participation of countries, which have concluded agreements with the European Community by virtue of which they have adopted and applied Community legislation in the field covered by this Regulation.

2. Arrangements shall be made under the relevant provisions of those agreements, specifying in particular the nature, extent and manner in which these countries will participate in the Agency's work, including provisions relating to participation in the initiatives undertaken by the Agency, financial contributions and staff.

---

[22] OJ 17, 6.10.1958, p. 385/58. Regulation as last amended by the 1994 Act of Accession.
[23] Council Regulation (EC) No 2965/94 of 28 November 1994 setting up a Translation Centre for bodies of the European Union (OJ L 314, 7.12.1994, p. 1). Regulation as last amended by Regulation (EC) No 1645/2003 (OJ L 245, 29.9.2003, p. 13).

SECTION 6

FINAL PROVISIONS

Article 25

Review clause

1. By 17 March 2007, the Commission, taking into account the views of all relevant stakeholders, shall carry out an evaluation on the basis of the terms of reference agreed with the Management Board. The Commission shall undertake the evaluation, notably with the aim to determine whether the duration of the Agency should be extended beyond the period specified in Article 27.

2. The evaluation shall assess the impact of the Agency on achieving its objectives and tasks, as well as its working practices and envisage, if necessary, the appropriate proposals.

3. The Management Board shall receive a report on the evaluation and issue recommendations regarding eventual appropriate changes to this Regulation to the Commission. Both the evaluation findings and recommendations shall be forwarded by the Commission to the European Parliament and the Council and shall be made public.

Article 26

Administrative control

The operations of the Agency are subject to the supervision of the Ombudsman in accordance with the provisions of Article 195 of the Treaty.

Article 27

Duration

The Agency shall be established from 14 March 2004 for a period of five years.

Article 28

Entry into force

This Regulation shall enter into force on the day following that of its publication in the Official Journal of the European Union.

This Regulation shall be binding in its entirety and directly applicable in all Member States.

———————————

Editors' Notes:

a OJ L 77, 13.3.2004, p. 1

AGREEMENT ON THE EUROPEAN ECONOMIC AREA

Editors' Note

The EC Member States and the Republic of Iceland, the Principality of Liechtenstein and the Kingdom of Norway entered into the "EEA Agreement" on 17 March 1993. Article 1 of the Agreement states as follows:

"1. The aim of this Agreement of association is to promote a continuous and balanced strengthening of trade and economic relations between the Contracting Parties with equal conditions of competition, and the respect of the same rules, with a view to creating a homogeneous European Economic Area, hereinafter referred to as the EEA."

The EEA Agreement prohibits, inter alia, restrictions on freedom of nationals of the Contracting Parties to provide services to persons in the territory of another Contracting Party, "within the framework of the provisions of [the EEA] Agreement." See in particular Articles 1,2(c) and 36. In furtherance of this aim, the original text of the EEA Agreement contained a series of Annexes listing measures already adopted by the EC which the Contracting Parties agreed would apply in the territories of the Contracting Parties. These Annexes included Annex XI relating to "Telecommunications Services." Annex XI included all of the main measures of the EC regulatory framework of the time. Provision was made in the EEA Agreement for the establishment of an EEA Joint Committee with responsibility for "ensur[ing] the effective implementation and operation of [the] Agreement:" Article 92,1. The Joint Committee is given express power to make amendments to the Annexes: Article 98. As a consequence of decisions of the EEA Joint Committee, Annex XI has been amended from time to time to include new measures adopted by the EU relating to telecommunications services, including the measures comprising the 2002 regulatory framework for electronic communications.

We have reproduced here the pertinent parts of Annex XI but, because of space limitations, omitted the text of the main body of the EEA Agreement. For a copy of the full text of the EEA Agreement, see http://secretariat.efta.int/Web/LegalCorner/

AGREEMENT ON THE EUROPEAN ECONOMIC AREA

of 17 March 1993

ANNEX XI - TELECOMMUNICATION SERVICES

List provided for in Article 36(2)

[as amended to 29 April 2006]

[excerpt]ᵃ

INTRODUCTION

When the acts referred to in this Annex contain notions or refer to procedures which are specific to the Community legal order, such as:

–   preambles;

–   the addressees of the Community acts;

–   references to territories or languages of the EC;

–   references to rights and obligations of EC Member States, their public entities, undertakings or individuals in relation to each other; and

–   references to information and notification procedures;

Protocol 1 on horizontal adaptations shall apply, unless otherwise provided for in this Annex.

ACTS REFERRED TO

Telecommunication services[1]

1.   **387 L 0372:** Council Directive 87/372/EEC of 25 June 1987 on the frequency bands to be reserved for the coordinated introduction of public pan-European cellular digital land-based mobile communications in the European Community (OJ No L 196, 17.7.1987 p. 85).

2.   [ ][2]

3.   [ ][3]

4.   **390 L 0544:** Council Directive 90/544/EEC of 9 October 1990 on the frequency bands designated for the coordinated introduction of pan-European land-based public radio paging in the Community (OJ No L 310, 9.11.1990, p. 28).

---

[1]   Subheading inserted by Decision No 91/98 (OJ No L 189, 22.7.1999, p. 64 and EEA Supplement No 32, 22.7.1999, p. 141), e.i.f. 1.5.1999.
[2]   Point deleted by Decision No 11/2004 (OJ No L 116, 22.4.2004, p. 60 and EEA Supplement No 20, 22.4.2004, p. 14), e.i.f. 1.11.2004.
[3]   Point deleted with effect from 25 July 2003 by Decision No 153/2003 (OJ No L 41, 12.02.2004, p. 45 and EEA Supplement No 7, 12.02.2004, p. 32), e.i.f. 1.11.2004.

5.   **391 L 0287:** Council Directive 91/C 287/EEC of 3 June 1991 on the frequency band to be designated for the coordinated introduction of digital European cordless telecommunications (DECT) into the Community (OJ No L 144, 8.6.1991, p. 45)

5a. – 5c. [ ][4]

5ca.[5][b] **397 D 0710:** Decision No 710/97/EC of the European Parliament and of the Council of 24 March 1997 on a coordinated authorisation approach in the field of satellite personal-communication services in the Community (OJ L 105, 23.4.1997, p. 4), as amended by:

–[6]   **32000 D 1215:** Decision No 1215/2000/EC of the European Parliament and of the Council of 16 May 2000 (OJ L 139, 10.6.2000, p. 1).

The provisions of the Decision shall, for the purposes of the present Agreement, be read with the following adaptations:

as regards relations with third countries described in Article 9 of the Decision, the following shall apply:

1.   With a view to achieving a maximum degree of convergence in the application of a third-country regime in relation to satellite personal-communication services, the Contracting Parties shall exchange information as described in Article 9(1) and consultations shall be held regarding matters referred to in Articles 9(2) within the framework of the EEA Joint Committee and according to specific procedures to be agreed by the Contracting Parties.

2.   Whenever the Community negotiates with a third country on the basis of Article 9(2), in order to obtain effective and comparable access for its organisations, it shall endeavour to obtain equal treatment for organisations of the EFTA-States.

5cb. – 5cc. [ ][7]

5cd.[8] **399 D 0128:** Decision No 128/1999/EC of the European Parliament and of the Council of 14 December 1998 on the coordinated introduction of a third-generation mobile and wireless communications system (UMTS) in the Community (OJ L 17, 22.1.1999, p. 1).

The provisions of the Decision shall, for the purposes of the present Agreement, be read with the following adaptations:

Article 9 shall be without prejudice to the right of an EFTA State to take measures relating to UMTS services and UMTS equipment in third countries or to negotiate bilateral and multilateral agreements applicable to UMTS with third countries and international organisations on its own behalf. The Commission and the EFTA States shall keep each other informed and, upon request, shall hold consultations regarding such measures or negotiations within the framework of the EEA Joint Committee.

---

[4]   Points deleted by Decision No 11/2004 (OJ No L 116, 22.4.2004, p. 60 and EEA Supplement No 20, 22.4.2004, p. 14), e.i.f. 1.11.2004.

[5]   Point inserted by Decision No 6/1999 (OJ No L 35, 10.2.2000, p. 35, and EEA Supplement No 7, 10.2.2000, p. 34), e.i.f. 30.1.1999.

[6]   Indent, and words "as amended by" above, added by Decision No 90/2000 (OJ No L 7, 11.1.2001, p. 11 and EEA Supplement No 2, 11.1.2001, p. 7), e.i.f. 28.10.2000.

[7]   Points deleted by Decision No 11/2004 (OJ No L 116, 22.4.2004, p. 60 and EEA Supplement No 20, 22.4.2004, p. 14), e.i.f. 1.11.2004.

[8]   Point inserted by Decision No 119/1999 (OJ No L 325, 21.12.2000, p. 34 and EEA Supplement No 60, 21.12.2000, p. 425 (Icelandic) and p. 426 (Norwegian)), e.i.f. 25.9.1999.

5ce.[9] **32000 R 2887**: Regulation (EC) No 2887/2000 of the European Parliament and of the Council of 18 December 2000 on unbundled access to the local loop (OJ L 336, 30.12.2000, p. 4).

5cf.[10] **32002 D 0676**: Decision No 676/2002/EC of the European Parliament and of the Council of 7 March 2002 on a regulatory framework for radio spectrum policy in the European Community (Radio Spectrum Decision) (OJ L 108, 24.4.2002, p. 1).

The provisions of the Decision shall, for the purposes of the present Agreement, be read with the following adaptations:

The following paragraphs shall be added to Article 6:

4. Without prejudice to paragraphs 5 and 6, paragraphs 1 to 4 shall not apply to the EFTA States.

5. As regards the EFTA States, the EFTA States shall carry out the tasks of the Commission mentioned in paragraph 1 and inform the Standing Committee of any difficulties created, de jure or de facto, by third countries or international organisations for the implementation of this Decision, which shall draw up a report.

6. This Article shall be without prejudice to the EFTA States' rights and obligations under relevant international agreements.

5cg.[11] **32002 L 0077**: Commission Directive 2002/77/EC of 16 September 2002 on competition in the markets for electronic communications networks and services (OJ L 249, 17.9.2002, p. 21) (1).

(1) Listed here for purposes of information only. For application, see Annex XIV.

The provisions of the Directive shall, for the purposes of the present Agreement, be read with the following adaptations:

In Article 7(2), the words "competition rules of the EC Treaty" shall read "the competition rules of the EEA Agreement".

5ch.[12] **32002 D 0622**: Commission Decision 2002/622/EC of 26 July 2002 establishing a Radio Spectrum Policy Group (OJ L 198, 27.7.2002, p. 49).

Procedures for the association of Liechtenstein, Iceland and Norway in accordance with Article 101 of the Agreement:

Each EFTA State may, in accordance with Article 3 of Commission Decision 2002/622/EC, appoint persons to participate as observers in the meetings of the Radio Spectrum Policy Group.

The EC Commission shall, in due time, inform the participants of the dates of the meetings of the Group and transmit to them the relevant documentation.

---

[9] Point inserted by Decision No 47/2001 (OJ L 158, 14.6.2001, p. 62 and EEA Supplement No 30, 14.6.2001, p.42 (Norwegian) p. 20 (Icelandic)), e.i.f. 31.10.2001.
[10] Point inserted by Decision No 79/2003 (OJ No L 257, 9.10.2003, p. 29 and EEA Supplement No 51, 9.10.2003, p.18), e.i.f. 1.8.2004.
[11] Point inserted by Decision No 153/2003 (OJ No L 41, 12.02.2004, p. 45 and EEA Supplement No 7, 12.02.2004, p. 32), e.i.f. 1.11.2004.
[12] Point inserted by Decision No 9/2004 (OJ No L 116, 22.4.2004, p. 56 and EEA Supplement No 20, 22.4.2004, p. 12), e.i.f. 7.2.2004.

5ci.[13] **32002 D 0627**: Commission Decision 2002/627/EC of 29 July 2002 establishing the European Regulators Group for Electronic Communications Networks and Services (OJ L 200, 30.7.2002, p. 38).

Procedures for the association of Liechtenstein, Iceland and Norway in accordance with Article 101 of the Agreement:

Each EFTA State may, in accordance with Article 4(1) of Commission Decision 2002/627/EC, appoint persons to participate as observers in the meetings of the European Regulators Group for Electronic Communications Networks and Services.

The EC Commission shall, in due time, inform the participants of the dates of the meetings of the Group and transmit to them the relevant documentation.

5cj.[14] **32002 L 0019**: Directive 2002/19/EC of the European Parliament and of the Council of 7 March 2002 on access to, and interconnection of, electronic communications networks and associated facilities (Access Directive) (OJ L 108, 24.4.2002, p. 7).

The provisions of the Directive shall, for the purposes of the present Agreement, be read with the following adaptation:

Whereas Liechtenstein and its national regulatory authority shall make all reasonable endeavours to apply the provisions of this Directive, the assessment of their compliance shall take due account of the specific situation of Liechtenstein and the particular circumstances of its very small telecommunications network, its market structure, its limited number of customers, its market potential and the possibility of market failure.

5ck.[14] **32002 L 0020**: Directive 2002/20/EC of the European Parliament and of the Council of 7 March 2002 on the authorisation of electronic communications networks and services (Authorisation Directive) (OJ L 108, 24.4.2002, p. 21).

5cl.[14] **32002 L 0021**: Directive 2002/21/EC of the European Parliament and of the Council of 7 March 2002 on a common regulatory framework for electronic communications networks and services (Framework Directive) (OJ L 108, 24.4.2002, p. 33).

The provisions of the Directive shall, for the purposes of the present Agreement, be read with the following adaptations:

(a) In Article 5(2), the word 'Treaty' shall read 'Agreement'.

(b) In Article 5(3), the word 'Commission' shall read 'Commission, Standing Committee, EFTA Surveillance Authority'.

(c) The following sub-paragraph shall be added to Article 7(3):

'The exchange of information between the national regulatory authorities of the EFTA States on the one hand and the national regulatory authorities of the EC Member States on the other hand shall pass through the EFTA Surveillance Authority and the Commission.'

(d) The following sub-paragraphs shall be added to Article 15(4):

---

[13] Point inserted by Decision No 10/2004 (OJ No L 116, 22.4.2004, p. 58 and EEA Supplement No 20, 22.4.2004, p. 13), e.i.f. 7.2.2004.
[14] Point inserted by Decision No 11/2004 (OJ No L 116, 22.4.2004, p. 60 and EEA Supplement No 20, 22.4.2004, p. 14), e.i.f. 1.11.2004.

'After consultation with national regulatory authorities the EFTA Surveillance Authority may adopt a Decision identifying transnational markets between two or more EFTA States.

If either the EFTA Surveillance Authority or the Commission intends to identify a transnational market, which affects both an EFTA State and an EC Member State, they shall co-operate with a view to agreeing on identical Decisions identifying a transnational market, which affects both an EFTA State and an EC State. Article 109 shall apply *mutatis mutandis.*'

5cm.[14] **32002 L 0022**: Directive 2002/22/EC of the European Parliament and of the Council of 7 March 2002 on universal service and users' rights relating to electronic communications networks and services (Universal Service Directive) (OJ L 108, 24.4.2002, p. 51).

The provisions of the Directive shall, for the purposes of the present Agreement, be read with the following adaptations:

Whereas Liechtenstein and its national regulatory authority shall make all reasonable endeavours to apply the provisions of this Directive, the assessment of their compliance shall take due account of the specific situation of Liechtenstein and the particular circumstances of its very small telecommunications network, its market structure, its limited number of customers, its market potential and the possibility of market failure.

Liechtenstein shall notify to the EFTA Surveillance Authority any factors that may need to be taken into account in applying the parameters, definitions and measurement methods set out in Annex III.

After the notification, the designated undertakings may refer to such factors in the publications required by Article 11(1).

5cn.[15] **32003 D 0548**: Commission Decision 2003/548/EC of 24 July 2003 on the minimum set of leased lines with harmonised characteristics and associated standards referred to in Article 18 of the Universal Service Directive (OJ L 186, 25.7.2003, p. 43).

5co.[16] **32003 H 0558**: Commission Recommendation 2003/558/EC of 25 July 2003 on the processing of caller location information in electronic communication networks for the purpose of location-enhanced emergency call services (OJ L 189, 29.7.2003, p. 49).

5cp.[17] **32004 R 0460**: Regulation (EC) No 460/2004 of the European Parliament and of the Council of 10 March 2004 establishing the European Network and Information Security Agency (OJ L 77, 13.3.2004, p. 1).

The text of the Regulation shall, for the purposes of this Agreement, be read with the following adaptations:

(a) Unless otherwise stipulated below, and notwithstanding the provisions of Protocol 1 to the Agreement, the term 'Member State(s)' and other terms referring to their public entities contained in the Regulation shall be understood to include, in addition

---

[15] Point inserted by Decision No 39/2004 (OJ No L 277, 26.08.2004), e.i.f. 24.4.2004.
[16] Point inserted by Decision No 74/2004 (OJ No L [to be published]), e.i.f. 9.6.2004.
[17] Point inserted by Decision No 103/2005 (OJ No L 306, 24.11.2005, p. 36 and EEA Supplement No 60, 24.11.2005, p. 23), e.i.f. 1.2.2006.

to its meaning in the Regulation, the EFTA States and their public entities. Paragraph 11 of Protocol 1 shall apply.

(b) As regards the EFTA States, the Agency shall, as and when appropriate, assist the EFTA Surveillance Authority or the Standing Committee, as the case may be, in the performance of their respective tasks.

(c) The following paragraph shall be added to Article 6:

'11. The EFTA States shall participate fully in the Management Board and shall within it have the same rights and obligations as EU Member States, except for the right to vote.'

(d) The following paragraph shall be added to Article 14:

'4. Regulation (EC) No 1049/2001 shall, for the application of this Regulation, apply to any documents of the Agency regarding the EFTA States as well.'

(e) The following paragraph shall be added to Article 15:

'12. The EFTA States shall participate in the contribution from the Community referred to in paragraph 1. For this purpose, the procedures laid down in Article 82(1)(a) and Protocol 32 to the Agreement shall apply *mutatis mutandis*.'

(f) The following paragraph shall be added to Article 19:

'3. By way of derogation from Article 12(2)(a) of the Conditions of employment of other servants of the European Communities, nationals of the EFTA States enjoying their full rights as citizens may be engaged under contract by the Executive Director of the Agency.'

(g) The following shall be added to Article 20:

'EFTA States shall apply to the Agency and to its staff the Protocol on the Privileges and Immunities of the European Communities and applicable rules adopted pursuant to that Protocol.'

5cq.[18] **32004 D 0545**: Commission Decision 2004/545/EC of 8 July 2004 on the harmonisation of radio spectrum in the 79 GHz range for the use of automotive short-range radar equipment in the Community (OJ L 241, 13.7.2004, p. 66).

5cr.[19] **32005 D 0050**: Commission Decision 2005/50/EC of 17 January 2005 on the harmonisation of the 24 GHz range radio spectrum band for the time-limited use by automotive short-range radar equipment in the Community (OJ L 21, 25.1.2005, p. 15).

---

[18] Point inserted by Decision No 148/2005 (OJ No L 53, 23.2.2006, p. 46 and EEA Supplement No 10, 23.2.2005, p. 20), e.i.f. 3.12.2005.
[19] Point inserted by Decision No 148/2005 (OJ No L 53, 23.2.2006, p. 46 and EEA Supplement No 10, 23.2.2005, p. 20), e.i.f. 3.12.2005.

[...]

Data Protection[20]

[...]

5ha.[21] **32002 L 0058**: Directive 2002/58/EC of the European Parliament and of the Council of 12 July 2002 concerning the processing of personal data and the protection of privacy in the electronic communications sector (Directive on privacy and electronic communications) (OJ L 201, 31.7.2002, p. 37).

The provisions of the Directive shall, for the purposes of the present Agreement, be read with the following adaptations:

(a) In Article 1(3), the words 'the Treaty establishing the European Community' shall be replaced with the words 'EEA Agreement'.

(b) In Article 15(1), the words 'general principles of Community law, including those referred to in Article 6(1) and (2) of the Treaty on European Union' shall be replaced with the words 'general principles of EEA law'.

Procedures for the association of Liechtenstein, Iceland and Norway in accordance with Article 101 of the Agreement:

The person appointed by each EFTA State to participate as observer in the meetings of the Working Party on the Protection of individuals with regard to the Processing of Personal Data may, under the same terms and conditions as set out in point 5e (Directive 95/46/EC of the European Parliament and of the Council), also participate in the meetings when the Working Party on the Protection of individuals with regard to the Processing of Personal Data carries out the tasks laid down in Article 30 of Directive 95/46/EC of the European Parliament and of the Council with regard to matters covered by this Directive, namely the protection of fundamental rights and freedoms and of legitimate interests in the electronic communications sector.

Information Society Services[22]

5i. **398 L 0034**: Directive 98/34/EC of the European Parliament and of the Council of 22 June 1998 laying down a procedure for the provision of information in the field of technical standards and regulations (OJ L 204, 21.7.1998, p. 37), as amended by:

— **398 L 0048**: Directive 98/48/EC of the European Parliament and of the Council of 20 July 1998 (OJ L 217, 5.8.1998, p. 18),

—[23] **1 03 T**: Act concerning the conditions of accession of the Czech Republic, the Republic of Estonia, the Republic of Cyprus, the Republic of Latvia, the Republic of Lithuania, the Republic of Hungary, the Republic of Malta, the Republic of Poland, the Republic of Slovenia and the Slovak Republic and the adjustments to the Treaties on which the European Union is founded adopted on 16 April 2003 (OJ L 236, 23.9.2003, p. 33).

---

[20] Heading and point inserted by Decision No 83/1999 (OJ No L 296, 23.11.2000, p. 41 and EEA Supplement No 43, 23.11.2000, p. 112 (I) and p. 81 Del 2 (N)), e.i.f. 1.7.2000.

[21] Point inserted by Decision No 80/2003 (OJ No L 257, 9.10.2003, p. 31 and EEA Supplement No 51, 9.10.2003, p. 19), e.i.f. 1.8.2004.

[22] Heading and point inserted by Decision No 16/2001 (OJ L 117, 26.4.2001, p. 16 and EEA Supplement No 22, 26.4.2001, p.10), e.i.f. 1.3.2001.

[23] Indent added by the EEA Enlargement Agreement (OJ L 130, 29.4.2004, p. 3 and EEA Supplement No 23, 29.4.2004, p. 1), e.i.f. 1.5.2004.

The provisions of the Directive shall, for the purposes of the present Agreement, be read with the following adaptations:

(a)   the second subparagraph of Article 1(3) is replaced by the following:

"The term 'technical specification' also covers production methods and processes used in respect of products intended for human and animal consumption, and in medicinal products as defined in Article 1 of Directive 65/65/EEC (point 1 of Chapter XIII of Annex II to the Agreement), as well as production methods and processes relating to other products, where these have an effect on their characteristics.";

(b)   the following shall be added to the end of the first subparagraph of Article 8(1):

"A full text of the draft technical regulation notified shall be made available in the original language as well as in a full translation into one of the official languages of the European Community.";

(c)   the following shall be added to the fourth subparagraph of Article 8(1):

"The Community, on the one side, and the EFTA Surveillance Authority or the EFTA States through the EFTA Surveillance Authority, on the other side, may ask for further information on a draft technical regulation notified.";

(d)   the following shall be added to Article 8(2):

"The comments of the EFTA States shall be forwarded by the EFTA Surveillance Authority to the EC Commission in the form of a single coordinated communication and the comments of the Community shall be forwarded by the Commission to the EFTA Surveillance Authority. The Contracting Parties shall, when a six-month standstill is invoked according to the rules of their respective internal systems, and when a four-month standstill is invoked according to the internal system of the European Community or, in respect of the EFTA States, according to the following two paragraphs, inform each other thereof in a similar manner.

The competent authorities of the EFTA States shall postpone for four months the adoption of any draft rule on services, from the date of receipt of the text of the draft regulation by the EFTA Surveillance Authority, if another EFTA State delivers a detailed opinion, within three months, to the effect that the measure envisaged may create obstacles to the free movement of services or to the freedom of establishment of service operators within the markets of the EFTA States.

With regard to draft rules on services, detailed opinions from EFTA States may not affect any cultural policy measures, in particular in the audiovisual sphere, which EFTA States might adopt in accordance with EEA law, taking account of their linguistic diversity, their specific national and regional characteristics and their cultural heritages.";

(e)   Article 9 shall be replaced by the following:

"1.   The competent authorities of the EC Member States and the EFTA States shall postpone the adoption of draft technical regulations notified for three months from the date of receipt of the text of the draft regulation

       —   by the EC Commission in case of drafts notified by Member States of the Community

      –   by the EFTA Surveillance Authority for drafts notified by the EFTA States.

2.   The standstill periods of paragraph 1 and adaptation (d), paragraph 1, shall not apply in those cases where,

      –   for urgent reasons relating to the protection of public health or safety, the protection of health and life of animals or plants, and for rules on services, also for public policy, notably the protection of minors, the competent authorities are obliged to prepare technical regulations in a very short space of time in order to enact and introduce them immediately without any consultations being possible or where,

      –   for urgent reasons occasioned by serious circumstances relating to the protection of the security and integrity of the financial system, notably the protection of depositors, investors and insured persons, the competent authorities are obliged to enact and implement rules on financial services immediately.

The reasons which warrant the urgency of the measures taken shall be given. The justification for urgent measures shall be detailed and clearly explained with particular emphasis on the unpredictability and the seriousness of the danger confronting the concerned authorities as well as the absolute necessity for immediate action to remedy it.";

(f)   the following shall be added to Annex II:

"ICELAND

STRI

Staðlaráð Íslands

LIECHTENSTEIN

TPMN

Liechtensteinische Technische Prüf-, Mess- und Normenstelle

NORWAY

NSF

Norges Standardiseringsforbund

NEK

Norsk Elektroteknisk Komite

PT

Post- og teletilsynet";

(g)   for the application of the Directive, the following communications by electronic means are considered necessary:

    (1)   notification slips. They may be communicated before or together with the transmission of the full text;

(2)   acknowledgement of receipt of draft text, containing inter alia, the relevant expiry date of the standstill determined according to the rules of each system;

(3)   messages requesting supplementary information;

(4)   answers to request for supplementary information;

(5)   comments;

(6)   requests for ad hoc meetings;

(7)   answers to requests for ad hoc meetings;

(8)   requests for final texts;

(9)   information that a four-month or a six-month standstill has been called;

the following communications may, for the time being, be transmitted by normal mail, however electronic means are preferable:

(10) the full text of the draft notified;

(11) basic legal texts or regulatory provisions;

(12) the final text;

(h)   administrative arrangements concerning the communications shall be jointly agreed by the Contracting Parties.

[...]

ACTS OF WHICH THE CONTRACTING PARTIES SHALL TAKE NOTE

The Contracting Parties take note of the contents of the following Acts:

Telecommunication services[24]

6.   **388 Y 1004(01):** Council Resolution 88/C 257/01 of 30 June 1988 on the development of the common market for telecommunications services and equipment up to 1992 (OJ No C 257, 4.10.1988, p. 1).

7.   **389 Y 0511(01):** Council Resolution 89/C 117/01 of 27 April 1989 on standardization in the field of information technology and telecommunications (OJ No C 117, 11.5.1989, p. 1).

8.   **389 Y 0801:** Council Resolution 89C/ 196/04 of 18 July 1989 on the strengthening of the coordination for the introduction of the Integrated Services Digital Network (ISDN) in the European Community up to 1992 (OJ No C 196, 1.8.1989, p. 4).

9.   **390 Y 0707(02):** Council Resolution 90/C 166/02 of 28 June 1990 on the strengthening of the Europewide cooperation on radio frequencies in particular with regard to services with a pan-European dimension (OJ No C 166, 7.7.1990, p. 4).

---

[24] Heading inserted by Decision No 28/94 (OJ No L 339, 29.12.1994, p. 87 and EEA Supplement No 53, 29.12.1994, p. 18), e.i.f. 1.2.1995.

10. **390 Y 3112(01):** Council Resolution 90C/ 329/25 of 14 December 1990 on the final stage of the coordinated introduction of pan-European land-based public digital mobile cellular communications in the Community (GSM) (OJ No C 329, 31.12.1990, p. 25).

11. **384 X 0549:** Council Recommendation 84/549/EEC of 12 November 1984 concerning the implementation of harmonization in the field of telecommunications (OJ No L 298, 16.11.1984, p. 49).

12. **384 X 0550:** Council Recommendation 84/550/EEC of 12 November 1984 concerning the first phase of opening up access to public telecommunications contract (OJ No L 298, 16.11.1984, p. 51).

13. **386 X 0659:** Council Recommendation 86/659/EEC of 22 December 1986 on the coordinated introduction of the Integrated Services Digital Network (ISDN) in the European Community (OJ No L 382, 31.12.1986, p. 36).

14. **387 X 0371:** Council Recommendation 87/371/EEC of 25 June 1987 on the coordinated introduction of public pan-European cellular digital and land-based mobile communications in the Community (OJ No L 196, 17.7.1987, p. 81).

15. **390 X 0543:** Council Recommendation 90/543/EEC on the coordinated introduction of pan-European land-based public radio paging in the Community (OJ No L 310, 9.11.1990, p. 23).

16. **391 X 0288:** Council Recommendation 91/C 288/EEC on the coordinated introduction of digital European cordless telecommunications (DECT) into the Community (OJ No L 144, 8.6.1991, p. 47).

17.[25] **392 Y 0114(01):** Council Resolution 92/C 8/01 of 19 December 1991 on the development of the common market for satellite communications services and equipment (OJ No C 8, 14. 1. 1992, p. 1).

18.[25] **392 X 0382:** Council Recommendation of 5 June 1992 on the harmonized provision of a minimum set of packet-switched data services (PSDS) in accordance with open network provision (ONP) principles (OJ No L 200, 18.7. 1992, p. 1).

19.[25] **392 X 0383:** Council Recommendation of 5 June 1992 on the provision of harmonized integrated services digital network (ISDN) access arrangements and a minimum set of ISDN offerings in accordance with open network provision (ONP) principles (OJ No L 200, 18. 7. 1992, p. 10).

20.[25] **392 Y 0625(01):** Council Resolution of 5 June 1992 on the development of the integrated services digital network (ISDN) in the Community as a European-wide telecommunications infrastructure for 1993 and beyond (OJ No C 158, 25. 6. 1992, p. 1).

21.[25] **392 Y 1204(02):** Council Resolution of 19 November 1992 on the promotion of Europe-wide cooperation on numbering of telecommunications services (OJ No C 318, 4. 12. 1992, p. 2).

22.[25] **393 Y 0106(01):** Council Resolution of 17 December 1992 on the assessment of the situation in the Community telecommunications sector (OJ No C 2, 6. 1. 1993, p. 5).

---

[25] Point inserted by Decision No 7/94.

23.[25] **392 Y 1204(01):** Council Resolution of 19 November 1992 on the implementation of the European Radiocommunications Committee decisions (OJ No C 318, 4. 12. 1992, p. 1).

24.[25] **393 Y 0806(01):** Council Resolution of 22 July 1993 on the review of the situation in the telecommunications sector and the need for further development in that market (OJ No C 213, 6. 8. 1993, p. 1).

25.[25] **393 Y 1216(01):** Council Resolution of 7 December 1993 on the introduction of satellite personal communication services in the Community (OJ No C 339, 16. 12. 1993, p. 1).

26.[26] **394 Y 0216(01):** Council Resolution 94/C 48/01 of 7 February 1994 on the universal service principles in the telecommunications sector (OJ No C 48, 16.2.1994, p. 1).

26a.[27] **394 Y 1222(03):** Council Resolution 94/C 379/03 of 22 December 1994 on the principles and timetable for the liberalization of telecommunications infrastructures (OJ No C 379, 31.12.1994, p. 4).

26b.[27] **394 Y 0122(04):** Council Resolution 94/C 379/04 of 22 December 1994 on further development of the Community's satellite communications policy, especially with regard to the provision of, and access to, space segment capacity (OJ No C 379, 31.12.1994, p. 5).

26c.[28] **395 Y 0722(02):** Council Resolution 95/C 188/02 of 29 June 1995 on the further development of mobile and personal communications in the European Union (OJ No C 188, 22.7.1995, p. 3).

26d.[29] **395 Y 1003(01):** Council Resolution 95/C 258/01 of 18 September 1995 on the implementation of the future regulatory framework for telecommunications (OJ No C 258, 3.10.1995, p. 1).

26e.[30] **395 Y 1219(03):** Council Resolution 95/C 341/03 of 27 November 1995 on the industrial aspects for the European Union in the development of the information society (OJ No C 341, 19.12.1995, p. 5).

26f.[31] **397 Y 1004(01):** Council Resolution 97/C 303/01 of 22 September 1997 on the further development of a numbering policy for telecommunications services in the European Community (OJ C 303, 4.10.1997, p. 1).

26g.[32] **398 X 0195:** Commission Recommendation 98/195/EC of 8 January 1998 on interconnection in a liberalised telecommunications market (Part 1 - Interconnection pricing) (OJ L 73, 12.3.1998, p. 42), as amended by:

---

[26] Point inserted by Decision No 28/94 (OJ No L 339, 29.12.1994, p. 87 and EEA Supplement No 53, 29.12.1994, p. 18), e.i.f. 1.2.1995.

[27] Point inserted by Decision No 26/95 (OJ No L 273, 16.11.1995, p. 47 and EEA Supplement No 43, 16.11.1995, p. 1), e.i.f. 1.6.1995.

[28] Point inserted by Decision No 5/96 (OJ No L 102, 25.4.1996, p. 48 and EEA Supplement No 18, 25.4.1996, p. 14), e.i.f. 1.3.1996.

[29] Point inserted by Decision No 6/96 (OJ No L 102, 25.4.1996, p. 49 and EEA Supplement No 18, 25.4.1996, p. 17), e.i.f. 1.3.1996.

[30] Point inserted by Decision No 41/96 (OJ No L 291, 14.11.1996, p. 30 and EEA Supplement No 51, 14.11.1996, p. 10), e.i.f. 1.7.1996.

[31] Point inserted by Decision No 75/98 (OJ No L 172, 8.7.1999, p. 54 and EEA Supplement No 30, 8.7.1999, p. 138), e.i.f. 1.8.1998.

[32] Point inserted by Decision No 93/98 (OJ No L 189, 22.7.1999, p. 67 and EEA Supplement No 32, 22.7.1999, p. 157), e.i.f. 26.9.1998.

$-^{33}$ **398 X 0511:** Commission Recommendation 98/511/EC of 29 July 1998 (OJ L 228, 15.8.1998, p. 30),

$-^{34}$ **32000 X 0263:** Commission Recommendation 2000/263/EC of 20 March 2000 (OJ L 83, 4.4.2000, p. 30),

$-^{35}$ **32002 H 0175:** Commission Recommendation 2002/175/EC of 22 February 2002 (OJ L 58, 28.2.2002, p. 56).

26h.[36] **398 X 0322:** Commission Recommendation 98/322/EC of 8 April 1998 on interconnection in a liberalised telecommunications market (Part 2 - Accounting separation and cost accounting) (OJ L 141, 13.5.1998, p. 6).

26i.[37] **32000 X 0417:** Commission Recommendation 2000/417/EC of 25 May 2000 on unbundled access to the local loop: enabling the competitive provision of a full range of electronic communications services including broadband multimedia and high-speed Internet (OJ L 156, 29.6.2000, p. 44).

[...]

Editors' Notes:

^{a} Sub-section on Postal Services [5d] omitted; sub-section on Data Protection [5e, 5f, 5g, 5h] reproduced only in so far as it relates to electronic communications; sub-section on Information Society Services [5i, 5j, 5k] reproduced only in so far as it relates to subject matter covered by the scope of this Handbook.

---

[33] Indent, and words ", as amended by:" above, added by Decision No 120/98 (OJ No L 297, 18.11.1999, p. 49 and EEA Supplement No 50, 18.11.1999, p. 70), e.i.f. 19.12.1998.

[34] Indent added by Decision No 67/2000 (OJ No L 250, 5.10.2000, p. 50 and EEA Supplement No 44, 5.10.2000, p. 3), e.i.f. 3.8.2000.

[35] Indent added by Decision No 104/2002 (OJ No L 298, 31.10.2002, p. 21 and EEA Supplement No 54, 31.10.2002, p. 16), e.i.f. 13.7.2002.

[36] Point inserted by Decision No 111/98 (OJ No L 277, 28.10.1999, p. 48 and EEA Supplement No 46, 28.10.1999, p. 126), e.i.f. 28.11.1998.

[37] Point inserted by Decision No 92/2000 (OJ No L 7, 11.1.2001, p. 1 and EEA Supplement No 2, 11.1.2001, p. 1), e.i.f. 28.10.2000.

GENERAL AGREEMENT ON TRADE IN SERVICES

Editors' Note

We have reproduced here the text of the Annex on Telecommunications, which forms part of the General Agreement on Trade in Services ("the GATS"), and Council Decision 97/838/EC, which authorises execution of the Fourth Protocol to the GATS by the European Communities. Because of space limitations, we have not included the main body of the GATS.[1] The following provides an outline of key aspects of the GATS and supplies some of the context relevant to the Annex and the Council Decision.

The GATS is one of a series of related agreements on international trade concluded in Marrakesh on 15 April 1994 as part of the Agreement establishing the World Trade Organization (the "WTO Agreement"). 140 countries are parties to the GATS. Under the terms of the GATS, parties agree to abide by certain defined "disciplines" in relation to services within the scope of the GATS.

Prior to 1998, the GATS had limited relevance to trade in telecommunications services because parties restricted the services subject to the full range of GATS disciplines to the provision of capacity for secondary applications, such as the supply of corporate networks and enhanced and value-added services. The parties did agree, however, the terms of the Annex on Telecommunications, the object of which is to elaborate upon the provisions of the GATS and provide some specifics concerning GATS Members' obligation to provide access to and use of their "public telecommunications transport networks and services."

In 1998, a protocol to the GATS ("the Fourth Protocol") entered into force under which 69 (now more than 80) Members agreed for the first time to extend the application of GATS to their basic telecommunications services. (The Fourth Protocol and the annexes to it are sometimes referred to as the "Basic Telecommunications Services Agreement.") The EC and most of its major trading partners became parties to the Fourth Protocol. As noted above, it is Council Decision 97/838/EC which authorised EC execution of the Fourth Protocol.

The GATS establishes a general legal framework for trade in services. Part II of the GATS set out rules that apply to essentially all services provided by service suppliers of Members. Part II includes Articles II - XV. Of special importance is Article II, entitled "Most-Favoured-Nation Treatment." The MFN obligation is the cornerstone of the GATS. Article II:1 stipulates that each Member (i.e., each signatory of the WTO Agreement) shall, "[w]ith respect to any measure covered by [the] Agreement, ... accord immediately and unconditionally to services and service suppliers of any other Member, treatment no less favourable than that it accords to like services and service suppliers of any other country." The other provisions of Part II are all aimed at either carrying this obligation into effect, or, in certain cases, limiting its application. Falling into the first category are Articles III (Transparency), VI (Domestic Regulation), VIII (setting out special rules relating to maintenance of national monopolies) and IX (governing unfair business practices). Certain provisions limit the application of Article II: Articles II:2 and 3 (providing for MFN exemptions), X and XIV (relating to emergency economic safeguards and security issues), VII (governing recognition of foreign licences and qualifications) and XIII (Government Procurement).

Part III (entitled "Specific Commitments") defines additional obligations which apply to a service sector or service of a Member only if the relevant sector or service has been listed by that Member in a Schedule of Specific Commitment. The contents of these Schedules are typically arrived at through multilateral negotiations. (The EU's Schedule of Specific

---

[1] For a copy of the full text of the GATS, see http://www.wto.org/english/docs_e/legal_e/legal_e.htm.

Commitments is included in the annex to Council Decision 97/838/EC.) Specific commitments may be made subject to any conditions or qualifications stipulated by the Member. As required by Article II:1, once Specific Commitments are made, they must be extended to all Members on an MFN basis (subject only to the exceptions permitted by Part II). The Specific Commitments provided for in Part III include the following:

Article XVI - Market Access: Under Article XVI, Members bind themselves not to maintain or adopt certain types of quantitative restrictions on market access by foreign suppliers (or similar measures such as foreign ownership   limits) except as otherwise specified in their Schedules.

Article XVII - National Treatment: Under Article XVII, each Member undertakes to accord "treatment no less favourable than it accords to its own like services and service suppliers" to services and service suppliers of any other Member (subject to any applicable conditions or qualifications in its Schedule). This is a level of commitment that goes beyond the MFN commitment, which merely requires that a particular Member treat no one Member better than any other Member.

Article XVIII - Additional Commitments: Article XVIII provides for the negotiation of commitments additional to those provided for in Articles XVI and XVII.

The EC's Schedule of Specific Commitments includes commitments with respect to market access and national treatment. In 1997, the EC was still in the process of liberalising its internal markets for telecommunications services, and the commitments on market access and national treatment made in the EC's Schedule were phased in over time to reflect the timetable for liberalisation of internal markets.

Most of the parties to the Fourth Protocol, including the European Communities, agreed to subscribe, as an "additional commitment," to the terms of a common "Reference Paper" defining key elements of the regulatory regime they will maintain in their jurisdictions. The text of the Reference Paper as agreed to by the EU is attached to its Schedule and can therefore be found in the documents annexed to Council Decision 97/838/EC.

GENERAL AGREEMENT ON TRADE IN SERVICES

ANNEX ON TELECOMMUNICATIONS

1. **Objectives**

   Recognizing the specificities of the telecommunications services sector and, in particular, its dual role as a distinct sector of economic activity and as the underlying transport means for other economic activities, the Members have agreed to the following Annex with the objective of elaborating upon the provisions of the Agreement with respect to measures affecting access to and use of public telecommunications transport networks and services. Accordingly, this Annex provides notes and supplementary provisions to the Agreement.

2. **Scope**

   (a) This Annex shall apply to all measures of a Member that affect access to and use of public telecommunications transport networks and services.[1]

   (b) This Annex shall not apply to measures affecting the cable or broadcast distribution of radio or television programming.

   (c) Nothing in this Annex shall be construed:

   (i) to require a Member to authorize a service supplier of any other Member to establish, construct, acquire, lease, operate, or supply telecommunications transport networks or services, other than as provided for in its Schedule; or

   (ii) to require a Member (or to require a Member to oblige service suppliers under its jurisdiction) to establish, construct, acquire, lease, operate or supply telecommunications transport networks or services not offered to the public generally.

3. **Definitions**

   For the purposes of this Annex:

   (a) "Telecommunications" means the transmission and reception of signals by any electromagnetic means.

   (b) "Public telecommunications transport service" means any telecommunications transport service required, explicitly or in effect, by a Member to be offered to the public generally. Such services may include, *inter alia*, telegraph, telephone, telex, and data transmission typically involving the real-time transmission of customer-supplied information between two or more points without any end-to-end change in the form or content of the customer's information.

   (c) "Public telecommunications transport network" means the public telecommunications infrastructure which permits telecommunications between and among defined network termination points.

---

[1] This paragraph is understood to mean that each Member shall ensure that the obligations of this Annex are applied with respect to suppliers of public telecommunications transport networks and services by whatever measures are necessary.

(d)   "Intra-corporate communications" means telecommunications through which a company communicates within the company or with or among its subsidiaries, branches and, subject to a Member's domestic laws and regulations, affiliates. For these purposes, "subsidiaries", "branches" and, where applicable, "affiliates" shall be as defined by each Member. "Intra-corporate communications" in this Annex excludes commercial or non-commercial services that are supplied to companies that are not related subsidiaries, branches or affiliates, or that are offered to customers or potential customers.

(e)   Any reference to a paragraph or subparagraph of this Annex includes all subdivisions thereof.

4. Transparency

In the application of Article III of the Agreement, each Member shall ensure that relevant information on conditions affecting access to and use of public telecommunications transport networks and services is publicly available, including: tariffs and other terms and conditions of service; specifications of technical interfaces with such networks and services; information on bodies responsible for the preparation and adoption of standards affecting such access and use; conditions applying to attachment of terminal or other equipment; and notifications, registration or licensing requirements, if any.

5. Access to and use of Public Telecommunications Transport Networks and Services

(a)   Each Member shall ensure that any service supplier of any other Member is accorded access to and use of public telecommunications transport networks and services on reasonable and non-discriminatory terms and conditions, for the supply of a service included in its Schedule. This obligation shall be applied, *inter alia*, through paragraphs (b) through (f).[2]

(b)   Each Member shall ensure that service suppliers of any other Member have access to and use of any public telecommunications transport network or service offered within or across the border of that Member, including private leased circuits, and to this end shall ensure, subject to paragraphs (e) and (f), that such suppliers are permitted:

     (i)   to purchase or lease and attach terminal or other equipment which interfaces with the network and which is necessary to supply a supplier's services;

     (ii)   to interconnect private leased or owned circuits with public telecommunications transport networks and services or with circuits leased or owned by another service supplier; and

     (iii)   to use operating protocols of the service supplier's choice in the supply of any service, other than as necessary to ensure the availability of telecommunications transport networks and services to the public generally.

---

[2]   The term "non-discriminatory" is understood to refer to most-favoured-nation and national treatment as defined in the Agreement, as well as to reflect sector-specific usage of the term to mean "terms and conditions no less favourable than those accorded to any other user of like public telecommunications transport networks or services under like circumstances".

(c) Each Member shall ensure that service suppliers of any other Member may use public telecommunications transport networks and services for the movement of information within and across borders, including for intra-corporate communications of such service suppliers, and for access to information contained in data bases or otherwise stored in machine-readable form in the territory of any Member. Any new or amended measures of a Member significantly affecting such use shall be notified and shall be subject to consultation, in accordance with relevant provisions of the Agreement.

(d) Notwithstanding the preceding paragraph, a Member may take such measures as are necessary to ensure the security and confidentiality of messages, subject to the requirement that such measures are not applied in a manner which would constitute a means of arbitrary or unjustifiable discrimination or a disguised restriction on trade in services.

(e) Each Member shall ensure that no condition is imposed on access to and use of public telecommunications transport networks and services other than as necessary:

   (i) to safeguard the public service responsibilities of suppliers of public telecommunications transport networks and services, in particular their ability to make their networks or services available to the public generally;

   (ii) to protect the technical integrity of public telecommunications transport networks or services; or

   (iii) to ensure that service suppliers of any other Member do not supply services unless permitted pursuant to commitments in the Member's Schedule.

(f) Provided that they satisfy the criteria set out in paragraph (e), conditions for access to and use of public telecommunications transport networks and services may include:

   (i) restrictions on resale or shared use of such services;

   (ii) a requirement to use specified technical interfaces, including interface protocols, for inter-connection with such networks and services;

   (iii) requirements, where necessary, for the inter-operability of such services and to encourage the achievement of the goals set out in paragraph 7(a);

   (iv) type approval of terminal or other equipment which interfaces with the network and technical requirements relating to the attachment of such equipment to such networks;

   (v) restrictions on inter-connection of private leased or owned circuits with such networks or services or with circuits leased or owned by another service supplier; or

   (vi) notification, registration and licensing.

(g) Notwithstanding the preceding paragraphs of this section, a developing country Member may, consistent with its level of development, place reasonable conditions on access to and use of public telecommunications transport networks and services necessary to strengthen its domestic telecommunications infrastructure and service capacity and to increase its participation in international trade in telecommunications services. Such conditions shall be specified in the Member's Schedule.

6. **Technical Cooperation**

(a) Members recognize that an efficient, advanced telecommunications infrastructure in countries, particularly developing countries, is essential to the expansion of their trade in services. To this end, Members endorse and encourage the participation, to the fullest extent practicable, of developed and developing countries and their suppliers of public telecommunications transport networks and services and other entities in the development programmes of international and regional organizations, including the International Telecommunication Union, the United Nations Development Programme, and the International Bank for Reconstruction and Development.

(b) Members shall encourage and support telecommunications cooperation among developing countries at the international, regional and sub-regional levels.

(c) In cooperation with relevant international organizations, Members shall make available, where practicable, to developing countries information with respect to telecommunications services and developments in telecommunications and information technology to assist in strengthening their domestic telecommunications services sector.

d) Members shall give special consideration to opportunities for the least-developed countries to encourage foreign suppliers of telecommunications services to assist in the transfer of technology, training and other activities that support the development of their telecommunications infrastructure and expansion of their telecommunications services trade.

7. **Relation to International Organizations and Agreements**

(a) Members recognize the importance of international standards for global compatibility and inter-operability of telecommunication networks and services and undertake to promote such standards through the work of relevant international bodies, including the International Telecommunication Union and the International Organization for Standardization.

(b) Members recognize the role played by intergovernmental and non-governmental organizations and agreements in ensuring the efficient operation of domestic and global telecommunications services, in particular the International Telecommunication Union. Members shall make appropriate arrangements, where relevant, for consultation with such organizations on matters arising from the implementation of this Annex.

COUNCIL DECISION 97/838/EC

of 28 November 1997[a]

concerning the conclusion on behalf of the European Community, as regards matters within its competence, of the results of the WTO negotiations on basic telecommunications services

THE COUNCIL OF THE EUROPEAN UNION,

Having regard to the Treaty establishing the European Community, and in particular Articles 57, 66, 90, 99, 100, 100a and 113, in conjunction with Article 228 (2) and the first subparagraph of Article 228 (3) thereof,

Having regard to the proposal from the Commission[1],

Having regard to the opinion of the European Parliament[2],

Whereas the Marrakesh Agreement establishing the World Trade Organization and its related agreements, the Ministerial Decisions and Declarations, including the Ministerial Decision on Negotiations on Basic Telecommunications, as well as the Annex on Telecommunications and the Annex on Negotiations on Basic Telecommunications were approved by Council Decision 94/800/EC of 22 December 1994[3];

Whereas the overall commitments in basic telecommunications services negotiated by the Commission, on behalf of the European Community and its Member States, constitutes a satisfactory and balanced outcome;

Whereas on 30 April 1996 the Council authorized the Commission to approve, on behalf of the European Community and its Member States, the Decision of the Negotiating Group on Basic Telecommunications and the WTO Council for Trade in Services adopting the Fourth Protocol to the General Agreement on Trade in Services and the Decision of the Council for Trade in Services on Commitments in Basic Telecommunications;

Whereas on 14 February 1997 the Council authorized the Commission to submit to the WTO the final schedule of commitments on behalf of the European Community and its Member States;

Whereas the competence of the Community to conclude international agreements does not derive only from explicit conferral by the Treaty but may also derive from other provisions of the Treaty and from acts adopted pursuant to those provisions by Community institutions;

Whereas where Community rules have been adopted in order to achieve the aims of the Treaty, Member States may not, outside the framework of the common institutions, enter into commitments liable to affect those rules or alter their scope;

Whereas some commitments on basic telecommunications services fall within the competence of the Community under Article 113 of the Treaty; whereas, furthermore, other commitments on basic telecommunications services affect Community rules adopted on the basis of Articles 57, 66, 90, 99, 100 and 100a and may therefore only be entered into by the Community alone;

---

[1]   OJ C 267, 3. 9. 1997, p. 80.
[2]   OJ C 339, 10. 11. 1997.
[3]   OJ L 336, 23. 12. 1994, p. 1.

Whereas the use of Article 100 of the Treaty as a legal base for this Decision is justified also by the fact that the aforementioned commitments on basic telecommunications services are likely to affect Council Directive 90/434/EEC of 23 July 1990 on the common system of taxation applicable to mergers, divisions, transfers of assets and exchanges of shares concerning companies of different Member States[4] and Council Directive 90/435/EEC of 23 July 1990 on the common system of taxation applicable in the case of parent companies and subsidiaries of different Member States[5], which are based on Article 100 of the Treaty;

Whereas, by their nature, the Agreement establishing the World Trade Organization and the Protocols to the General Agreement on Trade in Services, are not susceptible to being directly invoked in Community or Member States courts,

HAS DECIDED AS FOLLOWS:

Sole Article

1. The Fourth Protocol to the General Agreement on Trade in Services concerning basic telecommunications services is hereby approved on behalf of the European Community with regard to that portion of it which falls within the competence of the Community.

2. The text of the Fourth Protocol is attached to this Decision, as are also the following:

    -   the schedule of specific commitments of the Community and the Member States, which is part of the overall package of commitments reached at the WTO on 15 February 1997,

    -   the decision of the Council for Trade in Services on commitments in basic telecommunications, and

    -   the report of 15 February 1997 by the Group on Basic Telecommunications to the Council for Trade in Services.

3. The President of the Council is hereby authorized to designate the person(s) empowered to sign the Fourth Protocol to the General Agreement on Trade in Services in order to bind the Community with regard to that portion of the Protocol falling within its competence.

Editors' Notes:

[a] OJ L 347, 18.12.97, p. 45.

---

[4]   OJ L 225, 20. 8. 1990, p. 1.
[5]   OJ L 225, 20. 8. 1990, p. 6.

FOURTH PROTOCOL
TO THE GENERAL AGREEMENT ON TRADE IN SERVICES

Members of the World Trade Organization (hereinafter referred to as the 'WTO') whose Schedules of Specific Commitments and Lists of Exemptions from Article II of the General Agreement on Trade in Services concerning basic telecommunications are annexed to this Protocol (hereinafter referred to as 'Members concerned'),

Having carried out negotiations under the terms of the Ministerial Decision on Negotiations on Basic Telecommunications adopted at Marrakesh on 15 April 1994,

Having regard to the Annex on Negotiations on Basic Telecommunications,

Agree as follows:

1. Upon the entry into force of this Protocol, a schedule of specific commitments and a list of exemptions from Article II concerning basic telecommunications annexed to this Protocol relating to a Member shall, in accordance with the terms specified therein, supplement or modify the schedule of specific commitments and the list of Article II exemptions of that Member.

2. This Protocol shall be open for acceptance, by signature or otherwise, by the Members concerned until 30 November 1997.

3. The Protocol shall enter into force on 1 January 1998 provided it has been accepted by all Members concerned. If by 1 December 1997 the Protocol has not been accepted by all Members concerned, those Members which have accepted it by that date may decide, prior to 1 January 1998, on its entry into force.

4. This Protocol shall be deposited with the Director-General of the WTO. The Director-General of the WTO shall promptly furnish to each Member of the WTO a certified copy of this Protocol and notifications of acceptances thereof.

5. This Protocol shall be registered in accordance with the provisions of Article 102 of the Charter of the United Nations.

Done at Geneva this fifteenth day of April one thousand nine hundred and ninety-seven, in a single copy in the English, French and Spanish languages, each text being authentic, except as otherwise provided for in respect of the Schedules annexed hereto.

---

[1]   The Annex is authentic in English, French and Spanish.

THE EUROPEAN COMMUNITIES AND THEIR MEMBER STATES – SCHEDULE OF SPECIFIC COMMITMENTS

Modes of Supply: 1. Cross-border supply   2. Consumption abroad   3. Commercial presence   4. Presence of natural persons

Sector or subsector	Limitations on market access	Limitations on national treatment	Additional commitments
2.C Telecommunications services Telecommunications services are the transport of electromagnetic signals - sound, data image and any combinations thereof, excluding broadcasting.¹ Therefore. Commitments in this schedule do not cover the economic activity consisting of content provision which require telecommunications services for its transport. The provision of that content, transported via a telecommunications service, is subject to the specific commitments undertaken by the European Communities and their Member States in other relevant sectors. All sub-sectors	FIN: The general horizontal requirements for legal entities in GATS/SC/33 shall not apply to the telecommunications sector except as: - half of the founders, half of the members of the board of directors and the managing director must have permanent residence in the European Economic Area. If the founder is a legal person , it must have residence in the EEA. 1. None except for: P: basic services can be supplied only by companies established in Portugal. GR: access through SA and the company must be exclusively engaged in the supply of telecommunication services.	FIN: The general horizontal requirements for legal entities in GATS/SC/33 shall not apply to the telecommunications sector. Requirements concerning the Aland islands shall continue to apply. 1. None	The European Communities and their Member States undertake additional commitments as contained in the attachment, all parts of which are equally binding. B: Licensing conditions may address the need to guarantee universal service including through financing, in a transparent, nondiscriminatory and competitively neutral manner and will not be more burdensome than necessary.

Modes of Supply: 1. Cross-border supply   2. Consumption abroad   3. Commercial presence   4. Presence of natural persons

Sector or subsector	Limitations on market access	limitations on national treatment	Additional commitments
Domestic and international Domestic and international services provided using any network technology, on a facilities based or resale basis, for public and non-public use, in the following market segments (these correspond to the following CPC numbers: 7521, 7522, 7523, 7524**, 7525, 7526 and 7529***, broadcasting is excluded): a. Voice telephone services b. Packet switched data transmission services c. Circuit-switched data transmissions services d. Telex services	2. None 3. None except for:* GR: access through SA and the company must be exclusively engaged in the supply of telecommunication services. P: The direct or indirect participation of natural persons, who are non-nationals of EC Member States or non-EC companies or firms in the capital of companies supplying basic telecommunications services cannot exceed 25 %. F: Indirect: none. Non-EC natural or juridical persons may not hold directly more than 20 % of the shares or voting rights of companies authorised to establish and operate radio-based infrastructure for the provision of telecommunications services to the general public. For the application of this provision, companies or firms legally established according to the laws of a Member State of the EC are considered EC juridical persons. 4. Unbound except as indicated in the horizontal section 1. None except for:[2] E: none, except that the liberalisation calendar will be as follows: one additional nation-wide licence in January 1998; full liberalisation as from 30 November 1998.[3]	2. None 3. None 4. Unbound except as indicated in the horizontal section 1. None	P: The Government of Portugal has the intention of presenting to the Parliament draft legislation aiming at removing partially the present limitations on foreign equity participation in the capital of companies supplying basic telecommunication services no later than in 1998. In case of approval, the new legislation will be bound no later than in 1999.

Modes of Supply:	1. Cross-border supply	2. Consumption abroad	3. Commercial presence	4. Presence of natural persons
Sector or subsector	Limitations on market access		limitations on national treatment	Additional commitments
e. Telegraph services f. Facsimile services g. Leased circuit services	IRL: None except for public voice telephony and facilities-based service where none as of 1 January 2000. P: None, except for public voice telephony, telex and telegraph where none as from 1 January 2000, and facilities-based services where none as from 1 July 1999. GR: None except for public-voice telephony and facilities-based services where none as of 1 January 2003. 2. None 3. None except for:[2] E: none, except that the liberalisation calendar will be as follows: one additional nation wide licence in January 1998; full liberalisation as from 30 November 1998.[3] IRL: None except for public voice telephony and facilities-based services where none as of 1 January 2000. P: None, except for public voice telephony, telex and telegraph where none as from 1 January 2000 and facilities-based services where none as from 1 July 1999. GR: None except for public voice telephony and facilities-based services where none as of 1 January 2003. 4. Unbound except as indicated in the horizontal section		2. None 3. None 4. Unbound except as indicated in the horizontal section	

Modes of Supply: 1. Cross-border supply 2. Consumption abroad 3. Commercial presence 4. Presence of natural persons

Sector or subsector	Limitations on market access	limitations on national treatment	Additional commitments
o. Other services: Mobile and personal communications services and systems.	1. None except for: IRL, P: international interconnection of mobile networks with other mobile or fixed networks where none as of 1 January 1999.	1. None	
	2. None	2. None	
	3. None except for: IRL, P: international interconnection of mobile networks with other mobile or fixed networks where none as of 1 January 1999.	3. None	
	4. Unbound except as indicated in the horizontal section	4. Unbound except as indicated in the horizontal section	

[1] Broadcasting is defined as the uninterrupted chain of transmission required for the distribution of TV and radio programme signals to the general public, but does not cover contribution links between operators.

[2] Luxembourg has requested a delayed date for the liberalisation of telecommunications until 1 January 2000. The EC decision on this request is still pending.

[3] Applications for further licences to be received as from 1 August 1998.

* Footnote for clarification purposes: Some EC Member States maintain public participation in certain telecommunication operators. EC Member States reserve their rights to maintain such public participation in the future. This is not a market access limitation. In Belgium, government participation and voting rights in Belgacom are freely determined under legislative powers as is presently the case under the law of 21 March 1 991 on the reform of government-owned economic enterprises.

ADDITIONAL COMMITMENT BY THE EUROPEAN COMMUNITIES
AND THEIR MEMBER STATES

Scope

The following are definitions and principles on the regulatory framework for the basic telecommunications services underpinning the market access commitments by the European Communities and their Member States.

Definitions

Users mean service consumer and service suppliers.

Essential facilities mean facilities of a public telecommunications transport network and service that

(a)   are exclusively or predominantly provided by a single or limited number of suppliers; and

(b)   cannot feasibly be economically or technically substituted in order to provide a service.

A *major supplier* is a supplier which has the ability to materially affect the terms of participation (having regard to price and supply) in the relevant market for basic telecommunications services as a result of:

(a)   control over essential facilities; or

(b)   use of its position in the market.

1.   COMPETITIVE SAFEGUARDS

1.1. Prevention of anti-competitive practices in telecommunications

Appropriate measures shall be maintained for the purpose of preventing suppliers who, alone or together, are a major supplier from engaging in or continuing anti-competitive practices.

1.2. Safeguards

The anti-competitive practices referred to above shall include in particular:

(a)   engaging in anti-competitive cross-subsidization;

(b)   using information obtained from competitors with anti-competitive results; and

(c)   not making available to other services suppliers on a timely basis technical information about essential facilities and commercially relevant information which are necessary for them to provide services.

2.   INTERCONNECTION

2.1. This section applies to linking with suppliers providing public telecommunications transport networks or services in order to allow the users of one supplier to communicate with users of another supplier and to access services provided by another supplier.

2.2. Interconnection to be ensured

Within the limits of permitted market access, interconnection with a major supplier will be ensured at any technically feasible point in the network. Such interconnection is provided[1]:

(a)   under non-discriminatory terms, conditions (including technical standards and specifications) and rates and of a quality no less favourable than that provided for its own like services or for like services of non-affiliated service suppliers or for its subsidiaries or other affiliates[2];

(b)   in a timely fashion, on terms, conditions (including technical standards and specifications) and cost-oriented rates that are transparent, reasonable, having regard to economic feasibility, and sufficiently unbundled so that the supplier need not pay for network components or facilities that it does not require for the service to be provided; and

(c)   upon request, at points in addition to the network termination points offered to the majority of users, subject to charges that reflect the cost construction of necessary additional facilities.

2.3. Public availability of the procedures for interconnection negotiations

The procedures applicable for interconnection to a major supplier will be made publicly available.

2.4. Transparency of interconnection arrangements

It is ensured that a major supplier will make publicly available either its interconnection agreements or a reference interconnection offer.

2.5. Interconnection: dispute settlement

A service supplier requesting interconnection with a major supplier will have recourse, either:

(a)   at any time; or

(b)   after a reasonable period of time which has been made publicly known

to an independent domestic body, which may be a regulatory body as referred to in paragraph 5 below, to resolve disputes regarding appropriate terms, conditions and rates for interconnection within a reasonable period of time, to the extent that these have not been established previously.

3.   UNIVERSAL SERVICE

Any Member has the right to define the kind of universal service obligation it wishes to maintain. Such obligations will not be regarded as anti-competitive per se, provided

---

[1]   Suppliers of services or networks not generally available to the public, such as closed user groups, have guaranteed rights to connect with the public telecommunications transport network or services on terms, conditions and rates which are non-discriminatory, transparent and cost-oriented. Such terms, conditions and rates may, however, vary from the terms, conditions and rates applicable to interconnection between public telecommunications networks or services.

[2]   Different terms, conditions and rates may be set in the Community for operators in different market segments, on the basis of non-discriminatory and transparent national licensing provisions, where such differences can be objectively justified because these services are not considered 'like services'.

they are administered in a transparent, non-discriminatory and competitively neutral manner and are not more burdensome than necessary for the kind of universal service defined by the Member.

4. PUBLIC AVAILABILITY OF LICENSING CRITERIA

Where a licence is required, the following will be made publicly available:

(a) all the licensing criteria and the period of time normally required to reach a decision concerning an application for a licence and

(b) the terms and conditions of individual licences.

The reasons for the denial of a licence will be made known to the applicant upon request.

5. INDEPENDENT REGULATORS

The regulatory body is separate from, and not accountable to, any supplier of basic telecommunications services. The decisions of and the procedures used by regulators shall be impartial with respect to all market participants.

6. ALLOCATION AND USE OF SCARCE RESOURCES

Any procedures for the allocation and use of scarce resources, including frequencies, numbers and rights of way, will be carried out in an objective, timely, transparent and non-discriminatory manner. The current state of allocated frequency bands will be made publicly available, but detailed identification of frequencies allocated for specific government uses is not required.

DECISION ON COMMITMENTS IN BASIC TELECOMMUNICATIONS

THE COUNCIL FOR TRADE IN SERVICES,

HAVING REGARD to the Annex on negotiations on basic telecommunications,

HAVING REGARD to the results of the negotiations conducted under the terms of the decision on negotiations on basic telecommunications adopted at Marrakesh on 15 April 1994,

ACTING upon the final report of the negotiating group on basic telecommunications,

DECIDES as follows:

1. To adopt the text of the 'Fourth Protocol to the General Agreement on Trade in Services' (hereinafter referred to as the Protocol) and to take note of the schedules of commitments and lists of exemptions from Article II listed in the attachment to the final report of the negotiating group on basic telecommunications.

2. Commencing immediately and continuing until the date of entry into force of the Protocol Members concerned shall, to the fullest extent consistent with their existing legislation and regulations, not take measures which would be inconsistent with their undertakings resulting from these negotiations.

3. During the period from 15 January to 15 February 1997, a Member which has a schedule of commitments annexed to the Protocol, may supplement or modify such schedule or its list of Article II exemptions. Any such Member which has not annexed to the Protocol a list of Article II exemptions may submit such a list during the same period.

4. A Group on basic telecommunications reporting to the Council for Trade in Services shall conduct consultations on the implementation of paragraph 3 above commencing its work no later than 90 days from the adoption of the decision.

5. The Council for Trade in Services shall monitor the acceptance of the Protocol by Members concerned and shall, at the request of a Member, examine any concerns raised regarding the application of paragraph 2 above.

6. Members of the World Trade Organization which have not annexed to the Protocol schedules of commitments or lists of exemptions from Article II may submit, for approval by the Council, schedules of commitments and lists of exemptions from Article II relating to basic telecommunications prior to 1 January 1998.

REPORT OF THE GROUP ON BASIC TELECOMMUNICATIONS

1.   This report is made in accordance with paragraph 4 of the Decision on Commitments in Basic Telecommunications, adopted by the Council for Trade in Services on 30 April 1996 (S/L/19). In paragraph 1 of this Decision, the Council also adopted the text of the Fourth Protocol to the General Agreement on Trade in Services and took note of the schedules of commitments and lists of exemptions from Article II listed in the attachment to the final report of the negotiating group on basic telecommunications (S/NGBT/18).

2.   The Decision on commitments on basic telecommunications established the Group on Basic telecommunications to 'conduct consultations on the implementation of paragraph 3 of the Decision'. Paragraph 3 states that 'during the period from 15 January to 15 February 1997, a Member which has a schedule of commitments annexed to the Protocol, may supplement or modify such schedule or its list of Article II exemptions' and that 'any such Member which has not annexed to the Protocol a list of Article II exemptions may submit such a list during the same period'.

3.   At the Group's first meeting in July 1996, participants suggested that the principal issues before the GBT included the desirability of improving the quantity and quality of schedules offered, and the need to address certain issues which had been left unresolved in April. Subsequently, the Group sponsored frequent rounds of bilateral negotiations on offers and regularly included discussion of outstanding issues in its meetings. In November participants began submitting revised draft offers of commitments on basic telecommunications for consideration. The Group's Report to the Council on Trade in Services (S/GBT/2), which formed part of the Report to the Singapore Ministerial Conference, recommended that Ministers 'stress their commitment to bring the negotiations on basic telecommunications to a successful conclusion by 15 February 1997, urge all WTO Members to strive for significant, balanced and non-discriminatory liberalization commitments on basic telecommunications by that date and recognize the importance of resolving the principal issues before the GBT'. The Declaration adopted by Ministers in Singapore (WT/MIN(96)/DEC) contained a commitment to 'achieve a successful conclusion to the negotiations on basic telecommunications in February 1997'. Ministers also stated 'We are determined to obtain a progressively higher level of liberalization in services on a mutually advantageous basis with appropriate flexibility for individual developing country members, as envisaged in the agreement, in the continuing negotiations and those scheduled to begin no later than 1 January 2000. In this context, we look forward to full MFN agreements based on improved market access commitments and national treatment'.

4.   In its discussions on outstanding issues, the Group considered the following matters: ways to ensure accurate scheduling of commitments - particularly with respect to supply of services over satellites and to the management of radio spectrum; potential anti-competitive distortion of trade in international services; the status of intergovernmental satellite organizations in relation to GATS provisions; and the extent to which basic telecommunications commitments include transport of video and/or broadcast signals within their scope.

5.   The Chairman issued notes reflecting his understanding of the position reached in discussion of the scheduling of commitments and management of radio spectrum. The first such note set out a number of assumptions applicable to the scheduling of commitments and was intended to assist in ensuring the transparency of commitments (S/GBT/W/2/Rev. 1 of 16 January 1997). The second addressed the allocation of radio spectrum, suggesting that the inclusion of references to the availability of spectrum in schedules was unnecessary and that such references should be deleted (S/GBT/W/3 of 3 February 1997). These notes are attached to this Report.

6.   By 15 February 1997 the total number of schedules submitted had reached 55 (counting as one the offer of the European Communities and their Member States). Nine governments had submitted lists of Article II Exemptions.

7.   The Group noted that five countries had taken Article II exemptions in respect of the application of differential accounting rates to services and service suppliers of other Members. In the light of the fact that the accounting rate system established under the International Telecommunications Regulations is the usual method of terminating international traffic and by its nature involves differential rates, and in order to avoid the submission of further such exemptions, it is the understanding of the Group that:

-    the application of such accounting rates would not give rise to action by Members under dispute settlement under the WTO, and

-    that this understanding will be reviewed not later than the commencement of the further Round of negotiations on services commitments due to begin not later than 1 January 2000.

8.   The Group also recalled paragraph 6 of the Decision of 30 April 1996, which stated that Members of the World Trade Organization which have not annexed to the Protocol schedules of commitments or lists of exemptions from Article II may submit, for approval by the Council, schedules of commitments and lists of exemptions from Article II relating to basic telecommunications prior to 1 January 1998.

9.   At its meeting of 15 February 1997, the Group adopted this report and the attached list of the Schedules of Commitments and Lists of Article II Exemptions, which, in accordance with paragraph 3 of the Decision on commitments in basic telecommunications, will be attached to the Fourth Protocol to the General Agreement on Trade in Services in replacement of those attached on 30 April 1996.

NOTE BY THE CHAIRMAN

Revision

It has been suggested by a number of delegations that it might be helpful to produce a brief and simple note on assumptions applicable to the scheduling of commitments in basic telecoms. The purpose of the attached note is to assist delegations in ensuring the transparency of their commitments and to promote a better understanding of the meaning of commitments. This note is not intended to have or acquire any binding legal status.

NOTES FOR SCHEDULING BASIC TELECOM SERVICES COMMITMENTS

1. Unless otherwise noted in the sector column, any basic telecom service listed in the sector column:

    (a) encompasses local, long distance and international services for public and non-public use;

    (b) may be provided on a facilities-basis or by resale; and

    (c) may be provided through any means of technology (e.g., cable[3], wireless, satellites).

2. Subsector (g) - private leased circuit services - involves the ability of service suppliers to sell or lease any type of network capacity for the supply of services listed in any other basic telecom service subsector unless otherwise noted in the sector column. This would include capacity via cable, satellite and wireless network.

3. In view of points 1 and 2 above, it should not be necessary to list cellular or mobile services as a separate subsector. However, a number of Members have done so, and a number of offers have commitments only in these subsectors. Therefore, in order to avoid extensive changes in schedules, it would seem appropriate for Members to maintain separate entries for these subsectors.

CHAIRMAN'S NOTE

Editors' Note:

This Chairman's Note relates to technicalities for the scheduling of Specific Commitments and has been omitted.

---

[3] Including all types of cable.

REGULATION (EC) NO 2887/2000
OF THE EUROPEAN PARLIAMENT AND OF THE COUNCIL

of 18 December 2000[a]

on unbundled access to the local loop[b]

THE EUROPEAN PARLIAMENT AND THE COUNCIL OF THE EUROPEAN UNION,

Having regard to the Treaty establishing the European Community, and in particular Article 95 thereof,

Having regard to the proposal from the Commission,

Having regard to the opinion of the Economic and Social Committee[1],

Acting in accordance with the procedure laid down in Article 251 of the Treaty[2],

Whereas:

(1) The conclusions of the European Council of Lisbon of 23 and 24 March 2000 note that, for Europe to fully seize the growth and job potential of the digital, knowledge-based economy, businesses and citizens must have access to an inexpensive, world-class communications infrastructure and a wide range of services. The Member States, together with the Commission, are called upon to work towards introducing greater competition in local access networks before the end of 2000 and unbundling the local loop, in order to help bring about a substantial reduction in the costs of using the Internet. The Feira European Council of 20 June 2000 endorsed the proposed "e-Europe" Action Plan which identifies unbundled access to the local loop as a short-term priority.

(2) Local loop unbundling should complement the existing provisions in Community law guaranteeing universal service and affordable access for all citizens by enhancing competition, ensuring economic efficiency and bringing maximum benefit to users.

(3) The "local loop" is the physical twisted metallic pair circuit in the fixed public telephone network connecting the network termination point at the subscriber's premises to the main distribution frame or equivalent facility. As noted in the Commission's Fifth Report on the implementation of the telecommunications regulatory package, the local access network remains one of the least competitive segments of the liberalised telecommunications market. New entrants do not have widespread alternative network infrastructures and are unable, with traditional technologies, to match the economies of scale and the coverage of operators designated as having significant market power in the fixed public telephone network market. This results from the fact that these operators rolled out their metallic local access infrastructures over significant periods of time protected by exclusive rights and were able to fund investment costs through monopoly rents.

(4) The European Parliament Resolution of 13 June 2000 on the Commission communication on the 1999 Communications review stresses the importance of enabling the sector to develop infrastructures which promote the growth of electronic communications and e-commerce and the importance of regulating in a way that supports this growth. It notes that the unbundling of the local loop currently concerns

[1] [OJ C 14, 16.1.2001, p. 99].
[2] Opinion of the European Parliament of 26 October 2000 [OJ C 197, 12.7.2001, p. 355] and Decision of the Council of 5 December 2000.

mainly the metallic infrastructure of a dominant entity and that investment in alternative infrastructures must have the possibility of ensuring a reasonable rate of return, since that might facilitate the expansion of these infrastructures in areas where their penetration is still low.

(5) The provision of new loops with high capacity optical fibre directly to major users is a specific market that is developing under competitive conditions with new investments. This Regulation therefore addresses access to metallic local loops, without prejudice to national obligations regarding other types of access to local infrastructures.

(6) It would not be economically viable for new entrants to duplicate the incumbent's metallic local access infrastructure in its entirety within a reasonable time. Alternative infrastructures such as cable television, satellite, wireless local loops do not generally offer the same functionality or ubiquity for the time being, though situations in Member States may differ.

(7) Unbundled access to the local loop allows new entrants to compete with notified operators in offering high bit-rate data transmission services for continuous Internet access and for multimedia applications based on digital subscriber line (DSL) technology as well as voice telephony services. A reasonable request for unbundled access implies that the access is necessary for the provision of the services of the beneficiary, and that refusal of the request would prevent, restrict or distort competition in this sector.

(8) This Regulation mandates unbundled access to the metallic local loops only of notified operators that have been designated by their national regulatory authorities as having significant market power in the fixed public telephone network supply market under the relevant Community provisions (hereinafter referred to as "notified operators"). Member States have already notified to the Commission the names of those fixed public network operators which have significant market power under Annex I, Part 1, of Directive 97/33/EC of the European Parliament and of the Council of 30 June 1997 on interconnection in telecommunications with regard to ensuring universal service and interoperability through application of the principles of open network provision (ONP)[3], and Directive 98/10/EC of the European Parliament and of the Council of 26 February 1998 on the application of open network provision to voice telephony and on universal service for telecommunications in a competitive environment[4].

(9) A notified operator cannot be required to provide types of access which are not within its powers to provide, for example where fulfilment of a request would cause a violation of the legal rights of an independent third party. The obligation to provide unbundled access to the local loop does not imply that notified operators have to install entirely new local network infrastructure specifically to meet beneficiaries' requests.

(10) Although commercial negotiation is the preferred method for reaching agreement on technical and pricing issues for local loop access, experience shows that in most cases regulatory intervention is necessary due to imbalance in negotiating power between the new entrant and the notified operator, and lack of other alternatives. In certain circumstances the national regulatory authority may, in accordance with Community law, intervene on its own initiative in order to ensure fair competition, economic efficiency and maximum benefit for end-users. Failure of the notified operator to meet lead times should entitle the beneficiary to receive compensation.

---

[3] OJ L 199, 26.7.1997, p. 32. Directive as amended by Directive 98/61/EC (OJ L 268, 3.10.1998, p. 37).
[4] OJ L 101, 1.4.1998, p. 24.

(11) Costing and pricing rules for local loops and related facilities should be transparent, non-discriminatory and objective to ensure fairness. Pricing rules should ensure that the local loop provider is able to cover its appropriate costs in this regard plus a reasonable return, in order to ensure the long term development and upgrade of local access infrastructure. Pricing rules for local loops should foster fair and sustainable competition, bearing in mind the need for investment in alternative infrastructures, and ensure that there is no distortion of competition, in particular no margin squeeze between prices of wholesale and retail services of the notified operator. In this regard, it is considered important that competition authorities be consulted.

(12) Notified operators should provide information and unbundled access to third parties under the same conditions and of the same quality as they provide for their own services or to their associated companies. To this end, the publication by the notified operator of an adequate reference offer for unbundled access to the local loop, within a short time-frame and ideally on the Internet, and under the supervisory control of the national regulatory authority, would contribute to the creation of transparent and non-discriminatory market conditions.

(13) In its Recommendation 2000/417/EC of 25 May 2000 on unbundled access to the local loop enabling the competitive provision of a full range of electronic communications services including broadband multimedia and high-speed Internet[5] and its Communication of 26 April 2000[6], the Commission set out detailed guidance to assist national regulatory authorities on the fair regulation of different forms of unbundled access to the local loop.

(14) In accordance with the principle of subsidiarity as set out in Article 5 of the Treaty, the objective of achieving a harmonised framework for unbundled access to the local loop in order to enable the competitive provision of an inexpensive, world-class communications infrastructure and a wide range of services for all businesses and citizens in the Community cannot be achieved by the Member States in a secure, harmonised and timely manner and can therefore be better achieved by the Community. In accordance with the principle of proportionality as set out in that Article, the provisions of this Regulation do not go beyond what is necessary in order to achieve this objective for that purpose. They are adopted without prejudice to national provisions complying with Community law which set out more detailed measures, for example dealing with virtual collocation.

(15) This Regulation complements the regulatory framework for telecommunications, in particular Directives 97/33/EC and 98/10/EC. The new regulatory framework for electronic communications should include appropriate provisions to replace this Regulation,

HAVE ADOPTED THIS REGULATION:

Article 1

Aim and Scope

1. This Regulation aims at intensifying competition and stimulating technological innovation on the local access market, through the setting of harmonised conditions for unbundled access to the local loop, to foster the competitive provision of a wide range of electronic communications services.

---

[5]   OJ L 156, 29.6.2000, p. 44.
[6]   OJ C 272, 23.9.2000, p. 55.

2. This Regulation shall apply to unbundled access to the local loops and related facilities of notified operators as defined in Article 2(a).

3. This Regulation shall apply without prejudice to the obligations for notified operators to comply with the principle of non-discrimination, when using the fixed public telephone network in order to provide high speed access and transmission services to third parties in the same manner as they provide for their own services or to their associated companies, in accordance with Community provisions.

4. This Regulation is without prejudice to the rights of Member States to maintain or introduce measures in conformity with Community law which contain more detailed provisions than those set out in this Regulation and/or are outside the scope of this Regulation inter alia with respect to other types of access to local infrastructures.

Article 2

Definitions

For the purposes of this Regulation the following definitions apply:

(a) "notified operator" means operators of fixed public telephone networks that have been designated by their national regulatory authority as having significant market power in the provision of fixed public telephone networks and services under Annex I, Part 1, of Directive 97/33/EC or Directive 98/10/EC;

(b) "beneficiary" means a third party duly authorised in accordance with Directive 97/13/EC[7] or entitled to provide communications services under national legislation, and which is eligible for unbundled access to a local loop;

(c) "local loop" means the physical twisted metallic pair circuit connecting the network termination point at the subscriber's premises to the main distribution frame or equivalent facility in the fixed public telephone network;

(d) "local sub-loop" means a partial local loop connecting the network termination point at the subscriber's premises to a concentration point or a specified intermediate access point in the fixed public telephone network;

(e) "unbundled access to the local loop" means full unbundled access to the local loop and shared access to the local loop; it does not entail a change in ownership of the local loop;

(f) "full unbundled access to the local loop" means the provision to a beneficiary of access to the local loop or local sub loop of the notified operator authorising the use of the full frequency spectrum of the twisted metallic pair;

(g) "shared access to the local loop" means the provision to a beneficiary of access to the local loop or local sub loop of the notified operator, authorising the use of the non-voice band frequency spectrum of the twisted metallic pair; the local loop continues to be used by the notified operator to provide the telephone service to the public;

(h) "collocation" means the provision of physical space and technical facilities necessary to reasonably accommodate and connect the relevant equipment of a beneficiary, as mentioned in Section B of the Annex;

---

[7] Directive 97/13/EC of the European Parliament and of the Council of 10 April 1997 on a common framework for general authorisations and individual licences in the field of telecommunications services (OJ L 117, 7.5.1997, p. 15).

(i)   "related facilities" means the facilities associated with the provision of unbundled access to the local loop, notably collocation, cable connections and relevant information technology systems, access to which is necessary for a beneficiary to provide services on a competitive and fair basis.

Article 3

Provision of unbundled access

1.   Notified operators shall publish from 31 December 2000, and keep updated, a reference offer for unbundled access to their local loops and related facilities, which shall include at least the items listed in the Annex. The offer shall be sufficiently unbundled so that the beneficiary does not have to pay for network elements or facilities which are not necessary for the supply of its services, and shall contain a description of the components of the offer, associated terms and conditions, including charges.

2.   Notified operators shall from 31 December 2000 meet reasonable requests from beneficiaries for unbundled access to their local loops and related facilities, under transparent, fair and non-discriminatory conditions. Requests shall only be refused on the basis of objective criteria, relating to technical feasibility or the need to maintain network integrity. Where access is refused, the aggrieved party may submit the case to the dispute resolution procedure referred to in Article 4(5). Notified operators shall provide beneficiaries with facilities equivalent to those provided for their own services or to their associated companies, and with the same conditions and time-scales.

3.   Without prejudice to Article 4(4), notified operators shall charge prices for unbundled access to the local loop and related facilities set on the basis of cost-orientation.

Article 4

Supervision by the national regulatory authority

1.   The national regulatory authority shall ensure that charging for unbundled access to the local loop fosters fair and sustainable competition.

2.   The national regulatory authority shall have the power to:

(a)   impose changes on the reference offer for unbundled access to the local loop and related facilities, including prices, where such changes are justified; and

(b)   require notified operators to supply information relevant for the implementation of this Regulation.

3.   The national regulatory authority may, where justified, intervene on its own initiative in order to ensure non-discrimination, fair competition, economic efficiency and maximum benefit for users.

4.   When the national regulatory authority determines that the local access market is sufficiently competitive, it shall relieve the notified operators of the obligation laid down in Article 3(3) for prices to be set on the basis of cost-orientation.

5.   Disputes between undertakings concerning issues included in this Regulation shall be subject to the national dispute resolution procedures established in conformity with Directive 97/33/EC and shall be handled promptly, fairly and transparently.

Article 5

Entry into force

This Regulation shall enter into force on the third day following that of its publication in the Official Journal of the European Communities.[c]

This Regulation shall be binding in its entirety and directly applicable in all Member States.

Editors' Notes:

[a] OJ L 336, 30.12.2000, p. 4. Some citations in the original text have been updated to the current and complete Official Journal citation.

[b] The subject matter of Regulation 2887/2000 is also covered by the Access Directive. Regulation 2887/2000 will become obsolete once the Access Directive has been fully implemented in all Member States. This progress will be reviewed (see Recital 12 of the Access and Interconnection Directive), and Regulation 2887/2000 will eventually be repealed (see Recital 43 of the Framework Directive).

[c] The Regulation was published in the Official Journal on 30/12/2000.

ANNEX

Minimum List of Items to be Included in a Reference Offer for Unbundled Access to the
Local Loop to be Published by Notified Operators

A.   Conditions for unbundled access to the local loop

    1.   Network elements to which access is offered covering in particular the following elements:

        (a)   access to local loops;

        (b)   access to non-voice band frequency spectrum of a local loop, in the case of shared access to the local loop;

    2.   Information concerning the locations of physical access sites[1], availability of local loops in specific parts of the access network;

    3.   Technical conditions related to access and use of local loops, including the technical characteristics of the twisted metallic pair in the local loop;

    4.   Ordering and provisioning procedures, usage restrictions.

B.   Collocation services

    1.   Information on the notified operator's relevant sites[1];

    2.   Collocation options at the sites indicated under point 1 (including physical collocation and, as appropriate, distant collocation and virtual collocation);

    3.   Equipment characteristics: restrictions, if any, on equipment that can be collocated;

    4.   Security issues: measures put in place by notified operators to ensure the security of their locations;

    5.   Access conditions for staff of competitive operators;

    6.   Safety standards;

    7.   Rules for the allocation of space where collocation space is limited;

    8.   Conditions for beneficiaries to inspect the locations at which physical collocation is available, or sites where collocation has been refused on grounds of lack of capacity.

C.   Information systems

Conditions for access to notified operator's operational support systems, information systems or databases for pre-ordering, provisioning, ordering, maintenance and repair requests and billing.

---

[1]   Availability of this information may be restricted to interested parties only, in order to avoid public security concerns.

D. Supply conditions

    1.   Lead time for responding to requests for supply of services and facilities; service level agreements, fault resolution, procedures to return to a normal level of service and quality of service parameters;

    2.   Standard contract terms, including, where appropriate, compensation provided for failure to meet lead times;

    3.   Prices or pricing formulae for each feature, function and facility listed above.

PROVISIONS OF OLD REGULATORY FRAMEWORK WITH TRANSITIONAL RELEVANCE

Editors' Note:

The legislative measures comprising the old regulatory framework were, as a general rule, repealed with effect from 25 July 2003, the date by which Member States were required to apply the national measures implementing the new framework: see Article 26 of the Framework Directive. As an exception, certain obligations existing under the old framework will continue until the new regime is fully implemented: see Recital 12 of the Access Directive and Recital 28 of the Universal Service and User's Rights Directive. Under Article 27 of the Framework Directive, Member States are obliged to maintain all obligations referred to in Article 7 of the Access Directive and Article 16 of the Universal Service Directive until such time as they are withdrawn following a review pursuant to Article 16 of the Framework Directive. The provisions of the old framework to which Article 7 of the Access Directive and Article 16 of the Universal Service Directive refer are reproduced below.

DIRECTIVE 97/33/EC OF THE EUROPEAN PARLIAMENT AND OF THE COUNCIL of 30 June 1997 on interconnection in Telecommunications with regard to ensuring universal service and interoperability through application of the principles of Open Network Provision (ONP), as amended by Directive 98/61/EC of the European Parliament and of the Council of 24 September 1998

(excerpt)

Article 4

Rights and obligations for interconnection

1. Organizations authorized to provide public telecommunications networks and/or publicly available telecommunications services as set out in Annex II shall have a right and, when requested by organizations in that category, an obligation to negotiate interconnection with each other for the purpose of providing the services in question, in order to ensure provision of these networks and services throughout the Community. On a case-by-case basis, the national regulatory authority may agree to limit this obligation on a temporary basis and on the grounds that there are technically and commercially viable alternatives to the interconnection requested, and that the requested interconnection is inappropriate in relation to the resources available to meet the request. Any such limitation imposed by a national regulatory authority shall be fully reasoned and made public in accordance with Article 14 (2).

2. Organizations authorized to provide public telecommunications networks and publicly available telecommunications services as set out in Annex I which have significant market power shall meet all reasonable requests for access to the network including access at points other than the network termination points offered to the majority of end-users.

3. An organization shall be presumed to have significant market power when it has a share of more than 25 % of a particular telecommunications market in the geographical area in a Member State within which it is authorized to operate.

    National regulatory authorities may nevertheless determine that an organization with a market share of less than 25 % in the relevant market has significant market power. They may also determine that an organization with a market share of more than 25 %

in the relevant market does not have significant market power. In either case, the determination shall take into account the organization's ability to influence market conditions, its turnover relative to the size of the market, its control of the means of access to end-users, its access to financial resources and its experience in providing products and services in the market.

Article 6

Non-discrimination and transparency

For interconnection to public telecommunications networks and publicly available telecommunications services as set out in Annex I provided by organizations which have been notified by national regulatory authorities as having significant market power, Member States shall ensure that:

(a) the organizations concerned adhere to the principle of non-discrimination with regard to interconnection offered to others. They shall apply similar conditions in similar circumstances to interconnected organizations providing similar services, and shall provide interconnection facilities and information to others under the same conditions and of the same quality as they provide for their own services, or those of their subsidiaries or partners;

(b) all necessary information and specifications are made available on request to organizations considering interconnection, in order to facilitate conclusion of an agreement; the information provided should include changes planned for implementation within the next six months, unless agreed otherwise by the national regulatory authority;

(c) interconnection agreements are communicated to the relevant national regulatory authorities, and made available on request to interested parties, in accordance with Article 14 (2), with the exception of those parts which deal with the commercial strategy of the parties. The national regulatory authority shall determine which parts deal with the commercial strategy of the parties. In every case, details of interconnection charges, terms and conditions and any contributions to universal service obligations shall be made available on request to interested parties;

(d) information received from an organization seeking interconnection is used only for the purpose for which it was supplied. It shall not be passed on to other departments, subsidiaries or partners for whom such information could provide a competitive advantage.

Article 7

Principles for interconnection charges and cost accounting systems

1. Member States shall ensure that the provisions of paragraphs 2 to 6 apply to organizations operating the public telecommunications networks and/or publicly available telecommunications services as set out in Parts 1 and 2 of Annex I, which have been notified by national regulatory authorities as having significant market power.

2. Charges for interconnection shall follow the principles of transparency and cost orientation. The burden of proof that charges are derived from actual costs including a reasonable rate of return on investment shall lie with the organization providing interconnection to its facilities. National regulatory authorities may request an organization to provide full justification for its interconnection charges, and where appropriate shall require charges to be adjusted. This paragraph shall also apply to organizations set out in Part 3 of Annex I which have been notified by national

regulatory authorities as having significant market power on the national market for interconnection.

3. National regulatory authorities shall ensure the publication, in accordance with Article 14 (1), of a reference interconnection offer. The reference interconnection offer shall include a description of the interconnection offerings broken down into components according to market needs, and the associated terms and conditions including tariffs.

    Different tariffs, terms and conditions for interconnection may be set for different categories of organizations which are authorized to provide networks and services, where such differences can be objectively justified on the basis of the type of interconnection provided and/or the relevant national licensing conditions. National regulatory authorities shall ensure that such differences do not result in distortion of competition, and in particular that the organization applies the appropriate interconnection tariffs, terms and conditions when providing interconnection for its own services or those of its subsidiaries or partners, in accordance with Article 6 (a).

    The national regulatory authority shall have the ability to impose changes in the reference interconnection offer, where justified.

    Annex IV provides a list of examples of elements for further elaboration of interconnection charges, tariff structures and tariff elements. Where an organization makes changes to the published reference interconnection offer, adjustments required by the national regulatory authority may be retrospective in effect, from the date of introduction of the change.

4. Charges for interconnection shall, in accordance with Community law, be sufficiently unbundled, so that the applicant is not required to pay for anything not strictly related to the service requested.

5. The Commission shall, acting in accordance with the procedure laid down in Article 15, draw up recommendations on cost accounting systems and accounting separation in relation to interconnection. National regulatory authorities shall ensure that the cost accounting systems used by the organizations concerned are suitable for implementation of the requirements of this Article, and are documented to a sufficient level of detail, as indicated in Annex V.

    National regulatory authorities shall ensure that a description of the cost accounting system, showing the main categories under which costs are grouped and the rules used for the allocation of costs to interconnection, is made available on request. Compliance with the cost accounting system shall be verified by the national regulatory authority or another competent body, independent of the telecommunications organization and approved by the national regulatory authority. A statement concerning compliance shall be published annually.

6. Where they exist, charges related to the sharing of the cost of universal service obligations, as described in Article 5, shall be unbundled and identified separately.

Article 8

Accounting separation and financial reports

1. Member States shall require organizations providing public telecommunications networks and/or publicly available telecommunications services which have special or exclusive rights for the provision of services in other sectors in the same or another Member State to keep separate accounts for the telecommunications activities, to the extent that would be required if the telecommunications activities in question were carried out by legally independent companies, so as to identify all elements of cost

and revenue, with the basis of their calculation and the detailed attribution methods used, related to their telecommunications activities including an itemized breakdown of fixed asset and structural costs, or to have structural separation for the telecommunications activities.

Member States may choose not to apply the requirements referred to in the first subparagraph to these organizations where their annual turnover in telecommunications activities in the Community is less than the limit set in Part 1 of Annex VI.

2.   Member States shall require organizations operating public telecommunications networks and/or publicly available telecommunications services as set out in Parts 1 and 2 of Annex I and notified by national regulatory authorities as organizations having significant market power which provide public telecommunications networks and/or telecommunications services available for users and which offer interconnection services to other organizations, to keep separate accounts for, on the one hand, their activities related to interconnection - covering both interconnection services provided internally and interconnection services provided to others - and, on the other hand, other activities, so as to identify all elements of cost and revenue, with the basis of their calculation and the detailed attribution methods used, related to their interconnection activity, including an itemized breakdown of fixed asset and structural costs.

Member States may choose not to apply the requirements referred to in the first subparagraph to organizations where their annual turnover in telecommunications activities in the Member States is less than the limit set in Part 2 of Annex VI.

3.   Organizations providing public telecommunications networks and/or publicly available telecommunications services shall provide financial information to their national regulatory authority promptly on request and to the level of detail required. National regulatory authorities may publish such information as would contribute to an open and competitive market, while taking account of considerations of commercial confidentiality.

4.   The financial reports of organizations providing public telecommunications networks or publicly available telecommunications services shall be drawn up and submitted to independent audit and published. The audit shall be carried out in accordance with the relevant rules of national legislation.

The first subparagraph shall also apply to the separate accounts required in paragraphs 1 and 2.

Article 11

Collocation and facility sharing

Where an organization providing public telecommunications networks and/or publicly available telecommunications services has the right under national legislation to install facilities on, over or under public or private land, or may take advantage of a procedure for the expropriation or use of property, national regulatory authorities shall encourage the sharing of such facilities and/or property with other organizations providing telecommunications networks and publicly available services, in particular where essential requirements deprive other organizations of access to viable alternatives.

Agreements for collocation or facility sharing shall normally be a matter for commercial and technical agreement between the parties concerned. The national regulatory authority may intervene to resolve disputes, as provided for in Article 9.

Member States may impose facility and/or property sharing arrangements (including physical collocation) only after an appropriate period of public consultation during which all interested parties must be given an opportunity to express their views. Such arrangements may include rules for apportioning the costs of facility and/or property sharing.

Article 12

Numbering

1. Member States shall ensure the provision of adequate numbers and numbering ranges for all publicly available telecommunications services.

2. In order to ensure full interoperability of Europe-wide networks and services, Member States in accordance with the Treaty shall take all necessary steps to ensure the coordination of their national positions in international organizations and fora where numbering decisions are taken, taking into account possible future developments in numbering in Europe.

3. Member States shall ensure that national telecommunications numbering plans are controlled by the national regulatory authority, in order to guarantee independence from organizations providing telecommunications networks or telecommunications services and facilitate number portability. In order to ensure effective competition, national regulatory authorities shall ensure that the procedures for allocating individual numbers and/or numbering ranges are transparent, equitable and timely and the allocation is carried out in an objective, transparent and non-discriminatory manner. National regulatory authorities may lay down conditions for the use of certain prefixes or certain short codes, in particular where these are used for services of general public interest (e.g. freephone services, kiosk billed services, directory services, emergency services), or to ensure equal access.

4. National regulatory authorities shall ensure that the main elements of the national numbering plans, and all subsequent additions or amendments to them, are published in accordance with Article 14 (1), subject only to limitations imposed on the grounds of national security.

5. National regulatory authorities shall encourage the earliest possible introduction of operator number portability whereby subscribers who so request can retain their number(s) on the fixed public telephone network and the integrated services digital network (ISDN) independent of the organisation providing service, in the case of geographic numbers at a specific location and in the case of other than geographic numbers at any location, and shall ensure that this facility is available by 1 January 2000 at the latest or, in those countries which have been granted an additional transition period, as soon as possible after, but no later than two years after any later date agreed for full liberalisation of voice telephony services.

6. National regulatory authorities shall ensure that numbering plans and procedures are applied in a manner that gives fair and equal treatment to all providers of publicly available telecommunications services. In particular, Member States shall ensure that an organization allocated a range of numbers shall avoid undue discrimination in the number sequences used to give access to the services of other telecommunications operators.

7. National regulatory authorities shall require at least organisations operating public telecommunications networks as set out in Part 1 of Annex I and notified by national regulatory authorities as organisations having significant market power, to enable their subscribers, including those using ISDN, to access the switched services of any interconnected provider of publicly available telecommunications services. For this

purpose facilities shall be in place by 1 January 2000 at the latest or, in those countries which have been granted an additional transition period, as soon as possible thereafter, but no later than two years after any later date agreed for full liberalisation of voice telephony services, which allow the subscriber to choose these services by means of pre-selection with a facility to override any pre-selected choice on a call-by-call basis by dialling a short prefix.

National regulatory authorities shall ensure that pricing for interconnection related to the provision of this facility is cost-orientated and that direct charges to consumers, if any, do not act as a disincentive for the use of this facility.

Article 14

Publication of and access to information

1. With regard to the information identified in Article 7 (3), Article 9 (2), Article 10 and Article 12 (4), national regulatory authorities shall ensure that up-to-date information is published in an appropriate manner in order to provide easy access to that information for interested parties. Reference shall be made in the national Official Gazette of the Member State concerned to the manner in which this information is published.

2. With regard to the information identified in Article 4 (1), Article 5 (3), Article 5 (5), Article 6 (c) and Article 9 (3), national regulatory authorities shall ensure that up-to-date specific information referred to in those Articles is made available on request to interested parties, free of charge, during normal working hours. Reference shall be made in the national Official Gazette of the Member State concerned to the times and location(s) at which the information is available.

3. Member States shall notify to the Commission before 1 January 1998 - and immediately thereafter in case of any change - the manner in which the information referred to in paragraphs 1 and 2 is made available. The Commission shall regularly publish a corresponding reference to such notifications in the Official Journal of the European Communities.

COUNCIL DIRECTIVE 92/44/EEC of 5 June 1992 on the application of open network provision to leased lines, as amended by Directive 97/51/EC of the European Parliament and of the Council of 6 October 1997

(excerpt)

Article 3

Availability of information

1. Member States shall ensure that information in respect of leased lines, offerings on technical characteristics, tariffs, supply and usage conditions, licensing and declaration requirements, and the conditions for the attachment of terminal equipment is published in accordance with the presentation given in Annex I. Changes in existing offerings and information on new offerings shall be published as soon as possible. The national regulatory authority may lay down a suitable period of notice.

2. The information referred to in paragraph 1 shall be published in an appropriate manner so as to provide easy access for users to that information. Reference shall be

made in the national Official Journal of the Member State concerned to the publication of this information.

Member States shall notify to the Commission before 1 January 1993, and thereafter in case of any change, the manner in which the information is made available. The Commission will regularly publish reference to such notifications.

Article 4

Information on supply conditions

The supply conditions to be published pursuant to Article 3 shall include at least:

—   information concerning the ordering procedure

—   the typical delivery period, which is the period, counted from the date when the user has made a firm request for a leased line, in which 95 % of all leased lines of the same type have been put through to the customers.

This period will be established on the basis of the actual delivery periods of leased lines during a recent time interval of reasonable duration. The calculation must not include cases where late delivery periods were requested by users. For new types of leased lines a target delivery period shall be published instead of the typical delivery period,

—   the contractual period, which includes the period which is in general foreseen for the contract and the minimum contractual period which the user is obliged to accept,

—   the typical repair time, which is the period, counted from the time when a failure message has been given to the responsible unit within the organization notified in accordance with Article 11(1)(a) up to the moment in which 80 % of all leased lines of the same type have been re-established and in appropriate cases notified back in operation to the users. For new types of leased lines a target repair time period shall be published instead of the typical repair time. Where different classes of quality of repair are offered for the same type of leased lines, the different typical repair times shall be published,

—   any refund procedure.

Article 6

Access conditions, usage conditions and essential requirements

1.   Member States shall ensure that when access to and use of leased lines is restricted in accordance with Community law those restrictions are imposed by the national regulatory authorities through regulatory means.

No technical restrictions shall be introduced or maintained for the interconnection of leased lines among each other or for the interconnection of leased lines and public telecommunications networks.

2.   Where access to and use of leased lines are restricted on the basis of essential requirements, Member States shall ensure that the relevant national provisions identify which of the essential requirements listed in paragraph 3 are the basis of such restrictions.

3. The essential requirements specified in Article 3 (2) of Directive 90/387/EEC shall apply to leased lines in the following manner:

(a) *Security of network operations*

An organization notified in accordance with Article 11(1) (a) may take the following measures in order to safeguard the security of network operations during the period when an emergency situation prevails:

— the interruption of the service,
— the limitation of service features,
— the denial of access to the service.

An emergency situation in this context shall mean an exceptional case of force majeure, such as extreme weather, earthquakes, flood, lightning or fire.

In an emergency situation the organization notified in accordance with Article 11 (1) (a) .shall make every endeavour to ensure that service is maintained to all users. The Member States shall ensure that the organization notified in accordance with Article 11(1)(a) immediately notifies to the users and to the national regulatory authority the beginning and the end of the emergency as well as the nature and extent of temporary service restrictions;

(b) Maintenance of network integrity

The user has the right to be provided with a fully transparent service, in conformity with the specifications of the network termination point, which he can use in an unstructured manner as he wants, e.g. where no channel allocations are forbidden or prescribed. There shall be no restrictions on the use of leased lines on the ground of the maintenance of network integrity, as long as the access conditions related to terminal equipment are fulfilled;

(c) *Interoperability of services*

Without prejudice to the application of Article 3(5) and Article 5(3) of Directive 90/387/EEC, the use of a leased line shall not be restricted on the grounds of the interoperability of services, when the access conditions related to terminal equipment are fulfilled;

(d) *Protection of data*

In respect of data protection, Member States may restrict the use of leased lines only to the extent necessary to ensure compliance with relevant regulatory provisions on the protection of data including protection of personal data, the confidentiality of information transmitted or stored, as well as the protection of privacy compatible with Community law.

4. Access conditions related to terminal equipment

Access conditions relating to terminal equipment shall be considered to be fulfilled when the terminal equipment complies with the approval conditions laid down for its connection to the network-termination point of the type of leased line concerned in accordance with Directive 91/263/EEC[1] or 93/97/EEC[2].

---

[1] OJ L 128, 23.5.1991, p. 1.
[2] OJ L 290, 24.11.1993, p. 1.

In the case where a user's terminal equipment does not comply or no longer complies with these conditions, the provision of the leased line may be interrupted until the terminal is disconnected from the network termination point.

Member States shall ensure that the organization notified in accordance with Article 11(1)(a) immediately informs the user about the interruption, giving the reasons for the interruption. As soon as the user has ensured that the non-complying terminal equipment is disconnected from the network termination point, the provision of the leased line shall be restored.

Article 7

Provision of a minimum set of leased lines in accordance with harmonized technical characteristics

1. Member States shall ensure that the respective organizations notified in accordance with Article 11 (1) (a) separately or jointly provide a minimum set of leased lines in accordance with Annex II, in order to guarantee a harmonized offering throughout the Community.

2. Where leased lines which implement the standards listed in Annex II are not yet available, Member States shall take the necessary measures to ensure that these types of leased lines will be implemented by the date resulting from the application of Article 15.

2a. Member States shall encourage provision of the additional types of leased lines specified in Annex III, taking into account market demand and progress with standardization.

3. The amendments necessary to adapt Annexes II and III to new technical developments and to changes in market demand, including the possible deletion of certain types of leased lines from the Annexes, shall be adopted by the Commission under the procedure provided for in Article 10 of Directive 90/387/EEC, taking into account the state of development of national networks.

4. The provision of other leased lines beyond the minimum set of leased lines which must be provided by Member States shall not impede the provision of this minimum set of leased lines.

Article 8

Control by the national regulatory authority

1. Member States shall ensure that the national regulatory authority lays down the procedures whereby it decides, on a case-by-case basis and in the shortest time period, to allow or not organizations notified in accordance with Article 11 (1) (a) to take measures such as the refusal to provide a leased line, the interruption of the provision of leased lines or the reduction of the availability of leased line features for reasons of alleged failure to comply with the usage conditions by users of leased lines. These procedures may also foresee the possibility for the national regulatory authority to authorize, a priori, specified measures in the case of defined infringements of usage conditions.

Member States shall ensure that these procedures provide for a transparent decision-making process in which due respect is given to the rights of the parties. The decision shall be taken after having given the opportunity to both parties to state their case. The decision shall be motivated and notified to the parties within one week of its adoption: it shall not be enforced before its notification.

This provision shall not prejudice the right of the parties concerned to apply to the courts.

2.   The national regulatory authority shall ensure that the organizations notified in accordance with Article 11 (1) (a) adhere to the principle of non-discrimination when providing leased lines. Those organizations shall apply similar conditions in similar circumstances to organizations providing similar services, and shall provide leased lines to others under the same conditions and of the same quality as they provide for their own services, or those of their subsidiaries or partners, where applicable.

3.   Where, in response to a particular request, a telecommunications organization considers it unreasonable to provide a leased line under its published tariffs and supply conditions, it must seek the agreement of the national regulatory authority to vary those conditions in that case.

Article 10

Tariffing principles and cost accounting

1.   Member States shall ensure that tariffs for leased lines follow the basic principles of cost orientation and transparency in accordance with the following rules:

(a)   tariffs for leased lines shall be independent of the type of application which the users of the leased lines implement, without prejudice to the principle of non-discrimination set out in Article8(2);

(b)   tariffs for leased lines shall normally contain the following elements:

— an initial connection charge,
— a periodic rental charge, i.e. a flat-rate element.

When other tariff elements are applied, these must be transparent and based on objective criteria;

(c)   tariffs for leased lines apply to the facilities provided between network termination points at which the user has access to the leased lines.

For leased lines provided by more than one organization notified in accordance with Article 11 (1) (a) half-circuit tariffs, i.e. from one network termination point to a hypothetical mid-circuit point, can be applied.

2.   Member States shall ensure that their organizations notified in accordance with Article 11 (1) (a) formulate and put in practice, by 31 December 1993 at the latest, a cost accounting system suitable for the implementation of paragraph 1.

Without prejudice to the last subparagraph, the system referred to in the first subparagraph shall include the following elements:

(a)   the costs of leased lines shall in particular include the direct costs incurred by the organizations notified in accordance with Article 11(1)(a) for setting up, operating and maintaining leased lines, and for marketing and billing of leased lines;

(b)   common costs, that is costs which can neither be directly assigned to leased lines nor to other activities, are allocated as follows:

(i)   whenever possible, common cost categories shall be allocated based upon direct analysis of the origin of the costs themselves;

(ii) when direct analysis is not possible, common cost categories shall be allocated based upon an indirect linkage to another cost category or group of cost categories for which a direct assignment or allocation is possible. The indirect linkage shall be based on comparable cost structures;

(iii) when neither direct nor indirect measures of cost allocation can be found, the cost category shall be allocated on the basis of a general allocator computed by using the ratio of all expenses directly assigned or allocated to leased lines, on the one hand, to those allocated to other services, on the other hand.

After 31 December 1993, other cost accounting systems may be applied only if they are suitable for the implementation of paragraph 1 and have as such been approved by the national regulatory authority for application by the organization notified in accordance with Article 11(1)(a), subject to the Commission being informed prior to their application.

3. The national regulatory authority shall keep available, with an adequate level of detail, information on the cost accounting systems applied by the organizations notified in accordance with Article 11(1)(a) pursuant to paragraph 2. It shall submit this information to the Commission on request.

4. The national regulatory authority shall not apply the requirements of paragraph 1 where an organization does not have significant market power in respect of a specific leased-lines offering in a specific geographical area.

The national regulatory authority may decide not to apply the requirements of paragraph 1 in a specific geographical area where it is satisfied that there is effective competition in the relevant leased-lines market as evidenced by tariffs that already comply with those requirements.

DIRECTIVE 98/10/EC OF THE EUROPEAN PARLIAMENT AND OF THE COUNCIL of 26 February 1998 on the application of open network provision (ONP) to voice telephony and on universal service for telecommunications in a competitive environment

(excerpt)

Article 16

Special network access

1. National regulatory authorities shall ensure that organisations with significant market power in the provision of fixed public telephone networks deal with reasonable requests from organisations providing telecommunications services for access to the fixed public telephone network at network termination points other than the commonly provided network termination points referred to in Annex II, part 1. This obligation may only be limited on a case-by-case basis and on the grounds that there are technically and commercially viable alternatives to the special access requested, and if the requested access is inappropriate in relation to the resources available to meet the request.

2. The organisation making such a request shall be granted an opportunity to put its case to the national regulatory authority before a final decision is taken to restrict or deny access in response to a particular request.

Where a request for special network access is denied, the organisation making the request should be given a prompt and justified explanation of why the request has been refused.

3. Technical and commercial arrangements for special network access shall be a matter for agreement between the parties involved, subject to intervention by the national regulatory authority as laid down in paragraphs 2, 4 and 5.

The agreement may include reimbursement to the organisation of its costs incurred in providing the network access requested; these charges shall fully respect the principles of cost orientation set out in Annex II to Directive 90/387/EEC.

4. National regulatory authorities may intervene on their own initiative at any time, where justified, in order to ensure effective competition and/or interoperability of services and shall do so, if requested by either party, in order to set conditions which are non-discriminatory, fair and reasonable for both parties and offer the greatest benefit to all users.

5. National regulatory authorities shall also have the right, in the interest of all users, to ensure that the agreements include conditions which meet the criteria set out in paragraph 4, are entered into and implemented in an efficient and timely manner and include conditions on conformity with relevant standards, compliance with essential requirements and/or the maintenance of end-to-end quality.

6. Conditions set by national regulatory authorities in accordance with paragraph 5 shall be published in the manner laid down in Article 11(4).

7. National regulatory authorities shall ensure that organisations with significant market power referred to in paragraph 1 adhere to the principle of non-discrimination when they make use of the fixed public telephone network and, in particular, use any form of special network access, for providing publicly available telecommunications services. Such organisations shall apply similar conditions in similar circumstances to organisations providing similar services and shall provide special network access facilities and information to others under the same conditions and of the same quality as they provide for their own services or those of their subsidiaries or partners.

8. Where appropriate, the Commission shall, in consultation with the ONP Committee, acting in accordance with the procedure laid down in Article 29, request the European Telecommunications Standards Institute (ETSI) to draw up standards for new types of network access. Reference to such standards shall be published in the Official Journal of the European Communities in accordance with Article 5 of Directive 90/387/EEC.

9. Details of agreements for special network access shall be made available to the national regulatory authority on request. Without prejudice to the rights and obligations referred to in Article 20(2) of Directive 97/13/EC on Licensing, national regulatory authorities shall keep confidential those parts of the agreements referred to in paragraph 3 which deal with the commercial strategy of the parties.

Article 17

Tariff principles

1. Without prejudice to the specific provisions of Article 3 in relation to affordability or to paragraph 6, national regulatory authorities shall ensure that organisations providing voice telephony services which either have significant market power or have been designated in accordance with Article 5 and have significant market power comply with the provisions of this Article.

2.   Tariffs for use of the fixed public telephone network and fixed public telephone services shall follow the basic principles of cost orientation set out in Annex II to Directive 90/387/EEC.

3.   Without prejudice to Article 7(3) of Directive 97/33/EC on Interconnection, tariffs for access to and use of the fixed public telephone network shall be independent of the type of application which the users implement, except to the extent that they require different services or facilities.

4.   Tariffs for facilities additional to the provision of connection to the fixed public telephone network and fixed public telephone services shall, in accordance with Community law, be sufficiently unbundled so that the user is not required to pay for facilities which are not necessary for the service requested.

5.   Tariff changes shall be implemented only after an appropriate public notice period, set by the national regulatory authority, has been observed.

6.   Without prejudice to Article 3 in relation to affordability, a Member State may authorize its national regulatory authority not to apply paragraphs 1, 2, 3, 4 or 5 of this Article in a specific geographical area where it is satisfied that there is effective competition in the fixed public telephone services market.